McGraw-Hill
netw⊙rks™
A Social Studies Learning System

WORLD
HISTORY
& GEOGRAPHY
Modern Times

Jackson J. Spielvogel, Ph.D.

Mc Graw Hill Education

Bothell, WA • Chicago, IL • Columbus, OH • New York, NY

McGraw-Hill networks ™ meets you anywhere—takes you everywhere. Go online. 1. Go to connected.mcgraw-hill.com. 2. Get your User Name and Password from your teacher and enter them. 3. Click on your *networks* book. 4. Select your chapter and lesson.

www.mheonline.com/networks

Send all inquiries to:
McGraw-Hill Education
8787 Orion Place
Columbus, OH 43240

ISBN: 978-0-07-664738-5
MHID: 0-07-664738-2

Printed in the United States of America.

4 5 6 7 8 9 DOW 17 16 15 14

AUTHORS

Jackson Spielvogel, Ph.D., is associate professor emeritus of history at the Pennsylvania State University. He received his Ph.D. from the Ohio State University, where he specialized in Reformation history under Harold J. Grimm. His articles and reviews have been published in several scholarly publications. He is co-author (with William Duiker) of *World History,* published in 1994 (5ᵗʰ edition, 2007). Professor Spielvogel has won five major university-wide wards, and in 2000, he became the first winner of the Schreyer Institute's Student Choice Award for innovative and inspired teaching.

Contributing Author

Jay McTighe has published articles in a number of leading educational journals and has co-authored ten books, including the best-selling *Understanding By Design* series with Grant Wiggins. Jay also has an extensive background in professional development and is a featured speaker at national, state, and district conferences and workshops. He received his undergraduate degree from The College of William and Mary, earned a Masters degree from The University of Maryland and completed post-graduate studies at The Johns Hopkins University.

CONSULTANTS AND REVIEWERS

ACADEMIC CONSULTANTS

David Berger, Ph.D.
Ruth and I. Lewis Gordon Professor of Jewish
   History
Dean, Bernard Revel Graduate School
Yeshiva University
New York, New York

Michael C. Brose, Ph.D.
Associate Professor
Department of History
University of Wyoming
Laramie, Wyoming

Steven Cunha, Ph.D.
Professor
Department of Geography
Humboldt State University
Arcata, California

Richard Golden, Ph.D.
Professor of History and Director of Jewish
   Studies Program
University of North Texas
Denton, Texas

Farid Mahdavi, Ph.D.
Lecturer
Department of History
San Diego State University
San Diego, California

Guy R. Welbon, Ph.D.
Associate Professor Emeritus
South Asia Studies and
   Religious Studies
University of Pennsylvania
Philadelphia, Pennsylvania

TEACHER REVIEWERS

Elizabeth M. Bernard
Social Studies Teacher
Edgewood High School
Harford County Public Schools
Edgewood, Maryland

Christopher Bryant
Social Studies Teacher
Lake Forest High School
District 115
Lake Forest, Illinois

Penny Buckley
History Teacher
Sahuaro High school
Tucson Unified School District
Tucson, Arizona

Christine Conrad
Social Studies Department Chair
Olympia High School
Orange County Public Schools
Orlando, Florida

Stanley De Cusatis
Social Studies Teacher
Harford Technical High School
Harford County Public Schools
Belair, Maryland

Robin Depugh
Social Studies Teacher
Sahuaro High School
Tucson Unified School District
Tucson, Arizona

Dr. Jane Carter Eason
Secondary Social Studies
   Consultant
Richland County School
   District One
Columbia, South Carolina

Nadia Gunter
Social Studies Teacher
R.T. Cream
Camden, New Jersey

Loyd Henderson
Social Studies Department Chair
Travelers Rest High School
Travelers Rest, South Carolina

William Hocking
Social Studies Department
   Chair 6–12
Mansfield High School
Mansfield Public Schools
Mansfield, Massachusetts

Scott E. Jones
Social Studies Teacher
Hazelwood West High School
Hazelwood School District
Hazelwood, Missouri

Lisa McBride
Social Studies Teacher
Owasso Mid High School
Owasso Public Schools
Owasso, Oklahoma

Andre' McConico
Social Studies Teacher
The Pathway School
Mobile County Public Schools
Mobile, Alabama

Julie Peterson
Social Studies Chair
Carbondale Community High
   School
District 165
Carbondale, Illinois

Jacalyn A. Roche
History Teacher
Waukegan High School
CUSD #60
Waukegan, Illinois

Laura Snow
Social Studies Specialist, Retired
Escambia County School District
Pensacola, Florida

Gail S. Stockard
Teacher
Olympia High School
Orange County Public Schools
Orlando, Florida

CONTENTS

PHOTO: ©Gianni Dagli Orti/CORBIS

PHOTO: Leonardo da Vinci/The Bridgeman Art Library/Getty Images

PHOTO: The Image Works

 This icon indicates where reading skills and writing skills from the *Common Core State Standards for English Language Arts & Literacy in History/Social Studies, Science, and Technical Subjects* are practiced and reinforced.

CONTENTS

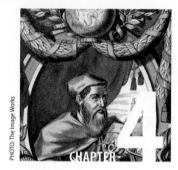

PHOTO: The Image Works

PHOTO: Sotheby / akg-images

PHOTO: The Granger Collection, NYC, All rights reserved

CONTENTS

CONTENTS

CONTENTS

PHOTO: Bettman/CORBIS

CHAPTER 12

The Reach of Imperialism, 1800–1914

PHOTO: Stringer/Fotosearch/Getty Images

CHAPTER 13

Challenges and Transition in East Asia, 1800–1914

CONTENTS

CONTENTS

CONTENTS

CONTENTS

PHOTO: ©Bettmann/Corbis

CHAPTER **20**

PHOTO: ullstein bild / The Granger Collection, NYC, All rights reserved

CHAPTER **21**

CONTENTS

PHOTO: ©Phillipe Lissa/Codong/Corbis

CHAPTER **22**

FEATURES

Analyzing PRIMARY SOURCES

BIOGRAPHY

Connections to TODAY...

Thinking like a HISTORIAN

POLITICAL CARTOON

MAPS, CHARTS AND GRAPHS

MAPS, CHARTS AND GRAPHS

Interactive White Board Activities

Interactive Time Lines

 ## Analyzing Primary Sources

Interactive Slide Shows

Chapter 2, Lesson 2	Art of the Italian Renaissance
Chapter 2, Lesson 2	Art of the Northern European Renaissance
Chapter 5, Lesson 3	The Westernization of Russia by Peter the Great
Chapter 5, Lesson 4	Virtual Field Trip: Museum
Chapter 5, Lesson 4	Virtual Field Trip: Music
Chapter 5, Lesson 4	Virtual Field Trip: Theater
Chapter 6, Lesson 1	Ottoman Architecture and Arts
Chapter 6, Lesson 2	The Art of the Safavid

Chapter 7, Lesson 1	Chinese Art and Literature During the Ming and Qing Dynasties
Chapter 8, Lesson 2	The Enlightenment and the Arts
Chapter 9, Lesson 4	Napoleon's Final Days
Chapter 11, Lesson 1	Inventions of the Second Industrial Revolution
Chapter 11, Lesson 4	Modern Painting and Architecture
Chapter 15, Lesson 4	Modern Art of Latin America
Chapter 17, Lesson 4	The Holocaust

Infographics

Chapter 1, Lesson 1	India's Caste System
Chapter 2, Lesson 2	Gutenberg and the Spread of Literacy
Chapter 3	Interactive Nations of the World Atlas
Chapter 4, Lesson 1	Spanish Conquest of the Aztec and Inca
Chapter 5, Lesson 1	The Voyage of the Spanish Armada

Chapter 5, Lesson 3	Versailles: A Palace Fit for the Sun King
Chapter 11, Lesson 4	Advancements in Chemistry and Physics
Chapter 14, Lesson 2	The Technology of Trench Warfare
Chapter 15, Lesson 3	The Hitler Youth
Chapter 17, Lesson 2	Pearl Harbor

Interactive Self-Check Quizzes

Chapter 1	Two Quizzes, One Per Lesson
Chapter 2	Two Quizzes, One Per Lesson
Chapter 3	Two Quizzes, One Per Lesson
Chapter 4	Three Quizzes, One Per Lesson
Chapter 5	Four Quizzes, One Per Lesson
Chapter 6	Three Quizzes, One Per Lesson
Chapter 7	Three Quizzes, One Per Lesson
Chapter 8	Four Quizzes, One Per Lesson
Chapter 9	Four Quizzes, One Per Lesson
Chapter 10	Five Quizzes, One Per Lesson
Chapter 11	Four Quizzes, One Per Lesson

Chapter 12	Four Quizzes, One Per Lesson
Chapter 13	Three Quizzes, One Per Lesson
Chapter 14	Four Quizzes, One Per Lesson
Chapter 15	Three Quizzes, One Per Lesson
Chapter 16	Four Quizzes, One Per Lesson
Chapter 17	Five Quizzes, One Per Lesson
Chapter 18	Three Quizzes, One Per Lesson
Chapter 19	Four Quizzes, One Per Lesson
Chapter 20	Three Quizzes, One Per Lesson
Chapter 21	Four Quizzes, One Per Lesson
Chapter 22	Four Quizzes, One Per Lesson

PRIMARY SOURCES AND POLITICAL CARTOONS

PRIMARY SOURCES AND POLITICAL CARTOONS

SCAVENGER HUNT

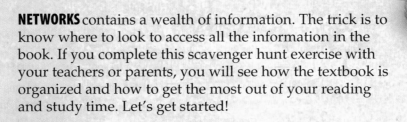

NETWORKS contains a wealth of information. The trick is to know where to look to access all the information in the book. If you complete this scavenger hunt exercise with your teachers or parents, you will see how the textbook is organized and how to get the most out of your reading and study time. Let's get started!

1 How many chapters and how many lessons are in this book?

2 Where do you find the glossary and the index? What is the difference between them?

3 Where can you find primary sources in the textbook?

4 If you want to quickly find all the maps, charts, and graphs about World War II, where do you look?

5 How can you find information about Constantine the Great?

6 Where can you find a graphic organizer that lists the causes of the French Revolution discussed in Chapter 9?

7 Where and how do you find the content vocabulary for Chapter 7, Lesson 3?

8 What are the online resources listed for Chapter 14, Lesson 2?

9 You want to read about the age of exploration. How will you find it?

10 What time period does Chapter 3 cover? How do you know?

The World Before Modern Times

Prehistory–A.D.1500

ESSENTIAL QUESTIONS · *What are the characteristics of a civilization?*
· *How did patterns of civilization differ between the ancient and medieval worlds?*

networks

There's More Online! about the world before modern times.

CHAPTER 1

Lesson 1
Ancient Civilizations

Lesson 2
New Patterns of Civilization

The Story Matters...

The history of the ancient world is filled with the rise and fall of civilizations. While some fell into obscurity, others continue to influence today's world. The civilization of ancient Greece had an enormous impact not only on the ancient world but also on the medieval and modern worlds. One of its most lasting contributions is the organized system of thought called philosophy. The Greek word for philosophy means "love of wisdom." As the Greek philosopher Socrates puts it (in one of the *Dialogues* of his pupil Plato), "The unexamined life is not worth living."

◄ Plato was one of the most influential thinkers in human history. Plato, along with his teacher Socrates and his pupil Aristotle, established the foundations of all subsequent Western philosophy. This marble portrait bust of Plato, from the Capitoline Museums in Rome, is a Roman copy of a Greek original sculpted in the fourth century B.C.

PHOTO: ©Gianni Dagli Orti/CORBIS

1

Place and Time: The World: PREHISTORY—A.D. 500

Fertile river valleys in Mesopotamia, Egypt, India, and China could support a large population in permanent settlements. These farming villages grew into culture hearths, early centers of culture whose ideas and practices spread to surrounding areas. At different points after about 3000 B.C., cities within these culture hearths became centers of the complex societies known as civilizations. Different empires rose and fell within these early civilizations, and some were more influential than others. Empire builders, such as the rulers of Han China or of Rome, created long-lasting empires that witnessed their own classical ages.

Step Into the Place

View the map to answer the following question.

 Analyzing Historical Documents From which early cultural centers did these early empires emerge?

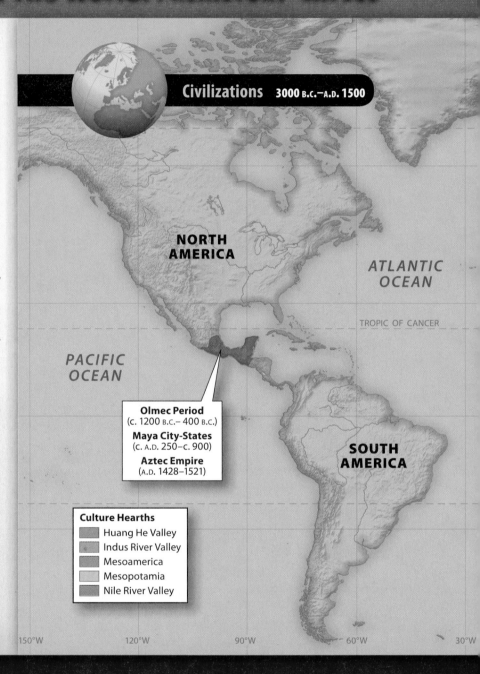

Civilizations 3000 B.C.–A.D. 1500

NORTH AMERICA

ATLANTIC OCEAN

TROPIC OF CANCER

PACIFIC OCEAN

Olmec Period
(c. 1200 B.C.– 400 B.C.)
Maya City-States
(c. A.D. 250–c. 900)
Aztec Empire
(A.D. 1428–1521)

SOUTH AMERICA

Culture Hearths
- Huang He Valley
- Indus River Valley
- Mesoamerica
- Mesopotamia
- Nile River Valley

150°W   120°W   90°W   60°W   30°W

Step Into the Time

Making Connections Research two events from the time line to explain their role in the development of civilization.

THE WORLD   3000 B.C.   2000 B.C.

c. 3000 B.C. Sumerian cities emerge; cuneiform writing is invented

c. 2340 B.C. Sargon of Akkad creates world's first empire

c. 1750 B.C. Mesopotamian Code of Hammurabi, early legal system

c. 3000 B.C. Cities are built in Indus River valley

c. 2560 B.C. Egypt's Great Pyramid is built

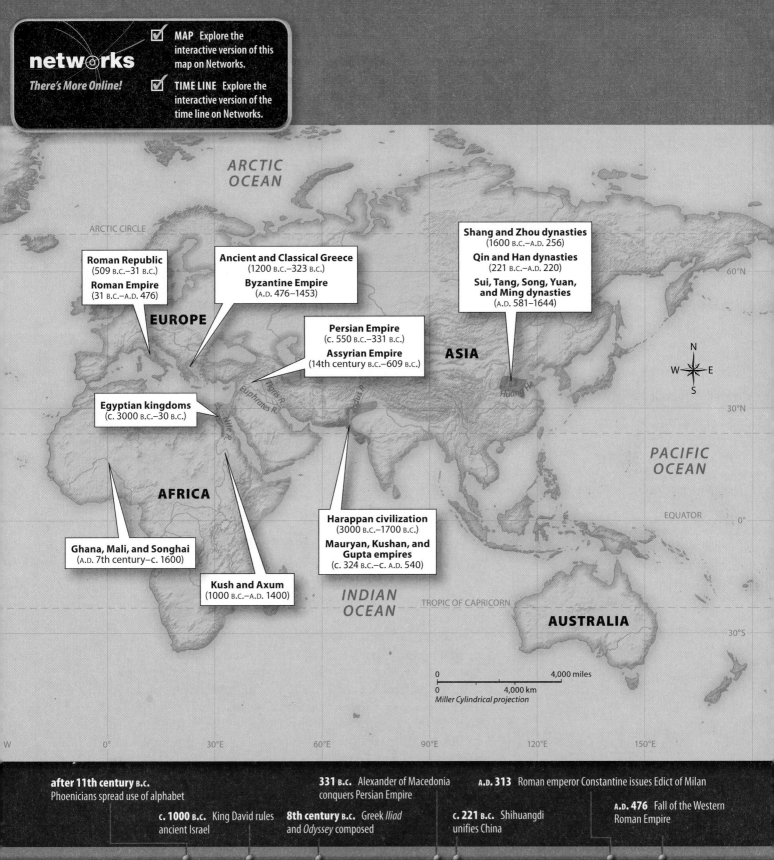

ARCTIC OCEAN

ARCTIC CIRCLE

Roman Republic
(509 B.C.–31 B.C.)
Roman Empire
(31 B.C.–A.D. 476)

EUROPE

Ancient and Classical Greece
(1200 B.C.–323 B.C.)
Byzantine Empire
(A.D. 476–1453)

Shang and Zhou dynasties
(1600 B.C.–A.D. 256)
Qin and Han dynasties
(221 B.C.–A.D. 220)
Sui, Tang, Song, Yuan, and Ming dynasties
(A.D. 581–1644)

Persian Empire
(c. 550 B.C.–331 B.C.)
Assyrian Empire
(14th century B.C.–609 B.C.)

ASIA

Egyptian kingdoms
(c. 3000 B.C.–30 B.C.)

Euphrates R.
Tigris R.
Nile R.
Indus R.
Huang He

AFRICA

PACIFIC OCEAN

EQUATOR

Harappan civilization
(3000 B.C.–1700 B.C.)
Mauryan, Kushan, and Gupta empires
(c. 324 B.C.–c. A.D. 540)

Ghana, Mali, and Songhai
(A.D. 7th century–c. 1600)

Kush and Axum
(1000 B.C.–A.D. 1400)

INDIAN OCEAN

TROPIC OF CAPRICORN

AUSTRALIA

N W E S

60°N
30°N
0°
30°S

0   4,000 miles
0   4,000 km
Miller Cylindrical projection

W   0°   30°E   60°E   90°E   120°E   150°E

after 11th century B.C.
Phoenicians spread use of alphabet

331 B.C. Alexander of Macedonia conquers Persian Empire

A.D. 313 Roman emperor Constantine issues Edict of Milan

c. 1000 B.C. King David rules ancient Israel

8th century B.C. Greek *Iliad* and *Odyssey* composed

c. 221 B.C. Shihuangdi unifies China

A.D. 476 Fall of the Western Roman Empire

1000 B.C.   **A.D. 1**   **A.D. 500**

c. 1500 B.C. Indus Valley civilization declines

5th century B.C. Classical era of Greece

447–432 B.C. Parthenon is built on the Acropolis in Athens

c. 27 B.C. Octavian becomes first Roman emperor

200 B.C. Travel begins on the Silk Road

Reading **HELP**DESK ⓒⒸⓈⓈ

Academic Vocabulary

- **culture**
- **cycle**
- **classical**

Content Vocabulary

- **monotheism**
- **Mandate of Heaven**
- **oligarchy**
- **republic**
- **democratic**

TAKING NOTES:

Key Ideas and Details

Identifying As you read, create a table like the one below identifying the six major characteristics of a civilization.

Civilization	
1	4
2	5
3	6

LESSON 1
Ancient Civilizations

ESSENTIAL QUESTIONS

- *What are the characteristics of a civilization?*
- *How did patterns of civilization differ between the ancient and medieval worlds?*

IT MATTERS BECAUSE

Around 3000 B.C., civilizations began to emerge in four different areas—Western Asia, Egypt, India, and China—that gave rise to the great empires of the ancient world. These included the Persian and Assyrian Empires, the empire of Alexander the Great, the Roman Empire, the Mauryan and Gupta Empires in India, and a unified Chinese Empire.

The First Humans

GUIDING QUESTION *What factors contributed to the establishment of organized communities?*

Historians rely mostly on written records to understand the past. However, no written records exist for the prehistory of humankind. In fact, *prehistory* means the time before writing was developed. Prehistoric analysis relies on archaeology, the study of past societies through an analysis of what people left behind. Archaeologists dig up and examine artifacts such as tools, weapons, and art. They also use physics and chemistry to date human fossils and artifacts, through such tools as radiocarbon dating and thermoluminescence. Tools of forensic chemistry, such as the analysis of deoxyribonucleic acid (DNA), also provide information about early humans.

Humanlike creatures first emerged in Africa more than 3 to 4 million years ago. Over a long period of time, Paleolithic people learned to create more sophisticated tools, how to use fire, and how to adapt to and even change their physical environment. Paleolithic people were primarily nomads who hunted animals and gathered wild plants for survival. Their chief work was finding food, and men and women were responsible for it. Despite this consuming task, they created a human **culture** that included cave paintings.

The agricultural revolution of the New Stone Age, which began around 10,000 B.C., dramatically changed human patterns of living. The planting of grains and vegetables provided a regular supply of food, and the domestication of animals added a steady source of meat, milk, and fibers such as wool for clothing. This Neolithic Revolution made it possible for humans to stop their nomadic ways of living. Instead, they began to settle down and form more permanent settlements. These organized communities gradually gave rise to more complex human societies.

These more complex human societies, which we call the first civilizations, emerged around 3000 B.C. in the river valleys of Mesopotamia, Egypt, India, and China. An increase in food production in these regions led to a significant growth in human population and the growth of cities. Efforts to control the flow of water for farming also led to organized governments in these new urban civilizations. A civilization is a complex culture in which large numbers of human beings share a number of common elements. Six of the most important basic characteristics of civilizations are cities, government, religion, social structure, writing, and art. The emergence of civilizations was a dramatic new stage in the story of world history.

✔ **READING PROGRESS CHECK**

Determining Cause and Effect What were the effects of the Neolithic Revolution?

The First Civilizations: The Peoples of Western Asia and Egypt

GUIDING QUESTION *What were the first ancient civilizations to emerge?*

The peoples of Mesopotamia and Egypt built the first civilizations. They developed cities and struggled with the problems of organized states. They invented writing to keep records and also created literature. Mesopotamians and Egyptians constructed monumental buildings to please their gods, giving witness to the gods' power and preserving their culture for all time. They developed new political, military, social, and religious structures to deal with the basic problems of human existence and organization. These first civilizations left detailed records that allow us to view how they grappled with three of the fundamental problems that humans have thought about: the nature of human relationships, the nature of the universe, and the role of divine forces in that universe. Although later peoples would provide different answers from those of the Mesopotamians and Egyptians, it was they who first posed the questions, gave answers, and wrote them down.

By 1500 B.C., much of the creative impulse of the Mesopotamian and Egyptian civilizations was beginning to decline. By 1200 B.C., the decline of the Hittites and Egyptians had created a power vacuum that allowed a number of small states to emerge and flourish for a short while. One example are the Phoenicians, who created a trading empire in the Mediterranean and an alphabet that was later adapted by the Greeks and Romans.

Of these small states, perhaps the most important was that of the Israelites, who created a kingdom under Saul, David, and Solomon. By the tenth century B.C., the inhabitants of Israel had divided into a northern kingdom of Israel and a southern kingdom of Judah. Larger states in the region, however, eventually conquered them. Although the Israelites created no empire, they left

▼ Constructed under King Khufu around 2560 B.C., the Great Pyramid at Giza is the largest and most magnificent of all the pyramids.

▶ **CRITICAL THINKING**
Analyzing Pyramids were tombs for the mummified bodies of pharaohs. What symbolic importance did they serve?

Societies developed calendars to measure time and to record significant events. Most societies have adopted the Gregorian calendar for civil affairs. This Christian calendar was introduced in the late 1500s. On this calendar, the era after the birth of Jesus is labeled A.D., Latin for *anno Domini,* "in the year of our Lord." The years before Jesus' birth are referred to as B.C., for "before Christ." Alternatively, some label those eras, or large divisions of time, as B.C.E. "Before the Common Era" and C.E. "Common Era."

Scientists divide the past into time periods to help categorize information. Archaeologists often describe the past based on tool-making technology. For example, they named the Bronze Age for its prominent use of bronze tools. Historians often analyze the past by dividing time into fixed periods and periods based on events, such as the Age of the Enlightenment. They describe the world in terms of decades, periods of ten years, and centuries, periods of 100 years. For example, a historian might refer to the 1910s as the second decade of the twentieth century.

monotheism the belief in one God, rather than many

a spiritual legacy that influenced much of the later development of Western civilization. The evolution of Israelite **monotheism** established Judaism as a major world religion. Judaism influenced the development of Christianity and Islam. The Judeo-Christian heritage of Western civilization refers not only to the concept of monotheism, but also to the ideas of law, morality, and social justice that have become important parts of Western culture.

These small states were eventually overshadowed by the rise of the great empires of the Assyrians and Persians. The Assyrian Empire, built upon the effective use of military force, had been the first to unite almost all of the ancient Middle East. The empire of the Great Kings of Persia, however, was even larger. Although the Persian Empire owed much to the administrative organization developed by the Assyrians, the Persian Empire had peculiar strengths. Persian rule was tolerant as well as efficient. Conquered peoples were allowed to keep their religions, customs, and methods of doing business. The many years of peace that the Persian Empire brought to the Middle East aided trade and the general well-being of its peoples. It is no wonder that many peoples expressed their gratitude for being subjects of the Great Kings of Persia.

✓ READING PROGRESS CHECK

Making Connections What structures did early civilizations create to deal with problems of organization and questions about their existence?

The First Civilizations: Ancient India

GUIDING QUESTION *How did civilization develop in ancient India?*

As in Mesopotamia and Egypt, early civilizations in India emerged in river valleys. The Indus River valleys supported a thriving civilization between 3000 B.C. and 1500 B.C. that was based on two major cities, Harappa and Mohenjo-Daro. An advanced civilization—known as Harappan or Indus civilization—prospered in these cities for hundreds of years and made significant political and social achievements. Internal decline, however, weakened this civilization in the Indus River valley. The final blow to the cities might have been an influx of new peoples.

The Aryans were an Indo-European-speaking nomadic people who moved south across the Hindu Kush mountain range into the plains of northern India. The ongoing migrations and interaction between the Aryans and the Dravidians—descendents of the Indus Valley people—resulted in a new and unique culture. A rigid caste system, in which people were clearly divided into distinct classes, became a chief feature of the new Indian civilization.

Two of the world's major religions, Hinduism and Buddhism, began in India. Hinduism was an outgrowth of the religious beliefs of the Aryan peoples who settled in India. With its belief in reincarnation, Hinduism provided justification for the rigid caste system of India.

In the sixth century B.C., a new doctrine called Buddhism appeared in northern India. Buddhism was the product of one man, Siddhārtha Gautama. He claimed that he had awakened and seen the world in a new way. His simple message of achieving wisdom created a new spiritual philosophy that came to rival Hinduism.

For most of the time between 325 B.C. and A.D. 500, India was a land of many states. Two major empires, however, were able to create large, unified Indian states and an Indian civilization that set the standard for centuries.

The first of these empires, the Mauryan Empire in northern India, lasted from 324 B.C. until 183 B.C. The Mauryan Empire was at its height during the reign of Aśoka, who ruled from 269 B.C. until 232 B.C. Aśoka, who used Buddhist ideals to guide his rule, is considered to be the greatest ruler in the history of India.

In 183 B.C., the Mauryan Empire collapsed. India then fell back into disunity until a new empire arose. The Gupta Empire prospered from A.D. 320 until the invasion of the Huns reduced its power in the late fifth century. Both Indian empires experienced strong central government and artistic achievements. Indian civilization was extensive and eventually, in the form of Hinduism and Buddhism, spread to China and Southeast Asia.

☑ READING PROGRESS CHECK

Identifying Which two major religions began in India, and how did they influence society?

The First Civilizations: Ancient China

GUIDING QUESTION *What was significant about the first civilizations in China?*

Of the great civilizations we have discussed so far, China was the last to fully emerge. By the time the Shang dynasty began to display the first signs of an organized state, the societies in Mesopotamia, Egypt, and India had already reached an advanced level of civilization. Not enough is known about the early stages of any of these civilizations to allow us to determine why some developed earlier than others. One likely reason for China's late arrival was that it was virtually isolated from other emerging centers of culture elsewhere in the world. It was forced to develop on its own.

The Shang dynasty created the first flourishing Chinese civilization. Under the Shang, China developed organized government, a system of writing, a lunar calendar, and advanced skills in the making of bronze vessels. During the Zhou dynasty, China began to adopt many of the features that characterized Chinese civilization for centuries. Especially important politically was the **Mandate of Heaven**, which supposedly gave kings a divine right to rule. This was closely tied to the pattern of dynastic **cycles**. Up to A.D. 1912, China was ruled by a series of dynasties. The Zhou dynasty lasted for almost 800 years. Others did not last as long, but the king of each dynasty ruled with the Mandate of Heaven. The family, with its ideal of filial piety, emerged as a powerful economic and social unit during the Zhou dynasty.

Between 500 B.C. and 200 B.C., three major schools of thought emerged in China—Confucianism, Daoism, and Legalism. All three sought to spell out the principles that would create a stable order in society. All three came to have an impact on Chinese civilization that lasted until the twentieth century.

After 200 years of civil war, a new dynasty known as the Qin created a new era of Chinese unity. But the first Qin emperor was also the last of his dynasty. A new dynasty—the Han—established a vast empire that lasted more than 400 years. During the glory years of the Han dynasty, China extended the boundaries of its empire far into the sands of Central Asia and southward along the coast of the South China Sea into what is modern-day Vietnam. Chinese culture appeared unrivaled, and its scientific and technological achievements were unsurpassed.

Mandate of Heaven claim by Chinese kings of the Zhou dynasty that they had direct authority from heaven to rule and keep order in the universe

cycle a series of events that recur regularly and usually lead back to the starting point

▼ This Shang dynasty bronze vessel decorated with the heads of rams was used to store wine.

▶ CRITICAL THINKING
Inferring What might this artifact have conveyed to historians about life in ancient China?

One reason for China's striking success was that, unlike other civilizations of its time, it was for a long time able to fend off the danger from nomadic peoples along the northern frontier. By the end of the second century B.C., however, the presence of the Xiongnu was becoming a threat, and tribal warriors began to nip at the borders of the empire. Although the dynasty was strong and the problem was manageable, when internal difficulties began to weaken the unity of the state, China became vulnerable to the threat from the north and entered a time of troubles.

✓ READING PROGRESS CHECK

Outlining What differentiated the first three major dynasties in China?

The Civilization of the Greeks

GUIDING QUESTION *What contributed to the rise and fall of the civilization of the ancient Greeks?*

Unlike the great centralized empires of the Persians and the Chinese, ancient Greece consisted of a large number of small, independent city-states. The *polis*, or city-state, was a community of citizens ruled by its male citizens. The two most famous city-states were Sparta, a militaristic polis ruled by an **oligarchy**, and Athens, which became known for its **democratic** institutions in spite of the fact that many slaves and women had no political rights.

The Greek city-states thrived and reached their height in the **Classical** era of the fifth century B.C. The century began with the Persian wars, which temporarily unified the Greeks, who were victorious against the powerful Persian Empire. But the growth of an Athenian empire in that same century led to a mighty conflict with Sparta—the Great Peloponnesian War. This led to a weakening of the Greek city-states that led to an invasion by Philip II of Macedonia that put an end to the freedom of the Greeks in 338 B.C.

Despite the small size of their city-states, these ancient Greeks created a civilization that was the source of Western culture. Socrates, Plato, and Aristotle established the foundations of Western philosophy. Western literary forms are largely derived from Greek poetry and drama. Greek notions of harmony, proportion, and beauty have remained the touchstones for all subsequent Western art. A rational method of inquiry, important to modern science, was conceived in ancient Greece. Many political terms are Greek in origin, as are the concepts of the rights and duties of citizenship, especially as they were conceived in Athens, the first great democracy the world had seen. Especially during the Classical era, the Greeks raised and debated fundamental questions about the purpose of human existence, the structure of human society, and the nature of the universe that have concerned thinkers ever since.

The Greeks were unable to rise above the rivalries that caused them to fight each other and undermine their civilization. Although the Greeks lost their freedom to Philip II, Greek culture did not die. A new age, known as the Hellenistic era, eventually came into being.

That era began with the conquest of the Persian Empire by Alexander the Great, the young successor to his father, Philip II. Alexander, vowing to avenge the Persian attacks on Greece, crossed into Asia Minor with his army in 334 B.C. Within four years, the Persian Empire was defeated. Alexander, never at rest, moved eastward into India. There, a mutiny by his exhausted troops forced him to return to Babylon, where he died in 323 B.C. Alexander was a great military leader, but not a good political administrator. He failed to establish any definite structure for the empire. Four Hellenistic kingdoms emerged as the successors to Alexander.

oligarchy "the rule of the few"; a form of government in which a select group of people exercises control

democratic when people are governed by the "rule of many," or by the people, either directly or through their elected representatives

classical authoritative, traditional; relating to the literature, art, architecture, and ideals of the ancient Greek and Roman world

▲ This bronze helmet and breastplate are from the time of the Peloponnesian War in the fifth century B.C.

▶ **CRITICAL THINKING**
Drawing Conclusions What purpose might these artifacts have served?

PHOTO: Erich Lessing/Art Resource, NY

Within those kingdoms, the resulting society is known as Hellenistic, meaning to "imitate Greeks." The Greek language became dominant as Greek ideas became influential. Greek merchants, artists, philosophers, and soldiers found opportunities and rewards throughout the Middle East, now a world of kingdoms rather than independent city-states.

The Hellenistic period was, in its own way, a vibrant one. New cities arose and flourished. New philosophical doctrines—such as Epicureanism and Stoicism—captured the minds of many. Significant achievements occurred in literature and science, and Greek culture spread throughout the Middle East and made an impact wherever it was carried. Although the Hellenistic era achieved a degree of political stability, by the late third century B.C., signs of decline were beginning to multiply, and the growing power of Rome eventually endangered the Hellenistic world.

☑ READING PROGRESS CHECK

Recognizing Relationships What was the legacy of the Greeks to Western civilization?

The World of the Romans

GUIDING QUESTION *What characteristics defined Roman rule?*

Sometime in the eighth century B.C., a group of Latin-speaking people built a small community called Rome on the Tiber River in Italy. Between 509 and 264 B.C., this city expanded and united almost all of Italy under its control. Roman diplomacy was as important as its armies in achieving this goal. Roman rule was made acceptable by allowing local autonomy and gradually granting Roman citizenship to non-Romans. During this time of conquest, Rome also developed the political institutions of a **republic** ruled by an aristocratic oligarchy.

Although Rome had no master plan for expansion, its relationship with its neighbors outside of Italy soon led to involvement in new wars. Its first challenge was Carthage and the Carthaginian Empire in Spain and Africa. Rome was victorious after the three long and bloody Punic Wars. In the east, Rome conquered Macedonia and also took control of the Greek states. Between 264 and 133 B.C., Rome expanded to the west and east and became master of the Mediterranean Sea.

After 133 B.C., Rome's republican institutions proved to be inadequate for the task of ruling an empire. In the breakdown that ensued, ambitious individuals such as Pompey, Crassus, and Julius Caesar saw opportunities for power unparalleled in Roman history and succumbed to the temptations. At the beginning of the first century, military reforms had made possible the creation of professional armies that were loyal to the generals who recruited them, rather than to the state. Bloody civil war ensued as powerful individuals jockeyed for power. Peace was finally achieved when Octavian defeated Antony and Cleopatra.

After a series of bloody civil wars, Octavian, who came to be known by the title of Augustus, created a new order that began the Roman Empire. He did not declare the Republic dead and continued to give the Senate a role in governing. But most of the political power remained in the hands of Augustus. He became the first Roman emperor. The army swore loyalty to him, and the return of peace soon made the new political order acceptable to most people in the empire. In the second century, five "good emperors"

▲ *The Winged Victory of Samothrace,* a marble statue dated circa 190 B.C., embodies the artistic movement of Hellenistic Greece.

republic a form of government in which the leader is not a king and certain citizens have the right to vote

maintained a period of peace and prosperity in which trade flourished and the provinces were governed efficiently. The Roman Empire developed a remarkable series of achievements that were bequeathed to the future.

These achievements were fundamental to the development of Western civilization, a civilization that consisted largely of lands in Europe conquered by the Romans, in which Roman culture and political ideals were gradually spread. The Romance languages of today—French, Italian, Spanish, Portuguese, and Romanian—are based on Latin. Western practices of impartial justice and trial by jury owe much to Roman law. As great builders, the Romans left monuments to their skills throughout Europe, some of which, including aqueducts and roads, are still in use today. Other monuments provided models for public buildings in the West for hundreds of years. Aspects of Roman administrative practices survived in the Western world for centuries. The Romans also preserved the intellectual heritage of the Greco-Roman world of antiquity.

By the third century, however, the Roman world was suffering an era of decline. Generals fought each other in civil wars. German tribes and Persian armies invaded the empire. There were plagues, population decline, and economic problems. At the same time, a new religion—Christianity— was spreading throughout the empire. Like Judaism, Christianity was monotheistic. Beginning among the followers of Jesus of Nazareth, Christianity, with its promise of salvation and its universality as a religion for all, slowly gained acceptance. In Rome's last 200 years, as Christianity with its ideals of spiritual equality and respect for human life grew, a slow transformation of the Roman world took place. The Germanic invasions hastened this process and brought an end to the Western Roman Empire in A.D. 476. Many aspects of the Roman world continued, but a new civilization was emerging that carried on another stage in the development of human society.

▼ Gladiatorial games were held in amphitheaters throughout the Roman world. The most famous was the Colosseum in Rome.

▶ **CRITICAL THINKING**
Making Connections What types of modern buildings resemble the Colosseum?

PHOTO: ©Image Source/PunchStock

✓ **READING PROGRESS CHECK**

Summarizing How and why did Rome make the transition from a republic to an empire?

LESSON 1 REVIEW

Reviewing Vocabulary
1. ***Making Connections*** How did rule differ under oligarchies, democracies, and republics?

Using Your Notes
2. ***Identifying*** Use your notes to identify the characteristics of a civilization.

Answering the Guiding Questions
3. ***Drawing Conclusions*** What factors contributed to the establishment of organized communities?

4. ***Inferring*** What were the first ancient civilizations to emerge?

5. ***Making Generalizations*** How did civilization develop in ancient India?

6. ***Analyzing*** What was significant about the first civilizations in China?

7. ***Explaining*** What contributed to the rise and fall of the civilization of the ancient Greeks?

8. ***Evaluating*** What characteristics defined Roman rule?

Writing Activity
9. **NARRATIVE** Imagine you are a nomad, moving from place to place to survive. Which factors would you need to settle in one place, start a community, and eventually form a successful civilization?

Reading **HELP** DESK CCSS

Academic Vocabulary

- **prospered** • **traditional**
- **revival**

Content Vocabulary

- **lineage group**
- **landed aristocrats**
- **sultanate**
- **Crusades**
- **feudalism**

TAKING NOTES:
Key Ideas and Detail

Categorizing As you read, use a graphic organizer like the one below to help identify characteristics of societies in the Islamic world, Africa, Asia, Europe and the Americas.

	Characteristics
Islamic World	
Africa	
Asia	
Europe	
Americas	

LESSON 2
New Patterns of Civilization

ESSENTIAL QUESTION
How did patterns of civilization differ between the ancient and medieval worlds?

IT MATTERS BECAUSE

By the beginning of the first millennium A.D., the great states of the ancient world were mostly in decline or at the point of collapse. On the ruins of these ancient empires, new patterns of civilization began to take shape between 400 and 1500. At the same time, new civilizations were also beginning to appear in Japan, in Southeast Asia, in Africa, and in the Americas. All these states were increasingly linked by trade into the first "global civilization."

The World of Islam

GUIDING QUESTION *What factors contributed to the development of the Arab Empire?*

In the seventh century, a new force arose in the Arabian Peninsula and spread rapidly throughout the region of the Middle East. This new force was a new religion called Islam, meaning "peace through submission to the will of Allah,"—and it was founded by a man named Muhammad. Islam, like Judaism and Christianity, is a monotheistic religion. After Muhammad's death, his successors—known as caliphs—organized the Arabs and set in motion a great expansion. Arab armies moved westward across North Africa and into Spain and eastward into the Persian Empire, conquering Syria and Mesopotamia.

In 661 this Arab Empire came under the control of the Umayyad dynasty. Under the Umayyads, the capital of the empire was moved from Madinah to Damascus, in Syria. In 750 Abū al-'Abbās, a descendant of Muhammad's uncle, overthrew the Umayyad dynasty and set up the Abbasid dynasty. Twelve years later, the Abbasids built a new capital city at Baghdad on the Tigris River, taking advantage of trading routes. The Abbasids were weakened by the Seljuk Turks and in 1258 fell to the Mongols.

Islamic civilization was built upon the teachings of the Quran, the holy book of Islam. Eventually, caliphs came to rule more like kings than spiritual leaders. Much of the prosperity of the Islamic civilization was based on trade within the Islamic world and with

▲ The Islamic calendar is lunar, or based on the phases of the moon. Astronomy was used to identify Islamic holy days and the beginning and ending of holy months.

▶ **CRITICAL THINKING**
Making Inferences Why might astronomers have played an important role in Islamic and other societies?

China, the Byzantine Empire, India, and Southeast Asia. Trade was carried both by ship and by camel caravan.

Muslim Arabs absorbed many scientific and technological achievments of the people they conquered. At the same time, they made advances of their own, especially in mathematics and the natural sciences, such as astronomy and medicine. In literature and art, the Muslim world combined Islamic ideals with pre-Islamic traditions to create original works. Mosques from this period that remain standing today are visible symbols of the greatness of Islamic art and architecture.

Like other empires in the Middle East, the Arab Empire did not last. Nevertheless, it made an impact. Islam brought a code of law and a written language to societies that were previously without these features. By creating a renewed trade network stretching from West Africa to East Asia, it brought untold wealth to thousands of people and a better life to millions.

By the end of the thirteenth century, the Arab Empire was no more than a memory. But it left a powerful legacy in Islam, which remains one of the major religions of the world. The spread of Islam to Africa and other parts of Asia ensured that it would affect more than just the Middle East.

☑ **READING PROGRESS CHECK**

Understanding Relationships How did Islam influence the rule of the Arab Empire?

Early African Civilizations

GUIDING QUESTION *What defined the economies and societies of trading states in Africa?*

The mastery of agriculture gave rise to three early civilizations in Africa—Egypt, Kush, and Axum. Later, new states emerged in different parts of Africa, some of them strongly influenced by the spread of Islam. Zimbabwe, which emerged around 1300, was important in southern Africa.

Ghana, Mali, and Songhai were three flourishing trading states in West Africa. Mali and Songhai were especially important. One of the most powerful kings of Mali was Mansa Mūsā, who ruled from 1312 to 1337. Mansa Mūsā doubled the size of Mali. As a devout Muslim, he made a pilgrimage to Makkah. He also made his capital city at Timbuktu a center of Islamic learning and culture. By the fifteenth century, a new kingdom—Songhai—was beginning to surpass Mali. The Songhai Empire reached the height of its power during the reign of Muhammad Ture. The chief cities of the empire **prospered** as never before from the salt and gold trade until the end of the sixteenth century.

The African continent was also an active participant in emerging regional and global trade with the Mediterranean world and across the Indian Ocean. Although the state-building process in Africa south of the Sahara was still in its early stages compared with the ancient civilizations of India, China, and Mesopotamia, in many respects these new states were as impressive and sophisticated as their counterparts elsewhere in the world.

Due to a lack of written records, we know little about early African society and culture. The relationship between king and subjects was often less rigid in African society than in other civilizations. Family, especially **lineage groups**, were basic units in African society. Religious beliefs in many African societies focused on many gods, nature spirits, the role of diviners, and the importance of ancestors. Africans produced a distinctive

prosper to succeed in an activity; to have economic success

lineage group an extended family unit within a larger community

culture in wood carving, sculpture, music, and architecture.

In the fifteenth century, a new factor came to affect Africa. Fleets from Portugal began to probe southward along the coast of West Africa. At first, the Portuguese were in search of gold and slaves, but when their ships rounded the southern coast of Africa by 1500, they began to seek domination of the Indian Ocean trade as well. The new situation posed a threat to the peoples of Africa, whose new states would be severely tested by the demands of the Europeans.

The peoples of Africa were not the only ones to confront a new threat from Europe at the beginning of the sixteenth century. When the Portuguese sailed across the Indian Ocean, they sought to reach India, where the Mogul Empire was in the throes of creation.

☑ **READING PROGRESS CHECK**

Explaining How did trade play a role in the development of early African states?

The Medieval Asian World

GUIDING QUESTION *What were the successes and challenges of medieval Asia?*

China fell into chaos after the Han dynasty ended. In 581 a new Chinese dynasty known as the Sui was established. During the Sui, Tang, and Song dynasties, which together ruled for almost 700 years, Chinese civilization flourished once again. A mature political system based on principles first put into practice during the Qin and Han dynasties gradually emerged in China. As in the Han era, China was a monarchy with a large bureaucracy. Confucian ideals were still the cement that held the system together. The Mongols overthrew the Song dynasty and established a new dynasty in 1279. Although Mongol rulers adapted to the Chinese political system, this dynasty also failed to last, and in 1369 a new Ming dynasty came into power.

During the thousand years of these five dynasties, China advanced in many ways. Industry and trade grew in size and technological capacity, while in the countryside a flourishing agriculture bolstered China's economic prosperity. In Chinese cities, technological developments added new products and stimulated trade. During the Tang dynasty, for example, the Chinese began to make steel for swords and sickles and invented gunpowder, which was used for explosives.

Chinese society also achieved a level of development and stability that was the envy of observers from other lands, near and far. The civil service provided for a stable government bureaucracy and an avenue of upward mobility that was virtually unknown elsewhere in the world. China's achievements were unsurpassed throughout the world, making it a civilization that was the envy of its neighbors and of the world. It also influenced other states in the region, including Japan.

Few societies in Asia have historically been as isolated as Japan. Cut off from the mainland by 120 miles of ocean, the Japanese had little contact with the outside world during most of their early development. However, after the Japanese became acquainted with Chinese culture, they were quick to take advantage of the opportunity. In the space of a few decades, the young state adopted many features of Chinese society and culture and thereby introduced major changes into the Japanese way of life. Nevertheless, although early Japanese rulers such as Shōtoku Taishi (a prince of the Yamato clan) tried to create a centralized political system like that of China,

▲ This ceremonial ivory armlet was worn by kings of Benin.

▲ This piece of art portrays the samurai hero, Kumagai Naozane, at the Battle of Ichinotani in Japan in 1184.

landed aristocrats an upper class whose wealth is based on land and whose power is passed on from one generation to another

sultanate a state whose military and political power is held by the sultan

traditional established; customary

the power of **landed aristocrats** ensured a weak central authority. The result was a society that was able to make use of ideas imported from beyond its borders without endangering customs, beliefs, and institutions inherited from the past.

Between 500 and 1500, civilization in India faced a number of severe challenges. One was an ongoing threat from beyond the mountains in the northwest. A group of rebellious Turkish slaves founded a new Islamic state called Ghazna, located in present-day Afghanistan. In 997 a new leader, Maḥmūd of Ghazna, began to attack neighboring Hindu kingdoms to the southeast. By 1200, Muslim power encompassed the entire plain of northern India, creating a new Muslim state known as the **sultanate** of Delhi. The impact of Islam on Indian civilization is still evident today in the division of the Indian subcontinent into mostly Hindu India and two Islamic states, Pakistan and Bangladesh.

A second challenge to India came from the tradition of internal rivalry that had marked Indian civilization for hundreds of years. After the fall of the Guptas, that tradition continued almost without interruption down to the sixteenth century. The third challenge appeared in the religious divisions (originally between Hindus and Buddhists and later between Hindus and Muslims) that took place throughout much of this period. In India, Hinduism was able to absorb Buddhism and reassert its dominant position in Indian society. But that victory was short-lived. One result of the Turkish conquest of northern India was the introduction of Islam into the region. The new religion became a serious rival to **traditional** beliefs among the Indian people.

Situated at the crossroads between two oceans and two great civilizations, Southeast Asia has long served as a bridge linking peoples and cultures. Despite the central position that Southeast Asia occupied in the ancient world, complex societies were slow to take form in the region. When they began to appear, they were strongly influenced by the older civilizations of neighboring China and India. In Vietnam, the Chinese imposed their culture by conquest. Elsewhere, merchants and missionaries brought Indian influence. Whatever the means, all the young states throughout the region—Vietnam, Angkor, Thailand, the Burmese kingdom of Pagan, and several states on the Malay peninsula and Indonesian archipelago—were heavily affected by foreign ideas and adopted them as a part of their own cultures. And yet, the Southeast Asian peoples, like the Japanese, put their unique stamp on the ideas that they adopted. The result was a region marked by cultural richness and diversity that was rooted in the local culture.

✓ **READING PROGRESS CHECK**

Summarizing How did the various societies in medieval Asia interact with each other?

Europe in the Middle Ages

GUIDING QUESTION *How did a new European civilization develop after the fall of the Roman Empire?*

After the collapse of the Roman Empire and the establishment of the Germanic states, a new European civilization slowly began to emerge in the Early Middle Ages. The coronation of Charlemagne—a descendant of a Germanic tribe converted to Christianity—as Roman emperor in 800 symbolized the fusion of the three chief components of the new European civilization: the German tribes, the Roman legacy, and the Christian church.

In the long run, the creation of Charlemagne's empire, the Carolingian Empire, fostered the idea of a distinct European identity. The lands north of the Alps now became the political center of Europe. Increasingly, Europe emerged as the focus and center of Western civilization.

With the disintegration of the Carolingian Empire, new forms of political institutions began to develop in Europe. **Feudalism** put power into the hands of many different lords, who came to constitute a powerful group of nobles that dominated the political, economic, and social life of Europe.

The new European civilization that had emerged in the ninth and tenth centuries began to come into its own in the eleventh and twelfth centuries, and Europeans established new patterns that reached their high point in the thirteenth century. The High Middle Ages, from around 1000 to around 1300, was a period of growth for Western civilization, characterized by a burst of energy and enthusiasm. An increase in agricultural production helped sustain a dramatic rise in population that was physically apparent in the expansion of towns and cities.

The development of trade, the expansion of towns and cities, and the development of a money economy added a dynamic new element to European civilization. Although these developments did not mean the end of a mostly rural European society, they opened the door to new opportunities for people to expand and enrich their lives. Eventually, they created the foundations for the development of a mostly urban industrial society.

During the High Middle Ages, European society was dominated by a landed aristocracy whose primary function was to fight. These nobles built innumerable castles that gave a distinctive look to the countryside. Over time, however, medieval kings began to exert a centralizing authority and to develop new kinds of monarchical states. Although they could not know it then, their actions laid the foundations for the European kingdoms that have dominated the European political scene ever since.

During the High Middle Ages, the power of nobles and kings was often overshadowed by the authority of the Catholic Church. It was perhaps the dominant institution of the era. The High Middle Ages witnessed a spiritual **revival** that transformed European society. Spiritual renewal during the period led to many and sometimes divergent paths: strong papal leadership, a dramatic increase in the number and size of churches, new religious orders, and the "Holy Warrior" in the **Crusades**—a military effort to recover the Holy Land of the Near East from the Muslims. All these paths seemed to reflect a greater concern for salvation.

A burst of intellectual and artistic activity also characterized the High Middle Ages. An intellectual revival led to new centers of learning in universities and to the use of reason to develop new ways of thought in theology. At the same time, a boom in the construction of religious buildings—especially evident in the great Romanesque and Gothic cathedrals—left Europe covered with churches. They were the visible symbols of Christian Europe's vitality.

European society in the fourteenth century, however, was challenged by an overwhelming number of disastrous forces. A devastating plague known as the Black Death that wiped out one-third of the European population, a decline in trade and industry, constant warfare, political instability, a decline of church power, and the spectacle of two popes

feudalism political and social order that developed during the Middle Ages when royal governments were no longer able to defend their subjects; nobles offered protection and land in return for service.

revival renewed attention to, or interest in, something

Crusades military expeditions carried out by European Christians in the Middle Ages to regain the Holy Land from the Muslims

▼ In this fourteenth-century English text, a priest blesses monks who have the bubonic plague.

▶ CRITICAL THINKING
Speculating How might it have been interpreted that religious figures died from the plague?

condemning each other seemed to overpower Europeans. No doubt, to some people it appeared that the last days of the world were at hand. But out of the collapse of medieval civilization came a rebirth of culture known as the Renaissance.

☑ **READING PROGRESS CHECK**

Making Connections What was the role of the Catholic Church in medieval Europe?

The Byzantine Empire

GUIDING QUESTION *What factors contributed to the emergence and success of the Byzantine Empire?*

After the collapse of Roman power in Western Europe, the Late Roman Empire in the East, or the Eastern Roman Empire, continued in the eastern Mediterranean. It eventually emerged as the Byzantine Empire, which prospered for hundreds of years. While a new Christian civilization arose in Europe, the Byzantine Empire created a unique Christian civilization. And while Europe struggled in the Early Middle Ages, the Byzantine world continued to prosper and flourish. Especially during the ninth, tenth, and eleventh centuries under the Macedonian emperors, the Byzantine Empire expanded and achieved an economic prosperity that was evident to foreign visitors who frequently praised the size, wealth, and physical surroundings of the central city of Constantinople.

▲ This early eleventh-century Byzantine mosaic depicts the Christian figures of Mary and her child, Jesus.

During its heyday, Byzantium was a multicultural and multi-ethnic world empire that ruled a remarkable number of peoples who spoke different languages. Byzantine cultural and religious forms spread to the Balkans, parts of central Europe, and Russia. Byzantine scholars spread the study of the Greek language to Italy, expanding Renaissance humanism with an interest in classical Greek civilization. The Byzantine Empire interacted with the world of Islam to its east and the new European civilization of the west. Both interactions proved costly and ultimately fatal. Although European civilization and Byzantine civilization shared a common bond in Christianity, the bond proved incapable of keeping them in harmony politically. Indeed, the west's Crusades to the Palestine region, for claimed religious motives, led to western control of the Byzantine Empire from 1204 to 1261. Although the empire technically was restored, it limped along. Ultimately its other inter-action—with the Muslim world—led to its demise when the Ottoman Turks conquered the city of Constantinople and made it the center of their empire.

☑ **READING PROGRESS CHECK**

Identifying In what way was the Byzantine Empire multicultural?

The World of the Americas

GUIDING QUESTION *Which civilizations flourished in the Americas before the arrival of Europeans?*

Around 5000 B.C., farming settlements began to appear in river valleys and upland areas in Central and South America. Not long afterward, organized communities developed along the coast of the Gulf of Mexico and the western slopes of the central Andes Mountains.

The Olmec, the first-known civilization in Mesoamerica, appeared around 1200 B.C. Aspects of their tradition influenced later Mesoamerican societies. For example, the Olmec played a ceremonial game on a stone ball court that was later played by the Zapotec and Maya. The Maya and the Aztec were especially successful in developing advanced and prosperous civilizations. Both cultures built elaborate cities that had pyramids, temples, and palaces. Both were polytheistic, worshiping many gods and goddesses. Mayan civilization collapsed in the ninth century, and the Aztecs fell to Spanish invaders in the sixteenth century.

In the fifteenth century the Inca Empire thrived in South America along the Andes. It was carefully planned and regulated, which is especially evident in the extensive network of roads that connected all parts of the empire. Despite this, the Inca eventually fell to Spanish invaders, due to a lack of advanced weaponry. Years before the Inca, around 900 B.C., the Chavin emerged in the Andean region of modern-day Peru. Their stone temples provide evidence of this early South American people.

While the Maya, Aztec, and Inca were developing their civilizations, the peoples of North America were creating a remarkable number of different cultures. The Inuit, Mound Builders, Anasazi, Plains Amerindians, and Iroquois developed societies that responded in unique ways to the environmental conditions that they faced.

All these societies in the Americas developed in apparently total isolation from their counterparts elsewhere in the world. This deprived them of access to developments taking place in Africa, Asia, and Europe, such as the wheel. Also their written languages were not as sophisticated as those in other parts of the world. But in other respects, their cultural achievements were equal to those realized elsewhere. When the first European explorers arrived in the Americas at the beginning of the sixteenth century, they described much that they observed in glowing terms. One need only point to the awed comments of early Spanish visitors who said that the cities of the Aztecs were the equal of any found in Spain.

Unfortunately for their own needs, one development that the peoples of America lacked was the knowledge of firearms. In a few short years, tiny bands of Spanish explorers were able to conquer the magnificent civilizations of the Americas and turn them into ruins.

▲ A figurine of Huitzilopochtli, the Aztec god of the sun and of war.

▶ **CRITICAL THINKING**
Determining Importance Why might Huitzilopochtli have been particularly important to the Aztecs?

 READING PROGRESS CHECK

Making Inferences What factors indicate that the peoples of Central and South America had organized societies?

LESSON 2 REVIEW (CCSS)

Reviewing Vocabulary
1. ***Contrasting*** What is the difference in authority between an aristocracy and a sultanate?

Using Your Notes
2. ***Summarizing*** Use your notes to summarize the characteristics of two major civilizations that emerged in Africa, Asia, Europe, and the Americas after the collapse of ancient empires.

Answering the Guiding Questions
3. ***Analyzing*** What factors contributed to the development of the Arab Empire?

4. ***Identifying*** What defined the economies and societies of trading states in Africa?

5. ***Evaluating*** What were the successes and challenges of medieval Asia?

6. ***Making Connections*** How did a new European civilization develop after the fall of the Roman Empire?

7. ***Describing*** What factors contributed to the emergence and success of the Byzantine Empire?

8. ***Identifying*** Which civilizations flourished in the Americas before the arrival of Europeans?

Writing Activity
9. **ARGUMENT** In what ways did the civilizations described in this lesson interact with and influence each other? Which civilization do you think had the greatest impact on society? Write an essay arguing your choice. Provide evidence to support your claims.

Directions: On a separate sheet of paper, answer the questions below. Make sure you read carefully and answer all parts of the questions.

Lesson Review

Lesson 1

❶ **STATING** Which civilization had the first great democracy in the world? How has this civilization influenced the politics of Western culture?

❷ **DRAWING CONCLUSIONS** Explain the social structure of the new Indian civilization. How did belief in the process of reincarnation provide a justification for this system?

Lesson 2

❸ **SUMMARIZING** Under what group of emperors did the Byzantine Empire expand and prosper? What city in particular attracted the attention of foreign visitors? Why?

❹ **IDENTIFYING** What political institution began to emerge in Europe after the Carolingian Empire? Who gained power as a result?

21st Century Skills

❺ **IDENTIFYING CAUSE AND EFFECT** Which other major world religions were influenced by Judaism? In what other ways did Judaism influence Western culture?

❻ **ECONOMICS** Under whose reign did the Songhai Empire reach its height? What was the key factor that allowed it to prosper?

❼ **COMPARE AND CONTRAST** How are the major beliefs and principles of Judaism, Christianity, and Islam similar? What are their major differences?

❽ **CREATE AND AND ANALYZE ARGUMENTS** Create an argument that explains the similarities between the decline of Rome and fall of the Qin dynasty. Then write an essay that analyzes the argument and explains why it is or is not valid.

Exploring the Essential Questions

❾ **SYNTHESIZING** Write an essay explaining the characteristics of a civilization. Then create a two-column table to contrast patterns of civilization between the ancient and medieval worlds. Be prepared to present your paper and table and to give examples for each element contrasted in the table.

DBQ Analyzing Historical Documents

Use the document to answer the following questions.

The following is an excerpt from *The Early History of Rome*, written by Roman historian Livy. Livy was interested in what could be learned from history in terms of moral lessons, so his stories were not always factually accurate. The following tale is about a simple farmer, Cincinnatus, who the Senate names dictator to save Rome.

PRIMARY SOURCE

❝ A mission from the city found him [Cincinnatus] at work on his land—digging a ditch, maybe, or ploughing. Greetings were exchanged, and he was asked . . . to put on his toga and hear the Senate's instructions . . . he told his wife . . . to run to their cottage and fetch his toga . . . and wiping the grimy sweat from his hands and face he put it on; at once the envoys from the city saluted him, with congratulations, as Dictator. . . . ❞

—Livy, from *The Early History of Rome*

❿ **INTERPRETING** What is Livy's opinion of Cincinnatus?

⓫ **DISCUSSING** Is it important to be factually accurate as a historian? What is the value in teaching moral lessons through history?

Extended-Response Question

⓬ **INFORMATIVE/EXPLANATORY** Write a paragraph that explains how Greek and Roman civilizations impacted western civilization. Your response should include specific examples.

Need Extra Help?

If You've Missed Question	❶	❷	❸	❹	❺	❻	❼	❽	❾	❿	⓫	⓬
Go to page	8	6	16	15	6	12	6	7	5	18	18	8

The Renaissance in Europe

1350–1600

ESSENTIAL QUESTIONS
- *How can trade lead to economic prosperity and political power?*
- *How can ideas be reflected in art, sculpture, and architecture?*

networks

There's More Online! about the Renaissance in Europe.

CHAPTER 2

Lesson 1
The Italian States

Lesson 2
Ideas and Art of the Renaissance

The Story Matters...

The word *renaissance* means "rebirth." What was reborn during this period? One of the most enduring innovations of Renaissance culture was a new view of human beings. This outlook, embodied in the intellectual movement known as humanism, celebrated the extraordinary individual. The Italian artist Leonardo da Vinci, who was also an architect, inventor, and mathematician, was seen by those around him as a model of this humanist ideal.

◄ Depicting Mary, Jesus's mother in Christian tradition, Leonardo's painting *Virgin of the Rocks* shows the influence of Renaissance humanism in portraying a realistic form, but also takes it a step further to depict human perfection.

PHOTO: Leonardo da Vinci/The Bridgeman Art Library/Getty Images

19

Place and Time: Europe 1350–1600

The Renaissance began in northern Italy in the late fourteenth century and then spread throughout Europe. Renaissance culture developed in the unique political, social, and economic environment of Italy's small, independent states. Located on major trade routes, cities such as Milan and Florence were ideal places to receive and spread ideas. Florence, controlled by the Medici family, was perhaps the most influential city. Its scholars, writers, artists, and architects defined the culture of the Renaissance.

Step Into the Place

Read the quotes and review the information presented on the panorama of Renaissance Florence.

 Analyzing Historical Documents Why do you think the Medici family spent large amounts of money on the patronage of the arts in Florence?

PRIMARY SOURCE

❝Lorenzo [de' Medici, shown at right] showed the same favor to poetry in the vernacular, to music, architecture, painting, sculpture, and to all the arts of mind and hand, so that the city [of Florence] overflowed with all these exquisite things. And these arts flourished all the more because Lorenzo, a universal man, could pass judgment and distinguish among men, so that they competed with one another to please him.❞

—Francesco Guicciardini, from *History of Florence*

PRIMARY SOURCE

❝In the time of the elder Lorenzo de' Medici, Lorenzo the Magnificent, truly a golden age for men of talent, there flourished an artist called Alessandro . . . Botticelli.

. . . [Botticelli] carried out many works in the house of the Medici for Lorenzo the Magnificent, notably a life-size Pallas [Athena] on a shield wreathed with fiery branches, and a St Sebastian [a painting created for Florence's Santa Maria Maggiore church]. . . . As an old man, Botticelli found himself so poor that if Lorenzo de' Medici . . . and then his friends and other worthy men who loved him for his talent had not come to his assistance, he would have almost died of hunger.❞

—Giorgio Vasari, from *The Lives of the Artists*

Step Into the Time

Determining Cause and Effect Research one or more publications from the time line. Write a short essay explaining how the publication(s) increased political unrest in Italy and around the world.

ITALY

THE WORLD

1350	1400	1450

1434 Cosimo de' Medici takes control of Florence

1450 Sforzas become rulers of Milan

1452 Leonardo da Vinci is born

1352 Arab traveler Ibn Battuta visits African kingdom of Mali

1405 Zheng He begins a series of voyages

after 1438 Inca ruler Pachacuti expands empire

1453 Constantinople falls to Ottoman forces

networks
There's More Online!

☑ **MAP** Explore the interactive version of this map on Networks.

☑ **TIME LINE** Explore the interactive version of the time line on Networks.

FIORENZA

Panorama of Florence c. 1500

Cosimo de' Medici was a patron of architect Filippo Brunelleschi, who designed the Florence cathedral's dome.

Textile makers and bankers, such as the Medici family, dominated the economy of Florence.

In the Medici Palace Chapel, Benozzo Gozzoli's *Procession of the Magi* included portraits of his patrons.

Botticelli included Medici portraits in his *Adoration of the Magi* in the church of Santa Maria Novella.

Dante, Florence's greatest poet, claimed its people were motivated by envy and pride.

1455 Gutenberg Bible becomes the earliest book printed from moveable type in Europe

1492 Lorenzo de' Medici dies

1494 French king Charles VIII leads an army into Italy

1513 Machiavelli's *The Prince* is completed

1527 German troops of Charles I pillage Rome

1559 Italian Wars end

1500

1550

1600

1492 Columbus reaches the West Indies

1498 Portuguese expedition under Vasco da Gama reaches India

1520 Süleyman I becomes Ottoman sultan

1530 Bābur, first Mogul emperor of India, dies at Agra

1558 Elizabeth I becomes queen of England

1571 Christian forces defeat Ottomans in naval battle at Lepanto

netw⊙rks

There's More Online!

BIOGRAPHY Lorenzo de' Medici

BIOGRAPHY Niccolò Machiavelli

IMAGE Procession of the Magi

INTERACTIVE SELF-CHECK QUIZ

MAP Italy, 1500

PRIMARY SOURCE The Book of the Courtier

TIME LINE Italian Wars

VIDEO The Italian States

Reading **HELP**DESK (CCSS)

Academic Vocabulary

• **dominate** • **decline**

Content Vocabulary

• **mercenary** • **burgher**
• **republic**

TAKING NOTES:

Key Ideas and Details

Identifying Use a graphic organizer like this one to identify the major principles of Machiavelli's work, *The Prince.*

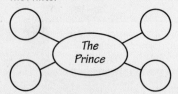

The Prince

LESSON 1
The Italian States

ESSENTIAL QUESTION
How can trade lead to economic prosperity and political power?

IT MATTERS BECAUSE

The Renaissance served as a bridge between the Middle Ages and modern times. Beginning in the prosperous states of Italy, the Renaissance marked the emergence of a new urban culture that was largely spread by trade. This culture had a more worldly outlook than that of the Middle Ages.

The Major Italian States

GUIDING QUESTIONS *What contributed to the rise of the Italian states during the Renaissance? How did Machiavelli's work influence political power in the Western world?*

In the late Middle Ages, Italy was much more urban than the rest of Europe, and a thriving trade network was based in Italy's many cities. The energy that trade gave to Italy's urban environment encouraged an exchange of ideas that helped stimulate the development of Renaissance culture.

Italy had prospered from a flourishing trade that had expanded during the Middle Ages. Italian cities such as Venice had taken the lead in establishing merchant fleets and trading with the Byzantine and Islamic civilizations to the east. High demand for Middle Eastern goods enabled Italian merchants to set up trading centers in eastern ports. There they obtained silks, sugar, and spices, which were sent back to Europe.

Italian trading ships had also moved into the western Mediterranean and then north along the Atlantic seaboard. These ships exchanged goods with merchants in England and the Netherlands. Goods, however, were not the only cargo. The ideas of the Renaissance, developed in Italy, spread north along trade routes to the rest of Europe.

During the Middle Ages, Italy had failed to develop a centralized monarchical state. The lack of a single strong ruler made it possible for a number of city-states in northern and central Italy to remain independent. By early in the fifteenth century, five major territorial states had come to **dominate** the peninsula. These were the city-states of Milan, Venice, and Florence, the Papal States centered on Rome, and the Kingdom of Naples. Because of their economic power, these states played crucial roles in Italian politics and culture.

Economics and Politics in the Major Italian States

Each of the five major territorial states dominated the economic and political life of its region. Milan, Venice, and Florence were located in northern Italy. One of the richest city-states, Milan stood at the crossroads of the main trade routes from Italian coastal cities to the Alpine passes. In the fourteenth century, members of the Visconti family established themselves as dukes of Milan. They extended their power over the surrounding territory of Lombardy. The last Visconti ruler of Milan died in 1447. Francesco Sforza (SFAWRT • sah) led a band of **mercenaries**—soldiers who fought primarily for money. Sforza conquered the city and became its duke. The Visconti and Sforza rulers built a strong centralized state. Using an efficient tax system, the Sforzas generated huge revenues for the government.

Another major northern Italian city-state, Venice, served as a commercial link between Asia and Western Europe. The city drew traders from around the world. Officially, Venice was a **republic** with an elected

dominate to influence or control

mercenary a soldier who fights primarily for pay

republic a form of government in which the leader is not a king and certain citizens have the right to vote

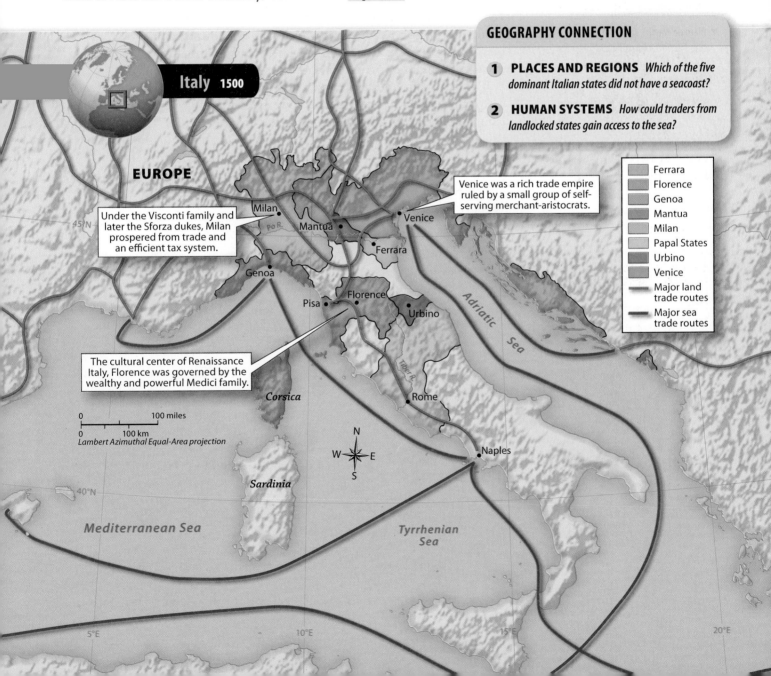

GEOGRAPHY CONNECTION

1 **PLACES AND REGIONS** *Which of the five dominant Italian states did not have a seacoast?*

2 **HUMAN SYSTEMS** *How could traders from landlocked states gain access to the sea?*

Italy 1500

EUROPE

Under the Visconti family and later the Sforza dukes, Milan prospered from trade and an efficient tax system.

Venice was a rich trade empire ruled by a small group of self-serving merchant-aristocrats.

The cultural center of Renaissance Italy, Florence was governed by the wealthy and powerful Medici family.

Ferrara
Florence
Genoa
Mantua
Milan
Papal States
Urbino
Venice
Major land trade routes
Major sea trade routes

leader called a doge (DOHJ). In reality, a small group of wealthy merchant-aristocrats ran the government of Venice for their benefit. Venice's trade empire was tremendously profitable and made the city-state an international power.

The republic of Florence dominated the northern Italian region of Tuscany. During the fourteenth century, a small, wealthy group of merchants established control of the Florentine government. They waged a series of successful wars against their neighbors and established Florence as a major city-state.

In 1434 Cosimo de' Medici (MEH • duh • chee) took control of the city. The wealthy Medici family ran the government from behind the scenes. Using their wealth and personal influence, Cosimo, and later his grandson Lorenzo de' Medici, dominated the city when Florence was the cultural center of Italy.

As the Italian states grew wealthier, the power of the Church began to **decline** slightly. Some church doctrines, such as the sinfulness of usury, or charging borrowers a fee on money loaned to them, were openly ignored. Many Italian leaders borrowed and loaned money without fear of reprisal.

During the late 1400s, Florence experienced an economic decline. Most of its economy was based on the manufacturing of cloth. Increased competition from English and Flemish cloth makers drove down profits.

During this time, a Dominican preacher named Girolamo Savonarola began condemning the corruption and excesses of the Medici family. Rejecting Medici rule and frustrated by economic events, citizens turned to Savonarola. His attacks weakened the power of the Medici, and a French invasion of Italy in 1494 resulted in their exile from Florence.

Eventually the Florentines tired of Savonarola's strict regulation of gambling, horseracing, swearing, painting, music, and books. He also attacked the corruption of the Church, which angered the pope. In 1498 Savonarola was accused of heresy and sentenced to death. The Medici family returned to power in Florence.

decline a change to a lower state or level

▼ Piero de' Medici, father of Lorenzo, hired Benozzo Gozzoli in 1459 to paint frescoes in the chapel of the Medici Palace. In this part of his *Procession of the Magi*, Gozzoli included portraits of the Medici, such as Lorenzo (shown as a young king on horseback).

▶ **CRITICAL THINKING**
Drawing Conclusions Why do you think Gozzoli included portraits of the Medici?

PHOTO: Massimo Listri/CORBIS

The two other dominant centers in Renaissance Italy were the Papal States and the Kingdom of Naples. Located in central Italy, Rome was the capital of the Papal States. These territories were officially under the control of the Catholic Church at this time. By contrast, the Kingdom of Naples, which dominated southern Italy, was the only one of the five major states ruled by a hereditary monarch.

The growth of monarchial states in the rest of Europe led to trouble for the Italian states. The riches of Italy attracted the French king, Charles VIII. He led an army of 30,000 men into Italy in 1494. The French occupied the Kingdom of Naples. Northern Italian states turned for help to the Spanish, who gladly agreed to send soldiers to Italy. For the next 30 years, the French and the Spanish battled in Italy as they sought to dominate the region.

A turning point in this struggle came in 1527. On May 5, thousands of troops arrived at the city of Rome. This army belonged to Charles I, king of Spain and ruler of the Holy Roman Empire. It included mercenaries from different countries. They had not been paid for months. When they yelled, "Money! Money!" their leader responded, "If you have ever dreamed of pillaging a town and laying hold of its treasures, here now is one, the richest of them all, queen of the world."

The next day the invading forces smashed the gates and pushed into the city. The troops went berserk in a frenzy of bloodshed and looting. The terrible sack of Rome in 1527 by the armies of Charles I left the Spanish a dominant force in Italy. The Italian Wars would continue for another quarter-century, ending only in 1559.

Machiavelli on Power

Political power fascinated the people of the Italian Renaissance. No one gave better expression to this interest than Niccolò Machiavelli (MA • kee • uh • VEH • lee). His book *The Prince* is one of the most influential works on political power in the Western world.

Machiavelli's central thesis in *The Prince* is the issue of how to get—and keep—political power. He dedicated his study of practical politics to the grandson of Lorenzo de' Medici. Machiavelli offered him rules on how to govern. In the Middle Ages, many writers on political power had emphasized the duty of rulers to follow Christian moral principles. Machiavelli, however, rejected this popular approach. He believed that morality was unrelated to politics.

From Machiavelli's point of view, a prince's attitude toward power must be based on an understanding of human nature. He believed human beings were motivated by self-interest. He said, "...this is to be asserted in general of men, that they are ungrateful, fickle, false, cowardly, covetous, and as long as you succeed they are yours entirely." Based on such an assessment, therefore, political activity should not be restricted by moral principles. A prince acts on behalf of the state. According to Machiavelli, for the state's sake, a leader must do good when possible, but be ready to do evil when necessary. Machiavelli abandoned morality as the basis for analyzing political activity and argued that the ends justify the means. His views have had a profound influence on later political leaders. His influence on politics has continued to the present day.

☑ **READING PROGRESS CHECK**

Explaining Why might Machiavelli have argued that political activity should not be restricted by moral principles?

Analyzing PRIMARY SOURCES

Machiavelli on Trust

❝Everyone realizes how praiseworthy it is for a prince to honor his word and to be straightforward rather than crafty in his dealings; none the less, contemporary experience shows that princes who have achieved great things have been those who have given their word lightly, who have known how to trick men with their cunning, and who, in the end, have overcome those abiding by honest principles.❞

—Niccolò Machiavelli, from *The Prince*

DBQ **INTERPRETING** What does Machiavelli use as the basis for his argument about how a prince should act?

Renaissance Society

GUIDING QUESTION *How was society characterized during the Renaissance?*

In the Middle Ages, society had been divided into three social classes: the clergy, the nobility, and the peasants and townspeople. Although this social order continued into the Renaissance, some changes became evident.

The Nobility

During the Renaissance, nobles, or aristocrats, continued to dominate society. Making up only a tiny portion of the population in most countries, nobles held important political posts and served as advisers to the king.

Nobles were expected to fulfill certain ideals in Renaissance society. The characteristics of a perfect Renaissance noble were expressed in *The Book of the Courtier,* written by the Italian diplomat Baldassare Castiglione (kahs • teel • YOH • nay) and published in 1528. One of the key ideals of the Renaissance was the well-developed individual. In Castiglione's interpretation, this ideal became the social goal of the aristocracy. A noble was born, not made. He must have character, grace, and talent. The noble had to be a warrior, but also needed a classical education and an interest in the arts. Finally, a noble had to follow certain standards of conduct. What was the purpose of these standards?

> **PRIMARY SOURCE**
>
> ❝The aim of the perfect Courtier . . . is so to win . . . the favor and mind of the prince whom he serves that he may be able to tell him . . . the truth about everything he needs to know . . . and that when he sees the mind of his prince inclined to a wrong action, he may dare to oppose him . . . so as to dissuade him of every evil intent and bring him to the path of virtue.❞
>
> —Baldassare Castiglione, from *The Book of the Courtier*

Thus, the aim of the perfect noble, by Renaissance standards, was to serve his prince in an effective and honest way. Nobles would aspire to Castiglione's principles for hundreds of years while they continued to dominate European social and political life.

Peasants and Townspeople

During the Renaissance, peasants still constituted the vast majority of the total European population. Serfdom continued to decrease with the decline of the manorial system. By 1500, especially in Western Europe, more and more peasants became legally free.

At the top of urban society were the patricians. With their wealth from trade, industry, and banking, they dominated their communities. Below them were the **burghers**—the shopkeepers, artisans, guild masters, and guild members. Below the burghers were the workers, who earned low wages, and the unemployed. Both of the latter groups lived miserable lives and made up a significant portion of the urban population.

During the late 1300s and the 1400s, urban poverty increased dramatically throughout Europe. One rich merchant, who had little sympathy for the poor, wrote:

> **PRIMARY SOURCE**
>
> ❝Those that are lazy in a way that does harm to the city, and who can offer no just reason for their condition, should either be forced to work or expelled from the [city]. The city would thus rid itself of that most harmful part of the poorest class.❞
>
> —quoted in *Renaissance Europe: Age of Recovery and Reconciliation*

▲ This portrait of Baldassare Castiglione was painted by the Renaissance artist Raphael in 1516.

burgher a member of the middle class who lived in a city or town

Family and Marriage

The family bond was a source of great security during the Renaissance. Parents carefully arranged marriages to strengthen business or family ties. In upper-class families, parents often worked out the details when their children were only two or three years old. These marriage contracts included a dowry, a sum of money that the wife's family gave to the husband upon marriage.

The father-husband was the center of the Italian family. He managed all finances, since his wife had no share in his wealth. He also made the decisions that determined the path of his children's lives.

The mother's chief role was to supervise the household and raise her children, which might include their moral education. For example, the fifteenth-century Florentine noblewoman Alessandra Strozzi wrote a letter to one of her grown sons commending him for acting charitably to the son of an enemy:

PRIMARY SOURCE

❝You gave Brunetto's son food to eat and clothes to wear, and you gave him shelter and money and sent him back here; out of the seven acts of mercy you have performed three.❞

—quoted in *Selected Letters of Alessandra Strozzi*

A father had absolute authority over the children living under his roof. Males became adults when they left home, reached a certain age—which varied from place to place—or were emancipated (legally freed) by their fathers. Women never became legal adults while the father lived unless they were emancipated.

✓ **READING PROGRESS CHECK**

Contrasting How does Castiglione's view of the responsibilities of a ruling class differ from Machiavelli's?

▼ Raphael's *Marriage of the Virgin* (1504) presents biblical figures in a contemporary Renaissance setting.

▶ **CRITICAL THINKING**
Synthesizing What view of the role of marriage in Renaissance society does the composition of this work present?

LESSON 1 REVIEW (CCSS)

Reviewing Vocabulary

1. **Comparing** Write a paragraph comparing a republic to a monarchical state. Give examples of each type of government from Renaissance Italy.

Using Your Notes

2. **Summarizing** Use your graphic organizer identifying the major principles of Machiavelli's work to write a paragraph summarizing his political views.

Answering the Guiding Questions

3. **Identifying Cause and Effect** What contributed to the rise of the Italian states during the Renaissance?

4. **Making Connections** How did Machiavelli's work influence political power in the Western world?

5. **Identifying Central Issues** How was society characterized during the Renaissance?

Writing Activity

6. **INFORMATIVE/EXPLANATORY** Write a paragraph explaining how trade encouraged the development of the Renaissance.

Reading **HELP**DESK (CCSS)

Academic Vocabulary
- **attain**
- **core**
- **style**
- **circumstance**

Content Vocabulary
- **humanism** • **fresco**
- **vernacular** • **perspective**

TAKING NOTES:
Key Ideas and Details

Organizing Use a chart like the following one to identify how Renaissance education was affected by humanism.

Area:
Effect:
Effect:
Effect:

LESSON 2
Ideas and Art of the Renaissance

ESSENTIAL QUESTION
- How can ideas be reflected in art, sculpture, and architecture?

IT MATTERS BECAUSE

Renaissance humanism focused European culture on the individual, marking a major change from the religion-centered view of the Middle Ages. The goal of the humanists was to educate the whole person, much as modern educators seek to do. Today's liberal arts curriculum began during the Renaissance.

Italian Renaissance Humanism

GUIDING QUESTION *How did humanism help define the Italian Renaissance?*

Secularism and an emphasis on the individual characterized the Renaissance. These characteristics are most noticeable in the intellectual and artistic accomplishments of the period. A key intellectual movement of the Renaissance was **humanism**.

Development of Humanism

Humanism was based on the study of the classics, the literature of ancient Greece and Rome. Humanists studied grammar, rhetoric, poetry, moral philosophy, and history. Today these subjects are called the humanities.

The humanists approached the classics in new ways. In the Middle Ages, writers had quoted the surviving classical texts in order to give authority to their religious writings. The humanists had a different goal. They wanted to use classical values to revitalize their culture. The humanists also felt a different relationship with the writers of antiquity. They saw the ancient Greek and Roman writers as their intellectual equals.

Francesco Petrarch (PEE • TRAHRK) is often called the father of Italian Renaissance humanism. He did more than any other individual in the fourteenth century to foster its development. He looked for forgotten Latin manuscripts and set in motion a search for similar manuscripts in monastic libraries throughout Europe.

Petrarch also began the humanist emphasis on using pure classical Latin. This meant Latin as it was used by the ancient Romans, rather than medieval Latin. Humanists used the works of two Roman writers as models—Cicero for prose and Virgil for poetry.

Fourteenth-century humanists such as Petrarch had described the intellectual life as one of solitude. They rejected family and a life of action in the community. In contrast, humanists in the early fifteenth century took a new interest in civic life. They believed that intellectuals had a duty to live an active civic life and to put their study of the humanities to the state's service. It is no accident that they served as secretaries in the Italian states and to princes and popes.

Byzantine and Islamic influences were also important to the development of Renaissance humanism. Byzantine scholars provided knowledge of the ancient Greek language, and Islamic scholars served as transmitters of ancient Greek culture.

Vernacular Literature

The humanist emphasis on classical Latin led to its widespread use in the writings of scholars, lawyers, and religious writers. However, some writers wrote in the **vernacular**, the local spoken language. People in different parts of Italy spoke different Italian dialects. In the fourteenth and fifteenth centuries, the literary works of Dante (DAHN • tay) Alighieri and Christine de Pizan helped make vernacular literature popular.

Dante wrote his masterpiece, the *Divine Comedy*, in the dialect of his native Florence, which would later become the Italian language. The *Divine Comedy* is a long poem describing the soul's journey to **attain** Paradise. Dante defended his use of the vernacular in the *Divine Comedy*, arguing that if he had written in Latin, only scholars would have understood him.

humanism an intellectual movement of the Renaissance based on the study of the humanities, which included grammar, rhetoric, poetry, moral philosophy, and history

vernacular the language of everyday speech in a particular region

attain to gain or achieve

> ### PRIMARY SOURCE
>
> ❝The Latin could only have explained them to scholars; for the rest would have not understood it. Therefore, as among those who desire to understand them there are many more illiterate than learned, [it follows that the Latin would not have fulfilled this behest as well as the vulgar tongue, which is understood both by the learned and the unlearned.]❞
>
> —Dante Alighieri, from *De vulgari eloquentia* ("Of Literature in the Vernacular")

PHOTO: SuperStock.

◀ In this painting by Domenico di Michelino, Dante stands outside the walls of Florence and holds a copy of his *Divine Comedy*.

▶ **CRITICAL THINKING**
Making Connections How does this painting reflect Renaissance humanism's emphasis on the individual?

Gutenberg (c. 1400–1468)

Johannes Gutenberg was born in Mainz, Germany. Beginning in the 1440s, and borrowing from several existing technologies, he developed a method of printing using blocks of movable type set on a mechanical press. This process took more than a decade, and Gutenberg borrowed heavily to finance his printing press. In 1455 the Gutenberg Bible became the earliest book printed from movable type in Europe.

▶ **CRITICAL THINKING**
Drawing Conclusions Why might Gutenburg have chosen the Bible as a first project for his printing press?

core basic or essential part

Another writer who used the vernacular was Christine de Pizan, an Italian who lived in France and wrote in French. She is best known for her works written in defense of women. In *The Book of the City of Ladies*, written between 1404 and 1405, she denounced the many male writers who had argued that women, by their very nature, are unable to learn. Women, de Pizan argued, could attain learning as well as men if they could attend the same schools, since "a woman's nature is clever and quick enough to learn speculative sciences as well as to discover them, and likewise the manual arts..."

✔ **READING PROGRESS CHECK**

Explaining How did the Renaissance contribute to the rediscovery of classical civilization and the development of vernacular literature?

Renaissance Education

GUIDING QUESTION *How was education during the Renaissance shaped by humanism?*

The humanist movement had a profound effect on education in the fourteenth and fifteenth centuries. Education during this time became increasingly secular—less focused on religion. Renaissance humanists believed that education could change human beings. They wrote books on education and opened schools based on their ideas.

At the **core** of humanist schools were the liberal studies. These form the basis of today's liberal arts. According to the humanists, students should learn history, ethics, public speaking, grammar, logic, poetry, mathematics, astronomy, and music. Humanists believed that liberal studies enabled individuals to reach their full potential. The purpose of a liberal education was to produce individuals who follow a path of virtue and wisdom. These individuals should also possess rhetorical skills so they could persuade others to take this same path.

Humanist educators thought that education was a practical preparation for life. Its aim was to create well-rounded citizens, not great scholars. Humanist education was also considered necessary for preparing the sons of aristocrats for leadership roles. Following the classical ideal of a sound mind in a sound body, humanist educators also emphasized physical education. Students learned the skills of javelin throwing, archery, and dancing. They ran, wrestled, hunted, and swam. The few female students who attended humanist schools studied the classics and were encouraged to know some history as well as how to ride, dance, sing, play the lute, and appreciate poetry.

The development of printing affected not only education, but eventually all aspects of Renaissance culture. Beginning in the mid-fifteenth century, the use of movable type was pioneered by the German printer Johannes Gutenberg (GOO • tehn • BURG). This innovation started a revolution that has affected how knowledge is distributed ever since. As the number of printing presses multiplied, the effects of new technology were felt in every area of European life. The printing of books encouraged scholarly research and stimulated an ever-expanding reading public's desire to gain knowledge.

✔ **READING PROGRESS CHECK**

Identifying Central Ideas What was the focus of education for the Renaissance humanists?

Italian Renaissance Art

GUIDING QUESTION *How did humanism influence the works of Renaissance artists and authors?*

Renaissance artists sought to imitate nature. They wanted viewers to be convinced of the reality of their subjects. At the same time, these artists were developing a new, human-focused worldview. To emphasize this, many artists painted the human body.

New Techniques in Painting

The works of the fourteenth-century Italian painter Giotto anticipated some of the innovations of the Renaissance. His style focused on depicting human beings and their realities and dramas.

However, the Renaissance period in art truly began with Tommaso di Giovanni, called Masaccio (muh • ZAH • chee • OH). His frescoes are the first masterpieces of Early Renaissance (1400–1490) art. A **fresco** is a painting done on fresh, wet plaster with water-based paints. Human figures in medieval paintings look flat, but Masaccio's figures have depth and "come alive." By mastering the laws of **perspective**, Masaccio could create the illusion of three dimensions, leading to a new, realistic **style**. One of his most famous works is *The Tribute Money,* which depicts the story of the life of Peter, s Christian saint. It is one of many frescoes Masaccio was commissioned to paint in the Brancacci Chapel in Florence.

Other fifteenth-century Florentine painters used and modified this new, or Renaissance, style. Especially important were two major developments. One development stressed the technical side of painting. This included understanding the laws of perspective and the organization of outdoor space and light through geometry. The second development was the investigation of movement and human anatomy. Realistic portrayal of the individual, especially the human nude, became one of the chief aims of Italian Renaissance art.

Sculpture and Architecture

The Renaissance produced equally stunning advances in sculpture and architecture. Like painters, Renaissance sculptors and architects sought to express a human-centered world. The sculptor Donatello studied the statues of the Greeks and Romans. His works included a realistic, free-standing marble figure of George, a Christian saint.

The buildings of classical Rome inspired the work of architect Filippo Brunelleschi (BROO • nuh • LEHS • kee). His design of the church of San Lorenzo in Florence reflects this. The classical columns and rounded arches in the church's interior design create an environment that does not overwhelm the worshiper, as Gothic cathedrals might. The church creates an open airy space to fit human, and not divine, needs. Using his mathematical and artistic skills, Brunelleschi came up with a way to build the large exterior dome. Likewise, he rediscovered the classical principles of linear-perspective construction, which had disappeared from use during the Middle Ages. These principles helped Renaissance artists create realistic imagery.

fresco painting done on fresh, wet plaster with water-based paints

perspective artistic techniques used to give the effect of three-dimensional depth to two-dimensional surfaces

style having a distinctive quality or form

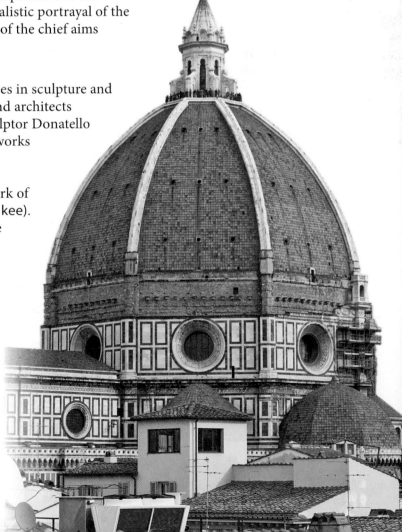

▼ Architect Filippo Brunelleschi's technical achievements mark the design and construction of the dome for the Cathedral of Florence as one of the major artistic landmarks of the Renaissance.

▶ CRITICAL THINKING
Drawing Conclusions Why might an architect be an appropriate model for the humanist ideal of the universal Renaissance person?

▲ The first casual portrait, Leonardo's *Mona Lisa* revolutionized art.

▶ **CRITICAL THINKING**
Making Inferences Why would portraiture be a natural development for a Renaissance culture shaped by humanism?

circumstance a determining condition

High Renaissance Masters

The final stage of Italian Renaissance painting flourished from about 1490 to 1520. Called the High Renaissance, this period is associated with Leonardo da Vinci, Raphael Sanzio, and Michelangelo Buonarroti and their works.

Leonardo da Vinci was the model "Renaissance man." He was an artist, scientist, inventor, and visionary. Leonardo mastered the art of realistic painting, even dissecting human bodies to better understand their workings. However, he wanted to go beyond such realism to create idealized forms that captured the perfection of nature in the individual. Leonardo could not express his vision of perfection fully in a realistic style.

At age 25, Raphael Sanzio was already one of Italy's best painters. He was admired for his numerous madonnas (paintings of Mary, the mother of Jesus). In these, he achieved an ideal of beauty far surpassing human standards. Raphael is also well known for his frescoes in the Vatican Palace. His *School of Athens* reveals a world of balance, harmony, and order—the underlying principles of classical Greek and Roman art.

Michelangelo Buonarroti, an accomplished painter, sculptor, and architect, was another master of the High Renaissance. Fiercely driven by his desire to create, he worked with great passion and energy on a remarkable number of projects. Michelangelo's figures on the ceiling of the Sistine Chapel in Rome depict an ideal type of human being with perfect proportions. The beauty of this idealized human being is meant to be a reflection of divine beauty—the more beautiful the body, the more godlike the figure.

☑ **READING PROGRESS CHECK**

Specifying In what ways did Italian artists use the ideas of the humanist movement in their works?

The Northern Artistic Renaissance

GUIDING QUESTION *How did the works of northern European artists differ from those of Italian artists?*

Like the Italian artists, the artists of northern Europe sought to portray their world realistically. However, their approach was different from that of the Italians. This was particularly true of the artists of the Low Countries (present-day Belgium, Luxembourg, and the Netherlands).

Circumstance played a role in the differences. The large wall spaces of Italian churches had encouraged the art of fresco painting. Italian artists used these spaces to master the technical skills that allowed them to portray humans in realistic settings. In the north, the Gothic cathedrals of the Middle Ages, with their stained glass windows, did not allow enough space for frescoes. Instead, northern European artists painted illustrations for books and wooden panels for altarpieces. Great care was needed to depict each object on a small scale.

The most important northern school of art in the 1400s was in Flanders, one of the Low Countries. Flemish artists typically placed their subjects among everyday objects, as in Robert Campin's *Merode Altarpiece*. Campin, one of the earliest Flemish masters of painting, used shadows to create depth and the smallest details to reflect reality. The Flemish painter Jan van Eyck (EYEK) was among the first to use and perfect the technique of oil painting. He used a varnish made of linseed oil and nut oils mixed with resins. This medium enabled van Eyck to use a wide variety of brilliant colors. With his oil paints, he could create striking realism in fine details, as

in his painting *Giovanni Arnolfini and His Bride.* Like other Northern Renaissance artists, however, van Eyck imitated nature not by using perspective, as the Italians did, but by simply observing reality and portraying details as best he could.

By 1500, artists from the north had begun to study in Italy and to be influenced by what artists were doing there. One German artist who was greatly affected by the Italians was Albrecht Dürer. He made two trips to Italy and absorbed most of what the Italians could teach on the laws of perspective. Like the Italian artists of the High Renaissance, Dürer tried to achieve a standard of ideal beauty that was based on a careful examination of the human form. He did not reject the use of minute details typical of northern artists. However, he did try to fit those details more harmoniously into his works in accordance with Italian artistic theories.

✓ READING PROGRESS CHECK

Contrasting What was a key difference between the northern European artists and the Italian artists?

▼ This central pa[...]
Altarpiece by Fle[...]ert
Campin (c. 1378–[...]44) shows the
Annunciation, when the archangel
Gabriel told Mary she was to be the
mother of Jesus.

► CRITICAL THINKING
Making Connections For the people who first saw this painting, what effect might have been created by the placement of this religious scene in an everyday setting?

PHOTO: © Francis G. Mayer/CORBIS.

LESSON 2 REVIEW (CCSS)

Reviewing Vocabulary

1. *Explaining* Write a paragraph explaining why vernacular literature eventually became the preferred way to produce books.

Using Your Notes

2. *Explaining* Using your chart on the effects of humanism on a Renaissance education, write a brief paragraph explaining these effects.

Answering the Guiding Questions

3. *Finding the Main Idea* How did humanism help define the Italian Renaissance?

4. *Evaluating* How was education during the Renaissance shaped by humanism?

5. *Making Connections* How did humanism influence the works of Renaissance artists and authors? Give specific examples.

6. *Contrasting* How did the works of northern European artists differ from the works of Italian artists?

Writing Activity

7. INFORMATIVE/EXPLANATORY Write a paragraph describing one of the works of art in the lesson. Pay particular attention to how the image is representative of the humanist movement of the Renaissance. Be sure to use descriptive words that will help your reader visualize the work of art.

Directions: On a separate sheet of paper, answer the questions below. Make sure you read carefully and answer all parts of the questions.

Lesson Review

Lesson 1

1 **ANALYZING** How did the lack of a single strong ruler benefit Italy during the Renaissance? How might Italy have evolved differently if it had been ruled by one powerful monarch?

2 **DETERMINING CAUSE AND EFFECT** How did consumers' demand for goods affect the power of the Italian states and the power of the Catholic Church?

3 **DRAWING CONCLUSIONS** How did the fact that other countries in Europe had strong rulers affect Italy's fate? Compare and contrast the king of Spain's treatment of Italy with that of the king of France.

Lesson 2

4 **ASSESSING** Why is Christine de Pizan's argument for women's intelligence so convincing?

5 **CONTRASTING** What were fresco artists able to convey that medieval painters could not? How does their accomplishment embody characteristics of humanism?

6 **IDENTIFYING** What stages did Leonardo da Vinci go through in learning to paint the human form? What goal did he share with other High Renaissance artists like Raphael and Michelangelo?

21st Century Skills

7 **IDENTIFYING CAUSE AND EFFECT** Why did Florence enjoy a flourishing of the arts in the fifteenth century?

8 **GEOGRAPHY SKILLS** Look at the map in Lesson 1 and locate the cities of Milan, Florence, Venice, Rome, and Naples. Which of these cities appear most accessible to trade routes? What other advantages did their locations provide?

9 **ECONOMICS** How could urban poverty increase while the Italian states grew wealthier?

10 **IDENTIFYING CONTINUITY AND CHANGE** How did Early Renaissance artists learn to create more realistic art than their predecessors?

Exploring the Essential Questions

11 **SYNTHESIZING** Work with a partner to create a multimedia presentation showing three pieces of art that reflect ideas that shaped the Renaissance. Provide a photo or reproduction of each piece of art, an audio analysis of its features, and a written explanation of how it was shaped by Renaissance ideas. Primary sources may also be used.

DBQ Analyzing Historical Documents

Use the document to answer the following questions.

Filippo Brunelleschi was the first architect since the ancient Greeks to successfully design and construct a large dome. A few years later, one of his students, Leon Battista Alberti, praised the dome:

PRIMARY SOURCE

❝ Within, one breathes the perpetual freshness of spring. Outside there may be frost, fog or wind, but in this retreat, closed to every wind, the air is quiet and mild. What a pleasant refuge from the hot blasts of summer and autumn! And if it is true that delight resides where our senses receive all that they can demand of nature, how can one hesitate to call this temple a nest of delights? ❞

—quoted in *Brunelleschi's Dome: How a Renaissance Genius Reinvented Architecture*

12 **DRAWING CONCLUSIONS** Alberti was one of Brunelleschi's students. How might this relationship have influenced Alberti's opinion?

13 **MAKING CONNECTIONS** Medieval architects were anonymous. Brunelleschi became famous throughout Italy. What humanist principle does this shift in attitude reflect?

Extended-Response Question

14 **ARGUMENT** Explain how the Renaissance was a rebirth. Analyze the ways in which it imitated and differed from the cultures that inspired it.

Need Extra Help?

If You've Missed Question	1	2	3	4	5	6	7	8	9	10	11	12	13	14
Go to page	22	24	25	30	31	32	31	23	26	31	28	31	28	28

The Reformation in Europe

1517–1600

ESSENTIAL QUESTIONS · *What conditions can encourage the desire for reform?*
· *How can reform influence society and beliefs?*

Lesson 1
The Protestant Reformation

Lesson 2
The Spread of Protestantism

The Story Matters...

The Protestant Reformation is the name given to the religious reform movement that divided western Christianity into Catholic and Protestant groups. Martin Luther's bold attempts to reform the Church led to new forms of Christianity. Although Luther did not see himself as a rebel, the spread of Protestantism ignited decades of bloody religious conflict and ended a thousand years of domination by the Catholic Church.

◄ Based on an earlier portrait, Charles Wagstaff's nineteenth-century engraving depicts Martin Luther, whose studies and determination drove him to defy the power of the Church and the Holy Roman Empire in order to assert his religious principles.

PHOTO: North Wind Picture Archives/The Image Works

CHAPTER 3

Place and Time: Europe 1517–1600

In the sixteenth century, Europe was undergoing rapid change as economies expanded, cities grew, and a recent invention, the printing press, helped spread new ideas. New ideas appeared in the movement known as the Reformation, which began in Germany with Martin Luther's protest against what he saw as abuses within the Catholic Church. The Reformation movement he started soon spread throughout Europe. In Switzerland, John Calvin created a center of Reformation thought in Geneva. King Henry VIII made himself head of the Protestant Church of England.

Step Into the Place

Read the quotes and look at the information presented on the map.

 Analyzing Historical Documents How was the struggle between Protestantism and the Catholic Church a war of ideas?

PRIMARY SOURCE

❝Unless I am convicted by Scripture and plain reason—I do not accept the authority of popes and councils, for they have contradicted each other—my conscience is captive to the Word of God. I cannot and I will not recant anything, for to go against conscience is neither right nor safe. Here I stand, I cannot do otherwise. God help me. Amen.❞

—Martin Luther, before the Diet of Worms in 1521

PRIMARY SOURCE

❝Now, in order that true religion may shine on us, we ought to hold that it must take its beginning from heavenly doctrine and that no one can get even the slightest taste of right and sound doctrine, unless he be a pupil of Scripture.❞

—John Calvin, from *Institutes of the Christian Religion*

PHOTO: (l)© The Art Archive / Superstock, (r)© Image Asset Managemen/AgeStock.

Step Into the Time

Determining Cause and Effect Organize the European events on the time line into two groups: (1) actions by Protestants and (2) reactions by the Catholic Church.

1521 Church excommunicates Luther; Edict of Worms outlaws him within the Holy Roman Empire

October 31, 1517 Martin Luther displays his Ninety-five Theses

1534 Act of Supremacy begins creation of Church of England

1536 John Calvin publishes *Institutes of the Christian Religion*

1540 Catholic Church recognizes the Society of Jesus, or Jesuits

EUROPE

THE WORLD

1510 — **1525** — **1540**

1520 Ferdinand Magellan sails into the Pacific Ocean

1526 Afonso I, king of Congo, attempts to restrict Portuguese slave trade

1529 Ottoman siege of Vienna fails

1542 Bartolomé de Las Casas writes his *Short Account of the Destruction of the Indies*

networks
There's More Online!

☑ **MAP** Explore the interactive version of this map on Networks.

☑ **TIME LINE** Explore the interactive version of the time line on Networks.

Christian Europe, 1600

Legend:
- Anabaptist
- Anglican
- Calvinist
- Eastern Orthodox Christian
- Lutheran
- Roman Catholic

Note: Colored squares indicate localized religious communities.

NORWAY
SWEDEN
SCOTLAND
IRELAND
North Sea
DENMARK
ENGLAND
NETHERLANDS
Baltic Sea
Canterbury
Wittenberg
SPANISH NETHERLANDS
GERMAN STATES
POLAND
RUSSIA
ATLANTIC OCEAN
Paris
Worms
BOHEMIA
Augsburg
BAVARIA
FRANCE
Zürich
Geneva
SWITZERLAND
AUSTRIA
Trent
HUNGARY
PORTUGAL
SPAIN
Avignon
PAPAL STATES
Black Sea
Rome
ITALY
OTTOMAN EMPIRE
AFRICA
Mediterranean Sea

0 400 miles
0 400 km
Lambert Azimuthal Equal-Area projection

20°W · 10°W · 0° · 10°E · 20°E · 30°E · 40°E · 50°E
50°N · 40°N · 30°N

1545 Council of Trent begins; concludes in 1563

1554 Catholic ruler Mary I begins persecution of Protestants in England

1555 Peace of Augsburg divides Christianity in Germany

1562 Teresa of Ávila founds reformed Carmelite Convent

1555 · 1570 · 1585 · 1600

1549 Jesuit missionary Francis Xavier arrives in Japan

1566 Ottoman Sultan Süleyman I dies

1570 Mogul emperor Akbar begins new capital at Fatehpur Sikri; abandoned in 1586

1587 "Lost Colony" of Roanoke founded in Virginia

1588 'Abbās becomes Shah of Persian Safavid Dynasty

networks

There's More Online!

☑ **BIOGRAPHY** Charles V

☑ **BIOGRAPHY** Desiderius Erasmus

☑ **BIOGRAPHY** Martin Luther

☑ **IMAGE** The True Church and the False Church

☑ **INFOGRAPHIC** Martin Luther and the Ninety-Five Theses

☑ **INTERACTIVE SELF-CHECK QUIZ**

☑ **TIME LINE** Christianity in Northern Europe

☑ **VIDEO** The Protestant Reformation

Reading **HELP**DESK (CCSS)

Academic Vocabulary
- **fundamental**
- **external** • **valid**

Content Vocabulary
- **Christian humanism**
- **salvation**
- **indulgence**
- **Lutheranism**

TAKING NOTES:

Key Ideas and Details

Determining Cause and Effect Use a graphic organizer like this one to identify steps that led to the Reformation.

Step
Step
Step
Reformation

LESSON 1
The Protestant Reformation

ESSENTIAL QUESTION

What conditions can encourage the desire for reform?

IT MATTERS BECAUSE

The humanist ideas of the Renaissance, in addition to perceived worldly and corrupt practices in the Catholic Church, gave rise to a widespread call for Church reform. The Protestant faith that resulted gave new directions to European history and culture by fragmenting western Christianity and reshaping political power.

Prelude to Reformation

GUIDING QUESTION *How did Christian humanism and Desiderius Erasmus pave the way for the Protestant Reformation in Europe?*

A German priest and professor named Martin Luther began the Protestant Reformation in the early 1500s. Prior developments, such as widespread intellectual changes during the preceding century, had already set the stage for religious change.

Christian Humanism

During the second half of the fifteenth century, the new classical learning that was part of Italian Renaissance humanism spread to northern Europe. From that came a movement called **Christian humanism**, or Northern Renaissance humanism. The major goal of this movement was the reform of the Catholic Church. The Christian humanists believed in the ability of human beings to reason and improve themselves. They thought that if people read the classics, and especially the **fundamental** teachings of Christianity in the Bible, they would become more sincerely religious. This religious feeling would bring about a reform of the Church and society.

The best-known Christian humanist was Desiderius Erasmus (ih • RAZ • muhs). Erasmus believed that Christianity should show people how to live good lives on a daily basis, not just provide beliefs that might help them be saved. He also thought that the

PHOTO: (l to r) SuperStock / SuperStock, Foto Marburg/Art Resource, NY, Private Collection/Bridgeman Art Library, © Bettmann/CORBIS, Image Asset Managemen.

Catholic Church needed to return to the simpler days of early Christianity. Stressing the inwardness of religious feeling, Erasmus thought the **external** forms of medieval religion, such as pilgrimages, fasts, and relics, were not all that important.

Erasmus wanted to educate people in the works of Christianity and worked to criticize the abuses in the Church. In his satire *The Praise of Folly*, written in 1509, Erasmus humorously criticized society's moral and religious state and called for a simpler, purer faith. In this passage, he satirizes what he views as the folly of clergy who encourage the practice of visiting the shrines of saints:

PRIMARY SOURCE

❝[They] attribute strange virtues to the shrines and images of saints and martyrs, and so would make their credulous proselytes believe, that if they pay their devotion to St. Christopher in the morning, they shall be guarded and secured the day following from all dangers and misfortunes: if soldiers, when they first take arms, shall come and mumble over such a set prayer before the picture of St. Barbara, they shall return safe from all engagements.❞

—from *The Praise of Folly*

▲ A portrait of Erasmus, painted in 1523 by Hans Holbein the Younger.

Erasmus sought reform within the Catholic Church. His intention was not to have people break away from it. His ideas, however, prepared the way for the Reformation. As people of his day said, "Erasmus laid the egg that Luther hatched."

Need for Reform

Erasmus and the Christian humanists were not the only ones calling for reform. Popular songs and printed images from the era, as well as court records, show that ordinary people, humanists, and some Church leaders were critical of the Church. For example, from 1450 to 1520 a series of Renaissance popes were viewed as more concerned with Italian politics and worldly interests than with the spiritual needs of their people. Church officials were viewed as using their church offices to advance their careers and their wealth. At the same time, many ordinary parish priests appeared to their parishioners as ignorant of their spiritual duties. People wanted to know how to save their souls, but many parish priests appeared unwilling or unable to offer them advice or instruction.

While the leaders of the Church were failing to meet their responsibilities, ordinary people desired meaningful religious expression and assurance of their **salvation**, or acceptance into Heaven. As a result, for some, the process of obtaining salvation became almost mechanical.

According to Church practice at that time, venerating a relic, such as a scrap of a saint's clothing, could gain someone an **indulgence**. An indulgence was a document sold by the Church and signed by the pope or another church official that released the bearer from all or part of the punishment for sin. Making pilgrimages to view relics grew popular as a way to acquire indulgences and, therefore, salvation.

As more people sought certainty of salvation through veneration of relics, collections of such objects grew. Frederick III, also known as Frederick the Wise, Luther's prince, had amassed more than 5,000 relics. Some people believed the indulgences attached to them could reduce time spent in purgatory by 1,443 years. The Church also sold indulgences.

Other people sought certainty of salvation in the popular mystical movement known as the Modern Devotion. The Modern Devotion downplayed Church practices and stressed the need to follow the teachings

Christian humanism
a movement that developed in northern Europe during the Renaissance, combining classical learning and individualism with the goal of reforming the Catholic Church

fundamental basic or essential

external outward or observable

salvation the state of being saved (that is, going to heaven) through faith alone or through faith and good works

indulgence a release from all or part of punishment for sin by the Catholic Church, reducing time in purgatory after death

▲ This image depicts Luther publicly displaying his Ninety-five Theses.

▶ **CRITICAL THINKING**
Interpreting Significance How might art be a useful weapon in a war of ideas such as the Protestant Reformation?

valid well-grounded or justifiable

of Jesus. This deepening of religious life was done within the Catholic Church. It also helps explain the tremendous impact of Luther's ideas.

☑ **READING PROGRESS CHECK**

Identifying Central Issues Why, according to Erasmus, other Christian humanists, and other critics, did the Church need reform?

Martin Luther

GUIDING QUESTION *What role did Martin Luther and his ideas play in the Reformation?*

Martin Luther was a monk in the Catholic Church and a professor at the University of Wittenberg, in Germany, where he lectured on the Bible. Through his study of the Bible, Luther arrived at an answer to a problem that had bothered him since he had become a monk. He wanted to know about the certainty of salvation.

Catholic teaching had stressed that faith and good works were needed to gain personal salvation. In Luther's opinion, human beings were powerless in the sight of an almighty God and could never do enough good works to earn salvation. Through his study of the Bible, Luther came to believe that humans are not saved through their good works but through their faith in God. This idea, called justification by faith alone, became the chief teaching of the Protestant Reformation.

Because Luther had arrived at his understanding of salvation by studying the Bible, the Bible became for Luther, as for all later Protestants, the only **valid** source of religious truth.

The Ninety-five Theses

Luther did not see himself as a rebel, but he was greatly upset by the widespread selling of indulgences. Especially offensive in his eyes was the monk Johann Tetzel. The Catholic Church had authorized Tetzel to sell indulgences to raise money to build St. Peter's Basilica in Rome. Tetzel told the faithful that their purchases would free the souls of their loved ones from purgatory. His slogan was: "As soon as coin in the coffer [money box] rings, the soul from purgatory springs." This enraged Luther, who believed that indulgences only soothed the conscience. They did not forgive sins.

On October 31, 1517, Luther, angered by the Church's practices, made his Ninety-five Theses public, perhaps by posting them on the door of the Castle Church in Wittenberg. The act of posting may be a legend, but posting topics to discuss was a common practice of the time. In any case, his theses were a stunning attack on abuses in the sale of indulgences. Thousands of copies of the Ninety-five Theses were printed and spread to all parts of Germany.

A Break With the Church

By 1520, Luther began to move toward a more definite break with the Catholic Church. He called on the German princes to overthrow the papacy in Germany and establish a reformed German church.

Luther also attacked the Church's system of sacraments. In his view, they were the means by which the pope and the Catholic Church had destroyed the real meaning of the Gospel for a thousand years. He kept only two sacraments—baptism and the Eucharist, which is also known as Communion. Luther also called for the clergy to marry. This went against the long-standing requirement of the Catholic Church that its clergy remain celibate, or unmarried.

Through all these calls for change, Luther continued to emphasize his new doctrine of salvation. It is faith alone, he said, and not good works, that justifies and brings salvation through Jesus.

Unable to accept Luther's ideas, the pope excommunicated him in January 1521, excluding him from Church membership. He was also summoned to appear before the imperial diet—or legislative assembly—of the Holy Roman Empire, which was called into session in the city of Worms by the newly elected emperor Charles V. The emperor believed he could convince Luther to change his ideas. However, Luther refused.

The young emperor was outraged. "A single friar who goes counter to all Christianity for a thousand years," he declared, "must be wrong." By the Edict of Worms, Martin Luther was made an outlaw within the empire. His works were to be burned, and Luther was to be captured and delivered to the emperor. However, Frederick III, the elector (or prince) of Saxony, was unwilling to see his subject killed. He sent Luther into hiding and then protected him when Luther returned to Wittenberg at the beginning of 1522.

The Rise of Lutheranism

During the next few years, Luther's religious movement became a revolution. Luther was able to gain the support of many of the German rulers among the approximately three hundred states that made up the Holy Roman Empire. These German rulers, motivated as much by politics and economics as by any religious feeling, quickly took control of the Catholic churches in their territories, forming state churches supervised by the government. The political leaders, not the Roman pope, held the last word. As part of the development of these state-dominated churches, Luther also set up new religious services to replace the Catholic mass. These services consisted of Christian Bible readings, preaching the word of God, and song. Luther also married a former nun, Katharina von Boren, providing a model of married and family life for the new Protestant ministers. Luther's doctrine soon became known as **Lutheranism** and the churches as Lutheran churches. Lutheranism was the first Protestant faith.

A series of crises soon made it apparent, however, that spreading the word of God was not an easy task for Luther. The Peasants' War was Luther's greatest challenge. In June 1524, German peasants revolted against their lords and looked to Luther to support their cause. Instead, Luther supported the lords. To him, the state and its rulers were called by God to maintain the peace necessary to spread the Gospel, the first four books of the New Testament in the Christian Bible. It was the duty of princes to stop all revolts. By the following spring, the German princes had crushed the peasant revolts. Luther found himself even more dependent on state authorities for the growth of his reformed church.

✔ **READING PROGRESS CHECK**

Interpreting How did Luther's ideas lead to a break with the Church and to a new faith?

▲ Summoned to the imperial assembly at Worms, Luther refused to change his ideas.

▶ **CRITICAL THINKING**
Predicting Consequences If Luther had agreed to change his ideas, what do you think would have been the consequences for the development of Protestantism? Explain.

Lutheranism the religious doctrine that Martin Luther developed; it differed from Catholicism in the doctrine of salvation, which Luther believed could be achieved by faith alone, not by good works; Lutheranism was the first Protestant faith

Politics in the German Reformation

GUIDING QUESTION *Why was the Holy Roman Empire forced to seek peace with the Lutheran princes?*

From its beginning, the fate of Luther's movement was tied closely to political affairs. Charles V, the Holy Roman emperor, ruled an immense empire consisting of Spain and its colonies, the Austrian lands, Bohemia, Hungary, the Low Countries, the duchy of Milan in northern Italy, and the kingdom of Naples in southern Italy.

Religious authorities primarily saw the Reformation as a challenge to Church power. Rulers such as Charles also saw the Reformation as a force that disrupted the political and social order. Charles hoped to preserve his empire's unity by keeping it Catholic and under the control of his dynasty, the Hapsburgs. However, a number of problems cost him his dream and his health. These same problems helped Lutheranism survive by giving Lutherans time to organize before facing Catholic forces.

The chief political concern of Charles V was his rivalry with the king of France, Francis I. Their conflict over a number of disputed territories led to a series of wars that lasted more than 20 years. Invasions by Ottoman Turks forced Charles to send forces into the eastern part of his empire as well.

Finally, the internal political situation in the Holy Roman Empire was not in Charles's favor. Germany was a land of several hundred territorial states. Although all owed loyalty to the emperor, many rulers of the German states supported Luther as a way to assert their authority and dislike of papal control. By the time Charles V brought military forces to Germany, the Lutheran princes were well organized. Unable to defeat them, Charles was forced to seek peace.

An end to religious warfare in Germany came in 1555 with the Peace of Augsburg. This agreement formally accepted the division of Christianity in Germany. The German states were now free to choose between Catholicism and Lutheranism. Lutheran states would have the same legal rights as Catholic states. Subjects did not choose their religion. German rulers determined that for them.

▲ A portrait by Lucas Cranach the Younger depicting Frederick III, Elector of Saxony. He sent Luther into hiding to protect him.

☑ READING PROGRESS CHECK

Evaluating How were the goals of Charles and the Holy Roman Empire at odds with the desires of Lutheran princes?

PHOTO: SuperStock / SuperStock

LESSON 1 REVIEW

Reviewing Vocabulary

1. *Analyzing* Write a paragraph that reports on indulgences by telling what they were, what people did to get them, who might buy or sell them, when or how they were given, and why they were considered desirable.

Using Your Notes

2. *Gathering Information* Use your notes on the steps leading to the Reformation and other insights you gathered while reading the lesson to explain that Luther did not start the Reformation on his own.

Answering the Guiding Questions

3. *Identifying Cause and Effect* How did Desiderius Erasmus and Christian humanism pave the way for the Protestant Reformation in Europe?

4. *Assessing* What role did Martin Luther and his ideas play in the Reformation?

5. *Drawing Conclusions* Why was the Holy Roman Empire forced to seek peace with the Lutheran princes?

Writing Activity

6. NARRATIVE Write a narrative paragraph based on the events surrounding Luther's possible posting of his Ninety-five Theses on the church door at Wittenberg. Be sure to use chronological order to present the events, and try to introduce literary techniques of conflict, characterization, and setting to strengthen your narrative.

Reading **HELP**DESK (CCSS)

Academic Vocabulary

- **community**
- **publish**

Content Vocabulary

- **justification**
- **predestination**
- **annul**
- **ghetto**

TAKING NOTES:

Key Ideas and Details

LISTING Use a graphic organizer like this one to list the characteristics of the Reformation in Switzerland and England.

Switzerland	England

LESSON 2
The Spread of Protestantism

ESSENTIAL QUESTION *How can reform influence society and beliefs?*

IT MATTERS BECAUSE

Different forms of Protestantism emerged in Europe during the 1500s. Calvinism challenged Lutheranism with new ideas about salvation, England's Henry VIII created a national church, and Anabaptists challenged both Catholics and other Protestants with ideas about separation of church and state. In response to Protestantism, the Catholic Church also underwent a reformation.

Protestantism in Switzerland

GUIDING QUESTION *Why did Calvinism become an important form of Protestantism by the mid-sixteenth century?*

By permitting German states to choose between Catholicism and Lutheranism, the Peace of Augsburg officially ended Christian unity in Europe. Previously, however, divisions had appeared within Protestantism. One of these new groups arose in Switzerland.

Ulrich Zwingli was a priest in the Swiss city of Zürich. The city council of Zürich, strongly influenced by Zwingli, began to introduce religious reforms. All paintings and decorations were removed from the churches and replaced by whitewashed walls. A new church service consisting of Scripture reading, prayer, and sermons replaced the Catholic mass.

As Zwingli's movement began to spread to other cities in Switzerland, he sought an alliance with Luther and the other German reformers. The German and Swiss reformers saw the need for unity to defend themselves against Catholic authorities, but they could not agree on certain Christian rites.

In October 1531, war broke out between the Protestant and Catholic states in Switzerland. Zürich's army was routed, and Zwingli was found wounded on the battlefield. His enemies killed him, cut up his body, burned the pieces, and scattered the ashes. The leadership of Protestantism in Switzerland passed to John Calvin.

PHOTO: (l to r) © Art Archive, The / SuperStock, NY; Image Asset Management/Age Fotostock America, Classic Vision/Age Fotostock America, Hoberman Collection/Corbis

John Calvin was educated in his native France. As a reformer and convert to Protestantism, Calvin had fled France for the safety of Switzerland. In 1536 he **published** his *Institutes of the Christian Religion,* a summary of his understanding of Protestant thought. Because of the recent invention of the printing press, Calvin's work and the writings of other Protestant leaders could be distributed widely. This helped spread the ideas of the Protestant Reformation. Publication of Calvin's work immediately gained him a reputation as one of the new leaders of Protestantism.

Like Luther, Calvin believed that faith alone was sufficient for **justification**, the process of being deemed worthy of salvation by God. However, Calvin's belief in the all-powerful nature of God led him to other ideas, such as **predestination**. This meant that God had selected some people to be saved and others to be damned. According to Calvin, "God has once for all determined, both whom he would admit to salvation, and whom he would condemn to destruction." Although Calvin stressed that no one could ever be absolutely certain of salvation, his followers did not always heed this warning.

The belief in predestination gave later Calvinists the firm conviction that they were doing God's work on Earth. This conviction made them determined to spread their faith to other people. Calvinism became a dynamic and activist faith.

Calvin created a type of theocracy, or government by divine authority, in the city of Geneva. This government used church leaders and non-clergy in the service of his church. John Knox, the Calvinist reformer of Scotland, called Geneva "the most perfect school of Christ on earth...." Missionaries trained in Geneva went to all parts of Europe. Calvinism was established in France, the Netherlands, Scotland, and central and eastern Europe.

☑ READING PROGRESS CHECK

Describing How did divisions in Protestantism take place in Switzerland?

Reformation in England

GUIDING QUESTION *What made the English Reformation different from the Reformation in the rest of Europe?*

The English Reformation was rooted in politics. King Henry VIII wanted to divorce his wife, Catherine of Aragon, with whom he had a daughter, Mary. He wanted to have a male heir and to marry a new wife, Anne Boleyn. The pope was unwilling to **annul** the king's marriage, so Henry turned to England's highest church courts.

Archbishop of Canterbury Thomas Cranmer ruled in May 1533 that the king's first marriage was "null and absolutely void." At the beginning of June, Henry's new wife, Anne, was made queen. Three months later their child, the future Queen Elizabeth I, was born.

In 1534 at Henry's request, Parliament finalized England's break with the pope and the Catholic Church. The Act of Supremacy of 1534 declared that the king was "the only supreme head on earth of the [new] Church of England." The king now had control over religious doctrine, clerical appointments, and discipline. Thomas More, a Christian humanist and devout Catholic, opposed the king's action and was beheaded.

Henry used his new powers to close monasteries. He sold their lands and possessions to landowners and merchants. The English nobility had

publish to print for distribution

justification process of being justified, or deemed worthy of salvation, by God

predestination belief that God has determined in advance who will be saved (the elect) and who will be damned (the reprobate)

▲ This gold half sovereign shows Henry VIII as king and head of the Church of England.

PHOTO: © Hoberman Collection/Corbis

disliked papal control of the Church, and now they had a financial interest in the new order. Additionally, the king received a boost to his treasury. In most matters of doctrine, however, Henry stayed close to Catholic teachings.

When the king died in 1547, he was succeeded by Edward VI, his nine-year-old son by his third wife. During the brief reign of King Edward VI, church officials who favored Protestant doctrines moved the Church of England, or the Anglican Church, in a Protestant direction. New acts of Parliament gave clergy the right to marry and created a Protestant church service. Before he turned 16, Edward died of tuberculosis.

The rapid changes in doctrine and policy during Edward's reign aroused opposition. When Henry VIII's daughter Mary I came to the throne in 1553, England was ready for a reaction. Mary was a Catholic who wanted to restore England to Roman Catholicism, but her efforts had the opposite effect. Among other actions, she ordered the burning of almost 300 Protestants as heretics, earning her the nickname "Bloody Mary." As a result of her policies, England was even more committed to Protestantism by the end of Mary's reign.

✔ **READING PROGRESS CHECK**

Identifying Cause and Effect What caused the Protestant Reformation in England, and what resulted from it?

▲ This image shows the execution of Thomas Cranmer, Protestant Archbishop of Canterbury, which was ordered by Mary I in 1556.

▶ **CRITICAL THINKING**
Drawing Conclusions Why would Protestants want to circulate images of events such as the execution of Cranmer?

Anabaptists

GUIDING QUESTION *Why did both Catholics and Protestants consider Anabaptists dangerous radicals?*

Reformers such as Luther had allowed the state to play an important, if not dominant, role in church affairs. However, some people strongly disliked giving such power to the state. These were radicals known as Anabaptists. Most Anabaptists believed in the complete separation of church and state. Not only was government to be kept out of the realm of religion, it was not supposed to have any political authority over "real" Christians. Anabaptists refused to hold political office or bear arms because many took literally the biblical commandment "Thou shall not kill."

To Anabaptists, the true Christian church was a voluntary **community** of adult believers who had undergone spiritual rebirth and then had been baptized. This belief in adult baptism separated the Anabaptists from Catholics and other Protestants, who baptized infants.

Anabaptists also believed in following the practices and the spirit of early Christianity. They considered all believers to be equal. Anabaptists based this belief on the accounts of early Christian communities in the New Testament of the Bible. Each Anabaptist church chose its own minister, or spiritual leader. Because all Christians were considered to be priests, any member of the community was eligible to be a minister—though women were often excluded.

Their political beliefs, as much as their religious beliefs, caused the Anabaptists to be regarded as dangerous radicals who threatened the very fabric of sixteenth-century society. The chief thing other Protestants and Catholics could agree on was the need to persecute Anabaptists.

Many of the persecuted Anabaptists settled in Münster, a city in Westphalia in modern-day Germany, in the 1530s. Under John of Leiden, the city

annul declare invalid

community a group of people with common interests and characteristics living together within a larger society

became a sanctuary for Anabaptists. In 1534 an army of Catholics and other Protestants surrounded the city. Then in 1535, they captured it, torturing and killing the Anabaptist leaders.

✓ READING PROGRESS CHECK

Discussing What beliefs did the Anabaptists have that alarmed the other Protestants and Catholics?

ghetto formerly a district in a city in which Jews were required to live

Reformation and Society

GUIDING QUESTION *How did the Reformation affect European society?*

The Protestant Reformation had an important effect on the development of education in Europe. Protestant teachers were very effective in using humanist methods in new Protestant secondary schools and universities. Protestant schools were aimed at a much wider audience than the humanist schools, which were mostly for the elite.

Convinced of the need to provide the church with good Christians, Martin Luther believed that all children should have an education provided by the state. To that end, he urged the cities and villages of German states to provide schools paid for by the public. Protestants in Germany then established secondary schools, where teaching in Greek and Latin was combined with religious instruction.

To some extent, Protestantism also modified the traditional view of marriage. Protestants had abolished monasticism and the requirement of celibacy for their clergy. The mutual love between man and wife in marriage could be praised. However, reality more often reflected the traditional roles of husband as the ruler and wife as the obedient servant and bearer of children. Calvin and Luther saw this role of women as part of the divine plan.

Other traditional features of European society were unaffected by the Reformation. Anti-Semitism, which is hostility or discrimination against Jews, remained common in Europe after the Reformation. Martin Luther expected Jews to convert to Lutheranism. When they resisted, Luther wrote that Jewish houses of worship and homes should be destroyed. The Catholic Church was no more tolerant. In Italy's Papal States, which were controlled by the popes, Jews who would not convert were forced to live in segregated areas called **ghettos**.

✓ READING PROGRESS CHECK

Analyzing What was Luther's view about women's role in society?

Catholic Reformation

GUIDING QUESTION *What prompted the Catholic Reformation during the sixteenth century?*

The situation in Europe did not appear favorable for the Catholic Church. Lutheranism had become rooted in Germany and Scandinavia, and Calvinism had taken hold in Switzerland, France, the Netherlands, and Eastern Europe. In England, the split from Rome had resulted in the creation of a national church. However, the Catholic Church was revitalized in the sixteenth century. It found new strength and regained much that it had lost to the Protestant Reformation. Three elements supported this

Catholic Reformation, which is also called the Counter-Reformation. The first was the establishment of a new religious order, the Jesuits. The second was the reform of the papacy. The third element was the Council of Trent.

A Spanish nobleman, Ignatius of Loyola, founded the Society of Jesus, or Jesuits. Pope Paul III recognized Loyola's small group of followers as a religious order in 1540. All Jesuits took a special vow of absolute obedience to the pope, making them an important instrument for papal policy. Jesuits used education to spread their message and established schools. Jesuit missionaries were very successful in restoring Catholicism to parts of Germany and eastern Europe and in spreading it to other parts of the world.

Later in the century, a Spanish nun, Teresa of Ávila, promoted the reform of the Carmelite order. The Carmelites were one of the four major religious orders founded in the Middle Ages who took a vow of complete poverty. In 1562 Teresa founded a small convent at Ávila where the nuns followed a very strict way of life.

Reform of the papacy was another important element in the Catholic Reformation. The participation of Renaissance popes in dubious financial transactions and in Italy's politics and wars had encouraged corruption. It took the jolt of the Protestant Reformation to change the Catholic Church.

Pope Paul III saw the need for reform. He took the bold step of naming a Reform Commission in 1535 to determine the Church's ills. The commission blamed the Church's problems on the popes' corrupt policies.

Pope Paul III also called the Council of Trent. Beginning in March 1545, a group of cardinals, archbishops, bishops, abbots, and theologians met off and on for 18 years in the city of Trent in modern-day Italy near the Swiss border.

The final decrees of the Council reaffirmed traditional Catholic teachings in opposition to Protestant beliefs. Both faith and good works were declared necessary for salvation. The seven sacraments, the Catholic view of the Eucharist, and clerical celibacy were all upheld. Belief in purgatory and in the use of indulgences was strengthened, although the selling of indulgences was forbidden. The Roman Catholic Church now possessed a clear body of doctrine. It was unified under the pope's supreme leadership. Catholics were now more confident as defenders of their faith.

BIOGRAPHY

Teresa of Ávila (1515–1582)

Displeased with the relaxed lifestyle at the Carmelite convent at Ávila, Teresa began thinking of ways to return the order to its former strict way of life. In her reforms, she required nuns to meditate and practice penance. With Pope Pius IV's approval, she opened the first convent of the Carmelite Reform in 1562. She went on to found 16 more convents throughout Spain.

▶ **CRITICAL THINKING**
Drawing Conclusions How did Teresa of Ávila combine the spiritual and the practical in her life?

☑ **READING PROGRESS CHECK**

Exploring Issues What were the three key elements of the Catholic Reformation, and why were they so important to the Catholic Church in the sixteenth century?

PHOTO: Getty Images

LESSON 2 REVIEW

Reviewing Vocabulary

1. ***Explaining*** Explain why England's King Henry VIII needed the pope to annul his marriage to Queen Catherine of Aragon.

Using your Notes

2. ***Distinguishing*** Use your notes to identify the characteristics of the Protestant Reformation in Switzerland and England.

Answering the Guiding Questions

3. ***Explaining*** Why did Calvinism become an important form of Protestantism by the mid-sixteenth century?

4. ***Contrasting*** What made the English Reformation different from the Reformation in the rest of Europe?

5. ***Analyzing*** Why were Anabaptists considered by both Catholics and Protestants to be dangerous radicals?

6. ***Finding the Main Idea*** How did the Reformation affect European society?

7. ***Making Connections*** What prompted the Catholic Reformation during the sixteenth century?

Writing Activity

8. **INFORMATIVE/EXPLANATORY** Explain how political and economic issues played a role in the Protestant Reformation in Europe.

Directions: On a separate sheet of paper, answer the questions below. Make sure you read carefully and answer all parts of the questions.

Lesson Review

Lesson 1

1 **CONTRASTING** How did humanism contradict medieval attitudes toward Christianity?

2 **IDENTIFYING** What was the Modern Devotion?

3 **CONTRASTING** How did Martin Luther's attitude toward good works contradict Erasmus's philosophy of Christ?

4 **ASSESSING** Why did it take 38 years from the time Luther wrote his Ninety-five Theses until Lutheranism was accepted at the Peace of Augsburg?

Lesson 2

5 **DRAWING CONCLUSIONS** How is the concept of predestination tied to the dynamic growth of the Calvinist faith?

6 **IDENTIFYING CENTRAL ISSUES** What were the Anabaptists' core beliefs?

7 **SUMMARIZING** What role did the Bible play in Protestant faiths? In the Roman Catholic faith?

8 **IDENTIFYING** What was the Council of Trent?

21st Century Skills

9 **IDENTIFYING PERSPECTIVES** What were Protestants protesting against?

10 **UNDERSTANDING RELATIONSHIPS AMONG EVENTS** Why did the German peasants expect Luther to support their revolt?

11 **IDENTIFYING CAUSE AND EFFECT** One can never predict all the effects of one's actions. How does the experience of Queen Mary I as she tried to restore Catholicism as the sole religion of England illustrate this?

12 **UNDERSTANDING RELATIONSHIPS AMONG EVENTS** What benefits, if any, did the revolt against the Catholic Church lead to for Catholicism?

Exploring the Essential Questions

13 **SEQUENCING INFORMATION** Work with a small group to create a time line showing at least six events in the Reformation and the Catholic Reformation. Label each event explaining how it influenced society and beliefs. Include visuals such as portraits, drawings of events, and maps.

DBQ Analyzing Historical Documents

Use the document to answer the following questions.

Teresa of Ávila wrote several books, including a treatise on prayer called *The Interior Castle,* addressed to the nuns in her convent. This excerpt is from the epilogue to *The Interior Castle.*

PRIMARY SOURCE

❝ In return for my strong desire to aid you in serving Him, my God and my Lord, I implore you, whenever you read this, to praise His Majesty fervently in my name and to beg Him to prosper His Church, to give light to the Lutherans, to pardon my sins and to free me from purgatory, where perhaps I shall be, by the mercy of God, when you see this book (if it is given to you after having been examined by theologians). If these writings contain any error, it is through my ignorance; I submit in all things to the teachings of the holy Catholic Roman Church, of which I am now a member, as I protest and promise I will be both in life and death. ❞

14 **ANALYZING PRIMARY SOURCES** What is Teresa's opinion of her religion?

15 **MAKING INFERENCES** Why does Teresa pray for God to give light to the Lutherans?

Extended-Response Question

16 **INFORMATIVE/EXPLANATORY** Discuss the links between politics and religion during the fifteenth and sixteenth centuries. Explain which political, economic, and social factors led to religious reform.

Need Extra Help?

If You've Missed Question	1	2	3	4	5	6	7	8	9	10	11	12	13	14	15	16
Go to page	38	39	40	40	44	45	38	47	39	41	45	46	39	48	48	38

The Age of Exploration

1500–1800

ESSENTIAL QUESTION *What are the effects of political and economic expansion?*

The Story Matters...

During the Age of Exploration that began in the late fifteenth century, European explorers made voyages in search of wealth, new lands, and converts for Christianity. They found all of these things and more, including civilizations undreamed of by Europeans. They also established the first global trading empires. One of these European explorers was Amerigo Vespucci, an Italian navigator who made several voyages to the Western Hemisphere.

◄ Reading of Vespucci's voyages, a German mapmaker proposed using a form of the name Amerigo for the newly found lands. In 1507 he published the first map with the name "America" on the still unknown lands of the Western Hemisphere. This portrait of Vespucci appeared in a geographical work published in 1673.

PHOTO: The Image Works.

Place and Time: The Age of Exploration 1500–1800

The Age of Exploration led to great cultural and economic changes, both in Europe and throughout the world. The European explorers of the fifteenth and sixteenth centuries pioneered new trade routes that would link regions previously isolated. New global political and economic relations developed, and a new interconnected world began to emerge. However, this large-scale European expansion often had negative side effects for the indigenous peoples, including war, disease, and cultural devastation.

Step Into the Place

Read the quotes and look at the information presented on the map.

DBQ **Analyzing Historical Documents** What different motivations affected European explorers of this time?

PRIMARY SOURCE

❝And [the Portuguese explorer Vasco da Gama] told [the Indian ruler of Calicut]... [kings of Portugal] had annually sent out vessels to make discoveries in the direction of India, ... not because they sought for gold or silver, for of this they had such abundance that they needed not what was to be found in this country. He further stated that the captains sent out traveled for a year or two, until their provisions were exhausted, and then returned to Portugal...❞

—from *Journal of the First Voyage of Vasco da Gama*, 1497–1499

PRIMARY SOURCE

❝[Hernán Cortés] said to [the Aztec ruler] Montezuma through our interpreter, half laughing: 'Señor Montezuma, I do not understand how such a great Prince and wise man as you are has not come to the conclusion, in your mind, that these idols of yours are not gods, but evil things that are called devils'...

Montezuma replied half angrily...'Señor [Cortés],... we consider [our gods] to be very good, for they give us health and rains and good seed times and seasons and as many victories as we desire, and we are obliged to worship them and make sacrifices, and I pray you not to say another word in their dishonour.'❞

—from *The Discovery and Conquest of Mexico*, Bernal Díaz del Castillo, 1552–1568

PHOTO: (l)Master of Saldana/Getty Images, (r)Pedro Barretto de Resende/The Bridgeman Art Library

Step Into the Time

Demonstrating Understanding Choose an event from the time line and explain how it shows a consequence of the European voyages of discovery.

EUROPE AND THE AMERICAS				
1500 Pedro Cabral of Portugal reaches South America	**1519** Hernán Cortés of Spain arrives in Mexico; by 1521 he has conquered the Aztec Empire	**1520** Commanding a Spanish fleet, Ferdinand Magellan sails into the Pacific Ocean	**1533** Francisco Pizarro of Spain conquers the Inca Empire	**1538** Fewer than 500 Native Americans survive on Hispaniola	**1608** Samuel de Champlain of France founds Quebec

THE WORLD

1500   **1550**   **1600**

1520 Süleyman I takes control of the Ottoman Empire.

circa 1526 West African ruler Afonso I attempts to restrict slave trade

1590 Toyotomi Hideyoshi takes control of Japan

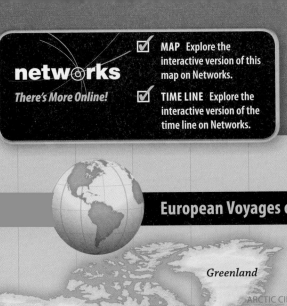
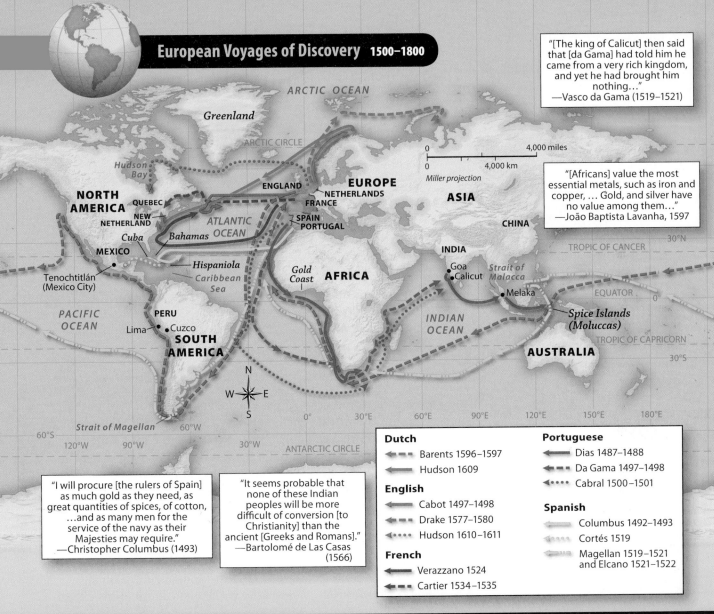

European Voyages of Discovery 1500–1800

"[The king of Calicut] then said that [da Gama] had told him he came from a very rich kingdom, and yet he had brought him nothing…"
—Vasco da Gama (1519–1521)

"[Africans] value the most essential metals, such as iron and copper, … Gold, and silver have no value among them…"
—João Baptista Lavanha, 1597

"I will procure [the rulers of Spain] as much gold as they need, as great quantities of spices, of cotton, …and as many men for the service of the navy as their Majesties may require."
—Christopher Columbus (1493)

"It seems probable that none of these Indian peoples will be more difficult of conversion [to Christianity] than the ancient [Greeks and Romans]."
—Bartolomé de Las Casas (1566)

Dutch
- ◄--- Barents 1596–1597
- ◄— Hudson 1609

English
- ◄— Cabot 1497–1498
- ◄--- Drake 1577–1580
- ◄···· Hudson 1610–1611

French
- ◄— Verazzano 1524
- ◄--- Cartier 1534–1535

Portuguese
- ◄— Dias 1487–1488
- ◄--- Da Gama 1497–1498
- ◄···· Cabral 1500–1501

Spanish
- ◄— Columbus 1492–1493
- ◄···· Cortés 1519
- ◄--- Magellan 1519–1521 and Elcano 1521–1522

1664 England seizes New Netherland colony from the Dutch and renames it New York

1740 War of Austrian Succession begins

1756 Seven Years' War between Britain and France begins

1787 Northwest Ordinance bans slavery in the Northwest Territory of the United States

1650   **1700**   **1750**   **1800**

1612 Tokugawa Shogunate begins closing of Japan to foreign missionaries

1644 End of China's Ming Dynasty; succeeded by Qing Dynasty

1632 Building of Taj Mahal begins

1687 Ottoman Sultan Süleyman II comes to power

1707 Decline of Mogul empire in India begins

1736 End of Safavid rule in Iran

networks

There's More Online!

- ☑ **BIOGRAPHY** Christopher Columbus
- ☑ **BIOGRAPHY** Hernán Cortés
- ☑ **IMAGE** Aztec Warriors Defend Tenochtitlán
- ☑ **INFOGRAPHIC** Spanish Conquest of the Aztec and Inca
- ☑ **INTERACTIVE SELF-CHECK QUIZ**
- ☑ **PRIMARY SOURCE** Letter from Hernán Cortés
- ☑ **PRIMARY SOURCE** Rights Granted to Columbus by Spain
- ☑ **VIDEO** European Exploration and Expansion

Reading HELP DESK CCSS

Academic Vocabulary

- overseas

Content Vocabulary

- caravel • colony
- conquistador

TAKING NOTES:

Key Ideas and Details

Summarizing Use a graphic organizer like this one to identify which European nations and individuals explored which region(s).

Nation	Explorer	Region(s)

LESSON 1
European Exploration and Expansion

ESSENTIAL QUESTION
What are the effects of political and economic expansion?

 ## IT MATTERS BECAUSE

European explorers traveled east and west driven by a variety of motives, including desire for wealth, political ambition, religious zeal, and the call of adventure. These connections between Europe and the rest of the world were crucial to forming the modern world.

Motives and Means

GUIDING QUESTION *What were the motivations behind European exploration of distant lands?*

For almost a thousand years, most Europeans had remained in their small region of the world. Then, between 1500 and 1800, European explorers used improved sailing ships to travel and explore the rest of the world. First Portugal and Spain, and then later the Netherlands, England, and France, reached to new economic heights through their travels and resulting trading activity. At the end of the fifteenth century, they set out on a remarkable series of **overseas** journeys. What caused them to undertake such dangerous voyages?

European explorers had long been attracted to Asia. In the late thirteenth century, Marco Polo traveled from Venice with his father and uncle to the Chinese court of the great Mongol ruler Kublai Khan (KOO • bluh KAHN). Marco Polo wrote an account of his experiences, entitled *The Travels*. Many Europeans read the book and were fascinated by what they imagined as the exotic East. In the fourteenth century, conquests by the Ottoman Turks reduced the ability of Westerners to travel by land to the East. People then spoke of gaining access to Asia by sea.

Economic motives loom large in European expansion. Merchants, adventurers, and state officials had high hopes of expanding trade, especially for the spices of the East. The spices, which were needed to preserve and flavor food, were very expensive after Arab middlemen shipped them to Europe. Europeans also had hopes of finding precious metals.

It has been said that "Gold, glory, and God" were the key motives for European expansion. This statement suggests another reason for the overseas voyages: religious zeal. Many people shared the belief of Hernán Cortés, the Spanish conqueror of Mexico, that they must ensure that indigenous people were "introduced into and instructed in the holy Catholic Faith."

Spiritual and secular affairs were connected in the sixteenth century. Many Europeans wanted to convert indigenous people to Christianity, but grandeur, glory, and a spirit of adventure also played a major role in European expansion.

New sailing technology made the voyages of discovery possible. Europeans had now reached a level of ship design that enabled them to make long-distance voyages beyond Europe. The Portuguese invented a ship, called the **caravel**, that was faster than previous models. It made long voyages of exploration possible and lowered the cost of transport. The caravel's design included a large cargo hold. It used triangular, or lateen, sails, taken from Arab designs, which allowed it to sail against the wind.

European explorers also had more accurate maps because of advances in cartography, the art and science of mapmaking. Sailors used the astrolabe, an invention of Greek astronomers, to plot their latitude using the sun or stars. The magnetic compass, invented in China, also helped sailors chart a course across the ocean.

Another factor assisting European explorers was their increasing knowledge of wind patterns of the Atlantic Ocean. The winds, ocean currents, and climate influenced the journeys of the early sailing vessels that depended on them. The Atlantic, Pacific, and Indian Oceans have spiraling currents, called gyres, that result from global winds and other forces. The winds blowing south and west in the North Atlantic, known as the trade winds, and the winds blowing from the west to the east, known as westerlies, were studied and utilized to the explorers' benefit.

overseas beyond or across the sea

caravel a small, fast, maneuverable ship that had a large cargo hold and usually three masts with lateen sails

✅ **READING PROGRESS CHECK**

Explaining What does the phrase "Gold, glory, and God" mean?

A Race for Riches

GUIDING QUESTION *How were Spain and Portugal able to take the lead in discovering new lands?*

During the fifteenth century, European explorers sailed into the world in new directions. Portuguese ships took the lead when they sailed southward along the West African coast.

Portuguese Explorers

Beginning in 1420, under the sponsorship of Prince Henry the Navigator, Portuguese fleets began probing southward along the western coast of Africa. There, they discovered a new source of gold. The southern coast of West Africa became known to Europeans as the Gold Coast.

Portuguese sea captains heard reports of a route to India around the southern tip of Africa. In 1488 Bartholomeu Dias reached the tip, later called the Cape of Good Hope, and returned. Next, Vasco da Gama went around Africa and cut across the Indian Ocean to the coast of India. In May 1498, he arrived off the port of Calicut. After da Gama returned to Portugal, he made a large profit from the cargo of spices he obtained in India.

▼ A Portuguese caravel

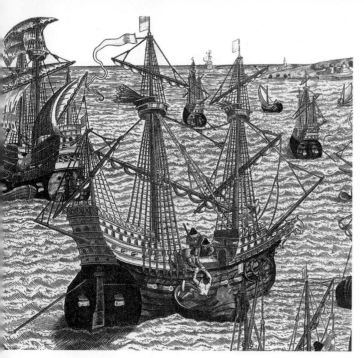

▲ An engraving from 1592 shows the harbor of Lisbon full of ships coming from and going to Portugal's overseas colonies.

▶ **CRITICAL THINKING**
Analyzing What does this image suggest about Portugal's role in international trade at the end of the sixteenth century?

Portuguese fleets returned to the area to take control of the spice trade from the Muslims. The Portuguese Admiral Afonso de Albuquerque (AL • buh • KUR • kee) established a port at Goa, India. Later, Albuquerque sailed into Melaka, a thriving spice trade port on the Malay Peninsula. By taking over Melaka, the Portuguese destroyed Arab control of the spice trade and gained a stopping place on the long journey to the Moluccas, then known as the Spice Islands.

A Portuguese treaty signed with the local Moluccan ruler established Portuguese control of the spice trade. The Portuguese had a limited empire of trading posts on the coasts of India and China. They did not have the power, people, or the desire to colonize these regions.

Spanish Explorers

Educated Europeans knew the world was round but had no idea of its circumference, the size of the Asian continent, or that another continent was located to the west between Europe and Asia. While the Portuguese sailed south along the coast of Africa, then east through the Indian Ocean, the Spanish sailed west across the Atlantic Ocean to find the route to Asia.

Christopher Columbus believed he could reach Asia by sailing west instead of east around Africa. Columbus persuaded Queen Isabella of Spain to finance an exploratory expedition. In October 1492, he reached the Americas, where he explored the coastline of Cuba and the island of Hispaniola in the Caribbean.

Columbus believed he had reached Asia. After three voyages, he had still not found a route through the outer islands to what he believed was the Asian mainland. In his four voyages, Columbus reached all the major Caribbean islands and Honduras in Central America—all of which he called the Indies.

Another important explorer funded by Spain was Ferdinand Magellan. In September 1519, he set sail from Spain in search of a sea passage through the Americas. In October 1520, Magellan passed through a waterway along the tip of South America, later called the Strait of Magellan, into the Pacific Ocean. The fleet reached the Philippines, but indigenous people there killed Magellan. Although only one of Magellan's ships returned to Spain, as the leader of the expedition, he is remembered as the first person to sail completely around the globe.

New Lands to Explore

Spain and Portugal each feared that the other would claim some of its newly discovered territories. They resolved their concerns over control of the Americas with the Treaty of Tordesillas, signed in 1494. The treaty called for a boundary line extending from north to south through the Atlantic Ocean and the easternmost part of the South American continent. Unexplored territories east of the line would be controlled by Portugal, and those west of the line by Spain. This treaty gave Portugal control over its route around Africa, and it gave Spain rights to almost all of the Americas.

Soon, government-sponsored explorers from many European countries joined the race to the Americas. A Venetian seaman, John Cabot, explored the New England coastline of the Americas on behalf of England in 1497. The Portuguese sea captain Pedro Cabral landed in South America in 1500,

Connections to TODAY

Mapping Ocean Winds

A contemporary use of ocean winds is to drive wind turbines producing electricity. To harness this resource, scientists first need to identify areas in the oceans that have strong winds, using data from NASA satellites. Then, scientists can prepare maps that indicate potential sites for wind farms.

PHOTO: Giraudon / The Bridgeman Art Library International

which established Portugal's claim to the region later named Brazil. Amerigo Vespucci (veh • SPOO • chee), a Florentine, went along on several voyages. His letters describing the lands he saw led to the use of the name America (after Amerigo) for the new lands.

✔ **READING PROGRESS CHECK**

Interpreting How were the first explorations of Spain and Portugal similar and different?

The Spanish Empire

GUIDING QUESTION *What were the results of Spanish and Portuguese conquests in the Americas?*

The Spanish conquerors of the Americas—known as **conquistadors**—were individuals whose firearms, organizational skills, and determination brought them extraordinary success. With their resources, the Spanish were able to establish an overseas empire that was quite different from the Portuguese trading posts.

conquistador a leader in the Spanish conquest of the Americas

Conquest of the Aztec

For a century, the Aztec ruled much of central Mexico from the Gulf of Mexico to the Pacific coast. Most local officials accepted the authority of the Aztec king in the capital Tenochtitlán, which was located at the site of modern-day Mexico City.

In 1519 a Spanish force under the command of Hernán Cortés landed at Veracruz, on the Gulf of Mexico. Cortés marched to Tenochtitlán with a small number of troops—550 soldiers and 16 horses. As he went, he made alliances with city-states that had tired of the oppressive rule of the Aztec. Particularly important was the alliance with Tlaxcala. In November, Cortés arrived at Tenochtitlán and was welcomed by the Aztec monarch Montezuma (Moctezuma). The Aztec were astounded to see the unfamiliar sight of men on horseback with firearms, cannons, and steel swords. These weapons gave the Spaniards a great advantage in fighting the Aztec.

▲ Aztec warriors defending Tenochtitlán against the Spanish

▶ **CRITICAL THINKING**
Drawing Conclusions How did the differences between Aztec and Spanish methods of waging war affect the outcome of the Spanish invasion?

PRIMARY SOURCE

❝We arrived at a broad causeway, when we saw many towns and villages built in the lake, and other large towns on the land, with the level causeway running in a straight line to [Tenochtitlán]. We were astounded and told one another that the majestic towers and houses, all of massive stone and rising out of the waters, were like enchanted castles we had read of in books. Indeed, some of our men even asked if what we saw was not a dream.❞

— Bernal Díaz del Castillo, from *The True History of the Conquest of New Spain*

Eventually, tensions arose between the Spaniards and the Aztec. The Spanish took Montezuma hostage and began to pillage the city. In the fall of 1520, one year after Cortés had first arrived, the local population revolted and drove the invaders from the city. Many of the Spaniards were killed.

However, the Aztec soon experienced new disasters. With no natural immunity to European diseases, many Aztec fell sick and died, especially from smallpox carried to the Americas by the Spaniards. Meanwhile, Cortés received fresh soldiers from his new allies in city-states such as Tlaxcala. After four months, the Aztec surrendered.

The forces of Cortés leveled pyramids, temples, and palaces and used the stones to build Spanish government buildings and churches. They filled in Aztec canals to make roads. The magnificent city of Tenochtitlán was no more. During the 30 years after the fall of the Aztec Empire, the Spanish expanded their control to all of Mexico.

Conquest of the Inca

When the first Spanish expeditions arrived in the central Andes of South America, they encountered a flourishing empire ruled by indigenous people, the Inca. In early 1531, Francisco Pizarro landed on the Pacific coast of South America with only a small band of about 180 men. Like Cortés, Pizarro brought steel weapons, gunpowder, and horses. The Inca had never before seen these things.

The Spanish also brought smallpox. Like the Aztec, the Inca had no immunities to European diseases. Smallpox soon devastated entire villages. Even the Inca emperor was a victim.

When the emperor died, both of his sons claimed the throne. This led to a civil war. Taking advantage of the situation, Pizarro captured Atahuallpa, the new emperor. With their stones, arrows, and light spears, Inca warriors provided little challenge to Spanish technology.

After executing Atahuallpa, Pizarro, his soldiers, and their Inca allies sacked Cuzco, the Inca capital. By 1535, Pizarro had established a new capital at Lima for a new **colony** of the Spanish Empire.

colony a settlement of people living in a new territory, linked with the parent country by trade and direct government control

✅ **READING PROGRESS CHECK**

Comparing and Contrasting How were the conquests of the Aztec and the Inca similar and different?

European Rivals

GUIDING QUESTION *Which other European countries explored and settled in the Americas?*

By the end of the sixteenth century, several new European rivals—the Dutch, French, and English—had begun to challenge the Portuguese and the Spanish for colonial dominance. Motivated by the promise of gold and other precious goods, these countries sent explorers to the Americas to search for new sources of wealth and trade opportunities.

The Dutch formed the West India Company. Although it made some temporary inroads in Portuguese Brazil and the Caribbean, the company lacked the resources and power to maintain these gains.

In the early seventeenth century, Dutch settlements were established on the North American continent and named New Netherland. The colony extended from the mouth of the present-day Hudson River as far north as present-day Albany, New York. This settlement and others never flourished because of the West India Company's commercial goals. Fur trading, with its remote outposts, did not encourage settlement.

After 1660, the Dutch commercial empire in the Americas fell to its rivals, the English and the French. In 1664 the English seized the colony of New Netherland from the Dutch and renamed it New York. The Dutch West India Company soon went bankrupt.

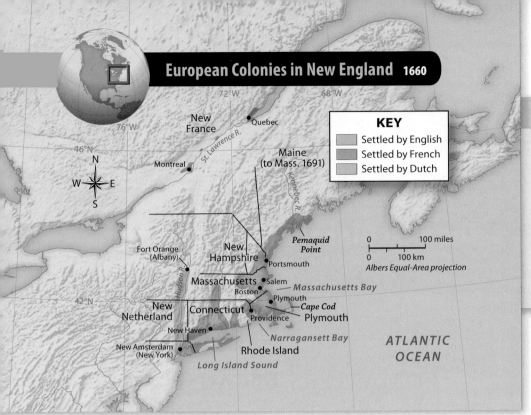

European Colonies in New England 1660

KEY
Settled by English
Settled by French
Settled by Dutch

New France
Quebec
Maine (to Mass. 1691)
Montreal
St. Lawrence R.
Kennebec R.
Pemaquid Point
Fort Orange (Albany)
New Hampshire
Portsmouth
Hudson R.
Massachusetts
Salem
Boston
Massachusetts Bay
Plymouth
Cape Cod
New Netherland
Connecticut
Providence
Plymouth
New Haven
Narragansett Bay
New Amsterdam (New York)
Rhode Island
Long Island Sound
ATLANTIC OCEAN

0   100 miles
0   100 km
Albers Equal-Area projection

GEOGRAPHY CONNECTION

1 ENVIRONMENT AND SOCIETY On which waterways did the early Dutch and French fur trappers depend?

2 PLACES AND REGIONS How did the pattern of English settlement differ from that of the Dutch and the French?

During the seventeenth century, the French colonized parts of what is now Canada, then named New France, and Louisiana. In 1608 Samuel de Champlain founded Quebec, the first permanent French settlement in the Americas. When New France became a royal province in 1663, with its own governor, military commander, and soldiers, the population grew and the colony developed. Meanwhile, English settlers were founding Virginia and the Massachusetts Bay Colony.

By the end of the seventeenth century, the English had established control over most of the eastern seaboard of North America. They had also set up sugar plantations on several Caribbean islands. Nevertheless, compared to the enormous Spanish empire in Latin America, the North American colonies were of minor importance to the English economy.

✔ **READING PROGRESS CHECK**

Locating Where were the earliest settlements of the Dutch, French, and English in the Americas?

LESSON 1 REVIEW ⓒⒸⓈⓈ

Reviewing Vocabulary

1. *Identifying* Write a paragraph explaining why the caravel was an important development for European explorers.

Using Your Notes

2. *Summarizing* Use your graphic organizer on European exploration to write a paragraph summarizing the major explorers and the regions each nation explored.

Answering the Guiding Questions

3. *Identifying Cause and Effect* What were the motivations behind European exploration of distant lands?

4. *Making Connections* How were Spain and Portugal able to take the lead in discovering new lands?

5. *Identifying Cause and Effect* What were the results of Spanish and Portuguese conquests in America?

6. *Naming* Which other European countries explored and settled in the Americas?

Writing Activity

7. **INFORMATIVE/EXPLANATORY** Write an essay explaining how the Spanish succeeded in conquering much of the Americas. Identify the various factors that enabled them to overthrow such long-standing and extensive empires as the Aztec and the Inca.

netw⊙rks
There's More Online!

☑ **BIOGRAPHY** King Afonso I

☑ **CHART/GRAPH** Age of Exploration Economic Concepts

☑ **INTERACTIVE SELF-CHECK QUIZ**

☑ **PRIMARY SOURCE** Grant for Encomienda

☑ **PRIMARY SOURCE** King Afonso's Letter to the King of Portugal

☑ **TIME LINE** From Africa's Shores to America's Plantations

☑ **VIDEO** The First Global Economic Systems

Reading **HELP**DESK

Academic Vocabulary

- **culture**
- **export**
- **regime**

Content Vocabulary

- **mercantilism**
- **plantations**
- **Middle Passage**

TAKING NOTES:

Key Ideas and Details

Identifying Use a graphic organizer like this one to note how plants, animals, and diseases moved between Europe, Africa, and Asia and the Americas as a result of the Columbian Exchange.

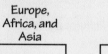

Europe, Africa, and Asia		The Americas
	⟷	

LESSON 2
The First Global Economic Systems

ESSENTIAL QUESTION
What are the effects of political and economic expansion?

IT MATTERS BECAUSE

As the number of European colonies grew in the 1500s and 1600s, so did the volume and area of European trade, beginning a process that led to a world economy. An Atlantic slave trade also brought as many as 10 million enslaved Africans to the Americas between 1500 and the late 1800s. Species of plants and animals, along with diseases, spread between the continents. These exchanges had a lasting effect on the world's peoples.

Trade, Colonies, and Mercantilism

GUIDING QUESTION *What economic theories were put into practice during the age of exploration?*

In less than 300 years, the European age of exploration changed the world. In some areas, such as the Americas and the Spice Islands, it led to the destruction of local **cultures** and the establishment of European colonies. In others, such as Africa and mainland Southeast Asia, it left native **regimes** intact but had a strong impact on local societies and regional trade patterns. European expansion affected Africa with a dramatic increase in the slave trade, which became a key part of European trade.

European colonial expansion around the world produced a great increase in European trade. This growth was one of the first steps in the development of the world economy. The nations of Europe were creating trading empires, causing dramatic shifts in the economies and cultures of the Americas, Africa, and Asia.

Led by Portugal and Spain, European nations established many trading posts and colonies in the Americas and in the East. The establishment of these colonies played a role in the theory of **mercantilism** that dominated economic thought throughout the seventeenth century.

Mercantilists believed that the prosperity of a nation depends on a large supply of bullion, or gold and silver. To bring in gold and silver payments, nations tried to have a favorable balance of trade. The balance of trade is the difference in value between what a nation imports and hat it **exports** over time. Imports are goods brought into a country; exports are goods shipped out of a country. When the balance is favorable, the exported goods are of greater value than the imported goods.

To encourage exports, governments stimulated the growth of industries and trade. They granted subsidies to new industries. Subsidies are payments made to support enterprises a government thinks are beneficial. Governments also improved transportation systems by building roads, bridges, and canals. They placed high tariffs, or taxes, on foreign goods to keep the balance of trade favorable. Tariffs make foreign goods less attractive because they raise the price of imports. European colonies were considered to be important as sources of raw materials and were viewed as markets for exports of manufactured goods.

☑ READING PROGRESS CHECK

Making Inferences How might mercantilism have encouraged colonial expansion abroad?

The Columbian Exchange

GUIDING QUESTION *How did the Columbian Exchange affect the Americas and Europe?*

A major goal of European exploration was to gain wealth. European nations sought to increase their wealth by exploiting sources of precious metals and raw materials in their colonies. They also tried to build wealth by increasing exports of goods from producers at home to colonial markets overseas. All of this economic activity created an immense trade network. The resulting exchange of plants and animals between Europe and the Americas is known as the Columbian Exchange. This name recognizes the explorer Christopher Columbus's key role in bringing Europe into contact with the Americas. This complex process had far-reaching results, both good and bad, on peoples around the world.

culture the customary beliefs, social forms, and material traits of a racial, religious, or social group

regime a government in power

mercantilism a set of principles that dominated economic thought in the seventeenth century; it held that the prosperity of a nation depended on a large supply of gold and silver

export to send a product or service for sale to another country

GOLD IMPORTS TO SPAIN IN THE SIXTEENTH CENTURY		CHARTS/GRAPHS

Period	Gold Imports (In grams)
1503–1510	4,965,180
1511–1520	9,153,220
1521–1530	4,889,050
1531–1540	14,466,360
1541–1550	24,957,130
1551–1560	42,620,080
1561–1570	11,530,940
1571–1580	9,429,140
1581–1590	12,101,650
1591–1600	19,451,420
Total	153,564,170

Source: Earl J. Hàmilton, *American Treasure and the Price Revolution in Spain, 1501–1650*

Gold and silver from the Americas increased Spain's economic power.

▶ CRITICAL THINKING

1 *Analyzing* About how many times greater were gold imports in 1551–1560 than they had been at the beginning of the century?

2 *Identifying* How does this pattern of change show mercantilist goals?

PHOTO: Giraudon

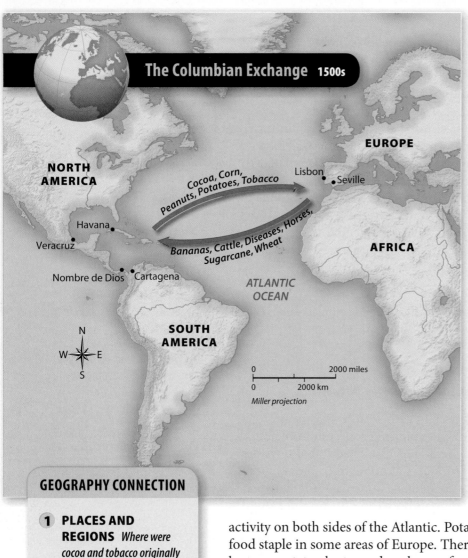

The Columbian Exchange 1500s

Cocoa, Corn, Peanuts, Potatoes, Tobacco

Bananas, Cattle, Diseases, Horses, Sugarcane, Wheat

NORTH AMERICA

EUROPE

Lisbon • Seville

Havana

Veracruz

Nombre de Dios • Cartagena

SOUTH AMERICA

AFRICA

ATLANTIC OCEAN

N W E S

0   2000 miles
0   2000 km
Miller projection

GEOGRAPHY CONNECTION

1. **PLACES AND REGIONS** *Where were cocoa and tobacco originally grown?*

2. **HUMAN SYSTEMS** *How did diseases spread as a result of the Columbian Exchange?*

plantation a large agricultural estate

Colonization and trade drove the Columbian Exchange. Colonists established **plantations** to grow sugar, cotton, vanilla, and other crops introduced to the Americas. Colonists established ranches where they raised livestock brought from Europe. Much of what the colonists grew and raised was exported to Europe. Europeans brought such plants and animals as wheat, citrus fruit, honeybees, horses, and cattle to the Americas. Horses significantly altered the lifestyles of Native Americans on the Great Plains. Horses enabled them to travel faster and over greater distances. This made hunting more effective, as they could follow the roaming bison herds. Agricultural products native to the Americas, such as potatoes, cocoa, corn, tomatoes, and tobacco, were shipped to Europe.

The exchange of plants and animals between Europe and the Americas transformed economic activity on both sides of the Atlantic. Potatoes, for example, became a basic food staple in some areas of Europe. There was a rapid increase in population because potato plants produced more food per acre than foods that had been grown there before. Elsewhere in the world, new food crops from the Americas not only supported population growth, but also changed tastes and created new markets. For example, the export of American crops such as maize and sweet potatoes to China encouraged a population explosion during the Qing dynasty, which began in 1644.

Some aspects of the Columbian Exchange proved deadly. With no immunity to European diseases, the native peoples of Mexico and Central and South America, such as the Aztec and the Inca, were ravaged by smallpox, measles, and typhus. Many of them died. Hispaniola, for example, had a population of 250,000 when Columbus arrived in 1492. By 1538, fewer than 500 Native Americans had survived. In Mexico, the population dropped from 25 million in 1500 to 1 million in 1630. Similar devastation occurred elsewhere in the region. In North America, entire communities of Native Americans died in epidemics of smallpox and other diseases brought by European settlers.

Colonization had other negative effects, such as the *encomienda* granted by Spain to Spanish settlers. This was the right to use Native Americans as laborers on plantations. The holders of an *encomienda* were supposed to protect the Native Americans, but they often abused them.

☑ READING PROGRESS CHECK

Evaluating How did the introduction of European livestock, foods, and diseases affect people in the Americas?

European Rivals in the East

GUIDING QUESTION *How did the nature of European exploration change by the seventeenth century?*

The Spanish and Portuguese were not the only European trading powers. The Dutch, English and French also expanded their activities into Asia. The first Dutch fleet had arrived in India in 1595. Shortly after, the Dutch formed the East India Company and gradually pushed the Portuguese out of the spice trade in Southeast Asia. The Dutch domination of the spice trade led to massive profits for Dutch merchants. These profits helped make the seventeenth century a Golden Age for the Dutch as they surpassed the Spanish and Portuguese in world trade.

The English soon followed. During the first half of the seventeenth century, the English presence in India steadily increased. By 1650, the British had established a number of trading posts. From them, English ships carried Indian-made cotton goods to the East Indies. There they were bartered for spices, which were shipped back to England.

English success in India attracted rivals. While the Dutch focused on the spice trade, the French established forts along the coast of India. British efforts, however, limited the French, who were soon restricted to a handful of small territories on the southeastern coast of the subcontinent. During the Seven Years' War, the British forced the French to withdraw completely from India. The British East India Company then began to expand, ultimately giving it complete control of India.

✅ **READING PROGRESS CHECK**

Drawing Conclusions How was the Dutch form of mercantilism different from that of Portugal or Spain?

▲ Turkey and citrus fruits show the range of Dutch trade.

The Atlantic Slave Trade

GUIDING QUESTION *How did European expansion affect Africa and the slave trade?*

European expansion led to a dramatic increase in the slave trade. Traffic in enslaved people was not new. As in other areas of the world, slavery had been practiced in Africa since ancient times. However, the demand for enslaved Africans increased with the European settlement of the Americas in the 1490s and the planting of sugarcane there.

Plantations were established in the 1500s along the coast of Brazil and on Caribbean islands to grow sugarcane. Growing cane sugar demands many laborers. Already devastated by European diseases, the surviving population of Native Americans could not supply the labor needed. So enslaved Africans were shipped to the Americas to relieve a labor shortage on plantations.

In 1518 a Spanish ship carried the first enslaved Africans directly from Africa to the Americas. During the next two centuries, the trade in enslaved people grew dramatically. It became part of the triangular trade that connected Europe, Africa, and the American continents.

The triangular trade functioned as follows: European merchant ships carried European manufactured goods, such as guns and cloth, to Africa where they were traded for enslaved people. The enslaved Africans were then sent to the Americas and sold. European merchants then bought tobacco, molasses, sugar, and raw cotton in the Americas and shipped them back to Europe.

As a result of this triangular trade, as many as 10 million enslaved Africans were brought to the Americas between the early sixteenth century and the late nineteenth century. Their journey from Africa to the Americas became known as the **Middle Passage**, the middle portion of the triangular trade route. Many enslaved Africans died on the journey. Those who survived often died from diseases to which they had little or no immunity.

Death rates were higher for newly arrived enslaved Africans than for those born and reared in the Americas. The new generation gradually developed at least a partial immunity to many diseases. Slaveholders, however, rarely encouraged enslaved people to have children. Many slaveholders, especially on islands in the Caribbean, believed that buying a new enslaved person was less expensive than rearing a child from birth to working age.

Sources of Enslaved Africans

Before Europeans arrived in the fifteenth century, most enslaved persons in Africa were prisoners of war. Europeans first bought enslaved people from African merchants at slave markets in return for gold, guns, or other European goods. Local slave traders first obtained their supplies of enslaved persons from nearby coastal regions. As demand grew, they had to move farther inland to find their victims. Local rulers became concerned about the impact of the slave trade on their societies. King Afonso of Congo (Bakongo) attempted to describe the extent of the crisis in his country.

PRIMARY SOURCE

❝[W]e cannot reckon how great the damage is, since the [slave traders] are taking every day our natives, sons of the land and the sons of our noblemen and vassals and our relatives,... [S]o great, Sir, is the corruption and licentiousness that our country is being completely depopulated....❞

—Afonso of Congo, from a letter to the king of Portugal, 1526

Europeans and other Africans, however, generally ignored such protests. Local rulers who traded in enslaved people viewed the slave trade as a source of income. Many sent raiders into defenseless villages.

Effects of the Atlantic Slave Trade

The slave trade was a tragedy for the victims and their families. Its broader effects varied from region to region. The slave trade depopulated some areas and deprived many African communities of their youngest and strongest men and women. The desire of slave traders to provide a constant supply of enslaved persons increased warfare in Africa. Coastal or near-coastal African chiefs and their followers, armed with guns acquired from the trade in enslaved people, increased raids and wars on neighboring peoples. Some Europeans lamented what they were doing to traditional African societies. One Dutch slave trader remarked:

PRIMARY SOURCE

❝From us they have learned... strife, quarrelling, drunkenness, trickery, theft,... unbridled desire for what is not one's own, misdeeds unknown to them before, and... the accursed lust for gold.❞

—From *Africa in History: Themes and Outlines*

The slave trade had a devastating effect on some African states. The case of Benin (buh • NEEN) in West Africa is a good example. A brilliant and creative society in the sixteenth century, Benin was pulled into the slave trade. As the population declined and warfare increased, the people of

▲ The growing demand for labor in the Americas fueled the slave trade in Africa. In this image, caravans of enslaved Africans are led by local slave traders.

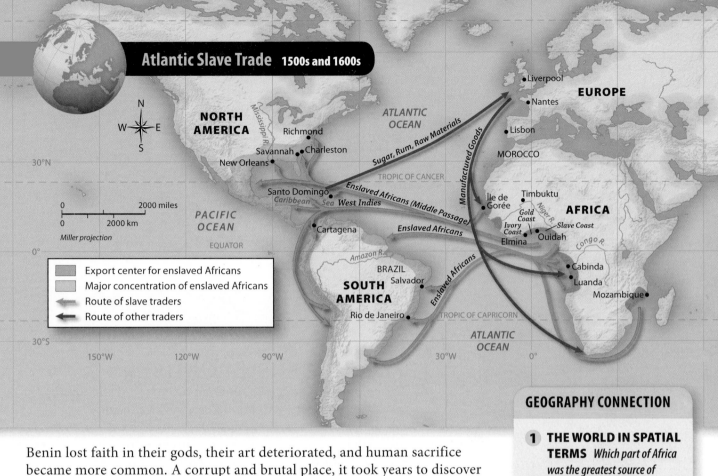

Atlantic Slave Trade 1500s and 1600s

Export center for enslaved Africans
Major concentration of enslaved Africans
Route of slave traders
Route of other traders

GEOGRAPHY CONNECTION

1 **THE WORLD IN SPATIAL TERMS** *Which part of Africa was the greatest source of enslaved people? Why?*

2 **HUMAN SYSTEMS** *What is the connection between the slave trade and the triangular trade?*

Benin lost faith in their gods, their art deteriorated, and human sacrifice became more common. A corrupt and brutal place, it took years to discover the brilliance of the earlier culture that was destroyed by slavery.

The use of enslaved Africans remained largely acceptable to European society. Europeans continued to view Africans as inferior beings fit chiefly for slave labor. Not until the Society of Friends, known as the Quakers, began to condemn slavery in the 1770s did feelings against slavery begin to build in Europe. Even then, it was not until the French Revolution in the 1790s that the French abolished slavery. The British ended the slave trade in 1807 and abolished slavery throughout the empire in 1833. Despite these reforms, slavery continued in the newly formed United States until the Civil War of the 1860s.

☑ **READING PROGRESS CHECK**

Determining Cause and Effect How did epidemics among the Native American populations contribute to an increase in the trade of enslaved Africans?

LESSON 2 REVIEW

Reviewing Vocabulary

1. *Summarizing* Write a paragraph explaining the function of colonies in increasing the wealth of European nations.

Using Your Notes

2. *Organizing* Use your graphic organizer on the Columbian Exchange to list the plants, animals, and diseases that were exchanged among Europe and Africa and the Americas.

Answering the Guiding Questions

3. *Identifying Central Issues* Which economic theory was put into practice during the age of exploration?

4. *Drawing Conclusions* How did the Columbian Exchange affect the Americas and Europe?

5. *Making Generalizations* How did European exploration change by the seventeenth century?

6. *Making Connections* How did European expansion affect Africa and the slave trade?

Writing Activity

7. INFORMATIVE/EXPLANATORY Write a paragraph describing the effects, both positive and negative, of European trade on the Americas. Be sure to refer to specific ideas and specific events.

Reading **HELP**DESK (CCSS)

Academic Vocabulary
- labor
- draft

Content Vocabulary
- *peninsulare*
- *creole*
- *encomienda*
- *mestizo*
- *mulatto*
- *mita*

TAKING NOTES:
Key Ideas and Details

Organizing Information Use a graphic organizer like this one to summarize the political, social, and economic characteristics of colonial Latin America.

LESSON 3
Colonial Latin America

ESSENTIAL QUESTION
What are the effects of political and economic expansion?

IT MATTERS BECAUSE
The colonization of Latin America by Portugal and Spain lasted from the early sixteenth century to the early nineteenth century. The Latin American colonies—rich in gold, silver, and other natural resources—proved to be very profitable for the two European nations. However, colonization led to many changes for both the indigenous peoples and the outsiders who settled there. The interactions of indigenous peoples, enslaved Africans, and the European colonists led to the formation of new social classes. The Catholic Church also had a great influence.

Colonial Empires in Latin America

GUIDING QUESTION *What were the social characteristics of colonial Latin America?*

In the sixteenth century, Spain and Portugal imposed their rule on the new lands they had conquered. Spain established an enormous colonial empire that included most of South America and parts of Central America and North America. At the same time, Portugal became the ruler of Brazil. Within the lands of Central and South America, a new civilization arose, which we call Latin America. This name comes from its principal languages, Spanish and Portuguese, both derived from Latin.

Social Classes

European colonies imitated the culture and social patterns of their parent countries. Colonial Latin America was divided by social classes that were based on status. At the top were **peninsulares**, Spanish and Portuguese officials born in Europe. They were called *peninsulares* because they came from the Iberian Peninsula, the part of Europe containing Spain and Portugal. The *peninsulares* held all the important government positions. Below the *peninsulares* were the **creoles**, descendants of Europeans born in Latin America.

The creoles resented the *peninsulares*, who retained power and regarded the creoles as second-class citizens.

Beneath the *peninsulares* and creoles were numerous multiracial groups. The Spanish and Portuguese in Latin America lived with Native Americans and Africans. Many Native Americans were forced to work in mines and on plantations. Because they were not able to do all the work that was required, however, enslaved Africans were also used for labor. Over a period of three centuries, as many as 8 million Africans were brought to Latin America.

Spanish rulers permitted intermarriage between Europeans and Native Americans. Their offspring became known as the **mestizos**. In addition, the offspring of Africans and Europeans—called **mulattoes**—became another social group. Other groups emerged as a result of unions between mestizos and mulattoes and between Native Americans and Africans. The coexistence of these various groups produced a unique multiracial society in Latin America.

The *peninsulares* and creoles considered all these multiethnic groups to be socially inferior. However, over a period of time, mestizos grew in status due to their increasing numbers. Some mestizos became artisans and merchants in cities, and others became small-scale farmers or ranchers. The groups at the very bottom of the social scale were the Africans and conquered Native Americans.

peninsulare a person born on the Iberian Peninsula; typically, a Spanish or Portuguese official who resided temporarily in Latin America for political and economic gain and then returned to Europe

creole a person of European descent born in Latin America and living there permanently

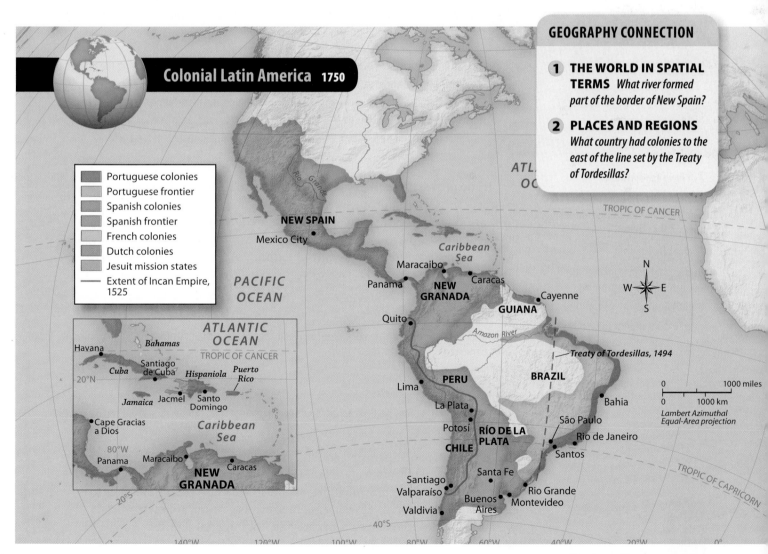

Colonial Latin America 1750

Portuguese colonies
Portuguese frontier
Spanish colonies
Spanish frontier
French colonies
Dutch colonies
Jesuit mission states
— Extent of Incan Empire, 1525

GEOGRAPHY CONNECTION

1 **THE WORLD IN SPATIAL TERMS** *What river formed part of the border of New Spain?*

2 **PLACES AND REGIONS** *What country had colonies to the east of the line set by the Treaty of Tordesillas?*

mestizo a person of mixed European and Native American descent

mulatto a person of mixed African and European descent

labor people with all their abilities and efforts

encomienda a system of labor the Spanish used in the Americas; Spanish landowners had the right, as granted by Queen Isabella, to use Native Americans as laborers

▲ A silver mine in Brazil

▶ **CRITICAL THINKING**
Evaluating How would Europeans find workers to mine silver?

mita a labor system that the Spanish administrators in Peru used to draft native people to work

draft to select for some purpose; to conscript

Economic Foundations

One source of wealth for the Portuguese and Spanish came from resource extraction, or the removal of natural resources from the land. The most important resource extraction was the mining of gold and silver. The abundant supply of those precious metals exported from Latin American colonies financed Spain's wars and stimulated further colonization.

Farming became a more enduring source of prosperity as Spanish and Portuguese landowners created immense estates. However, colonial farming practices also damaged the environment as a result of deforestation, overgrazing, and overcultivation of single export crops.

To maintain a supply of **labor**, the Spanish continued to make use of the **encomienda** system. In this system, Spanish landowners forced Native Americans to pay taxes and provide labor. In return, the landowners were expected to protect them and ensure they were instructed in the Catholic faith. In Peru, the Spanish used an arrangement known as the **mita**, which allowed authorities to **draft** indigenous labor to work in the silver mines.

This system of landowners and dependent peasants became a feature of Latin American society, and it could be an extremely damaging one. The harsh working conditions under the system contributed to a drastic decline in the Native American population. It was the population decline among Native Americans that spurred the importation of enslaved Africans. Catholic priest Bartolomé de Las Casas (bar • to • lo • MAY day lahs CAH • sahs) spoke out against the *encomienda* and its effects on the indigenous peoples.

PRIMARY SOURCE

❝[T]he Spaniards, from the beginning . . . were no more solicitous of promoting the preaching of the Gospel of Christ to [the Native Americans], than if they had been dogs or beasts, . . . laying many heavy [burdens] upon them, daily afflicting and persecuting them, that they might not have so much time and leisure at their own disposal, as to attend their preaching and divine service; for they looked upon that to be an impediment to their getting gold. ❞

—Bartolomé de Las Casas, from *A Brief Account of the Destruction of the Indies*, 1534

Trade provided another avenue for profit. Besides gold and silver, other products shipped to Europe were sugar, tobacco, diamonds, and animal hides. In turn, the Europeans supplied their colonists with manufactured goods. Spain and Portugal regulated the trade of their colonies to keep other European nations out. By the beginning of the eighteenth century, however, the British and French were too powerful to be kept out of these lucrative markets.

☑ **READING PROGRESS CHECK**

Drawing Conclusions What were the two key factors in determining status in colonial Latin America?

State and Church

GUIDING QUESTION *How did Portugal and Spain govern their colonies to promote economic gain and exert their authority?*

The Portuguese and Spanish colonial empires in Latin America lasted more than 300 years. Communication and travel between the Americas and Europe were difficult, making it impossible for the European monarchs to keep a close watch on their overseas empires. As a result, colonial officials in Latin America took liberties in carrying out imperial policies.

Beginning in the mid-sixteenth century, the Portuguese monarchy attempted to assert its control over Brazil by creating the position of governor-general. The governor-general (later called a viceroy) headed a bureaucracy that governed the colony. Such an official was in the colony as a representative of the monarch. But it was not a perfect system. At best, the governor-general had only loose control over the lesser officials who governed the districts into which Brazil was divided.

To rule his American empire, the Spanish king also appointed viceroys. The first was established for New Spain (Mexico) in 1535. Another viceroy was appointed for Peru in 1543. In the eighteenth century, two additional viceroyalties (colonies ruled by a viceroy) were added. Spaniards held all major government positions.

From the beginning of their conquest of the Americas, Spanish and Portuguese rulers were determined to Christianize the indigenous peoples. This policy gave the Catholic Church great influence upon the society and culture of the Americas.

Catholic missionaries—especially the Dominicans, Franciscans, and Jesuits—fanned out to different parts of the Spanish Empire. To make their efforts easier, the missionaries brought Native Americans together into villages, or missions. There, they could be converted, taught trades, and encouraged to grow crops.

Missions enabled missionaries to control the lives of the Native Americans and make them docile subjects of the empire. The Jesuits established more than 30 missions in the region of Paraguay. Well-organized, the Jesuits made their missions into profitable businesses.

Along with the missions, the Catholic Church also built cathedrals, hospitals, and schools in the colonies. These schools gave the Native American students a basic education in the Spanish or the Portuguese language and grammar while preparing them for a religious education.

The Catholic Church provided an outlet other than marriage for women. Women could enter convents and become nuns. Women in religious orders—many of them of aristocratic background—often lived well. Many nuns worked outside their convents by running schools and hospitals. Indeed, one of these women, the Mexican nun Juana Inés de la Cruz (WAHN • ah ee • NAYS de la KROOS), wrote poetry and prose and urged that women be educated.

✔ **READING PROGRESS CHECK**

Applying What role did the Catholic Church play in the colonization of Latin America?

BIOGRAPHY

Juana Inés de la Cruz (1651–1695)

Juana Inés de la Cruz was a Mexican poet and scholar. In 1664 she was invited to the Spanish court and later had her knowledge tested by scholars. She became a nun in 1667, largely in order to focus on her studies. At the Convent of Santa Paula in Mexico, in addition to reading and writing poetry, she served as an archivist and accountant. She became the unofficial poet of the court in the 1680s and was renowned in Mexico and Spain.

▶ **CRITICAL THINKING**
Analyzing What freedoms did becoming a nun afford Juana Inés de la Cruz?

LESSON 3 REVIEW (CCSS)

Reviewing Vocabulary

1. ***Summarizing*** Explain how the social status of mestizos changed over time.

Using Your Notes

2. ***Identifying*** Using your graphic organizer of characteristics of colonial Latin America, summarize the political and economic features.

Answering the Guiding Questions

3. ***Applying*** What were the social characteristics of colonial Latin America?

4. ***Analyzing*** How did Portugal and Spain govern their colonies to promote economic gain and exert their authority?

Writing Activity

5. **INFORMATIVE/EXPLANATORY** Indigenous populations of colonial Latin America were forced to work for years under the *encomienda* and *mita* systems. Write three paragraphs that explain how these systems were the result of economic and political expansion.

Directions: On a separate sheet of paper, answer the questions below. Make sure you read carefully and answer all parts of the questions.

Lesson Review

Lesson 1

1 **DESCRIBING** What events first sparked Europeans' interest in Asia and the Middle East, starting in the thirteenth century?

2 **CATEGORIZING** What were Europeans trying to achieve in North America in the sixteenth and seventeenth centuries? Who were some of the explorers, and where did they travel?

Lesson 2

3 **EXPLAINING** What is the theory of mercantilism? What did the governments of European nations do to encourage exports and favorable trade balances?

4 **IDENTIFYING CENTRAL ISSUES** What movement of people and goods was involved in the triangular slave trade?

Lesson 3

5 **INTERPRETING** What were the differences among *peninsulares*, creoles, mestizos, and mulattoes in Latin America? What was the main purpose of these distinctions?

6 **SPECIFYING** What natural resources did Spain find in Latin America? What did the Spanish government use those resources for?

21st Century Skills

7 **ECONOMICS** What is a country's balance of trade? What makes a trade balance favorable?

8 **GEOGRAPHY SKILLS** How would Columbus have used the ocean winds in his voyages to the Americas and home? Be specific.

9 **MAKING INFERENCES** Why do the people of Brazil speak Portuguese instead of Spanish? What event between Portugal and Spain ensured that they would?

10 **SPECULATING** If the instant communication of today had been available when European nations were exploring the world, how do you think it would have affected events?

Exploring the Essential Questions

11 Work with a partner to create a map showing places where the political and economic expansion of European states had negative effects on the indigenous peoples and/or the environment. Include visuals and primary sources of some of the people and places involved. Be prepared to draw conclusions about the effects of European expansion.

DBQ Analyzing Historical Documents

Use the document to answer the following questions.

Bartolomé de Las Casas took part in the Spanish colonization of the Americas. Shocked by the Spanish soldiers' treatment of the local people, he became a priest and worked in their defense.

PRIMARY SOURCE

" For God's sake and man's faith in him, is this the way to impose the yoke of Christ on Christian men? Is this the way to remove wild barbarism from the minds of barbarians? Is it not, rather, to act like thieves, cut-throats, and cruel plunderers and to drive the gentlest of people headlong into despair? The Indian race is not that barbaric, nor are they dull-witted or stupid, but they are easy to teach and very talented in learning all the liberal arts . . . "

—from Bartolomé de Las Casas, *In Defense of the Indians*, 1550

12 **SYNTHESIZING** Does Las Casas approve of the behavior of his countrymen in the Americas? Does he think the Spanish soldiers are good Christians?

13 **DRAWING CONCLUSIONS** Las Casas calls the Indians "the gentlest of people." Why then does he (or any European) also call them barbarians?

Extended-Response Question

14 **ARGUMENT** Who benefited the most from the first global economic system? Who lost the most?

Need Extra Help?

If You've Missed Question	1	2	3	4	5	6	7	8	9	10	11	12	13	14
Go to page	52	53	58	61	64	66	59	53	64	52	52	66	66	58

Conflict and Absolutism in Europe

1550–1715

netw⊙rks

There's More Online! about conflict and absolutism in Europe.

CHAPTER 5

ESSENTIAL QUESTIONS
• *What effect might social, economic, and religious conflicts have on a country?*
• *How would the exercise of absolute power affect a country?*

The Story Matters...

In seventeenth–century Europe, absolutism was a reaction to instability. In England, the desire of King James II to practice his Catholic faith openly was opposed by Parliament, ending in the creation of a constitutional monarchy under the joint rule of William III and Mary II. Mary's life mirrors the conflicts of her time. Raised as a Protestant, she reluctantly overthrew her own Catholic father, James II.

◄ Painted in 1677, years before Mary became queen, court painter Sir Peter Lely's portrait of her already conveys a regal pride and self-assurance.

PHOTO: Sotheby / akg-images.

Place and Time: Europe 1550–1715

During the sixteenth and seventeenth centuries, Europe was the scene of conflicts fueled by religious differences, along with political and economic rivalries. In some European nations, these conflicts led to the absolute power of a single ruler; in others, a constitutional monarchy developed. The cultural response by writers and artists of this period often reflected a spiritual search and an examination of the human condition.

Step Into the Place

Read the quotations and look at the information presented on the map.

 Analyzing Historical Documents Explain why Parliament would be threatened if the king in England took actions like those attributed to Louis XIV.

PRIMARY SOURCE

❝Whereas the late King James the Second [right image], by the assistance of diverse evil counselors, judges and ministers employed by him, did endeavor to subvert and extirpate the Protestant religion and the laws and liberties of this kingdom;...

That the freedom of speech and debates or proceedings in Parliament ought not to be impeached or questioned in any court or place out of Parliament;...❞

—from the English Bill of Rights, 1689

PRIMARY SOURCE

❝Louis XIV [left image] took great pains to be well informed of all that passed everywhere; in the public places, in the private houses, in society and familiar intercourse. His spies and tell-tales were infinite. He had them of all species; many who were ignorant that their information reached him; others who knew it; others who wrote to him direct, sending their letters through channels he indicated; and all these letters were seen by him alone, and always before everything else; others who sometimes spoke to him secretly in his cabinet, entering by the back stairs.❞

—Duc de Saint-Simon, from Memoirs, 1694–1723

Step Into the Time

Determining Cause and Effect

Choose an event from the European portion of the time line and predict its long-term political, social, or cultural consequences.

EUROPE

THE WORLD

1550   **1575**   **1600**

1562 French Wars of Religion begin

1598 Henry IV issues the Edict of Nantes; ends Wars of Religion

1555 Peace of Augsburg divides Christianity in Germany

1588 England defeats the Spanish Armada

1566 Ottoman Sultan Süleyman I dies

1588 Shāh 'Abbās becomes ruler of Persian Ṣafavid dynasty

1603 Tokugawa shogunate begins in Japan

1598 Rurik dynasty ends in Russia; Romanovs succeed in 1613

Europe 1650

20°W

50°N

N
W E
S

SCOTLAND

IRELAND

North Sea

SWEDEN

RUSSIA

DENMARK

ENGLAND
London •

UNITED PROVINCES

Baltic Sea

PRUSSIA
Berlin •

POLAND
Warsaw •

ATLANTIC OCEAN

SPANISH NETHERLANDS
Paris •

Prague •

KEY

	French Bourbon lands
	Spanish Hapsburg lands
	Austrian Hapsburg lands
	Prussian lands
	British Stuart lands
—	Boundary of Holy Roman Empire

0   400 miles
0   400 km
Lambert Azimuthal Equal-Area projection

Nantes •

Augsburg •

FRANCE

SWITZERLAND

Vienna •

10°W

40°N

PORTUGAL

SPAIN
Madrid •

Lisbon •

ITALIAN STATES

PAPAL STATES

Corsica

Rome •

OTTOMAN EMPIRE

Black Sea

Sardinia

Mediterranean Sea

THE TWO SICILIES

0°   10°E   20°E   30°E

1618 Start of the Thirty Years' War

1623 Shakespeare's *First Folio* is published

1661 Louis XIV begins absolutist rule in France

1690 John Locke publishes *Two Treatises of Government*

1697–1698 Peter the Great visits the West

1715 Louis XIV dies

1625   **1650**   **1675**   **1700**   **1725**

1644 China's Ming dynasty is overthrown; Qing dynasty succeeds

1630 English found Massachusetts Bay Colony

1680 Pueblo Rebellion temporarily overthrows Spanish rule in New Mexico

1682 La Salle claims Mississippi Valley for France

1707 Death of Aurangzeb, last great Mogul emperor

net**w**rks

There's More Online!

☑ **BIOGRAPHY** Elizabeth I

☑ **BIOGRAPHY** Philip II of Spain

☑ **CHART** The Thirty Years' War

☑ **IMAGE** The Thirty Years' War

☑ **INFOGRAPHIC** The Voyage of the Spanish Armada

☑ **INTERACTIVE SELF-CHECK QUIZ**

☑ **PRIMARY SOURCE** The Treaty of Westphalia

☑ **PRIMARY SOURCE** Account of a Witchcraft Trial in 1628

☑ **VIDEO** Europe in Crisis

Reading **HELP**DESK · CCSS

Academic Vocabulary

• **conflict** • **policy**

Content Vocabulary

• **heretic** • **inflation**
• **armada**

TAKING NOTES:

Key Ideas and Details

Monitoring As you read, complete the chart by filling in key details for each topic.

	Spain	England	France
Government			
Religion			
Conflicts			

LESSON 1
Europe in Crisis

ESSENTIAL QUESTION

What effect might social, economic, and religious conflicts have on a country?

IT MATTERS BECAUSE

During the sixteenth and seventeenth centuries, conflicts between Protestants and Catholics in many European nations resulted in wars for religious and political control. Social and economic crises also contributed to instability during these centuries.

Spain's Conflicts

GUIDING QUESTION *What roles did France and Spain play in religious conflicts?*

By 1560, Calvinism and Catholicism had become highly militant, or combative, religions. They were aggressive in winning converts and in eliminating each other's authority. Their struggle was the chief cause of the religious wars that plagued Europe in the sixteenth century. However, economic, social, and political forces also played an important role in these conflicts.

Spain's Militant Catholicism

The greatest supporter of militant Catholicism in the second half of the 1500s was King Philip II. He was the son of Charles V—the Holy Roman Emperor, King of Spain, and Archduke of Austria. Charles V's brother, Ferdinand I, succeeded him as Holy Roman Emperor. Philip II inherited the kingdoms of Milan, Naples, Sicily, the Netherlands, and Spain and its empire in the Americas from Charles V. Philip, who reigned from 1556 to 1598, ushered in an age of Spanish greatness. To strengthen his control, Philip insisted on strict conformity to Catholicism and strong monarchial authority. He also had the powerful Spanish navy at his command.

Around 1500, Catholic kingdoms in Spain had reconquered Muslim areas there and expelled Spanish Jews. Muslims were forced to convert or go into exile. Spain saw itself as a nation chosen by God to save Catholic Christianity from Protestant **heretics**. Philip II, the "Most Catholic King," championed Catholic causes. His actions led to spectacular victories and defeats. Spain's leadership of a Holy League against the Turks resulted in a stunning victory over the Turkish fleet in the Battle of Lepanto in 1571. Philip was not so fortunate in his other **conflicts**.

Resistance From the Netherlands

One of the richest parts of Philip's empire, the Spanish Netherlands, consisted of 17 provinces (modern-day Netherlands and Belgium). Philip's attempts to strengthen his control in this region caused resentment and opposition from the nobles of the Netherlands. Philip also tried to crush Calvinism in the Netherlands. When violence erupted in 1566, Philip sent 10,000 troops to crush the rebellion.

Philip faced growing resistance from the Dutch in the northern provinces led by William the Silent, the prince of Orange. The struggle dragged on until 1609 when a 12-year truce finally ended the war. The northern provinces began to call themselves the United Provinces of the Netherlands and became the core of the modern Dutch state. In fact, the seventeenth century has often been called the golden age of the Dutch Republic by scholars because the United Provinces held center stage as one of Europe's great powers.

Protestantism in England

Elizabeth Tudor ascended the English throne in 1558. During her reign, the small island kingdom became the leader of the Protestant nations of Europe and laid the foundations for a world empire.

Intelligent, careful, and self-confident, Elizabeth moved quickly to solve the difficult religious problem she inherited from her Catholic half-sister,

heretic one who does not conform to established doctrine

conflict opposition; a fight, battle, or war

GEOGRAPHY CONNECTION

Spain's Philip II ruled the world's largest empire at the time.

1 HUMAN SYSTEMS *How might the distribution of Philip's empire have made it difficult to administer?*

2 PLACES AND REGIONS *Why was Philip's relationship with the Holy Roman Emperor important?*

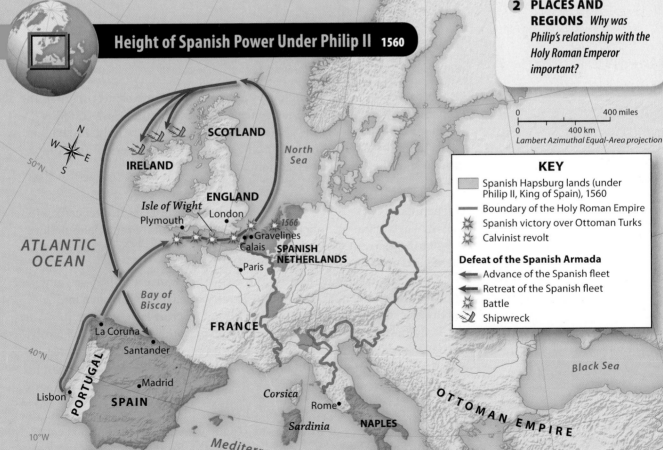

Height of Spanish Power Under Philip II 1560

KEY

Spanish Hapsburg lands (under Philip II, King of Spain), 1560
Boundary of the Holy Roman Empire
Spanish victory over Ottoman Turks
Calvinist revolt

Defeat of the Spanish Armada
Advance of the Spanish fleet
Retreat of the Spanish fleet
Battle
Shipwreck

0   400 miles
0   400 km
Lambert Azimuthal Equal-Area projection

▲ Queen Elizabeth I of England

policy an overall plan embracing the general goals and acceptable procedures of a governmental body

armada a fleet of warships

Queen Mary Tudor. Elizabeth repealed the laws favoring Catholics. A new Act of Supremacy named Elizabeth as "the only supreme governor" of both church and state. The Church of England under Queen Elizabeth followed a moderate Protestantism that kept most people satisfied.

Elizabeth was also moderate in her foreign **policy**. She tried to keep Spain and France from becoming too powerful by balancing power. If one nation seemed to be gaining in power, England would support the weaker nation. The queen feared that war would be disastrous for England and for her own rule; however, she could not escape a conflict with Spain.

Defeat of the Spanish Armada

In 1588, Philip II made preparations to send an **armada**—a fleet of warships—to invade England. A successful invasion of England would mean the overthrow of Protestantism. The fleet that set sail had neither the ships nor the manpower that Philip had planned to send.

The hoped-for victory never came. The armada was battered by the faster English ships and sailed back to Spain by a northern route around Scotland and Ireland where it was pounded by storms.

By the end of Philip's reign in 1598, Spain was not the great power that it appeared to be. Spain was the most populous empire in the world, but it was bankrupt. Philip II had spent too much on war. His successor spent too much on his court. The armed forces were out of date, and the government was inefficient. Spain continued to play the role of a great power, but the real power in Europe had shifted to England and France.

✔ **READING PROGRESS CHECK**

Drawing Conclusions Why might the overthrow of Protestantism in England have been important to Philip II?

The French Wars of Religion

GUIDING QUESTION *What fueled the French civil wars of the sixteenth century?*

Of the sixteenth-century religious wars, none was more shattering than the French civil wars known as the French Wars of Religion (1562–1598). Religious conflict was at the center of these wars. The Catholic French kings persecuted Protestants throughout the country, but the persecution did little to stop the spread of Protestantism.

Huguenots

Huguenots (HYOO • guh • nahts) were French Protestants influenced by John Calvin. They made up only about 7 percent of the total French population, but 40 to 50 percent of the nobility became Huguenots. This made the Huguenots a powerful political threat to the Crown.

An extreme Catholic party—known as the ultra-Catholics—strongly opposed the Huguenots. Having the loyalty of parts of northern and northwestern France, they could pay for and recruit large armies.

Religion was the most important issue, but other factors played a role in the ensuing French civil wars. Towns and provinces were willing to assist the nobles in weakening the growing power of the French monarchy.

Henry IV and the Edict of Nantes

For 30 years, battles raged in France between the Catholics and the Huguenots. In 1589, Henry of Navarre, the Huguenot political leader, succeeded to the throne as Henry IV. He realized that as a Protestant he would never

be accepted by Catholic France. Therefore, he converted to Catholicism. When Henry IV was crowned king in 1594, the fighting in France finally came to an end.

To solve the religious problem, Henry IV issued the Edict of Nantes in 1598. The edict recognized Catholicism as the official religion of France. It also gave the Huguenots the right to worship and to enjoy all political privileges such as holding public offices. This edict appeased both Catholics and Huguenots.

☑ **READING PROGRESS CHECK**

Identifying What was the purpose of the Edict of Nantes?

Crises in Europe

GUIDING QUESTION *How was Europe affected by social and economic crises in the seventeenth century?*

In addition to political upheaval and religious warfare, severe economic and social crises plagued Europe in the sixteenth and seventeenth centuries. One major economic problem was **inflation**, or rising prices. A growing population in the sixteenth century increased the demand for land and food and drove up prices for both.

inflation a rapid increase in prices

Economic and Social Crises

By 1600, an economic slowdown had begun in parts of Europe. Spain's economy, grown dependent on imported silver, was failing by the 1640s. Its mines were producing less silver. Its fleets were subject to pirate attacks. Also, the loss of Muslim and Jewish artisans and merchants hurt the economy. Italy, the financial center of Europe in the Renaissance, was also declining economically.

Population figures in the 1500s and 1600s reveal Europe's worsening conditions. The 1500s were a period of growing population, possibly due to a warmer climate and increased food supplies. Europe's population probably increased from 60 million in 1500 to 85 million by 1600. By 1620, the population had leveled off. It had begun to decline by 1650, especially in central and southern Europe. Warfare, plague, and famine all contributed to the population decline and to the creation of social tensions. One source of tension involved the witchcraft trials.

The Witchcraft Trials

A belief in witchcraft, or magic, had been part of traditional village culture for centuries. The religious zeal that led to the Inquisition and the hunt for heretics was extended to concern about witchcraft. During the sixteenth and seventeenth centuries, an intense hysteria affected the lives of many Europeans. Perhaps more than a hundred thousand people were charged with witchcraft. As more and more people were brought to trial, the fear of witches grew, as did the fear of being accused of witchcraft.

Common people—usually the poor and those without property—were the ones most often accused of witchcraft. More than 75 percent of those accused were women. Most of them were single or widowed and over 50 years old.

Under intense torture, accused witches usually confessed to a number of practices. For instance, many said that they had sworn allegiance to the devil and attended sabbats, nightly gatherings at which they feasted and danced. Others admitted to casting evil spells.

▲ A public execution of accused witches in England

By 1650, the witchcraft hysteria had begun to lessen. As governments grew stronger, fewer officials were willing to disrupt their societies with trials of witches. In addition, attitudes were changing. People found it unreasonable to believe in the old view of a world haunted by evil spirits.

✓ **READING PROGRESS CHECK**

Identifying What sources of social tension existed in Europe during the sixteenth and seventeenth centuries?

The Thirty Years' War

GUIDING QUESTION *What were the causes and effects of the Thirty Years' War?*

▲ A villager is attacked by a soldier during the Thirty Years' War.

Religious disputes continued in Germany after the Peace of Augsburg in 1555. One reason for the disputes was that the peace settlement had not recognized Calvinism. By the 1600s, Calvinism had spread through Europe.

Religion played an important role in the outbreak of the Thirty Years' War, called the "last of the religious wars." However, political and territorial motives were also evident. Beginning in 1618 in the Holy Roman Empire, the war first involved the struggle between Catholic forces, led by the Hapsburg Holy Roman emperors, and Protestant (primarily Calvinist) nobles in Bohemia. As Denmark, Sweden, France, and Spain entered the war, the conflict became more political. For instance, France, directed by the Catholic Cardinal Richelieu, fought against the Holy Roman Empire and Spain in an attempt to gain European leadership.

All major European powers except England were involved in the plundering and destruction of Germany during the Thirty Years' War. The Peace of Westphalia officially ended the war in 1648 and gave Sweden, France, and their allies new territories. Sweden's acquisitions in the Baltic Sea region increased its power in northern Europe. The peace settlement also divided the more than 300 states of the Holy Roman Empire into independent states, each with the freedom to determine their own religion and conduct foreign policy. The Holy Roman Empire ceased to be a political entity. Another 200 years would pass before German unification.

✓ **READING PROGRESS CHECK**

Stating Was the original motivation for the Thirty Years' War political or religious? State evidence.

LESSON 1 REVIEW (CCSS)

Reviewing Vocabulary
1. *Identifying* Explain why King Philip II viewed Protestants as heretics and why that view may have met with conflict.

Using Your Notes
2. *Comparing and Contrasting* Use your notes to choose one of the topics discussed in the lesson. Write several sentences comparing how the government, religion, or conflicts affected each power.

Answering the Guiding Questions
3. *Applying* What roles did England and Spain play in religious conflicts?

4. *Exploring Issues* What fueled the French civil wars of the sixteenth century?

5. *Examining* How was Europe affected by social and economic crises in the seventeenth century?

6. *Identifying Cause and Effect* What were the causes and effects of the Thirty Years' War?

Writing Activity
7. **INFORMATIVE/EXPLANATORY** In two or three paragraphs, compare Elizabeth I of England and King Philip II of Spain in terms of their personalities as rulers, their relationship to religion, and their foreign policy. Use descriptive language.

Reading **HELP**DESK ⓒⓒⓢⓢ

Academic Vocabulary

- **commonwealth**
- **restoration**
- **convert**

Content Vocabulary

- **divine right of kings**
- **Puritans**
- **Cavaliers**
- **Roundheads**
- **natural rights**

TAKING NOTES:

Key Ideas and Details

Summarizing As you read, use a chart like the one below to identify which conflicts were prompted by religious concerns.

Conflicts in England	Results

LESSON 2
War and Revolution in England

ESSENTIAL QUESTION
What effect might social, economic, and religious conflicts have on a country?

IT MATTERS BECAUSE

The seventeenth century was a period of great social and political change in England. These changes raised important questions about how to balance the power of government with the need to maintain order. England's answers eventually formed the basis of many modern democracies, including that of the United States.

Revolutions in England

GUIDING QUESTION *How did disagreements over rule between the Stuarts and Parliament lead to the English Civil War? What were the causes and effects of the Glorious Revolution?*

In addition to the Thirty Years' War, a series of rebellions and civil wars rocked Europe in the seventeenth century. By far the most famous struggle was the civil war in England known as the English Revolution. The war was between king and Parliament to determine what role each should play in governing England. It would take another revolution later in the century to finally reach a resolution.

The Stuarts and Divine Right

The Tudor dynasty ended with the death of Queen Elizabeth I in 1603. The Stuart line of rulers began when the king of Scotland, Elizabeth's cousin, ascended the English throne and became James I.

James believed that he received his power from and was only responsible to God. This is called the **divine right of kings**. Parliament did not think much of the divine right of kings. It had come to assume that the monarch and Parliament ruled England together.

Religion was an issue as well. The **Puritans**—Protestants in England inspired by Calvinist ideas—did not like the king's strong defense of the Church of England. While they were members of the Church of England, the Puritans wished to make the church more Protestant. Many of England's gentry, mostly well-to-do landowners, had become Puritans. The Puritan gentry formed an important

divine right of kings the belief that the king gets his power from God and not from his subjects

Puritans English Protestants who believed that the Church of England needed further reform and sought to simplify and regulate forms of worship

Cavaliers supporters of King Charles I in the English Civil War

Roundheads supporters of Parliament in the English Civil War

▲ Oliver Cromwell, Lord Protector of England during the Commonwealth

commonwealth a nation, state, or other political unit founded on law and united by agreement for and by the people

restoration a bringing back to a former position or condition

part of the House of Commons, the lower house of Parliament. It was not wise to alienate them.

The conflict that began during the reign of James came to a head during the reign of his son, Charles I. Charles, like his father, believed in the divine right of kings. In 1628, Parliament passed a Petition of Right. The petition placed limits on the king's ability to tax, imprison citizens without cause, quarter troops, and institute martial law. Although Charles initially accepted this petition, he later ignored it after realizing the limits it put on his power.

Charles also tried to impose more ritual on the Church of England. Thousands of Puritans went to America rather than accept his policy. Thus the struggles of the English Reformation influenced American history.

Civil War and Commonwealth

Complaints grew until England slipped into a civil war in 1642 between the supporters of the king (the **Cavaliers** or Royalists) and the parliamentary forces (called the **Roundheads**). Parliament proved victorious, due largely to the New Model Army of Oliver Cromwell, who was a military genius.

The New Model Army chiefly consisted of more extreme Puritans, known as the Independents. These men believed they were doing battle for God. As Cromwell wrote, "This is none other but the hand of God; and to Him alone belongs the glory." Some credit is due to Cromwell. His soldiers were well-disciplined and trained in the new military tactics of the 1600s.

The victorious New Model Army lost no time in taking control. Cromwell purged Parliament of any members who had not supported him. What was left—the so-called Rump Parliament—had Charles I executed on January 30, 1649. The execution of the king horrified much of Europe. Parliament next abolished the monarchy and the House of Lords and declared England a **commonwealth**, a type of republic.

Cromwell found it difficult to work with the Rump Parliament and finally dispersed it by force, exclaiming, "I have been forced to do this. I have sought the Lord, night and day, that He would slay me, than put upon me the doing of this work." After destroying both king and Parliament, Cromwell set up a military dictatorship.

The Restoration

Cromwell ruled until his death in 1658. The army, realizing how unpopular it had become, restored the monarchy in 1660 in the person of Charles II, the son of Charles I.

The **restoration** of the Stuart monarchy, known as the Restoration period, did not mean, however, that the work of the English Revolution was undone. Parliament kept much of the power it had won and continued to play an important role in government. The principle that Parliament must give its consent to taxation was also accepted. Charles, however, continued to push his own ideas, some of which were clearly out of step with many of the English people.

Charles was sympathetic to Catholicism. Moreover, his brother James, heir to the throne, did not hide the fact that he was a Catholic. Parliament's suspicions about their Catholic leanings were therefore aroused when Charles took the bold step of suspending the laws that Parliament had passed against Catholics and Puritans after the restoration of the monarchy. Parliament would have none of it and forced the king to back down. Driven by a strong anti-Catholic sentiment, Parliament then passed a Test Act, specifying that only Anglicans (members of the Church of England) could hold military and civil offices.

Arousing more suspicion, on his deathbed Charles II had decided to **convert** to Catholicism. After Charles died without a son, James II became king in 1685. James was an open and devout Catholic. He named Catholics to high positions in the government, army, navy, and universities. Religion once more became a cause of conflict between king and Parliament.

Parliament objected to James's policies but stopped short of rebellion. Members knew he was an old man and his Protestant daughters, Mary and Anne, born to his first wife, would succeed him. However, in 1688, James and his second wife, a Catholic, had a son. Now the possibility of a Catholic monarchy loomed large.

A Glorious Revolution

A group of English nobles invited the Dutch leader, William of Orange, to invade England. In their invitation, they informed William that most of the kingdom's people wanted a change. The invitation put William and his wife Mary, the daughter of James II, in a difficult position. It would be appalling for Mary to rise up against her father. However, William, a foe of France's Catholic king Louis XIV, welcomed this opportunity to fight France with England's resources.

William began making preparations to invade England in early 1688. It was not until early October that James realized William's intentions. In November 1688, William's forces landed at Torbay and began their march toward London. James responded by sending forward his army. Following the desertion of many of his soldiers and the defection of his daughter Anne and her husband, James retreated to London. There he made plans for his wife and son to flee to France where James later joined them.

With almost no bloodshed, England had undergone a "Glorious Revolution." The issue was not if there would be a monarchy but who would be monarch.

In January 1689, Parliament offered the throne to William and Mary. They accepted it, along with a Bill of Rights, which contained many of the same ideas as the Petition of Right. The Bill of Rights set forth Parliament's right to make laws and to levy taxes. It also made it impossible for kings to oppose or to do without Parliament by stating that standing armies could be raised only with Parliament's consent. The rights of citizens to keep arms and to have a jury trial were also confirmed. The Bill of Rights helped create a system of government based on the rule of law and a freely elected Parliament. This bill laid the foundation for a limited, or constitutional, monarchy.

Another important action of Parliament was the Toleration Act of 1689. This act granted Puritans, but not Catholics, the right of free public worship. It did mark a turning point in English history because few English citizens would ever again be persecuted for religion.

By deposing one king and establishing another, Parliament had destroyed the divine-right theory of kingship. William was, after all, king by the grace of Parliament, not by the grace of God. Parliament had asserted its right to be part of the government. Parliament did not have complete control of the government, but it now had the right to participate in affairs of state. Over the next century, Parliament would gradually prove to be the real authority in the English system of constitutional monarchy.

✔ READING PROGRESS CHECK

Identifying Central Issues In what important way was the monarchy of William and Mary different from the previous Stuart monarchy?

Analyzing CCSS
PRIMARY SOURCES

The English Bill of Rights

❝ …King James the Second having abdicated the government and the throne being thereby vacant, his Highness the prince of Orange (who it hath pleased Almighty God to make the glorious instrument of delivering this kingdom from popery and arbitrary power) did (by the advice of the Lords Spiritual and Temporal and divers principal persons of the Commons) cause letters to be written to the Lords Spiritual and Temporal…in order to such an establishment as that their religion, laws and liberties might not again be in danger of being subverted… ❞

—from English Bill of Rights

DBQ **ANALYZING** This document states James II abdicated the government. What does this mean, and how do the events of the Glorious Revolution support or not support this statement?

convert to change from one belief to another

Legal and Political Thought

GUIDING QUESTION *How did the English Revolution influence political thought?*

▲ Title page from *Leviathan*, by Thomas Hobbes, 1651

natural rights rights with which all humans are born, including the rights to life, liberty, and property

Concerns with order and power were reflected in English legal and political thought. William Blackstone, a judge and professor of law, wrote *Commentaries on the Laws of England*, arguing that political stability could be achieved by a revived emphasis on English common law. Two English political thinkers, Thomas Hobbes and John Locke, provided their own responses to the English revolutions of the seventeenth century.

Thomas Hobbes was alarmed by the revolutionary upheavals in England. In 1651, he published the political work *Leviathan* to try to deal with the problem of disorder. Hobbes argued that before organized society, humans were guided not by reason and moral ideals but by a ruthless struggle for self-preservation. To save themselves from destroying one another, people made a social contract and agreed to form a state. Hobbes called the state "that great LEVIATHAN . . . to which we owe . . . our peace and defense." People in the state agreed to be governed by an absolute ruler with unlimited power in order to suppress rebellion and to preserve order.

John Locke viewed the exercise of political power quite differently. His *Two Treatises of Government*, published in 1690, argued against the absolute rule of one person. Unlike Hobbes, Locke believed that before society was organized, humans lived in a state of equality and freedom rather than in a state of war. As a result, all humans had certain **natural rights**—rights with which they were born. These included rights to life, liberty, and property.

Like Hobbes, however, Locke believed people found it difficult to protect their natural rights. Thus, they agreed to establish a government to ensure the protection of their rights and to judge those who violated them. Government would protect the rights of the people, and the people would act reasonably. However, if a government broke the contract—for example, if a monarch failed to protect citizens' natural rights—the people would be within their rights to alter or remove and form a new government.

To Locke, *people* meant the landholding aristocracy. He was not an advocate of democracy, but his ideas proved important in the eighteenth century. These ideas were used to support demands for constitutional government, the rule of law, and the protection of rights. Locke's ideas can be found in both the American Declaration of Independence and the United States Constitution.

☑ **READING PROGRESS CHECK**

Drawing Inferences Did Hobbes or Locke have more trust in self-governance? Why?

PHOTO: North Wind Picture Archives

LESSON 2 REVIEW

Reviewing Vocabulary
1. *Defining* Outline the differences between the Roundheads and the Cavaliers.

Using Your Notes
2. *Discussing* Using your notes, describe the conflicts that occurred in England.

Answering the Guiding Questions
3. *Evaluating* How did disagreements over rule between the Stuarts and Parliament lead to the English Civil War?

4. *Identifying Cause and Effect* What were the causes and effects of the Glorious Revolution?

5. *Synthesizing* How did the English Revolution influence political thought?

Writing Activity
6. **ARGUMENT** Write a paragraph arguing either Locke's or Hobbes' position. Be sure to include specific ideas. You may use any of the material in the chapter to illustrate your argument.

networks

There's More Online!

- ☑ BIOGRAPHY Frederick William
- ☑ BIOGRAPHY Louis XIV
- ☑ BIOGRAPHY Peter the Great
- ☑ CHART/GRAPH Characteristics of an Absolute Monarch
- ☑ INFOGRAPHIC Versailles: A Palace Fit for the Sun King
- ☑ INTERACTIVE SELF-CHECK QUIZ
- ☑ MAP Expansion of Russia, 1505–1725
- ☑ SLIDE SHOW The Westernization of Russia by Peter the Great
- ☑ VIDEO Absolutism in Europe

Reading **HELP**DESK `CCSS`

Academic Vocabulary
- **stability**   • **emerge**
- **authority**

Content Vocabulary
- **absolutism** • **boyar**
- **czar**

TAKING NOTES:

Key Ideas and Details

Summarizing Information As you read, complete a chart like the one below summarizing the accomplishments of European leaders.

	Reforms
Louis XIV	
Frederick William	
Peter the Great	

PHOTO: (l to r)Giraudon/Bridgeman Art Library, Stringer/Hulton Archive/Getty Images, Hulton Archive/Hulton Royals Collection/Getty Images, Author's Image/Alamy Images.

LESSON 3
Absolutism in Europe

ESSENTIAL QUESTION
How does the exercise of absolute power affect a country?

IT MATTERS BECAUSE

In reaction to the crises of the seventeenth century, several European nations turned to absolute monarchy, with France's Louis XIV as its epitome. He waged many military campaigns and was extravagant. While Prussia, Austria, and Russia were emerging as great European powers under their monarchs' leadership, Spain was declining in power.

France Under Louis XIV

GUIDING QUESTION *Why is the reign of Louis XIV regarded as the best example of absolutism in the seventeenth century?*

One response to the crises of the seventeenth century was to seek more **stability** by increasing the power of the monarch. The result was what historians have called absolutism.

Absolutism is a system in which a ruler holds total power. In seventeenth-century Europe, absolutism was tied to the idea of the divine right of kings. This means that absolute monarchs supposedly received their power from God and were responsible to no one except God. They had the ability to make laws, levy taxes, administer justice, control officials, and determine foreign policy.

The reign of Louis XIV has long been regarded as the best example of absolutism in the seventeenth century. French culture, language, and manners reached into all levels of European society. French diplomacy and wars dominated the political affairs of Europe. The court of Louis XIV was imitated throughout Europe.

Richelieu

French history for the 50 years before Louis XIV was a period of struggle as governments fought to avoid the breakdown of the state. Louis XIII and Louis XIV were only boys when they came to the throne. The government was left in the hands of royal ministers. In France, two ministers, Cardinal Richelieu with Louis XIII and Cardinal Mazarin with Louis XIV, played important roles in preserving the **authority** of the monarchy.

stability the state of being stable; strong enough to endure

absolutism a political system in which a ruler holds total power

authority power; person in command

Cardinal Richelieu (RIH • shuh • loo), Louis XIII's chief minister, strengthened the monarchy's power. Because the Huguenots were seen as a threat to the king, Richelieu took away their political and military rights. He did preserve their religious rights. Richelieu also set up a network of spies to uncover and crush conspiracies by nobles, executing the conspirators.

Louis in Power

After his minister Cardinal Mazarin died in 1661, Louis XIV took over supreme power. The new king, at the age of 23, stated his desire to be a real king and the sole ruler of France. Well aware of her son's love of fun and games and his affairs with the maids, Louis's mother laughed at him. Louis was serious, however. He kept a strict routine and also fostered the myth of himself as the Sun King—the source of light for all of his people.

One key to Louis's power was his control of the central policy-making machinery of government. The royal court that Louis established at Versailles (vuhr • SY) served three purposes. The royal council was the personal household of the king. In addition, the chief offices of the state were located there. Finally, Versailles was the place powerful subjects came to find favors and offices for themselves.

The greatest danger to Louis's rule came from the highest nobles and royal princes. They believed they should play a role in the government. Instead, Louis removed them from the royal council. It was the king's chief administrative body, which supervised the government. At the same time, Louis enticed the nobles and royal princes to come to his court, where he kept them busy with court life and out of politics.

Louis's government ministers were to obey his every wish. Said Louis, "I had no intention of sharing my authority with them." Thus, Louis had complete authority over the traditional areas of royal power: foreign policy, the church, and taxes. Although Louis had absolute power over nationwide policy making, his power was limited at the local level. Nobles, local officials, and town councils had more influence than the king in the daily operation of local governments. As a result, the king bribed important people in the provinces to see that his policies were carried out.

Desiring to maintain religious harmony as part of the monarchical power in France, Louis pursued an anti-Protestant policy aimed at converting the Huguenots to Catholicism. Early in his reign, Louis ordered the destruction of Huguenot churches and the closing of their schools. As many as 200,000 Huguenots fled to England, the United Provinces, and the German states.

The cost of building palaces, maintaining his court, and pursuing his wars made finances a crucial issue for Louis XIV. He was most fortunate in having the services of Jean-Baptiste Colbert (kohl • BEHR) as controller-general of finances.

Colbert sought to increase France's wealth and power by following mercantilism. To decrease imports and increase exports, he granted subsidies to new industries. To improve communications and the transportation of goods within France, he built roads and canals. To decrease imports directly, Colbert raised tariffs on foreign goods and created a merchant marine to carry French goods.

To increase his royal power, Louis developed a standing army numbering 400,000 in time of war. He wished to achieve the military glory befitting the Sun King and ensure that his Bourbon dynasty dominated Europe. To achieve his goals, Louis waged four wars between 1667 and 1713. Many nations formed coalitions to prevent him from dominating Europe.

Analyzing **CCSS**
PRIMARY SOURCES

Louis XIV to his Chancellor (1661)

❝[Up] to this moment I have been pleased to entrust the government of my affairs to the late Cardinal. It is now time that I govern them myself. You [secretaries and ministers of state] will assist me with your counsels when I ask for them.... I request and order you to seal no orders except by my command.... I order you not to sign anything, not even a passport . . . without my command; to render account to me personally each day and to favour no one.❞

—Louis XIV, quoted in
Princes and Peoples

DBQ **INTERPRETING**
How do Louis XIV's instructions to his Chancellor exemplify absolutism?

82

Through his wars, Louis added some territory and set up a member of his own dynasty on the throne of Spain.

Legacy of Louis XIV

In 1715, the Sun King died. He left France surrounded by enemies and many of the French people in poverty. On his deathbed, the 76-year-old monarch seemed remorseful when he told his successor (his great- grandson), "You are about to become a great king. Do not imitate me either in my taste for building or in my love of war. Live in peace with the nations. . . . Strive to relieve the burdens of your people in which I have been so unfortunate as to fail."

Did Louis mean it? We do not know. In any event, his successor probably did not remember this advice; Louis's great-grandson was only five years old.

☑ **READING PROGRESS CHECK**

Classifying How was the monarchy of Louis XIV characteristic of absolutism?

The Spread of Absolutism

GUIDING QUESTION *How did Prussia and Austria emerge as great powers in seventeenth- and eighteenth- century Europe?*

Although absolutism largely failed in Spain, it was more successful in central and eastern Europe. After the Thirty Years' War, there were more than 300 German states. Of these, Prussia and Austria **emerged** in the seventeenth and eighteenth centuries as two great European powers.

The Decline of Spain

At the beginning of the seventeenth century, Spain was the most populous empire in the world. To most Europeans, Spain seemed the greatest power of the age. Reality was quite different, however.

The reign of Philip IV came closest to the practice of absolute monarchy. A program of political reform sought to centralize the government of Spain in the hands of the monarchy. However, unlike Louis XIV in France, the king was unable to curtail the power of the Spanish nobles. Expensive military campaigns led to revolts and the decline of Spain as a great power.

The Emergence of Prussia

Frederick William the Great Elector laid the foundation for the Prussian state. Realizing that Prussia was a small, open territory with no natural frontiers for defense, Frederick William built a large and efficient standing army. He had a force of 40,000 men, which made the Prussian army the fourth-largest in Europe.

To maintain the army and his own power, Frederick William set up the General War Commissariat to levy taxes for the army and oversee its growth. The Commissariat soon became an agency for civil government as well. The new bureaucratic machine became the elector's chief instrument to govern the state. Many of its officials were members of the Prussian landed aristocracy, or the Junkers, who also served as officers in the army.

In 1701, Frederick William's son Frederick officially gained the title of king. Elector Frederick III became King Frederick I.

The New Austrian Empire

The Austrian Hapsburgs had long played a significant role in European politics as emperors in the Holy Roman Empire. By the end of the Thirty

▲ *Triumph of King Louis XIV of France driving the Chariot of the Sun preceded by Aurora,* by Joseph Werner

emerge to become manifest; to become known

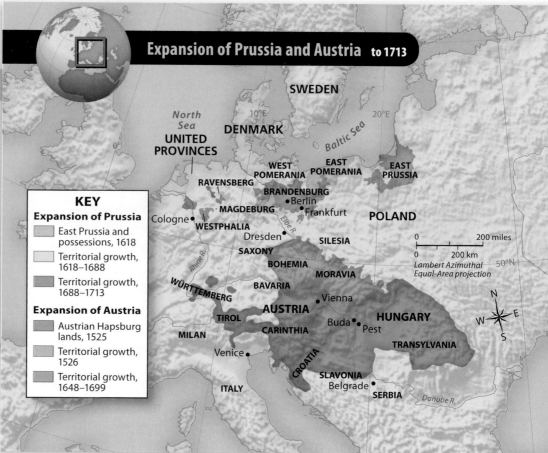

Expansion of Prussia and Austria to 1713

GEOGRAPHY CONNECTION

Prussia and Austria emerged as great European powers during the seventeenth and eighteenth centuries.

1 PHYSICAL SYSTEMS *What geographical features might account for Austria's expansion to the north and east?*

2 HUMAN SYSTEMS *What problems might Prussia have encountered in governing its territories?*

KEY

Expansion of Prussia
- East Prussia and possessions, 1618
- Territorial growth, 1618–1688
- Territorial growth, 1688–1713

Expansion of Austria
- Austrian Hapsburg lands, 1525
- Territorial growth, 1526
- Territorial growth, 1648–1699

Years' War, their hopes of creating an empire in Germany had been dashed. In the seventeenth century, however, the Hapsburgs created a new empire in eastern and southeastern Europe.

The core of the new Austrian Empire was the traditional Austrian lands in present-day Austria, the Czech Republic, and Hungary. After the defeat of the Turks at Vienna in 1683, Austria took control of all of Hungary, Transylvania, Croatia, and Slavonia. By the beginning of the eighteenth century, the Austrian Hapsburgs had gained a sizable new empire.

The Austrian monarchy, however, never became a highly centralized, absolutist state, chiefly because it was made of so many different national groups. The Austrian Empire remained a collection of territories held together by the Hapsburg emperor, who was archduke of Austria, king of Bohemia, and king of Hungary. Each of these areas had its own laws and political life. No common sentiment tied the regions together other than the ideal of service to the Hapsburgs.

✓ **READING PROGRESS CHECK**

Comparing How was the role of the military significant in Prussia and Austria?

Peter the Great

ESSENTIAL QUESTION *How did Russia emerge as a powerful state under Peter the Great?*

A new Russian state emerged in the fifteenth century under the principality of Muscovy and its grand dukes. In the sixteenth century, Ivan IV became the first ruler to take the title of **czar**, the Russian word for *caesar*.

Ivan expanded the territories of Russia eastward. He also crushed the power of the Russian nobility, or **boyars**. He was known as Ivan the

czar Russian for *caesar*; the title used by Russian emperors

boyar a Russian noble

84

Terrible because of his ruthless deeds, including stabbing his son to death in a heated argument. When Ivan's dynasty ended in 1598, a period of anarchy, the Time of Troubles, followed. This period ended when the *zemsky sobor*, or national assembly, chose Michael Romanov as the new czar in 1613.

The Romanov dynasty lasted until 1917. One of its most prominent members was Peter the Great, who became czar in 1689. Like other Romanov czars who preceded him, Peter was an absolute monarch who claimed the divine right to rule.

After becoming czar, Peter visited the West. Determined to westernize Russia, he was eager to borrow European technology. Modernization of the army and navy was crucial to make Russia a great power. Peter employed Russians and Europeans as officers. He drafted peasants for 25-year stints of service to build a standing army of 210,000 soldiers. By Peter's death in 1725, Russia was a great military power and an important European state.

Peter began to introduce Western customs, practices, and manners into Russia. He ordered the first Russian book of etiquette to teach Western manners. Men had to shave their beards and shorten their coats. Upper-class women were allowed to remove their traditional face-covering veils.

Along with making Russia into a great state and military power, Peter wanted to open a "window to the West," meaning a port with ready access to Europe. This could be achieved only on the Baltic Sea, which Sweden, the most important power in northern Europe, controlled. Peter acquired the lands he sought after a long war with Sweden. On the Baltic in 1703, Peter began construction of a new city, St. Petersburg, a base for the new Russian navy and a window to the West. St. Petersburg became Russia's most important port and remained the Russian capital until 1918.

To impose the rule of the central government more effectively, Peter divided Russia into provinces. He hoped to create a "police state," a well-ordered community governed by law. However, few bureaucrats shared his concept of honest service and duty to the state. Peter's personality created an atmosphere of fear. He wrote to one administrator, "According to these orders act, act, act. I won't write more, but you will pay with your head if you interpret orders again." Peter wanted the impossible—that his administrators be slaves and free persons at the same time.

 READING PROGRESS CHECK

Stating In what ways did Peter the Great modernize both the culture and the military of Russia?

BIOGRAPHY

Peter the Great (1672–1725)

As czar, Peter protected the interests of Russia's ruling class by creating a Table of Ranks, which modified the status of nobility. He also changed the rules so that the property of all landowners became hereditary instead of dependent on their service to the czar. In his appointments, Peter chose the most talented candidates, regardless of their level in society.

▶ **CRITICAL THINKING**
Drawing Conclusions How might Peter's policy make those he appointed more loyal to him?

LESSON 3 REVIEW (CCSS)

Reviewing Vocabulary

1. *Defining* Write a paragraph that relates the term *czar* to the term *absolutism* by giving two examples of czars and telling how they ruled absolutely.

Using Your Notes

2. *Identifying* Use your notes to write a paragraph that summarizes the reforms of absolutist rulers.

Answering the Guiding Questions

3. *Constructing Arguments* Why is the reign of Louis XIV regarded as the best example of absolutism in the seventeenth century?

4. *Comparing* How did Prussia and Austria emerge as great powers in seventeenth- and eighteenth-century Europe?

5. *Identifying Cause and Effect* How did Russia emerge as a powerful state under Peter the Great?

Writing Activity

6. **ARGUMENT** Write a paragraph that proves or disproves this thesis: Although absolutism was destructive in France, it had some positive effects in Russia.

networks

There's More Online!

☑ **BIOGRAPHY** Artemisia Gentileschi

☑ **BIOGRAPHY** El Greco

☑ **BIOGRAPHY** Miguel de Cervantes

☑ **BIOGRAPHY** William Shakespeare

☑ **IMAGE** The Globe Theater

☑ **INTERACTIVE SELF-CHECK QUIZ**

☑ **PRIMARY SOURCE** All Citizens are Soldiers

☑ **PRIMARY SOURCE** As You Like It

☑ **VIDEO** European Culture After the Renaissance

Reading **HELP**DESK (CCSS)

Academic Vocabulary

• decline   • creative
• drama

Content Vocabulary

• **Mannerism**
• **baroque**

TAKING NOTES:

Key Ideas and Details

Summarizing Use the following graphic organizer to identify one major figure and his or her country of origin in each of these areas of cultural expression: painting, architecture, music, and literature.

Medium	Artist	Country of Origin
Painting		
Architecture		
Music		
Literature		

LESSON 4
European Culture After the Renaissance

ESSENTIAL QUESTION
What effect might social, economic, and religious conflicts have on a country?

IT MATTERS BECAUSE
The religious and political conflicts of seventeenth-century Europe were reflected in the art, music, and literature of the time. Art produced during the Mannerist and baroque movements aroused the emotions, and the literature spoke of the human condition.

Art After the Renaissance

GUIDING QUESTION *How did art movements change in Europe after the Renaissance?*

The artistic movements of Mannerism and the baroque began in Italy and spread through Europe. The art produced during these movements reflected the tension of religious upheaval and the spirituality of religious revival.

Mannerism

The artistic Renaissance came to an end when a new movement, called **Mannerism**, emerged in Italy in the 1520s and 1530s. The Reformation's revival of religious values brought much political turmoil. Especially in Italy, the worldly enthusiasm of the Renaissance **declined** as people grew more anxious and uncertain and wished for spiritual experience.

Mannerism in art reflected this new environment by deliberately breaking down the High Renaissance principles of balance, harmony, and moderation. The rules of proportion were deliberately ignored as elongated figures were used to show suffering, heightened emotions, and religious ecstasy.

Mannerism spread from Italy to other parts of Europe and perhaps reached its high point in the work of El Greco, "the Greek." El Greco studied the elements of Renaissance painting in Venice. He also wrote many works on painting. From Venice, El Greco moved to Rome. His career as a painter stalled there possibly because he had criticized Michelangelo's artistic abilities. When he moved to Spain, El Greco met with success.

PHOTO: (l to r) Sylvain Grandadam/Age Fotostock, English School/Bridgeman Art Library/Getty Images, Library of Congress, Stringer/Archive Photos/Getty Images, The Granger Collection.

In El Greco's paintings, the figures are elongated or contorted and he sometimes used unusual shades of yellow and green against an eerie background of stormy grays. The mood of his works reflects well the tensions created by the religious upheavals of the Reformation.

Baroque Art

Mannerism eventually was replaced by a new movement—the **baroque**. This movement began in Italy at the end of the sixteenth century and eventually spread to the rest of Europe and Latin America. It was eagerly adopted by the Catholic reform movement as shown in the richly detailed buildings at Catholic courts, especially those of the Hapsburgs in Madrid, Prague, Vienna, and Brussels.

Baroque artists tried to bring together the classical ideals of Renaissance art and the spiritual feelings of the sixteenth-century religious revival. In large part, though, baroque art and architecture reflected a search for power. Baroque churches and palaces were magnificent and richly detailed. Kings and princes wanted others to be in awe of their power.

Perhaps the greatest figure of the baroque period was the Italian architect and sculptor Gian Lorenzo Bernini, who completed Saint Peter's Basilica in Vatican City, Rome. Saint Peter's Basilica is the church of the popes and a major pilgrimage site.

Action, exuberance, and dramatic effects mark the work of Bernini in the interior of Saint Peter's. For instance, his *Throne of Saint Peter* is a highly decorated cover for the pope's medieval wooden throne. It is considered by many to be Bernini's crowning achievement in Saint Peter's Basilica. The throne seems to hover in midair, held by the hands of the four great theologians of the early Catholic Church. Above the chair, rays of heavenly light drive a mass of clouds and angels toward the spectator.

The baroque painting style was known for its use of dramatic effects to arouse the emotions as shown in the work of another important Italian artist of the baroque period, Caravaggio. Similar to other baroque painters, Caravaggio used dramatic lighting to heighten emotions, to focus details, and to isolate the figures in his paintings. His work placed an emphasis on everyday experience. He shocked some of his patrons by depicting religious figures as common people in everyday settings, rather than in a traditional, idealized style.

Mannerism an artistic movement that emerged in Italy in the 1520s and 1530s; it marked the end of the Renaissance by breaking down the principles of balance, harmony, and moderation

decline a change to a lower state or level

baroque an artistic style of the seventeenth century characterized by complex forms, bold ornamentation, and contrasting elements

▼ *The Beheading of St. John the Baptist* by Caravaggio, 1607–1608

▶ CRITICAL THINKING
Interpreting Significance How is this biblical scene depicted and how might this style indicate a change in a way of thinking?

Artemisia Gentileschi is less well-known than the male artists who dominated the seventeenth-century art world in Italy but is prominent in her own right. Born in Rome, she studied painting with her father. In 1616 she moved to Florence and began a successful career as a painter. At the age of 23, she became the first woman to be elected to the Florentine Academy of Design. She was known internationally in her day as a portrait painter, but her fame now rests on a series of pictures of Hebrew Bible heroines.

The baroque style of art did not just flourish in Italy. Peter Paul Rubens embodied the baroque movement in Flanders (the Spanish Netherlands), where he worked most of his life. A scholar and a diplomat as well as an artist, Rubens used his classical education and connections with noble patrons in Italy, Spain, England, France, and Flanders to paint a variety of genres. He is best known for his depictions of the human form in action. These images are lavish and extravagant, much like the court life he experienced during the baroque period.

Baroque Music

In the first half of the eighteenth century, two composers—Johann Sebastian Bach and George Frideric Handel—perfected the baroque musical style and composed some of the world's most enduring music.

Bach, a renowned organist as well as a composer, spent his entire life in Germany. While he was music director at the Church of Saint Thomas in Leipzig, he composed his *Mass in B Minor* and other works that gave him the reputation of being one of the greatest composers of all time.

Handel was a German who spent much of his career in England. Handel wrote much secular music, but he is probably best known for his religious music. Handel's *Messiah* has been called a rare work that appeals immediately to everyone and yet is a masterpiece of the highest order.

☑ **READING PROGRESS CHECK**

Identifying Cause and Effect How did the Mannerist and baroque styles in art reflect the religious conflicts and revivals of their time?

Golden Age of Literature

GUIDING QUESTION *What characterized the Golden Age of literature in England and Spain?*

In both England and Spain, writing for the theater reached new heights between 1580 and 1640. Other forms of literature flourished as well.

England's Shakespeare

A cultural flowering took place in England in the late sixteenth and early seventeenth centuries. The period is often called the Elizabethan era, because so much of it fell within the reign of Queen Elizabeth I. Of all the forms of Elizabethan literature, none expressed the energy of the era better than **drama**. Of all the English dramatists, none is more famous than William Shakespeare.

When Shakespeare appeared in London in 1592, Elizabethans already enjoyed the stage. The theater was a very successful business. London theaters ranged from the Globe, a circular, unroofed structure holding 3,000 people, to the Blackfriars, a roofed structure that held only 500.

The Globe Theatre's admission charge of one or two pennies enabled even the lower classes of London to attend performances. The higher prices of the Blackfriars filled the audience with more well-to-do patrons. Because Elizabethan audiences for a single performance varied greatly, playwrights wrote works that were meant to please nobles, lawyers, merchants, and vagabonds alike.

drama a composition that tells a story, usually involving conflicts and emotions, through action and dialogue and typically designed for the theater

▶ **CRITICAL THINKING**
Drawing Conclusions How did the location and purpose of theaters like the Globe bring different classes together?

▼ The Globe Theatre in London was surrounded by other theaters holding entertainments such as plays, bear baitings, and sword-fighting displays.

William Shakespeare was a "complete man of the theater." Although best known for writing plays, he was also an actor and shareholder in the chief theater company of the time, the Lord Chamberlain's Men, which performed at the Globe.

Shakespeare has long been viewed as a universal genius. A master of the English language, he brought many new words into common usage. Shakespeare also wrote over 150 sonnets, a type of poetry popular during the Elizabethan era. He had a keen insight into human psychology. In his tragedies, comedies, and histories, Shakespeare showed a remarkable understanding of the human condition.

Spain's Cervantes and Vega

One of the crowning achievements of the golden age of Spanish literature was the work of Miguel de Cervantes (suhr • VAN • teez). His novel *Don Quixote* has been hailed as one of the greatest literary works of all time.

In the two main characters of this famous work, Cervantes presented the dual nature of the Spanish character. The knight, Don Quixote from La Mancha, is the visionary so involved in his lofty ideals that he does not see the hard realities around him. To him, for example, windmills appear to be our-armed giants. In contrast, the knight's fat and earthy squire, Sancho Panza, is a realist. Each of these characters finally comes to see the value of the other's perspective. The readers of *Don Quixote* are left with the conviction that both visionary dreams and the hard work of reality are necessary to the human condition.

The theater was also one of the most **creative** forms of expression during Spain's golden period of literature. The first professional theaters were created in Seville and Madrid. Soon, every large town had a public playhouse, including Mexico City in the Americas. Touring companies brought the latest Spanish plays to all parts of the Spanish Empire.

Beginning in the 1580s, the standard for playwrights was set by Lope de Vega. He wrote an extraordinary number of plays, perhaps 1,500 in all. Almost 500 of them survive to this day. Vega's plays are thought to be witty, charming, action-packed, and realistic. Lope de Vega made no apologies for the fact that he wrote his plays to please his audiences and to satisfy public demand. He remarked once that if anyone thought he had written his plays for the sake of fame, "undeceive him and tell him that I wrote them for money."

✔ **READING PROGRESS CHECK**

Explaining Why was the theater so popular in England, Spain, and the Spanish Empire between 1580 and 1640?

Analyzing CCSS
PRIMARY SOURCES

Don Quixote on the Windmills

❝[F]or you can see over there, good friend Sancho Panza, a place where stand thirty or more monstrous giants with whom I intend to fight a battle and whose lives I intend to take; and with the booty we shall begin to prosper. For this is a just war, and it is a great service to God to wipe such a wicked breed from the face of the earth.❞

—Miguel de Cervantes, from *Don Quixote*

DBQ **CONTRASTING**
How do Don Quixote's motives for attacking the windmills show a contrast?

creative imaginative

LESSON 4 REVIEW

Reviewing Vocabulary

1. *Defining* Write a paragraph defining Mannerism and the baroque in art. Be sure to describe the characteristics of each style.

2. *Comparing* Write a paragraph that defines the term *drama* and compares the qualities of drama to those of a novel, such as Cervantes' *Don Quixote*.

Using Your Notes

3. *Identifying* Use your notes to write a paragraph identifying one major figure in each of the following areas of cultural expression: painting, architecture, music, and literature. Briefly describe each figure's work.

Answering the Guiding Questions

4. *Identifying Central Issues* How did art movements change in Europe after the Renaissance?

5. *Drawing Conclusions* What characterized the Golden Age of literature in England and Spain?

Writing Activity

6. INFORMATIVE/EXPLANATORY Write a paragraph evaluating the effects of religious and political turmoil on sixteenth- and seventeenth-century art. Be sure to discuss specific artists.

Directions: On a separate sheet of paper, answer the questions below. Make sure you read carefully and answer all parts of the questions.

Lesson Review

Lesson 1

1 DESCRIBING What was King Philip II of Spain's religion? How did his political actions show his religious beliefs?

2 IDENTIFYING CAUSE AND EFFECT How did the number of people in Europe fluctuate in the sixteenth and seventeenth centuries? What effect did the change in population have on societies and their economies?

Lesson 2

3 EXPLAINING What did the Petition of Right limit? Who was responsible for it?

4 DIFFERENTIATING How did Thomas Hobbes and John Locke differ in the kind of government they thought would be best?

Lesson 3

5 EXPLORING ISSUES What steps did Louis XIV take to increase his royal power? What effects did his actions have on his country and his people?

6 STATING What inspired Frederick William to build a large standing army in Prussia?

Lesson 4

7 IDENTIFYING Who was Artemisia Gentileschi? Briefly describe her work.

8 MAKING CONNECTIONS What kind of audience did the Globe Theatre attract? How do you think Shakespeare may have taken this into account when writing his plays?

21st Century Skills

9 UNDERSTANDING RELATIONSHIPS AMONG EVENTS What were the effects of religious wars on Europe in the sixteenth and seventeenth centuries? How did the concept of heresy contribute to the issue?

10 COMPARE AND CONTRAST What were the roles of the English nobility, Parliament, and religion in the Glorious Revolution?

Exploring the Essential Questions

11 ORGANIZING Work with a partner to create a large chart on posterboard that lists social, economic, and religious conflicts in at least four European countries and shows the effects of those conflicts on each country and its culture. Include visuals such as sketches, maps, and photos of art.

DBQ Analyzing Historical Documents

Use the document to answer the following questions.

In 1589 King James I of England wrote, anonymously, a book in which he defended the divine right of kings to absolute power.

PRIMARY SOURCE

66 And as ye see it manifest that the king is over-lord of the whole land, so is he master over every person that inhabiteth the same, having power over the life and death of every one of them; for although a just prince will not take the life of any of his subjects without a clear law, yet the same laws whereby he taketh them are made by himself or his predecessors; and so the power flows always from himself 99

—from *True Law of Free Monarchies*

12 INTERPRETING What protection does James I claim subjects have against execution by their ruler?

13 DRAWING CONCLUSIONS Why does the king say that all kings are overlords of their whole lands?

Extended-Response Question

14 INFORMATIVE/EXPLANATORY What are the differences between an absolute monarchy and a constitutional monarchy? How did the type of monarchy a country had affect the satisfaction of its people?

If You've Missed Question	1	2	3	4	5	6	7	8	9	10	11	12	13	14
Go to page	72	75	79	80	82	83	88	88	72	79	72	90	90	79

The Muslim Empires

1450–1800

ESSENTIAL QUESTIONS • *What factors help unify an empire?*
• *How can the creation of a new empire impact the people and culture of a region?*

netw⊙rks
There's More Online! about the Muslim empires.

CHAPTER 6

Lesson 1
The Rise and Expansion of the Ottoman Empire

Lesson 2
The Ottomans and the Ṣafavids

Lesson 3
The Mogul Empire

The Story Matters...

Three Muslim empires, each united by the Islamic religion and its ruling dynasty, reached the height of their power at different times between 1450 and 1800. The Ottoman Empire dominated the eastern Mediterranean, threatening Europe. The Mogul Empire ruled most of what is now India and Pakistan. Centered in Persia between its two Muslim rivals was the Ṣafavid Empire. All three empires created brilliant cultures, as shown in this vivid painting of the Mogul ruler Akbar.

◀ Akbar was powerful as well as physically and mentally energetic. A tireless soldier, he conquered much of India. Although unable to read, he fostered a brilliant culture at his court.

Place and Time: The Muslim Empires 1450–1800

Each dedicated to extending Muslim power, the Ottoman, Ṣafavid, and Mogul dynasties were also alike in establishing what historians refer to as "gunpowder empires." Their success as conquerors was based on their mastery of the technology of firearms. These empires were also similar in sharing the influence of Persian culture in literature and the arts and in gaining strength from a growing world economy.

Step Into the Place

Read the quotes and look at the information presented on the map.

 Analyzing Historical Documents Compare the ruling styles of Akbar and Süleyman I. Predict the strengths and weaknesses of each style.

PRIMARY SOURCE

❝His Imperial Majesty [Akbar] does not let a month or year pass without devising good regulations or without providing the source of tranquility to the world through his far-seeing wisdom that mirrors truths, earthly and divine. At this time he cast his eyes far and wide to arrange better the conditions of the army and peasantry and secure the extension of the empire and enlargement of the Imperial resources, and instituted [for that purpose] wonderful regulations and firm rules.❞

—Abu-l-Fazl ʿAllāmī, from *Akbarnama*, 1574–1575

PRIMARY SOURCE

❝The Sultan's [Süleyman I] headquarters were crowded by numerous attendants, including many high officials . . . In all that great assembly no single man owed his dignity to anything but his personal merits and bravery; no one is distinguished from the rest by his birth, and honour is paid to each man according to the nature of the duty and offices which he discharges. . . . The Sultan himself assigns to all their duties, . . . pays no attention to wealth or the empty claims of rank, and takes no account of any influence or popularity which a candidate may possess; he only considers merit, and scrutinizes the character, natural ability, and disposition of each.❞

—Ogier Ghislain de Busbecq, from *The Turkish Letters*, 1555–1562

PHOTO: (l)eTrip/AgeFotostock, (r)Mughal School/The Bridgeman Art Library/Getty Images.

Step Into the Time

Determining Cause and Effect Choose an event from the time line and predict what consequences it may have had for the expansion of one of these Muslim empires.

April 6, 1453 Ottomans, led by Mehmed II, lay siege to Constantinople

1519 Mogul ruler Bābur crosses Khyber Pass into India

1526 Ottomans defeat Hungarians at Mohács

1556 Akbar, grandson of Bābur, takes over Mogul Empire

1571 Christian alliance destroys Ottoman fleet at Battle of Lepanto

THE MUSLIM EMPIRES
THE WORLD

1450   **1500**   **1550**

1464 The Sunni dynasty in Africa begins

1517 Martin Luther writes Ninety-Five Theses

1533 Francisco Pizarro conquers the Inca Empire

1534 Act of Supremacy makes Henry VIII head of the new Church of England

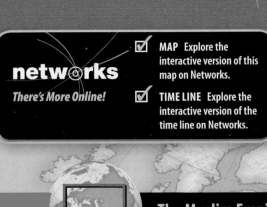
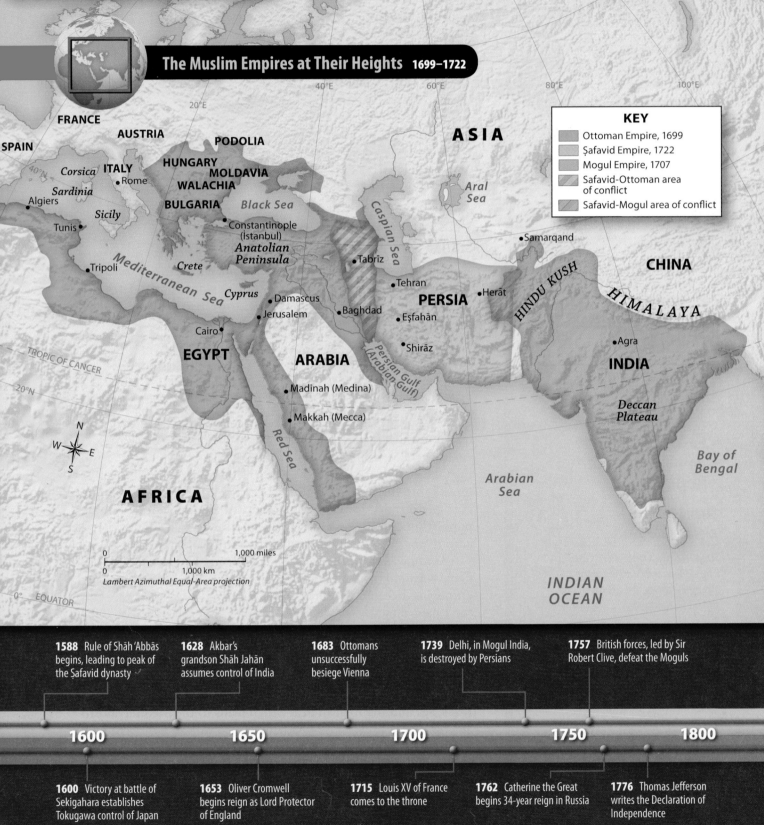

The Muslim Empires at Their Heights 1699–1722

KEY
- Ottoman Empire, 1699
- Ṣafavid Empire, 1722
- Mogul Empire, 1707
- Safavid-Ottoman area of conflict
- Safavid-Mogul area of conflict

FRANCE
AUSTRIA
SPAIN
PODOLIA
Corsica ITALY HUNGARY
Rome MOLDAVIA
Sardinia WALACHIA
Algiers Sicily BULGARIA Black Sea
Tunis Constantinople (İstanbul)
Tripoli Crete Anatolian Peninsula
Mediterranean Sea Cyprus Damascus
Jerusalem
Cairo
EGYPT ARABIA
Madinah (Medina)
Makkah (Mecca)
Red Sea
AFRICA

ASIA
Aral Sea
Caspian Sea
Tabrīz
Tehran Samarqand
PERSIA Herāt CHINA
Baghdad
Eṣfahān HINDU KUSH HIMALAYA
Shīrāz
Persian Gulf (Arabian Gulf)
Agra
INDIA
Deccan Plateau
Arabian Sea Bay of Bengal

TROPIC OF CANCER
20°N

N W E S

0 1,000 miles
0 1,000 km
Lambert Azimuthal Equal-Area projection

0° EQUATOR

INDIAN OCEAN

20°E 40°E 60°E 80°E 100°E
40°N

1588 Rule of Shāh 'Abbās begins, leading to peak of the Ṣafavid dynasty

1628 Akbar's grandson Shāh Jahān assumes control of India

1683 Ottomans unsuccessfully besiege Vienna

1739 Delhi, in Mogul India, is destroyed by Persians

1757 British forces, led by Sir Robert Clive, defeat the Moguls

1600   **1650**   **1700**   **1750**   **1800**

1600 Victory at battle of Sekigahara establishes Tokugawa control of Japan

1653 Oliver Cromwell begins reign as Lord Protector of England

1715 Louis XV of France comes to the throne

1762 Catherine the Great begins 34-year reign in Russia

1776 Thomas Jefferson writes the Declaration of Independence

The Muslim Empires **93**

networks

There's More Online!

- ☑ **BIOGRAPHY** Mehmed II
- ☑ **IMAGE** The Sacking of Constantinople
- ☑ **INTERACTIVE SELF-CHECK QUIZ**
- ☑ **MAP** Expansion of the Ottoman Empire to 1699
- ☑ **PRIMARY SOURCE** The Siege of Constantinople
- ☑ **SLIDE SHOW** Ottoman Architecture and Arts
- ☑ **VIDEO** The Rise and Expansion of the Ottoman Empire

Reading **HELP**DESK (CCSS)

Academic Vocabulary
- successor
- domain

Content Vocabulary
- janissary
- gunpowder empire
- sultan
- grand vizier
- harem
- pasha
- ulema

TAKING NOTES:

Key Ideas and Details

Organizing Create a chart like this one to show the structure of the Ottoman society. List the groups in order of importance.

Class	Description

LESSON 1
The Rise and Expansion of the Ottoman Empire

ESSENTIAL QUESTIONS · *What factors help unify an empire?*
· *How can the creation of a new empire impact the people and culture of a region?*

IT MATTERS BECAUSE

At its peak in the sixteenth century, the Ottoman Empire consisted of lands in western Asia, North Africa, and Europe. The Ottomans contributed new designs to world art, as seen in their magnificent mosques. They also practiced religious tolerance with their subjects.

Rise of the Ottoman Turks

GUIDING QUESTION *How did the Ottoman Turks establish power and expand their empire?*

In the late thirteenth century, a new group of Turks, under their leader Osman, began to build power in the northwest corner of the Anatolian Peninsula. As they expanded, the Osman Turks founded the Ottoman dynasty. In the fourteenth century, the Ottoman Turks moved into the Balkans, building a strong military by developing an elite guard called **janissaries**. Recruited from the local Christian population and converted to Islam, they trained as foot soldiers or administrators, serving the sultan, or Ottoman leader.

As knowledge of firearms spread during this period, the Ottomans began to master the new technology. With the janissaries, the Ottomans defeated the Serbs at the Battle of Kosovo in 1389. During the 1390s, they advanced northward and annexed Bulgaria.

Fall of the Byzantine Empire

In their expansion westward, the Ottomans came to control the Bosporus and the Dardanelles. These two straits (narrow water passageways), separated by the Sea of Marmara, connect the Black Sea and the Aegean Sea, which leads to the Mediterranean Sea. The Byzantine Empire had controlled this area for centuries.

Under Mehmed II, the Ottomans moved to end the Byzantine Empire. With 80,000 troops fighting against only 7,000 defenders, Mehmed laid siege to Constantinople.

The attack began on April 6, 1453, as the Ottomans bombarded Constantinople with massive cannons hurling stone balls weighing up to 1,200 pounds (545 kg) each. The Byzantines fought desperately for almost two months to save Constantinople. Finally, on May 29, the walls were breached, and Ottoman soldiers poured in. The Byzantine emperor died in the final battle, and an atrocious three-day sack of the city began.

In capturing Constantinople, the Turks now linked the European and Asian parts of the Ottoman Empire. Mehmed II renamed the city I˙stanbul. With the Ottoman Empire in control of this important crossroads, Europeans looked to the seas for trading routes to Asia. These explorations led Europeans to Africa and the Americas.

Expansion of the Ottoman Empire

From their new capital at I˙stanbul, the Ottoman Turks controlled the Balkans and the Anatolian Peninsula. From 1514 to 1517, Sultan Selim I conquered Mesopotamia, Egypt, and Arabia—the original heartland of Islam. Through these conquests, Selim I was now in control of several of Islam's holy cities. These cities included Jerusalem, Makkah (Mecca), and Madinah (Medina). Selim declared himself the new caliph, or defender of the faith and **successor** to Muhammad.

Ottoman forces advanced westward along the African coast almost to the Strait of Gibraltar. They also began to expand into other parts of Europe, back into the Balkans, and the Romanian territory of Walachia. The Hungarians, however, stopped their advance up the Danube Valley.

Under Süleyman I, whose reign began in 1520, the Ottomans advanced anew up the Danube, seized Belgrade, and won a major victory over the Hungarians in 1526 at the Battle of Mohács (MOH • hach). They then conquered most of Hungary and moved into Austria. Advancing to Vienna, they were defeated in 1529. They moved into the western Mediterranean until the Spanish destroyed a large Ottoman fleet at Lepanto in 1571.

During the first half of the seventeenth century, the Ottoman Empire in eastern Europe remained a "sleeping giant." Occupied with internal problems, the Ottomans kept the status quo. However, in the second half of the seventeenth century, they again went on the offensive, laying siege to Vienna. Repulsed by a European army, the Ottomans retreated and were pushed out of Hungary. Although they retained the core of their empire, the Ottoman Turks would never again be a threat to central Europe.

✓ **READING PROGRESS CHECK**

Explaining What was the role of the janissaries in the rise of the Ottoman Empire?

Life Under Ottoman Rule

GUIDING QUESTION *How was the Ottoman Empire ruled under a sultan? What were society and culture like in the Ottoman Empire?*

Like the Muslim empires in Persia and India, the Ottoman Empire is often labeled a "**gunpowder empire**." Gunpowder empires were formed by outside conquerors who unified their conquered regions. Such an empire's success was largely based on its mastery of firearms.

The Imperial Sultans

At the head of the Ottoman system was the **sultan**, who was the supreme authority in a political and a military sense. As the empire expanded, the status and prestige of the sultan increased. The position took on the trappings of imperial rule. A centralized administrative system was adopted, and the sultan became increasingly isolated from his people.

janissary a soldier in the elite guard of the Ottoman Turks

successor one who follows, especially one who takes over a throne, title, estate, or office

gunpowder empire an empire formed by outside conquerors who unified the regions that they conquered through their mastery of firearms

sultan "holder of power"; the military and political head of state under the Seljuk Turks and the Ottomans

domain place where one has absolute ownership of land or other property

harem "sacred place"; the private domain of an Ottoman sultan, where he and his wives resided

grand vizier the Ottoman sultan's chief minister who carried the main burdens of the state and who led the council meetings

pasha an appointed official of the Ottoman Empire who collected taxes, maintained law and order, and was directly responsible to the sultan's court

ulema a group of religious advisers to the Ottoman sultan; this group administered the legal system and schools for educating Muslims

▼ The Topkapi Palace overlooks the Bosporus and Sea of Marmara, part of an essential trade route connecting the Aegean and Black Seas.

▶ **CRITICAL THINKING**
Interpreting Significance What was the symbolic importance of where the Topkapi Palace was located?

The position of the sultan was hereditary. A son, although not necessarily the eldest, always succeeded the father. This practice led to struggles over succession upon the death of individual sultans. The losers in these struggles were often executed.

The private **domain** of the sultan was called the **harem** ("sacred place"). Here, the sultan and his wives resided. When a son became a sultan, his mother became known as the queen mother and acted as a major adviser to the throne. This tradition often gave considerable power to the queen mother in the affairs of state.

The sultan controlled his bureaucracy through an imperial council that met four days a week. The **grand vizier**, a chief minister who carried the main burdens of the state, led the meetings of the council. During the council meetings, the sultan sat behind a screen, overhearing the proceedings, and then privately indicated his desires to the grand vizier.

The empire was divided into provinces and districts, each governed by officials. They were assisted by bureaucrats known as **pashas**, who had been trained in a palace school for officials in I˙stanbul. The sultan gave land to the senior officials. They were then responsible for collecting taxes and supplying armies for the empire from this landed area.

The Topkapi ("iron gate") Palace in I˙stanbul was the center of the sultan's power. The palace was built in the fifteenth century by Mehmed II. Like Versailles in France, it had an administrative purpose but also served as the private residence of the ruler and his family.

Ottoman Society

Like most Turkic-speaking peoples in the Anatolian Peninsula and throughout western Asia, the Ottomans were Sunni Muslims. Ottoman sultans had claimed the title of caliph since the early sixteenth century. In theory, they were responsible for guiding the flock and maintaining Islamic law. In practice, the sultans gave their religious duties to a group of religious advisers known as the **ulema**. This group administered the legal system and schools for educating Muslims. Islamic law and customs were applied to all Muslims in the empire.

The Ottoman system was generally tolerant of non-Muslims, who made up a significant minority within the empire. Non-Muslims paid a tax, but they were allowed to practice their religion or to convert to Islam. Most people in the European areas of the empire remained Christian. In some areas, however, such as present-day Bosnia, large numbers of non-Muslims converted to the Islamic faith.

The subjects of the Ottoman Empire were divided by occupation. In addition to the ruling class, there were four main occupational groups: peasants, artisans, merchants, and pastoral peoples (nomadic herders). Peasants farmed land that the state leased to them. Ultimate ownership of all land resided with the sultan.

Artisans were organized according to craft guilds. Each guild provided financial services, social security, and training to its members. Outside the ruling elite, merchants were the most privileged class in Ottoman society. They were largely exempt from government regulations and taxes.

Technically, women in the Ottoman Empire were subject to the same restrictions as women in other Muslim societies. However, their position was somewhat better. As applied in the Ottoman Empire, Islamic law was more tolerant in defining the legal position of women. This relatively tolerant attitude was probably due to Turkish traditions that regarded women as almost equal to men. For instance, women were allowed to own and inherit property. They could not be forced into marriage and, in certain cases, were permitted to seek divorce. Women often gained considerable power within the palace. In a few instances, they served as senior officials.

Architecture and the Arts

The Ottoman sultans were enthusiastic patrons of the arts. Artists came from all over the world to compete for the sultans' generous rewards. They produced pottery; rugs, silk, and other textiles; jewelry; and arms and armor. All of these adorned the palaces of the rulers.

By far the greatest contribution of the Ottoman Empire to world art was in architecture, especially the magnificent mosques of the last half of the sixteenth century. The Ottoman Turks borrowed from the Byzantines and modeled their mosques on the open floor plan of Constantinople's Byzantine church of Hagia Sophia, creating a prayer hall with an open central area under one large dome.

In the mid-sixteenth century, the greatest of all Ottoman architects, Sinan, began building the first of his 81 mosques. One of Sinan's masterpieces was the Süleymaniye Mosque in İstanbul. Each of his mosques was topped by an imposing dome, and often the entire building was framed with four towers, or minarets.

The sixteenth century also witnessed the flourishing of textiles and rugs. The Byzantine emperor Justinian had introduced silk cultivation to the West in the sixth century. Under the Ottomans, the silk industry resurfaced. Factories produced silks for wall hangings and especially court costumes. Rugs were a peasant industry. The rugs were made of wool and cotton in villages from different regions.

☑ **READING PROGRESS CHECK**

Explaining What aspects of Ottoman life did the sultan control?

LESSON 1 REVIEW

Reviewing Vocabulary

1. *Describing* Write a paragraph describing the relationship between the sultan and the grand vizier.

Using Your Notes

2. *Explaining* Use your graphic organizer on Ottoman society to identify how the upper classes were supported by the lower classes.

Answering the Guiding Questions

3. *Evaluating* How did the Ottoman Turks establish power and expand their empire?

4. *Assessing* How was the Ottoman Empire ruled under the sultan?

5. *Summarizing* What were society and culture like in the Ottoman Empire?

Writing Activity

6. NARRATIVE Write a paragraph on Ottoman expansion or warfare from the point of view of a janissary in the Ottoman army.

Reading HELPDESK (CCSS)

Academic Vocabulary
• administrator • conform

Content Vocabulary
• shah • orthodoxy
• anarchy

TAKING NOTES:
Key Ideas and Details

Comparing and Contrasting Use the Venn diagram to compare and contrast the Ottoman and Ṣafavid Empires.

Ottoman Empire   Ṣafavid Empire

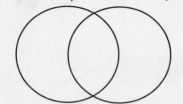

LESSON 2
The Ottomans and the Ṣafavids

ESSENTIAL QUESTIONS • *What factors help unify an empire?*
• *How can the creation of a new empire impact the people and culture of a region?*

IT MATTERS BECAUSE
The Ṣafavid Empire was the shortest lived of the three Muslim empires, but was nonetheless influential. The Shia faith, declared as the state religion, unified the empire, but also brought it into conflict with the Ottomans, who were Sunni Muslims.

Problems in the Ottoman Empire

GUIDING QUESTION *What led to the disintegration of the Ottoman Empire?*

The Ottoman Empire reached its high point under Süleyman I, known as the empire's greatest ruler. Süleyman (1520–1566) was also a great military leader, who led his army on 13 major military campaigns. He doubled the size of the Ottoman Empire. Europeans called him the "Grand Turk" and the "Magnificent."

To his own subjects, however, Süleyman was known as the "Lawgiver." Eager to provide justice for his subjects, he reorganized the government, regulated the laws of the empire, and saw that they were properly enforced. However, it might also have been during Süleyman's rule that problems began to occur. Having executed his two most able sons on suspicion of treason, Süleyman was succeeded by his only surviving son, Selim II (the Sot, or "the drunken sultan").

The problems of the Ottoman Empire did not become visible until 1699, when the empire began to lose some of its territory. However, signs of internal disintegration had already appeared in the early 1600s.

After the death of Süleyman, sultans became less involved in government. They allowed their ministers to exercise more power. The training of officials declined, and senior positions were increasingly assigned to the sons or daughters of elites. Members of the elite soon formed a privileged group seeking wealth and power. Earlier, the sultans had regarded members of the ruling class as the "sultan's slaves." Now the sultan became the servant of the ruling class. Moreover, the central bureaucracy lost its links with rural areas. Local officials became corrupt, taxes increased, and palace intrigue grew. Constant wars depleted the imperial treasury.

Another sign of change within the empire was a growing wealth and the impact of Western ideas and customs. Officials and merchants began to imitate the lifestyles of Europeans. They wore European clothing and bought Western furniture and art objects. During the sixteenth and early seventeenth centuries, coffee and tobacco were introduced into polite Ottoman society. Cafes, where both were consumed, began to appear in the major cities.

Some sultans attempted to counter this by outlawing such goods as coffee and tobacco. One sultan patrolled the streets of İstanbul at night, ordering the immediate execution of subjects he caught in illegal acts. Their bodies were left on the streets as an example to others.

The Ottoman Empire had economic problems reaching back to the closure of trade routes through its territories. The economy was also troubled by inflation and the trade imbalance between the empire and Europe. The Ottomans did not invest in manufacturing. Their guilds had strict price regulations and could not compete with inexpensive manufactured goods from Europe. This declining economy left little money for military expansion.

▲ The Süleymaniye Mosque in İstanbul, built between 1550–57

▶ CRITICAL THINKING
Interpreting Significance Why is it significant that the mosque design was inspired by the Byzantine church of Hagia Sophia?

✔ READING PROGRESS CHECK

Determining Cause and Effect How did some sultans respond to the influence of Western ideas in the Ottoman Empire?

The Ṣafavid Empire

GUIDING QUESTION *What was the source of conflict between the Ottomans and the Ṣafavids?*

After the empire of Timur Lenk (Tamerlane) collapsed in the early fifteenth century, the area extending from Persia into central Asia fell into anarchy. At the beginning of the sixteenth century, however, a new dynasty known as the Ṣafavids (sah • FAH • weedz) took control. Unlike many of their Islamic neighbors who were Sunni Muslims, the Ṣafavids became ardent Shias.

The Ṣafavid dynasty was founded by Shāh Esmāʿīl (ihs • MAH • eel), who, in 1501, used his forces to seize much of Iran and Iraq. He then called himself the **shah**, or king, of a new Persian state. Esmāʿīl sent Shia preachers into the Anatolian Peninsula to convert members of Turkish tribes in the Ottoman Empire. The Ottoman sultan tried to halt this activity, but Esmāʿīl refused to stop. Esmāʿīl also ordered the massacre of Sunni Muslims when he conquered Baghdad in 1508.

Alarmed by these activities, the Ottoman sultan, Selim I, advanced against the Ṣafavids in Persia. With their muskets and artillery, the Ottomans won a major battle near Tabrīz. However, a few years later, Esmāʿīl regained Tabrīz.

During the following decades, the Ṣafavids tried to consolidate their rule throughout Persia and in areas to the west. The Ṣafavids were faced with the problem of integrating various Turkish peoples with the settled Persian-speaking population of the urban areas. The Shia faith was used as a unifying force. Esmāʿīl made conversion to the Shia faith mandatory for the largely Sunni population. Many Sunnis were killed or exiled. Like the Ottoman sultan, the shah claimed to be the spiritual leader of all Islam.

shah king (used in Persia and Iran)

administrator one who manages the affairs of a government or a business

In the 1580s, the Ottomans went on the attack. They placed Azerbaijan under Ottoman rule and controlled the Caspian Sea with their fleet. This forced the new Ṣafavids shah, 'Abbās, to sign a peace treaty in which he lost much territory in the northwest. The capital of the Ṣafavids was moved from the northwestern city of Kazvin to the more centrally located city of Eşfahān. Eşfahān became one of the world's largest cities with a population of 1 million.

Under Shāh 'Abbās, who ruled from 1588 to 1629, the Ṣafavids reached the high point of their glory. Similar to the Ottoman Empire, **administrators** were trained to run the kingdom. Shāh 'Abbās also strengthened his army, which he outfitted with the latest weapons. In the early seventeenth century, Shāh 'Abbās moved against the Ottomans and returned Azerbaijan to the Ṣafavids.

After the death of Shāh 'Abbās in 1629, the Ṣafavid dynasty gradually lost its vigor. Most of 'Abbās's **successors** lacked his talent and political skills. Eventually, the power of Shia religious elements began to increase at court and in Ṣafavid society at large.

Intellectual freedom marked the height of the empire. However, the pressure to **conform** to traditional religious beliefs, called religious **orthodoxy**, increased. For example, Persian women had considerable freedom during the early empire. Now they were forced into seclusion and required to wear a veil. Treatment of non-Muslims deteriorated as well.

In the early eighteenth century, the Ṣafavid dynasty collapsed. The Turks took advantage of the situation to seize territories along the western border. Persia sank into a long period of political and social **anarchy**.

✅ READING PROGRESS CHECK

Analyzing What was the role of religion during the rule of Shāh Esmā'īl?

Life under the Ṣafavids

GUIDING QUESTION *What was life like under the Ṣafavids?*

Persia under the Ṣafavids was a mixed society. The combination of Turkish and Persian elements affected virtually all aspects of Ṣafavid society.

As Shia Islam was the state religion, the Ṣafavid rulers were eagerly supported by Shias. Shahs were more available to their subjects than were rulers elsewhere. "They show great familiarity . . . even to their own subjects, eating and drinking with them pretty freely," remarked one visitor.

Strong-minded shahs firmly controlled the power of the landed aristocracy. In addition, appointment to senior positions in the bureaucracy was based on merit rather than birth. For example, Shāh 'Abbās hired foreigners from neighboring countries for positions in his government.

The Ṣafavid shahs played an active part in trade and manufacturing activity. Across the empire, bazaars in regional capitals provided citizens with access to a variety of goods and merchandise. Merchants came from across Central Asia to trade in the Ṣafavid region.

The bazaar was the heart of their commerce. Many bazaars were enclosed and had high vaulted ceilings that covered narrow rows of stalls. Specific sections housed similar types of goods for shoppers' convenience. Spaces for manufacturing, storage, and merchants' offices stood alongside shops. Caravansaries attached to the bazaar received trains of camels or mules loaded with goods. In the caravansary, newly arrived trade goods were sold wholesale. In the bazaar, they were sold retail.

PHOTO:©Art Archive, The/SuperStock

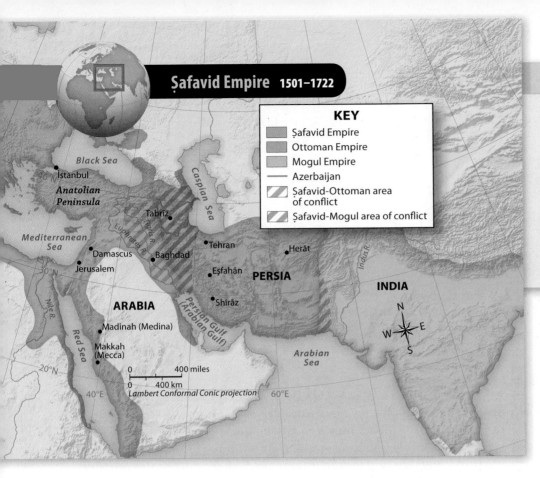

Safavid Empire 1501–1722

KEY
- Safavid Empire
- Ottoman Empire
- Mogul Empire
- Azerbaijan
- Safavid-Ottoman area of conflict
- Safavid-Mogul area of conflict

Black Sea
İstanbul
Anatolian Peninsula
Tabrīz
Mediterranean Sea
Damascus
Baghdad
Jerusalem
Tehran
Herāt
Eşfahān
PERSIA
Shīrāz
ARABIA
Madinah (Medina)
Makkah (Mecca)
Arabian Sea
INDIA
Caspian Sea
Persian Gulf (Arabian Gulf)
Red Sea
Nile R.
Euphrates R.
Tigris R.
Indus R.

0   400 miles
0   400 km
Lambert Conformal Conic projection
40°E   60°E
20°N
30°N

GEOGRAPHY CONNECTION

Differences between the Ṣafavids and the Ottomans led to conflict.

1 PLACES AND REGIONS *Which rivers flowed through the area disputed by the Ottomans and Ṣafavids?*

2 THE WORLD IN SPATIAL TERMS *Why would Tabrīz be a likely spot for a battle?*

Despite its trading activity, Ṣafavid Persia was probably not as prosperous as its neighbors to the east and west—the Moguls and the Ottomans. Hemmed in by European sea power to the south and the land power of the Ottomans to the west, the Ṣafavids found trade with Europe difficult.

In terms of culture, knowledge of science, medicine, and mathematics under the Ṣafavids was equal to that of other societies in the region. Persia also witnessed an extraordinary flowering of the arts during the reign of Shāh 'Abbās. Silk weaving and carpet weaving flourished, stimulated by the great demand for Persian carpets in the West. Persian painting enjoyed a long tradition. Riza-i-Abbasi, the most famous artist of this period, created exquisite works. Soft colors and flowing movement dominated the features of Ṣafavid painting.

conform to adhere to rules or standards; to fit in

orthodoxy traditional beliefs, especially in religion

anarchy political disorder; lawlessness

✓ **READING PROGRESS CHECK**

Differentiating What is the difference between a bazaar and a caravansary?

LESSON 2 REVIEW (CCSS)

Reviewing Vocabulary

1. *Identifying* Provide an example of a Persian shah and explain his duties and achievements.

Using Your Notes

2. *Comparing* Using your Venn diagram, discuss the similarities between the Ottoman and Ṣafavid empires.

Answering the Guiding Questions

3. *Explaining* What led to the disintegration of the Ottoman Empire?

4. *Interpreting* What was the source of the conflict between the Ottomans and the Ṣafavids?

5. *Summarizing* What was life like under the Ṣafavids?

Writing Activity

6. ARGUMENT Write a paragraph that supports or refutes this statement: Süleyman I was a cruel leader who was more interested in expanding his empire than in protecting or providing for his subjects.

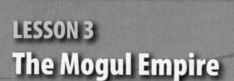

PHOTO: (l to r)Stapleton Collection/Victoria & Albert Museum, London/Bridgeman Art Library, Mughal School/The Bridgeman Art Library/Getty Images, ©Renaud Visage/age footstock, Gary Ombler/Dorling Kindersley/Getty Images.

networks

There's More Online!

Reading **HELP**DESK CCSS

Academic Vocabulary

- **intelligent** - **authority**
- **principle**

Content Vocabulary

- **zamindars** - **suttee**

TAKING NOTES:

Key Ideas and Details

Identifying Use a chart like this one to identify Akbar's accomplishments.

	Akbar's Accomplishments
Political	
Military	
Cultural	

102

LESSON 3
The Mogul Empire

ESSENTIAL QUESTIONS · *What factors help unify an empire?*
· *How can the creation of a new empire impact the people and culture of a region?*

IT MATTERS BECAUSE

Although they were not natives of India, the Moguls established a new dynasty by uniting the country under a single government with a common culture that blended Persian and Indian influences. The Mogul Empire reached its high point under the reign of Shāh Akbar.

The Mogul Dynasty

GUIDING QUESTION *How were the Moguls able to bring almost all of India under one rule?*

In 1500 the Indian subcontinent was still divided into a number of Hindu and Muslim kingdoms. The Moguls, who were not natives of India, established a new dynasty and brought a new era of unity to the region. They came from the mountainous region north of the Indus River valley. Their founder, Bābur, was descended from both Timur Lenk and Genghis Khan. Bābur had inherited a part of Timur Lenk's empire in an upland river valley of the Syr Dar'ya. As a youth, he led a group of warriors who seized Kabul in 1504. Thirteen years later, Bābur's forces crossed the Khyber Pass into India.

Bābur's forces were far smaller than those of his enemies, but with advanced weapons, including artillery, he captured Delhi. Establishing his power in the plains of North India, Bābur continued his conquests there until his death in 1530 at the age of 47.

Bābur's grandson Akbar was only 14 when he took the throne. **Intelligent** and industrious, by 1605 Akbar had brought Mogul rule to most of India. How was Akbar able to place almost all of India under his rule? By using heavy artillery, Akbar's armies were able to overpower the stone fortresses of their rivals. The Moguls also were successful negotiators. Akbar's conquests created the greatest Indian empire since the Mauryan dynasty. The empire appeared highly centralized but was actually a collection of semi-independent states held together by the power of the emperor.

Akbar was probably the greatest of the conquering Mogul monarchs, but he is best known for the humane character of his rule.

Like all Mogul rulers, Akbar was born a Muslim, but he showed a keen interest in other religions and tolerated Hindu practices. Akbar put his policy of religious tolerance into practice by taking a Hindu princess as one of his wives.

Akbar was also tolerant in his administration of the government. The upper ranks of the government bureaucracy were filled with nonnative Muslims, but many of the lower-ranking officials were Hindus. It became common practice to give the lower-ranking officials plots of farmland for their temporary use. These local officials, known as **zamindars**, kept a portion of the taxes paid by the peasants in lieu of a salary. They were then expected to forward the rest of the taxes from the lands under their control to the central government. Zamindars came to exercise considerable power and **authority** in their local districts.

The Akbar era was a time of progress, at least by the standards of the day. Indian peasants were required to pay about one-third of their annual harvest to the state, but the system was applied justly. When bad weather struck in the 1590s, taxes were reduced or suspended. Thanks to a long period of peace and political stability, trade and manufacturing flourished.

The era was an especially prosperous one in the area of foreign trade. Indian goods, notably textiles, tropical food products and spices, and precious stones, were exported in exchange for gold and silver. Arab traders handled much of the foreign trade because the Indians, like their Mogul rulers, did not care for travel by sea.

Akbar died in 1605 and was succeeded by his son Jahāngīr (juh • HAHN • gihr). During the early years of his reign, he continued to strengthen the central government's control over his vast empire. Eventually, however, his grip began to weaken when he fell under the influence of one of his wives, Persian-born Nūr Jahān. As Jahāngīr slowly lost interest in governing, he gave more authority to Nūr Jahān. The empress used her position to enrich her own family. She arranged the marriage of her niece to her husband's third son and successor, Shāh Jahān.

During his reign from 1628 to 1658, Shāh Jahān maintained the political system established by earlier Mogul rulers. He also expanded the boundaries of the empire through successful campaigns in the Deccan Plateau. Shāh Jahān's rule, however, was marred by his failure to deal with growing domestic problems. He had inherited a nearly empty treasury. His military campaigns and expensive building projects put a heavy strain on the imperial finances and compelled him to raise taxes. The peasants were even more deprived as a result of these taxes. The majority of Jahān's subjects lived in poverty.

Shāh Jahān's troubles worsened with his illness in the mid-1650s. It was widely reported that he had died. Such news led to a struggle for power among his sons. The victorious son, Aurangzeb, had his brother put to death and imprisoned his father. Aurangzeb then had himself crowned emperor in 1658.

Aurangzeb is one of the most controversial rulers in the history of India. During his reign, the empire reached its greatest physical size. He had expanded it along nearly all of its boundaries. Constant warfare and religious intolerance, however, made his subjects resentful.

As a man of high **principle,** Aurangzeb attempted to eliminate many of what he considered to be India's social evils. He forbade the custom of **suttee** (cremating a widow on her husband's funeral pyre), which was practiced by many Hindus, and he put a stop to the levying of illegal taxes. He tried to forbid gambling and drinking as well.

Analyzing CCSS
PRIMARY SOURCES

Jahāngīr on Akbar

66 In his actions and his movements, Akbar was not as ordinary men. The glory of God was manifest in him. He knew no fear and was always ready to risk his life in battle. With exquisite courtesy, he charmed all those that approached him. 99

—quoted in *A Brief History of India*

DBQ **DRAWING CONCLUSIONS**
How do the qualities Jahāngīr attributes to his father explain Akbar's success as a ruler?

intelligent having a high degree of understanding and mental capacity

zamindar a local official in Mogul India who received a plot of farmland for temporary use in return for collecting taxes for the central government

▼ Officials pay homage to Akbar in the *Akbarnama* (*History of Akbar*).

authority power; person in command

principle a fundamental law or idea; when said of people (e.g., someone is highly principled), it means a devotion to high codes or rules of conduct

suttee the Hindu custom of cremating a widow on her husband's funeral pyre

Aurangzeb was a devout Muslim and adopted a number of measures that reversed the Mogul policies of religious tolerance. For instance, he prohibited the building of new Hindu temples and forced Hindus to convert to Islam. Aurangzeb's policies led to Hindu outcries and a number of revolts against imperial authority.

After Aurangzeb's death in 1707, there were many contenders for the throne. Their reigns were short-lived, however. India was increasingly divided and vulnerable to attack from abroad. In 1739, Delhi was sacked by the Persians, who left it in ashes.

✅ **READING PROGRESS CHECK**

Contrasting What were some differences between the rules of Shāh Jahān and Aurangzeb?

Life in Mogul India

GUIDING QUESTION *What was life like in Mogul society?*

The Moguls were foreigners in India. In addition, they were Muslims ruling a largely Hindu population. The resulting blend of influences on the lives of ordinary Indians could be complicated. The treatment of women serves as a good example.

Women had long played an active role in Mogul tribal society. Mogul rulers often relied on female relatives for political advice. To a degree, these Mogul attitudes toward women affected Indian society. Women from aristocratic families frequently received salaries and were allowed to own land.

At the same time, the Moguls placed certain restrictions on women under their interpretations of Islamic law. These practices generally were adopted by Hindus. The practice of isolating women, for example, was followed by many upper-class Hindus.

In other ways, however, Hindu practices remained unchanged by Mogul rule. The custom of suttee continued in spite of efforts by the Moguls to abolish it. Child marriage also remained common.

The Mogul era saw the emergence of a wealthy nobility and a prosperous merchant class. During the late eighteenth century, this prosperity was shaken by the decline of the Moguls and the arrival of the British. However, many prominent Indians had trading ties with foreigners.

The Moguls brought together Persian and Indian influences in a new and beautiful architectural style. This style is best symbolized by the Taj Mahal, which Shāh Jahān built in Agra in the mid-seventeenth century. The project lasted more than twenty years. To finance it, the government raised land taxes, driving many Indian peasants into complete poverty.

The Taj Mahal is widely considered to be the most beautiful building in India, if not in the entire world. The building is monumental in size and boasts nearly blinding brilliance yet delicate lightness.

Another major artistic achievement of the Mogul period was in painting. Like architecture, painting in Mogul India resulted from the blending of two cultures: Persian and Indian. Akbar established a state workshop for artists, mostly Hindus, who worked under the guidance of Persian masters to create the Mogul school of painting. The "Akbar style" combined Persian with Indian motifs. It included the portrayal of humans in action, a characteristic not usually seen in Persian art.

✅ **READING PROGRESS CHECK**

Explaining What rights were enjoyed and what restrictions were imposed on upper-class women during the Mogul Empire?

Europeans Come to India

GUIDING QUESTION *What led to the decline of the Mogul Empire?*

The arrival of the British hastened the decline of the Mogul Empire. By 1650, British trading forts had been established at Surat, Fort William (which was renamed Calcutta and is now the city of Kolkata), and Madras (Chennai). British ships carried Indian-made cotton goods to the East Indies, where they were traded for spices.

British success in India attracted rivals, especially the French. The French established their own forts, many of them along the coast. For a brief period, the French went on the offensive, even capturing the British fort at Madras.

▲ The Taj Mahal in Agra is a classic example of Mogul architecture.

The British were saved by the military genius of Sir Robert Clive, an aggressive British empire builder. Clive served as the chief representative in India of the East India Company, a private company that acted on behalf of the British Crown. Clive's forces ultimately restricted the French to a few small territories.

While fighting the French, Clive was also consolidating British control in Bengal. The Indian ruler of Bengal had attacked Fort William in 1756. He had imprisoned the British garrison in the "Black Hole of Calcutta," an underground prison. Due to the intense heat in the crowded space, only 23 people (out of 146) survived.

In 1757 Clive led a small British force of about 3, 000 to victory over a Mogul-led army more than 10 times its size in the Battle of Plassey in Bengal. As part of the spoils of victory, the failing Mogul court gave the East India Company the power to collect taxes from lands in the area around Calcutta.

Britain's rise to power in India, however, was not a story of constant success. The arrogance and incompetence of many East India Company officials offended their Indian allies. Such behavior also alienated the local population, who were taxed heavily to meet the East India Company's growing expenses.

In the late eighteenth century, the East India Company moved inland from the bustling coastal cities. British expansion brought great riches to individual British merchants. British officials also became wealthy as they found they could obtain money from local rulers by selling trade privileges. The British were in India to stay.

✓ **READING PROGRESS CHECK**

Summarizing How did Sir Robert Clive increase the power of the British in India?

LESSON 3 REVIEW (CCSS)

Reviewing Vocabulary
1. ***Explaining*** Describe the duties and rewards of a zamindar in the Mogul system of governing.

Using Your Notes
2. ***Summarizing*** Describe the rule of Akbar using the information compiled in your graphic organizer.

Answering the Guiding Questions
3. ***Identifying*** How were the Moguls able to bring almost all of India under one rule?

4. ***Analyzing*** What was life like in Mogul society?

5. ***Identifying Cause and Effect*** What led to the decline of the Mogul Empire?

Writing Activity
6. **INFORMATIVE/EXPLANATORY** Using descriptive terms, write a paragraph on the reasons for the decline of the Mogul Empire beginning with Shāh Jahān.

Directions: On a separate sheet of paper, answer the questions below. Make sure you read carefully and answer all parts of the questions.

Lesson Review

Lesson 1

1 **ANALYZING** When a sultan died, how was a new sultan chosen? Why did the sultanate adopt a centralized administrative system?

2 **INTERPRETING** What did the Ottomans achieve artistically? What do these achievements signify?

Lesson 2

3 **IDENTIFYING** What happened to the Ottoman Empire under the reign of Süleyman I?

4 **CONTRASTING** How did attitudes between the Ottoman Empire and the Ṣafavid Dynasty differ toward religious tolerance?

Lesson 3

5 **EXAMINING** How did Shāh Akbar's religious beliefs affect his rule and his subjects?

6 **EVALUATING** What effects did Mogul rule have on women in India?

21st Century Skills

7 **TIME, CHRONOLOGY, AND SEQUENCING** How long did it take Mehmed II and the Ottoman forces to conquer Constantinople? How did they take over the city?

8 **CREATE AND ANALYZE ARGUMENTS** Do you agree that Aurangzeb was "a man of high principle"? Why or why not?

Exploring the Essential Questions

9 **ASSESSING** With a small group, role-play interviews with subjects of the three Muslim empires about their lives under each new rule. Choose a character and opinion, and write out what you will say. Then rehearse with a reporter, who should prepare questions on what daily life was like before, how it is now, and the advantages and disadvantages of each. Record your interview for the class.

DBQ Analyzing Historical Documents

Use the document to answer the following questions.

Sir John Chardin, a Frenchman, took two six-year trips through the Ṣafavid Empire, one during the reign of Shāh Abbās II and one after the death of Shāh Abbās II. Chardin described the changes between his two trips.

PRIMARY SOURCE

❝ Counting from that time to this, the riches seemed to be half diminished, with so little an interval as twelve years time only. Even the coin itself was altered. There was no such thing as good silver to be seen. The grandees being impoverished, exacted upon the people and peeled them of their fortunes. The people, to ward against the impressions of the great, were become cheats and sharpers, and from thence all the ill tricking ways that could be were introduced into the art of trade and commerce. There are too many examples throughout the world which show that even the fertility of the soil and the plenty of a country depends on the good order of a just and moderate government, and exactly regulated according to the laws. ❞

—from *Sir John Chardin's Travels in Persia*

10 **IDENTIFYING PERSPECTIVES** What changes in money and trade did Chardin observe during his two trips through the Ṣafavid Empire? Does his perception of when the dynasty lost its vigor agree with that of Lesson 2?

11 **MAKING INFERENCES** What does Chardin's final sentence imply about his opinion of the Ṣafavid Empire during his second trip?

Extended-Response Question

12 **INFORMATIVE/EXPLANATORY** What factors did the Ottoman, Ṣafavid, and Mogul Empires have in common that helped unify them? Give details that support your answer.

If You've Missed Question	**1**	**2**	**3**	**4**	**5**	**6**	**7**	**8**	**9**	**10**	**11**	**12**
Go to page	96	97	98	100	103	104	94	103	95	100	106	94

The East Asian World

1400–1800

ESSENTIAL QUESTIONS · *What factors help unify a kingdom or dynasty?*
· *How can external forces influence a kingdom or dynasty?*

The Story Matters...

In 1644 Manchu invaders from north of China founded the Qing dynasty. The Manchu were the most successful foreign conquerors in Chinese history and the Qing dynasty would rule China until 1911. Rulers such as Kangxi believed they were meant to restore China's greatness, and for two centuries they succeeded. It was during the Qing dynasty that Europeans gained their first in-depth look at the brilliance of Chinese civilization.

◀ This portrait shows Kangxi at about the age of 60, near the end of his reign. Although he was eager to learn about the science and technology of the West, he also feared the problems that contact with Europeans might bring to China.

PHOTO: CORBIS

107

Place and Time: East Asia 1400–1800

Strong rulers dominated East Asia between 1400 and 1800. Under the Ming and Qing dynasties, China flourished politically, economically, and culturally. At the end of the sixteenth century, powerful Japanese leaders reunified Japan and established the Tokugawa shogunate. The renowned Yi dynasty in Korea struggled to maintain its independence from China and Japan. In Southeast Asia, mainland and island kingdoms adopted different styles of ruling, depending on their religion and culture. Throughout East Asia, the arrival of European missionaries and merchants represented a social and cultural challenge.

Step Into the Place

Read the quotes and look at the information presented on the map.

DBQ **Analyzing Historical Documents** Draw a conclusion about the concerns East Asian governments had about contact with Europeans.

PRIMARY SOURCE

❝Since I discovered on the Southern Tour of 1703 that there were [Christian] missionaries wandering at will over China, I had grown cautious and determined to control them more tightly: to bunch them in the larger cities and in groups that included men from several different [European] countries, to catalogue their names and residences, and to permit no new establishments without my express permission. For with so many Westerners coming to China it has been hard to distinguish the real missionaries from other white men pretending to be missionaries.❞

—quoted in *Emperor of China: Self-portrait of K'ang-hsi* [Kangxi]

PRIMARY SOURCE

❝**1.** Japanese ships are strictly forbidden to leave for foreign countries.

2. No Japanese is permitted to go abroad. If there is anyone who attempts to do so secretly, he must be executed. . . .

3. If any Japanese returns from overseas after residing there, he must be put to death. . . .

7. If there are any Southern Barbarians [Europeans] who propagate the teachings of the priests, or otherwise commit crimes, they may be incarcerated in the prison. . . .❞

—Tokugawa Iemitsu, from Closed Country Edict of 1635

Step Into the Time

Demonstrating Understanding Research one or more publications from the time. Write a short essay explaining how the publication(s) influenced society

1405–1433 Zheng He leads seven Chinese voyages of exploration

1443 Korean phonetic alphabet is invented

1514 Portuguese fleet arrives in China

EAST ASIA **1400**

THE WORLD **1500**

after 1526 West African ruler Afonso I attempts to restrict slave trade

1533 Francisco Pizarro conquers the Inca Empire

Trade Centers and Trade Routes in Southeast Asia 1770

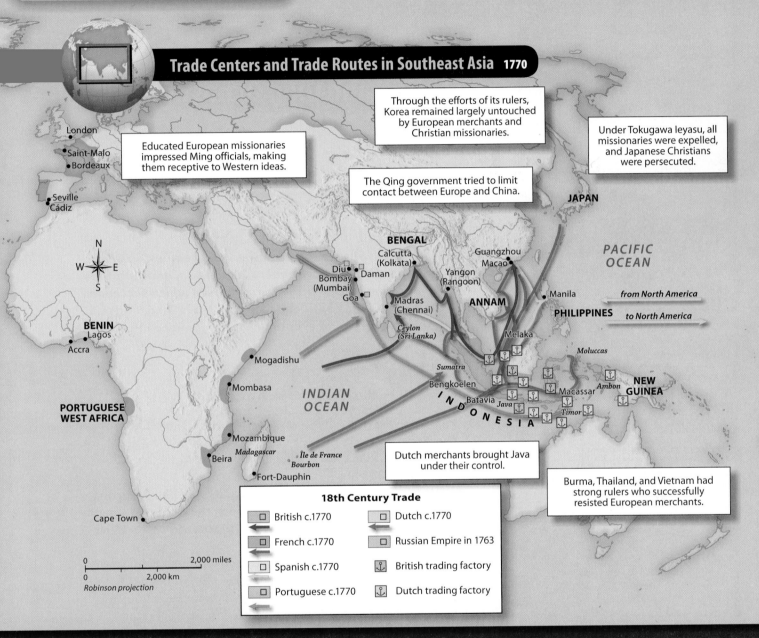

Educated European missionaries impressed Ming officials, making them receptive to Western ideas.

Through the efforts of its rulers, Korea remained largely untouched by European merchants and Christian missionaries.

Under Tokugawa Ieyasu, all missionaries were expelled, and Japanese Christians were persecuted.

The Qing government tried to limit contact between Europe and China.

Dutch merchants brought Java under their control.

Burma, Thailand, and Vietnam had strong rulers who successfully resisted European merchants.

18th Century Trade

- British c.1770
- French c.1770
- Spanish c.1770
- Portuguese c.1770
- Dutch c.1770
- Russian Empire in 1763
- ⚓ British trading factory
- ⚓ Dutch trading factory

0 — 2,000 miles
0 — 2,000 km
Robinson projection

1603 Tokugawa shogunate begins in Japan

1619 Dutch establish fort at Batavia on Java

1644 China's Ming dynasty is overthrown; Qing dynasty succeeds

1661 Kangxi, the greatest Qing emperor, comes to the throne

1679 Matsuo Bashō writes his first haiku in Japan

1791 Cao Xueqin's novel *The Dream of the Red Chamber* is published in China

1793 Lord Macartney leads British trade mission to China

1600

1700

1800

1555 Peace of Augsburg divides Christianity in Germany

1566 Ottoman sultan Süleyman I dies

1618 Thirty Years' War begins

1623 Shakespeare's First Folio is published

1661 Louis XIV begins absolutist rule in France

1664 England seizes Dutch New Netherland colony

1707 Aurangzeb, the last great Mogul emperor, dies

Reading HELPDESK (CCSS)

Academic Vocabulary

- series
- perspective

Content Vocabulary

- queue
- clan
- porcelain

TAKING NOTES:

Key Ideas and Details

Comparing and Contrasting Use a graphic organizer like this one to compare and contrast the achievements of the Ming and Qing dynasties.

Ming — Both — Qing

LESSON 1
The Ming and Qing Dynasties

ESSENTIAL QUESTIONS · *What factors help unify a kingdom or dynasty?*
· *How can external forces influence a kingdom or dynasty?*

IT MATTERS BECAUSE

The Ming dynasty began a new era of greatness in China, bringing effective government, expansion, and cultural advancements. Under the Qing dynasty, which succeeded the Ming, China continued to prosper, but Qing limits on foreign trade would eventually harm China economically.

The Ming Dynasty

GUIDING QUESTION *What were the achievements of the Ming dynasty?*

The Mongol dynasty in China was overthrown in 1368. The founder of the new dynasty took the title of Ming Hong Wu (the Ming Martial Emperor). This was the beginning of the Ming dynasty, which lasted until 1644.

Under Ming emperors, China extended its rule into Mongolia and central Asia. Along the northern frontier, the Chinese strengthened the Great Wall and made peace with the nomadic tribes that had troubled them for many centuries.

At home, Ming rulers ran an effective government using a centralized bureaucracy staffed with officials chosen by the civil service examination system. They set up a nationwide school system. Manufactured goods were produced in workshops and factories in vastly higher numbers. New crops were introduced, which greatly increased food production. The Ming rulers also renovated the Grand Canal, making it possible to ship grain and other goods from southern to northern China. The Ming dynasty truly began a new era of greatness in Chinese history.

Ming Hong Wu ruled from 1368 until 1398. After his death, his son Yong Le became emperor. In 1406 Yong Le began construction of the Imperial City in Beijing (BAY • JIHNG). In 1421 he moved the capital from Nanjing to Beijing. The Imperial City was created to convey power and prestige. It is an immense complex of palaces and temples surrounded by six and one-half miles of walls. Because it was off-limits to commoners, it was known as the Forbidden City.

During his reign, Yong Le also sent a **series** of naval voyages into the Indian Ocean that sailed as far west as the eastern coast of Africa. Led by the court official Zheng He (JUHNG • HUH), seven voyages were made between 1405 and 1433. The first fleet, consisting of 62 ships and nearly 28,000 men, passed through Southeast Asia, the western coast of India and the city-states of East Africa. It returned with items unknown in China and with information about the outside world.

In 1514 a Portuguese fleet arrived off the coast of China. It was the first direct contact between the Chinese Empire and Europe since the journeys of Marco Polo. At the time, the Ming government thought little of their arrival. China was at the height of its power, and from the **perspective** of the emperor, the Europeans were only an unusual form of barbarian. To the Chinese ruler, the rulers of all other countries were simply "younger brothers" of the Chinese emperor, who was seen as the Son of Heaven.

The Portuguese soon outraged Chinese officials with their behavior. They were expelled from Guangzhou (Canton) but were allowed to occupy Macao, a port on the southeastern coast of China.

At first, the Portuguese had little impact on Chinese society. Portuguese ships carried goods between China and Japan, but direct trade between Europe and China remained limited. Perhaps more important than trade, however, was the exchange of ideas.

Christian missionaries also made the long voyage to China on European merchant ships. Many of them were highly educated men who brought along instruments, such as clocks, that impressed Chinese officials and made them more receptive to Western ideas.

Both sides benefited from this early cultural exchange. Chinese scholars marveled at their ability to read better with European eyeglasses. Christian missionaries were impressed with the teachings of Confucius, the printing and availability of books, and Chinese architecture. When these reports began to circulate back home, Europeans became even more curious about this great civilization on the other side of the world.

After a period of prosperity and growth, the Ming dynasty gradually began to decline. During the late sixteenth century, internal power struggles led to a period of government corruption. High taxes, caused in part by this corruption, led to peasant unrest. Crop yields declined because of harsh weather. In the 1630s, a major epidemic greatly reduced the population in many areas. The suffering caused by the epidemic helped spark a peasant revolt led by Li Zicheng (LEE DZUH • CHUHNG). The revolt began in central China and then spread to the rest of the country. In 1644 Li and his forces occupied the capital of Beijing. When the capital fell, the last Ming emperor committed suicide in the palace gardens. Many officials took their own lives as well.

The overthrow of the Ming dynasty created an opportunity for the Manchus. They were a farming and hunting people who lived northeast of the Great Wall in the area known today as Manchuria. The forces of the Manchus conquered Beijing, and Li Zicheng's army fell. The victorious Manchus then declared the creation of a new dynasty called the Qing (CHIHNG), meaning "pure." This dynasty, created in 1644, remained in power until 1911.

☑ **READING PROGRESS CHECK**

Evaluating Explain the importance of three achievements of the Ming dynasty.

series a group of related things or events

perspective viewpoint

▼ A section of the Imperial City in Beijing, China

The Qing Dynasty

GUIDING QUESTION *How did the Qing dynasty adapt to become successful?*

queue the braided pigtail that was traditionally worn by Chinese males

When some Chinese resisted their new rulers and seized the island of Taiwan, the Manchu government prepared to attack them. To identify the rebels, the government ordered all males to adopt Manchu dress and hairstyles. They had to shave their foreheads and braid their hair into a pigtail called a **queue**. Those who refused were assumed to be rebels and were executed: "Lose your hair or lose your head."

Gradually accepted as legitimate rulers, the Qing flourished under a series of strong early rulers who pacified the country, corrected serious social and economic ills, and restored peace and prosperity. The Qing maintained the Ming political system but faced one major problem: the Manchus were ethnically and culturally different from their subject population. The Qing rulers dealt with this reality in two ways.

First, the Qing tried to preserve their distinct identity within Chinese society. The Manchus, only 2 percent of the population, were defined legally as distinct from everyone else in China. The Manchu nobility maintained large landholdings and received revenues from the state treasury. Second, the Qing dealt with this problem by bringing Chinese into the imperial administration to win their support. Chinese held more than 80 percent of lower posts, but a much smaller share of the top positions.

Kangxi (KAHNG • SHEE), who ruled from 1661 to 1722, was perhaps the greatest of the emperors who ruled China during the Ming and Qing dynasties. A person with political skill and a strong character, Kangxi took charge of the government while still in his teens and reigned for 61 years.

Kangxi rose at dawn and worked until late at night. He wrote: "One act of negligence may cause sorrow all through the country, and one moment of negligence may result in trouble for thousands of generations." Kangxi calmed the unrest along the northern and western frontiers by force. As a patron of the arts and letters, he gained the support of scholars in China.

In 1689, during Kangxi's reign, China and Russia signed the Treaty of Nerchinsk. Beginning in the 1620s, Russian traders had pushed eastward into land under China's protection in search of trade routes and goods. The treaty stopped Russia's push east, ended the frontier wars, and established trade between the two empires. This gave the Russians a special status with the Qing. Other European powers were limited to trade at certain ports.

Also during Kangxi's reign, the efforts of Christian missionaries reached their height. The emperor was quite tolerant of the Christians. Several hundred officials became Catholics, as did an estimated 300,000 ordinary Chinese. Ultimately, however, the Christian effort was undermined by squabbling among the Western religious orders. After the death of Kangxi, his successor began to suppress Christian activities.

☑ **READING PROGRESS CHECK**

Categorizing Explain how Kangxi exemplifies the adaptability of the Qing leaders.

Europeans in China

GUIDING QUESTION *How did the changing economy affect society during the Ming and Qing dynasties?*

Under Qianlong (CHEE • UHN • LUNG), who ruled from 1736 to 1795, the Qing dynasty experienced the greatest period of prosperity and reached its greatest physical size. It was during this great reign, however, that the first signs of decay appeared. Why did this happen?

As the emperor grew older, he fell under the influence of destructive elements at court. Corrupt officials and higher taxes led to unrest in rural areas. Population growth also exerted pressure on the land and led to economic hardship. In central China, unhappy peasants launched a revolt, the White Lotus Rebellion (1796–1804). The revolt was suppressed, but the expenses of war weakened the Qing dynasty.

Unfortunately for China, the Qing dynasty was declining just as Europe was seeking more trade. At first, the Qing government sold trade privileges to the Europeans, but to limit contacts between Europeans and Chinese, the Qing confined all European traders to a small island just outside Guangzhou. Traders could reside there only between October and March and only deal with a limited number of Chinese firms licensed by the government.

At first, the British accepted this system. By the end of the eighteenth century, however, some British traders had begun to demand access to additional cities, as Russian traders already enjoyed, along the Chinese coast. Likewise, the Chinese government was under pressure from its own merchants to open China to British manufactured goods.

Britain had an unfavorable, or negative, trade balance with China. That is, Britain imported more goods from China than it exported to the country. For years, Britain had imported tea, silk, and **porcelain** from the Chinese. To pay for these imports, Britain had sent Indian cotton to China, but this did not cover the entire debt, and the British had to pay for their imports with silver. The British sent ever-increasing quantities of silver to China, especially in exchange for tea, which was in great demand by the British.

In 1793 a British mission led by Lord George Macartney visited Beijing to seek more liberal trade policies. However, Emperor Qianlong responded that China had no need of "your country's manufactures."

☑ **READING PROGRESS CHECK**

Constructing a Thesis How did the Qing dynasty adapt to the presence of Europeans?

porcelain a ceramic material made of fine clay baked at very high temperatures

GEOGRAPHY CONNECTION

China expanded its borders during the Ming and Qing dynasties.

1. **THE WORLD IN SPATIAL TERMS** *How large was the Qing Dynasty in comparison to the Ming?*

2. **HUMAN SYSTEMS** *How did the location of the rebellion of Li Zicheng help the Qing conquest of Ming China?*

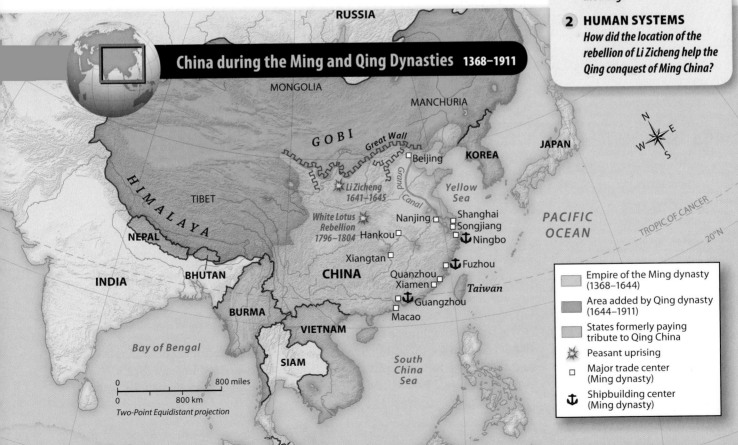

China during the Ming and Qing Dynasties 1368–1911

Empire of the Ming dynasty (1368–1644)

Area added by Qing dynasty (1644–1911)

States formerly paying tribute to Qing China

✳ Peasant uprising

◻ Major trade center (Ming dynasty)

⚓ Shipbuilding center (Ming dynasty)

Economy and Daily Life

GUIDING QUESTION *How did the changing economy affect society during the Ming and Qing dynasties?*

Between 1500 and 1800, China remained a mostly agricultural society. Nearly 85 percent of the people were small farmers. Nevertheless, the Chinese economy was changing.

The first change for China involved an increase in population, from less than 80 million in 1390 to more than 300 million at the end of the 1700s. The increase had several causes. These included a long period of stability under the early Qing dynasty and improvements in the food supply due to a faster growing species of rice from Southeast Asia.

The population increase meant that less land was available for each family. The imperial court tried to make more land available by limiting the amount wealthy landowners could hold. By the eighteenth century, however, almost all the land that could be was already being farmed. Rural land shortages led to unrest and revolts.

Another change in this period was a steady growth in manufacturing and increased trade between provinces. Taking advantage of the long era of peace and prosperity, merchants and manufacturers expanded their trade in silk, porcelain, cotton goods, and other products.

Despite the growth in trade and manufacturing, China did not develop the same attitude toward business that was emerging in Europe. Middle-class merchants and manufacturers in China were not as independent as those in Europe, The government controlled commercial activity and also saw business as inferior to farming. Due to Confucian ideals, merchants bought land rather than reinvesting their profits in their businesses.

Chinese society was organized around the family. The family was expected to provide for its members' needs, including the education of children, support of unmarried daughters, and care of the elderly. At the same time, all family members were expected to sacrifice their individual needs to benefit the family as a whole. This was based on Confucian ideals.

The ideal family unit in Qing China was the extended family, in which generations lived under the same roof. When sons married, their wives, no longer considered members of their original families, lived with them in the husband's family home. Unmarried daughters also remained in the house, as did parents and grandparents. Chinese society held the elderly in high regard. Aging parents knew they would be cared for in their home by their children.

Beyond the extended family was the **clan**, which consisted of dozens, or even hundreds, of related families. These families were linked by a clan council of elders and common social and religious activities. This system made it possible for wealthier families to help poorer relatives.

Women were considered inferior to men in Chinese society. Only males could have a formal education and pursue a career in government or scholarship. Within the family, Chinese women often played strong roles. Nevertheless, the wife was clearly subordinate to the husband. Legally, she could not divorce her husband or inherit property. The husband could divorce his wife if she did not produce sons. He could also take a second wife. Husbands were expected to support their wives and children.

A feature of Chinese society that restricted the mobility of women was the practice of footbinding. Scholars believe it began among the wealthy and was later adopted by all classes. Bound feet were a status symbol. Women who had bound feet were more marriageable than those who did

▲ Emperor Qianlong, in full ceremonial armor

clan a group of related families

not; thus, there was a status incentive as well as an economic incentive. An estimated one-half to two-thirds of the women in China bound their feet.

The process, begun in childhood, was very painful. Women who had their feet bound could not walk; they were carried. Not all clans looked favorably on footbinding. Women who worked in the fields or in occupations that required mobility did not bind their feet.

✔ **READING PROGRESS CHECK**

Summarizing How did population increases cause unrest?

Chinese Art and Literature

GUIDING QUESTION *What artistic advancements did China experience during the Ming and Qing dynasties?*

During the late Ming and the early Qing dynasties, traditional culture in China reached new heights. The Ming economic expansion increased standards of living, providing many Chinese with money to purchase books. Also, new innovations in paper manufacturing encouraged the growth of printing throughout China.

During the Ming dynasty, a new form of literature arose that evolved into the modern Chinese novel. Works in this literary form were quite popular, especially among well-to-do urban dwellers.

One Chinese novel, *The Golden Lotus,* is considered by many to be the first realistic social novel. *The Golden Lotus* depicts the corrupt life of a wealthy landlord in the late Ming period who cruelly manipulates those around him for sex, money, and power.

The Dream of the Red Chamber, by Cao Xueqin, is generally considered even today to be China's most distinguished popular novel. Published in 1791, it tells of the tragic love between two young people caught in the financial and moral disintegration of a powerful Chinese clan.

During the Ming and the early Qing dynasties, China experienced an outpouring of artistic brilliance. In architecture, the most outstanding example is the Imperial City in Beijing. The decorative arts also flourished in this period. Perhaps the most famous of all the arts of the Ming Era was blue-and-white porcelain. Europeans admired the beauty of this porcelain and collected it in great quantities. Different styles of porcelain were produced during the reign of individual emperors.

✔ **READING PROGRESS CHECK**

Identifying Relate advances in literature to economic advances during the period.

Analyzing CCSS PRIMARY SOURCES

Women in China

❝How sad it is to be a woman! Nothing on earth is held so cheap. . . . No one is glad when a girl is born: By *her* the family sets no store.❞

—Fu Hsüan, from "Woman"

DBQ **READING CLOSELY** Based on what you've read, does this seem like a fair assessment of the role of women in China?

▲ Porcelain vase from the Ming Dynasty, fifteenth century

LESSON 1 REVIEW CCSS

Reviewing Vocabulary

1. *Summarizing* Write a paragraph explaining how the queue functioned as an effective political tool during the Qing dynasty.

Using Your Notes

2. *Comparing and Contrasting* Use your notes on the Ming and Qing dynasties to write a paragraph comparing and contrasting their achievements.

Answering the Guiding Questions

3. *Listing* What were the achievements of the Ming dynasty?

4. *Synthesizing* How did the Qing dynasty adapt to become successful?

5. *Summarizing* How did the changing economy affect society during the Ming and Qing dynasties?

6. *Summarizing* What artistic advancements did China experience during the Ming and Qing dynasties?

Writing Activity

7. INFORMATIVE/EXPLANATORY Write a paragraph that evaluates the positive and negative features of the traditional family-centered values of Chinese society.

Reading **HELP**DESK (CCSS)

Academic Vocabulary

- process
- community

Content Vocabulary

- **daimyo**
- **hans**
- **hostage system**
- **eta**

TAKING NOTES:

Key Ideas and Details

Categorizing Use a graphic organizer like this one to categorize key elements of Japanese society and culture during the Tokugawa era.

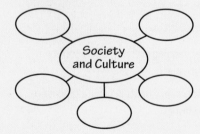

Society and Culture

LESSON 2
The Reunification of Japan

ESSENTIAL QUESTIONS • *What factors help unify a kingdom or dynasty?*
• *How can external forces influence a kingdom or dynasty?*

IT MATTERS BECAUSE

From the sixteenth century to the eighteenth century, Japan was unified through efforts of powerful leaders. It imposed restrictive social systems and enforced cultural isolation, while trade and industry increased.

Political Changes in Japan

GUIDING QUESTION *What changes took place in Japan after its political unification?*

At the end of the fifteenth century, Japan was in chaos. The centralized power of the shogunate had collapsed. **Daimyo**, heads of noble families, controlled their own lands and warred with their neighbors. Soon, however, a dramatic reversal would unify Japan.

The **process** of unification began in the late sixteenth century with three powerful political figures. The first was Oda Nobunaga (oh • dah noh • boo • nah • gah). Nobunaga seized the imperial capital of Kyōto and placed the reigning shogun under his control. By 1582 he had unified the central part of present-day Japan.

Nobunaga was succeeded by Toyotomi Hideyoshi (toh • yoh • toh • mee hee • day • yoh • shee), a farmer's son who had become a military commander. Hideyoshi located his capital at Ōsaka. By 1590 he had persuaded most of the daimyo on the Japanese islands to accept his authority.

After Hideyoshi's death in 1598, Tokugawa Ieyasu (toh • kuh • gah • wah ee • yah • soo), the powerful daimyo of Edo (modern-day Tokyo), took control of Japan. Ieyasu took the title of shogun in 1603. The Tokugawa rulers completed the restoration of central authority that had begun with Nobunaga and Hideyoshi. The Tokugawa shoguns remained in power at their capital of Edo until 1868. Tokugawa rule brought a period of peace known as the "Great Peace."

As the three great commanders were unifying Japan, the first Europeans began to arrive. Portuguese traders landed on the islands in 1543. In a few years, Portuguese ships began stopping regularly

might corrupt people's moral standards, forbade women to appear on stage. Thus a new profession was created—male actors who portrayed female characters on stage.

Art also reflected the changes in Japanese culture under the Tokugawa Era. The shogun's order that all daimyo and their families have residences in Edo sparked an increase in building. Nobles competed to erect the most magnificent mansions with lavish and beautiful furnishings.

Japanese art was enriched by ideas from other cultures. The Japanese studied Western medicine, astronomy, languages, and painting styles. In turn, Europeans wanted Japanese ceramics, which were prized as highly as the ceramics of the Chinese.

✔ **READING PROGRESS CHECK**

Summarizing Summarize the social structure that developed during the Tokugawa shogunate.

▼ Kabuki actors performing a play called *Soga Monogatari*

▶ **CRITICAL THINKING**
Comparing and Contrasting How does Kabuki theater appear similar to or different from Western theater?

LESSON 2 REVIEW

Reviewing Vocabulary

1. ***Explaining*** Write a paragraph explaining how the hostage system helped the shogunate control the daimyo.

Using Your Notes

2. ***Describing*** Use your notes to write a paragraph describing Japanese society and culture under the Tokugawa shogunate.

Answering the Guiding Questions

3. ***Identifying*** What changes took place in Japan under the Tokugawa shogunate?

4. ***Identifying*** What forms of art flourished under Tokugawa rule?

Writing Activity

5. ***NARRATIVE*** Write a narrative paragraph presenting an imaginary episode during the introduction of European goods to Japan. Present vivid details of the event in clear chronological order.

Reading **HELP**DESK CCSS

Academic Vocabulary

- **archipelago** • **network**
- **impose**

Content Vocabulary

- **isolationist**
- **mainland states**
- **bureaucracy**

TAKING NOTES:

Key Ideas and Details

Organizing As you read, use a chart like the one below to list and organize information about the kingdoms of Korea and Southeast Asia.

Korea	
Mainland states: Burma, Thailand, and Cambodia	
Vietnam	
Indonesian archipelago	
Malay Peninsula	

LESSON 3
The Kingdoms of Korea and Southeast Asia

ESSENTIAL QUESTIONS • *What factors help unify a kingdom or dynasty?* • *How can external forces influence a kingdom or dynasty?*

IT MATTERS BECAUSE

Beginning in the fourteenth century, the powerful Yi dynasty created a stable state in Korea. In Southeast Asia, Muslim merchants, attracted to the growing spice trade, established a workable trade network. In the sixteenth century, however, the Portuguese seized control of the spice trade, eventually attracting English and Dutch competition.

Korea: The Hermit Kingdom

GUIDING QUESTION *What characterized Korea's culture in the sixteenth and seventeenth centuries?*

The Yi dynasty in Korea began in 1392 when Yi Sŏng-gye (YEE • sung • jay), a renowned military strategist, ascended the throne by over-throwing the Koryo dynasty. Lasting for five centuries, the Yi dynasty was one of the world's longest-lasting monarchies.

From their capital at Hanseong (modern-day Seoul), Yi rulers consolidated their rule of Korea by adopting the Chinese example of a strong bureaucratic state. They patterned their society after the Chinese to the north but maintained their distinctive identity.

One distinctive Korean characteristic was its alphabet—Hangul. The first Korean and Japanese writing systems developed from Chinese characters, or symbols. Unlike Chinese, which uses thousands of symbols, the Korean Hangul is phonetically based. One symbol stands for each sound, similar to the English alphabet. Hangul is still largely the standard writing system in present-day Korea.

The Yi dynasty also experienced serious problems. During the late sixteenth and early seventeenth centuries, internal conflicts within the royal court weakened the dynasty. Japanese and Chinese invasions also devastated Korea.

A Japanese force under Toyotomi Hideyoshi invaded Korea in the late sixteenth century. Hideyoshi wanted to use Korea as the transit route for his conquest of China. Korean forces defeated the Japanese invaders, but victory came at a high price. Korean farmlands were devastated, and villages and towns were burned. The Japanese also killed or kidnapped skilled workers.

Korea was still recovering from the Japanese invasions when the Manchus attacked in the 1620s and 1630s. Korea recovered, however, and then began to experience a long period of peace.

In response to these events, the Korean rulers sought to limit contact with foreign countries and tried to keep the country isolated from the outside world. The country remained largely untouched by European merchants and Christian missionaries. Due to its **isolationist** practices, Korea received the name "Hermit Kingdom."

✔ READING PROGRESS CHECK

Explaining Why was Korea called the "Hermit Kingdom?"

isolationist a policy of national isolation by abstention from alliances and other international political and economic relations

Kingdoms in Southeast Asia

GUIDING QUESTION *What factors influenced the emerging kingdoms in Southeast Asia beginning in the sixteenth century?*

In 1500 mainland Southeast Asia was a relatively stable region. Throughout the region, from Burma in the west to Vietnam in the east, kingdoms with unique ethnic, linguistic, and cultural characteristics were being formed.

Nevertheless, conflicts erupted among the emerging states on the Southeast Asian mainland. One such conflict, over territory between the Thai and the Burmese, was bitter until a Burmese army sacked the Thai capital in 1767. The Thai then created a new capital at Bangkok, farther to the south.

GEOGRAPHY CONNECTION

Southeast Asia had a variety of kingdoms in the 1500s.

1 HUMAN SYSTEMS *Why was Islam present on the Indonesian islands?*

2 THE WORLD IN SPATIAL TERMS *What was the main style of kingship on the mainland?*

Southeast Asia and Political Systems 1500

Buddhist style of kingship
Javanese style of kingship
Islamic sultans
Vietnamese emperors

Across the mountains to the east, the Vietnamese had begun their "March to the South." By the end of the fifteenth century, they had subdued the rival state of Champa on the central coast. The Vietnamese then gradually took control of the Mekong Delta from the Khmer—the successor of the old Angkor kingdom. By 1800, the Khmer monarchy had virtually disappeared.

The situation was different in the Malay Peninsula and the Indonesian **archipelago**. Muslim merchants, who were attracted to the growing spice trade, gradually entered the area. The creation of an Islamic trade **network** had political results as new Islamic states arose along the spice route. The major impact of this trade network, however, came in the fifteenth century with the new Muslim sultanate at Melaka. Melaka owed its new power to its strategic location on the Strait of Malacca and to the rapid growth of the spice trade itself. Within a few years, Melaka had become the leading power in the region.

Religious beliefs changed in Southeast Asia during the period from 1500 to 1800. Particularly in the non-mainland states and the Philippines, Islam and Christianity began to attract converts. Buddhism advanced on the mainland, becoming dominant from Burma to Vietnam. Traditional beliefs, however, survived and influenced the new religions.

The political systems in Southeast Asian states evolved into four main types. Buddhist kings, Javanese kings, Islamic sultans, and Vietnamese emperors adapted foreign models of government to suit their particular local circumstances.

The Buddhist style of kingship became the chief form of government in the **mainland states** of Burma, Thailand, Laos, and Cambodia. In the Buddhist model, the king was considered superior to other human beings and served as the link between human society and the universe.

The Javanese style of kingship was rooted in the political traditions of India and shared many characteristics of the Buddhist system. Like Buddhist rulers, Javanese kings were believed to have a sacred quality. They maintained the balance between the sacred world and the material world. The royal palace was designed to represent the center of the universe. Its shape was like rays spreading outward to the corners of the Javanese realm.

Islamic sultans ruled on the Malay Peninsula and in the small coastal states of the Indonesian archipelago. In the Islamic pattern, the head of state was a sultan. Viewed as a mortal, he still possessed some special qualities. He was a defender of the faith and staffed his **bureaucracy** (nonelected government officials) mainly with aristocrats.

archipelago a chain of islands

network an interrelated or interconnected group or system

mainland states part of the continent, as distinguished from peninsulas or offshore islands

▼ This print depicts the port of Batavia (now Jakarta) on the island of Java in the Dutch East Indies.

▶ **CRITICAL THINKING**
Identifying Central Issues Why did the Dutch East India Company establish its headquarters at Batavia?

PHOTO: © The British Library/Heritage Images/Imagestate

In Vietnam, kingship followed the Chinese model. Like the Chinese emperor, the Vietnamese emperor ruled according to the teachings of Confucius. Confucius believed that a ruler should treat subjects with love and respect. The ruler was seen as an intermediary between Heaven and Earth. The emperor was appointed by Heaven to rule by his talent and virtue.

bureaucracy an administrative organization that relies on nonelective officials and regular procedures

✓ **READING PROGRESS CHECK**

Drawing Conclusions How did religion influence the forms of government in the kingdoms of Southeast Asia?

Europeans and the Spice Trade

GUIDING QUESTION *How did the arrival of Europeans affect Southeast Asia beginning in the sixteenth century?*

Since ancient times, spices had been highly valued. They were used as flavorings, medicines, and as food preservers. After bad harvests and in winter, meat preserved with salt and pepper kept many people from starving. Ginger, cloves, cinnamon, and nutmeg were also in high demand. European countries competed to find a sea route to the Indies. In particular, that hunt was for Melaka, the fabled gateway to the Spice Islands. Portugal found that gateway.

When Vasco da Gama and his crew came ashore at Calicut in 1498, they shouted, "For Christ and spices!" Most important were the spices. In 1511 the Portuguese seized Melaka and soon occupied the Moluccas. Known to Europeans as the Spice Islands, the Moluccas were the main source of spices that first attracted the Portuguese to the Indian Ocean. The Portuguese, however, lacked the military and financial resources to **impose** their authority over broad areas. They set up small settlements along the coast and used them as trading posts during travel to and from the Spice Islands.

impose to establish or apply

The situation changed with the arrival of the English and Dutch (Netherlands) traders, who were better financed than the Portuguese. The shift in power began in the early 1600s when the Dutch seized a Portuguese fort in the Moluccas and gradually pushed the Portuguese out of the spice trade.

During the next 50 years, the Dutch occupied most Portuguese coastal forts along the trade routes throughout the Indian Ocean. They drove the English traders out of the spice market. England was left with a single port on the southern coast of Sumatra.

✓ **READING PROGRESS CHECK**

Drawing Conclusions If the mainland states had been rich in spices like the Moluccas were, would they have faced the same fate? Explain your answer.

LESSON 3 REVIEW

Reviewing Vocabulary
1. ***Describing*** Write a paragraph about the trading networks in the mainland states and archipelagos of Southeast Asia.

Using Your Notes
2. ***Explaining*** Use your notes to write a paragraph describing the governments of Korea and Southeast Asia.

Answering the Guiding Questions
3. ***Making Generalizations*** What characterized Korea's culture in the sixteenth and seventeenth centuries?

4. ***Identifying the Central Issues*** How did Korea and the kingdoms of Southeast Asia respond to contact with foreign nations?

5. ***Identify Cause and Effect*** How did the arrival of Europeans affect Southeast Asia between the sixteenth and eighteenth centuries?

Writing Activity
6. **INFORMATIVE/EXPLANATORY** Write a paragraph comparing and contrasting Portuguese and Dutch activities in the spice trade in Southeast Asia. Be sure to link to specific facts and dates.

Directions: On a separate sheet of paper, answer the questions below. Make sure you read carefully and answer all parts of the questions.

Lesson Review

Lesson 1

1 **STATING** What was the Confucian ideal regarding families in China? What specific needs were families expected to meet?

2 **COMPARING AND CONTRASTING** How were the Ming and Qing dynasties similar in their treatment of the Europeans? How were they different?

Lesson 2

3 **IDENTIFYING** What political leaders brought about Japanese reunification? What did each accomplish?

4 **DRAWING CONCLUSIONS** What aspects of Japan's geography made it fairly easy to prohibit Europeans from entering the country?

Lesson 3

5 **MAKING CONNECTIONS** Why and how did Korea pursue an isolationist policy in the seventeenth century?

6 **EXPLORING ISSUES** How did the political systems of Southeast Asian kingdoms change from the sixteenth to the eighteenth centuries?

21st Century Skills

7 **IDENTIFYING CAUSE AND EFFECT** How did the Manchus, a small percentage of the population, maintain power over a much larger group of Chinese subjects?

8 **IDENTIFYING PERSPECTIVES** How did the Japanese treatment of and attitude toward Europeans change after Europeans first arrived on Japan's shores?

9 **UNDERSTANDING RELATIONSHIPS AMONG EVENTS** What kinds of conflicts developed among the mainland states of Southeast Asia? What were some of the reasons for these conflicts? Give two examples.

Exploring the Essential Questions

10 **GATHERING INFORMATION** Write an essay explaining how external factors influenced East Asian kingdoms and dynasties between 1400 and 1800. Include several examples from each lesson and discuss factors that had both negative and positive influences.

DBQ Analyzing Historical Documents

Use the document to answer the following questions.

Lord George Macartney was the British ambassador to China when Qianlong was emperor. In 1793 he visited Qianlong's palace.

PRIMARY SOURCE

❝ [The buildings are]...furnished in the richest manner, with pictures of the Emperor's huntings and progresses; with stupendous vases of jasper and agate; with the finest porcelains and japan, and with every kind of European toys and sing-songs; with spheres, orreries [models of the solar system], clocks and musical automatons of such exquisite workmanship, and in such profusion, that our presents must shrink from the comparison... ❞

—quoted in *The Fall of Imperial China*

11 **ANALYZING** How does Macartney's description of the court depict the economy of China under the Qing dynasty?

12 **MAKING INFERENCES** What does Macartney's statement that "our presents must shrink from the comparison" reveal about his likely success in improving Britain's negative trade balance with China?

Extended-Response Question

13 **INFORMATIVE/EXPLANATORY** What kinds of relationships did China, Japan, Korea, and Southeast Asia have with Europe in the sixteenth century? How did these relationships change over time? What can you conclude from these patterns about what causes countries to become allies and what causes conflict?

If You've Missed Question	**1**	**2**	**3**	**4**	**5**	**6**	**7**	**8**	**9**	**10**	**11**	**12**	**13**
Go to page	114	111	116	116	121	121	112	116	121	110	124	124	111

The Enlightenment and Revolutions

1550–1800

ESSENTIAL QUESTIONS · Why do new ideas often spark change?
· How do new ways of thinking affect the way people respond to their surroundings?

networks
There's More Online! about the Enlightenment and revolutions.

CHAPTER 8

The Story Matters...

The Scientific Revolution led to the Enlightenment, a major European intellectual movement that applied reason to all human experience. The English mathematician Sir Isaac Newton was a key figure in the Scientific Revolution. His fundamental scientific insight, that the physical world operated according to natural laws discovered through scientific investigation, influenced every area of Enlightenment thought.

◄ This engraving was based on a portrait of Newton by Sir Godfrey Kneller. The poet Alexander Pope summed up Newton's contribution to human understanding: "Nature and Nature's laws lay hid in night: / God said, Let Newton be! and all was light."

Place and Time: Europe and the World 1550–1800

The seventeenth and eighteenth centuries witnessed the Scientific Revolution and the Enlightenment. Philosophers and scientists produced new theories about the structure of the universe and humankind's relationship to it. As European powers explored the world and expanded their colonial empires, conflicts erupted. This first age of global warfare culminated in the Seven Years' War, fought in Europe, North America, and India.

Step Into the Place

Read the quotes and look at the information presented on the map.

DBQ **Analyzing Historical Documents** How would you generalize the attitude of the Enlightenment toward a conflict between colonial empires, such as the Seven Years' War? Reference specific primary sources in your answer.

PRIMARY SOURCE

❝Though . . . politics [cannot] be founded on any thing but the consent of the people . . . in the noise of war, which makes so great a part of the history of mankind, this consent is little taken notice of: and therefore many have mistaken the force of arms for the consent of the people, and reckon conquest as one of the originals of government. But conquest is as far from setting up any government, as demolishing an [sic] house is from building a new one in the place.... Without the consent of the people, [one] can never erect a new one.❞

—John Locke, from *Two Treatises of Government*, 1690

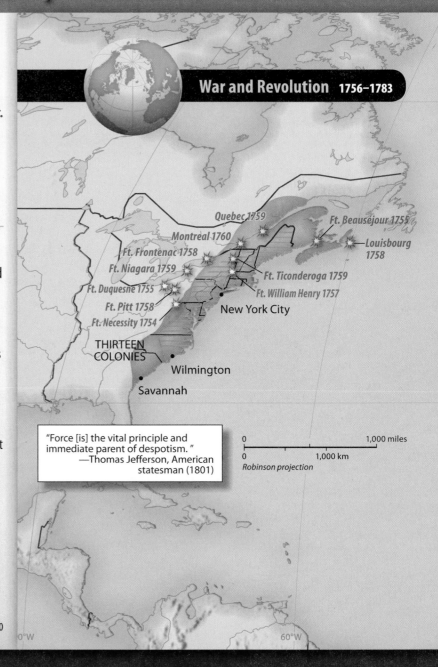

War and Revolution 1756–1783

Quebec 1759
Ft. Beausejour 1755
Montreal 1760
Louisbourg 1758
Ft. Frontenac 1758
Ft. Niagara 1759
Ft. Ticonderoga 1759
Ft. Duquesne 1755
Ft. William Henry 1757
Ft. Pitt 1758
New York City
Ft. Necessity 1754
THIRTEEN COLONIES
Wilmington
Savannah

"Force [is] the vital principle and immediate parent of despotism."
—Thomas Jefferson, American statesman (1801)

0   1,000 miles
0   1,000 km
Robinson projection

60°W   60°W

Step Into the Time

Making Connections

Choose several events from the time line and use them to write a paragraph summarizing the key interests of Enlightenment thinkers.

1610 Galileo Galilei publishes *The Starry Messenger*

1637 René Descartes publishes *Discourse on Method*

EUROPE

THE WORLD

1550

1600

1562 Beginning of Akbar's reign in India

1588 Shāh 'Abbās comes to power in Persia

1603 Tokugawa shogunate begins in Japan

1607 Founding of Jamestown Colony in Virginia

1632–53 Construction of Taj Mahal

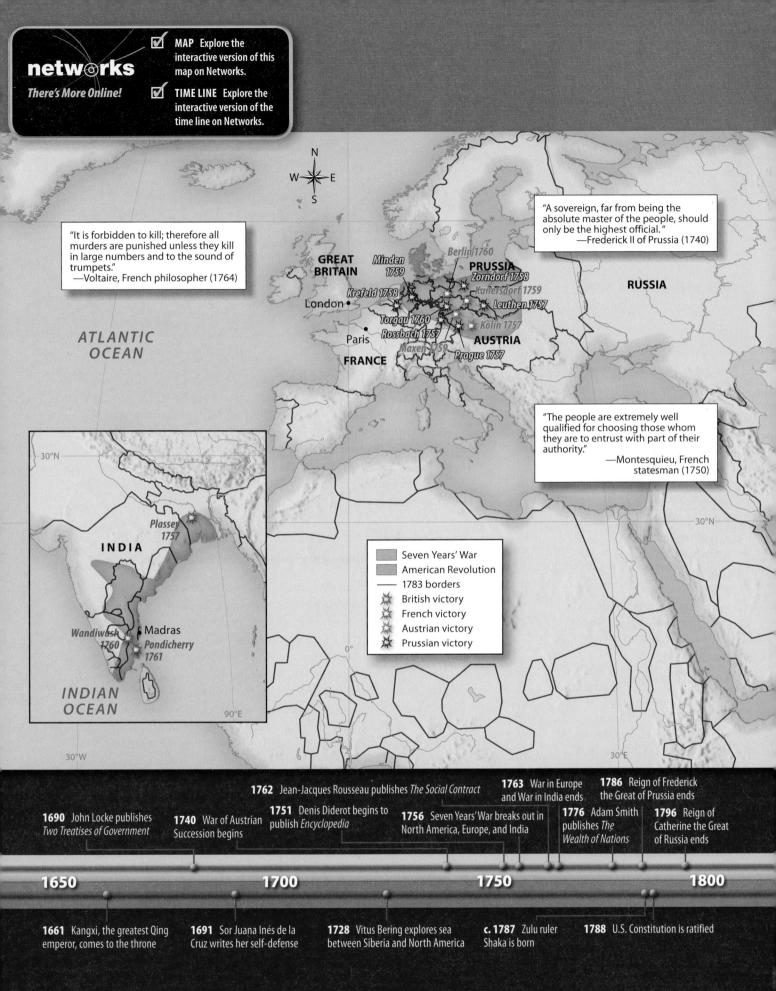

networks

There's More Online!

☑ **MAP** Explore the interactive version of this map on Networks.

☑ **TIME LINE** Explore the interactive version of the time line on Networks.

"It is forbidden to kill; therefore all murders are punished unless they kill in large numbers and to the sound of trumpets."
—Voltaire, French philosopher (1764)

"A sovereign, far from being the absolute master of the people, should only be the highest official."
—Frederick II of Prussia (1740)

"The people are extremely well qualified for choosing those whom they are to entrust with part of their authority."
—Montesquieu, French statesman (1750)

GREAT BRITAIN
London •

ATLANTIC OCEAN

Paris •

FRANCE

Minden 1759
Krefeld 1758
Torgau 1760
Rossbach 1757
Maxen 1759
Berlin 1760
PRUSSIA
Zorndorf 1758
Kunersdorf 1759
Leuthen 1757
Kolin 1757
AUSTRIA
Prague 1757

RUSSIA

INDIA
Plassey 1757
Wandiwash 1760
• Madras
Pondicherry 1761

INDIAN OCEAN

30°N
90°E
30°W
0°
30°E
30°N

	Seven Years' War
	American Revolution
—	1783 borders
✦	British victory
✦	French victory
✦	Austrian victory
✦	Prussian victory

1762 Jean-Jacques Rousseau publishes *The Social Contract*

1763 War in Europe and War in India ends

1786 Reign of Frederick the Great of Prussia ends

1690 John Locke publishes *Two Treatises of Government*

1740 War of Austrian Succession begins

1751 Denis Diderot begins to publish *Encyclopedia*

1756 Seven Years' War breaks out in North America, Europe, and India

1776 Adam Smith publishes *The Wealth of Nations*

1796 Reign of Catherine the Great of Russia ends

1650   **1700**   **1750**   **1800**

1661 Kangxi, the greatest Qing emperor, comes to the throne

1691 Sor Juana Inés de la Cruz writes her self-defense

1728 Vitus Bering explores sea between Siberia and North America

c. 1787 Zulu ruler Shaka is born

1788 U.S. Constitution is ratified

networks

There's More Online!

☑ **BIOGRAPHY** Francis Bacon

☑ **BIOGRAPHY** Galileo Galilei

☑ **BIOGRAPHY** Isaac Newton

☑ **CHART/GRAPH** Intellectuals of the Scientific Revolution

☑ **GAME** Terms from the Scientific Revolution

☑ **GRAPHIC ORGANIZER** The Scientific Method

☑ **INTERACTIVE SELF-CHECK QUIZ**

☑ **PRIMARY SOURCE** Meditations on First Philosophy

☑ **VIDEO** The Scientific Revolution

Reading **HELP**DESK (CCSS)

Academic Vocabulary
- philosopher • sphere

Content Vocabulary
- geocentric
- heliocentric
- universal law of gravitation
- rationalism
- scientific method
- inductive reasoning

TAKING NOTES:

Key Ideas and Details

Summarizing Use a table like this one to list the contributions of Copernicus, Kepler, Galileo, and Newton to a new concept of the universe.

Copernicus	
Kepler	
Galileo	
Newton	

LESSON 1
The Scientific Revolution

ESSENTIAL QUESTIONS • Why do new ideas often spark change?
• How do new ways of thinking affect the way people respond to their surroundings?

IT MATTERS BECAUSE

Of all the changes that swept Europe in the sixteenth and seventeenth centuries, the most widely influential was the Scientific Revolution. This revolution often is associated with the various scientific and technological changes made during this time. However, the Scientific Revolution was also about changes in the way Europeans looked at themselves and their world.

Causes of the Scientific Revolution

GUIDING QUESTION *What developments were the foundation of the Scientific Revolution?*

In the Middle Ages, many educated Europeans took great interest in the world around them. However, these "natural philosophers," as medieval scientists were known, did not make observations of the natural world. Instead they relied on a few ancient authorities— especially Aristotle—for their scientific knowledge. During the fifteenth and sixteenth centuries, a number of changes occurred that caused the natural philosophers to abandon their old views.

Renaissance humanists had mastered Greek as well as Latin. These language skills gave them access to newly discovered works by Archimedes and Plato. These writings made it obvious that some ancient thinkers had disagreed with Aristotle and other accepted authorities of the Middle Ages.

Other developments also encouraged new ways of thinking. Technical problems that required careful observation and accurate measurements, such as calculating the amount of weight that ships could hold, served to stimulate scientific activity. Then, too, the invention of new instruments, such as the telescope and microscope, made fresh scientific discoveries possible. Above all, the printing press helped spread new ideas quickly and easily.

Mathematics played a key role in the scientific achievements of the time. It was promoted in the Renaissance by the rediscovery of the works of ancient mathematicians. Moreover, mathematics was seen as the key to navigation, military science, and geography.

Renaissance thinkers also believed that mathematics was the key to understanding the nature of things in the universe. Nicolaus Copernicus, Johannes Kepler, Galileo Galilei, and Isaac Newton were all great mathematicians who believed that the secrets of nature were written in the language of mathematics. After studying, and sometimes discarding, the ideas of the ancient mathematicians, these intellectuals developed new theories that became the foundation of the Scientific Revolution.

✓ **READING PROGRESS CHECK**

Drawing Conclusions Why might new inventions such as the telescope and microscope change the way people saw the world?

Scientific Breakthroughs

GUIDING QUESTIONS *What role did scientific breakthroughs play during the Scientific Revolution? What obstacles did participants in the Scientific Revolution face?*

During the Scientific Revolution, discoveries in astronomy led to a new conception of the universe. Breakthroughs advanced medical knowledge and launched the field of chemistry as well.

The Ptolemaic System

Ptolemy, who lived in the A.D. 100s, was the greatest astronomer of antiquity. Using Ptolemy's ideas, as well as those of Aristotle and of Christianity, **philosophers** of the Middle Ages constructed a model of the universe known later as the Ptolemaic (TAH • luh • MAY • ihk) system. This system is **geocentric** because it places Earth at the center of the universe.

In the Ptolemaic system, the universe is seen as a series of concentric **spheres**—one inside the other. Earth is fixed, or motionless, at the center. The heavenly bodies—pure orbs of light—are embedded in the crystal-like, transparent spheres that rotate about Earth. The moon is embedded in the first sphere, Mercury in the second, Venus in the third, and the sun in the fourth. The rotation of the spheres makes these heavenly bodies rotate about Earth and move in relation to one another.

The tenth sphere in the Ptolemaic system is the "prime mover." This sphere moves itself and gives motion to the other spheres. Beyond the tenth sphere is Heaven, where God resides. God was at one end of the universe, then, and humans were at the center.

Copernicus and Kepler

In May 1543, Nicolaus Copernicus, a native of Poland, published his famous book, *On the Revolutions of the Heavenly Spheres*. Copernicus, a mathematician, thought that his **heliocentric**, or sun-centered, conception of the universe offered a more accurate explanation than did the Ptolemaic system. In his system, the sun, not Earth, was at the center of the universe. The planets revolved around the sun. The moon, however, revolved around Earth. Moreover, according to Copernicus, the apparent movement of the sun around Earth was caused by the rotation of Earth on its axis and its journey around the sun.

Johannes Kepler, a German mathematician, took the next step in destroying the Ptolemaic system. Kepler used detailed astronomical data to arrive at his laws of planetary motion. His observations confirmed that the

philosopher a person who seeks wisdom or enlightenment; a scholar or a thinker

geocentric Earth-centered; a system of planetary motion in which the sun, moon, and other planets revolve around the Earth

sphere any of the concentric, revolving, spherical transparent shells in which, according to ancient astronomy, the stars, sun, planets, and moon are set

heliocentric sun-centered; the system of the universe in which the Earth and planets revolve around the sun

▼ Diagram of the Copernican system, Andreas Cellarius, 1660

▶ **CRITICAL THINKING**
Analyzing Information How does this diagram illustrate the workings of the universe?

sun was at the center of the universe and also added new information. In his first law, Kepler showed that the planets' orbits around the sun were not circular, as Copernicus had thought. Rather, the orbits were elliptical (egg-shaped), with the sun toward the end of the ellipse instead of at the center. This finding, known as Kepler's First Law, contradicted the circular orbits and crystal-like spheres that were central to the Ptolemaic system.

Galileo's Discoveries

Scientists could now think in terms of planets revolving around the sun in elliptical orbits. Important questions remained unanswered, however. Of what are the planets made? How does one explain motion in the universe? An Italian scientist answered the first question. As the first European to make regular observations of the heavens using a telescope, mathematician Galileo Galilei made a series of remarkable discoveries: mountains on Earth's moon, four moons revolving around Jupiter, and sunspots.

Galileo's observations seemed to destroy another aspect of the Ptolemaic conception. Heavenly bodies had been seen as pure orbs of light. They now appeared to be composed of material substance, just as Earth was.

Galileo's discoveries, published in *The Starry Messenger* in 1610, did more to make Europeans aware of the new view of the universe than did the works of Copernicus and Kepler. But in the midst of his newfound fame, Galileo found himself under suspicion by the Catholic Church. The Church ordered him to abandon the Copernican idea, which threatened the Church's entire conception of the universe. In the Copernican view, humans were no longer at the center of the universe; God was no longer in a specific place.

In spite of the Church's position, by the 1630s and 1640s, most astronomers had accepted the heliocentric idea of the universe. However, motion in the universe had not been explained. The ideas of Copernicus, Kepler, and Galileo had yet to be tied together. An Englishman—Isaac Newton—would make this connection; he is considered the greatest genius of the Scientific Revolution.

▲ Galileo appears before officials in the Vatican in 1663.

▶ **CRITICAL THINKING**
Interpreting Significance Why would the Church be concerned that Galileo's ideas contradicted its worldview?

universal law of gravitation one of Newton's three rules of motion; it explains that planetary bodies continue in elliptical orbits around the sun because every object in the universe is attracted to every other object by a force called gravity

Newton's View of the Universe

Born in 1642, Isaac Newton attended Cambridge University and later became a professor of mathematics there. His major work was *Mathematical Principles of Natural Philosophy,* known simply as the *Principia*, from a shortened form of its Latin title.

In the *Principia*, Newton defined the three laws of motion that govern the planetary bodies, as well as objects on Earth. Crucial to his whole argument was the **universal law of gravitation**. This law explains why the planetary bodies continue their elliptical orbits about the sun. The law states, in mathematical terms, that every object in the universe is attracted to every other object by a force called gravity. This one universal law, mathematically proved, could explain all motion in the universe.

Newton's ideas created a new picture of the universe. It was now seen as one huge, regulated, uniform machine that worked according to natural laws. Newton's concept dominated the modern worldview until Albert Einstein's concept of relativity gave a new picture of the universe.

Breakthroughs in Medicine and Chemistry

The teachings of Galen, a Greek physician in the A.D. 100s, dominated medicine in the Late Middle Ages. Relying on animal, rather than human, dissection to picture human anatomy, Galen was wrong in many instances.

A revolution in medicine began in the sixteenth century. During this time Andreas Vesalius and William Harvey added to the understanding of human anatomy. By dissecting human bodies at the University of Padua, Vesalius accurately described the individual organs and general structure of the human body. William Harvey showed that the heart—not the liver, as Galen had thought—was the beginning point for the circulation of blood. He also proved that the same blood flows through the veins and arteries and makes a complete circuit through the body.

The French scientist Blaise Pascal experimented with how liquids behaved under pressure. This led him to the principle known as Pascal's Law. He applied this principle to the development of tools such as the syringe and the hydraulic press.

Robert Boyle was one of the first scientists to conduct controlled experiments in chemistry. His work on the properties of gases led to Boyle's Law, which states that the volume of a gas varies with the pressure exerted on it. In the eighteenth century, Antoine Lavoisier invented a system for naming chemical elements still used today. Many people consider him the founder of modern chemistry.

Women's Contributions

Although scholarship was considered the exclusive domain of men, there were women who contributed to the Scientific Revolution. Margaret Cavendish, a philosopher, and Maria Winkelmann, an astronomer, helped advance science through their work.

Margaret Cavendish came from an English aristocratic family and was tutored on subjects considered suitable for girls of proper upbringing—music, dancing, reading, and needlework. She was not formally educated in the sciences. However, Cavendish wrote a number of works on scientific matters, including *Observations Upon Experimental Philosophy*. In this work, Cavendish was especially critical of the growing belief that humans, through science, were the masters of nature:

PRIMARY SOURCE

❝We have no power at all over natural causes and effects...for man is but a small part, his powers are but particular actions of Nature, and he cannot have a supreme and absolute power.❞

—from *Observations Upon Experimental Philosophy*

Cavendish published under her own name at a time many female writers had to publish anonymously. Her contribution to philosophy is widely recognized today; however, many intellectuals of the time did not take her work seriously.

In Germany, many of the women who were involved in science were astronomers. These women had received the opportunity to become astronomers from working in family observatories where their fathers or husbands trained them. Between 1650 and 1710, women made up 14 percent of all German astronomers.

The most famous female astronomer in Germany was Maria Winkelmann. She received training in astronomy from a self-taught astronomer. When she married Gottfried Kirch, Prussia's foremost astronomer, she became his assistant and began to practice astronomy.

Connections to
TODAY

Women in Science

The important position of women in the sciences today can be traced back to the Enlightenment's ideas about human equality and natural rights. The careers of Enlightenment-era women like Margaret Cavendish and the astronomer Caroline Herschell (1750–1848), who was a pioneer in the study of nebulae and star clusters, gained acceptance for the female scientists who would follow them. For example, half of the engineers operating the Large Hadron Collider, a powerful particle accelerator, are women.

Winkelmann made some original contributions to astronomy, including the discovery of a comet. When her husband died, Winkelmann applied for a position as assistant astronomer at the Berlin Academy. She was highly qualified, but as a woman—with no university degree—she was denied the post. Members of the Berlin Academy feared that they would set a bad example by hiring a woman.

✅ **READING PROGRESS CHECK**

Speculating Why might changes in the way people saw the universe change the questions they asked about the natural world?

Philosophy and Reason

GUIDING QUESTION *How did the Scientific Revolution change people's worldview?*

New conceptions of the universe brought about by the Scientific Revolution strongly influenced the Western view of humankind.

Descartes and Rationalism

Nowhere is this more evident than in the work of the seventeenth-century French philosopher René Descartes (day • KAHRT), who brought a philosophical perspective to the natural sciences. He began by considering the doubt and uncertainty that seemed to be everywhere in the confusion of the seventeenth century. He ended with a philosophy that largely dominated Western thought until the twentieth century.

The starting point for Descartes's new system was doubt. In his most famous work, *Discourse on Method,* written in 1637, Descartes decided to set aside all that he had learned and to begin again. One fact seemed to him to be beyond doubt—his own existence.

Descartes emphasized the importance of his own mind, accepting only those things that his reason said were true. From his first principle—"I think, therefore I am"—Descartes used his reason to arrive at a second principle. He argued that because "the mind cannot be doubted but the body and material world can, the two must be radically different."

From this idea came the principle of the separation of mind and matter (and of mind and body). Descartes's idea that mind and matter were completely separate allowed scientists to view matter as dead or inert. That is, matter was something that was totally detached from the mind and that could be investigated independently by reason. Descartes has rightly been called the father of modern **rationalism**. This system of thought is based on the belief that reason is the chief source of knowledge.

Bacon and the Scientific Method

During the Scientific Revolution, people became concerned about how they could best understand the physical world. The result was the creation of the **scientific method**—a systematic procedure for collecting and analyzing evidence. The scientific method was crucial to the evolution of science in the modern world.

The person who developed the scientific method was not a scientist, but an English philosopher with few scientific credentials. Francis Bacon believed that scientists should not rely on the ideas of ancient authorities. Instead, they should learn about nature by using **inductive reasoning**— proceeding from the particular to the general. Knowledge of the natural world should be achieved through observation and experimentation.

Analyzing CCSS
PRIMARY SOURCES

Discourse on Method

❝But I immediately became aware that while I was thus disposed to think that all was false, it was absolutely necessary that I who thus thought should be something; and noting that this truth *I think, therefore I am,* was so steadfast and so assured . . . I concluded that I might without scruple accept it as being the first principle of the philosophy I was seeking.❞

—René Descartes, from *Discourse on Method*

DBQ **ANALYZING INFORMATION** What is the first principle of Descartes's philosophy?

Before beginning this reasoning, scientists try to free their minds of opinions that might distort the truth. Then they start with detailed facts and proceed toward general principles. From observing natural events, scientists propose hypotheses, or possible explanations, for the events. Then systematic observations and carefully organized experiments to test the hypotheses would lead to correct general principles.

Bacon was clear about what he believed his scientific method could accomplish. He stated that "the true and lawful goal of the sciences is none other than this: that human life be endowed with new discoveries and powers." He was much more concerned with practical matters than pure science. Bacon wanted science to benefit industry, agriculture, and trade. He said, "I am laboring to lay the foundation, not of any sect or doctrine, but of human utility and power."

Bacon believed this "human power" could be used to "conquer nature in action." The control and domination of nature became an important concern of science and the technology that accompanied it.

✔ READING PROGRESS CHECK

Describing What did Bacon believe was the purpose of the scientific method?

rationalism a system of thought expounded by René Descartes based on the belief that reason is the chief source of knowledge

scientific method a systematic procedure for collecting and analyzing evidence that was crucial to the evolution of science in the modern world

inductive reasoning the doctrine that scientists should proceed from the particular to the general by making systematic observations and carefully organized experiments to test hypotheses or theories, a process that will lead to correct general principles

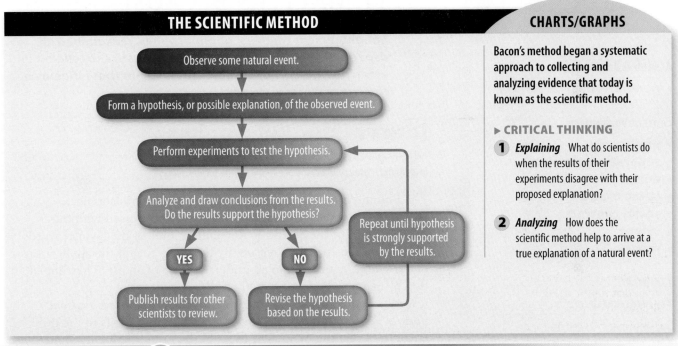

THE SCIENTIFIC METHOD

- Observe some natural event.
- Form a hypothesis, or possible explanation, of the observed event.
- Perform experiments to test the hypothesis.
- Analyze and draw conclusions from the results. Do the results support the hypothesis?
  - **YES** → Publish results for other scientists to review.
  - **NO** → Revise the hypothesis based on the results.
- Repeat until hypothesis is strongly supported by the results.

CHARTS/GRAPHS

Bacon's method began a systematic approach to collecting and analyzing evidence that today is known as the scientific method.

▶ **CRITICAL THINKING**

1 ***Explaining*** What do scientists do when the results of their experiments disagree with their proposed explanation?

2 ***Analyzing*** How does the scientific method help to arrive at a true explanation of a natural event?

LESSON 1 REVIEW

Reviewing Vocabulary

1. ***Making Connections*** Write a paragraph explaining how the scientific method exemplified the new emphasis on reason.

Using Your Notes

2. ***Summarizing*** Use your graphic organizer on Copernicus, Kepler, Galileo, and Newton to write a paragraph summarizing how each contributed to a new concept of the universe.

Answering the Guiding Questions

3. ***Identifying Central Issues*** What developments were the foundation of the Scientific Revolution?

4. ***Identifying Cause and Effect*** What role did scientific breakthroughs play during the Scientific Revolution?

5. ***Identifying*** What obstacles did participants in the Scientific Revolution face?

6. ***Drawing Conclusions*** How did the Scientific Revolution change people's worldview?

Writing Activity

7. **INFORMATIVE/EXPLANATORY** Write a paragraph analyzing the passage from Descartes's *Discourse on Method* from this lesson. Explain how his rationalism relates to the inductive reasoning used in the scientific method.

networks

There's More Online!

☑ **BIOGRAPHY** Adam Smith

☑ **BIOGRAPHY** Montesquieu

☑ **BIOGRAPHY** Voltaire

☑ **CHART/GRAPH** The Philosophes

☑ **IMAGE** The 18th-Century Salon

☑ **INTERACTIVE SELF-CHECK QUIZ**

☑ **PRIMARY SOURCE** The Social Contract

☑ **PRIMARY SOURCE** Vindication of the Rights of Woman

☑ **SLIDE SHOW** Enlightenment Arts

☑ **VIDEO** The Ideas of the Enlightenment

Reading HELPDESK (CCSS)

Academic Vocabulary

• generation   • arbitrary

Content Vocabulary

• philosophe
• separation of powers
• deism
• laissez-faire
• social contract
• salons
• rococo

TAKING NOTES:

Key Ideas and Details

Summarizing As you read, use a diagram like the one below to list some of the concepts introduced by intellectuals during the Enlightenment.

Major Ideas of the Enlightenment

LESSON 2
The Ideas of the Enlightenment

ESSENTIAL QUESTIONS • *Why do new ideas often spark change?* • *How do new ways of thinking affect the way people respond to their surroundings?*

IT MATTERS BECAUSE
Applying the scientific method to their physical world, Enlightenment thinkers, or philosophes, reexamined all aspects of life—from government and justice to religion and women's rights. They created a movement that influenced the entire Western world.

Ideas of the Philosophes

GUIDING QUESTIONS *What role did philosophes play in the Enlightenment? How did the belief in logic and reason promote the beginnings of the social sciences?*

The Enlightenment was an eighteenth-century philosophical movement of intellectuals who were greatly impressed with the achievements of the Scientific Revolution. One of the favorite words of these intellectuals was *reason*. By this, they meant the application of the scientific method to an understanding of all life. They hoped that by using the scientific method, they could make progress toward a better society than the one they had inherited. *Reason, natural law, hope, progress*—these were common words to the thinkers of the Enlightenment. The ideas of the Enlightenment would become a force for reform and eventually revolution.

The intellectuals of the Enlightenment were especially influenced by the ideas of two seventeenth-century Englishmen—John Locke and Isaac Newton. In his *Essay Concerning Human Understanding*, Locke argued that every person was born with a tabula rasa, or blank mind. Locke's ideas suggested that people were molded by the experiences that came through their senses from the surrounding world. Enlightenment thinkers began to believe that if environments were changed and people were exposed to the right influences, then they could be changed to create a new, and better, society.

The ideas of Isaac Newton also influenced eighteenth-century intellectuals. Newton believed that the physical world and everything in it was like a giant "world machine," operating according to natural laws that could be uncovered through systematic investigation.

The Enlightenment thinkers reasoned that if Newton was able to discover the natural laws that governed the physical world, then by applying his scientific methods, they would be able to discover the natural laws that governed human society. If all institutions would then follow these natural laws, the result would be an ideal society.

The Role of Philosophy

The intellectuals of the Enlightenment were known by the French word **philosophe** (FEE • luh • ZAWF), meaning "philosopher." Not all philosophers were French, however, and few were philosophers in the strict sense of the term. They were writers, professors, journalists, economists, and above all, social reformers. They came chiefly from the nobility and the middle class.

Most leaders of the Enlightenment were French, although the English had provided the philosophical inspiration for the movement. It was the French philosophes who affected intellectuals elsewhere and created a movement that influenced the entire Western world.

To the philosophes, the role of philosophy was to change the world. The use of reason and a spirit of rational criticism were to be applied to everything, including religion and politics. In the first half of the eighteenth century, three individuals dominated the intellectual landscape—Montesquieu (MAHN • tuhs • KYOO), Voltaire, and Diderot (dee • DROH).

Montesquieu

Charles-Louis de Secondat, the baron de Montesquieu, was a French noble. His famous work *The Spirit of the Laws* (1748) was a study of governments. In it, Montesquieu tried to find the natural laws that govern the social and political relationships of human beings.

Montesquieu stated that England's government had three branches: the executive (the monarch), the legislative (Parliament), and the judicial (the courts of law). The government functioned through a **separation of powers**. In this separation, the executive, legislative, and judicial powers of the government limit and control each other in a system of checks and balances. By preventing any one person or group from gaining too much power, this system provides the greatest freedom and security for the state.

The system of checks and balances through separation of powers was Montesquieu's most lasting contribution to political thought. Translation of his work into English made it available to American philosophes, who worked his principles into the United States Constitution.

Voltaire

The greatest figure of the Enlightenment was François-Marie Arouet, known simply as Voltaire. A Parisian, Voltaire came from a prosperous middle-class family. His numerous writings during the eighteenth century brought him both fame and wealth.

Voltaire was well known for his criticism of Christianity. He often challenged the actions of the Church, one of the most powerful institutions of the time. He had a strong belief in religious toleration, fighting against religious intolerance in France. Voltaire championed **deism**, an eighteenth-century religious philosophy based on reason and natural law. Deism built on the idea of the Newtonian world machine. In the Deists' view, a mechanic (God) had created the universe. To Voltaire and most other philosophes, the universe was like a clock. God, the clockmaker, had created it, set it in motion, and allowed it to run without his interference and according to its own natural laws.

philosophe French for "philosopher"; applied to all intellectuals during the Enlightenment

separation of powers a form of government in which the executive, legislative, and judicial branches limit and control each other through a system of checks and balances

deism an eighteenth-century religious philosophy based on reason and natural law

▼ Voltaire helped spread Enlightenment ideas through his writings.

▲ The press room of a print shop, from Diderot's *Encyclopedia*, 1751

▶ **CRITICAL THINKING**
Drawing Conclusions How did both printing and the *Encyclopedia* contribute to the promotion of Enlightenment ideas?

Diderot

Denis Diderot went to the University of Paris. His father hoped Denis would pursue a career in law or the Church. He did neither. Instead, he became a writer, covering many subjects. Diderot's most famous contribution to the Enlightenment was the *Encyclopedia, or Classified Dictionary of the Sciences, Arts, and Trades*, a 28-volume collection of knowledge that he edited. Published between 1751 and 1772, the purpose of the *Encyclopedia*, according to Diderot, was to "change the general way of thinking."

The *Encyclopedia* became a weapon against the old French society. Many of its articles attacked religious superstition and supported religious toleration. Others called for social, legal, and political reforms. Sold to doctors, clergymen, teachers, and lawyers, the *Encyclopedia* spread Enlightenment ideas.

✓ **READING PROGRESS CHECK**

Identifying Central Issues What are two ways in which philosophes sought to change the world?

New Social Sciences

GUIDING QUESTION *How did the belief in logic and reason promote the beginnings of the social sciences?*

The philosophes, as we have seen, believed that Newton's methods could be used to discover the natural laws underlying all areas of human life. This led to what we would call the social sciences—areas such as economics and political science.

The Physiocrats and Scottish philosopher Adam Smith have been viewed as the founders of the modern social science of economics. The Physiocrats, a French group, were interested in identifying the natural economic laws that governed human society. They maintained that if individuals were free to pursue their own economic self-interest, all society would benefit. The state, then, should not interrupt the free play of natural economic forces by imposing regulations on the economy. Instead, the state should leave the economy alone. This doctrine became known by its French name, **laissez-faire** (LEH • SAY • FEHR), meaning "to let (people) do (what they want)."

laissez-faire the concept that the state should not impose government regulations but should leave the economy alone

The best statement of laissez-faire was made in 1776 by Adam Smith in his famous work, *The Wealth of Nations*. Like the Physiocrats, Smith believed that the state should not interfere in economic matters. Indeed, Smith gave to government only three basic roles. First, it should protect society from invasion (the function of the army). Second, the government should defend citizens from injustice (the function of the police). And finally, it should keep up certain public works that private individuals alone could not afford—roads and canals, for example—but which are necessary for social interaction and trade.

✓ **READING PROGRESS CHECK**

Summarizing What roles did Adam Smith believe the government should fulfill in society?

The Spread of Ideas

GUIDING QUESTIONS *How did Enlightenment ideas influence society and culture?*

By the late 1760s, a new **generation** of philosophes had come to maturity. Ideas about liberty and the condition of women were spread through an increasingly literate society.

generation a group of individuals born and living at the same time

The Social Contract

The most famous philosophe of the later Enlightenment was Jean-Jacques Rousseau (ru • SOH). In his *Discourse on the Origins of the Inequality of Mankind*, Rousseau argued that people had adopted laws and government in order to preserve their private property. In the process, they had become enslaved by government and needed to regain their freedom.

In his major work *The Social Contract*, published in 1762, Rousseau presented his concept of the **social contract**. Through a social contract, an entire society agrees to be governed by its general will. Individuals who wish instead to follow their own self-interests must be forced to abide by the general will. "This means nothing less than that [they] will be forced to be free," said Rousseau. Thus, liberty is achieved by being forced to follow what is best for "the general will" because the general will represents what is best for the entire community.

Unlike many Enlightenment thinkers, Rousseau believed that emotions, as well as reason, were important to human development. He sought a balance between heart and mind, between emotions and reason.

social contract the concept that an entire society agrees to be governed by its general will and all individuals should be forced to abide by it since it represents what is best for the entire community

Women's Rights

For centuries, male intellectuals had argued that the nature of women made them inferior to men and made male domination of women necessary. By the eighteenth century, however, female thinkers began to express their ideas about improving the condition of women. Mary Wollstonecraft, an English writer, advanced the strongest statement for the rights of women. Many see her as the founder of the modern European and American movements for women's rights.

In *A Vindication of the Rights of Women*, Wollstonecraft identified two problems with the views of many Enlightenment thinkers. She noted that the same people who argued that women must obey men also said that government based on the **arbitrary** power of monarchs over their subjects was wrong. Wollstonecraft pointed out that the power of men over women was equally wrong.

Wollstonecraft further argued that the Enlightenment was based on an ideal of reason in all human beings. Therefore, because women have reason, they are entitled to the same rights as men. Women, Wollstonecraft declared, should have equal rights in education, as well as in economic and political life.

▲ Mary Wollstonecraft was an advocate of women's rights.

The Growth of Reading

Of great importance to the Enlightenment was the spread of its ideas to the literate elite of European society. The growth of both publishing and the reading public during the eighteenth century was noticeable. Books had previously been aimed at small groups of the educated elite. Now many books were directed at the new reading public of the middle classes, which included women and urban artisans. Especially appealing to these readers were the works of novelists who began to use realistic social themes. The English writer Henry Fielding wrote novels about people without morals

arbitrary at one's discretion; random

who survive by their wits. Fielding's best-known work is *The History of Tom Jones, a Foundling*, which describe the adventures of a young scoundrel.

An important aspect of the growth of publishing and reading in the eighteenth century was the development of magazines and newspapers for the general public. The first daily newspaper was printed in London in 1702. Newspapers were relatively cheap and were even provided free in many coffeehouses. Coffeehouses also served as gathering places for the exchange of ideas.

Enlightenment ideas were also spread through the salon. **Salons** were the elegant drawing rooms of the wealthy upper class's great urban houses. Invited guests gathered in these salons and took part in conversations that were often centered on the new ideas of the philosophes. The salons brought writers and artists together with aristocrats, government officials, and wealthy middle-class people. The women who hosted the salons were in a position to sway political opinion and helped spread the ideas of the Enlightenment.

▲ An eighteenth-century coffeehouse in London

► CRITICAL THINKING
Constructing Arguments Do the coffeehouses of today serve the same purpose as early ones? Why or why not?

salons the elegant urban drawing rooms where, in the eighteenth century, writers, artists, aristocrats, government officials, and wealthy middle-class people gathered to discuss the ideas of the philosophes

Religion in the Enlightenment

Although many philosophes attacked the Christian churches, most Europeans in the eighteenth century were still Christians. People also sought a deeper personal devotion to God. The desire of ordinary Protestants for greater depths of religious experience led to new religious movements.

In England, the most famous new religious and evangelical movement—Methodism—was the work of John Wesley, an Anglican minister. Wesley had a mystical experience in which "the gift of God's grace" assured him of salvation. This experience led him to become a missionary to the English people to bring them the "glad tidings" of salvation. Wesley often preached two or three times a day.

His sermons often caused people to have conversion experiences. Many converts then joined Methodist societies to do good works. One notable reform they influenced was the abolition of the slave trade in the early 1800s. After Wesley's death, Methodism became a separate Protestant group.

✓ READING PROGRESS CHECK

Evaluating How did Mary Wollstonecraft use the Enlightenment ideal of reason to advocate rights for women?

Enlightenment and the Arts

GUIDING QUESTION *How did Enlightenment ideas influence society and culture?*

The ideas of the Enlightenment also had an impact on the world of culture. Eighteenth-century Europe witnessed both traditional practices and important changes in art, music, and literature.

Architecture and Art

The palace of Louis XIV at Versailles, in France, had made an enormous impact on Europe as other European rulers also built grand residences. These palaces were modeled more on the Italian baroque style of the 1500s and 1600s than on the late seventeenth-century French classical style of Versailles.

One of the greatest architects of the eighteenth century was Balthasar Neumann. Neumann's two masterpieces are the Church of the Fourteen Saints in southern Germany and the Residence, the palace of the prince bishop of Würzburg. In these buildings, secular and spiritual become one, as lavish and fanciful ornament, light, bright colors, and elaborate detail greet the visitor. The baroque and neoclassical styles that had dominated seventeenth-century art continued into the eighteenth century. By the 1730s, however, a new artistic style, known as **rococo**, had spread all over Europe. Unlike the baroque style, which stressed grandeur and power, rococo emphasized grace, charm, and gentle action. Rococo made use of delicate designs colored in gold with graceful curves. The rococo style was highly secular. Its lightness and charm spoke of the pursuit of pleasure, happiness, and love.

Rococo's appeal is evident in the work of Antoine Watteau. In his paintings, gentlemen and ladies in elegant dress reveal a world of upper-class pleasure and joy. Underneath that exterior, however, is an element of sadness. The artist suggests such sadness in his paintings by depicting the fragility and passing nature of pleasure, love, and life. One of his masterpieces, the *Embarkation for Cythera*, shows French rococo at its peak.

▲ *The Swing,* by Jean-Honore Fragonard, 1767

Music

Eighteenth-century Europe produced some of the world's most enduring music. Two geniuses of the second half of the eighteenth century, Franz Joseph Haydn and Wolfgang Amadeus Mozart, were innovators who wrote classical music rather than the baroque music of Bach and Handel. Haydn spent most of his adult life as musical director for wealthy Hungarian princes. Visits to England introduced him to a world in which musicians wrote for public concerts rather than princely patrons. This "liberty," as he called it, led him to write two great works, *The Creation* and *The Seasons*.

Mozart was truly a child prodigy. He gave his first harpsichord concert at age six and wrote his first opera at twelve. His failure to get a regular patron to support him financially made his life miserable. Nevertheless, he wrote music passionately. His works *The Marriage of Figaro*, *The Magic Flute*, and *Don Giovanni* are three of the world's greatest operas. Haydn remarked to Mozart's father, "Your son is the greatest composer known to me . . ."

rococo an artistic style that replaced baroque in the 1730s; it was highly secular, emphasizing grace, charm, and gentle action

☑ **READING PROGRESS CHECK**

Making Inferences How do Haydn's interests as a composer reflect the influence of Enlightenment ideas?

LESSON 2 REVIEW

Reviewing Vocabulary

1. ***Explaining*** Write a paragraph explaining what Montesquieu meant by the phrase *separation of powers* and where he saw this principle applied.

Using Your Notes

2. ***Summarizing*** As you read, use your graphic organizer to list some of the main ideas introduced during the Enlightenment.

Answering the Guiding Questions

3. ***Identifying*** How did Enlightenment thinkers use the ideas of the Scientific Revolution?

4. ***Questioning*** What role did the philosophes play in the Enlightenment?

5. ***Understanding Relationships*** How did the belief in logic and reason promote the beginnings of the social sciences?

6. ***Interpreting*** How did Enlightenment ideas influence society and culture?

Writing Activity

7. **NARRATIVE** Write a paragraph giving your personal opinion of the ideas of one of the intellectuals discussed in this lesson. Explain why you agree or disagree with that person's work. Be sure to give specific details of the chosen topic as part of your response.

Reading **HELP**DESK **CCSS**

Academic Vocabulary

- **rigid**
- **eventually**

Content Vocabulary

- **enlightened absolutism**
- **successors**

TAKING NOTES:

Key Ideas and Details

Describing Use a graphic organizer like the one below to list details that help show the political philosophies of Frederick II, Joseph II, and Catherine II.

Ruler	Details That Show Political Philosophy
Frederick II	
Joseph II	
Catherine II	

LESSON 3
Enlightened Absolutism and the Balance of Power

ESSENTIAL QUESTIONS

- *Why do new ideas often spark change?*
- *How do new ways of thinking affect the way people respond to their surroundings?*

IT MATTERS BECAUSE

Enlightenment ideas had an impact on the politics of eighteenth-century Europe. While they liked to talk about enlightened reforms, most rulers were more interested in the power and stability of their nations. Their desire for balancing power, however, could also lead to war. The Seven Years' War became global as war broke out in Europe, India, and North America.

Enlightenment and Absolutism

GUIDING QUESTION *How were European rulers guided by Enlightenment thought?*

Enlightenment thought influenced European politics in the eighteenth century. The philosophes believed in natural rights for all people. These rights included equality before the law; freedom of religious worship; freedom of speech; freedom of the press; and the rights to assemble, hold property, and pursue happiness. To establish and preserve these natural rights, most philosophes believed that people needed to be governed by enlightened rulers. Enlightened rulers must allow natural rights and nurture the arts, sciences, and education. Above all, they must obey and enforce the laws fairly for all subjects. Only strong monarchs could bring about the enlightened reforms society needed.

Many historians once assumed that a new type of monarchy, **enlightened absolutism**, emerged in the later eighteenth century. In this system, rulers tried to govern by Enlightenment principles while maintaining their royal powers. Did Europe's rulers actually follow the advice of the philosophes and become enlightened? To answer this question, we examine three states—Prussia, Austria, and Russia.

Two able Prussian kings, Frederick William I and Frederick II, made Prussia a major European power in the eighteenth century. Frederick William I maintained a highly efficient bureaucracy of civil service workers.

They observed the supreme values of obedience, honor, and, above all, service to the king. As Frederick William asserted: "One must serve the king with life and limb, … and surrender everything except salvation. The latter is reserved for God. But everything else must be mine."

Frederick William's other major concern was the army. By the end of his reign in 1740, he had doubled the army's size. Although Prussia was a small state, it had the fourth-largest army after France, Russia, and Austria. The Prussian army, because of its size and its good reputation, was the most important institution in the state.

Members of the nobility, who owned large landed estates with many serfs, were the officers in the Prussian army. These officers, too, had a strong sense of service to the king or state. As Prussian nobles, they believed in duty, obedience, and sacrifice.

Frederick II, or Frederick the Great, who ruled from 1740 to 1786, was one of the best educated monarchs of the time. He was well versed in Enlightenment ideas and was also a dedicated ruler. He, too, enlarged the Prussian army by actively recruiting the nobility into civil service. Frederick kept a strict watch over the bureaucracy.

For a time, Frederick seemed quite willing to make enlightened reforms. He abolished the use of torture except in treason and murder cases. He also granted limited freedom of speech and press, as well as greater religious toleration. However, Frederick kept Prussia's serfdom and **rigid** social structure intact and avoided any additional reforms.

The Austrian Empire had become one of the great European states by the start of the eighteenth century. It was hard to rule, however, because it was a sprawling empire composed of many nationalities, languages, religions, and cultures. Empress Maria Theresa, who inherited the throne in 1740, worked to centralize and strengthen the state. While not open to the philosophes' calls for reform, she did work to improve the condition of the serfs.

Her son, Joseph II, believed in the need to sweep away anything standing in the path of reason: "I have made Philosophy the lawmaker of my empire." Joseph abolished serfdom and eliminated the death penalty. He established the principle of equality of all before the law and enacted religious reforms, including religious toleration.

Joseph's reform program largely failed, however. He alienated the nobles by freeing the serfs. He alienated the Catholic Church with his religious reforms. Even the serfs were unhappy because they could not understand the drastic changes. Joseph realized his failure when he wrote his own epitaph for his gravestone: "Here lies Joseph II who was unfortunate in all his enterprises." His **successors** undid almost all of Joseph II's reforms.

In Russia, Peter the Great was followed by six weak successors who were often put in power and deposed by the palace guard. A group of nobles murdered the last of these six successors, Peter III. His German wife emerged as ruler of all the Russians.

Catherine II, or Catherine the Great, ruled Russia from 1762 to 1796. She was an intelligent woman who was familiar with the works of the philosophes and seemed to favor enlightened reforms. She considered the idea of a new law code that would recognize the principle of equality of all people in the eyes of the law.

In the end, however, Catherine did nothing because she knew that her success depended on the support of the Russian nobility. Her policy of favoring the landed nobility led to worse conditions for the Russian peasants

enlightened absolutism a system in which rulers tried to govern by Enlightenment principles while maintaining their full royal powers

rigid inflexible, unyielding

▲ Maria Theresa, empress of Austria, and some of her children

successor one that follows, especially one who takes over a throne, title, estate, or office

eventually in the end

and **eventually** to rebellion. Led by an illiterate Cossack (a Russian warrior), Yemelyan Pugachov, the rebellion spread across southern Russia but soon collapsed. Catherine took stronger measures against the peasants. Rural reform was halted, and serfdom was expanded into newer parts of the empire.

Catherine proved to be a worthy successor to Peter the Great in her policies of territorial expansion. Russia spread southward to the Black Sea by defeating the Turks under Catherine's rule. To the west, Russia gained about 50 percent of Poland's territory, with the remainder split between Prussia and Austria. The Polish state disappeared until after World War I.

Of the rulers under discussion, only Joseph II sought truly radical changes based on Enlightenment ideas. Both Frederick II and Catherine II liked to talk about enlightened reforms. They even attempted some, but their priority was maintaining the existing system.

In fact, all three of these enlightened absolutists—Frederick, Joseph, and Catherine—were guided primarily by their interest in the power and welfare of their state. When they did manage to strengthen their position as rulers, they did not undertake enlightened reforms to benefit their subjects. Rather, their power was used to collect more taxes and thus to create armies, to wage wars, and to gain even more power.

The philosophes condemned war as a foolish waste of life and resources. Despite their words, the rivalry among states that led to costly struggles remained unchanged in eighteenth-century Europe. Europe's states were chiefly guided by their rulers' self-interest.

The eighteenth-century monarchs were concerned with the balance of power. This concept meant that states should have equal power in order to prevent any one from dominating the others. Large armies created to defend a state's security, however, were often used to conquer new lands as well. As Frederick II of Prussia said, "The fundamental rule of governments is the principle of extending their territories." This rule led to two major wars in the eighteenth century.

☑ **READING PROGRESS CHECK**

Comparing Describe two similarities between the reigns of Frederick II of Prussia and Catherine the Great of Russia.

▲ Catherine II (Catherine the Great) was a strong Russian ruler.

The Seven Years' War

GUIDING QUESTION *How did changing alliances in Europe lead to the Seven Years' War and how was the war carried out on a global scale?*

The stage was set for the Seven Years' War when, in 1740, a major war broke out over the succession to the Austrian throne. When the Austrian emperor Charles VI died without a male heir, his daughter, Maria Theresa, succeeded him. King Frederick II of Prussia took advantage of the confusion surrounding the succession of a woman to the throne by invading Austrian Silesia, a piece of land that he hoped to add to Prussia. By this action, Frederick refused to recognize the legitimacy of the empress of Austria. France then entered the war against Austria, its traditional enemy. In turn, Maria Theresa allied with Great Britain.

The War of the Austrian Succession (1740–1748) was fought in three areas of the world. In Europe, Prussia seized Silesia while France occupied some Austrian territory. In Asia, France took Madras (today called Chennai) in India from the British. In North America, the British captured the French fortress of Louisbourg at the entrance of the St. Lawrence River.

By 1748, all parties were exhausted and agreed to the Treaty of Aix-la-Chapelle. The treaty guaranteed the return of all occupied territories but Silesia to their original owners. Prussia's refusal to return Silesia meant yet another war, for Maria Theresa refused to accept the loss. She rebuilt her army while working diplomatically to separate Prussia from its chief ally, France. In 1756 Maria Theresa achieved what was soon labeled a diplomatic revolution.

The War in Europe

French-Austrian rivalry had been a fact of European diplomacy since the late sixteenth century. However, two new rivalries now replaced the old one: the rivalry of Britain and France over colonial empires and the rivalry of Austria and Prussia over Silesia.

France abandoned Prussia and formed an alliance with Austria. Russia, which saw Prussia as a major threat to Russian goals in central Europe, joined the new alliance with France and Austria. In turn, Britain allied with Prussia. This diplomatic revolution of 1756 led to another worldwide war. The war had three major areas of conflict: Europe, India, and North America.

Europe witnessed the clash of the two major alliances: the British and Prussians against the Austrians, Russians, and French. The superb army and military skill of Frederick the Great of Prussia enabled him at first to defeat the Austrian, French, and Russian armies. Under attack from three different directions, however, his forces were gradually worn down.

Frederick faced disaster until Peter III, a new Russian czar who greatly admired Frederick, withdrew Russian troops from the conflict. This withdrawal created a stalemate and led to the desire for peace. The European war ended in 1763. All occupied territories were returned to their original owners, except Silesia. Austria officially recognized Prussia's permanent control of Silesia.

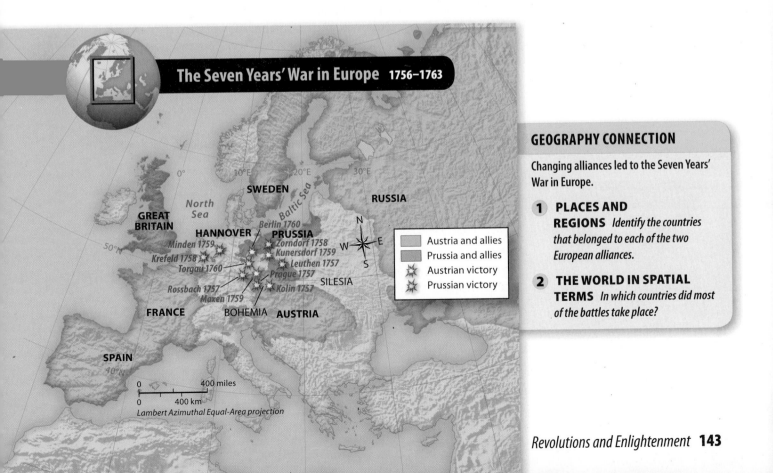

The Seven Years' War in Europe 1756–1763

Austria and allies
Prussia and allies
Austrian victory
Prussian victory

GEOGRAPHY CONNECTION

Changing alliances led to the Seven Years' War in Europe.

1. **PLACES AND REGIONS** *Identify the countries that belonged to each of the two European alliances.*

2. **THE WORLD IN SPATIAL TERMS** *In which countries did most of the battles take place?*

The War in India

The struggle between Britain and France that took place in the rest of the world had more decisive results. Known as the Great War for Empire, it was fought in India and North America. The French had returned Madras to Britain after the War of the Austrian Succession, but the struggle in India continued. The British ultimately won out, not because they had better forces but because they were more persistent. With the Treaty of Paris in 1763, the French withdrew and left India to the British.

The War in North America

The greatest conflicts of the Seven Years' War took place in North America. On the North American continent, the French and British colonies were set up differently. The French government administered French North America (Canada and Louisiana) as a vast trading area. It was valuable for its fur, leather, fish, and timber, but its colonies were thinly populated.

British North America consisted of thirteen prosperous colonies on the eastern coast of what is now the United States. Unlike the French colonies, the British colonies were more populated, containing more than one million people by 1750.

The British and French fought over two main areas in North America. One consisted of the waterways of the Gulf of St. Lawrence, which were protected by the fortress of Louisbourg and by forts that guarded French Quebec. The other area they fought over was the unsettled Ohio River valley. The French scored a number of victories at first. British fortunes were revived, however, by the efforts of William Pitt the Elder, Britain's prime minister. Pitt was convinced that the French colonial empire would have to be destroyed for Britain to create its own colonial empire.

A series of British victories soon followed. In 1759 British forces under General Wolfe defeated the French under General Montcalm on the Plains of Abraham, outside Quebec. Both generals died in the battle. The British went on to seize Montreal, the Great Lakes area, and the Ohio River valley. The French were forced to make peace. By the Treaty of Paris, the French transferred Canada and the lands east of the Mississippi to England. Spain, an ally of the French, transferred Spanish Florida to British control. In return, the French gave their Louisiana territory to the Spanish. By 1763, Great Britain had become the world's greatest colonial power.

▲ This painting by Benjamin West shows the death of the British General James Wolfe.

☑ **READING PROGRESS CHECK**

Explaining Explain the involvement of Great Britain and France in the Seven Years' War.

PHOTO: Phillips, Fine Art Auctioneers, New York, USA

LESSON 3 REVIEW

Reviewing Vocabulary

1. *Identifying* Write a paragraph defining the term *enlightened absolutism*. Discuss one example of an eighteenth-century monarch and explain how he or she fulfilled or failed to fulfill this ideal.

Using Your Notes

2. *Evaluating* Use your graphic organizer to write a paragraph evaluating the degree to which Frederick II, Joseph II, and Catherine II did or did not embrace Enlightenment ideas.

Answering the Guiding Questions

3. *Making Connections* How were European rulers guided by Enlightenment thought?

4. *Identifying Cause and Effect* How did changing alliances in Europe lead to the Seven Years' War and how was the war carried out on a global scale?

Writing Activity

5. NARRATIVE Narrate a series of events that help tell the story of both the War of the Austrian Succession and the Seven Years' War. Use transitional words and phrases to show a clear sequence.

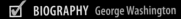

Reading **HELP**DESK (CCSS)

Academic Vocabulary

- **amendment**
- **guarantee**

Content Vocabulary

- **federal system**

Reading Strategy:
Key Ideas and Details

Summarizing As you read, use a chart like the one below to identify important elements of the government created by the American colonists.

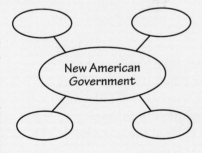

New American Government

LESSON 4
The American Revolution

PHOTO: PoodlesRock/Corbis; National Archives and Records Administration; David David Gallery / Super Stock; Super Stock.

ESSENTIAL QUESTIONS • *Why do new ideas often spark change?*
• *How do new ways of thinking affect the way people respond to their surroundings?*

IT MATTERS BECAUSE
The ideas of the Enlightenment clearly made an impact on the colonies in North America. In response to unfair taxation and other issues, the colonists revolted against British rule, formed their own army, and declared their independence. Many Europeans saw the American Revolution as the embodiment of the Enlightenment's political dreams.

Britain and the American Revolution

GUIDING QUESTION *What were the causes of and influences on the American Revolution?*

The United Kingdom of Great Britain came into existence in 1707, when the governments of England and Scotland were united. The term *British* came to refer to both the English and the Scots.

In 1688 the Glorious Revolution resulted in a Bill of Rights that affirmed Parliament's right to make laws. As a result, the monarch and Parliament shared power. The monarch chose ministers, who were responsible to the Crown. These ministers set policy and guided Parliament. Parliament's power to make laws, levy taxes, and pass the budget indirectly influenced the monarch's ministers.

In 1714 a new dynasty was established when the last Stuart ruler, Queen Anne, died without an heir. The crown was offered to her nearest relatives, Protestant rulers of the German state of Hannover. The first Hanoverian king, George I, did not speak English. Neither the first nor the second George knew the British system well, so their chief ministers were allowed to deal with Parliament.

In the meantime, growing trade and industry led to an ever-increasing middle class that favored the expansion of trade and of Britain's world empire. They found a spokesman in William Pitt the Elder, who became head of cabinet in 1757. He expanded the British Empire by acquiring Canada and India in the Seven Years' War.

In North America, then, Britain controlled Canada as well as the thirteen colonies on the eastern coast of what is now the United States. The British colonies were well populated, containing more than 1 million people by 1750. They were also prosperous.

▲ *The Declaration of Independence, 4 July, 1776,* by John Trumbull

▶ **CRITICAL THINKING**
Drawing Inferences What does this painting reveal about the process of the colonial break with Great Britain?

Analyzing PRIMARY SOURCES

Declaration of Independence

❝We hold these truths to be self-evident; that all men are created equal; that they are endowed by their Creator with certain inalienable rights; that among these are life, liberty and the pursuit of happiness; that to secure these rights, governments are instituted among men, deriving their just powers from the consent of the governed . . . ❞

—from the Declaration of Independence

DBQ ***PARAPHRASING***
Rewrite the excerpt from the Declaration of Independence in your own words.

In theory, the British Board of Trade, the Royal Council, and Parliament controlled the colonies. In actuality, the colonies had legislatures that often acted independently. Merchants in port cities such as Charleston, New York, and Boston did not want the British government to run their affairs.

The American Revolution Begins

After the Seven Years' War, British leaders wanted to get new colonial revenues from the colonies. These revenues would then be used to cover war costs. These would also pay for the expenses of maintaining an army to defend the colonies.

In 1765 Parliament imposed the Stamp Act on the colonies. The act required certain printed materials, such as legal documents and newspapers, to carry a stamp showing that a tax had been paid to Britain. Opposition was widespread and often violent. The act was repealed in 1766, ending the immediate crisis, but the cause of the dispute was not resolved.

Crisis followed crisis in the 1770s. To counteract British actions, the colonies organized the First Continental Congress, which met in Philadelphia in September 1774. Members urged colonists to take up arms and organize militias.

Fighting finally erupted between colonists and the British army in April 1775 in Lexington and Concord, Massachusetts. Meeting soon afterward, the Second Continental Congress set up an army, called the Continental Army. George Washington served as its commander in chief.

More than a year passed before the colonies declared independence from the British Empire. On July 4, 1776, the Second Continental Congress approved the Declaration of Independence written by Thomas Jefferson. With this stirring political document, the American Revolution had formally begun.

British Defeat

Support from foreign countries was important to the colonies' cause. These nations were eager to gain revenge for earlier defeats at the hands of the British. The French supplied arms and money to the rebels. French officers and soldiers also served in Washington's army. In February 1778, following a British defeat, the French granted diplomatic recognition to the new United States. When Spain and the Dutch Republic entered the war, the British faced war with the Europeans as well as the Americans.

When General Cornwallis was forced to surrender to the American and French forces under Washington at Yorktown in 1781, the British decided to end the war. In 1783 the Treaty of Paris recognized the independence of the American colonies. The treaty also granted the Americans control of the western territory from the Appalachians to the Mississippi River.

☑ **READING PROGRESS CHECK**

Explaining Why did some American colonists seek independence from Great Britain?

The Birth of a New Nation

GUIDING QUESTIONS *What were the effects of the American Revolution? Why did intellectuals believe the formation of the United States carried out Enlightenment thought?*

After overthrowing British rule, the former colonies feared the power of a strong central government. The states' first constitution, the Articles of Confederation (1781), created a weak central government that lacked the power to deal with the nation's problems. In 1787 delegates met in Philadelphia at the Constitutional Convention to revise the Articles of Confederation. The delegates decided to plan for an entirely new government.

The Constitution

The proposed Constitution created a **federal system** in which the national government and the state governments shared power. Based on Montesquieu's ideas, the national, or federal, government was separated into three branches: executive, legislative, and judicial. Each branch had power to check, or restrain, acts of the other branches.

A president served as the head of the executive branch, which is why it may be referred to as a presidential democracy. The legislative branch consisted of elected representatives in two houses—the Senate and the House of Representatives. The Supreme Court and other courts formed the judicial branch. After ratification by 9 of the 13 states, the Constitution took effect.

federal system a form of government in which power is shared between the national and state governments

The Bill of Rights

As promised during negotiations over ratification, the new Congress proposed 12 **amendments** to the Constitution. The states approved 10 of the amendments. Together, these amendments became known as the Bill of Rights. As we have seen, the Glorious Revolution of 1688 in England had also resulted in a Bill of Rights.

These 10 amendments **guaranteed** freedom of religion, speech, press, petition, and assembly. They gave Americans the right to bear arms and to be protected against unreasonable searches and arrests. They guaranteed trial by jury, due process of law, and the protection of property rights.

Many of the rights in the Bill of Rights were derived from the natural rights proposed by the eighteenth-century philosophes and John Locke. European intellectuals saw the American Revolution as the confirmation of the premises of the Enlightenment. A new age and a better world could be achieved.

amendment an alteration proposed or effected by parliamentary or constitutional procedure

guarantee to assure fulfillment of a condition

☑ **READING PROGRESS CHECK**

Analyzing What was the purpose of separating the federal government into three separate branches?

LESSON 4 REVIEW

Reviewing Vocabulary
1. *Explaining* Describe the federal system of government.

Using Your Notes
2. *Summarizing* Use your graphic organizer to write a paragraph identifying important elements of the government created by the American colonists.

Answering the Guiding Questions
3. *Identifying Cause and Effect* What were the causes of and influences on the American Revolution?

4. *Making Connections* Why did intellectuals believe the formation of the United States carried out Enlightenment thought?

5. *Drawing Conclusions* What were the effects of the American Revolution?

Writing Activity
6. **INFORMATIVE/EXPLANATORY** Write an essay discussing the influence of Enlightenment philosophy on the American Revolution, the Declaration of Independence, and the Constitution.

Directions: On a separate sheet of paper, answer the questions below. Make sure you read carefully and answer all parts of the questions.

Lesson Review

Lesson 1

1 **HYPOTHESIZING** Describe two inventions that helped spark the Scientific Revolution and their impact.

2 **DESCRIBING** In what model of the universe did philosophers of the Middle Ages believe? Give details.

Lesson 2

3 **IDENTIFYING CENTRAL ISSUES** What was the goal of the philosophes? Did their movement have an impact on our lives today?

4 **STATING** What did Adam Smith believe should be the three roles of government?

Lesson 3

5 **SPECIFYING** Why did countries create their particular alliances during the Seven Years' War?

6 **DIFFERENTIATING** Was Catherine the Great an enlightened ruler? Why or why not?

Lesson 4

7 **FINDING THE MAIN IDEA** How did the Constitution attempt to balance concerns over a strong central government and the weaknesses of the Articles of Confederation?

8 **NAMING** What countries helped the American colonists win their independence from Great Britain and why?

21st Century Skills

9 **IDENTIFYING CONTINUITY AND CHANGE** How were the discoveries of Copernicus, Kepler, Galileo, and Newton related to each other?

10 **COMPARE AND CONTRAST** What was unique about the U.S. Declaration of Independence? What did it have in common with documents and ideas from other countries?

Exploring the Essential Questions

11 **IDENTIFYING PERSPECTIVES** Work with a partner to create a word web showing how the Enlightenment changed ways of thinking. Start with a circle labeled "Enlightenment." Draw three circles beyond it labeled "politics," "religion," and "the arts." Add circles to these three describing changes in attitudes and behaviors. To the side, place a circle labeled "Scientific Revolution." Draw circles beyond it labeled "natural laws," "rational criticism," and "rights for all." Add lines connecting circles where the values of the Scientific Revolution overlap those of the Enlightenment. You may include artwork, maps, and primary sources in your web.

DBQ Analyzing Historical Documents

Use the document to answer the following questions.
John Locke grew up during the English Civil War. He disagreed strongly with the concept of absolute monarchy and wrote his treatises on government in response.

PRIMARY SOURCE

" . . . *But* Freedom of Men under Government, *is to have a standing Rule to live by, common to every one of that Society, and made by the Legislative Power erected in it; A Liberty to follow my own Will in all things where the Rule prescribes not; and not to be subject to the inconstant, uncertain, unknown, arbitrary Will of another Man . . .* "

—from *The Second Treatise of Government,* 1690

12 **ANALYZING** What does Locke believe true freedom is?

13 **THEORIZING** What is Locke's opinion of the kings making laws? Where did he acquire his distrust of rulers with absolute power?

Extended-Response Question

14 **INFORMATIVE/EXPLANATORY** Trace the belief in natural rights from its origins to 1776.

Need Extra Help?

If You've Missed Question	**1**	**2**	**3**	**4**	**5**	**6**	**7**	**8**	**9**	**10**	**11**	**12**	**13**	**14**
Go to page	128	129	135	136	142	141	147	146	129	137	129	148	148	134

The French Revolution and Napoleon

1789–1815

ESSENTIAL QUESTIONS • *What causes revolution?*
• *How does revolution change society?*

netw⦿rks

There's More Online! about the French Revolution and Napoleon.

The Story Matters...

The French Revolution was a major turning point in Western history. At its most essential, it was a struggle for representational government, equality of opportunity, and a response to the near collapse of the French economy. As a child of the revolution, Napoleon Bonaparte created a legal code for France that realized some of the dreams of the revolutionaries: economic freedom, legal equality, and religious toleration, at least in part.

◀ This detail from *Portrait of Napoleon Bonaparte in the Garb of the King of Italy,* by Andrea Appiani, shows Napoleon wearing a laurel wreath, a classical symbol of triumph.

PHOTO: Scala/White Images / Art Resource, NY

149

Place and Time: France 1785–1815

The political, economic, and social conflicts that led to the French Revolution changed the role of citizens and the structure of political systems in France. However, it was not the only conflict of the latter eighteenth century. Countries around the world engaged in conflict over territories, resources, or independence. This resulted in sweeping social and cultural change.

Step Into the Place

Read the quotes and look at the information presented on the map.

 Analyzing Historical Documents How do the concerns addressed in the quotes correspond to the styles of governments in Europe on the eve of the revolution?

PRIMARY SOURCE

" [A country] where certain areas are totally freed from burdens of which others bear the full weight, where the richest class contributes least, where privileges destroy all balance, where it is impossible to have either a constant rule or a common will, is necessarily a very imperfect kingdom, brimming with abuses, and one that is impossible to govern well. "

— Charles Alexandre de Calonne, France's finance minister, from a memorandum on reform to Louis XVI, 1786

PRIMARY SOURCE

" I conceive that there are two kinds of inequality among the human species; one, which I call natural or physical, because it is established by nature, and consists in a difference of age, health, bodily strength, and the qualities of the mind or of the soul: and another, which may be called moral or political inequality, because it depends on a kind of convention, and is established, or at least authorized by the consent of men. This latter consists of the different privileges, which some men enjoy to the prejudice of others; such as that of being more rich, more honoured, more powerful or even in a position to exact obedience. "

— Jean-Jacques Rousseau, from *A Dissertation on the Origin and Foundation of the Inequality of Mankind*, 1755

PHOTO: Stock Montage / Getty Images; Kean Collection / Getty Images

Step Into the Time

Integrating Information

Choose an event from the France portion of the time line and write a paragraph predicting the general social, political, or economic consequence that event might have on the world.

July 14, 1789 The Storming of the Bastille

August 26, 1789 The Declaration of the Rights of Man and the Citizen is approved

January 21, 1793 Louis XVI, King of France, is executed

November 1795 The Directory heads French government

September 1793 Reign of Terror begins

FRANCE

THE WORLD

1785 — 1790 — 1795

1789 George Washington inaugurated as first U.S. president

1792 English writer Mary Wollstonecraft writes *A Vindication of the Rights of Woman*

1794 American inventor Eli Whitney patents the cotton gin

1794 Persia's Qājār dynasty begins

1796 English physician Edward Jenner vaccinates first child against smallpox

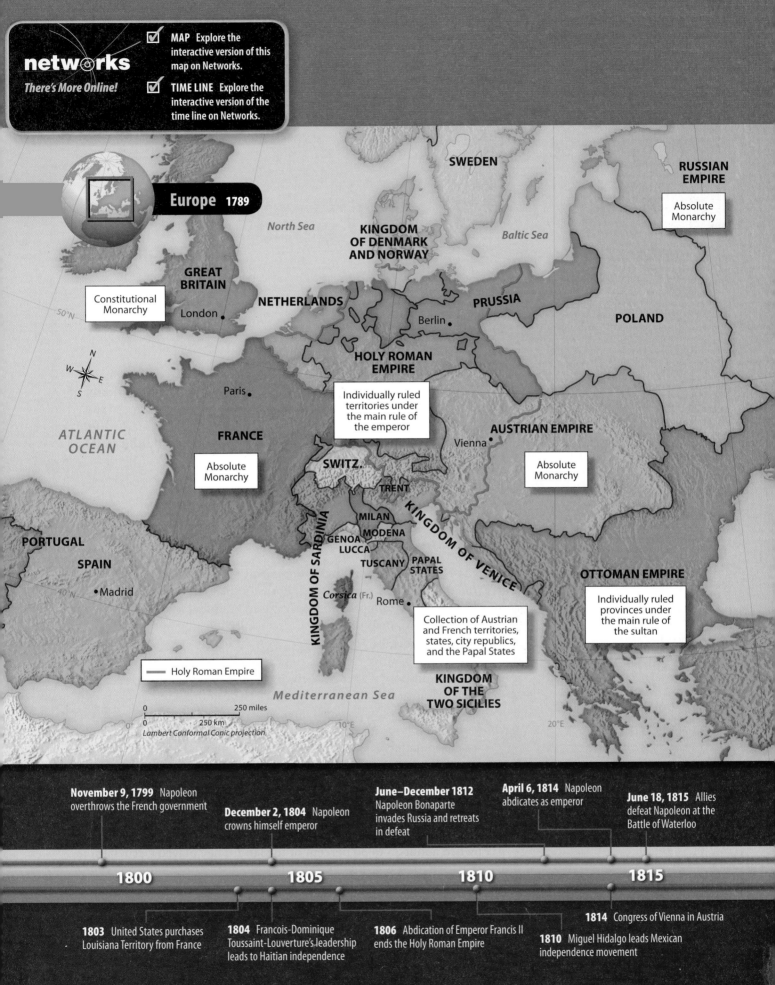

networks
There's More Online!

☑ MAP Explore the interactive version of this map on Networks.

☑ TIME LINE Explore the interactive version of the time line on Networks.

Europe 1789

North Sea

SWEDEN

RUSSIAN EMPIRE

Absolute Monarchy

Baltic Sea

KINGDOM OF DENMARK AND NORWAY

GREAT BRITAIN

Constitutional Monarchy

London

NETHERLANDS

PRUSSIA

Berlin

POLAND

HOLY ROMAN EMPIRE

50°N

Paris

Individually ruled territories under the main rule of the emperor

AUSTRIAN EMPIRE

Vienna

ATLANTIC OCEAN

FRANCE

Absolute Monarchy

SWITZ.

Absolute Monarchy

TRENT

MILAN

MODENA

GENOA
LUCCA

KINGDOM OF SARDINIA

KINGDOM OF VENICE

PORTUGAL

SPAIN

Madrid

40°N

TUSCANY

PAPAL STATES

OTTOMAN EMPIRE

Individually ruled provinces under the main rule of the sultan

Corsica (Fr.)

Rome

Collection of Austrian and French territories, states, city republics, and the Papal States

— Holy Roman Empire

Mediterranean Sea

KINGDOM OF THE TWO SICILIES

0 ——— 250 miles
0 ——— 250 km
Lambert Conformal Conic projection

10°E

20°E

November 9, 1799 Napoleon overthrows the French government

December 2, 1804 Napoleon crowns himself emperor

June–December 1812 Napoleon Bonaparte invades Russia and retreats in defeat

April 6, 1814 Napoleon abdicates as emperor

June 18, 1815 Allies defeat Napoleon at the Battle of Waterloo

1800　　　　**1805**　　　　**1810**　　　　**1815**

1803 United States purchases Louisiana Territory from France

1804 Francois-Dominique Toussaint-Louverture's leadership leads to Haitian independence

1806 Abdication of Emperor Francis II ends the Holy Roman Empire

1814 Congress of Vienna in Austria

1810 Miguel Hidalgo leads Mexican independence movement

networks

There's More Online!

☑ **BIOGRAPHY** Louis XVI

☑ **IMAGE** Bread Riot in Paris

☑ **IMAGE** Declaration of the Rights of Man and of the Citizen

☑ **IMAGE** Storming the Bastille

☑ **IMAGE** The Three Estates

☑ **INTERACTIVE SELF-CHECK QUIZ**

☑ **TIME LINE** The French Revolution

☑ **VIDEO** The French Revolution Begins

Reading HELPDESK (CCSS)

Academic Vocabulary

- consumer
- exclusion

Content Vocabulary

- estate
- taille
- bourgeoisie
- sans-culottes

TAKING NOTES:

Key Ideas and Details

Differentiating Use a graphic organizer like the one below to identify long-range and immediate causes of the French Revolution.

The French Revolution	
Long-Range	Immediate

LESSON 1
The French Revolution Begins

ESSENTIAL QUESTIONS • *What causes revolution?*
• *How does revolution change society?*

IT MATTERS BECAUSE

Two far-reaching events occurred in 1789: the beginning of a new United States of America and the beginning of the French Revolution. Compared with the American Revolution, the French Revolution was more complex and radical. It established a new political and social order.

Causes of the French Revolution

GUIDING QUESTIONS *How did the structure of social classes in France lead to discontent? How did the economic crises in France lead to the meeting of the Estates-General?*

The French Revolution has often been seen as a major turning point in European history. The institutions of the Old Regime were destroyed. A new order emerged, based on individual rights, representative institutions, and a concept of loyalty to the nation rather than the monarch.

The long-range causes of the French Revolution are to be found in the condition of French society. Before the Revolution, French society was based on inequality. Since the Middle Ages, France's population was divided into three orders, or **estates**.

The First Estate, or clergy, numbered about 130,000 (out of a total population of 27 million) and owned about 10 percent of the land. The clergy were radically divided. The higher clergy—cardinals, bishops, and heads of monasteries—were from noble families and shared their outlook and interests. The parish priests were often poor and from the class of commoners.

The Second Estate, or nobility, numbered about 350,000 and owned about 25 to 30 percent of the land. They played a crucial role in society in the 1700s. They held leading positions in the government, in the military, in the law courts, and in the Roman Catholic Church. Despite controlling most of the wealth, neither the clergy nor the nobles had to pay the **taille** (TAH • yuh), France's chief tax.

Unlike the First and Second Estates, the Third Estate was divided by vast differences in occupation, level of education, and wealth. Peasants made up 75 to 80 percent of the Third Estate and owned about 35 to 40 percent of the land. Middle class members of the Third Estate owned the rest. At least half the peasants had little or no land to live on.

Peasants owed certain duties to the nobles, which were a holdover from medieval times when serfdom was widespread. For example, a peasant had to pay a fee to grind his flour or press his grapes because the local lord controlled the flour mill and wine press. When the harvest time came, the peasant had to work a certain number of days harvesting the noble's crop. Peasants fiercely resented these duties.

Another part of the Third Estate consisted of urban craftspeople, shopkeepers, and workers. These people too were struggling to survive. In the 1700s, the price of **consumer** goods increased much faster than wages, which left these urban groups with decreased buying power.

The **bourgeoisie** (burzh • wah • ZEE), or middle class, was another part of the Third Estate. This group included about 8 percent of the population, or more than 2 million people. They owned about 20 to 25 percent of the land. The bourgeoisie included merchants, bankers, and industrialists, as well as professional people—lawyers, holders of public offices, doctors, and writers.

The middle class was unhappy with the privileges held by nobles. They did not want to abolish the nobility, however, but to better their own position. Some bourgeoisie had managed to become nobles by being appointed to public offices that conferred noble status. About 6,500 new nobles had been created by appointment during the 1700s.

The bourgeoisie also shared certain goals with the nobles. Both groups were increasingly upset with a monarchical system resting on privileges and on an old and rigid social order. Both were also drawn to the new political ideas of the Enlightenment.

Increased criticism of the old order of society had been part of the eighteenth-century Enlightenment. The philosophes did not advocate revolution. Their ideas, however, were widely spread among the

THE THREE ESTATES

POLITICAL CARTOON

This French political cartoon depicts the Three Estates. The circular object that pushes down on the middle figure represents the monarchy, who is burdening the people with taxes. The armored figure on the left side of the cartoon represents the nobility, the Second Estate. The robed figure on the right side of the cartoon represents the clergy, the First Estate. The crouched figure in the middle of the cartoon represents the commoners in France, the Third Estate.

▶ CRITICAL THINKING
Analyzing Information How are each of the three estates depicted? What is the commentary being made?

literate middle class and noble elites of France. When the revolution began, revolutionary leaders often quoted Enlightenment writers, especially Rousseau.

Social conditions and Enlightenment ideas, then, formed an underlying background to the French Revolution. The immediate cause of the revolution was the near collapse of the French budget. Although the economy had been expanding for 50 years, there were periodic crises. Bad harvests in 1787 and 1788 and a slowdown in manufacturing led to food shortages, rising prices for food, and unemployment.

On the eve of the revolution, the French economy was in crisis. Despite these problems, the French king and his ministers continued to spend enormous sums of money on wars and court luxuries. The queen, Marie Antoinette, was especially known for her extravagance and this too caused popular resentment. When the government decided to spend huge sums to help the American colonists against Britain, the budget went into total crisis.

With France on the verge of financial collapse, Louis XVI was forced to call a meeting of the Estates-General. This was the French parliament, and it had not met since 1614.

✔ **READING PROGRESS CHECK**

Identifying Cause and Effect How were economic problems a contributing cause of the French Revolution?

The National Assembly

GUIDING QUESTIONS *Why did the Third Estate declare itself to be the National Assembly? What were the French peasants reacting to in their rebellions of 1789?*

Louis XVI called a meeting of the Estates-General at Versailles on May 5, 1789. In the Estates-General, the First and Second Estates each had about 300 representatives. The Third Estate had almost 600 representatives. Most of the Third Estate wanted to set up a constitutional government that would make the clergy and nobility pay taxes, too.

From the start, there were arguments about voting. Traditionally, each estate had one vote—the First and Second Estates could outvote the Third Estate two to one. The Third Estate demanded instead that each deputy have one vote. Under this new system, with the help of a few nobles and clerics, the Third Estate would then have a majority vote. The king, however, stated that he favored the current system.

▶ **CRITICAL THINKING**
Drawing Conclusions David was a member of the Third Estate. How might his painting convey a biased view of the oath?

▼ *The Oath of the Tennis Court June 20th 1789,* by Jacques-Louis David

On June 17, 1789, the Third Estate boldly declared that it was the National Assembly and would draft a constitution. Three days later, on June 20, its deputies arrived at their meeting place, only to find the doors had been locked. They then moved to a nearby indoor tennis court and swore that they would continue meeting until they had a new constitution. The oath they swore is known as the Tennis Court Oath.

Louis XVI prepared to use force against the Third Estate. On July 14, 1789, about 900 Parisians gathered in the courtyard of the Bastille (ba • STEEL)—an old fortress used as a prison and armory. They stormed the Bastille, and after four hours of fighting, the prison warden surrendered. The rebels cut off the warden's head and demolished the Bastille brick by brick. Paris was abandoned to the rebels.

When King Louis XVI returned to his palace at Versailles after a day of hunting, the duc de la Rochefoucauld-Liancourt told him about the fall of the Bastille. Louis is said to have exclaimed, "Why, this is a revolt." "No, Sire," replied the duke. "It is a revolution."

Louis XVI was informed that he could no longer trust royal troops to shoot at the mob. The king's authority had collapsed in Paris. Meanwhile, all over France, revolts were breaking out. Popular hatred of the entire landholding system, with its fees and obligations, had finally spilled over into action.

Peasant rebellions became part of the vast panic known as the Great Fear. Rumors spread from village to village that foreign troops were on the way to put down the revolution. The peasants reacted by breaking into the houses of the lords to destroy the records of their obligations.

☑ **READING PROGRESS CHECK**

Making Connections What was the connection between the actions of the representatives of the Third Estate and the Estates-General and those of the peasants during the Great Fear?

Analyzing CCSS
PRIMARY SOURCES

Declaration of the Rights of Man and the Citizen

❝ **1.** Men are born and remain free and equal in rights; social distinctions can be established only for the common benefit.

7. No man can be accused, arrested, or detained except in cases determined by the law, and according to the forms which it has prescribed...

10. No one may be disturbed because of his opinions, even religious, provided that their public demonstration does not disturb the public order established by law. ❞

—from the Declaration of the Rights of Man and the Citizen, 1789

DBQ **IDENTIFYING** How does this document reflect Enlightenment thought?

End of the Old Regime

GUIDING QUESTION *How did the French Revolution enter a new phase after the storming of the Bastille?*

The National Assembly reacted to news of peasant rebellions and rumors of a possible foreign invasion. On August 4, 1789, the National Assembly voted to abolish all legal privileges of the nobles and clergy.

Declaration of the Rights of Man

On August 26, the National Assembly adopted the Declaration of the Rights of Man and the Citizen. Inspired by the English Bill of Rights of 1689 and by the American Declaration of Independence and Constitution, this charter of basic liberties began with "the natural and imprescriptible rights of man" to "liberty, property, security, and resistance to oppression."

Reflecting Enlightenment thought, the declaration proclaimed that all men were free and equal before the law, that appointment to public office should be based on talent, and that no group should be exempt from taxation. Freedom of speech and of the press were affirmed. The declaration raised an important issue. Should equal rights include women? Many deputies agreed, provided that, as one man said, "women do not [hope] to exercise political rights and functions." One writer, Olympe de Gouges, refused to accept this **exclusion** of women. Echoing the words of the official declaration, she wrote:

exclusion the act of excluding

"Believing that ignorance, omission, or scorn for the rights of woman are the only causes of public misfortunes and of the corruption of governments, the women have resolved to set forth in a solemn declaration the natural, inalienable, and sacred rights of woman in order that this declaration, constantly exposed before all the members of the society, will ceaselessly remind them of their rights and duties."

—from Declaration of the Rights of Woman and the Female Citizen, 1791

The King Concedes

In the meantime, Louis XVI remained quiet at Versailles. He refused to accept the National Assembly's decrees. On October 5, thousands of Parisian women armed with broomsticks, pitchforks, pistols, and other weapons marched to Versailles. Some of the women then met with the king. They told him that their children were starving because there was no bread. These women forced Louis to accept the new decrees.

The crowd insisted that the royal family return to Paris. On October 6, they did so. As a goodwill gesture, they carried wagonloads of flour from the palace storehouse. They were escorted by women who chanted: "We are bringing back the baker, the baker's wife, and the baker's boy." The king, the queen, and their son were now virtual prisoners in Paris.

Church Reforms

Under the old regime, the Catholic Church had been an important pillar of the old order. The revolutionaries felt they had to reform it, too. The new revolutionary government had another serious motivation, however: the need for money. By seizing and selling off Church lands, the National Assembly was able to increase the state's revenues.

Finally, the Church was formally brought under the control of the state. A new Civil Constitution of the Clergy said that bishops and priests were to be elected by the people, not appointed by the pope and the Church hierarchy. The state would also pay the salaries of the bishops and priests. Because of these changes, many Catholics became enemies of the revolution.

▶ **CRITICAL THINKING**

Identifying Central Ideas Why did the royal family attempt to leave France?

▼ The arrest of Louis XVI and his family at Varennes, July 1791

New Constitution and New Fears

The new Constitution of 1791 set up a limited monarchy. There was still a king, but a Legislative Assembly would make the laws. The Legislative Assembly was to consist of 745 representatives chosen in such a way that only the more affluent members of society would be elected.

By 1791, the old order had been destroyed, but the new government did not have universal support. Political radicals wanted more reform. The king detested the new order and his loss of absolute power. In June 1791, the royal family attempted to flee France in disguise. They almost succeeded but were recognized, captured, and brought back to Paris. In this unsettled situation, the new Legislative Assembly first met in October 1791. France's relations with the rest of Europe soon led to the king's downfall.

War With Austria

Over time, some European leaders began to fear that revolution would spread to their countries. The kings of Austria and Prussia even threatened to use force to restore Louis XVI to full power. Insulted by this threat and fearing attack, the Legislative

Assembly decided to strike first, declaring war on Austria in the spring of 1792. The French fared badly in the initial fighting. A frantic search for scapegoats began. One observer in France noted:

PRIMARY SOURCE

❝Everywhere you hear the cry that the king is betraying us, the generals are betraying us, that nobody is to be trusted; . . . that Paris will be taken in six weeks by the Austrians. . . . We are on a volcano ready to spout flames.❞

— quoted in *The Oxford History of the French Revolution*

Rise of the Paris Commune

In the spring of 1792, angry citizens demonstrated to protest food shortages and defeats in the war. In August, Paris radicals again decided the fate of the revolution. They declared themselves a commune—a popularly run city council—and attacked the royal palace and Legislative Assembly.

The French Revolution was entering a more radical and violent stage. Members of the new Paris Commune took the king captive. They forced the Legislative Assembly to suspend the monarchy and to call for a National Convention. This time they wanted a more radical change. All the representatives who would decide the nation's future would be elected through universal male suffrage, in which all adult males had the right to vote. This would broaden the group of voters to include men who did not meet the initial standards for citizenship established by the Assembly.

Many members of the Paris Commune proudly called themselves **sans-culottes**, meaning "without breeches." Wearing long trousers, not the knee-length breeches of the nobles, they identified themselves as ordinary patriots. Often, sans-culottes are depicted as poor workers, but many were merchants or artisans—the elite of their neighborhoods.

sans-culottes "without breeches"; members of the Paris Commune who considered themselves ordinary patriots (in other words, they wore long trousers instead of the fine knee-length breeches of the nobles)

 READING PROGRESS CHECK

Analyzing In what ways did the end of the old order move the revolution toward a more radical phase?

LESSON 1 REVIEW (CCSS)

Reviewing Vocabulary

1. *Describing* Write a paragraph describing all the types of people who made up the French bourgeoisie. Be sure to explain how people within this class might have different points of view about the French government.

Using Your Notes

2. *Comparing and Contrasting* Use your notes on the long-range and immediate causes of the French Revolution to compare and contrast one long-range and one immediate cause of the French Revolution.

Answering the Guiding Questions

3. *Evaluating* How did the structure of social classes in France lead to discontent?

4. *Identifying Central Issues* How did the economic crises in France lead to the meeting of the Estates-General?

5. *Drawing Conclusions* Why did the Third Estate declare itself to be the National Assembly?

6. *Making Connections* What were the French peasants reacting to in their rebellions of 1789?

7. *Theorizing* How did the French Revolution enter a new phase after the storming of the Bastille?

Writing Activity

8. INFORMATIVE/EXPLANATORY Write an essay exploring the influences on the Declaration of the Rights of Man and the Citizen. Be sure to include a discussion of influential documents from other countries. Also discuss influences specific to France, identifying cultural, political, and economic concerns the authors wanted to address.

networks

There's More Online!

☑ **BIOGRAPHY** Georges Danton

☑ **BIOGRAPHY** Jean Paul Marat

☑ **BIOGRAPHY** Marie Antoinette

☑ **CHART/GRAPH** Government Bodies of Revolutionary France

☑ **CHART/GRAPH** Political Groups of the French Revolution

☑ **INTERACTIVE SELF-CHECK QUIZ**

☑ **MAP** The Counterrevolution

☑ **TIME LINE** The Reign of Terror

☑ **VIDEO** Radical Revolution and Reaction

Reading **HELP**DESK `CCSS`

Academic Vocabulary

• **domestic** • **percent**

Content Vocabulary

• **electors** • **coup d'état**

TAKING NOTES:

Key Ideas and Details

Differentiating Use a graphic organizer like the one below to list actions taken by the National Convention.

Actions Taken by the National Convention
1.
2.
3.
4.

LESSON 2

Radical Revolution and Reaction

ESSENTIAL QUESTIONS • *What causes revolution?*
• *How does revolution change society?*

IT MATTERS BECAUSE

The French Revolution could be chaotic. The government repeatedly changed hands, foreign powers threatened to intervene, and economic conditions in France showed little improvement. This instability led to calls for new measures to be taken to secure the future of the revolution and to improve the living conditions of the people in France.

The Move to Radicalism

GUIDING QUESTION *Why did the French Revolution become more radical?*

In September 1792, the newly elected National Convention began meeting. The Convention had been called to draft a new constitution, but it also served as the ruling body of France. It was dominated by lawyers, professionals, and property owners. Two-thirds of its deputies were under the age of 45, but most had some political experience as a result of the revolution. Almost all distrusted the king. It was therefore no surprise that the National Convention's first major step on September 21 was to abolish the monarchy and to establish a republic.

After 1789, citizens had formed political clubs of varying social and political views. Many deputies belonged to these clubs. The Girondins (juh • RAHN • duhns) tended to represent areas outside Paris. They feared the radical mobs of Paris. The Mountain represented the interests of radicals in Paris, and many belonged to the Jacobin (JA • kuh • buhn) club. Increasingly they felt the king needed to be executed to ensure he was not a rallying point for opponents of the republic.

In early 1793, the Mountain convinced the Convention to pass a decree condemning Louis XVI to death. On January 21, the king was beheaded on the guillotine. Revolutionaries had adopted this machine because it killed quickly and, they thought, humanely. The king's execution created new enemies for the revolution, both at home and abroad. A new crisis was at hand.

The execution of King Louis XVI reinforced the trend toward a new radical phase. The local government in Paris—the Commune—had a number of working-class leaders who wanted radical change. Led by Georges Danton, it put constant pressure on the National Convention to adopt more radical measures. Moreover, the National Convention itself still did not rule all France. Peasants in western France, as well as many people in France's major cities, refused to accept the authority of the Convention.

A foreign crisis also loomed large. After Louis XVI was executed, a coalition of Austria, Prussia, Spain, Portugal, Britain, and the Dutch Republic took up arms against France. The French armies began to fall back. By late spring 1793, the coalition was poised to invade. It seemed possible that the revolution would be destroyed and the old regime reestablished.

✔ **READING PROGRESS CHECK**

Identifying What radical steps did the National Convention take?

The Reign of Terror

GUIDING QUESTION *How did the new French government deal with crises?*

To meet these crises, the National Convention gave broad powers to a special committee of 12 known as the Committee of Public Safety. It came to be dominated by the radical Jacobin Maximilien Robespierre. For approximately a year during 1793 and 1794, the Committee of Public Safety took control of the government. To defend France from **domestic** threats, the Committee adopted policies that became known as the Reign of Terror.

As a temporary measure, revolutionary courts were set up to prosecute counterrevolutionaries and traitors. Almost 40,000 people were killed during the French Reign of Terror. Of those, 16,000 people, including Marie Antoinette and Olympe de Gouges, died by the guillotine. Most executions occurred in towns that had openly rebelled against the Convention.

Revolutionary armies were set up to bring rebellious cities under the control of the Convention. The Committee of Public Safety decided to make an example of Lyon, a city that rebelled during a time when the Republic was in peril, and 1,880 citizens of Lyon were executed. When guillotining proved too slow, the condemned were shot with grapeshot (a cluster of small iron balls) into open graves. A foreign witness wrote:

PRIMARY SOURCE

❝Whole ranges of houses, always the most handsome, burnt. The churches, convents, and all the dwellings of the former patricians were in ruins. When I came to the guillotine, the blood of those who had been executed a few hours beforehand was still running in the street . . . I said to a group of sansculottes. . . that it would be decent to clear away all this human blood.— Why should it be cleared? one of them said to me. It's the blood of aristocrats and rebels. The dogs should lick it up.❞

—quoted in *The Oxford History of the French Revolution*

In western France, too, revolutionary armies were brutal and merciless in defeating rebels. Perhaps the most notorious violence occurred in the city

▲ This print by Faucher-Gudin depicts Louis XVI's execution on January 21, 1793.

▶ **CRITICAL THINKING**
Drawing Inferences Why might the method of the king's execution be significant?

domestic relating to or originating within one's country

f a whole

of Nantes, where victims were executed by being loaded onto and then sunk in barges in the Loire River.

People from all classes were killed during the Terror. Clergy and nobles made up about 15 **percent** of the victims, while the rest were from the Third Estate. The Committee of Public Safety held that all this bloodletting was only temporary. When the war and domestic crisis were over, the true "Republic of Virtue" would follow, and the Declaration of the Rights of Man and the Citizen would be realized.

In addition to the Terror, the Committee of Public Safety took other steps to control and shape a French society. Robespierre called this new order the Republic of Virtue—a democratic republic composed of good citizens. As outward signs of support for the republic, the titles "citizen" and "citizeness" were to replace "mister" and "madame." Women wore long dresses inspired by the clothing worn in the ancient Roman Republic.

Good citizens would be formed by good education. A law aimed at primary education for all was passed but not widely implemented. Another law abolished slavery in French colonies.

Because people were alarmed about high inflation, the Committee tried to control the prices of essential goods such as food, fuel, and clothing. The controls did not work well because the government had no way to enforce them.

From the beginning, women had been active participants in the revolution, although they had no official power. During the radical stage of the revolution, women observed sessions of the National Convention and were not shy about making their demands.

In 1793, two women founded the Society for Revolutionary Republican Women in Paris. Most members were working-class women who asserted that they were ready to defend the republic. Most men, however, believed that women should not participate in either politics or the military.

The Convention also pursued a policy of de-Christianization. Its members believed that the religion encouraged superstition, rather than the use of reason. The word *saint* was removed from street names, churches were looted and closed by revolutionary armies, and priests were encouraged to marry. In Paris, the cathedral of Notre Dame, the center of the Catholic religion in France, was designated a "temple of reason." In November 1793, a public ceremony dedicated to the worship of reason was held in the former cathedral. Patriotic young girls dressed in white dresses paraded before a temple of reason where the high altar had once stood.

► **CRITICAL THINKING**
Interpreting Significance Why, by 1793, would some Parisians hold a parade mocking the Church?

▼ **Parade in Paris ridiculing Christianity and the Church, 1793**

PHOTO: The Granger Collection, NYC

Another example of de-Christianization was the adoption of a new calendar. Years would no longer be numbered from the birth of Jesus but from September 22, 1792—the first day of the French Republic. The calendar contained 12 months. Each month consisted of three 10-day weeks, with the tenth day of each week a day of rest.

These changes in the calendar had a significant effect on religion in France, eliminating Sundays, Sunday worship services, and church holidays. Robespierre came to realize, however, that most French people would not accept these efforts at de-Christianization. France was still overwhelmingly Catholic.

☑ READING PROGRESS CHECK

Questioning Why did the French government use force against its own people?

A Nation in Arms

GUIDING QUESTION *How did the new French government deal with crises?*

As foreign troops gathered on its borders, the revolution seemed to be in danger. To save the republic, the Committee of Public Safety issued a decree to raise an army:

PRIMARY SOURCE

❝Young men will fight, young men are called to conquer. Married men will forge arms, transport military baggage and guns and will prepare food supplies. Women, who at long last are to take their rightful place in the revolution and follow their true destiny, will forget their futile tasks: their delicate hands will work at making clothes for soldiers; they will make tents and they will extend their tender care to shelters where the defenders of the *Patrie* [homeland] will receive the help that their wounds require. Children will make lint of old cloth. It is for them that we are fighting: children, those beings destined to gather all the fruits of the revolution, will raise their pure hands toward the skies. And old men, performing their missions again, as of yore, will be guided to the public squares of the cities where they will kindle the courage of young warriors and preach the doctrines of hate for kings and the unity of the Republic.❞

—from the mobilization decree, August 23, 1793

▲ The Battle of Valmy was a victory for the French over the Austrians.

▶ **CRITICAL THINKING**
Identifying Central Ideas What was the cause of the foreign crisis in the spring of 1793?

In less than a year, the new French government had raised a huge army—by September 1794, it had more than a million soldiers. It was the largest army ever seen in Europe, and it pushed the invaders back across the Rhine. It even conquered the Austrian Netherlands. In earlier times, wars were the business of rulers who fought rivals with professional soldiers. The new French army was created by a people's government. Its wars were now people's wars.

By the summer of 1794, the French had largely defeated their foreign foes. There was less need for the Reign of Terror, but it continued nonetheless. Robespierre was obsessed with ridding France of all the corrupt elements. Many in the National Convention who feared Robespierre decided to act, lest they be the next victims. They gathered enough votes to condemn him, and Robespierre was guillotined on July 28, 1794.

☑ READING PROGRESS CHECK

Summarizing How did the French army become the people's army?

The Directory

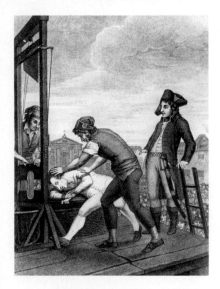

▲ Execution of Robespierre on July 28, 1794

GUIDING QUESTION *How did the constant transition within the French government influence its effectiveness?*

After the death of Robespierre, a reaction set in as more moderate middle-class leaders took control. The Reign of Terror came to a halt. The National Convention reduced the power of the Committee of Public Safety. Churches were allowed to reopen. Finally, a new constitution was created.

The Constitution of 1795 set up two legislative houses. A lower house, the Council of 500, drafted laws. An upper house of 250, the Council of Elders, accepted or rejected proposed laws. Members of both houses were chosen by **electors,** or qualified voters. Only those who owned or rented property worth a certain amount could be electors— only 30,000 people in the whole nation qualified. This was a significant change from the universal male suffrage the Paris Commune had demanded.

Under the new constitution, the executive was a committee of five called the Directory, chosen by the Council of Elders. The Directory, which lasted from 1795 to 1799, became known mainly for corruption. People reacted against the sufferings and sacrifices that had been demanded in the Reign of Terror. Some people made fortunes from government contracts or by loaning the government money at very high interest rates. They took advantage of the government's severe money problems during these difficult times.

At the same time, the government of the Directory faced political enemies from both conservatives and radicals. Some people wanted to bring back the monarchy, while others plotted to create a more radical regime like Robespierre's. Likewise, economic problems continued with no solution in sight. Finally, France was still conducting expensive wars against foreign enemies.

elector an individual qualified to vote in an election

coup d'état a sudden overthrow of the government

To stay in power, the Directory began to rely on the military, but one military leader turned on the government. In 1799 the successful and popular general Napoleon Bonaparte toppled the Directory in a **coup d'état** (KOO day • TAH), a sudden overthrow of the government. Napoleon then seized power.

☑ **READING PROGRESS CHECK**

Evaluating Did the transition from the Committee of Public Safety to the Directory help respond to the French people's needs?

PHOTO: ©BETTMANN/CORBIS

LESSON 2 REVIEW

Reviewing Vocabulary
1. *Examining* Explain how the coup d'état in which Napoleon took part differed from other transitions in the revolutionary French government.

Using Your Notes
2. *Applying* Use your notes to write a paragraph describing the actions taken by the National Convention and some of the consequences of these actions.

Answering the Guiding Questions
3. *Theorizing* Why did the French Revolution become more radical?

4. *Identifying* How did the new French government deal with crises?

5. *Analyzing* How did the constant transition within the French government influence its effectiveness?

Writing Activity
6. **INFORMATIVE/EXPLANATORY** Write an essay tracing the changes in the French government between the Constitution of 1791 and the Constitution of 1795. Include defining characteristics of each new form of government and how it led to the next change in leadership.

netw⊙rks

There's More Online!

☑ **CHART/GRAPH** Napoleon's Civil Law Code and Louisiana Civil Law

☑ **CHART/GRAPH** Napoleon's Domestic Policies

☑ **IMAGE** Napoleon's Civil Code

☑ **INTERACTIVE SELF-CHECK QUIZ**

☑ **MAP** Napoleonic Europe

☑ **PRIMARY SOURCE** The Concordat of 1801

☑ **VIDEO** The Rise of Napoleon and the Napoleonic Wars

Reading **HELP**DESK (CCSS)

Academic Vocabulary
- **capable**
- **liberal**

Content Vocabulary
- **consulate**
- **nationalism**

TAKING NOTES:
Key Ideas and Details

Differentiating As you read, create a diagram like the one below to list achievements of Napoleon's rule.

Achievements of Napoleon's Rule

PHOTO: (l to r)© The Gallery Collection / Corbis, The Art Gallery Collection/Alamy, Library of Congress, Library of Congress, © The Gallery Collection / Corbis

---

LESSON 3
The Rise of Napoleon and the Napoleonic Wars

ESSENTIAL QUESTIONS • *What causes revolution?*
• *How does revolution change society?*

IT MATTERS BECAUSE

Napoleon Bonaparte dominated French and European history from 1799 to 1815. During his reign, Napoleon built and lost an empire and also spread ideas about nationalism throughout much of Europe.

The Rise of Napoleon

GUIDING QUESTION *How did instability in the French government create an opportunity for Napoleon to take power?*

Napoleon Bonaparte's role in the French Revolution is complex. In one sense, he brought it to an end when he came to power in 1799. Yet he was a child of the revolution as well. Without it, he would never have risen to power, and he himself never failed to remind the French that he had preserved the best parts of the revolution during his reign as emperor.

Early Life

Napoleon was born in 1769 in Corsica, an island in the Mediterranean, only a few months after France had annexed the island. His father came from minor nobility in Italy, but the family was not rich. Napoleon was talented, however, and won a scholarship to a famous military school.

When he completed his studies, Napoleon was commissioned as a lieutenant in the French army. Although he became one of the world's greatest generals and a man beloved by his soldiers, there were few signs of his future success at this stage. He spoke with an Italian accent and was not popular with his fellow officers.

Napoleon devoted himself to his goals. He read what French philosophers had to say about reason, and he studied famous military campaigns. When revolution and war with Europe came about, there were many opportunities for Napoleon to use his knowledge and skills.

The French Revolution and Napoleon **163**

▲ *The Coronation of the Emperor Napoleon I* by Jacques-Louis David

▶ **CRITICAL THINKING**
Making Generalizations How does David portray Napoleon in this painting?

consulate government established in France after the overthrow of the Directory in 1799, with Napoleon as first consul in control of the entire government

Military Successes

Napoleon rose quickly through the ranks. In 1792 he became a captain. Two years later, at age 24, the Committee of Public Safety made him a brigadier general. In 1796 he became commander of the French armies in Italy. There Napoleon won a series of battles with speed, surprise, and decisive action. He also defeated the armies of the Papal States and their Austrian allies. These victories gave France control of northern Italy. Throughout the Italian campaigns, Napoleon's energy and initiative earned him the devotion of his troops. His personal qualities allowed him to win the support of those around him. In 1797 he returned to France as a hero. He was given command of an army in training to invade Britain, but he knew the French could not carry out that invasion. Instead, Napoleon suggested striking indirectly at Britain by taking Egypt.

Egypt lay on the route to India, one of Britain's most important colonies and a major source of its wealth. The British were a great sea power and controlled the Mediterranean. By 1799, the British had defeated the French naval forces supporting Napoleon's army in Egypt. Seeing certain defeat, Napoleon abandoned his army and returned to Paris.

Consul and Emperor

In Paris, Napoleon took part in the coup d'état of 1799 that overthrew the Directory and set up a new government, the **consulate**. In theory, it was a republic, but, in fact, Napoleon held absolute power. Napoleon was called first consul, a title borrowed from ancient Rome. He appointed officials, controlled the army, conducted foreign affairs, and influenced the legislature. In 1802 Napoleon was made consul for life. Two years later, he crowned himself Emperor Napoleon I.

Peace with the Church

One of Napoleon's first moves at home was to establish peace with the Catholic Church. In matters of religion, Napoleon was a man of the Enlightenment. He believed in reason and felt that religion was at most a social convenience. However, since most of France was Catholic, it was a good idea to mend relations with the Church.

In 1801 Napoleon came to an agreement with the pope, which recognized Catholicism as the religion of a majority of the French people. In return, the pope would not ask for the return of the church lands seized in the revolution.

With this agreement, the Catholic Church was no longer an enemy of the French government. It also meant that people who had acquired church lands in the revolution became avid supporters of Napoleon.

Codification of the Laws

Napoleon's most famous domestic achievement was to codify the laws. Before the revolution, France had almost 300 different legal systems. During the revolution, efforts were made to prepare a single law code for the nation. However, the work was not completed until Napoleon's reign.

Seven law codes were created, but the most important was the Civil Code, or Napoleonic Code, introduced in 1804. It preserved many of the principles that the revolutionaries had fought for: equality of all citizens before the law; the right of the individual to choose a profession; religious toleration; and the abolition of serfdom and all feudal obligations.

For women and children, the Civil Code was a step back. During the radical stage of the revolution, new laws had made divorce easier and allowed children, even daughters, to inherit property on an equal basis. The Civil Code undid these laws. Women were now "less equal than men." When they married, they lost control over any property they had. They could not testify in court, and it became more difficult for them to begin divorce proceedings. In general, the code treated women like children, who needed protection and who did not have a public role.

A New Bureaucracy

Napoleon also developed a powerful, centralized administrative machine. He focused on developing a bureaucracy of **capable** officials. Early on, the regime showed that it did not care about rank or birth. Public officials and military officers alike were promoted based on their ability. Opening careers to men of talent was a reform that the middle class had clamored for before the revolution.

capable having or showing ability

Napoleon also created a new aristocracy based on meritorious service to the nation. Between 1808 and 1814, Napoleon created about 3,200 nobles. Nearly 60 percent were military officers, while the rest were civil service or state and local officials. Socially, only 22 percent of this new aristocracy were from noble families of the old regime; about 60 percent were middle class in origin.

Preserver of the Revolution?

In his domestic policies, then, Napoleon did keep some major reforms of the French Revolution. Under the Civil Code, all citizens were equal before the law. The concept of opening government careers to more people was another gain of the revolution that he retained.

On the other hand, Napoleon destroyed some revolutionary ideals. Liberty was replaced by a despotism that grew increasingly arbitrary, in spite of protests by such citizens as the prominent writer Anne-Louise-Germaine de Staël. Napoleon shut down 60 of France's 73 newspapers and banned books, including de Staël's. He insisted that all manuscripts be subjected to government scrutiny before they were published. Even the mail was opened by government police.

✅ **READING PROGRESS CHECK**

Synthesizing How did Napoleon's Civil Code address the problems with the French legal system that were present before the revolution?

Napoleon's Empire

GUIDING QUESTIONS *Why would changes in France cause concern in other European countries? How did Napoleon's military background shape his perspective?*

Napoleon is, of course, known less for his domestic policies than for his military leadership. His conquests began soon after he rose to power.

Building the Empire

When Napoleon became consul in 1799, France was at war with a European coalition of Russia, Great Britain, and Austria. Napoleon realized the need for a pause in the war. "The French Revolution is not finished," he said, "so long as the scourge of war lasts …. I want peace, as much to settle the present French government, as to save the world from chaos." In 1802 a peace treaty was signed, but it did not last long. War with Britain broke out again in 1803. Gradually, Britain was joined by Austria, Russia, Sweden, and Prussia. In a

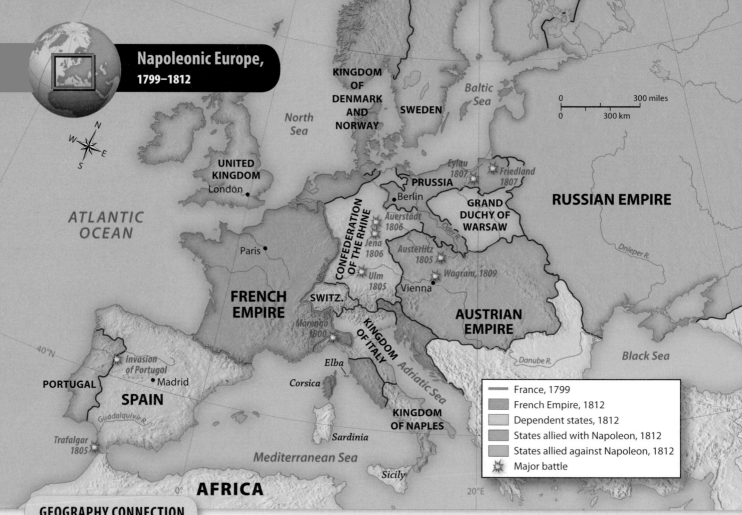

Napoleonic Europe, 1799–1812

Legend:
- France, 1799
- French Empire, 1812
- Dependent states, 1812
- States allied with Napoleon, 1812
- States allied against Napoleon, 1812
- ✶ Major battle

GEOGRAPHY CONNECTION

Napoleon's Grand Empire spread over much of Europe.

1 HUMAN SYSTEMS *Why might Napoleon have chosen to ally with states instead of taking them over?*

2 ENVIRONMENT AND SOCIETY *What do the countries allied against France have in common?*

liberal broad-minded; associated with ideals of the individual, especially economic freedom and greater participation in government

series of battles at Ulm, Austerlitz, Jena, and Eylau from 1805 to 1807, Napoleon's Grand Army defeated the Austrian, Prussian, and Russian armies.

From 1807 to 1812, Napoleon was the master of Europe. His Grand Empire was composed of three major parts: the French Empire, dependent states, and allied states. The French Empire was the inner core of the Grand Empire. It consisted of an enlarged France extending to the Rhine in the east and including the western half of Italy north of Rome.

Dependent states were kingdoms ruled by relatives of Napoleon. Eventually these included Spain, Holland, the kingdom of Italy, the Swiss Republic, the Grand Duchy of Warsaw, and the Confederation of the Rhine—a union of all German states except Austria and Prussia.

Allied states were countries defeated by Napoleon and then forced to join his struggle against Britain. These states included Prussia, Austria, Russia, and Sweden.

Spreading the Principles of the Revolution

Within his empire, Napoleon sought to spread some of the principles of the French Revolution, including legal equality, religious toleration, and economic freedom. In the inner core and dependent states of his Grand Empire, Napoleon tried to destroy the old order. The nobility and the clergy everywhere in these states lost their special privileges. Napoleon decreed equality of opportunity with offices open to those with ability, equality before the law, and religious toleration. The spread of French revolutionary principles was an important factor in the development of **liberal** traditions in these countries.

Like Hitler 130 years later, Napoleon hoped that his Grand Empire would last for centuries, but his empire collapsed almost as rapidly as it was formed. Two major reasons help explain this collapse: Britain's ability to resist Napoleon and the rise of nationalism.

British Resistance

Napoleon was never able to conquer Great Britain because of its sea power, which made it almost invulnerable. Napoleon hoped to invade Britain, but the British defeated the combined French-Spanish fleet at Trafalgar in 1805. This battle ended Napoleon's plans for invasion.

Napoleon then turned to his Continental System to defeat Britain. The aim of the Continental System was to stop British goods from reaching the European continent to be sold there. By weakening Britain economically, Napoleon would destroy its ability to wage war.

The Continental System also failed. Allied states resented being told by Napoleon that they could not trade with the British. Some began to cheat. Others resisted. Furthermore, new markets in the Middle East and in Latin America gave Britain new outlets for its goods. Indeed, by 1810, British overseas exports were at near-record highs.

Nationalism

A second significant factor in the defeat of Napoleon was **nationalism**. One of the most important forces of the nineteenth century, nationalism is the sense of unique identity of a people based on common language, religion, and national symbols. A new era was born when the French people decided that they were the nation.

Napoleon marched his armies through the Germanies, Spain, Italy, and Poland, arousing new ideas of nationalism in two ways. First, the conquered peoples became united in their hatred of the invaders. Second, the conquered peoples saw the power and strength of national feeling. It was a lesson not lost on them or their rulers.

✅ **READING PROGRESS CHECK**

Evaluating What were the consequences for a country conquered by Napoleon's Grand Army?

Analyzing CCSS
PRIMARY SOURCES

Napoleon's Reign

❝What is the throne?—a bit of wood gilded and covered with velvet—I am the state—I alone am here the representative of the people. Even if I had done wrong you should not have reproached me in public—people wash their dirty linen at home. France has more need of me than I of France.❞

—Napoleon, quoted in *The History of Napoleon Buonaparte*

DBQ **DRAWING CONCLUSIONS** How did Napoleon understand his role as leader of the French people?

nationalism the unique cultural identity of a people based on common language, religion, and national symbols

---

LESSON 3 REVIEW

Reviewing Vocabulary

1. *Identifying Central Issues* What is nationalism, and what role did it play in Napoleon's fall from power?

2. *Interpreting* Why do you think Napoleon used the ancient Roman term *first consul* to define his new role in the government?

Using Your Notes

3. *Comparing* Use your notes on the achievements of Napoleon to compare Napoleon's achievements to those of the French government during the Reign of Terror.

Answering the Guiding Questions

4. *Identifying* How did instability in the French government create an opportunity for Napoleon to take power?

5. *Drawing Conclusions* Why would changes in France cause concern in other European countries?

6. *Making Inferences* How did Napoleon's military background shape his perspective?

Writing Activity

7. ARGUMENT Write an essay analyzing whether Napoleon did or did not preserve the ideals of the French Revolution through his domestic and foreign policies. Demonstrate your knowledge of both sides of the argument, but ultimately choose one side using support from the text.

networks

There's More Online!

☑ **BIOGRAPHY** Duke of Wellington

☑ **BIOGRAPHY** Klemens von Metternich

☑ **IMAGE** The Congress of Vienna

☑ **INTERACTIVE SELF-CHECK QUIZ**

☑ **MAP** Europe after the Congress of Vienna, 1815

☑ **PRIMARY SOURCE** Napoleon's Retreat from Russia

☑ **SLIDE SHOW** Napoleon's Final Days

☑ **VIDEO** The Fall of Napoleon and the European Reaction

Reading **HELP**DESK **CCSS**

Academic Vocabulary

- civil   • constitution

Content Vocabulary

- **conservatism**
- **principle of intervention**
- **liberalism**

TAKING NOTES:

Key Ideas and Details

Differentiating As you read, use a diagram like the one below to summarize what led to Napoleon's downfall and how leaders in Europe attempted to restore order.

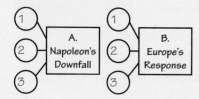

LESSON 4
The Fall of Napoleon and the European Reaction

ESSENTIAL QUESTIONS · *What causes revolution?*
· *How does revolution change society?*

IT MATTERS BECAUSE

After the turmoil of the French revolutionary years and the eventual fall of Napoleon, European rulers wanted to return to a conservative order, keeping a balance of power among nations. Liberals and nationalists, however, struggled to achieve more liberal governments and new nations.

The Fall of Napoleon

GUIDING QUESTION *How did Napoleon lose his empire?*

Napoleon's downfall began in 1812 when he decided to invade Russia. Within only a few years, his fall was complete.

The Russians had refused to remain in the Continental System, leaving Napoleon with little choice but to invade. He knew the risks in invading such a large country, but he also knew that if he did not punish the Russians for ignoring the Continental System, other nations would follow suit.

In June 1812, a Grand Army of more than 600,000 men entered Russia. Napoleon's hopes depended on a quick victory over the Russians, but they refused to do battle. Instead they retreated for hundreds of miles. As they retreated, they burned their own villages and countryside to keep Napoleon's army from finding food. When the Russians did fight at Borodino, Napoleon's forces won an indecisive victory, which cost many lives.

Finally reaching Moscow, the Grand Army found the city ablaze. With no food or supplies for his army, Napoleon abandoned the Russian capital in late October. As the winter snows began, Napoleon led the "Great Retreat" west across Russia. Thousands of soldiers starved and froze along the way. Fewer than 40,000 of the original 600,000 soldiers arrived back in Poland in January 1813.

This military disaster led other European states to rise up and attack the crippled French army. Paris was captured in March 1814. Napoleon was soon sent into exile on the island of Elba, off the northwest coast of Italy. The victorious powers restored monarchy to France in the person of Louis XVIII, brother of the executed king, Louis XVI.

The new king had little support, and the French people were not ready to surrender the glory of empire. Nor was Napoleon ready to give up. Restless in exile, he left the island of Elba and slipped back into France. The new king sent troops to capture Napoleon, who opened his coat and addressed them: "Soldiers of the 5th regiment, I am your Emperor. . . . If there is a man among you [who] would kill his Emperor, here I am!"

No one fired a shot. Shouting "Long live the Emperor!" the troops went over to his side. On March 20, 1815, Napoleon entered Paris in triumph.

Russia, Great Britain, Austria, and Prussia again pledged to defeat the man they called the "Enemy and Disturber of the Tranquility of the World." Meanwhile, Napoleon raised another French army of devoted veterans who rallied from all over France. He then readied an attack on the allied troops stationed across the border in Belgium.

At Waterloo in Belgium on June 18, 1815, Napoleon met a combined British and Prussian army under the Duke of Wellington and suffered a bloody defeat. This time, the victorious allies exiled him to St. Helena, a small island in the south Atlantic. Napoleon remained in exile until his death in 1821, but his memory haunted French political life for many decades.

✓ **READING PROGRESS CHECK**

Analyzing How did Napoleon's disaster in Russia affect both his Grand Army and the French nation?

▲ The burning of Moscow in October of 1812

European Reaction

GUIDING QUESTION *Why did the turmoil of the French revolutionary years result in a conservative European reaction?*

After the defeat of Napoleon, European rulers moved to restore the old order. This was the goal of the victors—Great Britain, Austria, Prussia, and Russia—when they met at the Congress of Vienna in September 1814 to arrange a final peace settlement.

The haughty Austrian foreign minister, Prince Klemens von Metternich (MEH • tuhr • nihk), was the most influential leader at that meeting in Vienna. Metternich claimed that the principle of legitimacy guided him. He meant that lawful monarchs from the royal families who had ruled before Napoleon would be restored to their positions of power. This, they believed, would ensure peace and stability in Europe. The victorious powers had already restored the Bourbon king to the French throne in 1814.

Practical considerations of power were addressed at the Congress of Vienna. The great powers rearranged territories in Europe, believing that this would form a new balance of power. The powers at Vienna wanted to keep any one country from dominating Europe. This meant balancing political and military forces that guaranteed the independence of the great powers. To balance Russian territorial gains, for example, new territories were given to Prussia and Austria.

The arrangements worked out at the Congress of Vienna were a victory for rulers who wanted to contain the forces of change that the French Revolution had unleashed. These rulers, such as Metternich, believed in the political philosophy known as **conservatism**.

conservatism a political philosophy based on tradition and social stability, favoring obedience to political authority and organized religion

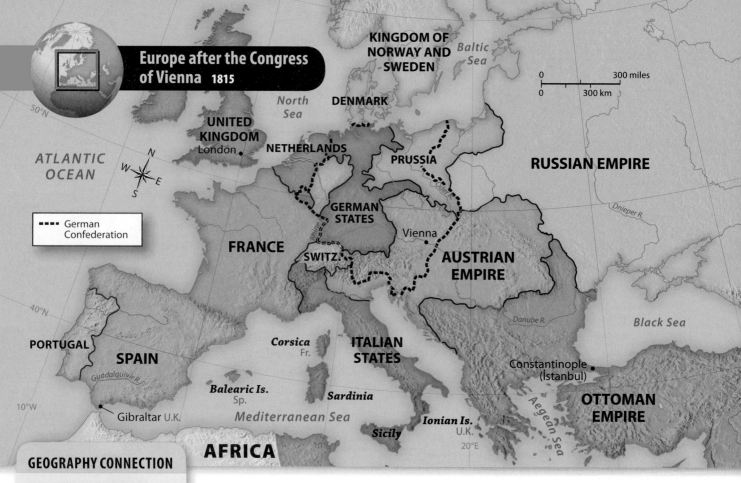

German Confederation

KINGDOM OF NORWAY AND SWEDEN

Baltic Sea

North Sea

DENMARK

UNITED KINGDOM
London

NETHERLANDS

PRUSSIA

RUSSIAN EMPIRE

ATLANTIC OCEAN

50°N

GERMAN STATES

Vienna

Dnieper R.

FRANCE

SWITZ.

AUSTRIAN EMPIRE

40°N

PORTUGAL

SPAIN

Guadalquivir R.

Corsica Fr.

ITALIAN STATES

Danube R.

Black Sea

Balearic Is. Sp.

Sardinia

Constantinople (İstanbul)

Gibraltar U.K.

Mediterranean Sea

Ionian Is. U.K.

Sicily

Aegean Sea

OTTOMAN EMPIRE

10°W

AFRICA

10°

20°E

GEOGRAPHY CONNECTION

The Congress of Vienna rearranged territories to maintain a balance of power.

1 **THE WORLD IN SPATIAL TERMS** *In what political boundaries is Vienna located?*

2 **HUMAN SYSTEMS** *Compare this map to the map of Napoleonic Europe in Lesson 3. What countries gained territory from France after the Congress of Vienna?*

Most conservatives at that time favored obedience to political authority. They also believed that religion was crucial to keep order in society. Conservatives hated revolutions and were unwilling to accept demands from people who wanted either individual rights or representative governments.

To maintain the new balance of power, Great Britain, Russia, Prussia, and Austria (and later France) agreed to meet in conferences to discuss their common interests and to maintain peace in Europe. These meetings came to be called the Concert of Europe.

The great powers adopted a **principle of intervention**. According to this principle, they had the right to send armies into countries in order to restore legitimate monarchs to their thrones. Britain argued that they should not interfere in the internal affairs of other states. However, the other great powers used military force to end revolutions in Spain and Italy.

☑ **READING PROGRESS CHECK**

Identifying Central Issues Why did European leaders think it was important to apply conservatism at the Congress of Vienna?

Forces of Change

GUIDING QUESTION *What happened to revolutionary ideas after the French Revolution was over?*

principle of intervention
idea that great powers have the right to send armies into countries where there are revolutions to restore legitimate governments

Between 1815 and 1830, conservative governments throughout Europe worked to maintain the old order. However, powerful forces for change—known as liberalism and nationalism—were also at work.

Liberalism is a political philosophy that grew out of the Enlightenment. **Liberalism** held that people should be as free as possible from government restraint. Liberal beliefs included the protection of **civil** liberties, the basic rights of all people. Civil liberties included equality before the law and freedom of assembly, speech, and the press. Liberals believed that freedoms should be guaranteed by a document such as the American Bill of Rights.

Many liberals favored a government ruled by a **constitution**—a concept called constitutionalism. For example, in a constitutional monarchy a king must follow the laws of the constitution. Liberals believed that written documents would help guarantee people's rights.

Most liberals wanted religious toleration for all, as well as separation of church and state. Liberals also demanded the right of peaceful opposition to the government. They believed that a representative assembly (legislature) elected by qualified voters should make laws. These liberal ideals were similar to republicanism, the belief that a government's power comes from the rule of law and the citizens who are allowed to vote.

Liberals did not believe everyone had a right to vote. They thought the right to vote and hold office should be open only to men of property. Liberalism was tied to middle-class men who wanted voting rights for themselves so they could share power with the landowning classes. The liberals feared mob rule and had little desire to let the lower classes share power.

Nationalism arose when people began to identify themselves as part of a community, a nation, defined by a distinctive language, common institutions, and customs. In earlier centuries, people's loyalty belonged to a king or to their town or region. In the nineteenth century, people began to feel that their chief loyalty was to the nation.

Nationalism did not become a popular force for change until the French Revolution. From then on, nationalists came to believe that each nationality should have its own government. Thus, the Germans, who were separated into many principalities, wanted national unity under one central government in a German nation-state. Subject peoples, such as the Hungarians, wanted the right to establish their own governments.

Nationalism was a threat to the existing order. A united Germany would upset the balance of power set up at the Congress of Vienna in 1815. An independent Hungarian state would mean the breakup of the Austrian Empire. Conservatives feared such change and tried to repress nationalism.

Nationalism found a strong ally in liberalism. Most liberals believed that freedom could only be possible in people who ruled themselves. Each group of people should have its own state.

✓ READING PROGRESS CHECK

Identifying Why did nationalism become popular after the French Revolution?

liberalism a political philosophy originally based largely on Enlightenment principles, holding that people should be as free as possible from government restraint and that civil liberties—the basic rights of all people—should be protected

civil involving the general public or civic affairs

constitution the basic principles and laws of a nation, state, or social group that determine the powers and duties of the government and guarantee certain rights to the people in it

---

LESSON 4 REVIEW (CCSS)

Reviewing Vocabulary

1. *Explaining* Write a paragraph explaining how the principle of intervention is an idea based on conservatism.

Using Your Notes

2. *Summarizing* Use your notes on Napoleon's downfall and Europe's response to list the various European responses to Napoleon's downfall.

Answering the Guiding Questions

3. *Drawing Conclusions* How did Napoleon lose his empire?

4. *Evaluating* Why did the turmoil of the French revolutionary years result in a conservative European reaction?

5. *Identifying the Main Idea* What happened to revolutionary ideas after the French Revolution was over?

Writing Activity

6. **INFORMATIVE/EXPLANATORY** Using the narrative and outside research, write an essay describing Napoleon's invasion of Russia. Be sure to cover his motivations for invasion, the logistical difficulties in carrying out the invasion, Russia's response, and the economic, political, and human toll of Napoleon's retreat.

Directions: On a separate sheet of paper, answer the questions below. Make sure you read carefully and answer all parts of the questions.

Lesson Review

Lesson 1

1 **CATEGORIZING** What was the Declaration of the Rights of Man and the Citizen?

2 **ANALYZING** What was the significance of the meeting of the Estates-General in 1789?

Lesson 2

3 **SUMMARIZING** What was the Reign of Terror and how did it end?

4 **ASSESSING** What effect did the Constitution of 1795 have?

Lesson 3

5 **IDENTIFYING CENTRAL ISSUES** What were four major principles that were reflected in the Napoleonic Civil Code?

6 **LISTING** What powers did Napoleon exercise as First Consul in France?

Lesson 4

7 **EXPLAINING** What was the significance of the Congress of Vienna?

8 **EXPLORING ISSUES** How did the great powers maintain the balance of power in Europe?

21st Century Skills

9 **IDENTIFYING CAUSE AND EFFECT** How did the Committee of Public Safety deal with opposition? What was the effect of its policies?

10 **ECONOMICS** What was the Continental System, and was it effective? Explain.

11 **COMPARE AND CONTRAST** How did the ideologies of liberalism and conservatism differ?

Exploring the Essential Questions

12 **SYNTHESIZING** Work with a partner to create an illustrated time line showing five pivotal events that occurred in France between 1789 and 1815. Include visuals such as photos, sketched images, and maps, along with primary sources. Be prepared to explain how the events you selected led to the exchange of new ideas.

DBQ Analyzing Historical Documents

Use the document to answer the following questions.

While emperor, Napoleon attempted to spread revolutionary ideals to other nations. He shares these ideas with his brother Jerome, the new king of Westphalia, in 1807:

PRIMARY SOURCE

❝ What the peoples of Germany desire most impatiently is that talented commoners should have the same right to your esteem and to public employments as the nobles, that any trace of serfdom and of an intermediate hierarchy between the sovereign and the lowest class of the people should be completely abolished. The benefits of the Code Napoléon, the publicity of judicial procedure, the creation of juries must be so many distinguishing marks of your monarchy. ❞

—**Napoleon in a letter to the king of Westphalia, 1807**

13 **DESCRIBING** What were Napoleon's views about how civil and military workers should be hired and promoted?

14 **MAKING PREDICTIONS** In the excerpt, Napoleon addresses "the peoples of Germany." How would the nobles of various German states be likely to respond and why?

Extended-Response Question

15 **INFORMATIVE/EXPLANATORY** How did the ideas of the Enlightenment help cause the French Revolution? How closely did the various factions of revolutionaries follow Enlightenment beliefs? How closely did Napoleon follow Enlightenment beliefs when he ruled France?

Need Extra Help?

If You've Missed Question	1	2	3	4	5	6	7	8	9	10	11	12	13	14	15
Go to page	155	154	159	162	164	164	169	170	159	167	169	154	172	172	153

Industrialization and Nationalism

1800–1870

ESSENTIAL QUESTIONS · *How can innovation affect ways of life?*
· *How does revolution bring about political and economic change?*

The Story Matters...

The ideals of the American and French Revolutions encouraged independence movements in other parts of the world. Napoleon's invasion of Spain weakened Spanish control of its Latin American colonies, resulting in nationalist uprisings there. These revolts were led by members of a Latin American-born elite of Spanish descent, such as Simón Bolívar, who vowed to bring freedom and independence to Latin America.

◀ Painted in about 1829 by Antonio Salas, this portrait of Bolívar, showing him as a dramatic figure posed against a dark background, presents the nationalist as a triumphant military leader.

PHOTO: Christie's Images/CORBIS.

Place and Time: Europe 1800–1870

The people of the nineteenth century witnessed the dramatic rise and fall of governments, the explosion of war and changing borders, and the rise of liberal economics and nationalist politics. The British government's support for free trade and its willingness to make political compromises to the middle classes helped it avoid the fate of many European nations where citizens took up arms for national identity in 1848. There were many causes of the Revolutions of 1848, including nationalism, the repressive nature of governments, and famines. The men and women of the middle classes and the urban working classes were discontented with their leaders.

Step Into the Place

Read the quotes and look at the information presented on the map.

 Analyzing Historical Documents Compare the lines from Shelley's poem to the excerpt from Macaulay's speech, focusing on their views of revolution. Use the map to draw a conclusion about which viewpoint dominated British politics in the nineteenth century.

PRIMARY SOURCE

"Men of England, wherefore plough
For the lords who lay ye low?
Wherefore weave with toil and care
The rich robes your tyrants wear? . . .

Sow seed,—but let no tyrant reap:
Find wealth,—let no imposter heap;
Weave robes,—let not the idle wear;
Forge arms,—in your defence to bear . . . "

—Percy Bysshe Shelley, from "A Song: 'Men of England,'" 1819

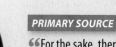 **PRIMARY SOURCE**

"For the sake, therefore, of the whole society, for the sake of the labouring classes themselves, I hold it to be clearly expedient that, in a country like this, the right of suffrage should depend on a pecuniary [monetary] qualification . . . I am opposed to Universal Suffrage, because I think that it would produce a destructive revolution. I support this plan [electoral reform], because I am sure that it is our best security against a revolution. "

—Thomas Babington Macaulay, from a speech in Parliament, March 2, 1831

PHOTO: (l)Hulton Archive/Getty images, (r)©Image Asset Management Ltd./SuperStock

Step Into the Time

Determining Understanding

Choose an event from the time line and explain how it shows a consequence of political unrest in Europe or a consequence of the Industrial Revolution.

EUROPE

1804 Richard Trevithick's steam locomotive runs on an industrial rail line in Britain

1807 Britain abolishes the slave trade

1814 Congress of Vienna meets

1830 French Revolution of 1830—Charles X flees the country to be replaced by the new constitutional monarchy of Louis-Philippe

THE WORLD

1800

1820

1789–1807 Selim III reigns as sultan of the Ottoman Empire and attempts reform efforts

1804 Haitians defeat French invasion and declare independence

1810–1825 Wars of independence in Latin America

1820 Mexico declares independence from Spain

☑ **MAP** Explore the interactive version of this map on Networks.

☑ **TIME LINE** Explore the interactive version of the time line on Networks.

Revolutionary Outbursts and Political Revolutions 1830–1848

SWEDEN

North Sea

IRELAND

GREAT BRITAIN

PRUSSIA

Berlin

Warsaw

RUSSIA

POLAND

BELGIUM

Paris

ATLANTIC OCEAN

Frankfurt

Prague

Vienna

Budapest

FRANCE

AUSTRIAN EMPIRE

Milan

Venice

PARMA

MODENA

PORTUGAL

SPAIN

Rome

PAPAL STATES

MONTENEGRO

OTTOMAN

EMPIRE

Black Sea

Naples

Mediterranean Sea

SICILY

GREECE

Baltic Sea

Legend	
✦	Revolutions of 1830s
✦	Revolutions of 1848

400 miles / 400 km

Lambert Azimuthal Equal-Area projection

1833 British Factory Act begins age of government regulations over factories

1848 Revolutions erupt in Europe, beginning with the overthrow of Louis-Philippe in France

1852 A year after a coup d'état overthrows the French Republic, Second Empire is proclaimed in France

1853–1856 Crimean War

1867 Dual monarchy of Austria-Hungary is created

1871 German unification achieved under William I

1840

1860

1880

1839 Opium War begins in China

1842 Treaty of Nanjing grants Hong Kong Island to Britain in perpetuity

1850 Taiping Rebellion begins in China

1865 Confederate forces surrender, ending the American Civil War

1867 French troops withdraw from Mexico

1868 Meiji Restoration in Japan

1869 Opening of the Suez Canal, ending overland route and reducing shipping costs

networks

There's More Online!

☑ **BIOGRAPHY** James Watt

☑ **BIOGRAPHY** Robert Fulton

☑ **IMAGE** The Rocket Steam Engine

☑ **IMAGE** Women Working in an English Cotton Mill

☑ **INTERACTIVE SELF-CHECK QUIZ**

☑ **MAP** Industry in Great Britain, 1850

☑ **PRIMARY SOURCE** A Miner's Story, 1842

☑ **PRIMARY SOURCE** Condition of the Working Class in England, 1844

☑ **VIDEO** The Industrial Revolution

Reading **HELP**DESK (CCSS)

Academic Vocabulary
• **labor**   • **derived**

Content Vocabulary
• **capital**
• **entrepreneur**
• **cottage industry**
• **puddling**
• **industrial capitalism**
• **socialism**

TAKING NOTES:

Key Ideas and Details

Categorizing As you read, use a table like the one below to name important inventors mentioned in this section and their inventions.

Inventors	Inventions

LESSON 1

The Industrial Revolution

ESSENTIAL QUESTIONS • *How can innovation affect ways of life?*
• *How does revolution bring about political and economic change?*

IT MATTERS BECAUSE
During the late eighteenth century, the Industrial Revolution began in Great Britain. An agricultural revolution and industrialization caused a shift from an economy based on farming and handicrafts to an economy based on manufacturing by machines in factories.

The Industrial Revolution in Great Britain

GUIDING QUESTIONS *What was the significance of the Agricultural Revolution in Great Britain? Why did the Industrial Revolution start in Great Britain?*

The Industrial Revolution began in Great Britain in the 1780s. However, it took decades to spread to other Western nations. Several factors contributed to make Great Britain the starting place.

First, an Agricultural Revolution beginning in the eighteenth century changed agricultural practices. Expansion of farmland, good weather, improved transportation, and new crops such as the potato dramatically increased the food supply. More people could be fed at lower prices with less **labor**. Now even ordinary British families could use some of their income to buy manufactured goods.

Second, with the increased food supply, the population grew. When Parliament passed enclosure movement laws in the eighteenth century, landowners fenced off common lands. This forced many peasants to move to towns, creating a labor supply for factories.

Third, Britain had a ready supply of money, or **capital**, to invest in new machines and factories. **Entrepreneurs** found new business opportunities and new ways to make profits.

Fourth, natural resources were plentiful in Britain. The country's rivers provided water power for the new factories and a means for transporting raw materials and finished products. Britain also had abundant supplies of coal and iron ore.

Finally, a supply of markets gave British manufacturers a ready outlet for their goods. Britain had a vast colonial empire, and British ships could transport goods anywhere in the world. Also, because of population growth and cheaper food at home, domestic markets increased. A growing demand for cotton cloth led British manufacturers to look for ways to increase production.

Cotton Production and New Factories

In the eighteenth century, Great Britain had surged far ahead in the production of inexpensive cotton goods. The manufacture of cotton cloth was a two-step process. First, spinners made cotton thread from raw cotton. Then, weavers wove the cotton thread into cloth on looms. In the eighteenth century, individuals did these tasks in their rural cottages. This production method was thus called a **cottage industry**.

A series of technological advances during this time made the cottage industry inefficient. In 1764 James Hargreaves had invented a machine called the spinning jenny, which made the spinning process much faster. In fact, spinners produced thread faster than weavers could use it.

The invention of a water-powered loom by Edmund Cartwright in 1787 made it possible for the weaving of cloth to catch up with the spinning of thread. It was now more efficient to bring workers to the new machines and have them work in factories near streams and rivers, which were used to power many of these early machines.

The cotton industry became even more productive when the steam engine was improved in the 1760s by James Watt, a Scottish engineer. In 1782 Watt made changes that enabled the engine to drive machinery. Steam power could now be used to spin and weave cotton. Before long, cotton mills using steam engines could be found throughout Britain. Because steam engines were fired by coal, not powered by water, they did not need to be located near rivers.

British cotton cloth production increased dramatically. In 1760 Britain had imported 2.5 million pounds (1.14 million kg) of raw cotton, which was used to produce cloth in cottage industries. By 1840, 366 million pounds (166 million kg) of cotton were imported each year. By this time, cotton cloth was Britain's most valuable product. Sold around the world, British cotton goods were produced mainly in factories.

The factory was another important element in the Industrial Revolution. From its beginning, the factory created a new labor system. Factory owners wanted to use their new machines constantly. So, workers were forced to work in shifts to keep the machines producing at a steady rate.

labor work performed by people that provides the goods or services in an economy

capital money available for investment

entrepreneur a person who finds new business opportunities and new ways to make profits

cottage industry a method of production in which tasks are done by individuals in their rural homes

▼ Titled *Carding, Drawing, and Roving*, this print shows girls and women working in an English cotton mill.

▶ CRITICAL THINKING
Analyzing Information In what way does this image depict factory work?

Early factory workers came from rural areas where they were used to periods of hectic work, such as harvest time, followed by periods of inactivity. Early factory owners therefore disciplined workers to a system of regular hours and repetitive tasks. For example, adult workers were fined for being late and were dismissed for more serious misconduct, especially being drunk. Child workers were often beaten with a rod or whipped to keep them at work. One early industrialist said that his aim was "to make such machines of the Men as cannot err."

Coal, Iron, and Railroads

The steam engine was crucial to Britain's Industrial Revolution. For fuel, the engine depended on coal, which seemed then to be unlimited in quantity. The success of the steam engine increased the need for coal and led to an expansion in coal production. New processes using coal aided the transformation of another industry—the iron industry.

Britain's natural resources included large supplies of iron ore. A better quality of iron was produced in the 1780s when Henry Cort developed a process called **puddling**. In this process, coke, which was **derived** from coal, was used to burn away impurities in crude iron, called pig iron, and to produce an iron of high quality.

The British iron industry boomed. In 1740 Britain had produced 17,000 tons (15,419 metric tons or t) of iron. After Cort's process came into use in the 1780s, production jumped to nearly 70,000 tons (63,490 t). In 1852 Britain produced almost 3 million tons (2.7 million t)—more iron than was produced by the rest of the world combined. High-quality iron was used to build new machines, especially trains.

In the eighteenth century, more efficient means of moving resources and goods developed. Railroads were particularly important to the success of the Industrial Revolution. Richard Trevithick, an English engineer, built the first steam locomotive. In 1804 Trevithick's locomotive ran on an industrial rail line in Britain. It pulled 10 tons (9 t) of ore and 70 people at 5 miles (8.05 km) per hour. Better locomotives soon followed. One called the *Rocket* was used on the first public railway line, which opened in 1830 and extended 32 miles (51.5 km) from the cotton-manufacturing town of Manchester to the thriving port of Liverpool.

The *Rocket* sped along at 16 miles (25.7 km) per hour while pulling a 40-ton (36-t) train. Within 20 years, locomotives were able to reach 50 miles (80.5 km) per hour, an incredible speed. In 1840 Britain had almost 2,000 miles (3,218 km) of railroads. In 1850 more than 6,000 miles (9,654 km) of railroad track crisscrossed much of the country.

Building railroads created new jobs for farm laborers and peasants. Less expensive transportation led to lower-priced goods, thus creating larger markets. More sales meant more demand and the need for more factories and more machinery. Business owners could reinvest their profits in new equipment, adding to the growth of the economy. This type of regular, ongoing economic growth became a basic feature of the new industrial economy.

✔ **READING PROGRESS CHECK**

Making Inferences Why might it be important to have fast, reliable transportation between Manchester and Liverpool?

puddling the process in which coke derived from coal is used to burn away impurities in crude iron to produce high quality iron

derived obtained from; came from

▼ The *Rocket* locomotive

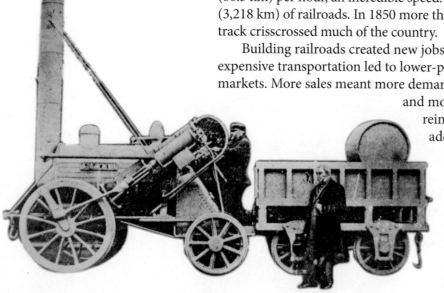

PHOTO: ©Science and Society/SuperStock

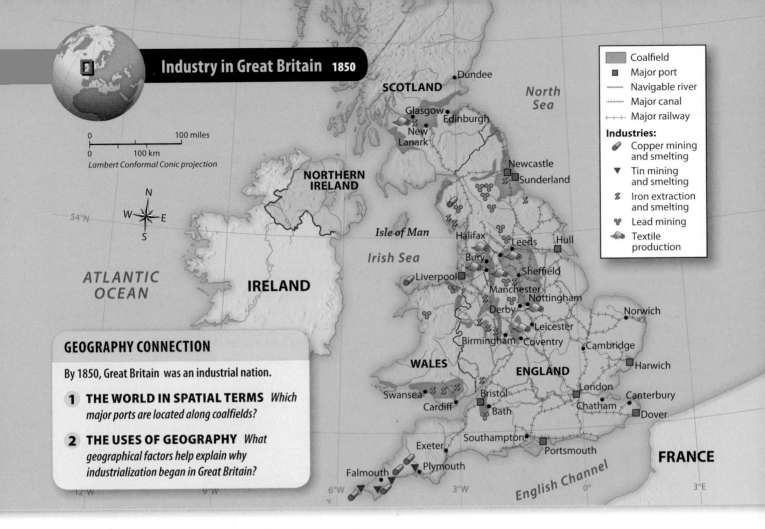

Industry in Great Britain 1850

Legend:
- Coalfield
- Major port
- Navigable river
- Major canal
- Major railway

Industries:
- Copper mining and smelting
- Tin mining and smelting
- Iron extraction and smelting
- Lead mining
- Textile production

Lambert Conformal Conic projection

GEOGRAPHY CONNECTION

By 1850, Great Britain was an industrial nation.

1 THE WORLD IN SPATIAL TERMS *Which major ports are located along coalfields?*

2 THE USES OF GEOGRAPHY *What geographical factors help explain why industrialization began in Great Britain?*

The Spread of Industrialization

GUIDING QUESTION *What factors fed the spread of industrialization in Europe and North America?*

By the mid-nineteenth century, Great Britain had become the world's first industrial nation. It had also become the world's richest nation. Great Britain produced one-half of the world's coal and manufactured goods. Its cotton industry alone in 1850 was equal in size to the industries of all other European countries combined.

The Industrial Revolution spread to the rest of Europe at different times and at different speeds. Belgium, France, and the German states were the first to be industrialized in continental Europe, and their governments actively encouraged such development. For example, governments provided funds to build roads, canals, and railroads. By 1850, a network of iron rails spread across Europe.

An Industrial Revolution also occurred in the United States during the first half of the nineteenth century. In 1800 more than 5 million people lived in the United States, and nearly 6 out of every 7 American workers were farmers. No city had more than 100,000 people. In contrast, the U.S. population had grown to more than 30 million people by 1860. Many of these people moved into the cities. Eight cities had populations over 100,000, and only about 50 percent of American workers were farmers.

A large country, the United States needed a good transportation system to move goods across the nation. Thousands of miles of roads and canals were built to link east and west. Robert Fulton built the first paddle-wheel steamboat, the *Clermont*, in 1807. Steamboats made transportation easier on the waterways of the United States.

On the conditions of child factory workers:

"Provided a child should be drowsy, the overlooker walks round the room . . . and he touches the child on the shoulder, and says, 'Come here.' In the corner of the room there is an iron cistern; it is filled with water . . . he takes this boy, and holding him up by the legs, dips him over head in the cistern, and sends him to work for the remainder of the day. . . . "

—from a British Parliament report, quoted in *The History of the Factory Movement, Vol I,* 1857

DBQ **MAKING INFERENCES**
Why might the British Parliament have examined the conditions of child factory workers?

industrial capitalism
an economic system based on industrial production or manufacturing

Most important in the development of an American transportation system was the railroad. By 1860, about 30,000 miles (48,270 km) of railroad track covered the continental United States. The railroad soon turned the country into a single massive market for the manufactured goods produced in the Northeast.

Labor for the growing number of factories in the Northeast came chiefly from the farm population. Women and girls made up a large majority of the workers in large textile (cotton and wool) factories.

☑ READING PROGRESS CHECK

Comparing How did the effects of industrialization in the United States compare with those in Great Britain?

Social Impact of Industrialization

GUIDING QUESTION *What was the social impact of industrialization in Europe?*

The Industrial Revolution drastically changed society. In the first half of the nineteenth century, cities grew and two new social classes—the industrial middle class and the industrial working class—emerged.

Population Growth and Urbanization

European population stood at an estimated 140 million in 1750. By 1850, the population had almost doubled to 266 million. The key to this growth was a decline in death rates, wars, and major epidemic diseases, such as smallpox and plague. Because of an increase in the food supply, people were better fed and more resistant to disease.

Famine and poverty were two factors that impacted global migration and urbanization. More than 1 million people died during the Irish potato famine, and poverty led a million more to migrate to the Americas. Industrialization also spurred urbanization, as large numbers of people migrated from the countryside to cities to work in factories.

In 1800 Great Britain had one major city, London, with a population of about 1 million. Six cities had populations between 50,000 and 100,000. By 1850, London's population had swelled to about 2.5 million. Nine cities had populations over 100,000. Also, more than 50 percent of the population lived in towns and cities.

The rapid growth of cities in the first half of the nineteenth century led to pitiful living conditions for many, leading urban reformers to call on local governments to clean up their cities. Reform would be undertaken in the second half of the nineteenth century.

New Social Classes

The Middle Ages saw the rise of commercial capitalism, an economic system based on trade. **Industrial capitalism**, an economic system based on industrial production, rose during the Industrial Revolution. This system produced a new middle-class group—the industrial middle class.

In the Middle Ages, the bourgeois, or middle-class person, was the burgher or town dweller. The bourgeois were merchants, officials, artisans, lawyers, or intellectuals. Later, the term *bourgeois* came to include people involved in industry and banking, as well as lawyers, teachers, or doctors. The new industrial middle class that emerged during the Industrial Revolution was made up of the people who built the factories, bought the machines, and developed the markets. They had initiative, vision, ambition, and often greed. One said, "Getting of money… is the main business of the life of Man. . . ."

The Industrial Revolution also created an industrial working class that faced wretched working conditions. Work hours ranged from 12 to 16 hours each day, 6 days per week. There was no security of employment, and there was no minimum wage.

Conditions in the coal mines were harsh. Steam-powered engines lifted the coal from the mines to the top, but the men inside the mines dug out the coal. Dangerous conditions, including cave-ins, explosions, and gas fumes, were a way of life. The cramped conditions in the mines and their constant dampness led to workers' deformed bodies and ruined lungs.

The worst conditions were in the cotton mills, which were also dirty, dusty, dangerous, and unhealthy. In Britain, women and children made up two-thirds of the cotton industry's workforce by 1830. However, the number of child laborers declined after the Factory Act of 1833. This act set nine as the minimum age for employment and limited hours for older children. After this, women came to make up 50 percent of the British labor force in textile factories. They were paid half or less than half of what men received. When the work hours of children and women were limited, a new pattern of work emerged. Men now earned most of the family income by working outside the home. Women took over daily care of the family and performed low-paying jobs that could be done at home.

Early Socialism

In the first half of the nineteenth century, the pitiful conditions created by the Industrial Revolution gave rise to a movement known as **socialism**. In this economic system, society—usually in the form of the government—owns and controls some means of production, such as factories and utilities.

Early socialism was largely the idea of intellectuals. To later socialists, especially the followers of Karl Marx, such ideas were impractical dreams. They contemptuously labeled the earlier reformers utopian socialists, a term that has lasted to this day. Robert Owen, a British cotton manufacturer, was one utopian socialist. He believed that humans would show their natural goodness if they lived in a cooperative environment. Owen transformed the squalid factory town of New Lanark, Scotland, into a flourishing community. He created a similar community at New Harmony, Indiana, in the United States in the 1820s, which failed.

 READING PROGRESS CHECK

Drawing Conclusions Why do you think the working conditions during the Industrial Revolution led some to argue for socialism?

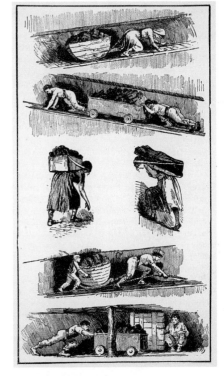

▲ Children and women working in an English coal mine

socialism a system in which society, usually in the form of the government, owns and controls the means of production

PHOTO: The Stapleton Collection/Bridgeman Art Library

LESSON 1 REVIEW (CCSS)

Reviewing Vocabulary

1. ***Summarizing*** Write a paragraph describing the importance of urbanization to the growth of industrial capitalism in Great Britain.

Using Your Notes

2. ***Organizing*** Use your graphic organizer to discuss the major inventors and inventions covered in this lesson.

Answering the Guiding Questions

3. ***Evaluating*** What was the significance of the Agricultural Revolution in Great Britain?

4. ***Identifying*** Why did the Industrial Revolution start in Great Britain?

5. ***Making Connections*** What factors fed the spread of industrialization in Europe and North America?

6. ***Drawing Conclusions*** What was the social impact of industrialization in Europe?

Writing Activity

7. **INFORMATIVE/EXPLANATORY** Using the information you collected in your graphic organizer, write a paragraph describing the impact the various inventions had on the Industrial Revolution.

Reading **HELP** DESK (CCSS)

Academic Vocabulary

- **radical**
- **temporary**

Content Vocabulary

- **universal male suffrage**
- **multinational empire**

TAKING NOTES:

Key Ideas and Details

Comparing and Contrasting Use your graphic organizer to compare and contrast the revolutions of 1830 and 1848.

	1830	1848
Governments/ countries in power		
Groups revolting		
Outcomes		

LESSON 2
Nationalism and Political Revolutions

ESSENTIAL QUESTIONS · *How can innovation affect ways of life?*
· *How does revolution bring about political and economic change?*

IT MATTERS BECAUSE

After the Napoleonic wars, European rulers sought to restore stability by reestablishing much of the old order. They also wanted to keep a balance of power among nations. New forces for change, however, especially liberalism and nationalism, had become too powerful to be contained. Revolts and revolutions soon shook Europe.

The Revolutions of the 1830s

GUIDING QUESTION *How did liberalism and nationalism present a challenge to conservatism in Europe during the 1830s and 1840s?ss*

Governments in Europe attempted to maintain the old order during the nineteenth century. Beginning in 1830, however, the forces of change—liberalism and nationalism—began to break through the conservative domination of Europe.

In France the Bourbon monarch Charles X, a reactionary, attempted to censor the press and take away voting rights from much of the middle class. In response, liberals overthrew Charles X in 1830 and established a constitutional monarchy. Louis-Philippe, a cousin of Charles X, took the throne. Political support for the new monarch came from the upper-middle class.

In the same year, three more revolutions occurred in Europe. Nationalism was the chief force in all three of them. Belgium, which had been annexed to the former Dutch Republic in 1815, rebelled and created an independent state. Both Poland and Italy, which were ruled by foreign powers, made efforts to break free. These efforts, however, were less successful. Russian troops crushed the Polish attempt to establish an independent Polish nation. Meanwhile, Austrian troops marched south and put down revolts in a number of Italian states.

☑ **READING PROGRESS CHECK**

Evaluating In what ways were liberalism and nationalism causes for the revolutions of the 1830s in Europe?

The Revolutions of 1848

GUIDING QUESTIONS *How did liberalism and nationalism present a challenge to conservatism in Europe during the 1830s and 1840s? What were the results of the revolutionary uprisings that occurred throughout Europe in 1848?*

Despite liberal and nationalist successes in France and Belgium, the conservative order still dominated much of Europe as the midpoint of the nineteenth century approached. However, the forces of liberalism and nationalism continued to grow. These forces of change erupted once more in the revolutions of 1848.

Another French Revolution

Revolution in France was again the spark for revolution in other countries. Severe economic problems beginning in 1846 brought untold hardship in France to the lower middle class, workers, and peasants. At the same time, members of the middle class clamored for the right to vote. The government of Louis-Philippe refused to make changes, and opposition grew.

The monarchy was finally overthrown in 1848. A group of moderate and **radical** republicans set up a provisional, or **temporary,** government. The republicans were people who wanted France to be a republic—a government in which leaders are elected.

The provisional government called for the election of representatives to a Constituent Assembly that would draw up a new constitution. Election would be determined by **universal male suffrage,** meaning all adult men could vote. The provisional government also set up national workshops to provide work for the unemployed. From March to June, the number of unemployed enrolled in the national workshops rose from about 66,000 to almost 120,000. This emptied the treasury and frightened the moderates, who reacted by closing the workshops on June 21, 1848.

The workers refused to accept this decision to close down the workshops. They poured into the streets in protest. In four days of bitter and bloody fighting, government forces crushed the working-class revolt. Thousands were killed and thousands more were sent to the French prison colony of Algeria in northern Africa.

The new French constitution, ratified on November 4, 1848, set up a republic called the Second Republic. The Second Republic had a single legislature elected by universal male suffrage. A president, also chosen by universal male suffrage, served for four years. In the elections for the presidency held in December 1848, Charles Louis Napoleon Bonaparte (called Louis-Napoleon), the nephew of the famous French ruler, won a resounding victory.

radical relating to a political group associated with views, practices, and policies of extreme change

temporary lasting for a limited time; not permanent

universal male suffrage the right of all males to vote in elections

▲ Burning the French throne at the Place de la Bastille, 1848

▶ **CRITICAL THINKING**
Drawing Inferences Describe the symbolic meaning of this painting.

PHOTO: The Stapleton Collection/Bridgeman Art Library

▲ The National Guard breaks up a labor uprising in Vienna, 1848.

▶ **CRITICAL THINKING**
Drawing Conclusions How does this image illustrate the chaos and level of participation in the 1848 revolts?

Revolt in the German States

News of the 1848 revolution in France led to upheaval in other parts of Europe. The Congress of Vienna, which lasted from 1814 to 1815, had recognized the existence of 38 independent German states (called the German Confederation). Of these, Austria and Prussia were the two great powers. The other states varied in size.

In 1848 cries for change led many German rulers to promise constitutions, a free press, jury trials, and other liberal reforms. In May 1848, an all-German parliament, called the Frankfurt Assembly, was held to fulfill a liberal and nationalist dream—the preparation of a constitution for a new united Germany. The Frankfurt Assembly's proposed constitution provided for a German state with a parliamentary government and a hereditary emperor ruling under a limited monarchy. The constitution also allowed for direct election of deputies to the parliament by universal male suffrage.

Ultimately, however, the Frankfurt Assembly failed to gain the support needed to achieve its goal. Frederick William IV of Prussia, to whom the throne was offered, refused to accept the crown from a popularly elected assembly. Thus, the assembly members had no real means of forcing the German rulers to accept their drafted constitution. German unification was not achieved.

Revolutions in Central Europe

multinational empire an empire in which people of many nationalities live

The Austrian Empire also had its problems. It was a **multinational empire**—a collection of different peoples including Germans, Czechs, Magyars (Hungarians), Slovaks, Romanians, Slovenes, Poles, Croats, Serbs, Ruthenians (Ukrainians), and Italians. Only the German-speaking Hapsburg dynasty held the empire together. The Germans, though only a quarter of the population, played a leading role in governing the Austrian Empire.

In March 1848, demonstrations erupted in the major cities. To calm the demonstrators, the Hapsburg court dismissed Metternich, the Austrian foreign minister, who fled to England. In Vienna, revolutionary forces took control of the capital and demanded a liberal constitution. To appease the revolutionaries, the government gave Hungary its own legislature. In Bohemia, the Czechs clamored for their own government.

Austrian officials had made concessions to appease the revolutionaries but were determined to reestablish their control over the empire. In June 1848, Austrian military forces crushed the Czech rebels in Prague. By the end of October, the rebels in Vienna had been defeated as well. With the help of a Russian army of 140,000 men, the Hungarian revolutionaries were finally subdued in 1849. The revolutions in the Austrian Empire had failed.

Revolts in the Italian States

The Congress of Vienna had set up nine states in Italy, which were divided among the European powers. These states included the Kingdom of Piedmont in the north; the Two Sicilies (Naples and Sicily); the Papal States; a handful of small states; and the northern provinces of Lombardy and Venetia, which were now part of the Austrian Empire.

In 1848 a revolt broke out against the Austrians in Lombardy and Venetia. Revolutionaries in other Italian states also took up arms and sought to create liberal constitutions and a unified Italy. By 1849, however, the Austrians had reestablished complete control over Lombardy and Venetia. The old order also prevailed in the rest of Italy.

The Failures of 1848

Throughout Europe in 1848, popular revolts started upheavals that led to liberal constitutions and liberal governments. But how could so many successes in 1848 soon be followed by so many failures? Two particular reasons stand out.

The unity of the revolutionaries had made the revolutions possible. However, moderate liberals and more radical revolutionaries were soon divided over their goals; therefore, conservative rule was reestablished.

In 1848 nationalities everywhere had also revolted in pursuit of self-government. However, little was achieved as divisions among nationalities proved disastrous. The Hungarians, for example, sought their freedom from the Austrians. At the same time, they refused the same to their minorities—the Slovenes, Croats, and Serbs. Instead of joining together to fight the old empire, minorities fought each other. The old order prevailed. Even with the reestablishment of conservative governments, however, the forces of nationalism and liberalism continued to influence political events.

✔ **READING PROGRESS CHECK**

Drawing Conclusions Why did the revolutions of 1848 fail?

Analyzing CCSS
PRIMARY SOURCES

Giuseppe Mazzini on Young Italy

❝Young Italy is a brotherhood of Italians who believe in a law of *Progress* and *Duty*, and are convinced that Italy is destined to become one nation. . .

Young Italy is *Unitarian*.

Because, without unity, there is no true nation.

Because without unity, there is no real strength; and Italy, surrounded as she is by powerful, united, and jealous nations, has need of strength before all things. . . . ❞

—Giuseppe Mazzini, from *General Instructions for the Members of Young Italy*, 1832

DBQ *MAKING INFERENCES*
Why would Italy's history have convinced Mazzini of the need for national unity?

LESSON 2 REVIEW

Reviewing Vocabulary

1. ***Describing*** Define the term *universal male suffrage* and give examples of when it affected the revolutions of 1848.

Using Your Notes

2. ***Comparing and Contrasting*** Use your graphic organizer to discuss the similarities and differences between the revolutions of the 1830s and 1848.

Answering the Guiding Questions

3. ***Determining Cause and Effect*** How did liberalism and nationalism present a challenge to conservatism in Europe during the 1830s and 1840s?

4. ***Making Observations*** What were the results of the revolutionary uprisings that occurred throughout Europe in 1848?

Writing Activity

5. **ARGUMENT** Write a paragraph that argues for or against the following statement: The revolutions of the 1830s ultimately failed.

Reading **HELP**DESK ⓒⒸⓈⓈ

Academic Vocabulary
- unification • regime

Content Vocabulary
- militarism
- kaiser
- plebiscite
- emancipation
- abolitionism

TAKING NOTES:

Key Ideas and Details

Summarizing Information As you read, use a table like the one below to list the changes that took place in the indicated countries during the nineteenth century.

Great Britain	France	Austrian Empire	Russia

LESSON 3
Nationalism, Unification, and Reform

ESSENTIAL QUESTIONS • *How can innovation affect ways of life?*
• *How does revolution bring about political and economic change?*

IT MATTERS BECAUSE

Although the revolutions of 1848 were unsuccessful, the forces of nationalism and liberalism remained powerful for the rest of the nineteenth century. Italy and Germany were eventually unified, and Great Britain and France became more liberal.

Toward National Unification

GUIDING QUESTION *What led to the unification of Italy and Germany after the revolution of 1848?*

The revolutions of 1848 had failed. By 1871, however, both Germany and Italy would be unified. The changes that made this possible began with the Crimean War.

Breakdown of the Concert of Europe

The Crimean War was the result of a long-term struggle between Russia and the Ottoman Empire. The Ottoman Empire had long controlled most of the Balkans in southeastern Europe. By 1800, however, the Ottoman Empire was in decline.

Russia was especially interested in expanding its power into Ottoman lands in the Balkans. This expansion would allow Russian ships to sail through the Dardanelles, the straits between the Black Sea and the Mediterranean Sea. If Russia could achieve this goal, it would become the major power in eastern Europe and challenge British naval control of the eastern Mediterranean. Other European nations feared Russian ambition and had their own interest in the decline of the Ottoman Empire.

In 1853 the Russians invaded the Turkish Balkan provinces of Moldavia and Walachia. In response, the Ottoman Turks declared war on Russia. Great Britain and France, fearful of Russian gains in this war, declared war on Russia the following year. This conflict came to be called the Crimean War. The Crimean War was poorly planned and poorly fought. Eventually, heavy losses caused the Russians to seek peace. By the Treaty of Paris, signed in March 1856,

Russia agreed to allow Moldavia and Walachia to be placed under the protection of all the great powers.

The effect of the Crimean War was to destroy the Concert of Europe. Austria and Russia, the chief powers maintaining the status quo before the 1850s, were now enemies. Austria, with its own interests in the Balkans, had refused to support Russia in the Crimean War. A defeated and humiliated Russia withdrew from European affairs for the next 20 years. Austria was now without friends among the great powers. This situation opened the door to the **unification** of Italy and Germany.

Italian Unification

In 1850 Austria was still the dominant power on the Italian Peninsula. After the failure of the revolution of 1848, people began to look to the northern Italian state of Piedmont for leadership in achieving the unification of Italy. The royal house of Savoy ruled the Kingdom of Piedmont. Included in the kingdom were Piedmont, the island of Sardinia, Nice, and Savoy. The ruler of the kingdom, beginning in 1849, was King Victor Emmanuel II.

The king named Camillo di Cavour his prime minister in 1852. As prime minister, Cavour pursued a policy of economic growth in order to equip a large army. Cavour, however, knew that Piedmont's army was not strong enough to defeat the Austrians. So he made an alliance with the French emperor Louis-Napoleon. Cavour then provoked the Austrians into declaring war in 1859.

unification the act, process, or result of making into a coherent or coordinated whole; the state of being unified

GEOGRAPHY CONNECTION

By 1871 Italy and Germany had unified.

1 **PLACES AND REGIONS** *Describe the sequence of events in Italian unification.*

2 **HUMAN SYSTEMS** *What provinces did Germany win in the Franco-Prussian War?*

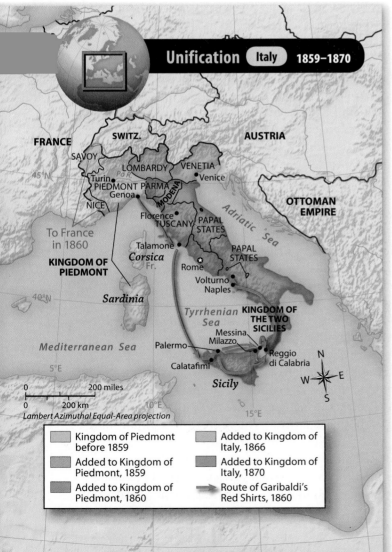

Unification Italy 1859–1870

Kingdom of Piedmont before 1859

Added to Kingdom of Piedmont, 1859

Added to Kingdom of Piedmont, 1860

Added to Kingdom of Italy, 1866

Added to Kingdom of Italy, 1870

→ Route of Garibaldi's Red Shirts, 1860

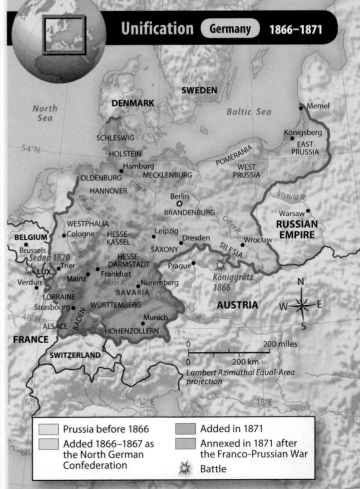

Unification Germany 1866–1871

Prussia before 1866

Added 1866–1867 as the North German Confederation

Added in 1871

Annexed in 1871 after the Franco-Prussian War

✸ Battle

Giuseppe Garibaldi (1807–1882)

Giuseppe Garibaldi, an Italian patriot and soldier, was instrumental in the unification of Italy. He raised an army of men called Red Shirts and seized Sicily and Naples. He handed over control of southern Italy to Victor Emmanuel II, whom he declared the first king of a united Italy. Garibaldi retired to the small island of Caprera but was soon called back into military service and continued fighting until Italy was completely free.

Otto von Bismarck (1815–1898)

Otto von Bismarck came from the class of aristocratic Prussian landowners known as *Junkers*. Under his leadership, Prussia won a series of European wars that united the German states under Prussian rule. Bismarck became a national hero. In 1871, when King William I of Prussia was proclaimed the German kaiser, Bismarck became chancellor of this new German empire.

▶ **CRITICAL THINKING**

Contrasting How did Bismarck's and Garibaldi's careers as unifiers differ?

Following that conflict, a peace settlement gave Nice and Savoy to the French. Lombardy, which had been under Austrian control, was given to Piedmont. Austria retained control of Venetia. Cavour's success caused nationalists in other Italian states (Parma, Modena, and Tuscany) to overthrow their governments and join their states to Piedmont.

Meanwhile, in southern Italy, a new Italian leader had arisen. Giuseppe Garibaldi, a dedicated patriot, raised an army of a thousand volunteers. A branch of the Bourbon dynasty ruled the Two Sicilies (Sicily and Naples), and a revolt had broken out in Sicily against the king. Garibaldi's forces landed in Sicily and, by the end of July 1860, controlled most of the island. In August, Garibaldi's forces crossed over to the mainland and began a victorious march up the Italian Peninsula. The entire Kingdom of the Two Sicilies fell in early September.

Garibaldi chose to turn over his conquests to Piedmont. On March 17, 1861, a new state of Italy was proclaimed under King Victor Emmanuel II. The task of unification was not yet complete, however. Austria still held Venetia in the north; and Rome was under the control of the pope, supported by French troops.

The Italians gained control of Venetia as a result of supporting Prussia in a war between Austria and Prussia. In 1870, during the Franco-Prussian War, French troops withdrew from Rome. Their withdrawal enabled the Italian army to annex Rome on September 20, 1870. Rome became the capital of the new European state.

German Unification

After the Frankfurt Assembly failed to achieve German unification in 1848 and 1849, Germans looked to Prussia for leadership in the cause of German unification. In the course of the nineteenth century, Prussia had become a strong, prosperous, and authoritarian state. The Prussian king had firm control over the government and the army. Prussia was also known for its **militarism**, or reliance on military strength.

In the 1860s, King William I tried to enlarge the Prussian army. When the Prussian legislature refused to levy new taxes for the proposed changes, William I appointed a new prime minister, Count Otto von Bismarck.

Bismarck has often been seen as the foremost nineteenth-century practitioner of realpolitik—the "politics of reality," a politics based on practical matters rather than on ethics. Bismarck openly voiced his strong dislike for anyone who opposed him. After his appointment, Bismarck ignored the legislative opposition to the military reforms. He proceeded to collect taxes and strengthen the army. From 1862 to 1866, Bismarck governed Prussia without approval of the parliament. In the meantime, he followed an active foreign policy, which soon led to war.

After defeating Denmark with Austrian help in 1864, Prussia gained control of the duchies of Schleswig and Holstein. Bismarck then goaded the Austrians into a war on June 14, 1866. The Austrians, no match for the well-disciplined Prussian army, were defeated on July 3.

Prussia now organized the German states north of the Main River into the North German Confederation. The southern German states, which were largely Catholic, feared Protestant Prussia. However, they also feared France, their western neighbor. As a result, they agreed to sign military alliances with Prussia for protection against France.

Prussia now dominated all of northern Germany, and the growing power and military might of Prussia worried France. In 1870 Prussia and France became embroiled in a dispute over the candidacy of a relative of the Prussian king for the throne of Spain. Taking advantage of the situation, Bismarck pushed the French into declaring war on Prussia on July 19, 1870—a conflict called the Franco-Prussian War.

Prussian armies advanced into France. At Sedan, on September 2, 1870, an entire French army and the French ruler, Napoleon III, were captured. Paris finally surrendered on January 28, 1871. An official peace treaty was signed in May. France had to pay 5 billion francs (about $1 billion) and give up the provinces of Alsace and Lorraine to the new German state. The loss of these territories left the French burning for revenge.

Even before the war had ended, the southern German states had agreed to enter the North German Confederation. On January 18, 1871, Bismarck and 600 German princes, nobles, and generals filled the Hall of Mirrors in the palace of Versailles, 12 miles (19.3 km) outside Paris. William I of Prussia was proclaimed **kaiser**, or emperor, of the Second German Empire (the first was the medieval Holy Roman Empire).

The Prussian monarchy and the Prussian army had achieved German unity. The authoritarian and militaristic values of Prussia were triumphant in the new German state. With its industrial resources and military might, Germany had become the strongest power in Europe.

☑ **READING PROGRESS CHECK**

Explaining How did the Crimean War destroy the Concert of Europe?

Nationalism and Reform in Europe

GUIDING QUESTION *What were the political climates in Great Britain, France, Austria, and Russia?*

While Italy and Germany were being unified, other states in Europe were also experiencing changes.

Great Britain

Great Britain managed to avoid the revolutionary upheavals of the first half of the nineteenth century. In 1815 aristocratic landowning classes, which dominated both houses of Parliament, governed Great Britain. In 1832 Parliament passed a bill that increased the number of male voters. The new voters were chiefly members of the industrial middle class. By giving the industrial middle class an interest in ruling, Britain avoided revolution in 1848. In the 1850s and 1860s, Parliament made social and political reforms that helped the country remain stable. Another reason for Britain's stability was its continuing economic growth. By 1850, industrialization had brought prosperity to the British middle class. After 1850, real wages of workers also rose significantly.

Queen Victoria, whose reign from 1837 to 1901 was the longest in English history, reflected perfectly the national pride of the British. Her sense of duty and moral respectability came to define the values and attitudes of her age, which was later called the Victorian Age.

France

In France, events after the revolution of 1848 moved toward the restoration of the monarchy. Four years after his election as president in 1848, Louis-Napoleon returned to the people to ask for the restoration of the empire. In this **plebiscite**, or popular vote, 97 percent responded with a yes vote. On December 2, 1852, Louis-Napoleon assumed the title of Emperor Napoleon III (Napoleon II was the son of Napoleon Bonaparte, but he never ruled France). The Second Empire had begun.

militarism the reliance on military strength

kaiser German for "caesar"; the title of the emperors of the Second German Empire

▲ Great Britain's Queen Victoria in her coronation robes, 1838

PHOTO: Popperfoto/Getty Images

plebiscite a popular vote

The government of Napoleon III was clearly authoritarian. As chief of state, Napoleon III controlled the armed forces, police, and civil service. Only he could introduce legislation and declare war. The Legislative Corps gave an appearance of representative government, because the members of the group were elected by universal male suffrage for six-year terms. However, they could neither initiate legislation nor affect the budget.

Napoleon III completely controlled the government and limited civil liberties. To distract the public from their loss of political freedom, he focused on expanding the economy. Government subsidies helped foster the rapid construction of railroads, harbors, roads, and canals.

In the midst of this economic expansion, Napoleon III also carried out a vast rebuilding of the city of Paris. The old Paris of narrow streets and walls was replaced by a modern Paris of broad boulevards, spacious buildings, public squares, an underground sewage system, a new public water supply system, and gaslights.

regime the government in power

In the 1860s, opposition to some of Napoleon's economic and governmental policies arose. In response, Napoleon III began to liberalize his **regime**. For example, he gave the legislature more power. After the French were defeated in the Franco-Prussian War in 1870, however, the Second Empire fell.

The Austrian Empire

Nationalism was a major force in nineteenth-century Europe. However, one of Europe's most powerful states—the Austrian Empire—was a multinational empire that had been able to frustrate the desire of its ethnic groups for independence.

After the Hapsburg rulers crushed the revolutions of 1848 and 1849, they restored centralized, autocratic government to the empire. Austria's defeat at the hands of the Prussians in 1866, however, forced the Austrians to make concessions to the fiercely nationalistic Hungarians. The result was the Compromise of 1867, which created the dual monarchy of Austria-Hungary. Each of these two components of the empire now had its own constitution, its own legislature, its own government bureaucracy, and its own capital (Vienna for Austria and Budapest for Hungary). Holding the two states together were a single monarch—Francis Joseph was emperor of Austria and king of Hungary—and a common army, foreign policy, and system of finances.

Russia

At the beginning of the nineteenth century, Russia was still rural, agricultural, and autocratic. The Russian czar was regarded as a divine-right monarch with unlimited power. In 1856, however, the Russians suffered a humiliating defeat in the Crimean War. Even conservatives realized that Russia was falling hopelessly behind the western European states. Czar Alexander II decided to make some reforms.

Serfdom was the largest problem in czarist Russia. On March 3, 1861, Alexander issued an **emancipation** edict, which freed the serfs. Peasants could now own property. The government provided land for the peasants by buying it from the landlords. The new land system, however, was not very helpful to the peasants. The landowners often kept the best lands for themselves. The Russian peasants had little good land to support themselves. Emancipation, then, led not to a free, landowning peasantry but to an unhappy, land-starved peasantry that followed old ways of farming.

▼ Russian peasants in the late nineteenth century

▶ **CRITICAL THINKING**
Making Generalizations How does this image convey the possible living conditions of Russian peasants?

Alexander II attempted other reforms as well, but he could please no one. Reformers wanted more changes, but conservatives thought that the czar was destroying Russia's basic institutions. When radicals assassinated Alexander II in 1881, his son, Alexander III, turned against reform and returned to the old methods of repression.

emancipation the act of setting free

☑ **READING PROGRESS CHECK**

Examining What concessions did the Hungarians gain from the Compromise of 1867?

Nationalism in the United States

GUIDING QUESTION *How did nationalism influence events in the United States during the 1800s?*

The U.S. Constitution committed the nation to liberalism and nationalism. Yet unity did not come easily. Two factions fought bitterly about the division of power in the new government. The Federalists favored a strong central government. The Republicans wanted the federal government to be subordinate to the state governments.

By the mid-nineteenth century, slavery had become a threat to American unity. Four million enslaved African Americans were in the South by 1860, compared with one million in 1800.

The South's economy was based on growing cotton on plantations, chiefly by slave labor. The South was determined to maintain the cotton economy and plantation-based slavery. **Abolitionism**, a movement to end slavery, arose in the North and challenged the Southern way of life. As opinions over slavery grew more divided, compromise became less possible. Abraham Lincoln said in a speech in 1858 that "this government cannot endure, permanently half slave and half free." When Lincoln was elected president in November 1860, war became certain. In April, fighting erupted between North and South—the Union and the Confederacy.

abolitionism a movement to end slavery

The American Civil War (1861–1865) was a bloody struggle. Lincoln's Emancipation Proclamation declared most of the nation's enslaved people "forever free." The Confederate forces surrendered on April 9, 1865. The United States remained united, "one nation, indivisible."

☑ **READING PROGRESS CHECK**

Identifying What issues divided Americans in the 1800s?

LESSON 3 REVIEW

Reviewing Vocabulary
1. ***Making Connections*** Write a paragraph about the Civil War in which you define the terms *emancipation* and *abolitionism*. Indicate relationships between these terms.

Using Your Notes
2. ***Describing*** Use your graphic organizer to write a paragraph describing the changes and conflicts that took place in Great Britain, France, the Austrian Empire, and Russia during the nineteenth century.

Answering the Guiding Questions
3. ***Identifying Cause and Effect*** What led to the unification of Italy and Germany after the revolution of 1848?

4. ***Describing*** What were the political climates in Great Britain, France, Austria, and Russia?

5. ***Identifying Central Issues*** How did nationalism influence events in the United States during the 1800s?

Writing Activity
6. **INFORMATIVE/EXPLANATORY** Write an essay evaluating the nineteenth-century social reforms that took place in Great Britain, Russia, and the United States. Were the reforms successful? Did they contribute to the stability of these nations?

networks

There's More Online!

☑ **BIOGRAPHY** Antonio López de Santa Anna

☑ **BIOGRAPHY** José de San Martín

☑ **BIOGRAPHY** Simón Bolívar

☑ **IMAGE** Monopoly in Latin America

☑ **IMAGE** San Martín Crossing the Andes in 1817

☑ **INTERACTIVE SELF-CHECK QUIZ**

☑ **MAP** European Colonies in Latin America

☑ **VIDEO** Nation Building in Latin America

Reading **HELP**DESK

Academic Vocabulary

• intervention • erupt

Content Vocabulary

• creole   • *peninsulare*
• mestizo   • caudillo
• cash crop

TAKING NOTES:

Key Ideas and Details

Categorizing Use a graphic organizer like this one to record places where revolts occurred and the leaders and the outcomes of these revolts. Add rows as needed.

Revolts in Latin America

Place	Leader	Outcome

LESSON 4

Nation Building in Latin America

ESSENTIAL QUESTIONS • How can innovation affect ways of life?
• How does revolution bring about political and economic change?

IT MATTERS BECAUSE

The success of the American Revolution and the ideals of the French Revolution spread throughout Latin America. One by one, the Portuguese and Spanish colonies rebelled and won their independence. Political independence, however, was achieved more easily in the new republics than political stability.

Nationalist Revolts

GUIDING QUESTION *How were nationalist revolts in Latin America influenced by the French and American Revolutions?*

By the end of the eighteenth century, the new political ideals stemming from the successful American Revolution were beginning to influence the creole elites. **Creoles** were the descendants of Europeans who had permanently settled in Latin America. They controlled land and business and were attracted to the principles of equality of all people in the eyes of the law, free trade, and a free press. The creoles especially disliked the domination of their trade by Spain and Portugal.

The creole elites soon began to use their new ideas to denounce the rule of the Spanish and Portuguese monarchs and their *peninsulares* (Spanish and Portuguese officials who resided temporarily in Latin America for political and economic gain and then returned to their homeland). The creole elites resented the *peninsulares,* who dominated Latin America and drained the region of its wealth.

At the beginning of the nineteenth century, Napoleon's wars provided the creoles with an opportunity for change. When Napoleon overthrew the monarchies of Spain and Portugal, the authority of the Spaniards and Portuguese in their colonial empires was weakened. Then, between 1807 and 1825, a series of revolts enabled most of Latin America to become independent.

Revolt in Haiti

An unusual revolution occurred before the main independence movements. Saint Domingue—on the island of Hispaniola—was a French sugar colony. François-Dominique Toussaint-Louverture (too • SAN • loo • VUHR • TYUR) led more than 100,000 enslaved people in revolt. They seized control of all of Hispaniola. On January 1, 1804, the western part of Hispaniola, now called Haiti, became the first independent state in Latin America.

Revolt in Mexico

Beginning in 1810, Mexico also experienced a revolt. The first real hero of Mexican independence was Miguel Hidalgo. A parish priest, Hidalgo lived in a village about 100 miles (160 km) from Mexico City.

Hidalgo had studied the French Revolution. He roused the local Native Americans and **mestizos**, people of mixed European and Native American descent, to free themselves from the Spanish: "Will you be free? Will you make the effort to recover from the hated Spaniards the lands stolen from your forefathers, three hundred years ago?"

On September 16, 1810, Hidalgo led this ill-equipped army of thousands of Native Americans and mestizos in an attack against the Spaniards. His forces were soon crushed, and a military court later sentenced Hidalgo to death. However, his memory lives on even today. In fact, September 16, the first day of the uprising, is Mexico's Independence Day.

The role of Native Americans and mestizos in Mexico's revolt against Spanish control frightened the creoles and the *peninsulares*. Afraid of the masses, they cooperated in defeating the revolutionary forces. Creoles and *peninsulares* then decided to overthrow Spanish rule. These conservative elites wanted an independent nation ruled by a monarch. They selected a creole military leader, Agustín de Iturbide (EE • tur • BEE • thay), to set up a new government. In 1821 Mexico declared its independence from Spain. Iturbide named himself emperor in 1822 but was deposed in 1823. Mexico then became a republic.

Revolts in South America

José de San Martín of Argentina and Simón Bolívar of Venezuela, both members of the creole elite, were hailed as the "Liberators of South America." Bolívar began the struggle for Venezuelan independence in 1810. He also led revolts in New Granada (Colombia) and Ecuador. By 1819, these countries had formed Gran Colombia.

By 1810, the forces of San Martín had liberated Argentina from Spanish authority. In January 1817, San Martín led his forces over the Andes Mountains to attack the Spanish in Chile. The journey was an amazing feat. Two-thirds of the pack mules and horses died during the trip. Soldiers suffered from lack of oxygen and severe cold while crossing mountain passes more than two miles (3.2 km) above sea level.

The arrival of San Martín's forces in Chile completely surprised the Spanish forces there. As a result, they were badly defeated at the Battle of Chacabuco on February 12, 1817. Chile declared its independence in 1818. In 1821 San Martín advanced on Lima, Peru, the center of Spanish authority.

San Martín was convinced that he could not complete the liberation of Peru alone. He welcomed Simón Bolívar and his forces. Bolívar, the "Liberator of Venezuela," took on the task of crushing the last significant Spanish army at Ayacucho on December 9, 1824.

creole a person of European descent born in Latin America and living there permanently

peninsulare a person born on the Iberian Peninsula; typically, a Spanish or Portuguese official who resided temporarily in Latin America for political and economic gain and then returned to Europe

mestizo a person of mixed European and Native American descent

▼ General San Martín after crossing the Andes in 1817

By the end of 1824, Peru, Uruguay, Paraguay, Colombia, Venezuela, Argentina, Bolivia, and Chile had become free of Spain. Earlier, in 1822, the prince regent of Brazil had declared Brazil's independence from Portugal. The Central American states had become independent in 1823. In 1838 and 1839, they divided into five republics: Guatemala, El Salvador, Honduras, Costa Rica, and Nicaragua.

Threats to Independence

In the early 1820s, one major threat remained to the newly won independence of the Latin American states. Members of the Concert of Europe favored using troops to restore Spanish control in Latin America. The British, who wished to trade with Latin America, disagreed. They proposed joint action with the United States against any European moves against Latin America.

Distrustful of British motives, James Monroe, the president of the United States, acted alone in 1823. In the Monroe Doctrine, he declared that the Americas were off limits for any colonizational efforts, and strongly warned against any European **intervention** in the Americas.

More important to Latin American independence than American words, however, was the British navy. Other European powers feared the power of the British navy, which stood between Latin America and any planned European invasion force.

intervention the involvement in a situation to alter the outcome

☑ **READING PROGRESS CHECK**

Comparing What do Hidalgo, José de San Martín, and Simón Bolívar have in common?

Nation Building

GUIDING QUESTIONS *What difficulties did newly independent Latin American countries face? How did economic dependence on foreign investment influence Latin America through the mid-1800s?*

The new Latin American nations faced a number of serious problems between 1830 and 1870. The wars for independence had resulted in a staggering loss of people, property, and livestock. During the course of the nineteenth century, the new Latin American nations would become economically dependent on Western nations once again.

Rule of the Caudillos and Inequality

Most of the new nations of Latin America began with republican governments, but they had no experience in self-rule. Soon after independence, strong leaders known as **caudillos** gained power.

Caudillos ruled chiefly by military force and were usually supported by the landed elites. Many kept the new national states together. Some were also modernizers who built roads and canals, ports, and schools. Others were destructive.

Mexican General Antonio López de Santa Anna, for example, ruled Mexico from 1833 to 1855. He misused state funds, halted reforms, and created chaos. In 1835 American settlers in the Mexican state of Texas revolted against Santa Anna's rule. Texas gained its independence in 1836 and U.S. statehood in 1845. War between Mexico and the United States soon followed (1846–1848). Mexico was defeated and lost almost one-half of its territory to the United States.

Fortunately for Mexico, Santa Anna's disastrous rule was followed by a period of reform from 1855 to 1876. This era was dominated by Benito Juárez, a Mexican national hero. The son of Native American peasants,

caudillo in post-revolutionary Latin America, a strong leader who ruled chiefly by military force, usually with the support of the landed elite

President Juárez brought liberal reforms to Mexico, including separation of church and state, land distribution to the poor, and an educational system for all of Mexico.

Other caudillos, such as Juan Manuel de Rosas in Argentina, were supported by the masses. These caudillos became extremely popular and brought about radical change. Unfortunately, the caudillo's authority depended on his personal power. When he died or lost power, civil wars for control of the country often **erupted**.

A fundamental problem for all the new Latin American nations was the domination of society by the landed elites. Large estates remained a way of life in Latin America. By 1848, for example, the Sánchez Navarro family in Mexico possessed 17 estates made up of 16 million acres (6,480,000 ha).

Land remained the basis of wealth, social prestige, and political power throughout the nineteenth century. Landed elites ran governments, controlled courts, and kept a system of inexpensive labor. These landowners made enormous profits by growing single **cash crops**, such as coffee, for export. Most of the population had no land to grow basic food crops. As a result, the masses experienced dire poverty.

Imperialism and Economic Dependence

Political independence brought economic independence, but old patterns were quickly reestablished. Instead of Spain and Portugal, Great Britain now dominated the Latin American economy. British merchants moved into Latin America, and British investors poured in funds. Old trade relationships soon reemerged.

Latin America continued to serve as a source of raw materials and foodstuffs for the industrial nations of Europe and the United States. Exports included wheat, tobacco, wool, sugar, coffee, and hides. At the same time, Latin American countries imported finished consumer goods, especially textiles, and had limited industry.

The emphasis on exporting raw materials and importing finished products ensured the ongoing domination of the Latin American economy by foreigners. Latin American countries remained economically dependent on Western nations, even though they were no longer colonies.

☑ **READING PROGRESS CHECK**

Identifying Central Issues Why did Latin American countries continue to experience economic dependence after achieving political independence?

▲ Mexican General Antonio López de Santa Anna

erupt to suddenly become active or violent

cash crop a crop that is grown for sale rather than for personal use

PHOTO: ©North Wind Picture Archives/Alamy

LESSON 4 REVIEW

Reviewing Vocabulary
1. *Explaining* Give examples of three cash crops that were grown in Latin America and explain why they were cash crops.

Using Your Notes
2. *Generalizing* Use your graphic organizer on the revolts in Latin America to write a paragraph that makes a generalization about the successes or failures of the revolutions.

Answering the Guiding Questions
3. *Drawing Conclusions* How were nationalist revolts in Latin America influenced by the French and American Revolutions?

4. *Gathering Information* What difficulties did newly independent Latin American countries face?

5. *Identifying Cause and Effect* How did economic dependence on foreign investment influence Latin America through the mid-1800s?

Writing Activity
6. **NARRATIVE** Imagine you are a creole leader in Mexico at the time when Miguel Hidalgo is rousing the Native Americans and mestizos or leading them into battle. Write a diary entry that shows your feelings about the events you witness.

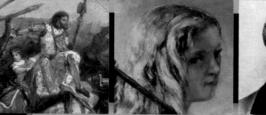

networks

There's More Online!

- ☑ **BIOGRAPHY** Charles Darwin
- ☑ **BIOGRAPHY** Charles Dickens
- ☑ **BIOGRAPHY** Louis Pasteur
- ☑ **BIOGRAPHY** Ludwig van Beethoven
- ☑ **IMAGE** Battle of Poitiers by Eugene Delacroix
- ☑ **IMAGE** Paris Opera House
- ☑ **IMAGE** The Old Mill by John Constable
- ☑ **INTERACTIVE SELF-CHECK QUIZ**
- ☑ **VIDEO** Romanticism and Realism

Reading **HELP**DESK

CCSS

Academic Vocabulary

- **individuality**
- **approach**

Content Vocabulary

- **romanticism**
- **secularization**
- **natural selection**
- **realism**

TAKING NOTES:

Key Ideas and Details

Listing Examples Use a table like this one to list examples of literature from the romantic and realist movements.

Romanticism	Realism

LESSON 5
Romanticism and Realism

ESSENTIAL QUESTIONS • *How can innovation affect ways of life?*
• *How does revolution bring about political and economic change?*

 IT MATTERS BECAUSE
Romanticism was a response to the Enlightenment and the Industrial Revolution. Romantics believed that emotions, rather than reason, should guide them. By the mid-nineteenth century, romanticism had given way to a new movement called realism. Realists focused on the everyday world and ordinary people.

Romanticism

GUIDING QUESTION *How did the idea of romanticism differ from those of the Enlightenment?*

At the end of the 1700s, a new intellectual movement, known as **romanticism**, emerged as a reaction to the ideas of the Enlightenment. The Enlightenment had stressed reason as the chief means for discovering truth. The romantics emphasized feelings, emotion, and imagination as sources of knowing.

Romantics valued individualism, or the belief in the uniqueness of each person. Many romantics rebelled against middle-class conventions. Male romantics grew long hair and beards, and men and women often wore outrageous clothes in order to express their **individuality**.

Many romantics had a passionate interest in past ages, especially the Middle Ages. Romantic architects revived medieval styles and built castles, cathedrals, city halls, parliamentary buildings, and railway stations in a style called neo-Gothic. The British Houses of Parliament in London are a prime example of this architectural style.

Romanticism in Art and Music

Romantic artists shared at least two features. First, to them, all art was a reflection of the artist's inner feelings. A painting should mirror the artist's vision of the world and be the instrument of the artist's imagination. Second, romantic artists abandoned classical reason for warmth and emotion.

Eugène Delacroix (DEH • luh • KWAH) was one of the most famous romantic painters from France. His paintings showed two chief characteristics: a fascination with the exotic and a passion for color. His works reflect his belief that "a painting is to be a feast to the eye."

In music, too, romantic trends dominated the first half of the nineteenth century. One of the most famous composers of this era was Ludwig van Beethoven. Beethoven's early work fell largely within the classical form of the eighteenth century. However, his *Third Symphony* embodied the elements of romanticism with powerful melodies that created dramatic intensity. For Beethoven, music had to reflect his deepest feelings: "I *must* write—for what weighs on my heart I *must* express."

Romanticism in Literature

The literary arts were deeply affected by the romantic interest in the past. Sir Walter Scott's *Ivanhoe*, for example, a best seller in the early nineteenth century, told of clashes between knights in medieval England. Many romantic writers chose medieval subjects and created stories that expressed their strong nationalism.

An attraction to the exotic and unfamiliar gave rise to Gothic literature. Chilling examples are Mary Shelley's novel *Frankenstein* in Britain and Edgar Allan Poe's short stories of horror in the United States. Some romantics even sought the unusual in their own lives. They explored their dreams and nightmares and sought to create altered states of consciousness.

The romantics viewed poetry as the direct expression of the soul. Romantic poetry gave expression to one of the most important characteristics of romanticism—its love of nature. Romantics believed that nature served as a mirror into which humans could look to learn about themselves. This is especially evident in the poetry of William Wordsworth, the foremost English romantic poet of nature. His experience of nature was almost mystical:

PRIMARY SOURCE

❝One impulse from a vernal wood
May teach you more of man,
Of moral evil and of good,
Than all the sages can.❞

—William Wordsworth, from *The Tables Turned*

The worship of nature also caused Wordsworth and other romantic poets to be critical of eighteenth-century science, which, they believed, had reduced nature to a cold object of study. To Wordsworth, the scientists' dry, mathematical **approach** left no room for the imagination or for the human soul. Many romantics were convinced that industrialization would cause people to become alienated, both from their inner selves and from the natural world.

☑ **READING PROGRESS CHECK**

Drawing Conclusions How did science and industrialization contribute to the development of romanticism's celebration of nature?

▲ *Battle of Poitiers* by Eugène Delacroix, 1830

▶ **CRITICAL THINKING**
Interpreting Significance Why might Delacroix have chosen to depict a scene from a French battle from 1356?

romanticism an intellectual movement that emerged at the end of the eighteenth century in reaction to the ideas of the Enlightenment; it stressed feelings, emotion, and imagination as sources of knowing

individuality a total character that distinguishes an individual from others

approach the way or method in which one examines or studies an issue or a concept

PHOTO: ©SuperStock/SuperStock

Dmitry Mendeleyev's discovery of recurring patterns in the properties of chemical elements is one of the foundations of modern chemistry. In 1869 when he proposed his periodic law, 70 elements were known. Before his death in 1907, Mendeleyev saw his predictions of the existence of several previously unknown elements confirmed. Since that time, many more elements have been discovered, bringing the total up to well over 100 today. Although electrons were discovered before Mendeleyev died, he had no idea of the complexity of the subatomic world, in which scientists have discovered more than 200 types of subatomic particles.

secularization indifference to or rejection of religion or religious consideration

natural selection the principle that some organisms are more adaptable to the environment than others

realism a mid-nineteenth century movement that rejected romanticism and sought to portray lower- and middle-class life as it actually was

New Age of Science

GUIDING QUESTION *How did advances in science influence life during the Industrial Revolution?*

The Scientific Revolution had created a modern, rational approach to the study of the natural world. For a long time, only the educated elite understood its importance. With the Industrial Revolution, however, came a heightened interest in scientific research. By the 1830s, new discoveries in science had led to benefits that affected all Europeans. Science came to have a greater and greater impact on people.

In biology, the Frenchman Louis Pasteur proposed the germ theory of disease, which was crucial to the development of modern scientific medical practices. In chemistry, the Russian Dmitry Mendeleyev in the 1860s classified all the material elements then known on the basis of their atomic weights. In physics, British scientist and inventor Michael Faraday put together a primitive generator that laid the foundation for the use of electric current.

Dramatic material benefits such as these led Europeans to have a growing faith in science. This faith, in turn, undermined the religious faith of many people. It is no accident that the nineteenth century was an age of increasing **secularization**, indifference to or rejection of religion in the affairs of the world. For many people, truth was now to be found in science and the concrete material existence of humans.

More than anyone else, it was Charles Darwin who promoted the idea that humans are material beings who are part of the natural world. In 1859 Darwin published *On the Origin of Species by Means of Natural Selection*. The basic idea of this book was that each species, or kind, of plant and animal had evolved over a long period of time from earlier, simpler forms of life. Darwin called this principle organic evolution.

How did this natural process work? According to Darwin, in every species, "many more individuals of each species are born than can possibly survive," which results in a "struggle for existence." Darwin believed that some organisms are born with variations, or differences, that make them more adaptable to their environment than other organisms, a process that Darwin called **natural selection**.

Those organisms that are naturally selected for survival reproduce and thrive. This is known as "survival of the fittest." In this process, the unfit do not survive. The fit that survive pass on the variations that enabled them to survive until, according to Darwin, a new, separate species emerges. In *The Descent of Man*, published in 1871, Darwin argued that human beings had animal origins and were not an exception to the rule governing the development of other species.

Darwin's ideas raised a storm of controversy. Some people did not take his ideas seriously. Other people objected that Darwin's theory made human beings ordinary products of nature rather than unique creations of God. Others were bothered by his idea of life as a mere struggle for survival. Some believers felt Darwin had not acknowledged God's role in creation. Some detractors scorned Darwin and depicted him unfavorably in cartoons. Gradually, however, many scientists and other intellectuals came to accept Darwin's theory. His theory changed thinking in countless fields from biology to anthropology.

✓ READING PROGRESS CHECK

Predicting Consequences Why might the scientific developments described in this lesson lead to increased secularization?

Realism

GUIDING QUESTION *What factors contributed to the movement known as realism?*

The belief that the world should be viewed realistically, a view often expressed after 1850, was closely related to the scientific outlook of the time. In politics, Bismarck practiced the "politics of reality." In the literary and visual arts, **realism** also became a movement.

The literary realists of the mid-nineteenth century rejected romanticism. They wanted to write about ordinary characters from life, not romantic heroes in exotic settings. They also tried to avoid emotional language by using precise description. They preferred novels to poems. Many literary realists combined their interest in everyday life with an examination of social issues. These artists expressed their social views through the characters in their novels.

The French author Gustave Flaubert, who was a leading novelist of the 1850s and 1860s, perfected the realist novel. His work *Madame Bovary* presents a critical description of small-town life in France. In Great Britain, Charles Dickens became a huge success with novels that showed the realities of life for the lower and middle classes in the early Industrial Age. Novels such as *Oliver Twist* and *David Copperfield* created a vivid picture of the brutal life of London's poor.

In art, too, realism became dominant after 1850. Realist artists sought to show the everyday life of ordinary people and the world of nature with photographic realism. The French became leaders in realist painting.

The French painter Gustave Courbet was the most famous artist of the realist school. He loved to portray scenes from everyday life. His subjects were factory workers and peasants. "I have never seen either angels or goddesses, so I am not interested in painting them," Courbet once commented. To Courbet, no subject was too ordinary.

☑ **READING PROGRESS CHECK**

Predicting Consequences Why might the work of realists, like Charles Dickens, have inspired social reform?

▲ *Girl with Seagulls* by Gustave Courbet, 1865

▶ **CRITICAL THINKING**
Comparing and Contrasting In what ways does this painting illustrate Courbet's rejection of romanticism?

LESSON 5 REVIEW

Reviewing Vocabulary
1. ***Describing*** How did the concepts of natural selection and secularization demonstrate a changing worldview?

Using Your Notes
2. ***Contrasting*** Using examples from your graphic organizer of literary works, write a paragraph contrasting the characteristics of romanticism and realism in literature.

Answering the Guiding Questions
3. ***Contrasting*** How did the ideas of romanticism differ from those of the Enlightenment?

4. ***Identifying Cause and Effect*** How did advances in science influence life during the Industrial Revolution?

5. ***Identifying Cause and Effect*** What factors contributed to the movement known as realism?

Writing Activity
6. **NARRATIVE** Write a paragraph describing some key event in your life using the style of the romantics or the realists.

Directions: On a separate sheet of paper, answer the questions below. Make sure you read carefully and answer all parts of the questions.

Lesson Review

Lesson 1

1 **DRAWING CONCLUSIONS** How might the working conditions in mines and mills have led the new industrial working class to support socialism?

Lesson 2

2 **SPECULATING** How did the Austrian government respond to demands for reform in early 1848, and how did its attitudes and actions change later?

Lesson 3

3 **IDENTIFYING CAUSE AND EFFECT** How did Britain's economic condition affect its political stability?

Lesson 4

4 **INTERPRETING** What were the motivations of Central and South American revolutionaries?

Lesson 5

5 **MAKING INFERENCES** In what ways did the individualism prized by the romantic movement differ from factory owners' attitudes toward workers?

21st Century Skills

6 **IDENTIFYING CAUSE AND EFFECT** Which were the first European countries to be industrialized after Great Britain and why?

7 **ECONOMICS** What benefits did foreign investors provide to newly independent Latin American countries? What were the drawbacks of foreign investment?

Exploring the Essential Questions

8 **SYNTHESIZING** With a partner, create a multimedia display of nineteenth-century changes and their causes in Europe, the United States, and Latin America. Include an example of technological, social, political, and economic change from each area. Provide a photo, drawing, or artifact that symbolizes each change and an audio or written explanation of the forces that led to it. You may also include primary sources.

DBQ Analyzing Historical Documents

Use the document to answer the following questions.

The British Parliament debated a bill that would ban factory owners from hiring children under the age of nine or working those children under sixteen longer than sixteen hours in a day.

PRIMARY SOURCE

" [Lord Kenyon] proceeded to enter into some detail of the evidence given before the committee, for the purpose of showing the injury that resulted to the health of the children, from being employed for 14, 15, or 16 hours a day in places heated to 80, 85 and nearly 90 degrees....

The Earl of Rosslyn said, . . . [it was] as an incontestible fact, that parents were the natural guardians of the health and prosperity of their own children, and that the legislature ought to be slow to interfere with free labour . . . "

—from the record of the House of Lords debate on the Cotton Factories Regulation Bill, June 14, 1819

9 **ANALYZING** What reason does the Earl of Rosslyn give for arguing against legislation that would protect child workers?

10 **EVALUATING** Is Lord Kenyon's evidence of children's working conditions in cotton mills believable?

Extended-Response Question

11 **INFORMATIVE/EXPLANATORY** How did the Industrial Revolution impact the formation of new economic and political systems in Europe? How did these systems compare with the absolutist and agricultural societies of the previous era?

Need Extra Help?

If You've Missed Question	**1**	**2**	**3**	**4**	**5**	**6**	**7**	**8**	**9**	**10**	**11**
Go to page	181	184	189	192	196	179	195	179	200	181	182

Mass Society and Democracy

1870–1914

ESSENTIAL QUESTIONS • *How can industrialization affect a country's economy?* • *How are political and social structures influenced by economic changes?*

The Story Matters...

The industrialization that began transforming Europe in the late 1700s had largely matured by a century later. Starting around 1850, the Second Industrial Revolution produced goods on a much larger scale. It created largely urban societies and a growing working class. This phase of industrialization also saw new advances in communications technology. A key figure was physicist and inventor Guglielmo Marconi.

◄ By applying research in electromagnetic waves, Marconi invented the wireless telegraph. Marconi is shown here with his invention, which became the basis of modern radio.

Place and Time: Europe 1870–1914

In the late 1800s, the European population increased in industrial areas. Workers migrated from the countryside to find employment in coal mines, factories, domestic service, and offices. Working-class families crowded into urban areas, where they struggled with insufficient housing and services. Urbanization often caused poverty, unemployment, the spread of disease, and political unrest. Between 1870 and 1914, Great Britain, France, and Germany gradually responded to the needs of their growing populace.

Step Into the Place

Read the quotes and look at the information presented on the map.

DBQ **Analyzing Historical Documents** What challenges did population growth and urbanization cause in Europe at the turn of the twentieth century?

PRIMARY SOURCE

❝For the next three months I was nearer to starvation than any time since. I learned the bitterness of a hopeless search for work….The best plan was to visit the wholesale firms in the City and get information about vacancies from the commercial travellers, and then journey as fast as the old horse buses allowed—perhaps right across London—only to find a queue of 150 to 200 applicants already there.❞

—Margaret Bondfield, from *A Life's Work*, on her unemployment before becoming one of the first female members of Parliament in Britain

PRIMARY SOURCE

❝It is like this in working-class families. The man, the one who after all has to work (*sic*), consumes the largest share of the available food. The children too have as much as possible. In most cases the mother is left out—she has to be satisfied with one or two mouthfuls if there is not enough to go round, and lives on bread, coffee, and potatoes. A working man's wife makes daily sacrifices for her family. She is happy if nobody shouts for more, even is [sic] she is still hungry herself.❞

—from Union of Construction Workers, Hamburg, Germany, 1908

Step Into the Time

Determining Cause and Effect
Choose an event from the time line and explain how it shows a consequence of the rise of mass society and democratic reforms.

1875 German Social Democratic Party emerges

1870 Women in Great Britain win the right to own some property

1876 Alexander Graham Bell invents telephone

1884 British Reform Act increases the number of adult male voters

EUROPE

THE WORLD

1870   1875   1880   1885

1876 Ottoman Empire's first Constitution

1884 Berlin West Africa conference opens

1885 Indian National Congress forms

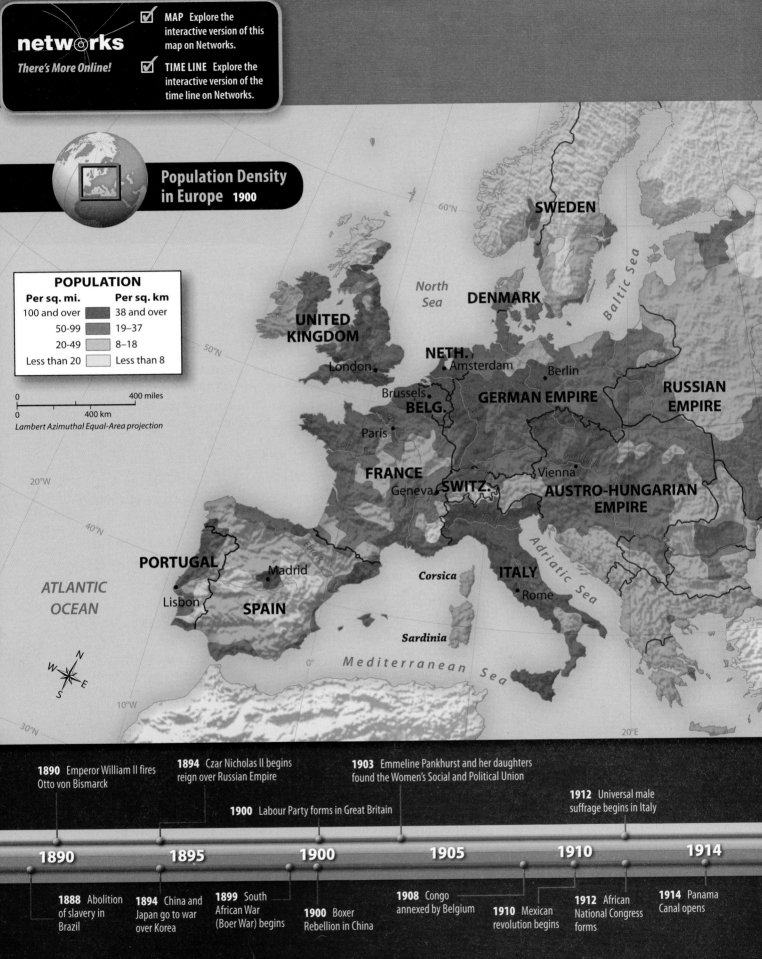

networks
There's More Online!

☑ **MAP** Explore the interactive version of this map on Networks.

☑ **TIME LINE** Explore the interactive version of the time line on Networks.

Population Density in Europe 1900

POPULATION

Per sq. mi.		Per sq. km
100 and over		38 and over
50-99		19–37
20-49		8–18
Less than 20		Less than 8

0 — 400 miles
0 — 400 km
Lambert Azimuthal Equal-Area projection

SWEDEN

North Sea

Baltic Sea

DENMARK

UNITED KINGDOM

London

NETH.

Amsterdam

Berlin

RUSSIAN EMPIRE

Brussels

BELG.

GERMAN EMPIRE

Paris

FRANCE

Geneva

SWITZ.

Vienna

AUSTRO-HUNGARIAN EMPIRE

20°W

40°N

PORTUGAL

Madrid

Corsica

ITALY

Rome

Adriatic Sea

ATLANTIC OCEAN

Lisbon

SPAIN

Sardinia

Mediterranean Sea

10°W

0°

20°E

30°N

1890 Emperor William II fires Otto von Bismarck

1894 Czar Nicholas II begins reign over Russian Empire

1903 Emmeline Pankhurst and her daughters found the Women's Social and Political Union

1912 Universal male suffrage begins in Italy

1900 Labour Party forms in Great Britain

1890 **1895** **1900** **1905** **1910** **1914**

1888 Abolition of slavery in Brazil

1894 China and Japan go to war over Korea

1899 South African War (Boer War) begins

1900 Boxer Rebellion in China

1908 Congo annexed by Belgium

1910 Mexican revolution begins

1912 African National Congress forms

1914 Panama Canal opens

Reading HELPDESK (CCSS)

Academic Vocabulary

• transition

Content Vocabulary

• **assembly line**
• **mass production**
• **bourgeoisie**
• **proletariat**
• **revisionists**

TAKING NOTES:

Key Ideas and Details

Identifying Cause and Effect As you read, use the organizer to show the effects of each innovation.

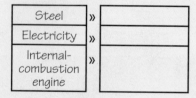

Steel	»	
Electricity	»	
Internal-combustion engine	»	

LESSON 1
The Growth of Industrial Prosperity

ESSENTIAL QUESTIONS
• *How can industrialization affect a country's economy?*
• *How are political and social structures influenced by economic changes?*

IT MATTERS BECAUSE

By the late 1800s, the Second Industrial Revolution transformed most of Europe into industrialized societies. However, the transition was not easy for workers. Many sought reform to improve their lives.

The Second Industrial Revolution

GUIDING QUESTION *What were the causes and effects of the Second Industrial Revolution in Western Europe?*

The first Industrial Revolution had given rise to textiles, railroads, iron, and coal. In the Second Industrial Revolution, steel, chemicals, electricity, and petroleum led the way to new industrial frontiers.

New Products and Patterns

In 1855 Sir Henry Bessemer patented a new process for making high-quality steel efficiently and cheaply known as the Bessemer process. Steel soon replaced iron and was used in the building of lighter, smaller, and faster machines and engines. It was also used in railways, ships, and weapons. In 1860 Great Britain, France, Germany, and Belgium produced 125,000 tons (112,500 t) of steel. By 1913, the total was an astounding 32 million tons (29 million t).

Electricity was a valuable new form of energy. It was easily converted into other energy forms, such as heat, light, and motion, and moved easily through wires. In the 1870s, the first practical generators of electrical current were developed. By 1910, hydroelectric power stations and coal-fired steam-generating plants connected homes and factories to a common source of power.

Electricity gave birth to a series of inventions. Homes and cities began to have electric lights when Thomas Edison in the United States and Joseph Swan in Great Britain created the lightbulb. A revolution in communications also began. Alexander Graham Bell invented the telephone in 1876. Guglielmo Marconi sent the first radio waves across the Atlantic Ocean in 1901.

By the 1880s, streetcars and subways powered by electricity had appeared in major European cities. Electricity transformed the factory as well. Conveyor belts, cranes, and machines could all be powered by electricity. With electric lights, factories could remain open 24 hours a day.

The development of the internal-combustion engine, fired by oil and gasoline, provided a new source of power in transportation. This engine gave rise to ocean liners with oil-fired engines, as well as to the airplane and the automobile. In 1903 Orville and Wilbur Wright made the first flight in a fixed-wing plane at Kitty Hawk, North Carolina. In 1919 the first regular passenger air service was established.

Industrial production grew at a rapid pace because of greatly increased sales of manufactured goods. Europeans could afford to buy more consumer products for several reasons. Wages for workers increased after 1870. In addition, prices for manufactured goods were lower because of reduced transportation costs. One of the biggest reasons for more efficient production was the **assembly line**, a new manufacturing method pioneered by Henry Ford in 1913. The assembly line allowed a much more efficient **mass production** of goods.

In the cities, the first department stores began to sell a new range of consumer goods. These goods—clocks, bicycles, electric lights, and typewriters, for example—were made possible by the steel and electrical industries.

Not everyone benefited from the Second Industrial Revolution. By 1900, Europe was divided into two economic zones. Great Britain, Belgium, France, the Netherlands, Germany, the western part of the

assembly line pioneered by Henry Ford in 1913, a manufacturing method that allowed much more efficient mass production of goods

mass production production of goods in quantity usually by machinery

GEOGRAPHY CONNECTION

1 **HUMAN SYSTEMS** What parts of Europe were the least industrialized?

2 **ENVIRONMENT AND SOCIETY** How do you think the environment was affected in areas of industrial concentration?

Industrialization in Europe 1914

Area of Industrial Concentration
• City
Industry:
Chemicals
Electricity
Petroleum
Steel

▲ Workers build Model T automobiles at a Ford assembly plant.

▶ **CRITICAL THINKING**
Making Connections How did the assembly line transform the car industry?

Connections to TODAY

Dependence on Raw Materials

Both the First and Second Industrial Revolution depended on vast imports of raw materials such as cotton (for textile manufacturing) and copper wire (for electricity). One legacy of the invention of the internal-combustion engine during the Second Industrial Revolution is today's dependence on a global trade in oil.

transition *changeover; the move from one form, stage, or style to another*

bourgeoisie *the middle class, including merchants, industrialists, and professional people*

proletariat *the working class*

Austro-Hungarian Empire, and northern Italy made up an advanced industrialized core. These nations had a high standard of living and adequate systems of transportation.

Another part of Europe to the south and east was still largely agricultural. It consisted of southern Italy, most of Austria-Hungary, Spain, Portugal, the Balkan kingdoms, and Russia. These countries provided food and raw materials for the industrial countries and had a much lower standard of living than the rest of Europe.

Toward a World Economy

The Second Industrial Revolution, combined with the growth of transportation by steamship and railroad, fostered a true world economy. By 1900, Europeans were receiving beef and wool from Argentina and Australia, coffee from Brazil, iron ore from Algeria, and sugar from Java.

European capital was also invested abroad to develop railways, mines, electrical power plants, and banks. Of course, foreign countries also provided markets for Europe's manufactured goods. With its capital, industries, and military might, Europe dominated the world economy by 1900.

☑ **READING PROGRESS CHECK**

Stating How were the effects of industrialization uneven across Europe?

Organizing the Working Classes

GUIDING QUESTION *How was socialism a response to industrialization?*

The **transition** to an industrialized society was very hard on workers. The desire to improve their working and living conditions led many industrial workers to form socialist political parties and socialist trade unions. The theory on which they were based had been developed by Karl Marx. One form of Marxist socialism was eventually called communism.

Marx's Theory

In 1848 *The Communist Manifesto* was published. It was written by two Germans, Karl Marx and Friedrich Engels, who were appalled at the horrible conditions in the industrial factories. They blamed the system of industrial capitalism for these conditions.

Marx believed that all of world history was a "history of class struggles." According to Marx, oppressor and oppressed have always "stood in constant opposition to one another." One group—the oppressors—owned the means of production, such as land, raw materials, and money. They controlled government and society. The other group—the oppressed—owned nothing and depended on the owners of the means of production.

Marx believed he saw a society that was "more and more splitting up into two great hostile camps, into two great classes directly facing each other: Bourgeoisie and Proletariat." The **bourgeoisie**—the middle class—were the oppressors. The **proletariat** (PROH • luh • TEHR • ee • uht)—the working class—were the oppressed.

PHOTO: © Culver Pictures, Inc. / SuperStock

Marx predicted that the struggle between the two groups would finally lead to a revolution. The proletariat would violently overthrow the bourgeoisie. After their victory, the proletariat would form a dictatorship to organize the means of production. However, because the proletariat victory would essentially abolish the economic differences that create separate social classes, Marx believed that the final revolution would ultimately produce a classless society. The state itself, which had been a tool of the bourgeoisie, would wither away.

Socialist Parties

In time, working-class leaders formed socialist parties based on Marx's ideas. Most important was the German Social Democratic Party (SPD), which emerged in 1875. Under the direction of its Marxist leaders, the SPD advocated revolution while organizing itself into a mass political party that competed in elections for the German parliament. When in parliament, SPD delegates worked to pass laws that would improve conditions for the working class. In spite of government efforts to destroy it, in 1912 the SPD became the largest single party in Germany.

Socialist parties also emerged in other European states. In 1889 leaders of the various socialist parties joined together and formed the Second International. This was an association of national socialist groups that would fight against capitalism worldwide.

Marxist parties were divided over their goals. Pure Marxists thought that capitalism could be defeated only by a violent revolution. Other Marxists, called **revisionists**, rejected the revolutionary approach. They argued that workers must continue to organize in mass political parties and even work with other parties to gain reforms. As workers received the vote, they could achieve their aims by working within democratic systems.

Trade Unions

Another force working for evolutionary, rather than revolutionary, socialism was the trade union, or labor union. To improve their conditions, workers organized in a union. The right to strike was an important part of the trade union movement. In a strike, a union calls on its members to stop work in order to pressure employers to meet their demands for higher wages or improved factory safety. At first, laws were passed that made strikes illegal under any circumstances. In Great Britain, unions won the right to strike in the 1870s. By 1914, there were almost 4 million workers in British trade unions. In the rest of Europe, trade unions had varying degrees of success in helping workers achieve a better life.

 READING PROGRESS CHECK

Identifying What issue divided pure Marxist socialists from revisionists?

▲ This German Social Democratic Party poster from 1904 proclaims "Proletarians of the World, Unite!"

▶ **CRITICAL THINKING**
Analyzing Visuals What does the poster convey about Marx's ideas?

revisionist a Marxist who rejected the revolutionary approach, believing instead in evolution by democratic means to achieve the goal of socialism

PHOTO: Bildarchiv Preussischer Kulturbesitz/Art Resource, NY

LESSON 1 REVIEW (CCSS)

Reviewing Vocabulary
1. *Speculating* What social and economic effects did mass production and the assembly line have on the bourgeoisie?

Using Your Notes
2. *Making Connections* Use your notes to write two paragraphs discussing the effects of technological breakthroughs on daily life and on world trade during the Second Industrial Revolution.

Answering the Guiding Questions
3. *Identifying Causes and Effects* What were the causes and effects of the Second Industrial Revolution in Western Europe?

4. *Inferring* How was socialism a response to industrialization?

Writing Activity
5. INFORMATIVE/EXPLANATORY Write a paragraph describing the obstacles that trade unions faced in their effort to improve labor conditions.

Mass Society and Democracy **207**

PHOTO: (l to r) Popperfoto/Getty Images, © Bettmann/CORBIS, The Granger Collection, NYC – All rights reserved, The Granger Collection, NYC.

networks

There's More Online!

☑ **IMAGE** Amusement Park in England, 1900

☑ **IMAGE** Emmeline Pankhurst

☑ **IMAGE** Domestic Servants, 1886

☑ **INTERACTIVE SELF-CHECK QUIZ**

☑ **VIDEO** The Emergence of Mass Society

Reading **HELP**DESK

Academic Vocabulary

• advocate

Content Vocabulary

• feminism • suffrage

TAKING NOTES:

Key Ideas and Details

Summarizing Use the graphic organizer to track the changes in each social class discussed in the lesson.

New Elite	Middle Class	Working Class

LESSON 2
The Emergence of Mass Society

ESSENTIAL QUESTIONS

• *How can industrialization affect a country's economy?*
• *How are political and social structures influenced by economic changes?*

IT MATTERS BECAUSE

By the end of the nineteenth century, the new industrial world had led to the emergence of a mass society in which the lower classes were demanding some governmental attention. Governments worked to improve public health and sanitation services in the cities. Women began to advocate for their rights, and many Western governments financed public education.

The New Urban Environment

GUIDING QUESTION *Why did European cities grow so quickly in the nineteenth century?*

With the emergence of a mass society, governments now had to consider how to appeal to the masses, rather than just to the wealthier citizens. Housing and public sanitation in the cities were two areas of great concern.

With few jobs available in the countryside, people from rural areas migrated to cities to find work in the factories. As a result, more and more people lived in cities. In the 1850s, urban dwellers made up about 40 percent of the English population, 15 percent in France, 10 percent in Prussia (Prussia was the largest German state), and 5 percent in Russia. By 1890, urban dwellers had increased to about 60 percent in England, 25 percent in France, 30 percent in Prussia, and 10 percent in Russia. In industrialized nations, cities grew tremendously. Between 1800 and 1900, the population in London grew from 960,000 to 6,500,000.

Cities also grew faster in the second half of the nineteenth century because of improvements in public health and sanitation. Improvements came in the 1840s after a number of urban reformers urged local governments to do something about the filthy living conditions that caused deadly epidemic diseases in the cities. Cholera (KAH • luh • ruh), for example, had ravaged Europe in the early 1830s and 1840s.

On the advice of reformers, city governments created boards of health to improve housing quality. City medical officers and building inspectors were authorized to inspect dwellings for public health hazards. Regulations required running water and internal drainage systems for new buildings.

Clean water and an effective sewage system were critical to public health. The need for freshwater was met by a system of dams and reservoirs that stored the water. Aqueducts and tunnels then carried water from the countryside to the city and into homes. Gas and electric heaters made regular hot baths possible. The treatment of sewage was improved by building underground pipes that carried raw sewage far from the city for disposal. A public campaign in Frankfurt, Germany, featured the slogan "from the toilet to the river in half an hour."

✓ **READING PROGRESS CHECK**

Theorizing Present three reasons for the growth of European cities in order of importance. Explain your answer.

Social Structure of Mass Society

GUIDING QUESTION *How did class divisions in Europe change during the nineteenth century?*

After 1871, most people enjoyed a higher standard of living. Still, great poverty remained in Western society. Between the few who were rich and the many who were poor existed several middle-class groups.

The New Elite

At the top of European society stood a wealthy elite. This group made up only 5 percent of the population but controlled from 30 to 40 percent of the wealth. During the 1800s, the most successful industrialists, bankers, and merchants—the wealthy upper-middle class—had joined with the landed aristocracy—the upper class—to form this new elite. Whether aristocratic or upper-middle class in background, members of the elite became leaders in the government and military.

The Diverse Middle Classes

While some members of the upper-middle class became part of the new elite, the rest of the middle class consisted of several groups at varying economic and social levels. Below the upper-middle class was a middle group that included lawyers, doctors, members of the civil service, business managers, engineers, architects, accountants, and chemists. Beneath this solid and comfortable middle group was a lower-middle class of small shopkeepers, traders, and prosperous farmers.

The Second Industrial Revolution produced a new group of white-collar workers between the lower-middle class and the lower classes. This group included traveling salespeople, bookkeepers, telephone operators, department store salespeople, and secretaries. Although not highly paid, these white-collar workers were often committed to middle-class ideals.

The middle classes shared a certain lifestyle with values that dominated much of nineteenth-century society. The European middle classes believed in hard work, which was open to everyone and guaranteed positive results. Outward appearances were also very important to the middle classes. The etiquette book *The Habits of Good Society* was a best seller.

The Working Classes

Below the middle classes on the social scale were the working classes—also referred to as the lower classes—which made up almost 80 percent of the

▲ These women and girls were domestic servants in a British home in 1886.

▶ **CRITICAL THINKING**
Drawing Conclusions To which social class did these women belong? What was the social class of their employer?

European population. These classes included landholding peasants, farm laborers, and sharecroppers.

The urban working class consisted of many different groups. They might be skilled artisans or semiskilled laborers, but many were unskilled day laborers or domestic servants. In Britain in 1900, one out of every seven employed persons was a domestic servant. Most servants were women.

After 1870, urban workers began to live more comfortably. Reforms created better living conditions in cities. In addition, a rise in wages, along with a decline in many consumer costs, made it possible for workers to buy extra clothes or pay to entertain themselves in their few leisure hours. In organizing and conducting strikes, workers had won the 10-hour workday with a Saturday afternoon off.

☑ **READING PROGRESS CHECK**

Categorizing Discuss the major social changes that occurred during the Second Industrial Revolution.

Women's Experiences

GUIDING QUESTION *How did the Second Industrial Revolution influence women's roles in society?*

In 1800 women were mainly defined by their families and household roles. In the nineteenth century, women struggled to change their status.

New Job Opportunities

During much of the nineteenth century, working-class groups maintained the belief that women should remain at home to bear and nurture children and should not be allowed in the industrial workforce.

The Second Industrial Revolution opened the door to new jobs for women. There were not enough men to fill the relatively low-paid, white-collar jobs being created. Both industrial plants and retail shops hired women as clerks, typists, secretaries, and salesclerks.

The expansion of government services also created job opportunities for women. Women took jobs in education, health, and social services. Middle-class women held these jobs, but they were mainly filled by the working class.

Marriage and the Family

As the chief family wage earners, men worked outside the home. Women were left to care for the family. Throughout the 1800s, marriage remained almost the only honorable and available career for most women. The number of children born to the average woman began to decline—the most significant development in the modern family. This decline was tied to improved economic conditions and increased use of birth control.

The family was the central institution of middle-class life. With fewer children in the family, mothers could devote more time to child care and domestic leisure. The middle-class family fostered an ideal of togetherness. The Victorians in Britain created the family Christmas with its Yule log, tree, songs, and exchange of gifts.

The lives of working-class women were different from those of their middle-class counterparts. Most working-class women had to earn money to help support their families. Their contributions made a big difference in the economic survival of their families. For the children of the working classes, childhood was over by the age of 9 or 10. By this age, children often became apprentices or were employed in odd jobs.

Between 1890 and 1914, family patterns among the working class began to change. Higher-paying jobs in heavy industry and improvements in the

standard of living made it possible for working-class families to depend on the income of husbands alone. By the early twentieth century, some working-class mothers could afford to stay at home, following the pattern of middle-class women. At the same time, working-class families aspired to buy new consumer products such as sewing machines and cast-iron stoves.

Women's Rights

Modern **feminism**, or the movement for women's rights, had its beginnings during the Enlightenment. At this time, some women **advocated** equality for women based on the doctrine of natural rights.

In the 1830s, a number of women in the United States and Europe argued for the right of women to own property. By law, a husband had almost total control over his wife's property. These early efforts were not very successful, however. Married women did not win the right to own some property until 1870 in Great Britain, 1900 in Germany, and 1907 in France.

The fight for property rights was only the beginning of the women's movement. Some middle- and upper-middle-class women fought for and gained access to universities. Others sought entry into occupations dominated by men. Although training to become doctors was largely closed to women, some entered the medical field by becoming nurses. The efforts of the British nurse Florence Nightingale, combined with those of Clara Barton in the U.S. Civil War, transformed nursing into a profession of trained, middle-class "women in white."

By the 1840s and 1850s, the movement for women's rights expanded as women called for equal political rights. They believed that **suffrage**, the right to vote, was the key to improving their overall position. Members of the women's movement, called suffragists, had one basic aim: the right of women to full citizenship in the nation-state.

The British women's movement was the most active in Europe. The Women's Social and Political Union, founded in 1903 by Emmeline Pankhurst and her daughters, used unusual publicity stunts to call attention to its demands. Its members pelted government officials with eggs, chained themselves to lampposts, and smashed department store windows. British police answered with arrests and brutal treatment of leading activists.

feminism the movement for women's rights

advocate to support; to speak in favor of

suffrage the right to vote

◀ Emmeline Pankhurst and her daughters try to enter Buckingham Palace to present a petition for women's rights to the King of England.

▶ **CRITICAL THINKING**
Drawing Conclusions Why did British police prevent the Pankhursts from entering Buckingham Palace?

PHOTO: © Bettmann/CORBIS

Mass Society and Democracy **211**

Before 1914, women had the right to vote in only a few nations, such as Norway and Finland, along with some American states. It took the upheaval of World War I to make governments give in on this basic issue.

☑ **READING PROGRESS CHECK**

Distinguishing How did the working-class family change in the late 1800s?

Education and Leisure

GUIDING QUESTION *How did society change as a result of urbanization and industrialization?*

Universal education was a product of the mass society of the late nineteenth and early twentieth centuries. Before that time, education was reserved mostly for the elite and the wealthier middle class. Between 1870 and 1914, most Western governments began to finance a system of primary education. Boys and girls between the ages of 6 and 12 were required to attend these schools.

Why did Western nations make this commitment to public education? One reason was industrialization. In the first Industrial Revolution, workers without training or experience were able to meet factory needs. The new firms of the Second Industrial Revolution needed trained, skilled workers.

The chief motive for public education was political. Giving more people the right to vote created a need for better-educated voters. Even more importantly, primary schools instilled patriotism.

Compulsory elementary education created a demand for teachers, and most of them were women. Many men saw teaching as a part of women's "natural role" as nurturers of children. Women were also paid lower salaries than men, which in itself was a strong incentive for states to set up teacher-training schools for women.

The Second Industrial Revolution allowed people to pursue new forms of leisure. Popular mass leisure both entertained large crowds and distracted them from the realities of work lives. Leisure came to be viewed as what people do for fun after work. The industrial system gave people new times—evening hours, weekends, and a week or two in the summer—to indulge in leisure activities. Amusement parks, dance halls, and organized team sports became enjoyable ways for people to spend their leisure hours.

☑ **READING PROGRESS CHECK**

Explaining What were some reasons governments promoted public education?

▼ At the turn of the twentieth century, Europeans enjoyed beaches and amusement parks such as this one at Blackpool on the Irish Sea in Lancashire, England.

▶ **CRITICAL THINKING**
Comparing and Contrasting Compare and contrast the amusement park at Blackpool with those of today.

PHOTO: The Granger Collection, NYC

LESSON 2 REVIEW (CCSS)

Reviewing Vocabulary
1. ***Determining Importance*** Why did members of the women's rights movement believe that suffrage was the key to improving the position of women in society?

Using Your Notes
2. ***Comparing*** Use your notes to write a paragraph detailing the changes in social structure that happened during the emergence of mass society.

Answering the Guiding Questions
3. ***Identifying Cause and Effect*** Why did European cities grow so quickly in the nineteenth century?

4. ***Identifying*** How did class divisions in Europe change during the nineteenth century?

5. ***Making Generalizations*** How did the Second Industrial Revolution influence women's roles in society?

6. ***Drawing Conclusions*** How did society change as a result of industrialization?

Writing Activity
7. **NARRATIVE** Assume the identity of a male member of the European middle class living in a big city in the year 1900. Write a diary entry in which you describe your day at work and what you looked forward to at home at the end of the day.

networks

There's More Online!

☑ **BIOGRAPHY** Czar Nicholas II

☑ **IMAGE** New York City, 1873

☑ **IMAGE** William II Fires Bismarck

☑ **INTERACTIVE SELF-CHECK QUIZ**

☑ **MAP** Europe, 1871

☑ **PRIMARY SOURCE** Labour Party Speech Before the House of Commons

☑ **PRIMARY SOURCE** Liberal Party Speech Before the House of Commons

☑ **VIDEO** The National State and Democracy

Reading HELPDESK CCSS

Academic Vocabulary

• insecure • controversy

Content Vocabulary

• **ministerial responsibility**
• **Duma**

TAKING NOTES:

Key Ideas and Details

Identifying As you read, use a table like the one below to list the different forms of European governments.

Nation	Form of Government
Great Britain	
France	
Germany	
Austria-Hungary	
Russia	

PHOTO: (l to r)© Bettmann/CORBIS, © A. H. C./Age Fotostock America, Library of Congress

LESSON 3
The National State and Democracy

ESSENTIAL QUESTION
How are political and social structures influenced by economic changes?

IT MATTERS BECAUSE

During the late 1800s and early 1900s, democracy expanded in Western Europe, while the old order preserved authoritarianism in central and eastern Europe. During this time, the United States recovered from the Civil War and became the world's richest nation. Meanwhile, international rivalries began to set the stage for World War I.

Western Europe: Political Democracy

GUIDING QUESTION *What happened with democracy in Western Europe in the late nineteenth century?*

By the late nineteenth century there were many signs that political democracy was expanding in Western Europe. First, universal male suffrage laws were passed. Second, the prime minister was responsible to the popularly elected legislative body, not to a king or president. This principle is called **ministerial responsibility** and is crucial for democracy. Third, mass political parties formed.

Great Britain had long had a working two-party parliamentary system. In a parliamentary system, the party with the greatest representation in parliament forms the government, the leader of which is the prime minister. The two parties—the Liberals and Conservatives—competed to pass laws that expanded the right to vote. Reform acts in 1867 and 1884 increased the number of adult male voters. By 1918, males over 21 and women over 30 could vote.

At the beginning of the twentieth century, then, political democracy was becoming well established in Britain. Social reforms for the working class soon followed. In 1900, a new Labour Party emerged and dedicated itself to the interests of workers. To retain the workers' support, the Liberals voted for social reforms, such as unemployment benefits and old-age pensions.

In France, the collapse of Louis-Napoleon's Second Empire left the country in confusion. Finally, in 1875, the Third Republic gained a republican constitution. The new government had a president and a two-house legislature. The upper house, or Senate, was elected by

Mass Society and Democracy **213**

Europe 1871

Legend:
- Austro-Hungarian Empire
- French Empire
- German Empire
- Kingdom of Italy
- Ottoman Empire
- Russian Empire

Lambert Azimuthal Equal-Area projection

GEOGRAPHY CONNECTION

In 1871 Europe was mostly controlled by large empires.

1 THE WORLD IN SPATIAL TERMS *Which empires had territory on more than one continent?*

2 HUMAN SYSTEMS *What do the country names tell you about democracy in Europe in 1871?*

ministerial responsibility the idea that the prime minister is responsible to the popularly elected legislative body and not to the king or president

high-ranking officials. All adult males voted for members of the lower house, the Chamber of Deputies. A premier (or prime minister), who led the government, was responsible to the Chamber of Deputies.

France failed to develop a strong parliamentary system. The existence of a dozen political parties forced the premier to depend on a coalition of parties to stay in power. Nevertheless, by 1914, the Third Republic had the loyalty of most voters.

Italy had emerged by 1870 as a united state. However, there was little national unity because of the gulf between the poverty-stricken south and the industrialized north. Turmoil between labor and industry weakened the social fabric of the nation. Even universal male suffrage, granted in 1912, did little to halt the widespread government corruption and weakness.

☑ READING PROGRESS CHECK

Comparing How did Italy's government in the 1870s compare to Great Britain's?

Central and Eastern Europe: The Old Order

GUIDING QUESTION *What political developments did Central and Eastern Europe experience in the late nineteenth century?*

Central and eastern Europe had more conservative governments than did Western Europe. In Germany, the Austro-Hungarian Empire, and Russia the old ruling groups continued to dominate politics.

The constitution of the new imperial Germany that Otto von Bismarck began in 1871 set up a two-house legislature. The lower house, the Reichstag, was elected on the basis of universal male suffrage. Ministers of government, however, were responsible not to the parliament but to the emperor, who controlled the armed forces, foreign policy, and the bureaucracy. As chancellor (prime minister), Bismarck worked to keep Germany from becoming a democracy.

By the reign of William II, kaiser from 1888 to 1918, Germany had become the strongest military and industrial power in Europe. With the expansion of industry and cities came demands for democracy.

Conservative forces—especially the nobility and big industrialists—tried to thwart the movement for democracy by supporting a strong foreign policy. They believed that expansion abroad would increase their profits and would also divert people from pursuing democratic reforms.

After the creation of the dual monarchy of Austria-Hungary in 1867, Austria adopted a constitution that, in theory, set up a parliamentary system with ministerial responsibility. In reality, the emperor, Francis Joseph, largely ignored this system. He appointed and dismissed his own ministers and issued decrees when the parliament was not in session.

The empire remained troubled by conflicts among its ethnic groups. A German minority governed Austria but felt increasingly threatened by Czechs, Poles, and other Slavic groups within the empire. Representatives of these groups in the parliament agitated for their freedom, which encouraged the emperor to ignore the parliament and govern by imperial decrees.

Unlike Austria, Hungary had a parliament that worked. It was controlled by landowners who dominated the peasants and ethnic groups.

In Russia, Nicholas II began his rule in 1894 believing that the absolute power of the czars should be preserved. Conditions were changing, however. By 1900, Russia had become the fourth-largest producer of steel. With industrialization came factories, an industrial working class, and pitiful working≈and living conditions. Socialist parties developed, but government repression forced them underground.

Growing discontent and opposition to the czarist regime finally exploded. On January 22, 1905, a massive procession of workers went to the Winter Palace in St. Petersburg to present a petition of grievances to the czar. Troops opened fire on the peaceful demonstration, killing hundreds. This "Bloody Sunday" caused workers throughout Russia to strike.

Nicholas II was eventually forced to grant civil liberties and to create a legislative assembly, the **Duma**. By 1907, the czar curtailed the power of the Duma and again used the army and bureaucracy to rule Russia.

☑ READING PROGRESS CHECK

Identifying Central Issues Did the government of Germany, Austria-Hungary, or Russia adhere to the principle of ministerial responsibility?

The United States

GUIDING QUESTION *How did the Second Industrial Revolution affect the United States?*

Four years of civil war had preserved the American nation, but the old South had been destroyed. In 1865 the Thirteenth Amendment to the Constitution was passed, abolishing slavery. Later, the Fourteenth and Fifteenth Amendments gave citizenship to African Americans and the right to vote to African American males. New state laws in the South, however, soon stripped African Americans of the right to vote. By 1880, supporters of white supremacy were back in power everywhere in the South.

Between 1860 and 1914, the United States shifted from a farm-based economy to an industrial economy. American steel and iron

Duma the Russian legislative assembly

▼ At the beginning of his rule, Czar Nicholas II said, "I shall maintain the principle of autocracy just as firmly and unflinchingly as did my unforgettable father."

▶ **CRITICAL THINKING**
Drawing Conclusions What changes in Russia challenged the autocracy of the czar?

production was the best in the world in 1900. Industrialization led to urbanization. By 1900, the United States had three cities with populations of more than 1 million, with New York reaching 4 million.

In 1900 the United States was the world's richest nation, but the richest 9 percent of Americans owned 71 percent of the wealth. Many workers labored in unsafe factories, and devastating cycles of unemployment made them **insecure**. Many tried to organize unions, but the American Federation of Labor represented only 8.4 percent of the labor force.

In the late 1800s, the United States began to expand abroad. The Samoan Islands in the Pacific were the first important U.S. colony. By 1887, Americans controlled the sugar industry on the Hawaiian Islands. As more Americans settled in Hawaii, they wanted political power. When Queen Liliuokalani (lih • LEE • uh • woh • kuh • LAH • nee) tried to strengthen the monarchy to keep the islands under her people's control, the United States sent military forces to the islands. The queen was deposed and the United States annexed Hawaii in 1898. In 1898 the United States defeated Spain in the Spanish-American War. As a result, the United States acquired the former Spanish possessions of Puerto Rico, Guam, and the Philippines.

✔ READING PROGRESS CHECK

Analyzing How did the U.S. Civil War affect African Americans?

International Rivalries

GUIDING QUESTION *How did international rivalries push Europe close to war?*

Otto von Bismarck realized that Germany's emergence in 1871 as the most powerful state in continental Europe had upset the balance of power established at Vienna in 1815. Fearing that France intended to create an anti-German alliance, Bismarck made a defensive alliance with Austria-Hungary in 1879. In 1882 Italy joined this alliance.

This Triple Alliance thus united the powers of Germany, Austria-Hungary, and Italy in a defensive alliance against France. At the same time, Bismarck maintained a separate treaty with Russia.

New Directions: William II

In 1890 Kaiser William II fired Bismarck and took control of Germany's foreign policy. The kaiser embarked on an activist policy dedicated to enhancing German power. He wanted, as he put it, to find Germany's rightful "place in the sun."

One of the changes William made in foreign policy was to drop the treaty with Russia. Almost immediately, in 1894, France formed an alliance with Russia. Germany thus had a hostile power on her western border and on her eastern border—exactly the situation Bismarck had feared!

Over the next decade, German policies caused the British to draw closer to

---

POLITICAL CARTOON

WILLIAM II FIRES BISMARCK

In this political cartoon, Emperor William II (seated) dismisses Otto von Bismarck (standing), while Germany, represented by the figure in the background, looks on.

▶ CRITICAL THINKING

1 *Analyzing Visuals* Of what is Wiilliam II's throne constructed?

2 *Determining Cause and Effect* According to the cartoonist, what consequences might result from the firing of Bismarck?

insecure uncertain, shaky; not adequately covered or sustained

France. By 1907, an alliance of Great Britain, France, and Russia—the Triple Entente—stood opposed to the Triple Alliance. Europe was now dangerously divided into two opposing camps unwilling to compromise.

Crises in the Balkans

In the 1800s, the Ottoman Empire began to fall apart. Most of its Balkan provinces gained their freedom. As this was happening, two Great Powers saw their chance to gain influence in the Balkans: Austria-Hungary and Russia. Their rivalry over the Balkans was one of the causes of World War I.

By 1878, Greece, Serbia, Romania, and Montenegro had become independent. Bulgaria was not independent but was allowed to operate autonomously under Russian protection. The Balkan territories of Bosnia and Herzegovina were placed under the protection of Austria-Hungary.

In 1908 Austria-Hungary took the drastic step of annexing Bosnia and Herzegovina. Serbia was outraged. The annexation of Bosnia and Herzegovina, two Slavic-speaking territories, led to an international **controversy** and dashed the Serbians' hopes of creating a large Serbian kingdom that would include most of the southern Slavs.

The Russians, self-appointed protectors of their fellow Slavs, supported the Serbs and opposed the annexation. Backed by the Russians, the Serbs prepared for war against Austria-Hungary. At this point, Emperor William II of Germany demanded that the Russians accept Austria-Hungary's annexation of Bosnia and Herzegovina or face war with Germany.

Weakened from their defeat in the Russo-Japanese War in 1905, the Russians backed down but vowed revenge. Two wars between Balkan states in 1912 and 1913 further embittered the inhabitants and created more tensions among the Great Powers.

The Serbs blamed Austria-Hungary for their failure to create a large Serbian kingdom. Austria-Hungary was convinced that Serbia and Serbian nationalism were mortal threats to its empire and must be crushed.

As Serbia's chief supporters, the Russians were angry and determined not to back down again in the event of another confrontation with Austria-Hungary or Germany in the Balkans. Finally, the allies of Austria-Hungary and Russia were determined to support their respective allies more strongly in another crisis. By the beginning of 1914, these countries viewed each other with suspicion. Europe was on the verge of war.

☑ **READING PROGRESS CHECK**

Sequencing Describe the events in the Balkans up through 1914.

Triple Alliance, 1882
• Germany
• Austria-Hungary
• Italy

Triple Entente, 1907
• Great Britain
• France
• Russia

▶ **CRITICAL THINKING**

1 *Transferring Knowledge* Create a political map that shows the Triple Alliance and the Triple Entente.

2 *Interpreting Significance* How did these alliances help create a crisis in the Balkans?

controversy a dispute or quarrel

LESSON 3 REVIEW

Reviewing Vocabulary
1. *Identifying* What is ministerial responsibility, and why is it important?

Using Your Notes
2. *Summarizing* Using the information in your notes, list the forms of government in Great Britain, France, Germany, Austria-Hungary, and Russia.

Answering the Guiding Questions
3. *Making Generalizations* What happened with democracy in Western Europe in the late nineteenth century?

4. *Drawing Conclusions* What political developments did Central and Eastern Europe experience in the late nineteenth century?

5. *Explaining* How did the Second Industrial Revolution affect the United States?

6. *Making Connections* How did international rivalries push Europe close to war?

Writing Activity
7. **INFORMATIVE/EXPLANATORY** Write a short paragraph about the impact of labor issues in Great Britain and Russia.

netw☺rks

There's More Online!

- ☑ **BIOGRAPHY** Marie Curie
- ☑ **BIOGRAPHY** Albert Einstein
- ☑ **BIOGRAPHY** Sigmund Freud
- ☑ **IMAGE** Id, Ego, and Superego
- ☑ **INFOGRAPHIC** Advancements in Chemistry and Physics
- ☑ **INTERACTIVE SELF-CHECK QUIZ**
- ☑ **PRIMARY SOURCE** J'accuse
- ☑ **SLIDE SHOW** Modern Painting and Architecture
- ☑ **VIDEO** Modern Ideas and Uncertainty

Reading **HELP**DESK (CCSS)

Academic Vocabulary

- abstract
- intensity

Content Vocabulary

- **modernism**
- **psychoanalysis**
- **Social Darwinism**
- **pogroms**
- **Zionism**

TAKING NOTES:

Key Ideas and Details

Organizing Use the following graphic organizer to name an artist and a characteristic of the art movement indicated.

Movement	Artist	Characteristic
Impressionist		
Post-impressionist		
Cubist		
Abstract		

LESSON 4
Modern Ideas and Uncertainty

ESSENTIAL QUESTION *How are political and social structures influenced by economic changes?*

IT MATTERS BECAUSE
During the late nineteenth and early twentieth centuries, people moved toward a modern consciousness. Their changing worldview was expressed in new art movements, while developments in the sciences also changed how people saw themselves and their world.

The Culture of Modernity

GUIDING QUESTION *How did innovation change literature, the visual arts, and music in the late 1800s and early 1900s?*

Between 1870 and 1914, many writers and artists rebelled against the traditional literary and artistic styles that had dominated European cultural life since the Renaissance. The changes they produced have since been called **modernism**.

Literature

Western novelists and poets who followed the naturalist style believed that literature should be realistic and address social problems. Henrik Ibsen and Émile Zola, for example, explored the role of women in society, alcoholism, and urban slums in their work.

The symbolist writers had a different idea about what was real. They believed the external world, including art, was only a collection of symbols reflecting the true reality—the human mind. Art, the symbolists believed, should function for its own sake, not criticize or seek to understand society.

Painting and Architecture

Since the Renaissance, Western artists had tried to represent reality as accurately as possible. By the late 1800s, artists were seeking new forms of expression to reflect their changing worldviews. Impressionism was a movement that began in France in the 1870s, when a group of artists rejected indoor studios and went to the countryside to paint nature directly. One important impressionist was Claude Monet (moh • NAY), who painted pictures that captured the interplay of light, water, and sky.

In the 1880s, a new movement, known as postimpressionism, arose in France and soon spread. For Vincent van Gogh, art was a spiritual experience. He was especially interested in color and believed that it could act as its own form of language. Van Gogh maintained that artists should paint what they feel.

By the early 1900s, artists were no longer convinced that their main goal was to represent reality. This was especially true in the visual arts. One reason for the decline of realism in painting was photography, which became popular after George Eastman created the Kodak camera in 1888.

Artists tended to focus less on mirroring reality, which the camera could do, and more on creating reality. Painters and sculptors, like the symbolist writers of the time, looked for meaning in individual consciousness. Between 1905 and 1914, this search for expression created modern art.

By 1905, Pablo Picasso, an important figure in modern art, was beginning his career. Picasso created a new artistic style—cubism. Cubism used geometric designs to re-create reality in the viewer's mind.

Abstract painting emerged around 1910. Wassily Kandinsky, a Russian, was one of the first to use an abstract style. Kandinsky sought to avoid visual reality altogether. He believed that art should speak directly to the soul. To do so, it must use only line and color.

Modernism in the arts revolutionized architecture and gave rise to functionalism. Functionalism was the idea that buildings, like the products of machines, should be functional, or useful. All unnecessary ornamentation should be stripped away. Architects, led by Louis H. Sullivan, used reinforced concrete, steel frames, and electric elevators to build skyscrapers virtually free of ornamentation.

modernism a movement in which writers and artists between 1870 and 1914 rebelled against the traditional literary and artistic styles that had dominated European cultural life since the Renaissance

abstract a style of art, emerging around 1910, that spoke directly to the soul and avoided visual reality by using only lines and color

ANALYZING PRIMARY SOURCES (CCSS)

▲ Claude Monet, *Haystacks*, 1891

▲ Pablo Picasso, *Houses on the Hill*, 1909

Impressionism and Cubism: Monet and Picasso

Contrast these two landscape paintings by impressionist Claude Monet (left) and cubist Pablo Picasso (right). Impressionists presented their impression of a scene at a specific moment in time. In Haystacks, *Monet captures the constantly shifting light and color of the natural world. Cubist painters built on the abstraction of impressionist art and took it considerably further. In* Houses on the Hill, *Picasso distills a landscape scene into its underlying geometric shapes.*

DBQ **Analyzing Historical Documents**

❶ *Examining* What techniques does Monet use to convey this rural landscape? Consider features of the painting such as Monet's brushstrokes as well as his choices of color, shape, and composition.

❷ *Comparing and Contrasting* In what ways are Impressionism and Cubism similar? In what ways are they different? Refer to these two paintings to defend your claims.

Music

At the beginning of the twentieth century, developments in music paralleled those in painting. The music of the Russian composer Igor Stravinsky exploited expressive sounds and bold rhythms.

Stravinsky's ballet *The Rite of Spring* revolutionized music. When it was performed in Paris in 1913, the sounds and rhythms of the music and dance caused a near riot by an outraged audience.

☑ READING PROGRESS CHECK

Explaining Why did modern artists turn away from realism?

Uncertainty Grows

GUIDING QUESTION *How did scientific discoveries in the late 1800s impact the way people saw themselves and their world?*

Science was one of the chief pillars supporting the worldview of many Westerners in the nineteenth century. Many believed that by applying scientific laws, humans could understand the physical world and reality.

Curie and the Atom

Throughout much of the 1800s, Westerners believed in a mechanical conception of the universe that was based on the ideas of Isaac Newton. The universe was viewed as a giant machine. Time, space, and matter were objective realities existing independently of those observing them. Matter was thought to be made of solid material bodies called atoms.

These views were seriously questioned at the end of the nineteenth century. The French scientist Marie Curie discovered that an element called radium gave off energy, or radiation, that apparently came from within the atom itself. Atoms were not just material bodies but small, active worlds.

Einstein and Relativity

In the early twentieth century, Albert Einstein, a German-born scientist, provided a new view of the universe. His special theory of relativity stated that space and time are not absolute but are relative to the observer.

According to this theory, neither space nor time has an existence independent of human experience. Moreover, matter and energy reflect the relativity of time and space. Einstein concluded that matter is just another form of energy. The vast energies contained within the atom were explained. To some, however, a relative universe was one without certainty.

Freud and Psychoanalysis

Sigmund Freud (FROYD), a doctor from Vienna, proposed theories regarding the nature of the human mind. His major theories were published in 1900 in *The Interpretation of Dreams*.

According to Freud, human behavior was strongly determined by past experiences and internal forces of which people were largely unaware. Repression of such experiences began in childhood, so he devised a method—known as **psychoanalysis**—by which a therapist could probe deeply into the patient's memory. In this way, they could retrace the repressed thoughts all the way back to their childhood origins. If the patient's conscious mind could be made aware of the unconscious and its repressed contents, the patient could be healed.

☑ READING PROGRESS CHECK

Explaining According to Freud, what determines much of human behavior?

▲ Marie Curie was the first woman to win a Nobel Prize. With her husband, she was awarded half the Nobel Prize for Physics in 1903 for their study in radiation.

▶ CRITICAL THINKING

Contrasting How was the practice of science different at the turn of the twentieth century than it is today?

psychoanalysis a method by which a therapist and patient probe deeply into the patient's memory; by making the patient's conscious mind aware of repressed thoughts, healing can take place

Extreme Nationalism

GUIDING QUESTION *What role did nationalism play in the late 1800s?*

Nationalism became more intense in many countries in the late 1800s. **Social Darwinism** was the radical belief that Darwin's theory of natural selection could be applied to modern human societies. A British philosopher, Herbert Spencer, argued that social progress came from "the survival of the fittest"—that is, the strong advanced while the weak declined. This kind of thinking allowed some people to reject the idea that they should take care of the less fortunate.

Extreme nationalists also used Social Darwinism. They said that nations, too, were engaged in a "struggle for existence" in which only the fittest nations would survive. This idea was also used to justify racism, or the belief that some peoples were superior to others.

The growth of extreme nationalism and racism also led to the growth of anti-Semitism, or hostility toward and discrimination against Jews. The **intensity** of anti-Semitism was evident from the Dreyfus affair in France. In 1894, a military court found Alfred Dreyfus, a Jewish captain in the French general staff, guilty of selling army secrets. After the trial, evidence emerged that proved Dreyfus innocent. A wave of public outcry finally forced the government to pardon Dreyfus in 1899.

The worst treatment of Jews at the turn of the century occurred in Russia. Persecutions and **pogroms**, or organized massacres, were widespread. Hundreds of thousands of Jews decided to emigrate to escape the persecution. Some Jews, probably about 25,000, immigrated to Palestine, which became home for a Jewish nationalist movement called **Zionism**.

For many Jews, Palestine, the land of ancient Israel, had long been the land of their dreams. A key figure in the growth of political Zionism was Theodor Herzl, who stated in his book *The Jewish State* (1896), "The Jews who wish it will have their state." Settlement in Palestine was difficult, however, because it was then part of the Ottoman Empire, which was opposed to Jewish immigration. Although 3,000 Jews went annually to Palestine between 1904 and 1914, the Zionist desire for a homeland in Palestine remained only a dream on the eve of World War I.

Social Darwinism theory used by Western nations in the late nineteenth century to justify their dominance; it was based on Charles Darwin's theory of natural selection, "the survival of the fittest," and applied to modern human activities

intensity extreme degree of strength, force, energy, or feeling

pogrom the organized massacre of a minority group, especially Jews

Zionism an international movement originally for the establishment of a Jewish national homeland in Palestine, where ancient Israel was located, and later for the support of modern Israel

☑ **READING PROGRESS CHECK**

Analyzing How did the Dreyfus affair illustrate anti-Semitism in France?

LESSON 4 REVIEW

Reviewing Vocabulary

1. *Synthesizing* Write a paragraph on European nationalism and persecution in the late nineteenth and early twentieth centuries in which you define the terms *pogrom* and *Zionism*.

Using Your Notes

2. *Identifying* Use your notes to name four artists and identify characteristics of the art movements in which they participated.

Answering the Guiding Questions

3. *Evaluating* How did innovation change literature, the visual arts, and music in the late 1800s?

4. *Identifying Central Issues* How did scientific discoveries in the late 1800s impact the way people saw themselves and their world?

5. *Drawing Conclusions* What role did nationalism play in the late 1800s?

Writing Activity

6. **INFORMATIVE/EXPLANATORY** Write a paragraph in which you explore how modern artistic and scientific ideas could lead to an understanding of the world as less certain than was previously believed but also, perhaps, as more exciting. Discuss at least one example of an artist and one example of a scientist.

Directions: On a separate sheet of paper, answer the questions below. Make sure you read carefully and answer all parts of the questions.

Lesson Review

Lesson 1

1 **COMPARING AND CONTRASTING** What did the first and second Industrial Revolutions have in common? In what ways did they differ?

2 **SUMMARIZING** What qualities of socialism appealed to working-class people?

Lesson 2

3 **EXPLORING ISSUES** What problems were created by the rapid population growth in cities?

4 **MAKING INFERENCES** When did public education become widespread and why had it not happened earlier?

Lesson 3

5 **EXPLAINING** How did ministerial responsibility relate to how power was distributed in Central Europe?

6 **IDENTIFYING CENTRAL ISSUES** How was wealth distributed among U.S. citizens?

Lesson 4

7 **CLASSIFYING** Describe two painting styles that became popular in the late nineteenth or early twentieth century.

8 **SPECULATING** How might extreme nationalists' perception of themselves lead them to believe in Social Darwinism?

21st Century Skills

9 **ECONOMICS** Why did some parts of Europe not share in the economic boom of the early twentieth century?

10 **UNDERSTANDING RELATIONSHIPS AMONG EVENTS** What were some of the signs that democracy was expanding in the late nineteenth century? What were some reasons for that expansion?

Exploring the Essential Questions

11 **SYNTHESIZING** Create a word web with *Industrialization* in the center. Draw arrows to two circles, labeled *Strong Economy* and *Weak Economy*. Draw arrows from them to circles showing which political and social structures were influenced by economic changes in 1870–1914. Explain each of the connections.

DBQ Analyzing Historical Documents

Use the document to answer the following questions.

Emmeline Pankhurst explained in a 1913 speech why it was so important for women to have a voice in their government.

> **PRIMARY SOURCE**
>
> " I wonder that women have the courage to take upon themselves the responsibilities of marriage and motherhood when I see how little protection the law of my country affords them. I wonder that a woman will face the ordeal of childbirth with the knowledge that after she has risked her life to bring a child into the world she has absolutely no parental rights over the future of that child. "
>
> —quoted in *Sources of the Western Tradition, Volume II: From the Renaissance to the Present*

12 **ANALYZING** What personality trait is Pankhurst amazed that women have? Why do they need that trait?

13 **DRAWING CONCLUSIONS** How does Pankhurst's description of women's lack of rights fit with the Lesson 2 discussion of women's experiences?

Extended-Response Question

14 **INFORMATIVE/EXPLANATORY** How do the living conditions of the masses of people affect how a nation is ruled? How does a move toward democracy affect the living conditions of the masses?

Need Extra Help?

If You've Missed Question	**1**	**2**	**3**	**4**	**5**	**6**	**7**	**8**	**9**	**10**	**11**	**12**	**13**	**14**
Go to page	204	206	208	212	213	216	218	221	206	213	204	222	222	208

The Reach of Imperialism

1800–1914

ESSENTIAL QUESTIONS • *What are the causes and effects of imperialism?*
• *How do some groups resist control by others?*

The Story Matters...

After 1870 the industrialized nations of Europe engaged in an unprecedented competition to acquire overseas colonies. A struggle for economic and military power largely motivated this intense rivalry, which historians refer to as the "new imperialism." The "Jewel in the Crown" of the vast British Empire was India. The British attempted to dominate every aspect of Indian life, including the culture. One Indian who resisted this cultural imperialism was the Bengali writer Rabindranath Tagore.

◄ This photograph shows Tagore in 1929, when he was nearly 70. Although a passionate nationalist, he nevertheless strove for a balance between modern Western influence and ancient Indian traditions. One expression of this effort was his habit of writing his poetry first in Bengali and then translating it into English.

PHOTO: Bettmann/CORBIS

223

Place and Time: Asia and Africa 1800–1914

The nineteenth century was known for a new wave of imperialism as European powers, Japan, and the United States seized control of new territories and conquered peoples in Asia and Africa. The race for new colonies was fueled by competition among the European powers, nationalism, demand for raw materials, superior technology, and a belief in racial hierarchies. In Latin America, independence movements struggling to throw off Spanish authority succeeded by the mid-nineteenth century.

Step Into the Place

Read the quotes and look at the information presented on the map.

 Analyzing Historical Documents In 1893 Frederick Lugard was arguing for more funding for African colonies, while journalists like Edmund Morel argued against the practice. What were the central motivations for imperialism, and what were the perceived costs to conquered peoples?

PRIMARY SOURCE

❝We owe to the instincts of colonial expansion of our ancestors, those vast and noble dependencies which are our pride and the outlets of our trade to-day; and we are accountable to posterity that opportunities which now present themselves of extending the sphere of our industrial enterprise are not neglected, for the opportunities now offered will never recur again.❞

—Frederick Lugard, British colonial administrator, from *The Rise of Our East African Empire*, 1893

PRIMARY SOURCE

❝What the partial occupation of his soil by the white man has failed to do; what the mapping out of European political 'spheres of influence' has failed to do; what the maxim and the rifle, the slave gang, labour in the bowels of the earth and the lash, have failed to do; what imported [diseases] have failed to do; what even the oversea slave trade failed to do, the power of modern capitalistic exploitation, assisted by modern engines of destruction, may yet succeed in accomplishing. For from the evils of the latter, scientifically applied and enforced, there is no escape for the African.❞

—Edmund D. Morel, British author, from *The Black Man's Burden*, 1920

PHOTO: (I)© Pictorial Press Ltd / Alamy, (r)Library of Congress, Prints & Photographs Division.

Step Into the Time

Demonstrating Understanding Choose an event from the time line and explain how it shows resistance to European imperialism.

AFRICA, ASIA, AND LATIN AMERICA			
1800	1815	1830	

1819 Great Britain sends Sir Thomas Raffles to Singapore.

1830 French take over Algeria

1830 Belgium creates an independent state

1841 Explorer David Livingstone arrives in Africa

THE WORLD

1807 Slave trade to British colonies outlawed

1812 Napoleon invades Russia

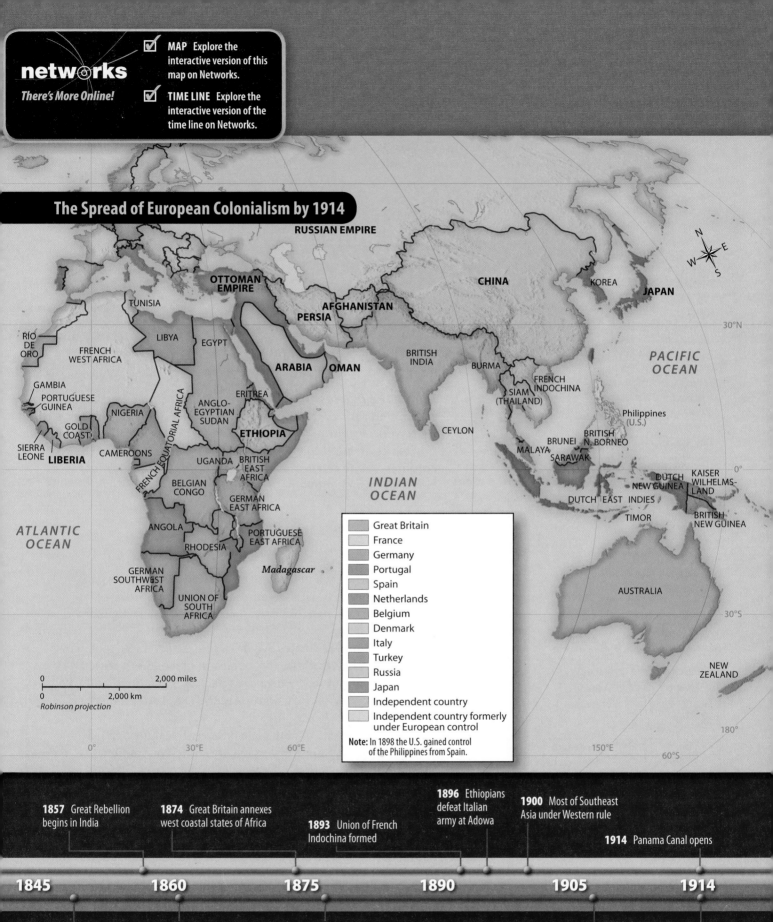

networks

There's More Online!

☑ **MAP** Explore the interactive version of this map on Networks.

☑ **TIME LINE** Explore the interactive version of the time line on Networks.

The Spread of European Colonialism by 1914

RUSSIAN EMPIRE

OTTOMAN EMPIRE

CHINA

KOREA

JAPAN

TUNISIA

RÍO DE ORO

FRENCH WEST AFRICA

LIBYA

EGYPT

AFGHANISTAN

PERSIA

ARABIA

OMAN

BRITISH INDIA

BURMA

FRENCH INDOCHINA

SIAM (THAILAND)

PACIFIC OCEAN

30°N

GAMBIA

PORTUGUESE GUINEA

NIGERIA

GOLD COAST

SIERRA LEONE

LIBERIA

CAMEROONS

FRENCH EQUATORIAL AFRICA

ERITREA

ANGLO-EGYPTIAN SUDAN

ETHIOPIA

UGANDA

BRITISH EAST AFRICA

CEYLON

Philippines (U.S.)

BRUNEI

MALAYA

BRITISH N. BORNEO

SARAWAK

KAISER WILHELMS-LAND

DUTCH NEW GUINEA

BRITISH NEW GUINEA

BELGIAN CONGO

GERMAN EAST AFRICA

INDIAN OCEAN

DUTCH EAST INDIES

TIMOR

0°

ATLANTIC OCEAN

ANGOLA

RHODESIA

PORTUGUESE EAST AFRICA

Madagascar

AUSTRALIA

GERMAN SOUTHWEST AFRICA

UNION OF SOUTH AFRICA

30°S

NEW ZEALAND

0   2,000 miles

0   2,000 km

Robinson projection

	Great Britain
	France
	Germany
	Portugal
	Spain
	Netherlands
	Belgium
	Denmark
	Italy
	Turkey
	Russia
	Japan
	Independent country
	Independent country formerly under European control

Note: In 1898 the U.S. gained control of the Philippines from Spain.

0°   30°E   60°E   150°E   180°

60°S

1857 Great Rebellion begins in India

1874 Great Britain annexes west coastal states of Africa

1893 Union of French Indochina formed

1896 Ethiopians defeat Italian army at Adowa

1900 Most of Southeast Asia under Western rule

1914 Panama Canal opens

1845	1860	1875	1890	1905	1914

1848 Demonstrations erupt in the Austrian Empire

1861 Jefferson Davis leads Confederacy as U.S. Civil War begins

1877 "Jim Crow" laws enforce segregation in southern United States

1907 France, Great Britain, and Russia create Triple Entente

1914 Assassination of Archduke Francis Ferdinand

Reading HELPDESK (CCSS)

Academic Vocabulary
• exploit • export

Content Vocabulary
• imperialism
• racism
• protectorate
• indirect rule
• direct rule

TAKING NOTES:

Key Ideas and Details

Identifying Use a graphic organizer like this one to identify the political status of various regions of Southeast Asia.

Region	Political Status
Burma	
Singapore	
Vietnam	
Thailand	
Philippines	

LESSON 1
Colonial Rule in Southeast Asia

ESSENTIAL QUESTIONS
• *What are the causes and effects of imperialism?*
• *How do some groups resist control by others?*

IT MATTERS BECAUSE

During the nineteenth century, many Western powers scrambled for new territories in Southeast Asia and Africa. Governing by either indirect or direct rule, the Western powers controlled the governments and economies of their colonies. Some territories resisted colonial rule, but most early resistance movements failed.

The New Imperialism

GUIDING QUESTION *What were the motivations for the new imperialism?*

In the nineteenth century, a new phase of Western expansion began. European nations began to view Asian and African societies as a source of industrial raw materials and a market for Western manufactured goods.

In the 1880s, European states began an intense scramble for overseas territory. **Imperialism**, the extension of a nation's power over other lands, was not new. Europeans had set up colonies and trading posts in North America, South America, and Africa by the sixteenth century.

However, the imperialism of the late nineteenth century, called the "new imperialism" by some historians, was different. Earlier, European states had been content, especially in the case of Africa and Asia, to set up a few trading posts where they could carry on trade and perhaps some missionary activity. Now they sought nothing less than direct control over vast territories.

Why did Westerners begin to increase their search for colonies after 1880? There was a strong economic motive. Capitalist states in the West were looking for both markets and raw materials such as rubber, oil, and tin for their industries. The issue was not simply an economic one, however. European nation-states were involved in heated rivalries. They acquired colonies abroad in order to gain an advantage over their rivals. Colonies were also a source of national prestige. To some people, in fact, a nation could not be great without colonies.

In addition, imperialism was tied to Social Darwinism and racism. Social Darwinists believed that in the struggle between nations, the fit are victorious. **Racism** is the belief that race determines traits and capabilities. Racists erroneously believe that particular races are superior or inferior.

Racist beliefs led to the use of military force against other nations. Some Europeans took a more religious and humanitarian approach to imperialism. They believed Europeans had a moral responsibility to civilize primitive people. They called this responsibility the "white man's burden." To some, this meant bringing the Christian message to the "heathen masses." To others, it meant bringing the benefits of Western democracy and capitalism to these societies.

imperialism the extension of a nation's power over other lands

racism the belief that race determines a person's traits and capabilities

☑ **READING PROGRESS CHECK**

Explaining How did Europeans justify imperialism?

Colonial Takeover

GUIDING QUESTION *What led to Western dominance in Southeast Asia?*

The new imperialism was evident in Southeast Asia. In 1800 the Europeans ruled only two societies in this area: the Spanish Philippines and the Dutch East Indies. By 1900 virtually the entire area was under Western rule.

Great Britain

The process began with Great Britain. In 1819 Great Britain sent Sir Thomas Stamford Raffles to found a new colony on a small island at the tip of the Malay Peninsula. Called Singapore ("city of the lion"), in the new age of steamships, it soon became a major stopping point for traffic traveling to or from China.

GEOGRAPHY CONNECTION

European countries used Southeast Asia as a source for raw materials.

1 **ENVIRONMENT AND SOCIETY** *Which territory was the primary source of spices?*

2 **HUMAN SYSTEMS** *Which raw materials did the United States have access to?*

Imperialism in Southeast Asia 1900

Possessions

British
Dutch
French
German
Portuguese
United States
Independent

Raw materials

Coffee
Palm oil
Rubber
Spices
Sugar
Tea
Timber
Tin

❝Mr. President, the times call for candor. The Philippines are ours forever. And just beyond the Philippines are China's illimitable markets. We will not retreat from either. We will not abandon an opportunity in [Asia]. We will not renounce our part in the mission of our race, trustee, under God, of the civilization of the world.❞

—Senator Albert Beveridge, from a speech before the U.S. Senate, January 9, 1900

DBQ **ANALYZING** How does Beveridge's statement reflect a mixture of moral idealism and a desire for profit?

protectorate a political unit that depends on another government for its protection

▼ This photograph shows King Norodom of Cambodia and his son being transported in a Western-style carriage in 1900.

▶ **CRITICAL THINKING**
Drawing Conclusions How did the French influence life in Cambodia?

During the next few decades, the British advance into Southeast Asia continued. Next to fall was the kingdom of Burma (modern Myanmar). Britain wanted control of Burma in order to protect its possessions in India. It also sought a land route through Burma into southern China. Although the difficult terrain along the frontier between Burma and China caused this effort to fail, British activities in Burma led to the collapse of the Burmese monarchy. Britain soon established control over the entire country.

France

France, which had some missionaries operating in Vietnam, nervously watched the British advance into Burma. The local Vietnamese authorities, who viewed Christianity as a threat to Confucian doctrine, persecuted the French missionaries. However, Vietnam failed to stop the Christian missionaries. Vietnamese internal rivalries divided the country into two separate governments—the north and the south.

France was especially alarmed by British attempts to monopolize trade. To stop any British movement into Vietnam, the French government decided in 1857 to force the Vietnamese to accept French protection.

The French eventually succeeded in making the Vietnamese ruler give up territories in the Mekong River delta. The French occupied the city of Saigon and, during the next 30 years, extended their control over the rest of the country. In 1883 France seized the city of Hanoi and later made the Vietnamese empire a French **protectorate**.

In the 1880s, France extended its control over neighboring Cambodia, Annam, Tonkin, and Laos. By 1887 France included all its new possessions in a new Union of French Indochina.

Thailand—The Exception

After the French conquest of Indochina, Thailand (then called Siam) was the only remaining free state in Southeast Asia. But the rivalry between the British and the French threatened to place Thailand under colonial rule, too.

Two remarkable rulers were able to prevent that from happening. One was King Mongkut (known to theatergoers as the king in *The King and I*), and the other was his son, King Chulalongkorn. Both promoted Western learning and maintained friendly relations with the major European powers. In 1896 Britain and France agreed to maintain Thailand as an independent buffer state between their possessions in Southeast Asia.

The United States

In 1898 during the Spanish-American War, U.S. naval forces under Commodore George Dewey defeated the Spanish fleet in Manila Bay in the Philippines. Believing it was his moral obligation to "civilize" other parts of the world, President William McKinley decided to turn the Philippines, which had been under Spanish control, into an American colony. This action would also prevent the area from falling into the hands of the Japanese. The islands gave the United States convenient access to trade with China.

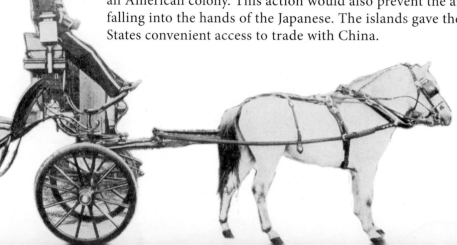

PHOTO: © Leonard de Selva/CORBIS

Many Filipinos did not wish to be under American control. Emilio Aguinaldo (AH • gee • NAHL • doh) was the leader of a movement for independence in the Philippines. He began his revolt against the Spanish and went into exile in 1898. When the United States acquired the Philippines, Aguinaldo continued the revolt and set himself up as the president of the Republic of the Philippines. Led by Aguinaldo, the guerrilla forces fought bitterly against the U.S. troops to establish their independence.

The fight for Philippine independence resulted in three years of bloody warfare. However, the United States eventually defeated the guerrilla forces, and President McKinley had his stepping-stone to the rich markets of China.

☑ **READING PROGRESS CHECK**

Identifying What prompted Britain to colonize Singapore and Burma?

Colonial Regimes

GUIDING QUESTION *How did colonial powers govern their colonies?*

Western powers governed their new colonial empires by either indirect or direct rule. Their chief goals were to **exploit** the natural resources of the lands and to open up markets for their own manufactured goods.

Indirect and Direct Rule

Sometimes a colonial power could realize its goals by cooperating with local political elites. For example, the Dutch East India Company used **indirect rule** in the Dutch East Indies. Under indirect rule, local rulers were allowed to keep their authority and status in a new colonial setting. This made access to the region's natural resources easier. Indirect rule was cheaper because fewer officials had to be trained. It also affected local culture less.

However, indirect rule was not always possible. Some local elites resisted foreign conquest. In these cases, the local elites were replaced with Western officials. This system was called **direct rule**. Great Britain administered Burma directly through its colonial government in India. In Indochina, France used both systems. It imposed direct rule in southern Vietnam but ruled indirectly through the emperor in northern Vietnam

To justify their conquests, Western powers spoke of bringing the blessings of Western civilization to their colonial subjects, including representative government. However, many Westerners came to fear the idea of native peoples (especially educated ones) being allowed political rights.

Colonial Economies

The colonial powers did not want their colonists to develop their own industries. Thus, colonial policy stressed the **export** of raw materials. This policy often led to the development of plantation agriculture. In this system, peasants worked as wage laborers on the foreign-owned plantations. Plantation owners kept wages at poverty levels to increase profits. Conditions on plantations were often so unhealthful that thousands died. Also, peasants bore the burden of high taxes.

Nevertheless, colonial rule did bring some benefits to Southeast Asia. A modern economic system began there. Colonial governments built railroads, highways, and other structures that benefited native peoples as well as colonials. The development of an export market helped create an entrepreneurial class in rural areas. In the Dutch East Indies, for example,

▲ Filipinos mount an insurrection against the Americans in Manila in February 1899.

▶ **CRITICAL THINKING**
Analyzing Visuals Contrast the depiction of the Filipinos with that of the American soldiers.

exploit to make use of meanly or unfairly for one's own advantage

indirect rule a colonial government in which local rulers are allowed to maintain their positions of authority and status

direct rule colonial government in which local elites were removed from power and replaced by a new set of officials brought from the colonizing country

export to send a product or service for sale to another country

small growers of rubber, palm oil, coffee, tea, and spices began to share in the profits of the colonial enterprise. Most of the profits, however, were taken back to the colonizing country.

✓ **READING PROGRESS CHECK**

Describing What kind of economic system did colonial rulers establish?

Resistance to Colonial Rule

GUIDING QUESTION *How did indigenous people in Southeast Asia respond to colonial rule?*

Many subject peoples in Southeast Asia resented colonization. At first, resistance came from the existing ruling class. In Burma, for example, the monarch himself fought Western domination. By contrast, in Vietnam, after the emperor had agreed to French control of his country, a number of government officials set up an organization called Can Vuong ("Save the King"). They fought against the French without the emperor's help.

Sometimes resistance to Western control took the form of peasant revolts. Peasants were often driven off the land to make way for plantation agriculture. Angry peasants then vented their anger at the foreign invaders. For example, in Burma, in 1930 the Buddhist monk Saya San led a peasant uprising against the British colonial regime.

Early resistance movements failed. They were overcome by Western powers. In the early 1900s, however, a new kind of resistance emerged that was based on nationalism. The leaders were often from a new class that the colonial rule had created: Westernized intellectuals in the cities. They were the first generation of Asians to embrace the institutions and values of the West. Many were educated in the West, spoke Western languages, and worked in jobs connected with the colonial regimes.

At first, many of the leaders of these movements did not focus clearly on the idea of nationhood. Instead, they simply tried to defend the economic interests or religious beliefs of the native peoples. In Burma, for example, students at the University of Rangoon formed an organization to protest against official persecution of the Buddhist religion and British lack of respect for local religious traditions. They protested against British arrogance and failure to observe local customs in Buddhist temples. Not until the 1930s, however, did these resistance movements, such as those begun in Burma, begin to demand national independence.

✓ **READING PROGRESS CHECK**

Analyzing Why were resistance movements often led by Southeast Asian people who had been educated in the West?

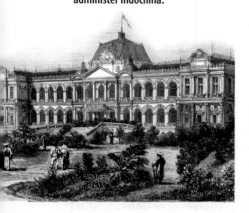

▼ This 1874 engraving depicts the government palace at Saigon, which the French constructed to administer Indochina.

PHOTO: The new government palace at Saigon, from 'L'Illustration', 1874 (engraving), French School, (19th century) / Private Collection / Archives Charmet / The Bridgeman Art Library

LESSON 1 REVIEW

Reviewing Vocabulary

1. Describing Write a paragraph describing different forms of colonial rule. Be sure to define *protectorate, direct rule,* and *indirect rule* and to discuss specific examples.

Using Your Notes

2. Summarizing Use your notes to write a paragraph summarizing the political situation of the regions of Southeast Asia by 1900.

Answering the Guiding Questions

3. Analyzing What were the motivations for the new imperialism?

4. Identifying Cause and Effect What led to Western dominance in Southeast Asia?

5. Explaining How did colonial powers govern their colonies?

6. Analyzing How did indigenous people in Southeast Asia respond to colonial rule?

Writing Activity

7. INFORMATIVE/EXPLANATORY Write an essay discussing the effects of colonial rule on the countries that were colonized. Be sure to discuss at least two specific examples.

Reading HELPDESK (CCSS)

Academic Vocabulary

• **uncharted** • **traditions**

Content Vocabulary

• **annex** • **indigenous**

TAKING NOTES:

Key Ideas and Details

Categorizing Use the graphic organizer to show which countries controlled different parts of Africa.

Western Power	Area of Africa
Belgium	
Britain	
France	
Germany	

PHOTO: (l to r) FPG/Archive Photos/Getty Images, The Stapleton Collection/The Bridgeman Art Library, akg-images, ©Classic Vision/Age Fotostock America

LESSON 2
Empire Building in Africa

ESSENTIAL QUESTIONS
• *What are the causes and effects of imperialism?*
• *How do some groups resist control by others?*

IT MATTERS BECAUSE

During the late nineteenth century, the major European powers scrambled to colonize Africa. Virtually all of Africa was under European rule by 1900. Maintaining that rule was not easy, however. African nationalism emerged during the early part of the twentieth century.

West Africa and North Africa

GUIDING QUESTION *Why were European countries interested in West Africa and North Africa?*

Before 1880, Europeans controlled little of the African continent directly. They were content to let African rulers and merchants represent European interests. Between 1880 and 1900, however, Great Britain, France, Germany, Belgium, Italy, Spain, and Portugal, spurred by intense rivalries among themselves, placed virtually all of Africa under European rule.

West Africa

Europeans had a keen interest in Africa's raw materials, especially those of West Africa—peanuts, timber, hides, and palm oil. Earlier in the nineteenth century, Europeans had profited from the slave trade in this region of Africa. By the late 1800s, however, trade in enslaved people had virtually ended. As the slave trade declined, Europe's interest in other forms of trade increased. The growing European presence in West Africa led to increasing tensions with African governments in the region.

For a long time, most African states were able to maintain their independence. However, in 1874 Great Britain **annexed** (incorporated a country within another country) the west coastal states as the first British colony of Gold Coast. At about the same time, Britain established a protectorate in Nigeria. By 1900, France had added the huge area of French West Africa to its colonial empire. This left France in control of the largest part of West Africa. In addition, Germany controlled Togo, Cameroon, German Southwest Africa, and German East Africa.

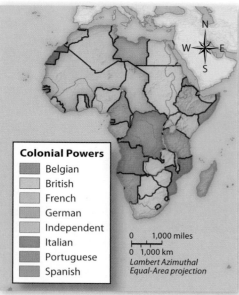

Colonial Powers
- Belgian
- British
- French
- German
- Independent
- Italian
- Portuguese
- Spanish

0   1,000 miles

0 1,000 km

Lambert Azimuthal Equal-Area projection

▶ **CRITICAL THINKING**

Drawing Conclusions Which colonial power controlled most of West Africa?

annex to incorporate into an existing political unit, such as a city or country

North Africa

Egypt had been part of the Ottoman Empire, but as Ottoman rule declined, the Egyptians sought their independence. In 1805 an officer of the Ottoman army named Muhammad Ali seized power and established a separate Egyptian state.

During the next 30 years, Muhammad Ali introduced a series of reforms to bring Egypt into the modern world. He modernized the army, set up a public school system, and helped create small industries that refined sugar, produced textiles and munitions, and built ships.

The growing economic importance of the Nile Valley in Egypt, along with the development of steamships, gave Europeans the desire to build a canal east of Cairo to connect the Mediterranean and Red Seas. Such a canal would allow transport between Europe and Asia, without traveling around Africa. In 1854 a French entrepreneur, Ferdinand de Lesseps, signed a contract to begin building the Suez Canal. The canal was completed in 1869.

The British took an active interest in Egypt after the Suez Canal was opened. Believing that the canal was its "lifeline to India," Great Britain tried to gain as much control as possible over the canal area.

In 1875 Britain bought Egypt's share in the Suez Canal. When an Egyptian army revolt against foreign influence broke out in 1881, Britain suppressed the revolt. Egypt became a British protectorate in 1914.

The British believed that they should also control Sudan, south of Egypt, to protect their interests in Egypt and the Suez Canal. In 1881 Muslim cleric Muhammad Ahmad, known as the Mahdi (in Arabic, "the rightly guided one"), launched a revolt that brought much of Sudan under his control.

Britain sent a military force under General Charles Gordon to restore Egyptian authority over Sudan. However, Muhammad Ahmad's troops wiped out Gordon's army at Khartoum in 1885. General Gordon himself died in the battle. Not until 1898 were British troops able to seize Sudan.

The French also had colonies in North Africa. In 1879 after about 150,000 French people had settled in the region of Algeria, the French government established control there. Two years later, France imposed a protectorate on neighboring Tunisia. In 1912 France established a protectorate over much of Morocco.

Italy joined the competition for colonies in North Africa by attempting to take over Ethiopia. In 1896, however, the Italian invading forces were defeated. Italy now was the only European state defeated by an African state. This humiliating loss led Italy to try again in 1911. Italy invaded and seized Turkish Tripoli, which it renamed Libya.

☑ **READING PROGRESS CHECK**

Summarizing What motivated the British to compete for control of Egypt?

Central and East Africa

GUIDING QUESTION *Why did European countries compete for colonies in Central Africa and East Africa?*

Central Africa

Central African territories were soon added to the list of European colonies. European explorers aroused popular interest in the dense tropical jungles of Central Africa.

David Livingstone was one such explorer. He arrived in Africa in 1841 as a 27-year-old medical missionary. During the 30 years he spent in Africa,

Livingstone trekked through **uncharted** regions. He sometimes traveled by canoe, but mostly Livingstone walked and spent much of his time exploring the interior of the continent.

During his travels through Africa, Livingstone made detailed notes of his discoveries. He sent this information back to London whenever he could. The maps of Africa were often redrawn based on Livingstone's eyewitness accounts and reports. A major goal of Livingstone's explorations was to find a navigable river that would open Central Africa to European commerce and to Christianity.

When Livingstone disappeared for a while, an American newspaper, the *New York Herald,* hired a young journalist, Henry Stanley, to find the explorer. Stanley did find him, on the eastern shore of Lake Tanganyika. Overwhelmed by finding Livingstone alive if not well, Stanley greeted the explorer with these now-famous words, "Dr. Livingstone, I presume?"

After Livingstone's death in 1873, Stanley decided to carry on the great explorer's work. Unlike Livingstone, however, Henry Stanley had a strong dislike of Africa. He once said, "I detest the land most heartily."

In the 1870s, Stanley explored the Congo River in Central Africa and sailed down it to the Atlantic Ocean. Soon, he was encouraging the British to send settlers to the Congo River basin. When Britain refused, Stanley turned to King Leopold II of Belgium.

King Leopold II was the real driving force behind the colonization of Central Africa. He rushed enthusiastically into the pursuit of an empire in Africa. "To open to civilization," he said, "the only part of our globe where it has yet to penetrate, to pierce the darkness which envelops whole populations, it is, I dare to say, a crusade worthy of this century of progress." Profit, however, was equally important to Leopold. In 1877 he hired Henry Stanley to set up Belgian settlements in the Congo.

Leopold's claim to the vast territories of the Congo aroused widespread concern among other European states. France, in particular, rushed to plant its flag in the heart of Africa. Leopold ended up with the territories around the Congo River. France occupied the areas farther north.

East Africa

By 1885 Britain and Germany had become the chief rivals in East Africa. Germany came late to the ranks of the imperialist powers. At first, the German chancellor Otto von Bismarck had downplayed the importance of colonies. As more and more Germans called for a German empire, however, Bismarck became a convert to colonialism. As he expressed it, "All this colonial business is a sham, but we need it for the elections."

In addition to its West African holdings, Germany tried to develop colonies in East Africa. Most of East Africa had not yet been claimed by any other power. However, the British were also interested in the area because control of East Africa would connect the British Empire in Africa from South Africa to Egypt. Portugal and Belgium also claimed parts of East Africa.

To settle conflicting claims, European countries met at the Berlin Conference in 1884 and 1885. The conference officially recognized both British and German claims for

uncharted not mapped; unknown

▼ This 1872 British illustration depicts the meeting between Stanley and Livingstone on November 19, 1872.

▶ **CRITICAL THINKING**
Analyzing Why did the phrase "Dr. Livingstone, I presume?" become so famous?

territory in East Africa. Portugal received a clear claim on Mozambique. No African delegates, however, were present at this conference.

☑ **READING PROGRESS CHECK**

Explaining How did Leopold's aggression promote Western imperialism in Africa?

South Africa

GUIDING QUESTION *How was European dominance different in South Africa?*

Nowhere in Africa did the European presence grow more rapidly than in the south. By 1865 the total white population of South Africa had risen to nearly 200,000 people. The Boers, or Afrikaners—as the descendants of the original Dutch settlers were called—had occupied Cape Town and surrounding areas in South Africa since the seventeenth century. During the Napoleonic Wars, however, the British seized these lands from the Dutch. Afterward, the British encouraged settlers to come to what they called Cape Colony.

The Boer Republics

In the 1830s, disgusted with British rule, the Boers moved from the coastal lands and headed northward on the Great Trek. Altogether one out of every five Dutch-speaking South Africans joined the trek. Their parties eventually settled in the region between the Orange and Vaal (VAHL) Rivers and in the region north of the Vaal River. In these areas, the Boers formed two independent republics—the Orange Free State and the Transvaal (later called the South African Republic).

The Boers believed that white superiority was ordained by God. They denied non-Europeans any place in their society, other than as laborers or servants. As they settled the lands, the Boers put many of the **indigenous** peoples, those native to a region, in these areas on reservations.

The Boers had frequently battled the indigenous Zulu people. In the early nineteenth century, the Zulu, under a talented ruler named Shaka, had carved out their own empire. Even after Shaka's death, the Zulu remained powerful. In the late 1800s, the Zulu were defeated when the British military joined the conflict.

Cecil Rhodes

In the 1880s, British policy in South Africa was influenced by Cecil Rhodes. Rhodes had founded diamond and gold mining companies that had made him a fortune. Rhodes was a great champion of British expansion. He said once, "I think what [God] would like me to do is to paint as much of Africa British red as possible." One of Rhodes's goals was to create a series of British colonies "from the Cape to Cairo"—all linked by a railroad.

When gold and diamonds were discovered in the Transvaal, British settlers swarmed in looking to make their fortunes. The Boer residents resented the settlers and they were sometimes mistreated.

Rhodes then secretly backed a raid that was meant to spark an uprising among British settlers against the Transvaal government. The raid failed, and the British government forced Rhodes to resign as head of the Cape Colony. This action was too late, however, to prevent a war between the British and the Boers.

indigenous native to a region

▶ CRITICAL THINKING
Analyzing Visuals What conditions did men endure in South African diamond mines?

▼ After diamonds were discovered in 1867, thousands of Europeans came to Africa to make their fortunes. In 1881 Cecil Rhodes formed the De Beers Mining Company, which still dominates the world diamond market.

The Boer War

This war, called the Boer War, dragged on from 1899 to 1902. Fierce guerrilla resistance by the Boers angered the British. They responded by burning crops and forcing about 120,000 Boer women and children into detention camps, where lack of food caused some 20,000 deaths. Eventually, the vastly larger British army won. A peace treaty was signed in 1902.

In 1910 the British created an independent Union of South Africa, which combined the old Cape Colony and the Boer republics. The new state would be a self-governing nation within the British Empire. To appease the Boers, the British agreed that only whites, with a few propertied Africans, would vote.

✓ **READING PROGRESS CHECK**

Identifying Central Issues What role did Cecil Rhodes play in promoting British imperialism in the south of Africa?

Effects of Imperialism

GUIDING QUESTION *How did European governance lead to African nationalism?*

By 1914 Great Britain, France, Germany, Belgium, Italy, Spain, and Portugal had divided up Africa. Only Liberia, which had been created as a homeland for the formerly enslaved persons of the United States, and Ethiopia remained free states. Native peoples who dared to resist were devastated by the Europeans' superior military force.

Colonial Rule in Africa

As was true in Southeast Asia, most European governments ruled their new territories in Africa with the least effort and expense possible. Indirect rule meant relying on existing political elites and institutions. The British especially followed this approach. At first, in some areas, the British simply asked a local ruler to accept British authority and to fly the British flag over official buildings.

The concept of indirect rule was introduced in the Islamic state of Sokoto, in northern Nigeria, beginning in 1903. This system of indirect rule in Sokoto had one good feature: It did not disrupt local customs and institutions. However, it did have some unfortunate consequences.

The system of indirect rule was basically a fraud because British administrators made all major decisions. The native authorities served chiefly to enforce those decisions.

Another problem was that the policy of indirect rule kept the old African elite in power. Such a policy provided few opportunities for ambitious and talented young Africans from outside the old elite. In this way British indirect rule sowed the seeds for class and ethnic tensions, which erupted after independence came in the twentieth century.

Most other European nations governed their African possessions through a form of direct rule. This was true in the French colonies. At the top was a French official, usually known as a governor-general. He was appointed from Paris and governed with the aid of a bureaucracy in the capital city of the colony.

The French ideal was to assimilate African subjects into French culture rather than preserve native **traditions**. Africans were eligible to run for office and even serve in the French National Assembly in Paris. A few were also appointed to high-powered positions in the colonial administration.

▲ The Zulu chief Cetewayo surrendered to the British after they captured the city of Ulundi in July 1879.

▶ **CRITICAL THINKING**
Drawing Conclusions Why was Zulu chief Cetewayo unable to maintain power?

traditions the established customs of a people

Imperialism in Africa

66Some time ago a party of men came to my country, the principal one appearing to be a man called Rudd. They asked me for a place to dig for gold, and said they would give me certain things for the right to do so. I told them to bring what they could give and I would show them what I would give. A document was written and presented to me for signature. I asked what it contained, and was told that in it were my words and the words of those men. I put my hand to it. About three months afterwards I heard from other sources that I had given by the document the right to all the minerals of my country.99

—Lobengula, a southern African king, in a letter to Queen Victoria, quoted in *The Imperialism Reader*

DBQ *IDENTIFYING*
How did the Europeans take advantage of Lobengula?

Rise of African Nationalism

A new class of leaders emerged in Africa by the beginning of the twentieth century. Educated in colonial schools or in Western nations, they were the first generation of Africans to know a great deal about the West.

The members of this new class admired Western culture and sometimes disliked the ways of their own countries. They were eager to introduce Western ideas and institutions into their own societies. Still, many of these new leaders came to resent the foreigners and their arrogant contempt for African peoples. These intellectuals recognized the gap between theory and practice in colonial policy. Westerners had exalted democracy, equality, and political freedom but did not apply these values in the colonies.

There were few democratic institutions. Native peoples could have only low-paying jobs in the colonial bureaucracy. To many Africans, colonialism had meant losing their farmlands or working on plantations or in factories run by foreigners. Some African leaders lost even more, such as the rights to mine the natural resources in their country.

Middle-class Africans did not suffer as much as poor African peasants. However, members of the middle class also had complaints. They usually qualified only for menial jobs in the government or business. Even then, their salaries were lower than those of Europeans in similar jobs.

Europeans expressed their assumed superiority over Africans in other ways. Segregated clubs, schools, and churches were set up as more European officials brought their wives and began to raise families. Europeans were also condescending in their relationships with Africans. For instance, Europeans had a habit of addressing Africans by their first names.

Such conditions led many members of the new urban educated class to feel great confusion toward their colonial rulers and the civilization the colonists represented. The educated Africans found many aspects of Western culture to be superior to their own. However, these intellectuals fiercely hated colonial rule and were determined to assert their own nationality and cultural destiny. Out of this mixture of hopes and resentments emerged the first stirrings of modern nationalism in Africa.

During the first quarter of the twentieth century, resentment turned to action. Across Africa, native peoples began to organize political parties and movements seeking the end of foreign rule. They wanted to be independent and self-governing.

☑ **READING PROGRESS CHECK**

Drawing Conclusions In what ways were Western nations hypocritical in their treatment of their colonies?

LESSON 2 REVIEW (CCSS)

Reviewing Vocabulary

1. ***Identifying*** While defining the terms, explain how the traditions of indigenous Africans influenced their relations with Europeans.

Using Your Notes

2. ***Summarizing*** Use your notes to indicate the predominant areas of Africa controlled by various European nations.

Answering the Guiding Questions

3. ***Determining Cause and Effect*** Why were European countries interested in West Africa and North Africa?

4. ***Analyzing Information*** Why did European countries compete for colonies in Central Africa and East Africa?

5. ***Identifying Central Issues*** How was European dominance different in South Africa?

6. ***Drawing Conclusions*** How did European governance lead to African nationalism?

Writing Activity

7. **INFORMATIVE/EXPLANATORY** In one or two paragraphs, explain the effects of the Berlin conference of 1884–1885 on the scramble for Africa.

Reading **HELP**DESK ⓒⓒⓢⓢ

Academic Vocabulary
- **civil**
- **estate**

Content Vocabulary
- **sepoys**
- **viceroys**

TAKING NOTES:
Key Ideas and Details

Determining Cause and Effect
Use a chart like this one to identify some causes and effects of British influence on India.

Causes	Effect
British manufactured goods	. . .
Cotton crops	
School system	
Railroad, telegraph, telephone services	

PHOTO: (l to r) The Granger Collection, ©Underwood & Underwood/CORBIS, ©Bettmann/CORBIS, Wallace Kirkland/Time & Life Pictures/Getty Images, V&A Images/Alamy

LESSON 3
British Rule in India

ESSENTIAL QUESTIONS
- *What are the causes and effects of imperialism?*
- *How do some groups resist control by others?*

IT MATTERS BECAUSE
The British brought order and stability to India, but India paid a high price for British rule. The mistrust and cultural differences between the British and Indians sparked an independence movement and renewed interest among Indians in their culture and history.

The Great Rebellion

GUIDING QUESTION *What was the source of conflict between the British and the Indian people?*

Over the course of the eighteenth century, British power in India had increased while the power of the Mogul rulers had declined. The British government gave a trading company, the British East India Company, power to become actively involved in India's political and military affairs. To rule India, the British East India Company had its own soldiers and forts. It also hired Indian soldiers, known as **sepoys**, to protect the company's interests in the region.

Events Leading to Rebellion

In 1857 a growing Indian distrust of the British led to a revolt. The British call the revolt the Sepoy Mutiny. Indians call it the First War of Independence. Neutral observers label it the Great Rebellion.

The major immediate cause of the revolt was a rumor that the troops' new rifle cartridges were greased with cow and pig fat. The cow was sacred to Hindus. The pig was taboo to Muslims. To load a rifle at that time, soldiers had to bite off the end of the cartridge. To the sepoys, touching these greased cartridges to their lips would mean that they were polluted.

A group of sepoys at an army post in Meerut, near Delhi, refused to load their rifles with the cartridges. The British charged them with mutiny, publicly humiliated them, and put them in prison. This treatment of their comrades enraged the sepoy troops in Meerut. They went on a rampage, killing 50 European men, women, and children. Soon other Indians joined the revolt, including princes whose land the British had taken.

The Reach of Imperialism **237**

▲ This engraving of the Battle of Kanpur (Cawnpore) shows sepoys on horseback fighting British soldiers.

▶ **CRITICAL THINKING**
Analyzing Visuals Which side had the military advantage in this battle? Why?

sepoy an Indian soldier hired by the British East India Company to protect the company's interests in the region

Within a year, however, Indian troops loyal to the British and fresh British troops had crushed the rebellion. Although Indian troops fought bravely and outnumbered the British by about 230,000 to 45,000, they were not well organized. Rivalries between Hindus and Muslims kept the Indians from working together.

Atrocities were terrible on both sides. At Kanpur (Cawnpore), Indians massacred 200 defenseless women and children in a building known as the House of the Ladies. Recapturing Kanpur, the British took their revenge before executing the Indians.

Effects of the Rebellion

As a result of the uprising, the British Parliament transferred the powers of the East India Company directly to the British government. In 1876 Britian's Queen Victoria took the title Empress of India. The people of India were now her colonial subjects, and India then became her "Jewel in the Crown."

Although the rebellion failed, it helped fuel Indian nationalism. The rebellion marked the first significant attempt by the people of South Asia to throw off British Raj (rule). Later, a new generation of Indian leaders would take up the cause.

☑ **READING PROGRESS CHECK**

Determining Cause and Effect What were the effects of the Great Rebellion in India?

British Colonial Rule

GUIDING QUESTION *What were the consequences of British rule in India?*

After the Sepoy Mutiny, the British government began to rule India directly. They appointed a British official known as a **viceroy** (a governor who ruled as a representative of a monarch). A British **civil** service staff assisted the viceroy. This staff of about 3,500 officials ruled almost 300 million people, the largest colonial population in the world. British rule involved both benefits and costs for Indians.

British rule in India had several benefits for colonial subjects. It brought order and stability to a society badly divided into many states with different, and sometimes opposing, political systems. It also led to a fairly honest, efficient government.

Through the efforts of the British administrator and historian Lord Thomas Macaulay, a new school system was set up. The new system used the English language, as Macaulay explained:

PRIMARY SOURCE

"What then shall [the language of education] be? [Some] maintain that it should be the English. The other half strongly recommend the Arabic and Sanskrit. The whole question seems to me to be, which language is the best worth knowing? ... It is, I believe, no exaggeration to say that all the historical information which has been collected from all the books written in the Sanskrit language is less valuable [than] what may be found in [short textbooks] used at preparatory schools in England."

—Lord Macaulay, from speech to Parliament, February 2, 1835

The goal of the new school system was to train Indian children to serve in the government and army. The new system served only elite, upper-class Indians, however. Ninety percent of the population remained uneducated and illiterate.

The British hired Indians and built roads, canals, universities, and medical centers. A postal service was introduced shortly after it appeared in Great Britain. India's first rail network, beginning in Bombay, opened in 1853. By 1900, 25,000 miles (40,225 km) of railroads crisscrossed India. Health and sanitation conditions were also improved.

But the Indian people paid a high price for the peace and stability brought by British rule. Perhaps the greatest cost was economic. British entrepreneurs and a small number of Indians reaped financial benefits from British rule, but it brought hardship to millions of others in both the cities and the countryside. British manufactured goods destroyed local industries. British textiles put thousands of women out of work and severely damaged the Indian textile industry.

In rural areas, the British sent the zamindars to collect taxes. The British believed that using these local officials would make it easier to collect taxes from the peasants. However, the zamindars in India took advantage of their new authority. They increased taxes and forced the less fortunate peasants to become tenants or lose their land entirely. Peasant unrest grew.

The British also encouraged many Indian farmers to switch from growing food to growing cotton. As a consequence, food supplies could not keep up with the growing population. Between 1800 and 1900, 30 million Indians died of starvation.

Finally, British rule was degrading, even for the newly educated upper classes who benefited the most from it. The best jobs and the best housing were reserved for Britons. Although many British colonial officials sincerely tried to improve the lot of the people in India, British arrogance and racial attitudes cut deeply into the pride of many Indians and led to the rise of an Indian nationalist movement.

☑ READING PROGRESS CHECK

Analyzing Information What was the price Indians had to pay for the increased stability of British rule?

Rabindranath Tagore on India

"The conditions which have prevailed in India from a remote antiquity have guided its history along a particular channel, which does not and cannot coincide with the lines of evolution taken by other countries under different sets of influences. It would be a sad misreading of the lessons of the past to tread too closely in the footsteps of any other nation, however successful in its own career.

I feel strongly that our country has been entrusted with a message which is not a mere echo of the living voices that resound from western shores ..."

—Rabindranath Tagore from a letter, January 4, 1909

 **DRAWING CONCLUSIONS**
What attitude would Tagore have had toward the opinion expressed by Macaulay about the use of English to educate Indians?

viceroy a governor who ruled as a representative of a monarch

civil involving the general public or civic affairs

Indian Nationalists

GUIDING QUESTION *What led to an Indian independence movement?*

The first Indian nationalists were upper-class and English-educated. Many of them were from urban areas, such as Bombay (Mumbai), Madras (Chennai), and Calcutta (Kolkata). Some were trained in British law and were members of the civil service.

At first, many Indian nationalists preferred reform to revolution. However, the slow pace of reform convinced many that relying on British goodwill was futile. In 1885 a small group of Indians met in Bombay to form the Indian National Congress (INC). The INC did not demand immediate independence. Instead, the group called for a share in the governing process.

The INC had difficulties because of religious differences. The INC sought independence for all Indians, regardless of class or religious background. However, many of its leaders were Hindu and reflected Hindu concerns. Later, Muslims called for the creation of a separate Muslim League. Such a league would represent the interests of the millions of Muslims in Indian society.

In 1914 the return of a young Hindu from South Africa brought new life to India's struggle for independence. Mohandas Gandhi was born in 1869 in Gujarat, in western India. He studied in London and became a lawyer. In 1893 Gandhi went to South Africa to work in a law firm serving Indian workers there. He soon learned of the racial exploitation of Indians living in South Africa.

On his return to India, Gandhi became active in the independence movement. Using his experience in South Africa, he began a movement based on nonviolent resistance. Its aim was to force the British to improve the lot of the poor and to grant independence to India. Ultimately, Gandhi's movement led to Indian independence.

☑ **READING PROGRESS CHECK**

Identifying Central Issues What difficulties did the Indian National Congress face?

Colonial Indian Culture

GUIDING QUESTION *How did British rule influence Indian culture?*

From the beginning of their rule, the British often showed disrespect for India's cultural heritage. The Taj Mahal, for example, was built as a tomb for the beloved wife of an Indian ruler. The British used it as a favorite site for weddings and parties. Many partygoers even brought hammers to chip off pieces as souvenirs.

The love-hate tension in India that arose from British domination led to a cultural awakening as well. The cultural revival began in the early nineteenth century with the creation of a British college in Calcutta. A local publishing house was opened. It issued textbooks on a variety of subjects, including the sciences, Sanskrit, and Western literature. The publisher also printed grammars and dictionaries in various Indian languages.

This revival soon spread to other regions of India. It led to a search for a new national identity and a modern literary expression. Indian novelists and poets began writing historical romances and epics. Some wrote in English, but most were uncomfortable with a borrowed colonial language. They preferred to use their own regional tongues.

Connections to
TODAY

Commonwealth Games

One legacy of imperialism is evident in the Commonwealth Games. Participation in the games is limited to amateur athletes who come from one of the countries of the British Commonwealth, the free association of states that includes many former parts of the British Empire. A more recent addition to the games is cricket, which the British brought to their colonies. Cricket is especially popular in India.

Printed in the various regional Indian languages, newspapers were a common medium used to arouse mass support for nationalist causes. These newspapers reached the lower-middle-class populations—tens of thousands of Indians who had never learned a word of English. In his newspaper *Kesari* ("The Lion"), journalist Balwantrao Gangadhar Tilak used innuendo (suggestion) to convey the negative feelings about the British without ever writing anything disloyal.

The most famous Indian author was Rabindranath Tagore, winner of the Nobel Prize in Literature in 1913. A great writer and poet, Tagore had many talents. He was also a social reformer, spiritual leader, educator, philosopher, singer, painter, and international spokesperson for the moral concerns of his age. Tagore liked to invite the great thinkers of the time to his expansive country home, or **estate**. There he set up a school that became an international university.

Tagore's life mission was to promote pride in a national Indian consciousness in the face of British domination. He wrote a widely read novel in which he portrayed the love-hate relationship of India toward its colonial mentor. The novel reflected an Indian people who admired and imitated the British but who agonized over how to establish their own national identity.

Rabindranath Tagore, however, was more than an Indian nationalist. His life's work was one long prayer for human dignity, world peace, and the mutual understanding and union of East and West. As Tagore once said,

estate a landed property usually with a large house

▼ Many Indians worked as domestic servants in the homes of British colonialists.

▶ **CRITICAL THINKING**
Making Connections Why might Indian domestic servants have become resentful of British rule?

PRIMARY SOURCE

66 It is my conviction that my countrymen will truly gain their India by fighting against the education that teaches them that a country is greater than the ideals of humanity. 99

—Rabindranath Tagore, from *Nationalism*

PHOTO: ©Underwood & Underwood/CORBIS

✓ **READING PROGRESS CHECK**

Drawing Conclusions How did newspapers and literature help shape the nationalist movement?

LESSON 3 REVIEW (CCSS)

Reviewing Vocabulary
1. *Identifying* What were the roles of viceroys and civil servants in India and whom did they represent?

Using Your Notes
2. *Summarizing* Use your notes on the causes and effects of British rule in India to write a paragraph summarizing its effects.

Answering the Guiding Questions
3. *Identifying* What was the source of conflict between the British and the Indian people?

4. *Evaluating* What were the consequences of British rule in India?

5. *Identifying Cause and Effect* What led to an Indian independence movement?

6. *Explaining* How did British rule influence Indian culture?

Writing Activity
7. **INFORMATIVE/EXPLANATORY** Write a short paragraph outlining the general British attitude toward the people of India and the consequences of that attitude.

netw⚙rks

There's More Online!

☑ **IMAGE** Construction of the Panama Canal

☑ **IMAGE** Leaders of the Mexican Revolution

☑ **IMAGE** The Roosevelt Corollary

☑ **INTERACTIVE SELF-CHECK QUIZ**

☑ **MAP** Sea Routes Before and After the Panama Canal

☑ **PRIMARY SOURCE** Mexican Constitution of 1917

☑ **VIDEO** Imperialism in Latin America

Reading **HELP**DESK (CCSS)

Academic Vocabulary
• **whereas** • **sector**

Content Vocabulary
• **dollar diplomacy**

TAKING NOTES:
Key Ideas and Details

Listing Use a graphic organizer like this one to list problems faced by Mexico after 1870 and reforms enacted in the constitution of 1917.

Problems

Reforms

LESSON 4
Imperialism in Latin America

ESSENTIAL QUESTIONS
• *What are the causes and effects of imperialism?*
• *How do some groups resist control by others?*

IT MATTERS BECAUSE

In the course of the nineteenth century, the new nations of Latin America found themselves dependent on the West. The United States was especially prominent in the economic and political affairs of its southern neighbors. Social and political inequalities also continued to characterize many Latin American nations.

The U.S. in Latin America

GUIDING QUESTION *What was the impact of U.S. involvement in Latin America in the early 1900s?*

In the late 1800s, the United States began to intervene in the affairs of its southern neighbors. In 1895 exile José Martí returned to Cuba to lead a revolt against Spanish rule. The brutality with which the Spanish crushed the rebellion shocked Americans and began a series of events that led the United States to declare war against Spain in 1898. As a result of the Spanish-American War, Cuba effectively became a protectorate of the United States. By the treaty that ended the war, Puerto Rico was also annexed to the United States.

In 1903 President Theodore Roosevelt supported a rebellion that allowed Panama to separate from Colombia and establish a new nation. In return, the United States was granted control of a 10-mile strip of land through the country. There the United States built the Panama Canal, which opened in 1914 and was one of the world's greatest engineering feats of its time. The canal connects the Atlantic and Pacific Oceans. On average, it takes a ship 8 to 10 hours to move through the canal passage.

In 1904 President Roosevelt expanded American involvement in Latin America. At the time, European powers threatened to send warships to Santo Domingo in the Dominican Republic to collect debts owed to them. In a statement that became known as the Roosevelt Corollary to the Monroe Doctrine, Roosevelt claimed that the United States could intervene in any Latin American nation guilty of "chronic misconduct" (such as the inability to repay debts). The United States then took control of debt collection in the Dominican Republic.

American investments in Latin America soon expanded. In the early 1900s, the United States began to pursue "**dollar diplomacy**," extending its influence by investing in Latin American development. The United States soon replaced Europe as the source of loans and investments. Direct U.S. investments reached $3.5 billion, out of a world total of $7.5 billion.

As American investments grew, so too did the resolve to protect those investments. U.S. military forces were sent to Cuba, Mexico, Guatemala, Honduras, Nicaragua, Panama, Colombia, Haiti, and the Dominican Republic to protect American interests. Some expeditions stayed for years. U.S. Marines were in Haiti from 1915 to 1934 and in Nicaragua from 1912 to 1933. Increasing numbers of Latin Americans began to resent this interference from the "big bully" to the north.

✔ **READING PROGRESS CHECK**

Analyzing Ethical Issues In what ways were U.S. actions in Latin America during the early 1900s imperialist?

Revolution in Mexico

GUIDING QUESTION *What were the causes and effects of the Mexican Revolution?*

After 1870, large landowners in Latin American began to take a more direct interest in national politics and even in governing. In Argentina and Chile, for example, landholding elites controlled the governments. They adopted constitutions similar to those of the United States and European democracies. The ruling elites, however, limited voting rights.

In some countries, large landowners supported dictators who looked out for the interests of the ruling elite. Porfirio Díaz, who ruled Mexico between 1877 and 1911, created a conservative, centralized government. The army, foreign capitalists, large landowners, and the Catholic Church supported Díaz. All these groups benefited from their alliance with Díaz. However, growing forces for change in Mexico led to a revolution.

dollar diplomacy
diplomacy that seeks to strengthen the power of a country or effect its purposes in foreign relations by the use of its financial resources

▼ Workers wait along the railroad tracks during the construction of the Panama Canal at Gatun, Panama. The canal changed commercial shipping patterns in the Western Hemisphere.

▶ CRITICAL THINKING
Making Connections How did ships travel before the opening of the Panama Canal?

whereas although

During Díaz's dictatorial reign, the wages of workers had declined. Ninety-five percent of the rural population owned no land, **whereas** about 1,000 families owned almost all of Mexico. A liberal landowner, Francisco Madero, forced Díaz from power in 1911. The door to a wider revolution then opened.

Madero made a valiant effort to handle the revolutionary forces. He put some of the best officials in his administration, and he sought a balance in dealing with foreign interests. However, his efforts proved ineffective.

The northern states were in near anarchy as Pancho Villa's armed masses of bandits swept the countryside. The federal army was full of hard-minded generals who itched to assert their power. Even the liberal politicians and idealists found fault with Madero for not solving all of the country's problems at once.

Francisco Madero's ineffectiveness created a demand for agrarian reform. This new call for reform was led by Emiliano Zapata. Zapata aroused the masses of landless peasants and began to seize and redistribute the estates of wealthy landholders. Although Madero tried to reach an agreement with him for land reforms, Zapata refused to disarm his followers.

Between 1910 and 1920, the Mexican Revolution caused great damage to the Mexican economy. Finally, a new constitution was enacted in 1917. This constitution set down many goals of the revolution. For revolutionary leaders, the goal was political reform. For peasants, it was about land reform. The constitution set up a government led by a president and elected by universal male suffrage. It also created land-reform policies, established limits on foreign investors, and set an agenda to help the workers. This agenda included the rights of workers to form unions, set a minimum wage, and limited working hours. Eventually, the revolution helped bring about a more democratic and politically stable Mexico.

The revolution also led to an outpouring of patriotism throughout Mexico. National pride was evident as intellectuals and artists sought to capture what was unique about Mexico with special emphasis on its past.

▲ Revolutionary leaders, such as Pancho Villa (seated left) and Emiliano Zapata (seated right), raised armies from the masses of discontented poor to fight for land reform in Mexico.

▶ **CRITICAL THINKING**
Analyzing Visuals What is the significance of this 1915 photograph of Mexican revolutionaries?

☑ **READING PROGRESS CHECK**

Identifying Central Issues How did Díaz, Madero, Villa, and Zapata help incite or prolong the Mexican Revolution?

Prosperity and Social Change

GUIDING QUESTION *How did prosperity change Latin America after 1870?*

After 1870, Latin America began an age of prosperity based to a large extent on the export of a few basic items. These included wheat and beef from Argentina, coffee from Brazil, coffee and bananas from Central America, and sugar and silver from Peru. These foodstuffs and raw materials were largely exchanged for finished goods—textiles, machines, and luxury items—from Europe and the United States.

After 1900, Latin Americans also increased their own industrialization. They built factories to produce textiles, foods, and construction materials. But because the growth of the Latin American economy came mostly from the export of raw materials, Latin America remained economically dependent on Western nations and their foreign investment.

Despite its economic growth, Latin America was still an underdeveloped region of the world. Old patterns still largely prevailed in Latin American societies. Rural elites dominated their estates and their workers. Slavery had been abolished by 1888, but former enslaved people and their descendants were at the bottom of society. The indigenous peoples were still poverty stricken.

One result of the prosperity of increased exports was growth in the middle **sectors** of Latin American society. Lawyers, merchants, shopkeepers, businesspeople, schoolteachers, professors, bureaucrats, and military officers increased in numbers.

Regardless of the country in which they lived, middle-class Latin Americans shared some common characteristics. They lived in cities and sought education and decent incomes. They also saw the United States as a model, especially in regard to industrialization. The middle class sought liberal reform, not revolution. After they had the right to vote, they generally sided with the landholding elites.

As Latin American export economies boomed, the working class grew. So too did the labor unions, especially after 1914. Radical unions often advocated the use of the general strike as an instrument for change. By and large, the governing elites were able to stifle the political influence of the working class by limiting their right to vote.

The need for industrial workers also led Latin American countries to seek immigrants from Europe. For example, between 1880 and 1914, 3 million Europeans, primarily Italians and Spaniards, settled in Argentina.

As in Europe and the United States, in Latin America industrialization led to urbanization. Buenos Aires (called "the Paris of South America") had 750,000 inhabitants by 1900 and 2 million by 1914. By that time, 53 percent of Argentina's population lived in cities.

✔ **READING PROGRESS CHECK**

Explaining How did an increase in exports change Latin America after 1870?

sector a sociological, economic, or political subdivision of society

Thinking Like a
HISTORIAN

Determining Cause and Effect

Historians look for patterns to determine causes and effects of important historical phenomena and events, such as industrialization. As it had earlier in Western Europe and the United States, industrialization caused changes in Latin American societies. Did the process of industrialization have the same effects on Latin American societies as it did on European societies? Use historical analysis skills to answer this question.

LESSON 4 REVIEW

Reviewing Vocabulary
1. *Explaining* Write a paragraph explaining why the term *dollar diplomacy* appears in quotation marks in the text.

Using Your Notes
2. *Differentiating* Use your notes listing problems in Mexico after 1870 to write a paragraph that outlines how the new constitution tried to address these problems.

Answering the Guiding Questions
3. *Identifying Cause and Effect* What was the impact of U.S. involvement in Latin America in the early 1900s?

4. *Identifying Cause and Effect* What were the causes and effects of the Mexican Revolution?

5. *Assessing* How did prosperity change Latin America after 1870?

Writing Activity
6. **ARGUMENT** Write a paragraph that supports or argues against this point of view: The United States was right to do whatever was necessary to build the Panama Canal because it is such an important and strategic waterway.

Directions: On a separate sheet of paper, answer the questions below. Make sure you read carefully and answer all parts of the questions.

Lesson Review

Lesson 1

1 **IDENTIFYING CENTRAL ISSUES** What is imperialism? What did it lead to in the late nineteenth century?

2 **MAKING INFERENCES** What new class did colonial rule create? How did this eventually lead to the end of colonialism?

Lesson 2

3 **SUMMARIZING** What raw materials did Europeans seize in West Africa?

4 **INTERPRETING** What was the goal of European missionaries as they traveled to the rain forests of Central Africa?

Lesson 3

5 **SPECULATING** Why didn't the British set up universal public education in India?

6 **FINDING THE MAIN IDEA** What was the spark for India's cultural revival? What are some examples of it?

Lesson 4

7 **SPECIFYING** What provisions did the Mexican Constitution of 1917 include?

8 **MAKING CONNECTIONS** What caused the increase in the number of Latin Americans in the middle class in the late nineteenth century?

21st Century Skills

9 **UNDERSTANDING RELATIONSHIPS AMONG EVENTS** Who were the Boers? How did they influence the European presence in South Africa?

10 **IDENTIFYING PERSPECTIVES AND DIFFERING INTERPRETATIONS** What can you deduce from the three different names for the rebellion of 1857 in India and the perspectives of the groups that use them?

Exploring the Essential Questions

11 Work with a partner to create a time line showing at least three causes and three effects of imperialism, as well as three examples of resistance to imperialism (successful or unsuccessful) between 1800 and 1914. Include visuals such as photos, sketches, and maps. You may also include primary sources. Be prepared to explain any connections you find.

DBQ Analyzing Historical Documents

Use the document to answer the following questions.

In 1893 Captain F. D. Lugard presented a justification for Great Britain's indirect rule of East Africa.

PRIMARY SOURCE

" There are some who say we have no right in Africa at all, that 'it belongs to the natives.' I hold that our right is the necessity that is upon us to provide for our ever-growing population—either by opening new fields for emigration, or by providing work.... In Africa, moreover, there is among the people a natural inclination to submit to a higher authority. That intense detestation of control which animates our Teutonic races does not exist among the tribes of Africa, and if there is any authority that we replace, it is the authority of the Slavers and Arabs, or the intolerable tyranny of the 'dominant tribe'. "

—quoted in *Civilization Past & Present*

12 **IDENTIFYING** What three reasons does Captain Lugard give to justify Great Britain's takeover of African nations?

13 **EVALUATING** How convincing do Captain Lugard's arguments seem today? Give details.

Extended-Response Question

14 **ARGUMENT** Compare and contrast the native peoples' resistance to colonization in Southeast Asia, Africa, India, and Latin America. Discuss who resisted, the tactics they used, and their successes or failures.

Need Extra Help?

If You've Missed Question	**1**	**2**	**3**	**4**	**5**	**6**	**7**	**8**	**9**	**10**	**11**	**12**	**13**	**14**
Go to page	226	230	231	232	239	240	244	245	234	237	226	231	231	230

Challenge and Transition in East Asia

1800–1914

ESSENTIAL QUESTIONS
- *How can new ideas accelerate economic and political change?*
- *How do cultures influence each other?*

The Story Matters...

In the nineteenth century, the Qing dynasty's growing weakness led to civil war, rebellion, and Western intervention. Followers of reformer Sun Yat-sen began an uprising in 1911 that ended the Qing dynasty and more than two thousand years of imperial rule. However, the new Chinese republic was not strong enough to maintain control, and China slipped into civil disorder and the rule of warlords. Throughout this period, Western economic and cultural influence on China continued to grow.

◄ Sun Yat-sen was a patriot and visionary dedicated to bringing China and its ancient traditions into the modern world. His political program was founded on principles of national self-determination, democracy, and equality. This photograph, taken around 1910, features Sun in European-influenced clothing. His knowledge of the Western world helped make him a symbol of modernization.

PHOTO: Stringer/Fotosearch/Getty Images

Place and Time: East Asia 1800–1914

The centuries-old Qing dynasty, China's last , finally fell as a result of many factors, including foreign pressures, social unrest, and the resistance of the autocratic government to the introduction of reforms. By contrast, Japan's empire expanded as its leaders embraced industrial development and commerce, undertook educational and governmental reform, and used Western ideas, institutions, and technology to create a new national order. Important victories over China and Russia secured Japanese military leadership in East Asia.

Step Into the Place

Read the quotes and look at the information presented on the map.

DBQ **Analyzing Historical Documents** How might attitudes toward change in China and Japan have affected the two countries' histories during this period?

PRIMARY SOURCE

66 Those who insist that there is no need for reform still say, 'Let us follow the ancients, follow the ancients.' They coldly sit and watch everything being laid to waste by following tradition, and there is no concern in their hearts. . . . Now there is a big mansion which has lasted a thousand years. The tiles and bricks are decayed and the beams and rafters are broken up, its fall is foredoomed. Yet the people in the house are still happily playing or soundly sleeping. Even some who have noted the danger know only how to weep bitterly, folding their arms and waiting for death without thinking of any remedy. . . . A nation is also like this. 99

—Liang Qichao, comment made in 1896 after China's defeat by Japan, quoted in *East Asia: A New History*

PRIMARY SOURCE

66 I am willing to admit my pride in Japan's accomplishments [in rapid modernization]. The facts are these: It was not until the sixth year of Kaei (1853) that a steamship was seen for the first time. . . . by 1860, the science was sufficiently understood to enable us to sail a ship across the Pacific. . . . I think we can without undue pride boast before the world of this courage and skill. . . . I feel convinced that there is no other nation which has the ability or the courage to navigate a steamship across the Pacific after a period of five years of experience in navigation and engineering. 99

—Fukuzawa Yukichi, from his autobiography, 1898

PHOTO: Fierce Fighting between Japanese and Chinese Troops in a Chinese City, an episode from the Sino-Japanese War, late 19th century (colour woodblock print), Japanese School, (19th century) / Private Collection / Archives Charmet / The Bridgeman Art Library

Step Into the Time

Synthesizing Information

Research an event from the time line and explain how it shows either the disintegration of the Qing dynasty in China or the expansion of Japan's imperialist power.

EAST ASIA

1800 China prohibits trade in opium

1800 Qing dynasty at the height of its power

1804 Russian ambassador arrives in Nagasaki

1839 Opium War begins in China

THE WORLD

1800

1820

1840

1804 Napoleon Bonaparte is crowned Emperor

1821 José de San Martín advances on Lima, Peru

1823 Monroe Doctrine is announced

networks
There's More Online!

☑ MAP Explore the interactive version of this map on Networks.

☑ TIME LINE Explore the interactive version of the time line on Networks.

Fall of the Qing Dynasty and the Rise of Japan 1850–1911

Legend:
- Rebellions in China
- Extent of Qing dynasty
- Area under Nationalist control, 1911
- Japanese expansion
- Japanese influence

Japan defeated Russia in the Russo-Japanese War. (1904–1905)

An allied force of Europeans, Americans, and Japanese crushed the Boxer Rebellion. (1900)

Sun Yat-sen's followers launched an uprising in central China, toppling the Qing dynasty. (1911)

Tai Ping rebels seized Nanjing and massacred 25,000 people. (1853)

Japan claimed control of the Ryukyu Islands, part of the Chinese Empire. (1874)

Japan defeated China in the First Sino-Japanese War, receiving Taiwan and the Liaodong Peninsula. (1894)

Map labels:
SIBERIA · RUSSIA · Lake Baikal · MANCHURIA · MONGOLIA · Amur R. · Sakhalin · Karafuto · Sea of Japan (East Sea) · JAPAN · Tokyo (Edo) · Kyōto · Ōsaka · KOREA · Beijing · Tianjin · Shimonoseki · Nagasaki · Northwestern Muslim Rebellion, 1863–1874 · Taiyuan · CHINA · Xi'an · Huang He (Yellow R.) · Nian Rebellion, 1851–1868 · Nanjing · Shanghai · Yellow Sea · TIBET · Chengdu · Chang Jiang (Yangtze R.) · Wuhan · Jiujiang · East China Sea · PACIFIC OCEAN · NEPAL · TROPIC OF CANCER · Yunnan and Sichuan Muslim Rebellion, 1855–1878 · Changsha · Miao Rebellion, 1850–1872 · Tai Ping Rebellion, 1850–1863 · BHUTAN · Tengchong · Kunming · GUANGDONG · Formosa (Taiwan) · INDIA · Red Turban Rebellion, 1854–1857 · Guangzhou · BURMA (MYANMAR) · LAOS · South China Sea · PHILIPPINES · Bay of Bengal · SIAM (THAILAND) · FRENCH INDOCHINA

0 — 800 miles
0 — 800 km
Two-Point Equidistant projection

Timeline:

1850 Tai Ping Rebellion begins in China

1848 Nationalist and liberal revolutions erupt in Europe

1853 U.S. asks Japan to open foreign relations

1856 Second Opium War begins

1865 American Civil War ends

1860

1868 Japanese emperor Mutsuhito begins Meiji rule

1899 U.S. establishes Open Door Policy with China

1879 Thomas Edison develops the electric light bulb

1880

1894 José Martí leads revolt against Spanish rule in Cuba

1910 Japan annexes Korea

1905 Russia grants Liaodong Peninsula to Japan

1902 Afrikaners are defeated in the Boer War

1900

1911 Followers of Sun Yat-sen launch Chinese rebellion

1914 World War I begins

1914

Reading **HELP**DESK (CCSS)

Academic Vocabulary
- **highlighted**
- **exclusive**

Content Vocabulary
- **extraterritoriality**
- **self-strengthening**
- **spheres of influence**
- **Open Door policy**
- **indemnity**

TAKING NOTES:

Key Ideas and Details

Comparing and Contrasting As you read, create a chart like the one below to compare and contrast the Tai Ping and Boxer Rebellions.

	Tai Ping	Boxer
Reforms Demanded		
Method Used		
Outcomes		

250

LESSON 1
The Decline of the Qing Dynasty

ESSENTIAL QUESTIONS
- *How can new ideas accelerate economic and political change?*
- *How do cultures influence each other?*

IT MATTERS BECAUSE
China preferred to keep its culture free of Western influences. However, as the Qing government grew more unstable, foreign powers created spheres of influence and pursued a policy to secure trading rights. The Chinese resisted but were eventually overcome, weakening the imperial government even more.

Causes of Decline

GUIDING QUESTION *What factors influenced the decline of the Qing Empire?*

In 1800, after a long period of peace and prosperity, the Qing dynasty of the Manchus was at the height of its power. A little more than a century later, however, humiliated and harassed by the Western powers, the Qing dynasty collapsed.

One important reason for the abrupt decline and fall of the Qing dynasty was the intense external pressure that the modern West applied to Chinese society. However, internal problems also played a role.

After an extended period of growth, the Qing dynasty began to suffer from corruption, peasant unrest, and incompetence. These weaknesses were made worse by rapid growth in the country's population. By 1900, there were 400 million people in China. Population growth created a serious food shortage. In the 1850s, one observer wrote, "Not a year passes in which a terrific number of persons do not perish of famine in some part or other of China."

The ships, guns, and ideas of foreigners **highlighted** the growing weakness of the Qing dynasty and probably hastened its end. By 1800, Europeans had been in contact with China for more than 200 years. Wanting to limit contact with outsiders, the Qing dynasty had restricted European merchants to a small trading outlet at Guangzhou (GWAHNG • JOH), or Canton. The merchants could deal with only a few Chinese firms. The British did not like this arrangement.

PHOTO: (l to r)Art Archive/Eileen Tweedy; Library of Congress; Hu Weibiao/Panorama/The Image Works.

Britain had a trade deficit, or an unfavorable trade balance, with China. That is, it imported more goods from China than it exported to China. Britain had to pay China with silver for the difference between its imports—tea, silk, and porcelain—from China and its exports—Indian cotton—to China. At first, the British tried to negotiate with the Chinese to improve the trade imbalance. When negotiations failed, the British turned to trading opium.

highlighted centered attention on

The Opium War

Opium was grown in northern India under the sponsorship of the British East India Company and then shipped directly to Chinese markets. Demand for opium—a highly addictive drug—in South China jumped dramatically. Soon, silver was flowing out of China and into the pockets of the officials of the British East India Company.

The Chinese reacted strongly. They appealed to the British government on moral grounds to stop the traffic in opium. Lin Zexu, a Chinese government official, wrote to Queen Victoria:

PRIMARY SOURCE

66 Suppose there were people from another country who carried opium for sale to England and seduced your people into buying and smoking it; certainly your honorable ruler would deeply hate it and be bitterly aroused. 99

—quoted in *The British Imperial Century, 1815–1914*

The British refused to halt their activity, however. As a result, the Chinese blockaded the foreign area in Guangzhou to force traders to surrender their opium. The British responded with force, starting the Opium War (1839–1842).

The Chinese were no match for the British. British warships destroyed Chinese coastal and river forts. When a British fleet sailed almost unopposed up the Chang Jiang (Yangtze River) to Nanjing, the Qing dynasty made peace.

In the Treaty of Nanjing in 1842, the Chinese agreed to open five coastal ports to British trade, limit taxes on imported British goods, and pay for the costs of the war. China also agreed to give the British ownership of the island of Hong Kong. Nothing was said in the treaty about the opium trade.

PHOTO: Art Archive / Eileen Tweedy

◄ This illustration by E. Duncan shows the British steamship *Nemesis* destroying Chinese war junks in Anson's Bay, 1841.

▶ **CRITICAL THINKING**
Transferring Use the information in the table to create a bar graph of the amount of opium imported into China.

Opium Imported into China*	
Year	**Number of Chests**
1729	200
1767	1,000
1830	10,000
1838	40,000

*(1 chest = approximately 135 pounds)

extraterritoriality living in a section of a country set aside for foreigners but not subject to the host country's laws

Moreover, in the five ports, Europeans lived in their own sections and were subject not to Chinese laws but to their own laws—a practice known as **extraterritoriality**.

The Opium War marked the beginning of the establishment of Western influence in China. For the time being, the Chinese dealt with the problem by pitting foreign countries against one another. Concessions granted to the British were offered to other Western nations, including the United States. Soon, thriving foreign areas were operating in the five treaty ports along the southern Chinese coast.

The Tai Ping Rebellion

In the meantime, the failure of the Chinese government to deal with pressing internal economic problems led to a peasant revolt, known as the Tai Ping (TIE PING) Rebellion (1850–1864). It was led by Hong Xiuquan, a Christian convert who viewed himself as a younger brother of Jesus.

Hong was convinced that God had given him the mission of destroying the Qing dynasty. Joined by great crowds of peasants, Hong captured the town of Yongan and proclaimed a new dynasty, the Heavenly Kingdom of Great Peace (*Tai Ping Tianguo* in Chinese—hence the name of the rebellion.)

In March 1853, the rebels seized Nanjing, the second largest city of the empire, and massacred 25,000 men, women, and children. The revolt continued for 10 more years but gradually began to fall apart. Europeans came to the aid of the Qing dynasty when they realized the destructive nature of the Tai Ping forces. One British observer noted there was "no hope of any good ever coming of the rebel movement. They do nothing but burn, murder, and destroy."

GEOGRAPHY CONNECTION

By 1900, parts of China were divided into separate spheres of influence.

1 **HUMAN SYSTEMS** *After Russia, which country had the largest sphere of influence?*

2 **THE USES OF GEOGRAPHY** *Why were countries able to maintain ports in other countries' spheres of influence?*

Spheres of Influence in China 1900

In 1864, Chinese forces, with European aid, recaptured Nanjing and destroyed the remaining rebel force. The Tai Ping Rebellion was one of the most devastating civil wars in history. As many as 20 million people died during the 14-year struggle.

China's ongoing struggle with the West prevented the Qing dynasty from dealing effectively with the internal unrest. Beginning in 1856, the British and the French applied force to gain greater trade privileges. As a result of the Treaty of Tianjin in 1858, the Chinese agreed to legalize the opium trade and to open new ports to foreign trade. They also surrendered the Kowloon Peninsula to Great Britain.

Efforts at Reform

By the late 1870s, the Qing dynasty was in decline. Unable to restore order themselves, government troops had relied on forces recruited by regional warlords to help fight the Tai Ping Rebellion. To finance their armies, the warlords had collected taxes from local people. After the revolt, many of these warlords kept their armies.

In its weakened state, the Qing court finally began to listen to the appeals of reform-minded officials. The reformers called for a new policy they called "**self-strengthening**." That is, China should adopt Western technology but keep its Confucian values and institutions.

Some reformers wanted to change China's traditional political institutions by introducing democracy. However, such ideas were too radical for most reformers. During the last quarter of the nineteenth century, the Chinese government tried to modernize China's military forces and build up industry without touching the basic elements of Chinese civilization. Railroads, weapons factories, and shipyards were built. However, the Chinese value system remained unchanged.

> **self-strengthening**
> a policy promoted by reformers toward the end of the Qing dynasty under which China would adopt Western technology while keeping its Confucian values and institutions

☑ **READING PROGRESS CHECK**

Analyzing Information Why do you think the Qing dynasty wanted to limit contact with foreign nations?

The Advance of Imperialism

GUIDING QUESTION *Why were spheres of influence established in China?*

In the end, however, the changes did not help the Qing stay in power. The European advance into China continued during the last two decades of the nineteenth century. Internal conditions also continued to deteriorate.

Mounting Pressures

In the north and northeast, Russia took advantage of the Qing dynasty's weakness to force China to give up territories north of the Amur River in Siberia. In Tibet, a struggle between Russia and Great Britain kept both powers from seizing the territory outright. This allowed Tibet to become free from Chinese influence.

Even more ominous changes were taking place in the Chinese heartland. European states began to create **spheres of influence**, areas in which the imperial powers had **exclusive** trading rights. After the Tai Ping Rebellion, warlords in the provinces began to negotiate directly with foreign nations. In return for money, the warlords granted these nations exclusive trading rights or railroad-building and mining privileges. In this way, Britain, France, Germany, Russia, and Japan all established spheres of influence in China.

> **spheres of influence**
> areas in which foreign powers have been granted exclusive rights and privileges, such as trading rights and mining privileges
>
> **exclusive** limited to a single individual or group

Ci Xi (1835–1908)

Though never the official ruler of China, Ci Xi was the power behind the throne for 47 years. Ci Xi was appointed regent when her son, the emperor's only heir, became emperor at age six. After her son died, she ruled for her three-year-old nephew, Guang Xu. Ci Xi officially retired when Guang Xu came of age. Later, however, when he tried to institute reforms, Ci Xi had him imprisoned and resumed the regency. In 1899 she supported the Boxer Rebellion, which ultimately failed, and fled Beijing after China's defeat. She did not return to Beijing until 1902.

▶ **CRITICAL THINKING**
Drawing Conclusions How did Ci Xi acquire and maintain power in a political system dominated by men?

In 1894, another blow furthered the disintegration of the Qing dynasty. The Chinese went to war with Japan over Japanese inroads into Korea, a land that the Chinese had controlled for a long time. The Chinese were soundly defeated. Japan demanded and received the island of Taiwan and the Liaodong (LYOW • DOONG) Peninsula. Fearing Japan's growing power, however, the European powers forced Japan to give the Liaodong Peninsula back to China.

New pressures for Chinese territory soon arose. In 1897, Chinese rioters murdered two German missionaries. Germany used this as a pretext to demand territories in the Shandong (SHON • DOONG) Peninsula. When the Chinese government approved the demand, other European nations made new claims on Chinese territory.

Internal Crisis

This latest scramble for territory took place at a time of internal crisis in China. In June 1898, the young emperor Guang Xu (GWANG SHYOO) launched a massive reform program based on changes in Japan. During the following weeks, known as the One Hundred Days of Reform, the emperor issued edicts calling for major political, administrative, and education reforms. With these reforms, Guang Xu intended to modernize government bureaucracy by following Western models; to adopt a new education system that would replace the traditional civil service examinations; and to adopt Western-style schools, banks, and a free press. Guang Xu also intended to train the military to use modern weapons and Western fighting techniques.

Many conservatives at court, however, opposed these reforms. They saw little advantage in copying the West. As one said, "An examination of the causes of success and failure in government reveals that . . . the adoption of foreignism leads to disorder." According to this conservative, traditional Chinese rules needed to be reformed and not rejected in favor of Western changes.

Most important, Empress Dowager Ci Xi (TSUH • SEE), the emperor's aunt, opposed the new reform program. Ci Xi became a dominant force at court and opposed the emperor's reforms. With the aid of the imperial army, she eventually imprisoned the emperor. Other supporters of the reforms were imprisoned, exiled, or prosecuted. These actions ended Guang Xu's reforms. Although Guang Xu's efforts aroused popular sympathy, they had limited support within Chinese society overall.

☑ **READING PROGRESS CHECK**

Drawing Conclusions Why did Guang Xu's reforms fail to achieve the modernization of the government and military?

Responses to Imperialism

GUIDING QUESTION *What were the responses to imperialism in China?*

As foreign pressure on the Qing dynasty grew stronger, both Great Britain and the United States feared that other nations would overrun the country should the Chinese government collapse.

Opening the Door to China

In 1899, U.S. secretary of state John Hay wrote a note to Britain, Russia, Germany, France, Italy, and Japan. Hay presented a proposal that ensured equal access to the Chinese market for all nations and preserved the unity of the Chinese empire. When none of the other imperialist governments expressed opposition to the idea, Hay proclaimed that all major states with economic interests in China had agreed that the country should have an Open Door policy.

In part, the **Open Door policy** reflected American concern for the survival of China. However, it also reflected the interests of some U.S. trading companies. These companies wanted to operate in open markets and disliked the existing division of China into separate spheres of influence dominated by individual countries.

The Open Door policy did not end the system of spheres of influence. However, it did reduce restrictions on foreign imports imposed by the dominating power within each sphere. The Open Door policy also helped reduce imperialist hysteria over access to the China market. The policy lessened fears in Britain, France, Germany, and Russia that other powers would take advantage of China's weakness and attempt to dominate the China market for themselves.

The Boxer Rebellion

The Open Door policy came too late to stop the Boxer Rebellion. Boxer was the popular name given to members of a secret organization called the Society of Harmonious Fists. Members practiced a system of exercise—a form of shadowboxing, or boxing with an imaginary opponent—that they thought would protect them from bullets.

The Boxers were upset by economic distress and the foreign takeover of Chinese lands. They wanted to push foreigners out of China. Their slogan was "destroy the foreigner." They especially disliked Christian missionaries and Chinese converts to Christianity who seemed to threaten Chinese traditions. At the beginning of 1900, Boxer bands roamed the countryside and slaughtered foreign missionaries and Chinese Christians. Foreign business people and the German envoy to Beijing were also victims.

Response to the killings was immediate and overwhelming. An allied army consisting of 20,000 British, French, German, Russian, American, and Japanese troops attacked Beijing in August 1900. The army restored order and demanded more concessions from the Chinese government. The Chinese government was forced to pay a heavy **indemnity** to the powers that had crushed the uprising. The imperial government was now weaker than ever.

✓ **READING PROGRESS CHECK**

Drawing Conclusions Did the Boxer Rebellion do anything to reduce the foreign presence in China? Explain your answer.

Open Door policy
a policy, proposed by U.S. secretary of state John Hay in 1899, that stated all powers with spheres of influence in China would respect equal trading opportunities with China and not set tariffs giving an unfair advantage to the citizens of their own country

indemnity the payment for damages

▶ **CRITICAL THINKING**
Making Inferences Why do you think the foreign response to the Boxer Rebellion was "immediate and overwhelming"?

▼ This photograph, from around 1901, shows Chinese men who took part in the Boxer Rebellion. They were captured and imprisoned by the American forces at Tientsin, China.

LESSON 1 REVIEW (CCSS)

Reviewing Vocabulary
1. *Identifying Cause and Effect* Write a short paragraph describing the Open Door policy and its effect on the existing spheres of influence in China.

Using Your Notes
2. *Comparing and Contrasting* Use your notes to answer the following questions. How were the Tai Ping and Boxer Rebellions different? How were they similar?

Answering the Guiding Questions
3. *Identifying* What factors influenced the decline of the Qing Empire?

4. *Theorizing* Why were spheres of influence established in China?

5. *Synthesizing* What were the responses to imperialism in China?

Writing Activity
6. INFORMATIVE/EXPLANATORY Write a short paragraph describing the major events in China related to imperialism during the nineteenth and early twentieth centuries.

netw🌐rks
There's More Online!

☑ **IMAGE** Chinese Emperor Henry Pu Yi at Age Three

☑ **IMAGE** Chinese Men Voluntarily Cut Their Pigtails

☑ **IMAGE** New Market in Hong Kong

☑ **IMAGE** The Revolution of 1911

☑ **INTERACTIVE SELF-CHECK QUIZ**

☑ **PRIMARY SOURCE** Sun Yat-sen

☑ **PRIMARY SOURCE** Yuan Shigai

☑ **VIDEO** Revolution in China

Reading **HELP**DESK (CCSS)

Academic Vocabulary
- **phase**
- **motive**

Content Vocabulary
- **provincial**
- **commodities**

TAKING NOTES:
Key Ideas and Details

Comparing and Contrasting Use the graphic organizer to compare and contrast the reforms of Empress Dowager Ci Xi with those proposed by Sun Yat-sen.

Empress Dowager Ci Xi	Sun Yat-sen

LESSON 2
Revolution in China

ESSENTIAL QUESTIONS
- *How can new ideas accelerate economic and political change?*
- *How do cultures influence each other?*

IT MATTERS BECAUSE
After the Boxer Rebellion failed, China made desperate reform efforts. However, when Empress Dowager Ci Xi died in 1908, the Qing dynasty was near collapse. China slipped into revolution and civil war.

The Fall of the Qing

GUIDING QUESTION *What led to the fall of the Qing dynasty?*

After the Boxer Rebellion, the Qing dynasty in China tried desperately to reform itself. Ci Xi, who had long resisted suggestions from her advisers for change, now embraced a number of reforms.

A new education system based on the Western model was adopted, and the civil service examination system was dropped. In 1909 legislative assemblies were formed at the **provincial**, or local, level. Elections for a national assembly were held in 1910.

The emerging new elite, composed of merchants, professionals, and reform-minded gentry, soon became impatient with the slow pace of political change. They were angry when they discovered that the new assemblies were not allowed to pass laws but could only give advice to the ruler. Moreover, the recent reforms had done nothing for the peasants, artisans, and miners, whose living conditions were getting worse as taxes increased. Unrest grew in the countryside as the dynasty continued to ignore deep-seated resentments.

The Rise of Sun Yat-sen

The first signs of revolution appeared during the 1890s when the young radical Sun Yat-sen formed the Revive China Society.

Sun Yat-sen believed that the Qing dynasty was in a state of decay and could no longer govern the country. Unless the Chinese were united under a strong government, they would remain at the mercy of other countries. Although Sun believed that China should follow the pattern of Western countries, he also knew that the Chinese people were hardly ready for democracy.

Sun instead developed a three-stage reform process. The first stage would be a military takeover. In the second stage, a transitional **phase**, Sun's own revolutionary party would prepare the people for democratic rule. The final stage called for establishment of a constitutional democracy.

At a convention in Tokyo in 1905, Sun united members of radical groups from across China and formed the Revolutionary Alliance, which eventually became the Nationalist Party. In presenting his program, Sun Yat-sen called for the following changes:

provincial local; of or relating to a province

phase a part in the development cycle

PRIMARY SOURCE

❝Establish the Republic: Now our revolution is based on equality, in order to establish a republican government. All our people are equal and all enjoy political rights.... Equalize land ownership: The good fortune of civilization is to be shared equally by all the people of the nation.... Its [the land's] present price shall be received by the owner ... after the revolution [it] shall belong to the state.❞

—quoted in *Sources of Chinese Tradition*, 1960

Sun's new organization advocated his Three People's Principles, which promoted nationalism, democracy, and the right for people to pursue their own livelihoods. Although the new organization was small, it beefited from the rising discontent generated by the Qing dynasty's failure to improve conditions in China.

The Revolution of 1911

The Qing dynasty was near its end. In 1908, Empress Dowager Ci Xi died. Her nephew Guang Xu, a prisoner in the palace, died one day before his aunt. The throne was now occupied by China's "last emperor," the infant Henry Pu Yi.

ANALYZING PRIMARY SOURCES CCSS

The End of the Qing Dynasty

As the Qing Dynasty was coming to an end, Sun Yat-sen and Yuan Shigai communicated via telegrams about who would assume the presidency of a new China. Even though he was a general in the Qing dynasty, Yuan Shigai became president of the new Chinese republic in 1911.

❝I beg to call the attention of Premier Yüan in Peking to the fact that when I reached Shanghai two days ago my comrades entrusted me with the responsibility of organizing a provisional government.... Although I have accepted this position for the time being, it is actually waiting for you, and my offer will eventually be made clear to the world. I hope that you will decide to accept this offer.❞

—telegram from Sun Yat-sen to Yuan Shigai, January 1, 1911, quoted in *The Political History of China, 1840–1928*

❝I have received your telegram of the first. The choice between monarchism and republicanism in the political system is to be decided by public opinion and there is no way to predict what the decision will be. I dare not participate in the provisional government. You have been kind to offer me such great honor, but I am sorry to say that I dare not accept it; I hope I shall be excused from doing so.❞

—telegram from Yuan Shigai to Sun Yat-sen, January 2, 1911, quoted in *The Political History of China, 1840–1928*

DBQ Analyzing Historical Documents

❶ *Paraphrasing* Summarize the excerpt from Sun Yat-sen's telegram to Yuan Shigai in your own words.

❷ *Making Inferences* Why do you think Yuan Shigai initially declined Sun Yat-sen's offer?

Historians look for general characteristics and particular patterns to classify events. Political revolutions are important phenomena that historians analyze. For example, a historian might classify one event as a revolution while another as an uprising. The author of this textbook notes that "the events of 1911 were less a revolution than a collapse of the old order." In other words, the revolution of 1911 was not really a revolution. Think about other revolutions you have learned about in your textbook and why this might be so.

motive a reason to take action

In October 1911, followers of Sun Yat-sen launched an uprising in central China. At the time, Sun was traveling in the United States. Thus, the revolt had no leader, but the government was too weak to react. The Qing dynasty collapsed, opening the way for new political forces.

Sun's party had neither the military nor the political strength to form a new government. The party was forced to turn to a member of the old order, General Yuan Shigai (YOO • AHN SHUR • GIE), who controlled the army.

Yuan was a prominent figure in military circles. He had been placed in charge of the imperial army sent to suppress the rebellion. However, he abandoned the government and negotiated with members of Sun Yat-sen's party. General Yuan agreed to serve as president of a new Chinese republic and to allow the election of a legislature. Sun arrived in China in January 1912, after reading about the revolution in a Denver, Colorado newspaper.

In the eyes of Sun Yat-sen's party, the events of 1911 were a glorious revolution that ended 2,000 years of imperial rule. However, the 1911 uprising was hardly a revolution. It produced no new political or social order. Sun Yat-sen and his followers still had much to accomplish.

The Revolutionary Alliance was supported mainly by an emerging urban middle class, and its program was based largely on Western liberal democratic principles. However, the urban middle class in China was too small to support a new political order. Most of the Chinese people still lived on the land, and few peasants supported Sun Yat-sen's party. In effect, then, the events of 1911 were less a revolution than a collapse of the old order.

An Era of Civil War

After the collapse of the Qing dynasty, the military took over. Sun Yat-sen and his colleagues had accepted General Yuan Shigai as president of the new Chinese republic in 1911 because they lacked the military force to compete with his control over the army. Many feared that if the revolt lapsed into chaos, the Western powers would intervene. If that happened, the last shreds of Chinese independence would be lost. However, even the general's new allies distrusted his **motives**.

Yuan understood little of the new ideas sweeping into China from the West. He ruled in a traditional manner and even tried to set up a new imperial dynasty. The reformers hated Yuan for using murder and terror to destroy the new democratic institutions. The traditionalists hated Yuan for being disloyal to the dynasty he had served.

Yuan's dictatorial efforts rapidly led to clashes with Sun's party, now renamed the *Guomindang*, or Nationalist Party. When Yuan dissolved the new parliament, the Nationalists launched a rebellion. The rebellion failed, and Sun Yat-sen fled to Japan.

Yuan was strong enough to brush off the challenge from the revolutionary forces, but he could not turn back history. He died in 1916 and was succeeded by one of his officers. Over the next several years, China slipped into civil war as the power of the central government disintegrated and military warlords seized power in the provinces. Their soldiers caused massive destruction throughout China.

☑ **READING PROGRESS CHECK**

Explaining Why did rebellions occur in China after Yuan Shigai became president of the new republic in 1911?

Cultural Changes

GUIDING QUESTION *How did Western influences change Chinese society and culture?*

Western influences forced the Chinese to adapt to new ways of thinking and living. Early twentieth-century Chinese culture reflected the struggle between Confucian social ideas and those of the West.

Society in Transition

When European traders began to move into China in greater numbers in the mid-1800s, Chinese society was in a state of transition. The growth of industry and trade was especially noticeable in the cities, where a national market for **commodities** such as oil, copper, salt, and tea had appeared.

The Chinese economy had never been more productive. Faster and more reliable transportation and a better system of money and banking had begun to create the foundation for a money economy. Foreign investments in China grew rapidly, and the money went into modernizing the Chinese economy. New crops brought in from abroad increased food production and encouraged population growth.

The coming of Westerners to China affected the Chinese economy in three ways. Westerners introduced modern means of transportation and communications, created an export market, and integrated the Chinese market into the nineteenth-century world economy.

To some, these changes were beneficial. Shaking China out of its old ways quickened a process of change that had already begun. Western influences forced the Chinese to adopt new ways of thinking and acting, and Western ideas stimulated the desire to modernize. Westerners also provided something else to the Chinese. They gave them a model, funds, and the technical knowledge to modernize.

At the same time, China paid a heavy price for the new ways. Imperialism imposed a state of dependence on China, and many Chinese were exploited. Imperialism condemned the country to a condition of underdevelopment. Its local industry was largely destroyed. Also, many of the profits in the new economy went to foreign countries rather than back into the Chinese economy.

During the first quarter of the twentieth century, the pace of change in China quickened even more. After World War I, which temporarily drew foreign investment out of the country, Chinese businesspeople began to develop new ventures. Shanghai became the bastion of the new bourgeoisie. People lived in Shanghai at the same rhythm they lived in other modern cities. Wuhan, Tianjin, and Guangzhou also became major industrial and commercial centers with a growing middle class and an industrial working class.

In 1800 daily life in China was the same as it had been for centuries. Most Chinese were farmers, living in millions of villages near rice fields and on hillsides throughout the countryside. A farmer's life was governed by the harvest cycle, village custom, and family ritual. A few men were educated in the Confucian classics. Women stayed at home or in the fields.

▲ As part of the changes to the Chinese economy, trade increased between China and the West, as shown in this circa 1900 photograph of the New Market in Hong Kong.

▶ **CRITICAL THINKING**
Analyzing Visuals How does this image show the mixture of Chinese and Western influence in Chinese society?

commodities agricultural, mined, and mass-produced marketable goods

Analyzing
PRIMARY SOURCES

Ba Jin on writing

Ba Jin once described his compulsion to express himself:

Before my eyes are many miserable scenes, the suffering of others and myself forces my hands to move. I become a machine for writing.**"**

—Ba Jin, *China Daily*

DBQ *DRAWING CONCLUSIONS*
What do you think motivated Ba Jin to write?

All children were expected to obey their parents, and wives were expected to submit to the wishes of their husbands.

A visitor to China 125 years later would have seen a different society, although it would still have been recognizably Chinese. The changes were most striking in the cities, among the urban middle class. Here the educated and wealthy had been visibly affected by the growing Western cultural presence. Confucian social ideas were declining rapidly in influence.

Culture in Transition

Nowhere in China was the struggle between old and new more visible than in the culture. Radical reformers wanted to eliminate traditional culture, condemning it as an instrument of oppression. They were interested in creating a new China that would be respected by the modern world.

The first changes in traditional culture came in the late nineteenth century. Intellectuals began to introduce Western books, art, and ideas to China. Soon, China was flooded by Western culture as intellectuals called for a new culture based on that of the modern West.

Western literature and art became popular in China, especially among the urban middle class. Traditional culture, however, remained popular, especially in rural areas. Most creative artists followed foreign trends, while traditionalists held on to Chinese culture.

Literature in particular was influenced by foreign ideas. Western novels and short stories began to attract a larger audience. Although most Chinese novels written after World War I dealt with Chinese subjects, they reflected the Western tendency toward a realistic portrayal of society. Often, they dealt with the new Westernized middle class. Most of China's modern authors showed a clear contempt for the past.

Mao Dun became known as one of China's best modern novelists. *Midnight*, Dun's most popular work, was also published in French and English. A naturalistic novel, *Midnight* described the changing customs of Shanghai's urban elites.

Ba Jin, the author of numerous novels and short stories, was one of China's foremost writers of the twentieth century. Born in 1904, Ba Jin was well attuned to the rigors and expected obedience of Chinese family life. In his trilogy, *Family, Spring,* and *Autumn,* he describes the disintegration of traditional Confucian ways as the younger members of a large family attempt to break away from their elders.

☑ **READING PROGRESS CHECK**

Identifying How did education reforms during the late Qing dynasty contribute to intellectual and cultural innovations following the revolution?

LESSON 2 REVIEW

Reviewing Vocabulary
1. *Making Generalizations* Write a paragraph in which you define the term *commodities* and discuss the impact of domestic and international trade on China in the late nineteenth and early twentieth century.

Using Your Notes
2. *Comparing and Contrasting* Use your notes to write a paragraph comparing the reforms undertaken by Ci Xi toward the end of her reign with those proposed by Sun Yat-sen.

Answering the Guiding Questions
3. *Identifying Cause and Effect* What led to the fall of the Qing dynasty?

4. *Making Connections* How did Western influences change Chinese society and culture?

Writing Activity
5. **INFORMATIVE/EXPLANATORY** In what ways did Sun Yat-sen and the intellectuals and writers who succeeded him embrace Western ideas? How did they adapt these ideas to the Chinese context?

Reading **HELP**DESK (CCSS)

Academic Vocabulary

- **subsidy**
- **context**

Content Vocabulary

- **concessions**
- **prefecture**

TAKING NOTES:

Key Ideas and Details

Organizing As you read, create a table like the one below listing the political, economic, and social reforms of the Meiji Restoration.

Political	Economic	Social

PHOTO: (l to r)/Asian Art & Archaeology/CORBIS, Asian Art & Archaeology/CORBIS, Buyenlarge/Archive Photos/Getty Images, ©Corbis.

LESSON 3
The Rise of Modern Japan

ESSENTIAL QUESTIONS

- *How can new ideas accelerate economic and political change?*
- *How do cultures influence each other?*

IT MATTERS BECAUSE

In the mid-nineteenth century, the United States forced Japan to open its doors to trade with Western nations. After the Sat-Cho alliance overthrew the shogun, the Meiji Restoration began. Japan emerged as a modern industrial society.

Japan Responds to Foreign Pressure

GUIDING QUESTION *How did Japan respond to foreign pressure to end its isolationist policies?*

By the end of the nineteenth century, Japan was emerging as a modern imperialist power. The Japanese followed the example of Western nations, while trying to preserve Japanese values.

By 1800, the Tokugawa shogunate had ruled Japan for 200 years. It had kept an isolationist policy, allowing only Dutch and Chinese merchants at its port at Nagasaki. Western nations wanted to end Japan's isolation, believing that the expansion of trade on a global basis would benefit all nations.

The first foreign power to succeed with Japan was the United States. In the summer of 1853, Commodore Matthew Perry arrived in Edo Bay (now Tokyo Bay) with an American fleet of four war-ships. Perry brought a letter from President Millard Fillmore, asking the Japanese for better treatment of sailors shipwrecked on the Japanese islands. (Foreign sailors shipwrecked in Japan were treated as criminals and exhibited in public cages.) He also asked to open foreign relations between the United States and Japan. Perry returned about six months later for an answer, this time with a larger fleet. Some shogunate officials recommended **concessions**, or political compromises. The guns of Perry's ships ultimately made Japan's decision.

Under military pressure, Japan agreed to the Treaty of Kana-gawa with the United States. The treaty provided for the return of shipwrecked American sailors, the opening of two Japanese ports to Western traders, and the establishment of a U.S. consulate in Japan.

concession a political compromise

In 1858 a more detailed treaty called for the opening of several new ports to U.S. trade and residence. Japan soon signed similar treaties with several European nations.

Resistance to opening foreign relations was especially strong among the samurai warriors in two southern territories, Satsuma and Choshu. In 1863 the Sat-Cho alliance (from Satsuma-Choshu) forced the shogun to promise to end relations with the West. In 1868, when the shogun refused, the Sat-Cho leaders attacked the shogun's palace in Kyōto. His forces collapsed, ending the shogunate system and beginning the Meiji Restoration.

☑ **READING PROGRESS CHECK**

Applying What led to the collapse of the shogunate system in Japan?

The Meiji Restoration

GUIDING QUESTION *How did the Meiji Restoration change Japan?*

The Sat-Cho leaders had genuinely mistrusted the West, but they soon realized that Japan must change to survive. The new leaders embarked on a policy of reform that transformed Japan into a modern industrial nation. The symbol of the new era was the young emperor Mutsuhito. He called his reign the Meiji (MAY • jee), or "Enlightened Rule." This period has thus become known as the Meiji Restoration.

Of course, the Sat-Cho leaders controlled the Meiji ruler, just as the shogunate had controlled earlier emperors. In recognition of the real source of political power, the capital was moved from Kyōto to Edo (now named Tokyo), the location of the new leaders.

Transformation of Japanese Politics

When in power, the new leaders moved to abolish the old order and to strengthen power in their hands. To undercut the power of the daimyo (the local nobles) the new leaders stripped them of their lands in 1871. In turn, the lords were named governors of the territories formerly under their control. The territories were now called **prefectures**.

The Meiji reformers set out to create a modern political system based on the Western model. During the next 20 years, the Meiji government carefully studied Western political systems. As the process evolved, two main factions appeared, the Liberals and the Progressives. The Liberals wanted political reform based on the Western liberal democratic model, which vested supreme authority in a parliament. The Progressives wanted power to be shared between the legislative and executive branches, with the executive branch having more control.

During the 1870s and 1880s, these factions fought for control. The Progressives won. The Meiji constitution, adopted in 1889, was modeled after that of Imperial Germany. It gave most authority to the executive branch.

In theory, the emperor exercised all executive authority, but in practice he was a figurehead. Real executive authority rested in the prime minister and his cabinet of ministers chosen by the Meiji leaders. The upper house included royal appointees and elected nobles, while the lower house was elected. The two houses were to have equal legislative powers.

The final result was a political system that was democratic in form but authoritarian in practice. Although modern in external appearance, it was still traditional because power remained in the hands of a ruling oligarchy (the Sat-Cho leaders). The system allowed the traditional ruling class to keep its influence and economic power.

▲ Japanese artist Hiroshige III created this woodblock print of the Tokyo-Yokohama railway just years after the Meiji Restoration opened the door to Western trade and ideas.

▶ **CRITICAL THINKING**

Identifying Bias Do you think the artist was biased in his depiction of the railway? Why or why not?

prefecture in the Japanese Meiji Restoration, a territory governed by its former daimyo lord

Meiji Economics

The Meiji leaders also set up a land reform program, which made the traditional lands of the daimyo the private property of the peasants. The daimyo were compensated with government bonds. The Meiji leaders then levied a new land tax, which was set at an annual rate of 3 percent of the estimated value of the land. The new tax was a great source of revenue for the government but a burden for farmers.

Under the old system, farmers had paid a fixed percentage of their harvest to the landowners. In bad harvest years, they had owed little or nothing. Under the new system, the farmers had to pay the land tax every year, regardless of the quality of the harvest. As a result, in bad years, many peasants were unable to pay their taxes. This forced them to sell their lands to wealthy neighbors and become tenant farmers who paid rent to the new owners. By the end of the nineteenth century, about 40 percent of all farmers were tenants.

With its budget needs met by the land tax, the government turned to the promotion of industry. The Meiji government gave **subsidies** to needy industries, provided training and foreign advisers, and improved transportation and communications. By 1900, Japan's industrial sector was beginning to grow. Besides tea and silk, other key industries were weapons and shipbuilding.

From the start, a unique feature of the Meiji model of industrial development was the close relationship between government and private business. The government encouraged new industries by giving businesspeople money and privileges. After an industry was on its feet, it was turned over entirely to private ownership.

Modern Institutions and Social Structures

The Meiji reformers also transformed other institutions. A new imperial army based on compulsory military service was formed in 1871. All Japanese men now served for three years. The new army was well equipped with modern weapons.

Education also changed. The Meiji leaders realized the need for universal education. In 1871 a new ministry of education adopted the American model of elementary schools, secondary schools, and universities. It brought foreign specialists to Japan to teach, and it sent students to study abroad.

Before the Meiji reforms, the lives of all Japanese people were determined by their membership in families, villages, and social classes. Japanese society was highly hierarchical. Belonging to a particular social class determined a person's occupation and social relationships. Women were especially limited by the "three obediences": child to father, wife to husband, and widow to son. Husbands could obtain a divorce; wives could not. Marriages were arranged, and the average marital age of females was 16 years. Females did not share inheritance rights with males. Few received any education outside the family.

The Meiji Restoration had a marked effect on the traditional social system in Japan. Special privileges for the aristocracy were abolished. For the first time, women were allowed to seek an education. As the economy shifted from an agricultural to an industrial base, many Japanese began to get new jobs and establish new social relationships.

Western fashions and culture became the rage. A new generation began to imitate the clothing styles, eating habits, and social practices of Westerners. The game of baseball was imported from the United States.

▲ These woodblock prints are part of a series called "Famous Places on the Tokaido: A Record of the Process of Reform" (1875).

▶ **CRITICAL THINKING**
Analyzing Visuals How do these prints show the effects of reform on Japanese society?

subsidy government payment to encourage or protect a certain economic activity

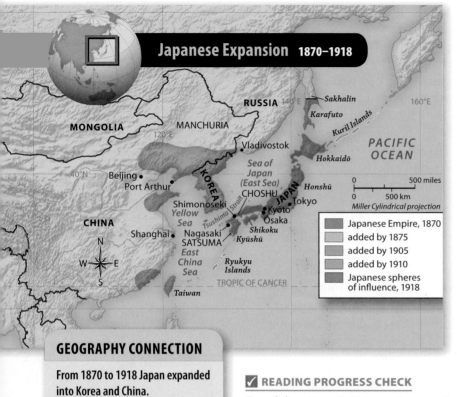

Japanese Expansion 1870–1918

RUSSIA 140°E · Sakhalin · 160°E

Karafuto

Kuril Islands

MONGOLIA · MANCHURIA

120°E

Vladivostok

PACIFIC OCEAN

Hokkaidō

40°N · Beijing · Sea of Japan (East Sea)

Port Arthur · CHOSHU · Honshū · 0 · 500 miles

Shimonoseki · JAPAN · Tokyo · 0 · 500 km

Yellow Sea · Kyoto · Miller Cylindrical projection

CHINA · Ōsaka

Shanghai · Nagasaki · Shikoku

SATSUMA · Kyūshū

East China Sea · Ryukyu Islands

TROPIC OF CANCER

Taiwan

KOREA

Tsushima Strait

	Japanese Empire, 1870
	added by 1875
	added by 1905
	added by 1910
	Japanese spheres of influence, 1918

GEOGRAPHY CONNECTION

From 1870 to 1918 Japan expanded into Korea and China.

1 THE WORLD IN SPATIAL TERMS *What lands did Japan take by 1905?*

2 HUMAN SYSTEMS *What countries did Japan come into conflict with as it expanded?*

context the circumstances surrounding a situation or event

The social changes brought about by the Meiji Restoration also had a less attractive side. Many commoners were ruthlessly exploited in the coal mines and textile mills. Workers labored up to 20 hours a day. Coal miners in some areas worked in temperatures up to 130 degrees Fahrenheit (54 degrees C). When they tried to escape, they were shot.

The transformation of Japan into a "modern society" did not detach the country entirely from its old values, however. Traditional values based on loyalty to the family and community were still taught in schools. Traditional Japanese values were also given a firm legal basis in the 1889 constitution, which limited the right to vote to men. The Civil Code of 1898 played down individual rights and placed women within the **context** of their family role.

✔ **READING PROGRESS CHECK**

Examining How did Meiji reforms reflect a mix of Western and traditional values?

Japanese Expansion

GUIDING QUESTION *Why did Japan turn itself into an imperialist power?*

The Japanese soon copied Western imperialism. The Japanese knew that Western nations had amassed some of their wealth and power because of their `colonies. Those colonies had provided sources of raw materials, inexpensive labor, and markets for manufactured products. To compete, Japan would also have to expand.

The Japanese began their program of territorial expansion close to home. In 1874 Japan claimed control of the Ryukyu (ree • YOO • kyoo) Islands, which belonged to the Chinese Empire. Two years later, Japan's navy forced the Koreans to open their ports to Japanese trade. The Chinese grew concerned by Japan's growing influence there.

In the 1880s, Chinese-Japanese rivalry over Korea intensified. In 1894, the two nations went to war, and Japan won. In the treaty ending the war, China recognized Korea's independence.

China also ceded Taiwan and the Liaodong Peninsula, with its strategic naval base at Port Arthur, to Japan. In time, the Japanese gave the Liaodong Peninsula back to China.

Rivalry with Russia over influence in Korea led to increasingly strained relations. The Russo-Japanese War began in 1904. Japan launched a surprise attack on the Russian naval base at Port Arthur, which Russia had taken from China in 1898. In the meantime, Russia had sent its Baltic fleet half-way around the world to East Asia, only to be defeated by the new Japanese navy off the coast of Japan. After their defeat, the Russians agreed to a humiliating peace in 1905. They gave the Liaodong Peninsula back to Japan, as well as the southern part of Sakhalin (SA • kuh • LEEN), an island north of Japan. The Japanese victory stunned the world. Japan had become one of the great powers.

When Japan established a sphere of influence in Korea, the United States recognized Japan's role there. In return, Japan recognized American authority in the Philippines. In 1910 Japan annexed Korea outright.

Some Americans began to fear Japan's power in East Asia. In 1907 President Theodore Roosevelt made a "gentlemen's agreement" with Japan that essentially stopped Japanese immigration to the United States.

✓ **READING PROGRESS CHECK**

Identifying How did Japan benefit from its imperialist strategy?

Culture in an Era of Transition

GUIDING QUESTION *How did contact between Japan and the West influence culture?*

The wave of Western technology and ideas that entered Japan after 1850 greatly altered traditional Japanese culture. Dazzled by European literature, Japanese authors began imitating the imported models. They began to write novels that were patterned after the French tradition of realism. Japanese authors presented social conditions and the realities of war as objectively as possible.

Other aspects of Japanese culture were also changed. The Japanese invited engineers, architects, and artists from Europe and the United States to teach their "modern" skills to Japanese students. The Japanese copied Western architectural styles. Huge buildings of steel and reinforced concrete, adorned with Greek columns, appeared in many Japanese cities.

A national reaction had begun by the end of the 1800s, and many Japanese artists began to return to older techniques. In 1889 the Tokyo School of Fine Arts was established to promote traditional Japanese art.

Cultural exchange also went the other way. Japanese arts and crafts, porcelains, textiles, fans, folding screens, and woodblock prints became fashionable in Europe and North America. Japanese gardens, with their close attention to the positioning of rocks and falling water, became especially popular in the United States.

✓ **READING PROGRESS CHECK**

Drawing Conclusions What inspired Japanese artists to return to traditional forms?

▶ **CRITICAL THINKING**
Making Inferences Why did aspects of Japanese culture become fashionable in the United States?

▼ This Japanese garden and tea house was showcased at the World's Fair in St. Louis, Missouri, in 1904.

PHOTO: Buyenlarge/Archive Photos/Getty Images

LESSON 3 REVIEW

Reviewing Vocabulary
1. ***Explaining*** Explain how the prefecture system affected the daimyo.

Using Your Notes
2. ***Identifying*** Use the information from your notes to help explain the results of the Meiji Restoration.

Answering the Guiding Questions
3. ***Drawing Conclusions*** How did Japan respond to foreign pressure to end its isolationist policies?

4. ***Analyzing*** How did the Meiji Restoration change Japan?

5. ***Identifying Cause and Effect*** Why did Japan turn itself into an imperialist power?

6. ***Making Connections*** How did contact between Japan and the West influence culture?

Writing Activity
7. **INFORMATIVE/EXPLANATORY** Write two descriptive paragraphs about the woodblock prints in this lesson. In your answer, cite the artist's use of color, texture, line, shape, space, and perspective.

Directions: On a separate sheet of paper, answer the questions below. Make sure you read carefully and answer all parts of the questions.

Lesson Review

Lesson 1

1 **THEORIZING** What were the goals of the Tai Ping Rebellion? Why do you think Western nations fought against the rebels?

2 **EXPLAINING** What were spheres of influence? How did Western nations and Japan acquire spheres of influence in China?

Lesson 2

3 **SUMMARIZING** Why were the Qing reforms after the Boxer Rebellion unsuccessful?

4 **DESCRIBING** How did Western ideas influence Chinese authors?

Lesson 3

5 **SPECIFYING** What was the Treaty of Kanagawa? Why did Japan sign it?

6 **EXPLORING ISSUES** Which Western values inspired Meiji reforms? Which did the Meiji not copy?

21st Century Skills

7 **UNDERSTANDING RELATIONSHIPS AMONG EVENTS** How did China respond to Western imperialism? How were the responses of the Qing government and the Boxers connected?

8 **ECONOMICS** Why did Britain begin selling opium to China? What was the intended effect, and what were some major unintended effects?

9 **EXPLAINING CONTINUITY AND CHANGE** What did the Meiji claim their land reforms would give the peasants? How did those reforms actually work out?

10 **IDENTIFYING CAUSE AND EFFECT** How did the Meiji reformers increase Japan's industrial sector?

Exploring the Essential Questions

11 **ANALYZING** Work with a partner to create two maps, one of China and one of Japan, showing places where new ideas accelerated economic or political change. Include labels explaining the ideas and the changes involved. Add visuals of people and places that represented change. Draw conclusions about why cultures change.

DBQ Analyzing Historical Documents

Use the document to answer the following questions.

In 1868, after ending the shogunate, the Sat-Cho reformers insisted that the new emperor sign the Charter Oath below.

> PRIMARY SOURCE

❝ Article 1. Deliberative assemblies shall be widely established and all matters decided by public discussion.
Article 2. All classes, high and low, shall unite in vigorously carrying out the administration of the affairs of state.
Article 3. The common people, no less than the civil and military officials, shall each be allowed to pursue his own calling so that there may be no discontent.
Article 4. Evil customs of the past shall be broken off and everything based upon the just laws of Nature.
Article 5. Knowledge shall be sought throughout the world so as to strengthen the foundation of imperial rule. ❞

—quoted in *East Asia: A New History*

12 **ANALYZING** Does the Charter Oath fit the mood of Japan in 1868? Explain.

13 **COMPARING AND CONTRASTING** What are the similarities and differences between the Meiji Charter Oath and Sun Yat-sen's Three People's Principles in China?

Extended-Response Question

14 **INFORMATIVE/EXPLANATORY** How did Western culture affect China and Japan? How did Chinese and Japanese culture affect Western nations?

Need Extra Help?

If You've Missed Question	**1**	**2**	**3**	**4**	**5**	**6**	**7**	**8**	**9**	**10**	**11**	**12**	**13**	**14**
Go to page	252	253	256	260	261	262	250	251	263	263	252	266	266	250

World War I and the Russian Revolution

1914–1919

ESSENTIAL QUESTIONS • Why do politics often lead to war?
• How can technology impact war?

networks

There's More Online! about World War I and the Russian Revolution.

CHAPTER 14

The Story Matters...

On June 28, 1914, an assassination in the Balkans created an international crisis, igniting a European powder keg created by nationalism, massive military buildups, complex alliances, and imperial rivalries. By August, Europe was at war. The widespread use of trench warfare on the Western Front in France created a destructive stalemate that lasted four years. The introduction of new weapons, including heavy artillery, tanks, machine guns, and poison gas, produced casualty levels that dwarfed those of previous wars.

◄ A young French infantryman pauses for a photograph during World War I. In France, the troops of the enemy armies lived in trenches in the ground and faced each other across the barbed wire marking the limits of the narrow, deadly strip known as "no-man's land."

PHOTO: Rue des Archives/The Granger Collection, NYC

267

Place and Time: Europe and Russia 1914–1919

In the years before World War I, European powers made use of the industrial innovations of the late nineteenth century to create new weapons. Most European nations also enlarged their armies. In 1882 Germany, Italy, and Austria-Hungary came together in the Triple Alliance, while in 1907 Great Britain, France, and Russia formed the Triple Entente. Retaliation against the 1914 assassination of Francis Ferdinand, Archduke of Austria-Hungary, tested those alliances and eventually drew Europe into World War I.

Step Into the Place

Read the quote and look at the information presented on the map.

 Analyzing Historical Documents Why did the assassination of Archduke Francis Ferdinand spark World War I?

PRIMARY SOURCE

"A note of genuine regret is that, deprived of the Archduke's strong personality, Austria inevitably will be more subject to German influence. Several journalists express the fear that the consequences will be sufficiently serious again to plunge the Balkans, if not Europe, into a conflict.

Apprehension lest the Sarajevo crime prove a dire blow to the stability of Europe almost overshadows the feeling of horror and reprobation over the assassination and deep sympathy for the aged Emperor in the comments of the morning papers."

—from a special cable from Paris to *The New York Times*, June 29, 1914

PHOTO: Henry Guttmann/Hulton Archive/Getty Images

Step Into the Time

Predicting Consequences

Choose a European event from the time line and write a paragraph predicting how it might influence the events of World War I.

June 1914 Assassination of Archduke Francis Ferdinand sparks World War I

August 1914 Germany is at war with Russia and France

EUROPE

THE WORLD

1914

1915

August 1914 Japan declares war on Germany

1915 Ottoman Turks commit genocide against Armenians

networks
There's More Online!

☑ **Map** Explore the interactive version of this map on Networks.

☑ **Time Line** Explore the interactive version of the time line on Networks.

Europe 1914

NORWAY
Christiania (Oslo)
St. Petersburg (Petrograd)
Stockholm
SWEDEN
Moscow •
North Sea
DENMARK
Copenhagen
Baltic Sea
RUSSIA
UNITED KINGDOM
50°N
London
NETH.
Amsterdam
Berlin
Elbe R.
English Channel
Brussels
BELG.
GERMANY
Rhine R.
Dnieper R.
ATLANTIC OCEAN
Seine R.
Paris
LUX.
Danube R.
Loire R.
Geneva
Vienna
Budapest
FRANCE
SWITZ.
AUSTRIA-HUNGARY
40°N
ROMANIA
Bucharest
Belgrade
Black Sea
PORTUGAL
Madrid
Sarajevo •
SERBIA
BULGARIA
Lisbon
Corsica
ITALY
Cetinje
Sofia
Constantinople (İstanbul)
SPAIN
Rome
MONT.
Durrës
ALB.
OTTOMAN EMPIRE
Sardinia
GREECE
Sicily
Athens
Cyprus U.K.
Mediterranean Sea
Crete

0 ——— 400 miles
0 ——— 400 km
Lambert Azimuthal Equal-Area projection

February–December 1916
German offensive at the Battle of Verdun

December 1917
The peace conference at Brest-Litovsk opens

November 11, 1918 Germany and Allies sign an armistice

1916 Germany engages in unrestricted submarine warfare

1917 Russian Revolution begins

1918 Germany agrees to truce

June 1919 Treaty of Versailles signed

1916

1917

1918

1919

1917 U.S. enters World War I

October, 1917 Brazil declares war on Germany

1919 U.S. president Woodrow Wilson helps form the League of Nations

1916 Germans flee Cameroon for Spanish Guinea

1918 Worldwide influenza epidemic begins

1919 Togo becomes a French mandate

netw⊕rks

There's More Online!

- ☑ **BIOGRAPHY** Archduke Francis Ferdinand
- ☑ **CHART/GRAPH** Estimated Army Size, 1914
- ☑ **IMAGE** German Mobilization
- ☑ **INTERACTIVE SELF-CHECK QUIZ**
- ☑ **MAP** Alliances in Europe, 1914
- ☑ **MAP** The Schlieffen Plan
- ☑ **PRIMARY SOURCE** The Assassination of Francis Ferdinand
- ☑ **TIME LINE** The Outbreak of World War I
- ☑ **VIDEO** World War I Begins

Reading **HELP**DESK (CCSS)

Academic Vocabulary

- military
- complex

Content Vocabulary

- conscription
- mobilization

TAKING NOTES:

Key Ideas and Details

Sequencing Use a sequence chain like the one below to list the events leading up to World War I.

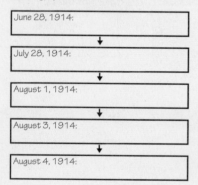

June 28, 1914:
↓
July 28, 1914:
↓
August 1, 1914:
↓
August 3, 1914:
↓
August 4, 1914:

LESSON 1
World War I Begins

ESSENTIAL QUESTIONS • *Why do politics often lead to war?*
• *How can technology impact war?*

It Matters Because

As European countries formed alliances and increased the sizes of their armed forces, they set the stage for a global war. All they needed was a good reason to mobilize troops. When a Serbian terrorist assassinated Archduke Francis Ferdinand and his wife, World War I soon followed.

Causes of the War

GUIDING QUESTION *What factors contributed to the start of World War I?*

Nineteenth-century liberals believed that if European states were organized along national lines, these states would work together and create a peaceful Europe. They were very wrong.

Nationalism, Imperialism, Militarism, and Alliances

The system of nation-states that emerged in Europe in the last half of the nineteenth century led not to cooperation but rather to competition. Each European nation-state regarded itself as subject to no higher interest or authority. Each state was guided by its own self-interests and success. Furthermore, most leaders thought that war was an acceptable way to preserve the power of their national states. These attitudes made war an ever-present possibility.

The imperialist expansion of the last half of the nineteenth century also played a role in the coming of war. The competition for lands abroad, especially in Africa, led to conflict and heightened the existing rivalries among European states.

Nationalism, along with imperialism, had another serious result. Not all ethnic groups had become nations in Europe. Slavic minorities in the Balkans and the Austro-Hungarian Empire still dreamed of their own national states. The Irish in the British Empire and the Poles in the Russian Empire had similar dreams.

Industrialization offered new methods of shipbuilding and the use of iron, steel, and chemicals for new weapons. The growth of mass armies and navies after 1900 heightened tensions in Europe. It was obvious that if war did come, it would be highly destructive.

Most Western countries had established **conscription**, a **military** draft, as a regular practice before 1914. European armies doubled in size between 1890 and 1914. With its 1.3 million men, the Russian army had grown to be the largest. The French and German armies were not far behind, with 900,000 soldiers each. The British, Italian, and Austro-Hungarian armies numbered between 250,000 and 500,000 soldiers each.

Militarism—the aggressive preparation for war—was growing. As armies grew, so did the influence of military leaders. They drew up vast and **complex** plans for quickly mobilizing millions of soldiers and enormous quantities of supplies in the event of war.

Fearing that any changes would cause chaos in the armed forces, military leaders insisted that their plans could not be altered. This left European political leaders with little leeway. In 1914 they had to make decisions for military instead of political reasons.

At the same time, a system of alliances intensified the dangers of militarism. Europe's great powers had been divided into two loose political alliances. Germany, Austria-Hungary, and Italy formed the Triple Alliance in 1882. France, Great Britain, and Russia created the Triple Entente in 1907.

In the early years of the twentieth century, a series of crises tested these alliances. Especially troublesome were the crises in the Balkans between 1908 and 1913. These events left European states angry at each other and eager for revenge. By 1914 the major European states had come to believe that their allies were important. They were willing to use war to preserve their power and the power of their allies.

conscription military draft

military relating to the armed forces or to soldiers, arms, or war

complex having many intricate parts

GEOGRAPHY CONNECTION

In 1914 Europe was divided into the Triple Alliance and Triple Entente.

1 **THE WORLD IN SPATIAL TERMS** *Which alliance controlled the most territory?*

2 **HUMAN SYSTEMS** *Which alliance had the most soldiers in 1914?*

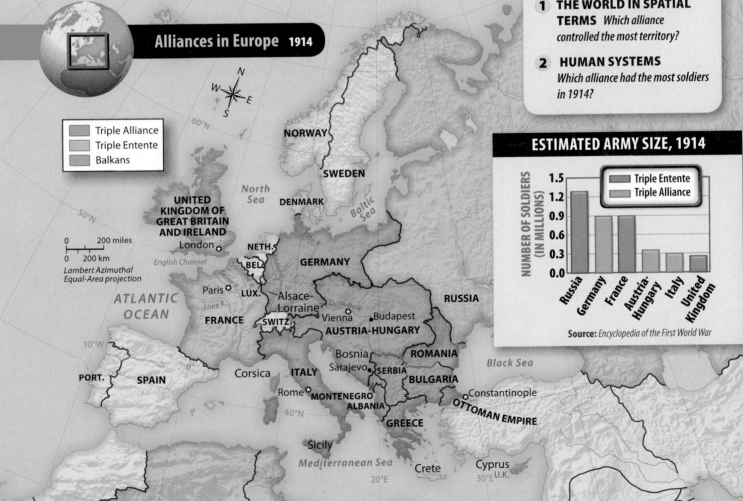

Alliances in Europe 1914

Triple Alliance
Triple Entente
Balkans

ESTIMATED ARMY SIZE, 1914

Triple Entente
Triple Alliance

NUMBER OF SOLDIERS (IN MILLIONS)

Russia · Germany · France · Austria-Hungary · Italy · United Kingdom

Source: *Encyclopedia of the First World War*

Internal Dissent

National desires were not the only source of internal strife at the beginning of the twentieth century. Socialist labor movements also had grown more powerful. The Socialists were increasingly inclined to use strikes, even violent ones, to achieve their goals.

Some conservative leaders, alarmed at the increase in labor strife and class division, feared that European nations were on the verge of revolution. This desire to suppress internal disorder might have encouraged various leaders to take the plunge into war in 1914.

☑ **READING PROGRESS CHECK**

Analyzing How might internal dissent in European states have led to World War I?

The Outbreak of War

GUIDING QUESTION *How did the assassination of Archduke Francis Ferdinand spark the outbreak of war?*

Nationalism and imperialism, militarism and alliances, and the desire to stifle internal dissent might all have played a role in starting World War I. However, it was the decisions that European leaders made in response to a crisis in the Balkans that led directly to the conflict.

Assassination in Sarajevo and Responses

By 1914 Serbia, supported by Russia, was determined to create a large, independent Slavic state in the Balkans. Austria-Hungary, which had its own Slavic minorities to contend with, was equally determined to prevent that from happening.

On June 28, 1914, Archduke Francis Ferdinand, the heir to the Hapsburg throne of Austria-Hungary, and his wife Sophia visited the city of Sarajevo (SAR • uh • YAY • voh) in Bosnia. A group of conspirators waited there in the streets.

In that group was Gavrilo Princip, a 19-year-old Bosnian Serb. Princip was a member of the Black Hand, a Serbian terrorist organization that wanted Bosnia to be free of Austria-Hungary and to become part of a large Serbian kingdom. An assassination attempt earlier that morning by one of the conspirators had failed. Later that day, however, Princip succeeded in fatally shooting the archduke and his wife.

The Austro-Hungarian government did not know if the Serbian government was directly involved in the archduke's assassination, but it did not care. It saw an opportunity to "render Serbia innocuous once and for all by a display of force," as the Austrian foreign minister put it. Austrian leaders wanted to attack Serbia but feared that Russia would intervene on Serbia's behalf. So, they asked for—and received—the backing of their German allies.

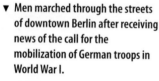

▼ Men marched through the streets of downtown Berlin after receiving news of the call for the mobilization of German troops in World War I.

▶ **CRITICAL THINKING**

Analyzing Visuals What words would you use to describe how these Berliners felt about the mobilization for war?

Emperor William II of Germany gave Austria-Hungary a "blank check," promising Germany's full support if war broke out between Russia and Austria-Hungary. On July 28, Austria-Hungary declared war on Serbia.

Russia was determined to support Serbia's cause. On July 28, Czar Nicholas II ordered partial mobilization of the Russian army against Austria-Hungary. **Mobilization** is the process of assembling troops and supplies for war. In 1914 mobilization was considered an act of war.

Leaders of the Russian army informed the czar that they could not partially mobilize. Their mobilization plans were based on a war against both Germany and Austria-Hungary. Mobilizing against only the one front of Austria-Hungary, they claimed, would create chaos in the army. Based on this claim, the czar ordered full mobilization of the Russian army on July 29, knowing that Germany would consider this order an act of war.

The Conflict Broadens

Indeed, Germany reacted quickly. The German government warned Russia that it must halt its mobilization within 12 hours. When Russia ignored this warning, Germany declared war on Russia on August 1.

Like the Russians, the Germans had a military plan. General Alfred von Schlieffen (SHLEE • fuhn) had helped draw up the plan, which was known as the Schlieffen Plan. It called for a two-front war with France and Russia because the two had formed a military alliance in 1894.

According to the Schlieffen Plan, Germany would conduct a small holding action against Russia while most of the German army would carry out a rapid invasion of France. This meant invading France by moving quickly along the level coastal area through Belgium. After France was defeated, the German invaders would move to the east against Russia.

Under the Schlieffen Plan, Germany could not mobilize its troops solely against Russia. Therefore, it declared war on France on August 3. At about the same time, it issued an ultimatum to Belgium demanding that German troops be allowed to pass through Belgian territory. Belgium, however, was a neutral nation.

On August 4, Great Britain declared war on Germany, officially for violating Belgian neutrality. In fact, Britain, which was allied with France and Russia, was concerned about maintaining its own world power. As one British diplomat put it, if Germany and Austria-Hungary won the war, "what would be the position of a friendless England?" By August 4, all the great powers of Europe were at war.

✔ **READING PROGRESS CHECK**

Interpreting What roles did the assassination of Francis Ferdinand and the existence of prior military plans play in leading quickly to the outbreak of World War I?

▲ The Schlieffen Plan had German troops attack France by quickly moving through Belgium.

▶ **CRITICAL THINKING**
Analyzing How did the implementation of the Schlieffen Plan broaden the conflict in Europe?

mobilization the process of assembling troops and supplies and making them ready for war

---

LESSON 1 REVIEW

Reviewing Vocabulary
1. **Making Connections** How is mobilization related to militarism?

Using Your Notes
2. *Constructing Arguments* Use your notes to discuss how alliances helped lead to the start of World War I.

Answering the Guiding Questions
3. *Identifying Causes* What factors contributed to the start of World War I?

4. *Interpreting* How did the assassination of Archduke Francis Ferdinand spark the outbreak of war?

Writing Activity
5. **NARRATIVE** Imagine you are an ordinary citizen of Germany. You have been reading the newspapers daily since the assassination of Francis Ferdinand, archduke of Austria. Write two or more journal entries on different days between the assassination on June 28, 1914, and August 4, 1914, reflecting on the events.

Reading **HELP**DESK (CCSS)

Academic Vocabulary

- target
- unrestricted

Content Vocabulary

- propaganda
- trench warfare
- war of attrition
- total war
- planned economies

TAKING NOTES:

Key Ideas and Details

Identifying Use a graphic organizer like the one below to identify how alliances shifted during World War I.

World War I Alliances

	Allied Powers	Central Powers
Pre-war name		
Original members		
Later additions		

LESSON 2
World War I

ESSENTIAL QUESTIONS · Why do politics often lead to war?
· How can technology impact war?

IT MATTERS BECAUSE

The war that many thought would be over in a few weeks lasted far longer, resulting in many casualties on both sides. The war widened, and the United States entered the fray in 1917. As World War I escalated, governments took control of their economies, rationing food and supplies and calling on civilians to work and make sacrifices for the war effort.

1914 to 1915: Illusions and Stalemate

GUIDING QUESTION *How did the war on the Eastern Front differ from war on the Western Front?*

Before 1914 many political leaders believed war to be impractical because it involved so many political and economic risks. Others believed that diplomats could easily prevent war. In August 1914 both ideas were shattered. However, the new illusions that replaced them soon proved to be equally foolish.

Government **propaganda**—ideas that are spread to influence public opinion for or against a cause—had stirred national hatreds before the war. Now, in August 1914, the urgent pleas of European governments for defense against aggressors fell on receptive ears in every nation that was at war. Most people seemed genuinely convinced that their nation's cause was just.

A new set of illusions also fed the enthusiasm for war. In August 1914 almost everyone believed that the war would be over in a few weeks. After all, almost all European wars since 1815 had, in fact, ended in a matter of weeks. The soldiers who boarded the trains for the war front in August 1914 and the jubilant citizens who saw them off believed that the warriors would be home by Christmas.

The Western Front

German hopes for a quick end to the war rested on a military gamble. The Schlieffen Plan called for the German army to make a vast encircling movement through Belgium into northern France. According to the plan, the German forces would sweep around Paris. This would enable them to surround most of the French army.

However, the German advance was halted a short distance from Paris at the First Battle of the Marne (September 6–10). To stop the Germans, French military leaders loaded 2,000 Parisian taxicabs with fresh troops and sent them to the front line.

The war quickly turned into a stalemate as neither the Germans nor the French could dislodge each other from the trenches they had dug for shelter. Two lines of trenches soon reached from the English Channel to the frontiers of Switzerland. The Western Front had become bogged down in **trench warfare**. Both sides were kept in virtually the same positions for four years.

The Eastern Front

Unlike the Western Front, the war on the Eastern Front was marked by mobility. The cost in lives, however, was equally enormous. At the beginning of the war, the Russian army moved into eastern Germany but was decisively defeated at the Battle of Tannenberg on August 30 and the Battle of Masurian Lakes on September 15. After these defeats, the Russians were no longer a threat to Germany.

Austria-Hungary, Germany's ally, fared less well at first. The Austrians had been defeated by the Russians in Galicia and thrown out of Serbia as well. To make matters worse, the Italians betrayed their German and Austrian allies in the Triple Alliance by attacking Austria in May 1915. Italy thus joined France, Great Britain, and Russia, who had previously been known as the Triple Entente, but now were called the Allied Powers, or Allies.

propaganda ideas spread to influence public opinion for or against a cause

trench warfare fighting from ditches protected by barbed wire, as in World War I

GEOGRAPHY CONNECTION

World War I took place along two main fronts.

1 **HUMAN SYSTEMS** *What generalizations can you make about the war based on the dates of important victories for the Allied and Central Powers?*

2 **THE USES OF GEOGRAPHY** *Why does the farthest advance of the Allied and Central Powers change more on the Eastern Front than the Western Front?*

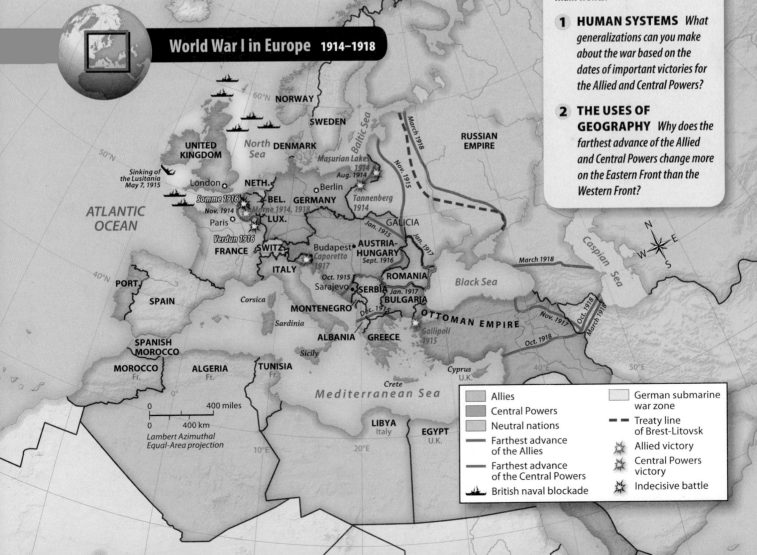

World War I in Europe 1914–1918

Allies	German submarine war zone
Central Powers	– – Treaty line of Brest-Litovsk
Neutral nations	Allied victory
Farthest advance of the Allies	Central Powers victory
Farthest advance of the Central Powers	Indecisive battle
British naval blockade	

0 400 miles
0 400 km
Lambert Azimuthal Equal-Area projection

▲ A boy delivers a newspaper to men living in the trenches during World War I.

▶ **CRITICAL THINKING**
Explaining What was unique about trench warfare?

By this time, the Germans had come to the aid of the Austrians. A German-Austrian army defeated the Russian army in Galicia and pushed the Russians far back into their own territory. Russian casualties stood at 2.5 million killed, captured, or wounded. The Russians were almost knocked out of the war.

Encouraged by their success against Russia, Germany and Austria-Hungary, joined by Bulgaria in September 1915, attacked and eliminated Serbia from the war. Their successes in the east would enable the German troops to move back to the offensive in the west.

☑ **READING PROGRESS CHECK**

Inferring Why did trench warfare develop on the Western Front but not on the Eastern Front?

Trench and Air Warfare

GUIDING QUESTION *What made World War I more devastating than any previous wars?*

On the Western Front, the trenches dug in 1914 had by 1916 become elaborate systems of defense. The Germans and the French each had hundreds of miles of trenches, which were protected by barbed-wire entanglements up to 5 feet (about 1.5 m) high and 30 yards (about 27 m) wide. Concrete machine-gun nests and other gun batteries, supported further back by heavy artillery, protected the trenches. Troops lived in holes in the ground, separated from each other by a strip of territory known as no-man's-land.

Trench warfare baffled military leaders who had been trained to fight wars of movement and maneuver. At times, the high command on either side would order an offensive that would begin with an artillery barrage to flatten the enemy's barbed wire and leave them in a state of shock. After "softening up" the enemy in this fashion, a mass of soldiers would climb out of their trenches with fixed bayonets and hope to work their way toward the enemy trenches.

The attacks rarely worked because men advancing unprotected across open fields could be fired at by the enemy's machine guns. In 1916 and 1917, millions of young men died in the search for the elusive breakthrough. In just 10 months at Verdun, France, 700,000 men lost their lives over a few miles of land. World War I had turned into a **war of attrition**, a war based on wearing down the other side with constant attacks and heavy losses.

By the end of 1915, airplanes appeared on the battlefront for the first time in history. Planes were first used to spot the enemy's position. Soon, planes also began to attack ground **targets**, especially enemy communications. Fights for control of the air space occurred, and then increased over time. At first, pilots fired at each other with handheld pistols. Later, machine guns were mounted on the noses of planes, which made the skies considerably more dangerous.

The Germans also used their giant airships—the zeppelins—to bomb London and eastern England. This caused little damage but frightened

war of attrition a war based on wearing down the other side with constant attacks and heavy losses, such as World War I

target something or someone marked for attack

many people. Germany's enemies, however, soon found that zeppelins, which were filled with hydrogen gas, quickly became raging infernos when hit by antiaircraft guns.

✔ **READING PROGRESS CHECK**

Drawing Conclusions Why did technology make it difficult for armies on the Western Front to mount a successful offensive attack?

A World War

GUIDING QUESTION *Why did the war widen to become a world conflict?*

Because of the stalemate on the Western Front, both sides sought to gain new allies. Each side hoped new allies would provide a winning advantage, as well as a new source of money and war goods.

Widening of the War

Bulgaria entered the war on the side of the Central Powers, as Germany, Austria-Hungary, and the Ottoman Empire were called. Russia, Great Britain, and France—the Allied Powers—declared war on the Ottoman Empire. The Allies tried to open a Balkan front by landing forces at Gallipoli (guh • LIH • puh • lee), southwest of Constantinople, in April 1915. However, the campaign was disastrous and the Allies withdrew.

By 1917 the war had truly become a world conflict. That year, while stationed in the Middle East, a British officer known as Lawrence of Arabia urged Arab princes to revolt against their Ottoman overlords. In 1918 British forces from Egypt mobilized troops from India, Australia, and New Zealand and worked to destroy the Ottoman Empire in the Middle East.

The Allies also took advantage of Germany's preoccupations in Europe and lack of naval strength to seize German colonies in the rest of the world. Japan, a British ally beginning in 1902, seized a number of German-held islands in the Pacific. Australia seized German New Guinea.

Entry of the United States

At first, the United States tried to remain neutral. As World War I dragged on, however, it became more difficult to do so. The immediate cause of the United States's involvement grew out of the naval war between Germany and Great Britain.

Britain had used its superior navy to set up a blockade of Germany. The blockade kept war materials and other goods from reaching Germany by sea. Germany, in turn, set up its own blockade of Britain and enforced it with the use of **unrestricted** submarine warfare, including the sinking of passenger liners.

On May 7, 1915, German forces sank the British ship *Lusitania*. About 1,100 civilians, including more than 100 Americans, died. After strong protests from the United States, the German government suspended unrestricted submarine warfare in September 1915 to avoid antagonizing the United States further. Only once did the Germans and British engage in direct naval battle—at the Battle of Jutland on May 31, 1916; neither side won a conclusive victory.

By January 1917, however, the Germans were eager to break the deadlock in the war. German naval officers convinced Emperor William II that resuming the use of unrestricted submarine warfare could starve the British into submission within six months. When the emperor expressed concern

▲ The sinking of the *Lusitania* made the front page of *The New York Herald*. Germany claimed that the British passenger ship was a fair target because it carried 173 tons of ammunitions as cargo.

▶ **CRITICAL THINKING**

Inferring Why did this event help lead to the U.S. entry in the war?

unrestricted having no restrictions or bounds

The pandemic of 1918 was caused by a type of the H1N1 influenza virus. A previously unknown strain of this virus appeared in 2009. First occurring in Mexico in February 2009, the disease spread rapidly worldwide, presumably due to high levels of air travel. In June, the World Health Organization (WHO) declared that H1N1 had become a pandemic, or an outbreak affecting a high proportion of the population over a wide geographic area. Unlike the 1918 outbreak, the H1N1 flu did not mutate into a more deadly form, and the death toll remained relatively low. In August 2010, the WHO announced that the H1N1 flu had moved into a post-pandemic stage.

total war a war that involved the complete mobilization of resources and people, affecting the lives of all citizens in the warring countries, even those remote from the battlefield

planned economy an economic system directed by government agencies

about the United States, German Admiral Holtzendorf assured him: "I give your Majesty my word as an officer that not one American will land on the continent."

The German naval officers were quite wrong. The British were not forced to surrender, and the return to unrestricted submarine warfare brought the United States into the war in April 1917. U.S. troops did not arrive in large numbers in Europe until 1918. However, the entry of the United States into the war gave the Allied Powers a psychological boost and a major new source of money and war goods.

☑ **READING PROGRESS CHECK**

Analyzing How did imperialism contribute to the widening of World War I?

The Impact of Total War

GUIDING QUESTION *What was the impact of total war?*

As World War I dragged on, it became a **total war** involving a complete mobilization of resources and people. It affected the lives of all citizens in the warring countries, however far from the battlefields. The home front was rapidly becoming a cause for as much effort as the war front.

Increased Government Powers

Most people had expected the war to be short. Little thought had been given to long-term wartime needs. Governments had to respond quickly, however, when the new war machines failed to achieve their goals. Many more men and supplies were needed to continue the war effort. To meet these needs, governments expanded their powers. Countries drafted tens of millions of young men, hoping for that elusive breakthrough to victory.

Wartime governments throughout Europe also expanded their power over their economies. Free-market capitalistic systems were temporarily put aside. Governments set up price, wage, and rent controls. They also rationed food supplies and materials; regulated imports and exports; and took over transportation systems and industries. In effect, in order to mobilize all the resources of their nations for the war effort, European nations set up **planned economies**.

As a result of total war mobilization, the differences between soldiers at war and civilians at home were narrowed. In the view of political leaders, all citizens were part of a national army that was dedicated to victory. Woodrow Wilson, president of the United States, said that the men and women "who remain to till the soil and man the factories are no less a part of the army than the men beneath the battle flags."

Manipulation of Public Opinion

As the war continued and casualties worsened, the patriotic enthusiasm that marked the early stages of the war began to wane. By 1916 signs indicated that civilian morale was beginning to crack. War governments, however, fought back against growing opposition to the war.

Authoritarian regimes, such as those of Germany, Russia, and Austria-Hungary, relied on force to subdue their populations. With the pressures of the war, however, even democratic states expanded their police powers to stop internal dissent. The British Parliament, for example, passed the Defence of the Realm Act (DORA). It allowed the government to arrest protesters as traitors. Newspapers were censored, and sometimes publication was suspended.

Wartime governments made active use of propaganda to increase enthusiasm for the war. As the war progressed and morale sagged, governments were forced to devise new techniques for motivating citizens.

Total War and Society

In the fall of 1918, a deadly influenza struck, adding to the horrors of World War I. Probably spread by soldiers returning from the front, influenza becamethe deadliest epidemic in history. An estimated total of 50 million people died worldwide.

Total war also had a significant impact on European society. World War I created new roles for women. Because so many men left to fight at the front, women were asked to take over jobs that were not available to them before. Women found themselves employed in jobs that once were considered beyond their capacity. These jobs included civilian occupations such as chimney sweeps, truck drivers, farm laborers, and factory workers in heavy industry. For example, 38 percent of the workers in the Krupp Armaments works in Germany in 1918 were women.

The place of women in the workforce was far from secure, however. Both men and women seemed to expect that many of the new jobs for women were only temporary.

At the end of the war, as men returned to the job market, governments quickly removed women from the jobs they were encouraged to take earlier. By 1919, 650,000 women in Great Britain were unemployed. Wages for the women who were still employed were lowered.

Nevertheless, in some countries the role women played in wartime economies had a positive impact on the women's movement for social and political emancipation. The most obvious gain was the right to vote, which was given to women in Germany, Austria, and the United States immediately after the war. British women over the age of 30 gained the right to vote, together with the right to stand for Parliament, in 1918.

Many upper- and middle-class women also gained new freedoms. In ever-increasing numbers, young women from these groups took jobs, lived in their own apartments, and relished their new independence.

✓ **READING PROGRESS CHECK**

Explaining Why did women in some countries receive the right to vote after the war?

▶ **CRITICAL THINKING**
Drawing Conclusions How might this poster have increased British support for the war?

▼ This British recruiting poster is an example of wartime propaganda.

Daddy, what did YOU do in the Great War?

LESSON 2 REVIEW (CCSS)

Reviewing Vocabulary
1. *Applying* Describe the steps that resulted in the development of trench warfare.

Using Your Notes
2. *Identifying* Use your notes to describe the ways in which alliances shifted during World War I.

Answering the Guiding Questions
3. *Contrasting* How did the war differ on the Western and Eastern Fronts?

4. *Drawing Conclusions* What made World War I more devastating than any previous wars?

5. *Identifying* Why did the war widen to become a world conflict?

6. *Determining Cause and Effect* What was the impact of total war?

Writing Activity
7. INFORMATIVE/EXPLANATORY Write a paragraph discussing the role that women played in World War I.

networks

There's More Online!

- ☑ **BIOGRAPHY** V.I. Lenin
- ☑ **IMAGE** Bolshevik Attack on the Winter Palace
- ☑ **IMAGE** The Red Army
- ☑ **IMAGE** The Romanov Family
- ☑ **INTERACTIVE SELF-CHECK QUIZ**
- ☑ **MAP** Russian Revolution and Civil War, 1917–1922
- ☑ **PRIMARY SOURCE** An Ambassador's Memoirs
- ☑ **TIME LINE** Russia and Europe, 1914–1918
- ☑ **VIDEO** The Russian Revolution

Reading HELPDESK (CCSS)

Academic Vocabulary
- revolution
- aid

Content Vocabulary
- soviet
- war communism
- abdicate

TAKING NOTES:
Key Ideas and Details

Categorizing Information As you read, use a chart like the one below to identify the factors and events that led to Lenin's rise to power in 1917.

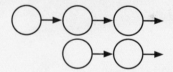

LESSON 3
The Russian Revolution

ESSENTIAL QUESTIONS · *Why do politics often lead to war?*
· *How can technology impact war?*

IT MATTERS BECAUSE

As the war dragged on, Russia stirred with unrest. The Romanov dynasty of Russia ended when Czar Nicholas II stepped down and a provisional government was put in power. Then the Bolsheviks under V. I. Lenin overthrew the government and by 1921 were in total command of Russia.

Background to Revolution

GUIDING QUESTION *What factors and events led to the Russian Revolution?*

After its defeat by Japan in 1905 and the Revolution of 1905, Russia was unprepared militarily and technologically for the total war of World War I. Russia had no competent military leaders. Even worse, Czar Nicholas II insisted on taking personal charge of the armed forces despite his lack of ability and training.

In addition, Russian industry was unable to produce the weapons needed for the army. Many soldiers trained using broomsticks. Others were sent to the front without rifles and told to pick one up from a dead comrade. Thus, it is not surprising that the Russian army suffered incredible losses. Two million soldiers were killed between 1914 and 1916, and another 4 to 6 million were wounded or captured. By 1917 the Russian will to fight had vanished.

An autocratic ruler, Czar Nicholas II relied on the army and bureaucracy to hold up his regime. He was further cut off from events when a man named Grigory Rasputin (ra • SPYOO • tuhn), known to be a mystic, began to influence the czar's wife, Alexandra. With the czar at the battlefront, it was rumored that Alexandra made all of the important decisions after consulting Rasputin. Rasputin's influence made him an important power behind the throne.

As the leadership stumbled its way through a series of military and economic disasters, the Russian people grew more upset with the czarist regime. Even conservative aristocrats who supported the monarchy felt the need to do something. They assassinated Rasputin in December 1916, but it was too late to save the monarchy.

At the beginning of March 1917, working-class women led a series of strikes in the capital city of Petrograd (formerly St. Petersburg), helping to change Russian history. A few weeks earlier, the Russian government had started bread rationing in Petrograd after the price of bread skyrocketed. Many of the women who stood in the lines waiting for bread were also factory workers who worked 12-hour days. Exhausted from standing in line, and distraught over their half-starving and sick children, the women finally revolted.

On March 8, about 10,000 women marched through the city of Petrograd demanding "Peace and Bread" and "Down with Autocracy." Soon the women were joined by other workers. Together they called for a general strike. The strike shut down all the factories in the city on March 10.

Alexandra wrote to her husband Nicholas II at the battlefront: "This is a hooligan movement. If the weather were very cold they would all probably stay at home." Nicholas ordered troops to break up the crowds by shooting them if necessary. Soon, however, large numbers of the soldiers joined the demonstrators and refused to fire on the crowds.

The Duma, or legislative body, which the czar had tried to dissolve, met anyway. On March 12, it established the provisional government, which mainly consisted of middle-class representatives. It urged the czar to step down. Because he no longer had the support of the army or even the aristocrats, Nicholas II reluctantly agreed and stepped down on March 15, ending the 300-year-old Romanov dynasty.

The provisional government, headed by Aleksandr Kerensky (keh • REHN • skee), decided to carry on the war to preserve Russia's honor. This decision to remain in World War I was a major blunder. It satisfied neither the workers nor the peasants, who were tired and angry from years of suffering and wanted an end to the war.

The government also faced a challenge to its authority—the **soviets**. The soviets were councils comprised of representatives from the workers and soldiers. The soviet of Petrograd was formed in March 1917. At the same time, soviets sprang up in army units, factory towns, and rural areas. The soviets, largely made up of Socialists, represented the more radical interests of the lower classes. One group—the Bolsheviks—came to play a crucial role.

☑ **READING PROGRESS CHECK**

Drawing Conclusions What grievances did the Russian people have with the provisional government?

Lenin and the Bolsheviks

GUIDING QUESTION *How did Russia move from a czarist regime to a Communist regime?*

The Bolsheviks began as a small faction of a Marxist party called the Russian Social Democrats. The Bolsheviks came under the leadership of Vladimir Ilyich Ulyanov (ool • YAH • nuhf), known to the world as V. I. Lenin. Under Lenin's direction, the Bolsheviks became a party dedicated to violent **revolution**. Lenin believed that only violent revolution could destroy the capitalist system. A "vanguard" (forefront) of activists, he said, must form a small party of well-disciplined, professional revolutionaries to accomplish the task.

Between the years 1900 and 1917, Lenin spent most of his time abroad. When the Russian provisional government was formed in March 1917, he saw an opportunity for the Bolsheviks to seize power. In April 1917,

— *Thinking Like a* —
HISTORIAN

How Important Was Rasputin?

In the introduction to his best-selling book *Nicholas and Alexandra*, historian Robert Massie quotes Aleksandr Kerensky's observation, "If there had been no Rasputin, there would have been no Lenin." The role of Rasputin in the history of Russia is one debated by historians. Was he such an important figure or was his influence merely the stuff of legends? How much influence can one man have to effect historical change? Use the Internet to find reliable sources about how much Rasputin contributed to the fall of the Russian monarchy.

soviets Russian councils composed of representatives from the workers and soldiers

revolution a overthrow of government

German military leaders, hoping to create disorder in Russia, shipped Lenin back to Russia. Lenin and his associates were sent in a sealed train to prevent their ideas from infecting Germany.

Lenin's arrival in Russia began a new phase of the Russian Revolution. Lenin maintained that the soviets of soldiers, workers, and peasants were ready-made instruments of power. He believed that the Bolsheviks should work toward gaining control of these groups and then use them to overthrow the provisional government.

At the same time, the Bolsheviks reflected the discontent of the people. They promised an end to the war. They also promised to redistribute all land to the peasants, to transfer factories and industries from capitalists to committees of workers, and to transfer government power from the provisional government to the soviets. Three simple slogans summed up the Bolshevik program: "Peace, Land, Bread," "Worker Control of Production," and "All Power to the Soviets."

✅ READING PROGRESS CHECK

Inferring Why did German military leaders return Lenin to Russia?

The Bolsheviks Seize Power

GUIDING QUESTION *How did Russia move from a czarist regime to a Communist regime?*

By the end of October 1917, Bolsheviks made up a slight majority in the Petrograd and Moscow soviets. The number of party members had grown from 50,000 to 240,000. With Leon Trotsky as head of the Petrograd soviet, the Bolsheviks were in a position to claim power in the name of the soviets. During the night of November 6, Bolshevik forces seized the Winter Palace, the seat of the provisional government. The government quickly collapsed with little bloodshed. This overthrow coincided with a meeting of the all-Russian Congress of Soviets, which represented local soviets countrywide. Outwardly, Lenin turned over the power of the provisional government to the Congress of Soviets. The real power, however, passed to a council headed by Lenin.

The Bolsheviks, who soon renamed themselves the Communists, still had a long way to go. Lenin had promised peace, yet he realized delivering that would not be easy. It would mean the humiliating loss of much Russian territory, but there was no real choice.

On March 3, 1918, Lenin signed the Treaty of Brest-Litovsk with Germany and gave up eastern Poland, Ukraine, Finland, and the Baltic provinces. To his critics, Lenin argued that it made no difference. The spread of the socialist revolution throughout Europe would make the treaty largely irrelevant. In any case, he had promised peace to the Russian people. Real peace did not come, however, because the country soon sank into civil war.

✅ READING PROGRESS CHECK

Making Generalizations Why might the promises of the Bolsheviks have been appealing to the Russian people?

▼ This painting depicts the Bolshevik attack on the Winter Palace during the October Revolution.

▶ CRITICAL THINKING
Analyzing Why did the Bolsheviks choose the Winter Palace as the place to attack?

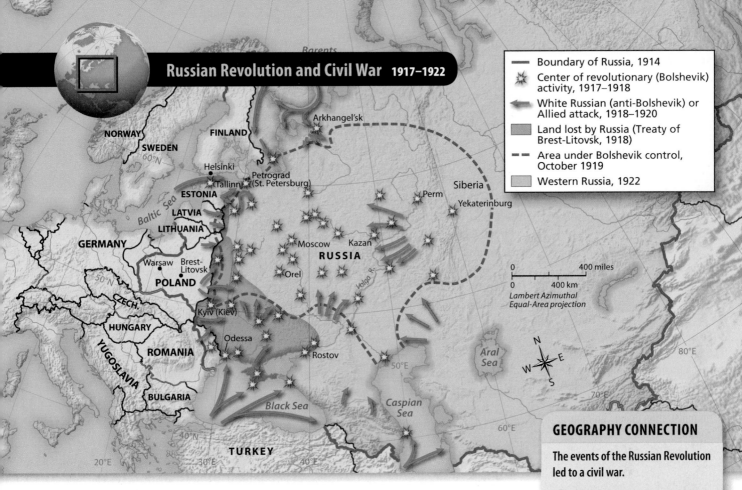

Russian Revolution and Civil War 1917–1922

- —— Boundary of Russia, 1914
- ✳ Center of revolutionary (Bolshevik) activity, 1917–1918
- ⬅ White Russian (anti-Bolshevik) or Allied attack, 1918–1920
- ▇ Land lost by Russia (Treaty of Brest-Litovsk, 1918)
- - - Area under Bolshevik control, October 1919
- ▇ Western Russia, 1922

Civil War in Russia

GUIDING QUESTION *What forces opposed the Communist government?*

Many people were opposed to the new Bolshevik, or Communist, government. These people included not only groups that were loyal to the czar but also liberal and anti-Leninist socialists. They were joined by the Allies, who were concerned about the Communist takeover. The Allies sent troops to Russia in the hope of bringing Russia back into the war. The Allies rarely fought on Russian soil, but they gave material **aid** to anti-Communists.

Between 1918 and 1921, the Communist, or Red, Army fought on many fronts. The first serious threat to the Communists came from Siberia. An anti-Communist, or White, force attacked and advanced almost to the Volga River before being stopped. Attacks also came from the Ukrainians and from the Baltic regions. In mid-1919, White forces swept through Ukraine and advanced almost to Moscow before being pushed back.

By 1920, however, the major White forces had been defeated and Ukraine retaken. The next year, the Communist regime regained control over the independent nationalist governments in Georgia, Russian Armenia, and Azerbaijan.

The royal family was another victim of the civil war. After the czar **abdicated**, he, his wife, and their five children had been held as prisoners. In April 1918, they were moved to Yekaterinburg, a mining town in the Urals. On the night of July 16, members of the local soviet murdered the czar and his family and burned their bodies in a nearby mine shaft.

✔ **READING PROGRESS CHECK**

Contrasting How were the White forces and the anti-Leninist socialists different?

GEOGRAPHY CONNECTION

The events of the Russian Revolution led to a civil war.

1 **THE WORLD IN SPATIAL TERMS** *Measure the distance from Russia's westernmost border in 1914 to the western border under Bolshevik control in October 1919.*

2 **HUMAN SYSTEMS** *Why were many of the White Russian or Allied attacks from outside of Russia?*

aid assistance such as money or supplies

abdicate to formally give up control of a country or state

Triumph of the Communists

GUIDING QUESTION *What factors helped the Communists win the Russian civil war?*

How did Lenin and the Communists triumph in the civil war over such overwhelming forces? One reason was that the Red Army was a well-disciplined fighting force. This was largely due to the organizational genius of Leon Trotsky. As commissar of war, Trotsky reinstated the draft and insisted on rigid discipline. Soldiers who deserted or refused to obey orders were executed on the spot.

Furthermore, the disunity of the anti-Communist forces weakened their efforts. Political differences created distrust among the Whites. Some Whites insisted on restoring the czarist regime. Others wanted a more liberal and democratic program. The Whites, then, had no common goal.

The Communists, in contrast, had a single-minded sense of purpose. Inspired by their vision of a new socialist order, the Communists had revolutionary zeal and strong convictions. They also were able to translate their revolutionary faith into practical instruments of power. A policy of **war communism**, for example, was used to ensure regular supplies for the Red Army. War communism meant the government controlled the banks and most industries, seized grain from peasants, and centralized state administration under Communist control.

Another instrument was Communist revolutionary terror. A new Red secret police—known as the Cheka—began a Red Terror. Aimed at destroying all those who opposed the new regime, the Red Terror added an element of fear to the Communist regime.

Finally, foreign armies on Russian soil enabled the Communists to appeal to the powerful force of Russian patriotism. At one point, more than 100,000 foreign troops—mostly Japanese, British, American, and French—were stationed in Russia in support of anti-Communist forces. Their presence made it easy for the Communist government to call on patriotic Russians to fight foreign attempts to control the country.

By 1921 the Communists were in total command of Russia. The Communist regime had transformed Russia into a centralized state dominated by a single party. The state was also largely hostile to the Allied Powers, because the Allies had tried to help the Communists' enemies in the civil war.

war communism in World War I Russia, government control of banks and most industries, the seizing of grain from peasants, and the centralization of state administration under Communist control

☑ **READING PROGRESS CHECK**

Identifying Central Issues What was war communism, and why was it important?

LESSON 3 REVIEW

Reviewing Vocabulary

1. *Making Generalizations* During the civil war that followed the revolution, why did the Allies give aid to the anti-Communist forces?

Using Your Notes

2. *Determining Cause and Effect* Using your notes, list the factors and events that brought Lenin to power in 1917.

Answering the Guiding Questions

3. *Identifying Central Issues* What factors and events led to the Russian Revolution?

4. *Determining Cause and Effect* How did Russia move from a czarist regime to a Communist regime?

5. *Analyzing Information* What forces opposed the Communist government?

6. *Drawing Conclusions* What factors helped the Communists win the Russian civil war?

Writing Activity

7. ARGUMENT Write a short paragraph arguing that the Russian Revolution was a result of World War I.

netw⊙rks

There's More Online!

☑ **IMAGE** The Treaty of Versailles

☑ **INTERACTIVE SELF-CHECK QUIZ**

☑ **MAP** Europe and the Middle East After WWI

☑ **PRIMARY SOURCE** Charter of the League of Nations

☑ **PRIMARY SOURCE** The Treaty of Versailles

☑ **PRIMARY SOURCE** Wilson's Fourteen Points

☑ **VIDEO** World War I Ends

Reading HELPDESK (CCSS)

Academic Vocabulary
- **psychological**
- **cooperation**

Content Vocabulary
- **armistice** • **mandate**
- **reparation**

TAKING NOTES:
Key Ideas and Details

Organizing Information As you read, use a chart like the one below to identify the national interests of each country as it approached the Paris Peace Conference.

France	Great Britain	United States

PHOTO: (l to r)©Hulton-Deutsch Collection/CORBIS, The Granger Collection, NYC, All rights reserved, Imperial War Museum/akg-images, Henry Miller/FPG/Hulton Archive/Getty Images.

LESSON 4
World War I Ends

ESSENTIAL QUESTIONS • *Why do politics often lead to war?*
• *How can technology impact war?*

IT MATTERS BECAUSE
Governments, troops, and civilians were weary as World War I continued through 1917. Shortly after the United States entered the war, Germany made its final military gamble on the Western Front and lost. The war finally ended on November 11, 1918. New nations were formed, and a League of Nations was created to resolve future international disputes.

The Last Year of the War

GUIDING QUESTION *How did World War I come to an end?*

The year 1917 was not a good one for the Allies. Allied offensives on the Western Front had been badly defeated. The Russian Revolution, which began in November 1917, led to Russia's withdrawal from the war a few months later. On the positive side, however, the entry of the United States into the war in 1917 gave the Allies a much-needed **psychological** boost. The United States also provided fresh troops and supplies.

For Germany, the withdrawal of the Russians offered new hope for a successful end to the war. Germany was then free to concentrate entirely on the Western Front. Erich Ludendorff, who guided German military operations, decided to make one final military gamble—a grand offensive in the west.

The German attack was launched in March 1918. By April German troops were within about 50 miles (80 km) of Paris. However, the German advance was stopped at the Second Battle of the Marne on July 18. French, Moroccan, and American troops (140,000 fresh American troops had just arrived), supported by hundreds of tanks, pushed the Germans back over the Marne. Ludendorff's gamble had failed.

With more than a million American troops pouring into France, Allied forces began an advance toward Germany. On September 29, 1918, General Ludendorff told German leaders that the war was lost. He demanded that the government ask for peace at once.

psychological mental; directed toward the will or mind

armistice a truce or an agreement to end fighting

Collapse and Armistice

German officials soon found that the Allies were unwilling to make peace with the autocratic imperial government of Germany. Reforms for a liberal government came too late for the tired, angry German people.

On November 3, 1918, sailors in the northern German town of Kiel mutinied. Within days, councils of workers and soldiers formed throughout northern Germany and took over civilian and military offices. Emperor William II gave in to public pressure and left the country on November 9. After his departure, the Social Democrats under Friedrich Ebert announced the creation of a democratic republic. Two days later, on November 11, 1918, the new German government signed an **armistice** to end the fighting.

Revolutionary Forces

The war was over, but the revolutionary forces that had been set in motion in Germany were not yet exhausted. A group of radical socialists, unhappy with the Social Democrats' moderate policies, formed the German Communist Party in December 1918. A month later, the Communists tried to seize power in Berlin.

The new Social Democratic government, backed by regular army troops, crushed the rebels and murdered Rosa Luxemburg and Karl Liebknecht (LEEP • KNEHKT), leaders of the German Communists. A similar attempt at Communist revolution in the city of Munich, in southern Germany, was also crushed. The new German republic had been saved. The attempt at revolution, however, left the German middle class with a deep fear of communism.

Austria-Hungary also experienced disintegration and revolution. As the empire grew war weary, ethnic groups increasingly sought to achieve their independence. By the time World War I ended, the Austro-Hungarian Empire had ceased to exist. The empire was replaced by the independent republics of Austria, Hungary, and Czechoslovakia, along with the large monarchical state called Yugoslavia.

✓ **READING PROGRESS CHECK**

Describing What happened in Germany after its military defeat?

▼ British cavalry pass the ruins of the Albert Cathedral. It was destroyed in the Second Battle of the Somme in France.

▶ **CRITICAL THINKING**
Explaining What does this photograph tell you about the changing nature of warfare in World War I?

The Peace Settlements

GUIDING QUESTION *How was a final settlement of World War I established?*

In January 1919, representatives of 27 victorious Allied nations met in Paris to make a final settlement of World War I. Over a period of years, the reasons for fighting World War I had changed dramatically. When European nations went to war in 1914, they sought territorial gains. By the beginning of 1918, however, they also were expressing more idealistic reasons for the war.

Wilson's Proposals

No one expressed these idealistic reasons for war better than the president of the United States, Woodrow Wilson. Even before the end of the war, Wilson outlined "Fourteen Points" to the U. S. Congress—his basis for a peace settlement that he believed justified the enormous military struggle being waged.

Wilson's proposals for a truly just and lasting peace included reaching the peace agreements openly rather than through secret diplomacy. His proposals also included reducing armaments (military forces or weapons) and ensuring self-determination (the right of each people to have their own nation).

Wilson portrayed World War I as a people's war against "absolutism and militarism." These two enemies of liberty, he argued, could be eliminated only by creating democratic governments and a "general association of nations." This association would guarantee "political independence and territorial integrity" to all states.

Wilson became the spokesperson for a new world order based on democracy and international **cooperation**. When he arrived in Europe for the peace conference, Wilson was cheered enthusiastically by many Europeans. President Wilson soon found, however, that more practical motives guided other states.

The Paris Peace Conference

Delegates met in Paris in early 1919 to determine the peace settlement. Complications soon arose at the Paris Peace Conference. For one thing, secret agreements that had been made before the war had raised the hopes of European nations for territorial gains. These hopes, however, conflicted with the principle of self-determination put forth by Wilson.

National interests also complicated the deliberations of the Paris Peace Conference. David Lloyd George, prime minister of Great Britain, had won a decisive victory in elections in December 1918. His platform was simple: make the Germans pay for this dreadful war.

France's approach to peace was chiefly guided by its desire for national security. To Georges Clemenceau (KLEH • muhn • SOH), the premier of France, the French people had suffered the most from German aggression. The French desired security against future German attacks. Clemenceau wanted Germany stripped of all weapons, vast German payments—**reparations**—to cover the costs of the war, and a separate Rhineland as a buffer state between France and Germany.

The most important decisions at the Paris Peace Conference were made by Wilson, Clemenceau, and Lloyd George, acting on behalf of the United States, France, and Great Britain (who were called the Big Three). Germany was not invited to attend, and Russia could not be present because of its civil war.

cooperation a common effort

reparation a payment made to the victor by the vanquished to cover the costs of war

▲ *The Signing of Peace in the Hall of Mirrors, Versailles, 28th June 1919* by Sir William Orpen depicts the major powers at Versailles. Wilson, Clemenceau, and Lloyd George (left to right) are seated at the table across from the German delegate.

▶ **CRITICAL THINKING**
Analyzing Visuals What is significant about the placement of the delegates around the table?

PHOTO: Imperial War Museum/akg-images

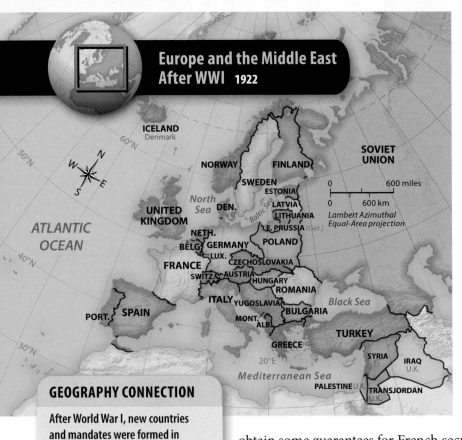

Europe and the Middle East After WWI 1922

ICELAND
Denmark

NORWAY   FINLAND   SOVIET UNION

SWEDEN
ESTONIA

North Sea   DEN.   LATVIA
LITHUANIA
E. PRUSSIA (Ger.)

UNITED KINGDOM

NETH.   POLAND

BELG.   GERMANY
LUX.

FRANCE   CZECHOSLOVAKIA
SWITZ.   AUSTRIA
HUNGARY
ROMANIA

ITALY   YUGOSLAVIA   Black Sea
BULGARIA
MONT.
ALB.

PORT.   SPAIN

TURKEY

GREECE

Mediterranean Sea   SYRIA
Fr.   IRAQ
U.K.

PALESTINE U.K.   TRANSJORDAN
U.K.

ATLANTIC OCEAN

0   600 miles
0   600 km
Lambert Azimuthal Equal-Area projection

GEOGRAPHY CONNECTION

After World War I, new countries and mandates were formed in Europe and the Middle East.

1 HUMAN SYSTEMS
Compare this map with the map on the Place and Time feature in this chapter. Which countries no longer existed after World War I?

2 ENVIRONMENT AND SOCIETY *Why do you think East Prussia was separated from the rest of Germany?*

In view of the conflicting demands that arose at the Paris Peace Conference, it was no surprise that the Big Three quarreled. Wilson wanted to create a world organization, the League of Nations, to prevent future wars. Clemenceau and Lloyd George wanted to punish Germany. In the end, only compromise made it possible to achieve a peace settlement.

Wilson's wish for the creation of an international peacekeeping organization to be the first order of business was granted. On January 25, 1919, the conference accepted the idea of a League of Nations. In return, Wilson agreed to make compromises on territorial arrangements among the countries. He did so because he believed that the League of Nations could later fix any unfair settlements.

Clemenceau also compromised to obtain some guarantees for French security. He gave up France's wish for a separate Rhineland and instead accepted a defensive alliance with Great Britain and the United States. However, the U.S. Senate refused to ratify this agreement, which weakened the Versailles peace settlement.

The Treaty of Versailles

The final peace settlement of Paris consisted of five separate treaties with the defeated nations of Germany, Austria, Hungary, Bulgaria, and Turkey. The Treaty of Versailles with Germany was by far the most important.

The Germans considered it a harsh peace. They were especially unhappy with Article 231, the so-called War Guilt Clause, which declared that Germany (and Austria) were responsible for starting the war. The treaty ordered Germany to pay reparations (financial compensation) for all damages that the Allied governments and their people had sustained as a result of the war.

The military and territorial provisions of the Treaty of Versailles also angered the Germans. Germany had to reduce its army to 100,000 men, cut back its navy, and eliminate its air force. Alsace and Lorraine, taken by the Germans from France in 1871, were returned. Sections of eastern Germany were awarded to a new Polish state.

German land along the Rhine River became a demilitarized zone, stripped of all weapons and fortifications. This, it was hoped, would serve as a barrier to any future German moves against France. Although outraged by the "dictated peace," Germany accepted the treaty.

The Legacies of the War

The war, the Treaty of Versailles, and the separate peace treaties made with the other Central Powers redrew the map of eastern Europe. Many of these changes had already taken place at the end of the war. The German and Russian empires lost considerable territory in eastern Europe. The Austro-Hungarian Empire disappeared.

New nation-states emerged from the lands of these three empires: Finland, Latvia, Estonia, Lithuania, Poland, Czechoslovakia, Austria, and Hungary. New territorial arrangements were also made in the Balkans. Romania acquired additional lands. Serbia formed the nucleus of a new state, called Yugoslavia, which combined Serbs, Croats, and Slovenes.

The principle of self-determination supposedly guided the Paris Peace Conference. However, the mixtures of peoples in eastern Europe made it impossible to draw boundaries along strict ethnic lines. As a result of compromises, almost every eastern European state was left with ethnic minorities: Germans in Poland; Hungarians, Poles, and Germans in Czechoslovakia; Hungarians in Romania; and Serbs, Croats, Slovenes, Macedonians, and Albanians in Yugoslavia. The problem of ethnic minorities within nations would lead to many conflicts later.

Yet another centuries-old empire—the Ottoman Empire—was broken up by the peace settlement. To gain Arab support against the Ottoman Turks during the war, the Western Allies had promised to recognize the independence of Arab states in the Ottoman Empire. Once World War I was over, however, the Western nations changed their minds. France controlled the territory of Syria, and Britain controlled the territories of Iraq and Palestine.

These acquisitions were officially called **mandates**. Woodrow Wilson opposed the outright annexation of colonial territories by the Allies. As a result, in the mandate system, a nation officially governed a territory on a temporary basis as a mandate on behalf of the League of Nations, but did not own the territory.

World War I shattered the liberal, rational society that had existed in Europe at that time. The deaths of nearly 10 million people, as well as the incredible destruction caused by the war, undermined the whole idea of progress. Entire populations had participated in a devastating slaughter.

World War I was a total war—one that involved a complete mobilization of resources and people. As a result, the power of governments over the lives of their citizens increased. Freedom of the press and speech were limited in the name of national security. World War I made the practice of strong central authority a way of life.

The turmoil created by the war also seemed to open the door to even greater insecurity. Revolutions broke up old empires and created new states, which led to new problems. The hope that Europe and the rest of the world would return to normalcy was soon dashed.

☑ **READING PROGRESS CHECK**

Explaining What did Wilson hope to accomplish by creating the League of Nations?

mandate a territory temporarily governed by another country on behalf of the League of Nations

---

LESSON 4 REVIEW CCSS

Reviewing Vocabulary

1. ***Defining*** Write a short paragraph defining the terms *armistice* and *reparations* and discussing their significance for Germany at the end of World War I.

Using Your Notes

2. ***Identifying*** Use your notes to write a paragraph identifying the national interests of Great Britain, France, and the United States as they entered the Paris Peace Conference.

Answering the Guiding Questions

3. ***Identifying Cause and Effect*** How did World War I come to an end?

4. ***Identifying Central Issues*** How was a final settlement of World War I established?

Writing Activity

5. **INFORMATIVE/EXPLANATORY** Write an essay discussing the elements of the World War I peace settlement that seemed likely to lead to future conflict.

World War I and the Russian Revolution **289**

Directions: On a separate sheet of paper, answer the questions below. Make sure you read carefully and answer all parts of the questions.

Lesson Review

Lesson 1

1 **EXPLAINING** Why did Austria-Hungary object to Serbia's desire to establish an independent state?

2 **MAKING INFERENCES** How were other countries pulled into the conflict between Serbia and Austria-Hungary? What effect did their alliances have on prospects for war?

Lesson 2

3 **DIFFERENTIATING** How did the way the war was fought differ on the Eastern and Western Fronts?

4 **SUMMARIZING** Why did the countries fighting the war seek new allies? Which countries joined the conflict on which side?

Lesson 3

5 **IDENTIFYING CENTRAL ISSUES** Why did a revolution occur in Russia in 1917?

6 **SPECULATING** If Lenin had not returned to Russia after the czar stepped down, what would have been the likely outcome of the revolution? Who would have held power?

Lesson 4

7 **DESCRIBING** What actions ended World War I?

8 **MAKING PREDICTIONS** What were Germany's objections to the Treaty of Versailles? What might you expect a defeated nation to do in the years after its humiliation?

21st Century Skills

9 **ECONOMICS** What did it mean in economic terms to say that World War I was a "total war"?

10 **UNDERSTANDING RELATIONSHIPS AMONG EVENTS** Who were the Bolsheviks, and how did they overthrow the provisional government?

Exploring the Essential Questions

11 **SYNTHESIZING** Work with a partner to create a multimedia display of political motives and technological advances that contributed to the destructiveness of World War I. Provide a photo, a drawing, or an artifact that symbolizes each contributing factor and an audio or a written explanation of the factor. You may also include primary sources.

DBQ Analyzing Historical Documents

Use the document to answer the following questions.

Many soldiers were exposed to chemical weapons during the war. Doctors could do nothing to help them. One nurse described the situation in a hospital near the Western Front.

PRIMARY SOURCE

“ I wish those people who write so glibly about this being a holy war and the orators who talk so much about going on no matter how long the war lasts and what it may mean could see a case—to say nothing of ten cases—of mustard gas in its early stages—could see the poor things burnt and blistered all over with great mustard-coloured suppurating [oozing] blisters, with blind eyes . . . all sticky and stuck together, and always fighting for breath, with voices a mere whisper, saying that their throats are closing and they know they will choke. ”

—quoted in *Eye-Deep in Hell: Trench Warfare in World War I*

12 **IDENTIFYING BIAS** What does the nurse imply limits the thinking of people who insist the war should go on at any cost?

13 **ANALYZING** What words used by the nurse tell the reader how she feels about the war?

Extended-Response Question

14 **INFORMATIVE/EXPLANATORY** In what ways was World War I a bigger and more destructive conflict than any previous conflicts?

Need Extra Help?

If You've Missed Question	1	2	3	4	5	6	7	8	9	10	11	12	13	14
Go to page	272	273	274	277	280	282	285	288	278	281	272	276	276	289

The West Between the Wars

1919–1939

ESSENTIAL QUESTIONS · *What can cause economic instability?*
· *How might political change impact society?*

The Story Matters...

Bitterness over the Treaty of Versailles and severe economic problems helped the rise of Adolf Hitler's Nazi movement in Germany. The Hitler Youth (*Hitlerjugend*) organization was created in 1926 to win young people over to the Nazi cause. When Hitler took power in 1933, the Hitler Youth had about 100,000 members. Boys and girls in the Hitler Youth were indoctrinated to be race-conscious, obedient, and put the needs of the nation above their own. By the early years of World War II, about 90 percent of the country's young people belonged to the Hitler Youth.

◄ Boys in the Hitler Youth participated in Nazi rallies and activities where they spent time with other children with minimal parental guidance. This photograph was taken circa 1939.

PHOTO: Heinrich Hoffmann/Time & Life Pictures/Getty Images

At the end of the First World War, world leaders attempted to craft a lasting peace. However, the 1920s and 1930s witnessed severe economic crises that led to political instability. Authoritarian political leaders used widespread fear of disorder to gain power. Once in power, they violently suppressed all opposition.

Step Into the Place

Read the quotes and look at the information presented on the map.

 Analyzing Historical Documents Discuss the differences between Adolf Hitler's and Joseph Stalin's ideas about the goal of government. Look at the map and draw conclusions about the success of both leaders' policies.

PRIMARY SOURCE

❝[T]he Soviet power is a *new form* of state organization, different in principle from the old bourgeois-democratic and parliamentary form, a *new type* of state, adapted not to the task of exploiting and oppressing the labouring masses, but to the task of completely emancipating them from all oppression and exploitation, to the task facing the dictatorship of the proletariat.❞

—Stalin, from *Foundations of Leninism,* 1939

PRIMARY SOURCE

❝The state is a means to an end. Its end lies in the preservation and advancement of a community of physically and psychically homogeneous creatures. This preservation itself comprises first of all existence as a race and thereby permits the free development of all the forces dormant in this race. Of them a part will always primarily serve the preservation of physical life, and only the remaining part the promotion of a further spiritual development.❞

—Hitler, from *Mein Kampf*

PHOTO: (l)©SuperStock/SuperStock, (r)©RIA Novosti/TopFoto/The Image Works

Step Into the Time

Determining Cause and Effect

Research an event on the time line, and explain how it was a direct or an indirect result of the Treaty of Versailles.

EUROPE

THE WORLD

1919

1925

1919 Treaty of Versailles

1922 Vladimir Lenin and the Communists create the USSR

1923 French and Belgian troops occupy the Ruhr Valley

1924 Joseph Stalin leads Soviet Union after Lenin's death

1926 Benito Mussolini establishes a Fascist dictatorship in Italy

1920 First meeting of the League of Nations

1922 League of Nations confirms British Mandate for Palestine

1923 Mustafa Kemal, Atatürk, proclaims Republic of Turkey

1923 Nationalists and Communists are allies in China

1926 Fidel Castro, future president of Cuba, is born

networks

There's More Online!

☑ **MAP** Explore the interactive version of this map on Networks.

☑ **TIME LINE** Explore the interactive version of the time line on Networks.

Rise of Dictatorships in Europe 1938

Legend:
- Dictatorships by 1938
- Remaining democracies in 1938

Lambert Azimuthal Equal-Area projection

0 — 400 miles
0 — 400 km

1933 Paul von Hindenburg appoints Adolf Hitler as Chancellor

1935 Nuremberg laws in Germany strip Jews of their citizenship

April 1, 1939 Francisco Franco overthrows the Spanish Republic

1930   **1935**   **1939**

1929 U.S. stock market crashes; Great Depression begins

1930 Gandhi's civil disobedience movement begins in India

1932 Ibn Sa'ūd establishes the kingdom of Saudi Arabia

1934 Beginning of the Long March by Chinese Communists

1938 Japan passes military draft law

networks

There's More Online!

- ☑ **BIOGRAPHY** Albert Einstein
- ☑ **CHART/GRAPH** Unemployment, 1928–1938
- ☑ **IMAGE** Hyperinflation in Germany
- ☑ **IMAGE** The Persistence of Memory
- ☑ **INTERACTIVE SELF-CHECK QUIZ**
- ☑ **MAP** The Ruhr Valley
- ☑ **PRIMARY SOURCE** Locarno Gives Hope of an Era of Peace
- ☑ **SLIDE SHOW** Photomontage, Dadaism, and Surrealism
- ☑ **VIDEO** Instability After World War I

Reading **HELP**DESK (CCSS)

Academic Vocabulary

- annual
- appropriate

Content Vocabulary

- depression
- collective bargaining
- deficit spending
- surrealism
- uncertainty principle

TAKING NOTES:

Key Ideas and Details

Organizing As you read, use a table like the one below to compare France's Popular Front with the New Deal in the United States.

Popular Front	New Deal

294

LESSON 1
Instability After World War I

ESSENTIAL QUESTIONS · *What can cause economic instability?*
· *How might political change impact society?*

IT MATTERS BECAUSE

The peace settlement of World War I left many nations unhappy. The brief period of prosperity that began in Europe during the early 1920s ended in 1929 with the beginning of the Great Depression. This economic collapse shook people's confidence in political democracy. The arts and sciences also reflected the insecurity of the age.

Uneasy Peace, Uncertain Security

GUIDING QUESTION *What led to new problems in the years after World War I?*

From the beginning, the peace settlement at the end of World War I left nations unhappy. President Woodrow Wilson had realized that the peace settlement included provisions that could serve as new causes for conflict. He had placed many of his hopes for the future in the League of Nations. This organization, however, was not very effective in maintaining the peace.

One problem was the failure of the United States to join the League. Most Americans wanted to avoid involvement in European affairs. The U.S. Senate, in spite of President Wilson's wishes, refused to ratify, or approve, the Treaty of Versailles. That meant the United States could not join the League of Nations. Without the United States, the League of Nations' effectiveness was weakened.

Between 1919 and 1924, desire for security led the French government to demand strict enforcement of the Treaty of Versailles. This tough policy began with the issue of reparations (payments) that the Germans were supposed to make for the damage they had done in the war. In April 1921, the Allied Reparations Commission determined that Germany owed 132 billion German marks (33 billion U.S. dollars) for reparations, payable in **annual** installments of 2.5 billion marks.

The new German republic made its first payment in 1921. One year later, the German government faced a financial crisis and announced that it could not pay any more reparations. Outraged,

France sent troops to occupy the Ruhr Valley, Germany's chief industrial and mining center. France planned to collect reparations by using the Ruhr mines and factories.

Inflation in Germany

The German government adopted a policy of passive resistance to this French occupation. German workers went on strike. The German government mainly paid their salaries by printing more paper money. This only added to the inflation (rise in prices) that had already begun in Germany by the end of the war. The German mark soon became worthless. In 1914, 4.2 marks equaled 1 U.S. dollar. By the end of November 1923, the ratio had reached an incredible 4.2 trillion marks to equal 1 dollar.

Both France and Germany began to seek a way out of the disaster. In August 1924, an international commission adopted a new plan for reparations. The Dawes Plan, named after the American banker who chaired the commission, first reduced reparations. It then coordinated Germany's annual payments with its ability to pay.

The Dawes Plan also granted an initial $200 million loan for German recovery. This loan soon opened the door to heavy American investment in Europe. A brief period of European prosperity followed.

The Treaty of Locarno

With prosperity came a new European diplomacy. The foreign ministers of Germany and France, Gustav Stresemann and Aristide Briand, fostered a spirit of cooperation. In 1925, they signed the Treaty of Locarno, which guaranteed Germany's new western borders with France and Belgium. Many viewed the Locarno pact as the beginning of a new era of European peace.

Three years later, the Kellogg-Briand Pact brought even more hope. Sixty-five nations signed this accord and pledged to "renounce [war] as an instrument of national policy." Nothing was said, however, about what would be done if anyone violated the pact.

✔ **READING PROGRESS CHECK**

Explaining What contributed to the German mark becoming worthless?

The Great Depression

GUIDING QUESTION *What triggered the Great Depression?*

The brief period of prosperity that began in Europe in 1924 ended in an economic collapse that came to be known as the Great Depression. A **depression** is a period of low economic activity and rising unemployment.

Two factors played a major role in the start of the Great Depression. First was a series of downturns in the economies of individual nations in the second half of the 1920s. For example, prices for farm products, especially wheat, fell rapidly due to overproduction. An increase in the use of oil and hydroelectricity led to a slump in the coal industry.

The second trigger was an international financial crisis involving the U.S. stock market. Much of the European prosperity between 1924 and 1929 was built on U.S. bank loans to Germany. During the 1920s, the U.S. stock market boomed. By 1928, American investors pulled money out of Germany to invest it in stocks. Then, in October 1929, the U.S. stock market crashed. Stock prices plunged.

▶ **CRITICAL THINKING**
Analyzing Why was the Ruhr Valley important to Germany?

annual yearly

▲ This woman uses German marks to light her stove during the Great Depression.

▶ **CRITICAL THINKING**
Explaining Why would this woman burn money during the Great Depression?

depression a period of low economic activity and rising unemployment

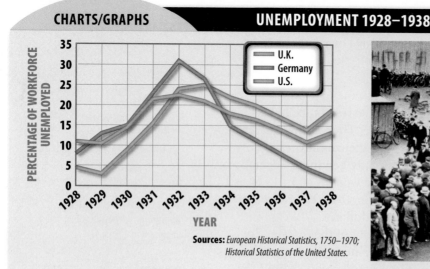

Sources: *European Historical Statistics, 1750–1970; Historical Statistics of the United States.*

▶ **CRITICAL THINKING**

1 *Drawing Conclusions* When was the height of the Great Depression?

2 *Transferring* Which country experienced the largest rise in unemployment?

▲ Long lines of unemployed workers sought food and jobs.

In a panic, U.S. investors withdrew more funds from Germany and other European markets. By 1931 trade was slowing, industrial production was declining, and unemployment was rising.

☑ **READING PROGRESS CHECK**

Applying Why were farmers hit hard at the onset of the Great Depression?

Responses to the Depression

GUIDING QUESTION *How did the Great Depression affect people's confidence in democracy?*

Economic depression was not new to Europe. However, the extent of the economic downturn after 1929 truly made this the Great Depression. During 1932, the worst year of the Depression, nearly 1 in every 4 British workers was unemployed. About 5.5 million Germans, or roughly 30 percent of the German labor force, had no jobs. The unemployed and homeless filled the streets.

Governments were unsure of how to deal with the crisis. They raised tariffs to exclude foreign goods from home markets. This worsened the crisis and had serious political effects.

One effect of the economic crisis was increased government activity in the economy. The Great Depression also led masses of people to follow political leaders who offered simple solutions in return for dictatorial power. Everywhere, democracy seemed on the defensive.

In 1919, most European states, both major and minor, had democratic governments. In a number of states, women could now vote. Male political leaders had rewarded women for their contributions to the war effort by granting them voting rights. (However, women could not vote until 1944 in France, 1945 in Italy, and 1971 in Switzerland.) In the 1920s, maintaining these democratic governments was not easy.

Germany

Imperial Germany ended in 1918 with Germany's defeat in the war. A German democratic state known as the Weimar (VY • mahr) Republic was then created.

PHOTO: Walter Ballhause/ akg-images.

296

The Weimar Republic was plagued by serious economic problems. Germany experienced runaway inflation in 1922 and 1923. With it came serious social problems. Families on fixed incomes watched their life savings disappear.

To make matters worse, after a period of relative prosperity from 1924 to 1929, Germany was struck by the Great Depression. In 1930, unemployment had grown to 3 million people by March and to 4.38 million by December. The Depression paved the way for fear and the rise of extremist parties.

France

France, too, suffered from financial problems after the war. Because it had a more balanced economy, France did not begin to feel the full effects of the Great Depression until 1932. The economic instability it then suffered soon had political effects. During a 19-month period in 1932 and 1933, six different cabinets were formed as France faced political chaos. Finally, in June 1936, a coalition of leftist parties—Communists, Socialists, and Radicals—formed the Popular Front government.

The Popular Front started a program for workers that some have called the French New Deal. This program was named after the New Deal in the United States. The French New Deal gave workers the right to **collective bargaining**, a 40-hour workweek in industry, and a minimum wage.

Great Britain

Although Britain experienced limited prosperity from 1925 to 1929, by 1929 it too faced the growing effects of the Great Depression. The Labour Party failed to solve the nation's economic problems and fell from power in 1931. A new government, led by the Conservatives, claimed credit for bringing Britain out of the worst stages of the Depression by using the traditional policies of balanced budgets and protective tariffs.

Political leaders in Britain largely ignored the new ideas of a British economist, John Maynard Keynes. Keynes argued that unemployment came from a decline in demand, not from overproduction. He believed governments could increase demand by creating jobs through **deficit spending**, or going into debt if necessary. Keynes's ideas differed from those who believed that depressions should be left to resolve themselves without government interference.

The United States

After Germany, no Western nation was more affected by the Great Depression than the United States. All segments of society suffered. By 1932, U.S. industrial production fell by almost 50 percent from its 1929 level. By 1933, there were more than 12 million unemployed. Under these conditions, Democrat Franklin D. Roosevelt won the presidential election in 1932 by a landslide. Believing in free enterprise, Roosevelt felt that capitalism must be reformed to save it. He pursued a policy of active governmental economic intervention known as the New Deal.

The New Deal included an increased program of public works. The Works Progress Administration (WPA), established in 1935, was a government organization employing about 3 million people at its peak. Workers built bridges, roads, post offices, and airports.

The Roosevelt administration instituted new social legislation that began the U.S. welfare system. In 1935, the Social Security Act created a system of old-age pensions and unemployment insurance.

These reforms may have prevented a social revolution in the United States, but they did not solve the unemployment problems. In 1938, U.S.

Connections to TODAY

Depression vs. Recession

When the United States experienced a recession in 2008, people worried unemployment would reach Great Depression levels. But in studying unemployment numbers, economists discovered that, while the economic downturn was the worst since World War II, it was nowhere near as bad as the Great Depression. In 1933, unemployment had reached 29.4 percent. In December 2010, 9.4 percent of the U.S. population was unemployed.

collective bargaining the right of unions to negotiate with employers over wages and hours

deficit spending when a government pays out more money than it takes in through taxation and other revenues, thus going into debt

appropriate suitable or compatible; fitting

surrealism an artistic movement that seeks to depict the world of the unconscious

uncertainty principle the idea put forth by Werner Heisenberg in 1927 that the behavior of subatomic particles is uncertain, suggesting that all of the physical laws governing the universe are based on uncertainty

▲ *The Persistence of Memory* (1931), a surrealist painting by Salvador Dalí

unemployment was more than 10 million. Only World War II and the growth of weapons industries brought U.S. workers back to full employment.

✓ **READING PROGRESS CHECK**

Defining How might collective bargaining have helped French workers?

Arts and Sciences

GUIDING QUESTION *How were the arts and sciences influenced by World War I?*

With political, economic, and social uncertainties came intellectual uncertainties. These were evident in the artistic and scientific achievements of the years following World War I. After 1918, the prewar fascination with the absurd and the unconscious content of the mind seemed even more **appropriate** in light of the nightmare landscapes of the World War I battlefronts.

"The world does not make sense, so why should art?" was a common remark. This sentiment gave rise to Dadaism and surrealism.

The dadaists were artists who were obsessed with the idea that life has no purpose. They tried to express the insanity of life in their art. A more important artistic movement than Dadaism was **surrealism**. By portraying the unconscious—fantasies, dreams, and even nightmares—the surrealists sought to show the greater reality that exists beyond the world of physical appearances. One of the world's foremost surrealist painters, the Spaniard Salvador Dalí, placed recognizable objects in unrecognizable relationships, thus making the irrational visible.

The prewar physics revolution begun by Albert Einstein continued in the 1920s and 1930s. In fact, some have called the 1920s the "heroic age of physics." Newtonian physics had made people believe that all phenomena could be completely defined and predicted. In 1927, German physicist Werner Heisenberg's **uncertainty principle** shook this belief. Physicists knew that atoms were made of smaller parts (subatomic particles). The uncertainty principle is based on the unpredictable behavior of these subatomic particles. Heisenberg's theory essentially suggests that all physical laws are based on uncertainty. This theory challenged Newtonian physics and represented a new worldview. The principle of uncertainty fit in well with the other uncertainties of the interwar years.

✓ **READING PROGRESS CHECK**

Assessing Why was non-realistic art popular after World War I?

LESSON 1 REVIEW

Reviewing Vocabulary

1. *Applying* Explain why John Maynard Keynes argued for the concept of deficit spending.

Using Your Notes

2. *Identifying* Use your notes to write a summary of the key points of the Popular Front and the New Deal.

Answering the Guiding Questions

3. *Exploring Issues* What led to new problems in the years after World War I?

4. *Discussing* What triggered the Great Depression?

5. *Evaluating* How did the Great Depression affect people's confidence in democracy?

6. *Identifying* How were the arts and sciences influenced by World War I?

Writing Activity

7. INFORMATIVE/EXPLANATORY Write an essay that explains how President Roosevelt's New Deal had immediate and far-reaching effects on the U.S. economy.

298

netw⊚rks

There's More Online!

- ☑ **BIOGRAPHY** Benito Mussolini
- ☑ **BIOGRAPHY** Francisco Franco
- ☑ **BIOGRAPHY** Joseph Stalin
- ☑ **CHART/GRAPH** Soviet Industry, 1927–1938
- ☑ **IMAGE** Guernica
- ☑ **INTERACTIVE SELF-CHECK QUIZ**
- ☑ **MAP** Politics in Europe, 1930s
- ☑ **MAP** Soviet Union, 1939
- ☑ **VIDEO** The Rise of Dictatorial Regimes

Reading **HELP**DESK (CCSS)

Academic Vocabulary
- media   • attitudes

Content Vocabulary
- totalitarian state
- fascism
- collectivization

TAKING NOTES:
Key Ideas and Details

Sequencing As you read, use a sequence chain like the one below to record the events leading up to Franco's authoritarian rule of Spain.

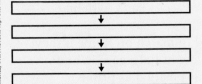

PHOTO: (l to r)© Bettmann/CORBIS, ©Jean, Baptiste, Greuz/Age Fotostock America, ©RIA Novosti/TopFoto/The Image Works.

LESSON 2
The Rise of Dictatorial Regimes

ESSENTIAL QUESTIONS • *What can cause economic instability?*
• *How might political change impact society?*

IT MATTERS BECAUSE
After World War I, European democracy was under threat. A new kind of dictatorship emerged with Mussolini's fascist state in Italy and Stalin's totalitarian rule in the Soviet Union. Other Western states such as Spain maintained authoritarian regimes.

The Rise of Dictators

GUIDING QUESTION *How did Mussolini create a dictatorial state in Italy?*

By 1939, only two major European states—France and Great Britain—remained democratic. Italy, the Soviet Union, Germany, and many other European states adopted dictatorial regimes. These regimes took both old and new forms.

A new form of dictatorship was the modern totalitarian state. In a **totalitarian state**, the government aims to control the political, economic, social, intellectual, and cultural lives of its citizens. Totalitarian regimes pushed the central state's power far beyond what it had been in the past. These regimes wanted more than passive obedience; they wanted to conquer the minds and hearts of their subjects. They achieved this goal through mass propaganda techniques and modern communications.

The totalitarian states were led by a single leader and a single party. They rejected the ideal of limited government power and the guarantee of individual freedoms. Instead, individual freedom was subordinated to the collective will of the masses as determined by the leader. The masses were expected to be actively involved in achieving the state's goals.

Fascism in Italy
In the 1920s, Benito Mussolini (MOO • suh • LEE • nee) set up the first European fascist movement in Italy. Mussolini began his political career as a Socialist. In 1919, he created a new political group, the *Fascio di Combattimento*, or League of Combat. *Fascism* comes from that name.

Politics in Europe 1930s

Legend:
- Authoritarian
- Communist
- Fascist
- Democratic
- Democratic, became Authoritarian
- Democratic, became Nazi

Map labels include: NORWAY (Oslo), SWEDEN (Stockholm), FINLAND (Helsinki), Leningrad, ESTONIA (Tallinn), LATVIA (Riga), Moscow, LITHUANIA (Kaunas), EAST PRUSSIA (Ger.), USSR, Stalingrad, IRELAND (Dublin), UNITED KINGDOM (London), DENMARK (Copenhagen), NETH. (Amsterdam), Berlin, GERMANY, Warsaw, POLAND, BELG. (Brussels), LUX., Prague, CZECHOSLOVAKIA, FRANCE (Paris), Munich, Vienna, AUSTRIA, Bern, SWITZ., Budapest, HUNGARY, ROMANIA, Bucharest, ANDORRA, ITALY, Belgrade, YUGOSLAVIA, Black Sea, PORTUGAL (Lisbon), SPAIN (Madrid), Corsica, Rome, Adriatic Sea, BULGARIA (Sofia), Angora (Ankara), Sardinia, ALBANIA, Tirane, TURKEY, GREECE, Athens, Sicily, Aegean Sea, Crete, Cyprus (U.K.), Mediterranean Sea, North Sea, Baltic Sea, ATLANTIC OCEAN

0 — 500 miles
0 — 500 km
Lambert Azimuthal Equal-Area projection

GEOGRAPHY CONNECTION

1. **THE WORLD IN SPATIAL TERMS** *Where were authoritarian governments located?*

2. **HUMAN SYSTEMS** *Which countries transitioned from democratic to nondemocratic in the 1930s?*

totalitarian state
a government that aims to control the political, economic, social, intellectual, and cultural lives of its citizens

fascism a political philosophy that glorifies the state above the individual by emphasizing the need for a strong central government led by a dictatorial ruler

As a political philosophy, **fascism** (FA • SHIH • zuhm) glorifies the state above the individual by emphasizing the need for a strong central government led by a dictatorial ruler. In a fascist state, the government controls the people and stifles any opposition.

By 1922, Mussolini's movement was growing quickly. The middle-class fear of socialism, communism, and disorder made the Fascists increasingly attractive to many people. Mussolini knew that many Italians were still angry over the failure to receive more land from the peace treaty. He knew nationalism was a powerful force and demanded more land for Italy. Mussolini converted thousands to the Fascist Party with his nationalistic appeals.

In 1922, Mussolini and the Fascists threatened to march on Rome if they were not given power. Victor Emmanuel III, the king of Italy, gave in and made Mussolini prime minister. Mussolini used his position as prime minister to create a Fascist dictatorship. He was made head of the government with the power to make laws by decree. The police were given unrestricted authority to arrest and jail anyone for either political or nonpolitical crimes. In 1926, the Fascists outlawed all other political parties in Italy and set up a secret police, known as the OVRA. By the end of the year, Mussolini ruled Italy as *Il Duce* (eel DOO • chay), "The Leader."

The Fascist State

Believing that the Fascist state should be totalitarian, Mussolini used various means to establish complete control over the Italian people. The OVRA watched citizens' political activities and enforced government policies. The Italian Fascists also tried to exercise control over the mass **media**, including newspapers, radio, and film. The media was used to spread propaganda. Simple slogans like "Mussolini Is Always Right" were used to mold Italians into a single-minded Fascist community.

The Fascists also used organizations to promote the ideals of fascism. For example, by 1939, about 66 percent of the population between the ages of 8 and 18 were members of Fascist youth groups. These youth groups particularly focused on military activities and values.

With these organizations, the Fascists hoped to create a nation of new Italians who were fit, disciplined, and war-loving. In practice, however, the Fascists largely maintained traditional social **attitudes**. This was especially evident in their policies on women. The Fascists portrayed the family as the pillar of the state. Seen as the foundation of the family, women were to be homemakers and mothers. According to Mussolini, these roles were "their natural and fundamental mission in life."

In spite of his attempts, Mussolini never achieved the degree of totalitarian control seen in Hitler's Germany or Stalin's Soviet Union. The Italian Fascist Party did not completely destroy the country's old power structure. Mussolini's compromise with the traditional institutions of Italy was evident in his dealings with the Catholic Church. In the Lateran Accords of February 1929, Mussolini's regime recognized the sovereign independence of a small area of 109 acres (about 44 hectares) within Rome known as Vatican City. The Church had claimed this area since Italian unification in 1870. Mussolini's regime also recognized Catholicism as the "sole religion of the State." In return, the Catholic Church urged Italians to support the Fascist regime.

☑ **READING PROGRESS CHECK**

Analyzing Why did many Italian people find fascism acceptable?

▲ Mussolini addressing a crowd of over 500,000 people

media channels or systems of communication

attitude a mental position regarding a fact or state

From Russia to the USSR

GUIDING QUESTION *How did Stalin gain and maintain power in the USSR?*

During the civil war in Russia, Lenin had followed a policy of war communism. The government controlled most industries and seized grain from peasants to ensure supplies for the army. When the war was over, peasants began to sabotage the Communist program by hoarding food. Moreover, drought caused a terrible famine between 1920 and 1922. As many as 5 million died. With agricultural disaster came industrial collapse. By 1921, industrial output was only 20 percent of its 1913 level. Russia was exhausted. A peasant banner proclaimed, "Down with Lenin and horseflesh. Bring back the czar and pork." As Leon Trotsky said, "The country, and the government with it, were at the very edge of the abyss."

Lenin's New Economic Policy

In March 1921, Lenin pulled Russia back from the abyss. He abandoned war communism in favor of his New Economic Policy (NEP). The NEP was a modified version of the old capitalist system. Peasants were allowed to sell their produce openly. Retail stores, as well as small industries that employed fewer than 20 workers, could be privately owned and operated. Heavy industry, banking, and mines, however, remained in the hands of the government.

Soviet Union 1939

Main area of collective farms

Labor camp

Forced labor region

Iron and steel production

Iron mining

Coal

Oil

GEOGRAPHY CONNECTION

By 1939, the Soviet Union was increasingly industrialized and collectivized.

1 **THE WORLD IN SPATIAL TERMS** *What resource was plentiful near the Caspian Sea?*

2 **HUMAN SYSTEMS** *Why do you think the forced labor region was located in the far east of Russia?*

The Soviet Union

In 1922, Lenin and the Communists formally created a new state called the Union of Soviet Socialist Republics. The state was also known as the USSR (its initials) or as the Soviet Union (its shortened form). By that time, a revived market and a good harvest had ended the famine. Soviet agricultural production climbed to 75 percent of its prewar level.

Overall, the NEP saved the Soviet Union from complete economic disaster. Lenin, however, intended the NEP to be only a temporary retreat from the goals of communism.

Lenin died in 1924. A struggle for power began at once among the seven members of the Politburo (PAH • luht • BYUR • OH)—the Communist Party's main policy-making body. The Politburo was severely divided over the future direction of the Soviet Union.

One group, led by Leon Trotsky, wanted to end the NEP and to launch Russia on a path of rapid industrialization, chiefly at the expense of the peasants. This group also wanted to spread communism abroad. It believed that the revolution in Russia would survive only with new communist states.

Another group in the Politburo rejected the idea of worldwide communist revolution. Instead, it wanted to focus on building a socialist state in Russia and to continue Lenin's NEP. This group believed that rapid industrialization would harm the living standards of the peasants.

Stalin and His Five-Year Plans

These divisions were further strained by an intense personal rivalry between Leon Trotsky and another Politburo member, Joseph Stalin. In 1924, Trotsky held the post of commissar of war. Stalin held the bureaucratic job of party general secretary. Stalin used his post as general secretary to gain complete control of the Communist Party. By 1926, Stalin had removed the Bolsheviks of the revolutionary era from the Politburo and had established a powerful dictatorship. Trotsky, pushed out of the party in 1927, eventually made his way to Mexico. There he was murdered in 1940, probably on Stalin's orders.

Stalin made a significant shift in economic policy in 1928 when he ended the NEP. That year he launched his First Five-Year Plan. The Five-Year Plans set economic goals for five-year periods. Their purpose was to transform Russia virtually overnight from an agricultural into an industrial country.

The First Five-Year Plan focused on production of military and capital goods (goods devoted to the production of other goods such as heavy machines). The plan quadrupled the production of heavy machinery and doubled oil production. Between 1928 and 1937, during the first two Five-Year Plans, steel production in Russia increased from 4 million to 18 million tons (3.6 to 16.3 million t) per year.

Costs of Stalin's Programs

The social and political costs of industrialization were enormous. The number of workers increased by millions between 1932 and 1940, but investment in housing actually declined after 1929. The result was that millions of workers and their families lived in miserable conditions. Real wages of industrial workers declined by 43 percent between 1928 and 1940.

With rapid industrialization came an equally rapid **collectivization** of agriculture—a system in which private farms were eliminated. Instead, the government owned all the land, and the peasants worked it. The peasants resisted by hoarding crops and killing livestock. In response, Stalin stepped up the program. By 1934, 26 million family farms had been collectivized into 250,000 units.

Collectivization was done at tremendous cost. Hoarding food and slaughtering livestock led to widespread famine. Stalin is supposed to have said that 10 million died in the famine of 1932 to 1933. Stalin gave the peasants only one concession. Each collective farm worker could have one tiny, privately owned garden plot.

Stalin's programs had other costs as well. To achieve his goals, Stalin strengthened his control over the party. Those who resisted were sent into forced labor camps in Siberia. During the time known as the Great Purge, Stalin expelled army officers, diplomats, union officials, intellectuals, and ordinary citizens. About 8 million were arrested and sent to labor camps; they never returned. Others were executed.

The Stalin era also overturned permissive social legislation enacted in the early 1920s. To promote equal rights for women, the Communists had made the divorce process easier. After Stalin came to power, the family was praised as a small collective. Parents were responsible for teaching the values of hard work, duty, and discipline to their children.

✓ READING PROGRESS CHECK

Stating Explain how Joseph Stalin used his position in the Communist Party and other means to gain control over the USSR.

Authoritarian States in the West

GUIDING QUESTION *What was the goal of authoritarian governments in the West?*

A number of governments in the Western world were not totalitarian but were authoritarian. These states adopted some of the features of totalitarian states, in particular, their use of police powers. However, these authoritarian governments did not want to create a new kind of mass society. Instead, they wanted to preserve the existing social order.

Analyzing CCSS
PRIMARY SOURCES

Stalin's Purge

Poet Anna Andreyevna Gorenko, who wrote under the pseudonym Anna Akhmatova, was silenced during the Great Purge and watched as loved ones and fellow writers were imprisoned and disappeared. In 1942, her poem "Courage" appeared:

❝We know that our fate in the balance is cast
And we are the history makers.
The hour for courage has sounded at last
And courage has never forsaken us.
We do not fear death where the wild bullets screech,
Nor weep over homes that are gutted,
For we shall preserve you our own Russian speech,
The glorious language of Russia!
Your free and pure utterance we shall convey
To new generations, unshackled you'll stay
Forever!❞

—quoted in *Anna Akhmatova and Her Circle*

 DRAWING CONCLUSIONS

According to this poem, what may be lost in the Great Purge that "we" must save?

collectivization a system in which private farms are eliminated and peasants work land owned by the government

Eastern Europe

At first, it seemed that political democracy would become well established in eastern Europe after World War I. Austria, Poland, Czechoslovakia, Yugoslavia (known as the kingdom of the Serbs, Croats, and Slovenes until 1929), Romania, Bulgaria, and Hungary all adopted parliamentary systems. However, authoritarian regimes soon replaced most of these systems.

Parliamentary systems failed in most eastern European states for several reasons. These states had little tradition of political democracy. In addition, they were mostly rural and agrarian. Large landowners still dominated most of the land. Powerful landowners, the churches, and even some members of the small middle class feared land reform. They also feared communist upheaval and ethnic conflict. These groups looked to authoritarian governments to maintain the old system. Only Czechoslovakia, which had a large middle class, a liberal tradition, and a strong industrial base, maintained its political democracy.

Spain

In Spain, too, political democracy failed to survive. Led by General Francisco Franco, Spanish military forces revolted against the democratic government in 1936. A brutal and bloody civil war began.

Foreign intervention complicated the Spanish Civil War. The fascist regimes of Italy and Germany aided Franco's forces with arms, money, and soldiers. Hitler used the Spanish Civil War as an opportunity to test the new weapons of his revived air force. German bombers destroyed the city of Guernica in April 1937. The Spanish republican government was aided by 40,000 foreign volunteers. The Soviet Union sent in trucks, planes, tanks, and military advisers.

The Spanish Civil War came to an end when Franco's forces captured Madrid in 1939. Franco established a dictatorship that lasted until his death in 1975. Because Franco's dictatorship favored traditional groups and did not try to control every aspect of people's lives, it is an example of an authoritarian rather than a totalitarian regime. Nevertheless, his rule was harsh. He relied on special police forces, and opponents to the regime who had not fled into exile were imprisoned.

▼ In his mural *Guernica* Spanish artist Pablo Picasso immortalized the horrible destruction of the city of Guernica in April 1937.

▶ **CRITICAL THINKING**
Analyzing Visuals What one word best describes your response to *Guernica*? Use details from the painting to explain how the artist creates this feeling.

PHOTO: Art Archive/Reina Sofia Museum, Madrid

☑ **READING PROGRESS CHECK**

Describing In what ways did Franco's government preserve the existing social order?

LESSON 2 REVIEW (CCSS)

Reviewing Vocabulary
1. *Describing* Describe the restriction of individual rights and the use of mass terror in Italy and the Soviet Union.

Using Your Notes
2. *Sequencing* Use your notes and details from the text to explain how Franco established an authoritarian government in Spain.

Answering the Guiding Questions
3. *Organizing* How did Mussolini create a dictatorial state in Italy?

4. *Identifying Cause and Effect* How did Stalin gain and maintain power in the USSR?

5. *Interpreting* What was the goal of authoritarian governments in the West?

Writing Activity
6. **ARGUMENT** Imagine you are a middle-class Italian in the 1920s. Write a letter to the editor of the local newspaper supporting Mussolini's new government.

Reading **HELP**DESK (CCSS)

Academic Vocabulary
• **require** • **prohibit**

Content Vocabulary
• **Nazi**
• **concentration camp**
• **Aryan**

TAKING NOTES:
Key Ideas and Details

Categorizing As you read, use a chart like the one below to list anti-Semitic policies enforced by the Nazi Party.

Anti-Semitic Policies

LESSON 3
Hitler and Nazi Germany

ESSENTIAL QUESTIONS • *What can cause economic instability?*
• *How might political change impact society?*

IT MATTERS BECAUSE

Recovering from the loss of World War I and from the Great Depression, Germans found extremist parties more attractive. Adolf Hitler's Nazi Party promised to build a new Germany, and his party's propaganda appealed to the German sense of national honor.

Hitler and Nazism

GUIDING QUESTION *What was the basis of Adolf Hitler's ideas?*

Adolf Hitler was born in Austria in 1889. A failure in school, he traveled to Vienna to become an artist but was rejected by the academy. Here he developed his basic political ideas. At the core of Hitler's ideas was racism, especially anti-Semitism (hostility toward Jews). Hitler was also an extreme nationalist who knew how political parties could effectively use propaganda and terror.

After serving four years on the Western Front during World War I, Hitler remained in Germany and entered politics. In 1919, he joined the little-known German Workers' Party, one of several right-wing extreme nationalist parties in Munich.

By the summer of 1921, Hitler had taken total control of the party. By then the party had been renamed the National Socialist German Workers' Party (NSDAP, an abbreviation of the German name), or **Nazi**, for short. Within two years, party membership had grown to 55,000 people, with 15,000 in the party militia. The militia was variously known as the SA, the Storm Troops, or the Brownshirts, after the color of their uniforms.

An overconfident Hitler staged an armed uprising against the government in Munich in November 1923. This uprising, called the Beer Hall Putsch, was quickly crushed, and Hitler was sentenced to prison, where he wrote *Mein Kampf*, or *My Struggle*, an account of his movement and its basic ideas.

In *Mein Kampf*, Hitler links extreme German nationalism, strong anti-Semitism, and anticommunism together by a Social Darwinian theory of struggle. This theory emphasizes the right of "superior"

Nazi shortened form of the German *Nazional,* or the National Socialist German Workers' Party; a member of such party

concentration camp a camp where prisoners of war, political prisoners, or members of minority groups are confined, typically under harsh conditions

Aryan a term used to identify people speaking Indo-European languages; Nazis misused the term, treating it as a racial designation and identifying the Aryans with the ancient Greeks and Romans and twentieth-century Germans and Scandinavians

nations to *Lebensraum* (LAY • buhnz • ROWM)—"living space"—through expansion. It also upholds the right of "superior" individuals to gain authoritarian leadership over the masses.

Rise of Nazism

In prison, Hitler realized that the Nazis would have to attain power legally, not by a violent overthrow of the Weimar Republic. This meant that the Nazi Party would have to be a mass party that could compete for votes.

When out of prison, Hitler expanded the Nazi Party in Germany. By 1929, it had a national party organization. Three years later, it had 800,000 members and had become the largest party in the Reichstag—the German parliament.

No doubt, Germany's economic difficulties were a crucial factor in the Nazi rise to power. Unemployment had risen dramatically, growing from 4.35 million in 1931 to about 5.5 million by the winter of 1932. Hitler also promised a new Germany that appealed to nationalism and militarism.

The Nazis Take Control

After 1930, the German government ruled by decree with the support of President Hindenburg. The Reichstag had little power. Increasingly, the right-wing elites of Germany—the industrial leaders, landed aristocrats, military officers, and higher bureaucrats—looked to Hitler for leadership. Under pressure, Hindenburg agreed to allow Hitler to become chancellor in 1933 and to create a new government.

Within two months, Hitler had laid the foundation for the Nazi Party's complete control over Germany. Hitler's "legal seizure" of power came on March 23, 1933, when a two-thirds vote of the Reichstag passed the Enabling Act. This law gave the government the power to ignore the constitution for four years while it issued laws to deal with the country's problems. It also gave Hitler's later actions a legal basis. He no longer needed the Reichstag or President Hindenburg. In effect, Hitler became a dictator appointed by the parliamentary body itself.

With their new power, the Nazis quickly brought all institutions under their control. They purged the civil service of democratic elements and of Jews—whom they blamed for Europe's economic woes. They set up prison camps called **concentration camps** for people who opposed them. All political parties except the Nazis were abolished.

By the end of the summer of 1933, only seven months after being appointed chancellor, Hitler had established the basis for a totalitarian state. When Hindenburg died in 1934, the office of president was abolished. Hitler became sole ruler of Germany. People took oaths of loyalty to their *Führer* (FYUR • uhr), or "Leader."

☑ **READING PROGRESS CHECK**

Identifying Central Issues How did the Enabling Act contribute to Hitler's rise to power?

The Nazi State, 1933–1939

GUIDING QUESTION *How did Hitler build a Nazi state?*

Hitler wanted to develop a totalitarian state. He had not simply sought power for power's sake. He had a larger goal—the development of an **Aryan** racial state that would dominate Europe and possibly the world for generations to come. (*Aryan* is a term used to identify people speaking Indo-European languages. The Nazis misused the term by treating it as a racial designation and identifying the Aryans with the ancient Greeks and Romans and twentieth-century Germans and Scandinavians.) The Nazis thought the Germans were the true descendants and leaders of the Aryans and would create an empire.

To achieve his goal, Hitler needed the active involvement of the German people. Hitler stated:

PRIMARY SOURCE

❝We must develop organizations in which an individual's entire life can take place. Then every activity and every need of every individual will be regulated by the collectivity represented by the party. There is no longer any arbitrary will, there are no longer any free realms in which the individual belongs to himself. . . . The time of personal happiness is over.❞

—quoted in *Hitler,* 2002

The Nazis pursued the creation of the totalitarian state in several ways. For one thing, they used mass demonstrations and spectacles to make the German people an instrument of Hitler's policies. These meetings, especially the Nuremberg party rallies that were held every September, usually evoked mass enthusiasm and excitement.

The State and Terror

As sole ruler of Nazi Germany, Hitler relied on instruments of terror to maintain control. The *Schutzstaffeln* ("Guard Squadrons"), known as the SS, were an important force for maintaining order. The SS was originally created as Hitler's personal bodyguard. Under the direction of Heinrich Himmler, the SS came to control not only the secret police forces that Himmler had set up but also the regular police forces.

The SS was based on two principles: terror and ideology. Terror included the instruments of repression and murder—secret police, criminal police, concentration camps, and later, execution squads and death camps (concentration camps in which prisoners are killed). For Himmler, the chief goal of the SS was to further the "Aryan master race".

▲ SS troops march through the streets of Berlin on Hitler's birthday in 1939.

▶ **CRITICAL THINKING**

Analyzing How did marches such as this one help create allegiance to the Nazi state?

Economics

In the economic sphere, Hitler used public works projects and grants to private construction firms to put people back to work and end the depression. A massive rearmament program, however, was the key to solving the unemployment problem. Unemployment, which had reached more than 5 million in 1932, dropped to less than 500,000 in 1937. The regime claimed full credit for solving Germany's economic woes. Its part in ending the depression was an important factor in leading many Germans to accept Hitler and the Nazis.

▲ This Nazi propaganda poster features a mother with her children. It says, "Now we again have a happy future. For that, we thank the Führer on December 4."

require to demand as being necessary

prohibit to prevent or to forbid

Women and Nazism

Women played a crucial role in the Aryan state as bearers of the children who, the Nazis believed, would bring about the triumph of the "Aryan race". The Nazis believed men were destined to be warriors and political leaders, while women were meant to be wives and mothers. In this way, each could best serve to maintain the entire community.

Nazi ideas determined employment opportunities for women. Jobs in heavy industry, the Nazis thought, might hinder women from bearing healthy children. Professions such as university teaching, medicine, and law were also considered unsuitable for women, especially married women. The Nazis instead encouraged women to pursue occupations such as social work and nursing. The Nazi regime pushed its campaign against working women with poster slogans such as "Get hold of pots and pans and broom and you'll sooner find a groom!"

Anti-Semitic Policies

From its beginning, the Nazi Party reflected the strong anti-Semitic beliefs of Adolf Hitler. When in power, the Nazis translated anti-Semitic ideas into anti-Semitic policies.

In September 1935, the Nazis announced new anti-Semitic laws at the annual party rally in Nuremberg. These Nuremberg laws defined who was considered a Jew—anyone with even one Jewish grandparent. They also stripped Jews of their German citizenship and civil rights, and forbade marriages between Jews and German citizens. Eventually, German Jews were also **required** to wear yellow Stars of David and to carry identification cards saying they were Jewish.

A more violent phase of anti-Jewish activity began on the night of November 9, 1938—*Kristallnacht,* or the "night of shattered glass." In a destructive rampage, Nazis burned synagogues and destroyed some 7,000 Jewish businesses. Thirty thousand Jewish males were arrested and sent to concentration camps. Jews were now barred from all public transportation and all public buildings, including schools and hospitals. They were **prohibited** from owning, managing, or working in any retail store. Finally, under the direction of the SS, Jews were encouraged to emigrate from Germany. The fortunate Jews were the ones who managed to escape from the country.

Culture and Leisure

A series of inventions in the late 1800s had led the way for a revolution in mass communications. Especially important was Marconi's discovery of wireless radio waves. By the end of the 1930s, there were 9 million radios in Great Britain. Full-length motion pictures appeared shortly before World War I. By 1939, about 40 percent of adults in the more developed countries were attending a movie once a week.

Of course, radio and the movies could be used for political purposes. Radio offered great opportunities for reaching the masses. The Nazi regime encouraged radio listening by urging manufacturers to produce inexpensive radios that could be bought on an installment plan.

Film, too, had propaganda potential, a fact not lost on Joseph Goebbels (GUHR • buhlz), the German propaganda minister. Believing that film was one of the "most modern and scientific means of influencing the masses," Goebbels created a special film division in his Propaganda Ministry. The film division supported the making of both feature films and documentaries—nonfiction films—that carried the Nazi message.

The Nazis also made use of the new mass leisure activities that had emerged by 1900. Mass leisure offered new ways for totalitarian states to control the people. The Nazi regime adopted a program called *Kraft durch Freude* ("Strength through Joy"). The program offered a variety of leisure activities to amuse the working class. These activities included concerts, operas, films, guided tours, and sporting events. Hitler used sporting events like the Olympic Games, which were held in Berlin in 1936, to show the world Germany's physical strength and prestige.

✔ **READING PROGRESS CHECK**

Predicting Consequences How do you think the Nazi control of media such as radio and film helped keep the regime in power?

PHOTO: ©CORBIS

Thinking Like a
HISTORIAN

Detecting Bias

In 1934 Adolf Hitler commissioned Leni Riefenstahl to film the 1934 Nazi party rally in Nuremberg. The resulting film, *Triumph of the Will*, is considered an important documentary—and a chilling piece of Nazi propaganda.

Ultimately, Riefenstahl was cleared of complicity in Nazi war crimes, but she was blacklisted as a director. Riefenstahl later said of the film, "It reflects the truth that was then, in 1934, history. It is therefore a documentary, not a propaganda film." As a record of an actual event that happened at a specific time, it is a documentary. However, Riefenstahl's powerful and positive images of Hitler as a kind of savior attempt to influence the audience's attitude toward the Nazis—which is the goal of propaganda.

◀ Director Leni Riefenstahl filming *Triumph of the Will* at the Luitpoldhain Arena in Nuremberg, 1934

LESSON 3 REVIEW (CCSS)

Reviewing Vocabulary

1. ***Identifying Central Issues*** What does the term *Aryan* mean and how did the Nazis misuse the term?

Using Your Notes

2. ***Categorizing Information*** Use your notes to identify the anti-Semitic policies enforced by the Nazi Party.

Answering the Guiding Questions

3. ***Analyzing Information*** What was the basis of Adolf Hitler's ideas?

4. ***Drawing Conclusions*** How did Hitler build a Nazi state?

Writing Activity

5. **INFORMATIVE/EXPLANATORY** Write a paragraph discussing how Hitler used the existing German political structure and the economic situation in Germany to rise to power.

Directions: On a separate sheet of paper, answer the questions below. Make sure you read carefully and answer all parts of the questions.

Lesson Review

Lesson 1

1 **EXPLAINING** What effects did the U.S. Senate's refusal to ratify the Treaty of Versailles have?

2 **MAKING CONNECTIONS** What outlook did the arts and physics share in the 1920s? What was a root cause for this outlook?

Lesson 2

3 **IDENTIFYING CENTRAL ISSUES** What were the main characteristics of the totalitarian states? How did they achieve their goals?

4 **SPECULATING** How do you think Americans would react today to propaganda that said, "Our leader is always right"? Why would people react that way?

Lesson 3

5 **SPECIFYING** What were the core beliefs on which Hitler's totalitarian state was based?

6 **HYPOTHESIZING** Hitler insisted that women should concentrate on keeping house and raising children, yet he chose a woman, Leni Riefenstahl, to direct the famous Nazi propaganda film *Triumph of the Will*. Why do you think Hitler chose to contradict his beliefs?

21st Century Skills

7 **CREATE AND ANALYZE ARGUMENTS** Examine the responses of European states to the challenges they faced after World War II. Pick one of the states and create an argument about why its method of dealing with the challenges was the most effective.

8 **TIME, CHRONOLOGY, AND SEQUENCING** In what order did Hitler's actions against Jews happen? What does this chronology show about the effects of escalating hate speech and behavior?

Exploring the Essential Questions

9 **GATHERING INFORMATION** Work with a small group to research first-person accounts of life in the 1920s and 1930s, with special attention to economic difficulties and the effects of political change on individuals and families. You may find accounts in books, online, or by interviewing people directly. Take turns reading accounts to your class.

DBQ Analyzing Historical Documents

Use the cartoon to answer the following questions.

This political cartoon by John Baer was published in 1932, shortly after Franklin Roosevelt first used the term *New Deal*.

PRIMARY SOURCE

10 **NAMING** Who are the card players demanding a new deal? Who is happy with the old deal?

11 **MAKING INFERENCES** What details in the cartoon provide insight into Baer's views on the distribution of wealth in the United States?

Extended-Response Question

12 **INFORMATIVE/EXPLANATORY** Use the actions of Mussolini, Stalin, and Hitler to identify five things to avoid in order to protect the United States from a dictator. Add a sentence or two of explanation to each list item.

Need Extra Help?

If You've Missed Question	1	2	3	4	5	6	7	8	9	10	11	12
Go to page	294	298	299	301	305	309	294	306	295	310	310	299

Nationalism Around the World

1919–1939

ESSENTIAL QUESTIONS · How can political control lead to nationalist movements?
· How does economic exploitation lead to nationalist movements?

The Story Matters...

World War I slowed the push toward independence among colonies in many parts of the world, but the end of the war gave a new strength to these efforts. Mohandas Gandhi was the charismatic leader of the Indian nationalist movement against British rule. He was committed to nonviolent action as a method for political and social change. Using peaceful methods, he eventually led India to independence. His actions inspired people to seek the end of colonialism, racism, and violence.

◄ This photograph shows Gandhi in his characteristic white garb woven of homespun cloth that he wore as a sign of solidarity with India's poor and as a rejection of foreign-made goods.

311

Place and Time: Africa and Asia 1919–1939

In the 1920s and 1930s, independence movements, already present before World War I, strengthened in many parts of the world. The collapse of the Ottoman Empire led to the creation of Turkey, Iraq, and Saudi Arabia. In Africa, a new generation educated abroad and African veterans of World War I often led protests to colonial governments, but independence would not be achieved until after World War II. Asian nationalists, including Mohandas Gandhi in British India and Ho Chi Minh in French Indochina, struggled against colonial rule. In China, an alliance against imperialists between Nationalists and Communists broke down, leading to civil war.

Step Into the Place

Read the quotes and look at the information presented on the map.

 Analyzing Historical Documents What did nationalist leaders hope to achieve? How did they differ in their approach to achieving their goals?

PRIMARY SOURCE

❝A revolution is not a dinner party, or writing an essay, or painting a picture, or doing embroidery; it cannot be so refined, so leisurely and gentle, so temperate, kind, courteous, restrained and magnanimous. A revolution is an insurrection, an act of violence by which one class overthrows another.❞

—Mao Zedong, from *Report on an Investigation of the Peasant Movement in Hunan*, 1927

PRIMARY SOURCE

❝Passive resistance is a method of securing rights by personal suffering; it is the reverse of resistance by arms. When I refuse to do a thing that is repugnant to my conscience, I use soul-force . . . If I do not obey the law and accept the penalty for its breach, I use soul-force. . . Everybody admits that sacrifice of self is infinitely superior to sacrifice of others.❞

—Mohandas Gandhi, from *Indian Home Rule*, 1909

Step Into the Time

Classifying Create a two-column chart. Analyze the time line and organize the events into either column "Decline of an Empire" or "Rise of Nationalism."

1919 British massacre of unarmed Indian protesters at Amritsar

1920–1922 Mohandas Gandhi's Non-Cooperation Movement

1921 Young Kikuyu Association protests British taxes in Africa

AFRICA AND ASIA

THE WORLD

1919

1924

1919 League of Nations formed at Paris Peace Conference

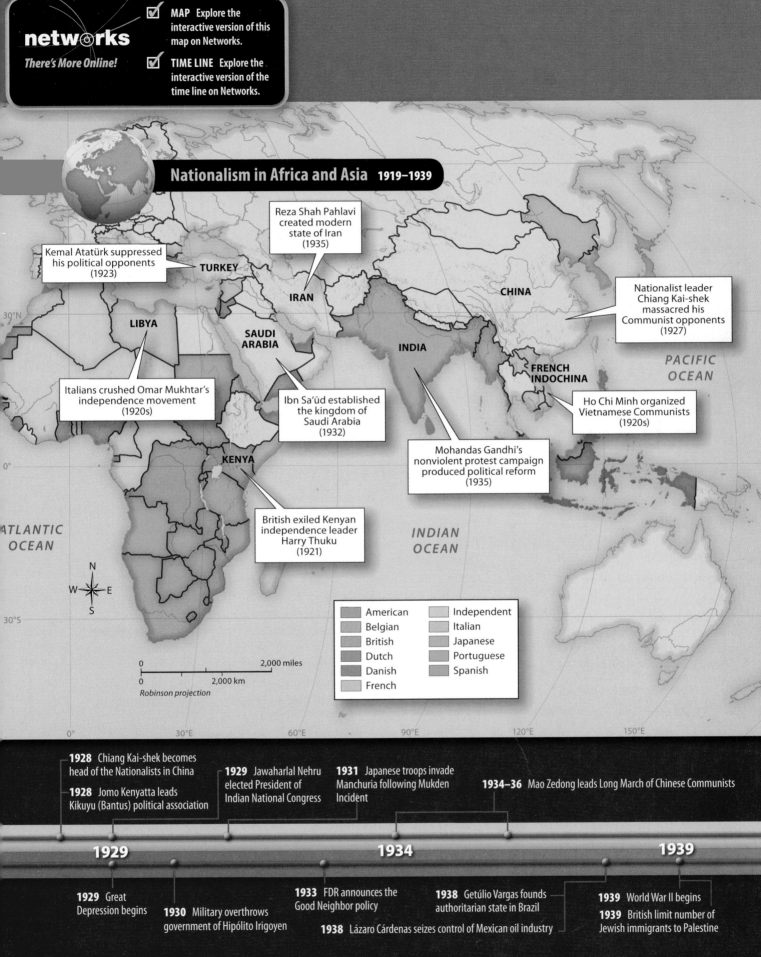

networks
There's More Online!

☑ **MAP** Explore the interactive version of this map on Networks.

☑ **TIME LINE** Explore the interactive version of the time line on Networks.

Nationalism in Africa and Asia 1919–1939

Kemal Atatürk suppressed his political opponents (1923)

Reza Shah Pahlavi created modern state of Iran (1935)

Nationalist leader Chiang Kai-shek massacred his Communist opponents (1927)

Italians crushed Omar Mukhtar's independence movement (1920s)

Ibn Sa'ūd established the kingdom of Saudi Arabia (1932)

Ho Chi Minh organized Vietnamese Communists (1920s)

Mohandas Gandhi's nonviolent protest campaign produced political reform (1935)

British exiled Kenyan independence leader Harry Thuku (1921)

TURKEY

IRAN

LIBYA

SAUDI ARABIA

CHINA

INDIA

FRENCH INDOCHINA

KENYA

PACIFIC OCEAN

ATLANTIC OCEAN

INDIAN OCEAN

30°N

0°

30°S

0°   30°E   60°E   90°E   120°E   150°E

N W E S

0   2,000 miles
0   2,000 km
Robinson projection

American	Independent
Belgian	Italian
British	Japanese
Dutch	Portuguese
Danish	Spanish
French	

1928 Chiang Kai-shek becomes head of the Nationalists in China

1928 Jomo Kenyatta leads Kikuyu (Bantus) political association

1929 Jawaharlal Nehru elected President of Indian National Congress

1931 Japanese troops invade Manchuria following Mukden Incident

1934–36 Mao Zedong leads Long March of Chinese Communists

1929

1929 Great Depression begins

1930 Military overthrows government of Hipólito Irigoyen

1934

1933 FDR announces the Good Neighbor policy

1938 Getúlio Vargas founds authoritarian state in Brazil

1938 Lázaro Cárdenas seizes control of Mexican oil industry

1939

1939 World War II begins

1939 British limit number of Jewish immigrants to Palestine

netw⊙rks

There's More Online!

☑ **CHART/GRAPH** Goals of the Young Turks

☑ **CHART/GRAPH** Oil Discovery in the Middle East

☑ **IMAGE** Atatürk

☑ **IMAGE** T. E. Lawrence

☑ **IMAGE** Young Turks

☑ **INTERACTIVE SELF-CHECK QUIZ**

☑ **MAP** Middle East, 1919–1935

☑ **VIDEO** Nationalism in the Middle East

Reading **HELP**DESK (CCSS)

Academic Vocabulary
- legislature
- element

Content Vocabulary
- genocide
- ethnic cleansing
- caliphate

TAKING NOTES:
Key Ideas and Details

Comparing and Contrasting As you read, make a graphic organizer like the one below comparing and contrasting the national policies of Atatürk and Reza Shah Pahlavi.

Atatürk   Both   Pahlavi

LESSON 1

Nationalism in the Middle East

ESSENTIAL QUESTIONS
- *How can political control lead to nationalist movements?*
- *How does economic exploitation lead to nationalist movements?*

IT MATTERS BECAUSE

The Ottoman Empire ended shortly after World War I. While the new Turkish Republic modernized, Persia evolved into the modern state of Iran and the kingdom of Saudi Arabia was established. In Palestine, tensions mounted as both Arabs and Jews viewed the area as their homeland.

Decline of the Ottoman Empire

GUIDING QUESTION *What led to the final decline and fall of the Ottoman Empire?*

The Ottoman Empire—which once included parts of eastern Europe, the Middle East, and North Africa—had been growing steadily weaker. The empire's size had decreased dramatically during the nineteenth century when it lost much of its European territory. Ottoman rule also ended in North Africa.

In 1876 Ottoman reformers seized control of the empire's government and adopted a constitution that set up a **legislature**. However, the sultan they placed on the throne, Abdülhamīd II, suspended the new constitution. Abdülhamīd paid a high price for his authoritarian actions—he lived in constant fear of assassination. He kept 1,000 loaded revolvers hidden throughout his guarded estate.

The suspended constitution became a symbol of change to a group of reformers named the Young Turks. This group forced the restoration of the constitution in 1908 and deposed the sultan the following year. However, the Young Turks lacked strong support for their government.

Impact of World War I

The final blow to the old empire came from World War I. After the Ottoman government allied with Germany, the British sought to undermine Ottoman rule in the Arabian Peninsula by supporting Arab nationalist activities there. The nationalists were aided by the dashing British adventurer T.E. Lawrence, popularly known as Lawrence of Arabia.

In 1916 Arabia declared its independence from Ottoman rule. British troops advanced from Egypt and seized Palestine. After suffering more than 300,000 deaths during the war, the Ottoman Empire made peace with the Allies in October 1918.

The Armenian Genocide

During the war the Ottoman Turks alienated the Allies with their policies toward minority subjects, especially the Armenians. The Christian Armenian minority had been pressing the Ottoman government for its independence for years. In 1915 the Ottoman government accused the Armenians of supporting the Russians and used those allegations to kill or exile all Armenians.

Within seven months, 600,000 Armenians were killed, and 500,000 were deported. Of those, 400,000 died while marching through the deserts and swamps of Syria and Mesopotamia. By September 1915, an estimated 1 million Armenians were dead. They were victims of **genocide**, the deliberate mass murder of a particular racial, political, or cultural group. (A similar practice would be called **ethnic cleansing** in the Bosnian War of 1993–1996.) One eyewitness to the 1915 Armenian deportation said:

> **PRIMARY SOURCE**
>
> ❝[She] saw vultures hovering over children who had fallen dead by the roadside. She saw beings crawling along, maimed, starving and begging for bread. . . . [S]he passed soldiers driving before them . . . whole families, men, women and children, shrieking, pleading, wailing . . . setting out for exile into the desert from which there was no return.❞
>
> —from *The Nili Spies*, by Anita Engle

By 1918, another 400,000 Armenians were massacred. Russia, France, and Britain denounced the Turkish actions as being "crimes against humanity and civilization." Because of the war, however, the killings continued.

☑ **READING PROGRESS CHECK**

Summarizing In what ways did the war effort affect the Ottoman government?

Middle East Changes

GUIDING QUESTION *How did the Middle East change after the fall of the Ottoman Empire?*

While Turkey, Iran, and Saudi Arabia emerged as modern states, tensions mounted between the Jewish and Muslim inhabitants in Palestine.

The Modernization of Turkey

At the end of World War I, the tottering Ottoman Empire collapsed. Great Britain and France made plans to divide Ottoman territories in the Middle East. Only the area of present-day Turkey remained under Ottoman control. Then, Greece invaded Turkey and seized the western parts of the Anatolian Peninsula.

The invasion alarmed key **elements** in Turkey, who were organized under the leadership of the war hero Colonel Mustafa Kemal. Kemal summoned a national congress calling for the creation of an elected government and a new Republic of Turkey. His forces drove the Greeks from the Anatolian Peninsula. In 1923 the last of the Ottoman sultans fled the country, which was then declared to be the Turkish Republic. The Ottoman Empire had finally come to an end.

legislature an organized body that makes laws

genocide the deliberate mass murder or physical extinction of a particular racial, political, or cultural group

ethnic cleansing a policy of killing or forcibly removing an ethnic group from its lands; used by the Serbs against the Muslim minority in Bosnia

element a distinct group within a larger group

President Kemal was now popularly known as Atatürk (AT • uh • TUHRK), or "father Turk." Over the next several years, he tried to transform Turkey into a modern state. A democratic system was put in place, but Atatürk did not tolerate opposition and harshly suppressed his critics.

Atatürk's changes went beyond politics. Many Arabic elements were eliminated from the Turkish language, which was now written in the Roman alphabet. Popular education was introduced, and all Turkish citizens were forced to adopt family (last) names, in the European style.

Atatürk also took steps to modernize Turkey's economy. Factories were established, and a five-year plan provided for state direction over the economy. Atatürk also tried to modernize farming, although he had little effect on the nation's peasants.

Perhaps the most significant aspect of Atatürk's reform program was his attempt to break the power of the Islamic religion. He wanted to transform Turkey into a secular state—a state that rejects religious influence on its policies. Atatürk said, "Religion is like a heavy blanket that keeps the people of Turkey asleep."

The **caliphate** was formally abolished in 1924. Men were forbidden to wear the fez, the brimless cap worn by Turkish Muslims. When Atatürk began wearing a Western panama hat, one of his critics remarked, "You cannot make a Turk into a Westerner by giving him a hat."

Women were strongly discouraged from wearing the veil, a traditional Islamic custom. New laws gave women marriage and inheritance rights equal to men's. In 1934 women received the right to vote. All citizens were also given the right to convert to other religions.

The legacy of Kemal Atatürk was enormous. In practice, not all of his reforms were widely accepted, especially by devout Muslims. However, most of the changes that he introduced were kept after his death in 1938. By and large, the Turkish Republic was the product of Atatürk's determined efforts.

The Beginnings of Modern Iran

A similar process of modernization was underway in Persia. Under the Qājār dynasty (1794–1925), the country had not been very successful in resolving its domestic problems. Increasingly, the dynasty turned to Russia and Great Britain to protect itself from its own people, which led to a growing foreign presence in Persia. The discovery of oil in the southern part of the country in 1908 attracted more foreign interest. Oil exports increased, and most of the profits went to British investors.

The growing foreign presence led to the rise of a native Persian nationalist movement. In 1921 Reza Khan, an officer in the Persian army, led a military mutiny that seized control of Tehran, the capital city. In 1925 Reza Khan established himself as shah, or king, and was called Reza Shah Pahlavi. The name of the new dynasty he created, Pahlavi, was the name of the ancient Persian language.

During the next few years, Reza Shah Pahlavi tried to follow the example of Kemal Atatürk in Turkey. He introduced a number of reforms to strengthen and modernize the government, the military, and the economic system. Persia became the modern state of Iran in 1935.

caliphate the office of the caliph

▲ The Young Turks rode through the streets of Turkey waving flags in 1908.

▶ **CRITICAL THINKING**
Analyzing Visuals What about this photograph suggests it is from before Atatürk's rule?

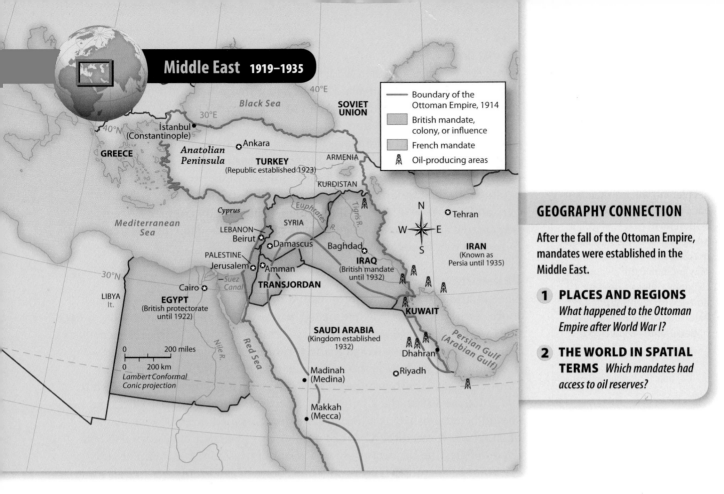

Middle East 1919–1935

- —— Boundary of the Ottoman Empire, 1914
- British mandate, colony, or influence
- French mandate
- ⚒ Oil-producing areas

Black Sea

SOVIET UNION

İstanbul (Constantinople)

Ankara

GREECE

Anatolian Peninsula

TURKEY (Republic established 1923)

ARMENIA

KURDISTAN

Cyprus

Euphrates R.

Tigris R.

Tehran

Mediterranean Sea

SYRIA

LEBANON
Beirut

Damascus

Baghdad

IRAN (Known as Persia until 1935)

PALESTINE
Jerusalem

Amman

IRAQ (British mandate until 1932)

TRANSJORDAN

LIBYA It.

Cairo

Suez Canal

EGYPT (British protectorate until 1922)

KUWAIT

SAUDI ARABIA (Kingdom established 1932)

Persian Gulf (Arabian Gulf)

Dhahran

Nile R.

Red Sea

0   200 miles
0   200 km
Lambert Conformal Conic projection

Madinah (Medina)

Riyadh

Makkah (Mecca)

N W E S

GEOGRAPHY CONNECTION

After the fall of the Ottoman Empire, mandates were established in the Middle East.

1 PLACES AND REGIONS *What happened to the Ottoman Empire after World War I?*

2 THE WORLD IN SPATIAL TERMS *Which mandates had access to oil reserves?*

Unlike Atatürk, Reza Shah Pahlavi did not try to destroy the power of Islamic beliefs. However, he did encourage the creation of a Western-style educational system and forbade women to wear the veil in public.

Foreign powers continued to harass Iran. To free himself from Great Britain and the Soviet Union, Reza Shah Pahlavi drew closer to Nazi Germany. During World War II, the shah rejected the demands of Great Britain and the Soviet Union to expel a large number of Germans from Iran. In response, Great Britain and the Soviet Union sent troops into the country. Reza Shah Pahlavi resigned and was replaced by his son, Mohammad Reza Pahlavi.

Arab Nationalism

World War I offered the Arabs an excellent opportunity to escape from Ottoman rule. However, what would replace that rule? The Arabs were not a nation, though they were united by their language and their Islamic cultural and religious heritage. However, efforts by generations of political leaders to create a single Arab nation have not succeeded.

Because Britain supported the efforts of Arab nationalists in 1916, the nationalists hoped this support would continue after the war. Instead, Britain agreed with France to create mandates in the area. These were former Ottoman territories that the new League of Nations now supervised. The League, in turn, granted its members the right to govern particular mandates. Iraq and Palestine (including Transjordan) were assigned to Great Britain; Syria and Lebanon were assigned to France.

For the most part, Europeans created these Middle Eastern states. The Europeans determined the nations' borders and divided the peoples. In general, the people in these states had no strong identification with their designated country. However, a sense of Arab nationalism remained.

Connections to
TODAY

World Oil Reserves

Saudi Arabia has the largest oil reserves in the world, possessing one-fifth of Earth's known supplies. The Saudi reserves are estimated to be more than 260 billion barrels. Saudi Arabia is also the location of the world's largest oil field, Al-Ghawār, which was discovered in 1948 and still holds 70 billion barrels after 60 years of production. Following Saudi Arabia in estimated oil reserves are Canada, Iran, Iraq, and Kuwait. The United States, with estimated reserves of 19 billion barrels, ranks only 14th, just behind China.

66His Majesty's Government view with favour the establishment in Palestine of a national home for the Jewish people, and will use their best endeavors to facilitate the achievement of this object, it being clearly understood that nothing shall be done which may prejudice the civil and religious rights of existing non-Jewish communities in Palestine, or the rights and political status enjoyed by Jews in any other country.99

—from the Balfour Declaration

 DRAWING CONCLUSIONS
How does the Balfour Declaration simultaneously acknowledge the Zionist desire for a Jewish state and the challenges in the region?

Saudi Arabia

In the early 1920s, a reform leader, Ibn Sa'ūd, united Arabs in the northern part of the Arabian Peninsula. Devout and gifted, Ibn Sa'ūd won broad support. He established the kingdom of Saudi Arabia in 1932.

At first, the new kingdom, which consisted mostly of the vast central desert of the Arabian Peninsula, was desperately poor. Its main source of income came from the Muslim pilgrims who visited Makkah (Mecca) and Madinah (Medina). During the 1930s, however, U.S. prospectors began to explore for oil. Standard Oil made a successful strike at Dhahran, on the Persian Gulf, in 1938. Soon, the Arabian-American oil company Aramco was created. The isolated kingdom was suddenly flooded with Western oil industries that brought the promise of wealth.

Palestine and the Balfour Declaration

The situation in Palestine complicated matters in the Middle East even more. Although Palestine had been the home of the Jews in antiquity, most Jews were forced into exile in the first century A.D. A Jewish presence always remained, but Muslim Arabs made up about 80 percent of the region's population. In Palestine, the nationalism of Jews and Arabs came into conflict because both groups viewed the area as a potential national state.

Since the 1890s, the Zionist movement had advocated that Palestine should be established as a Jewish state. Jews recalled that the ancient state of Israel was located there. Arabs pointed out that their ancestors also had lived in Palestine for centuries. As a result of the Zionist movement and growing anti-Semitism in Europe, more Jews began to migrate to Palestine. Then during World War I, the British government, hoping to win Jewish support for the Allies, issued the Balfour Declaration. It expressed support for a national home for the Jews in Palestine, but it also added that this goal should not undermine the rights of the non-Jewish peoples living there.

The Balfour Declaration drew even more Jews to Palestine. In 1933 the Nazi regime in Germany began policies that later led to the Holocaust and the murder of 6 million Jews. During the 1930s, many Jews fled to Palestine. Violence flared between Jewish and Muslim inhabitants.

Trying to end the violence, the British declared in 1939 that only 75,000 Jewish people would be allowed to immigrate to Palestine over the next five years; after that, no more Jews could do so. This decision, however, only intensified the tension and increased the bloodshed.

 **READING PROGRESS CHECK**

Contrasting Contrast the emergence of modern Turkey and Iran.

LESSON 1 REVIEW **CCSS**

Reviewing Vocabulary
1. *Analyzing* What role does the legislature or parliament fulfill in a constitutional monarchy?

Using Your Notes
2. *Making Connections* Why did the occupation of Kemal Atatürk and Reza Shah Pahlavi give them a shared outlook?

Answering the Guiding Questions
3. *Determining Cause and Effect* What led to the final decline and fall of the Ottoman Empire?

4. *Drawing Conclusions* How did the Middle East change after the fall of the Ottoman Empire?

Writing Activity
5. **INFORMATIVE/EXPLANATORY** Write a short paragraph that compares the original context of the Balfour Declaration with its role in subsequent decades.

netw⚙rks

There's More Online!

☑ **BIOGRAPHY** Jawaharlal Nehru

☑ **BIOGRAPHY** Mohandas Gandhi

☑ **IMAGE** Japanese Silk Factory

☑ **IMAGE** Women Protesting in Bombay

☑ **INTERACTIVE SELF-CHECK QUIZ**

☑ **MAP** Imperialism in Africa, 1914

☑ **PRIMARY SOURCE** Garveyism in Africa

☑ **PRIMARY SOURCE** Government of India Act of 1935

☑ **VIDEO** Nationalism in Africa and Asia

Reading **HELP**DESK 🄲🄲🅂🅂

Academic Vocabulary
- **volunteer**
- **compensation**

Content Vocabulary
- **Pan-Africanism**
- **civil disobedience**
- *zaibatsu*

TAKING NOTES:
Key Ideas and Details

Contrasting Use a table like the one below to contrast the backgrounds and values of Gandhi and Nehru.

Mohandas Gandhi	Jawaharlal Nehru

LESSON 2
Nationalism in Africa and Asia

ESSENTIAL QUESTIONS
- *How can political control lead to nationalist movements?*
- *How does economic exploitation lead to nationalist movements?*

IT MATTERS BECAUSE
Nationalism spread throughout Africa and Asia in the early twentieth century. In Africa, calls for independence came from a new generation of Western-educated African leaders. As communism spread in Asia, Mohandas Gandhi and Jawaharlal Nehru worked for the independence of India. Militarists gained control of the Japanese government.

African Independence Movements

GUIDING QUESTION *What motivated African independence movements after World War I?*

Black Africans fought in World War I in British and French armies. Many Africans hoped that independence after the war would be their reward. As one newspaper in the Gold Coast argued, if African **volunteers** who fought on European battlefields were "good enough to fight and die in the Empire's cause, they were good enough to have a share in the government of their countries." Most European leaders were not ready to give up their colonies.

The peace settlement after World War I was a huge disappointment. Germany was stripped of its African colonies, but these colonies were awarded to Great Britain and France to be administered as mandates for the League of Nations. Britain and France now governed a vast portion of Africa.

African Protests
After World War I, Africans became more active politically. The foreign powers that conquered and exploited Africa also introduced Western education. In educating Africans, the colonial system gave them visions of a world based on the ideals of liberty and equality. In Africa, the missionary schools taught these ideals to their pupils. The African students who studied abroad, especially in Britain and the United States, and the African soldiers who served in World War I learned new ideas about freedom and nationalism in the West. As more Africans became aware of the enormous gulf between Western ideals and practices, they decided to seek reform.

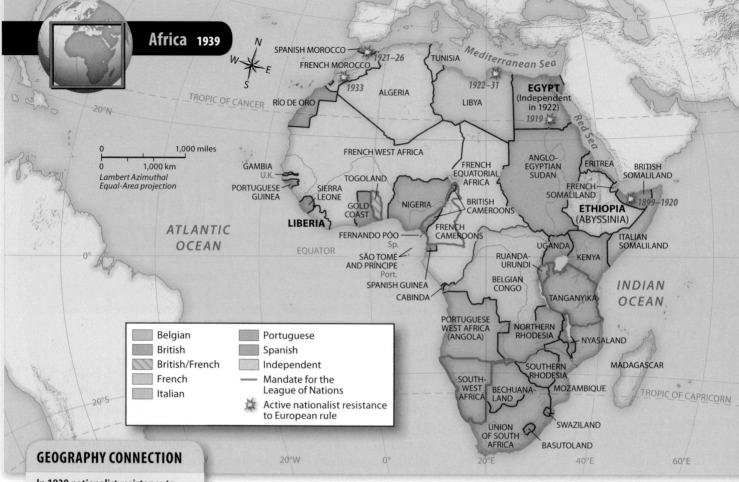

Africa 1939

SPANISH MOROCCO 1921–26
FRENCH MOROCCO
1933
RÍO DE ORO
TUNISIA
Mediterranean Sea
ALGERIA
LIBYA
1922–31
EGYPT (Independent in 1922)
1919
Red Sea

TROPIC OF CANCER
20°N

0   1,000 miles
0   1,000 km
Lambert Azimuthal Equal-Area projection

GAMBIA U.K.
PORTUGUESE GUINEA
SIERRA LEONE
GOLD COAST
FRENCH WEST AFRICA
TOGOLAND
NIGERIA
BRITISH CAMEROONS
FRENCH EQUATORIAL AFRICA
ANGLO-EGYPTIAN SUDAN
ERITREA
FRENCH SOMALILAND
BRITISH SOMALILAND
ETHIOPIA (ABYSSINIA)
1899–1920
ITALIAN SOMALILAND

LIBERIA
FERNANDO PÓO Sp.
FRENCH CAMEROONS
SÃO TOMÉ AND PRÍNCIPE Port.
SPANISH GUINEA
CABINDA
UGANDA
RUANDA-URUNDI
BELGIAN CONGO
KENYA
TANGANYIKA

ATLANTIC OCEAN
EQUATOR
0°

INDIAN OCEAN

PORTUGUESE WEST AFRICA (ANGOLA)
NORTHERN RHODESIA
NYASALAND
MADAGASCAR

Belgian
British
British/French
French
Italian
Portuguese
Spanish
Independent
Mandate for the League of Nations
Active nationalist resistance to European rule

SOUTH-WEST AFRICA
BECHUANA-LAND
SOUTHERN RHODESIA
MOZAMBIQUE
TROPIC OF CAPRICORN

20°S
UNION OF SOUTH AFRICA
BASUTOLAND
SWAZILAND

20°W   0°   20°E   40°E   60°E

GEOGRAPHY CONNECTION

In 1939 nationalist resistance to European rule spread across Africa.

1 PLACES AND REGIONS
Which countries had active nationalist resistance movements by 1939?

2 HUMAN SYSTEMS *Where did the first nationalist resistance movement shown on this map occur?*

volunteer one who enters the military voluntarily

compensation payment

Reform movements took different forms. One of the most important issues in Kenya concerned land redistribution. Large tracts of land were given to white settlers. Black Africans received little if any **compensation** for this land and became squatters on the land they believed was their own.

During the 1920s, moderate protest organizations, mostly founded by the Kikuyu, emerged in Kenya. The Kikuyu Association, founded in 1920 by farmers, was intent on blocking further land confiscation. This association was willing to work for reform within the existing colonial structure.

Some of the Kenyan protesters were more radical, however. The Young Kikuyu Association, organized by Harry Thuku in 1921, challenged European authority. Thuku, a telephone operator, protested against the high taxes levied by the British rulers. His message was simple:

PRIMARY SOURCE

❝Hearken, every day you pay ... tax to the Europeans of Government. Where is it sent? It is their task to steal the property of the Kikuyu people.❞

—quoted in *Africa: History of a Continent*

Thuku was arrested. When an angry crowd stormed the jail and demanded his release, government authorities fired into the crowd and killed at least 20 people. Thuku was sent into exile.

Libya also struggled against foreign rule in the 1920s. Forces led by Omar Mukhtar used guerrilla warfare against the Italians and defeated them a number of times. The Italians reacted ferociously. They established concentration camps and used all available modern weapons to crush the revolt. Mukhtar's death ended the movement.

Although colonial powers typically responded to such movements with force, they also began to make some reforms. They made these reforms in an effort to satisfy African peoples. Reforms, however, were too few and too late. By the 1930s, an increasing number of African leaders were calling for independence, not reform.

New Leaders

Calls for independence came from a new generation of young African leaders. Many had been educated abroad, in Europe and the United States. Those who studied in the United States were especially influenced by the ideas of W.E.B. Du Bois and Marcus Garvey.

Du Bois, an African American who was educated at Harvard University, was the leader of a movement that tried to make all Africans aware of their own cultural heritage. Garvey, a Jamaican who lived in Harlem in New York City, stressed the need for the unity of all Africans, a movement known as **Pan-Africanism**. His *Declaration of the Rights of the Negro Peoples of the World*, issued in 1920, had a strong impact on later African leaders.

Leaders and movements in individual African nations also appeared. Educated in Great Britain, Jomo Kenyatta of Kenya argued in his book *Facing Mount Kenya* that British rule was destroying the traditional culture of the peoples of Africa.

Léopold Senghor, who studied in France and wrote poetry about African culture, organized an independence movement in Senegal. Nnamdi Azikiwe of Nigeria began a newspaper, *The West African Pilot*, in 1937 and urged nonviolence as a method of gaining independence. These are just a few of the leaders who worked to end colonial rule in Africa. Success, however, would not come until after World War II.

☑ **READING PROGRESS CHECK**

Listing Name four African leaders and discuss their motivations for African independence.

Revolution in Southeast Asia

GUIDING QUESTION *Why was communism more accepted in Asia after World War I?*

Before World War I, the Marxist doctrine of social revolution had no appeal for Asian intellectuals. After all, most Asian societies were still agricultural and hardly ready for revolution. That situation changed after the revolution in Russia in 1917. Lenin and the Bolsheviks showed that a revolutionary Marxist party could overturn an outdated system—even one that was not fully industrialized—and begin a new one.

In 1920 Lenin adopted a new revolutionary strategy aimed at societies outside the Western world. He spread the word of Karl Marx through the Communist International, or Comintern, a worldwide organization of Communist parties formed in 1919 to advance world revolution. Agents were trained in Moscow and then returned to their countries to form Marxist parties. By the end of the 1920s, almost every colonial society in Asia had a Communist party.

How successful were these new parties? In some countries, the local Communists established a cooperative relationship with nationalist parties to struggle against Western imperialism. This was true in French Indochina. Moscow-trained Ho Chi Minh organized the Vietnamese Communists in

Pan-Africanism
the unity of all black Africans, regardless of national boundaries

the 1920s. The strongest Communist-nationalist alliance was formed in China. In most colonial societies, though, Communist parties of the 1930s failed to gain support among the majority of the population.

✓ READING PROGRESS CHECK

Summarizing How did communism spread to Asia after World War I?

Indian Independence

GUIDING QUESTION *Who and what shaped India's independence movement?*

Mohandas Gandhi was active in the Indian National Congress and the movement for Indian self-rule before World War I. The Indian people began to refer to him as India's "Great Soul," or Mahatma. After the war, Gandhi remained an important figure, and new leaders also arose.

Protest and Reform

Gandhi left South Africa in 1914. When he returned to India, he organized mass protests against British laws. A believer in nonviolence, Gandhi used the methods of **civil disobedience** to push for Indian independence.

In 1919 British troops killed hundreds of unarmed protesters in Amritsar, in northwestern India. Horrified at the violence, Gandhi briefly retreated from active politics but was later arrested and imprisoned for his role in protests.

In 1935 Britain passed the Government of India Act, which expanded the role of Indians in governing. Before, the Legislative Council could give advice only to the British governor. Now, it became a two-house parliament, and two-thirds of its Indian members were to be elected. Five million Indians (still a small percentage of the total population) were given the right to vote.

A Push for Independence

The Indian National Congress (INC), founded in 1885, sought reforms in Britain's government of India. Reforms, however, were no longer enough. Under its new leader, Motilal Nehru, the INC wanted to push for full independence from Britain.

Gandhi, now released from prison, returned to his earlier policy of civil disobedience. He worked hard to inform ordinary Indians of his beliefs and methods. It was wrong, he said, to harm any living being. He believed that hate could be overcome only by love, and love, rather than force, could win people over to one's position.

Nonviolence was central to Gandhi's campaign of noncooperation and civil disobedience. To protest unjust British laws, Gandhi told his people: "Don't pay your taxes or send your children to an English-supported school …. Make your own cotton cloth by spinning the thread at home, and don't buy English-made goods. Provide yourselves with home-made salt, and do not buy government-made salt."

Britain had increased the salt tax and prohibited Indians from manufacturing or harvesting their own salt. In 1930 Gandhi led a protest. He walked to the sea with his supporters in what was called the Salt March. On reaching the coast, Gandhi picked up a pinch of salt. Thousands of Indians followed his act of civil disobedience. Gandhi and many other members of the INC were arrested.

civil disobedience
refusal to obey laws that are considered to be unjust

New Leaders and Problems

In the 1930s, Jawaharlal Nehru entered the movement. The son of Motilal Nehru, Jawaharlal studied law in Great Britain. He was a new kind of Indian politician—upper class and intellectual.

The independence movement in India split into two paths. The one identified with Gandhi was religious, anti-Western, and traditional. The other, identified with Nehru, was secular, pro-Western, and modern. The two approaches created uncertainty about India's future path.

In the meantime, another problem arose in the independence movement. Hostility between Hindus and Muslims had existed for centuries. Muslims were dissatisfied with the Hindu dominance of the INC and raised the cry "Islam is in danger."

By the 1930s, the Muslim League was under the leadership of Mohammed Ali Jinnah. The league believed in the creation of a separate Muslim state of Pakistan ("the land of the pure") in the northwest.

✔ **READING PROGRESS CHECK**

Identifying What was Gandhi's role in the Indian independence movement?

A Militarist Japan

GUIDING QUESTION *What triggered the rise of militarism in Japan?*

Japanese society developed along a Western model. Meiji Era reforms led to increasing prosperity and a modern industrial and commercial sector.

A *Zaibatsu* Economy

In the Japanese economy, various manufacturing processes were concentrated within a single enterprise called the **zaibatsu**, a large financial and industrial corporation. These vast companies controlled major segments of the Japanese industrial sector. By 1937, the four largest *zaibatsu* (Mitsui, Mitsubishi, Sumitomo, and Yasuda) controlled 21 percent of the banking, 26 percent of the mining, 35 percent of the shipbuilding, and more than 60 percent of the paper manufacturing and insurance industries.

The concentration of wealth led to growing economic inequalities. City workers were poorly paid and housed. Economic crises added to this problem. After World War I, inflation in food prices led to food riots. A rapid increase in population led to food shortages. (The population of the Japanese islands increased from 43 million in 1900 to 73 million in 1940.) Later, when the Great Depression struck, workers and farmers suffered the most.

With hardships came calls for a return to traditional Japanese values. Traditionalists especially objected to the growing influence of Western ideas and values on Japanese educational and political systems. At the same time, many citizens denounced Japan's attempt to find security through cooperation with the Western powers. Instead, they demanded that Japan use its strength to dominate Asia.

zaibatsu in the Japanese economy, a large financial and industrial corporation

▼ Japanese women at a silk factory in 1913 check the unreeling of raw silk.

▶ **CRITICAL THINKING**
Contrasting Contrast the Japanese economy before and after World War I.

Japan and the West

In the early twentieth century, Japan had difficulty finding sources of raw materials and foreign markets for its manufactured goods. Until World War I, Japan fulfilled these needs by seizing territories, such as Taiwan (Formosa), Korea, and southern Manchuria. This policy succeeded but aroused the concern of the Western nations, especially the United States.

In 1922 the United States held a conference of nations with interests in the Pacific. This conference created a nine-power treaty that recognized the territorial integrity of China and the maintenance of the Open Door policy. Japan agreed, in return for recognition of its control of southern Manchuria. However, this agreement did not prove popular. Heavy industry, mining, and manufacture of appliances and automobiles require resources that are not found in abundance in Japan. The Japanese government came under pressure to find new sources for raw materials abroad.

The Rise of Militarism

During the early 1900s, Japan had moved toward a more democratic government. The parliament and political parties grew stronger. The influence of the old ruling oligarchy, however, remained strong.

At the end of the 1920s, a militant group within the ruling party gained control of the political system. Some militants were civilians who were convinced that Western ideas had corrupted the parliamentary system. Others were military members who were angered by the cuts in military spending and the government's pacifist policies of the early 1920s.

During the early 1930s, civilians formed extremist patriotic organizations such as the Black Dragon Society. Members of the army and navy created similar societies. One group of middle-level army officers invaded Manchuria without government approval in 1931. Within a short time, all of Manchuria had been conquered. The Japanese government opposed the conquest, but the Japanese people supported it. Unable to act, the government was soon dominated by the military.

Japanese society was put on wartime status. A military draft law was passed in 1938. Economic resources were placed under strict government control. All political parties were merged into the Imperial Rule Assistance Association, which called for Japanese expansion abroad. Labor unions were disbanded, and education and culture were purged of most Western ideas.

✓ **READING PROGRESS CHECK**

Making Connections Explain the relationship between the *zaibatsu* and militarism.

LESSON 2 REVIEW

Reviewing Vocabulary

1. *Naming* Name the different forms that civil disobedience took under Gandhi's leadership.

Using Your Notes

2. *Differentiating* Use your notes to write a paragraph explaining how Gandhi and Jawaharlal Nehru waged the same yet different battles for their nation.

Answering the Guiding Questions

3. *Exploring Issues* What motivated African independence movements after World War I?

4. *Identifying Causes and Effects* Why was communism more accepted in Asia after World War I?

5. *Gathering Information* Who and what shaped India's independence movement?

6. *Analyzing* What triggered the rise of militarism in Japan?

Writing Activity

7. NARRATIVE Imagine you were a participant in the Salt March in India. Write several paragraphs expressing the feelings you had as you and others reached the sea and picked up salt.

networks

There's More Online!

- ☑ **BIOGRAPHY** Mao Zedong
- ☑ **CHART/GRAPH** The Urban/Rural Divide in 1930s China
- ☑ **IMAGE** Chinese Refugees from the Northern Expedition
- ☑ **IMAGE** Rural Life in China
- ☑ **INTERACTIVE SELF-CHECK QUIZ**
- ☑ **MAP** China, 1926–1937
- ☑ **PRIMARY SOURCE** China's Destiny
- ☑ **VIDEO** Revolutionary Chaos in China

Reading HELPDESK CCSS

Academic Vocabulary

- ceased
- eventually

Content Vocabulary

- guerrilla tactics
- redistribution of wealth

TAKING NOTES:

Key Ideas and Details

Summarizing As you read, make a cluster diagram like the one below showing the Confucian values that Chiang Kai-shek used to bring modern Western ideas into a culturally conservative population.

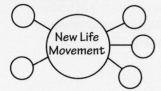

New Life Movement

PHOTO: (l to r)Keystone-France/Gamma-Keystone/Getty Images;Gamma-Keystone/Getty Images; ©Dean Fox/SuperStock; ©CORBIS.

LESSON 3
Revolutionary Chaos in China

ESSENTIAL QUESTIONS

- *How can political control lead to nationalist movements?*
- *How does economic exploitation lead to nationalist movements?*

IT MATTERS BECAUSE

In 1923 the Nationalist and Communist parties formed an alliance to drive the imperialists out of China. Tensions between the two parties grew, however. Sun Yat-sen's successor, Chiang Kai-shek, struck against the Communists. Many Communists went into hiding or fled to the mountainous north, where Mao Zedong set up a Communist base.

Nationalists and Communists

GUIDING QUESTION *What was the relationship between the Nationalists and the Communists?*

Revolutionary Marxism had its greatest impact in China. By 1920 central authority had almost **ceased** to exist in China. Two different political forces began to emerge as competitors for the right to rule China: Sun Yat-sen's Nationalist Party, which had been driven from the political arena several years earlier, and the Chinese Communist Party.

The Nationalist-Communist Alliance

In 1921 a group of young radicals, including several faculty and staff members from Beijing University, founded the Chinese Communist Party (CCP) in the commercial and industrial city of Shanghai. Comintern agents soon advised the new party to join with the more experienced Nationalist Party.

Sun Yat-sen, leader of the Nationalists, welcomed the cooperation. He needed the expertise and the diplomatic support that the Soviet Union could provide. His anti-imperialist words alienated many Western powers. One English-language newspaper in Shanghai wrote: "All his life, all his influence, all his energies are devoted to ideas that keep China in turmoil, and it is utterly undesirable and improper that he should be allowed to prosecute those aims here." In 1923 the Nationalists and Communists formed an alliance to oppose the warlords and drive the imperialist powers out of China.

Nationalism Around the World **325**

China 1926–1937

MONGOLIA

MANCHUKUO (MANCHURIA)

GOBI

Peking

Sea of Japan (East Sea)

KOREA

JAPAN 140°E

Mu Us Desert

Yan'an

Huang He (Yellow)

Wei He

Xi'an

QINLING SHANDI

CHINA

HENGDUAN SHAN

DAXUE SHAN

(Yangtze R.)

Wuhan

Chang Jiang

JIANGXI

Nanjing

Shanghai

Yellow Sea

East China Sea

PACIFIC OCEAN

TROPIC OF CANCER

Guangzhou

TAIWAN (FORMOSA)

Hainan

South China Sea

120°E

0   400 miles
0   400 km
Two-Point Equidistant projection

Northern Expedition against imperialist powers (1926–1928)
Communist base
Long March led by Communist Mao Zedong (1934–1935)
Communist base, 1935
Area controlled by Chiang Kai-shek's Nationalist government, 1937
Area occupied by Japan, 1937

GEOGRAPHY CONNECTION

After World War I, China was torn among Nationalists, Communists, and Japan.

1 **PLACES AND REGIONS** *Why would the occupation of Nanjing be significant for the Nationalists?*

2 **THE USES OF GEOGRAPHY** *What geographic features likely helped the Communists defend their 1935 base?*

cease to come to an end

eventually in the end

For more than three years, the two parties overlooked their mutual suspicions and worked together. They formed a revolutionary army to march north and seize control over China. The so-called Northern Expedition began in the summer of 1926. By the following spring, revolutionary forces had taken control of all of China south of the Chang Jiang (Yangtze River), including the major river ports of Wuhan and Shanghai.

Tensions between the parties **eventually** rose to the surface. Sun Yat-sen died in 1925, and General Chiang Kai-shek (JYAHNG KY • SHEHK), his military subordinate, succeeded him as head of the Nationalist Party. Chiang pretended to support the alliance with the Communists but actually planned to destroy them. In April 1927, he struck against the Communists in Shanghai, killing thousands. After the Shanghai Massacre, the Nationalist-Communist alliance ceased to exist.

In 1928 Chiang Kai-shek founded a new Chinese republic at Nanjing. During the next three years, he worked to reunify China. Although Chiang saw Japan as a serious threat, he believed that the Communists were more dangerous. He once remarked that "the Japanese are like a disease of the skin, but the Communists are like a disease of the heart."

The Communists in Hiding

After the Shanghai Massacre of April 1927, most of the Communist leaders went into hiding in the city. There, they tried to revive the Communist movement in its traditional urban base among the working class. Shanghai was a rich recruiting ground for the party. People were discontented and looking for leadership.

Some party members, however, fled to the mountainous Jiangxi (JYAHNG • SHEE) Province south of the Chang Jiang. They were led by the young Communist organizer Mao Zedong (MOW DZUH • DUNG). Unlike most other leading members of the Communist Party, Mao was convinced that a Chinese revolution would be driven by the poverty-stricken peasants in the countryside rather than by the urban working class. Mao, the son of a prosperous peasant, had helped organize a peasant movement in southern China during the early 1920s.

Chiang Kai-shek now tried to root the Communists out of their urban base in Shanghai and their rural base in Jiangxi Province. He succeeded in the first task in 1931. Most party leaders in Shanghai were forced to flee to Mao's base in southern China.

Chiang Kai-shek then turned his forces against Mao's stronghold in Jiangxi Province. Chiang's forces far outnumbered Mao's, but Mao made effective use of **guerrilla tactics**, using unexpected methods like sabotage and deception to fight the enemy. Four slogans by Mao describe his methods:

PRIMARY SOURCE

❝When the enemy advances, we retreat! When the enemy halts and camps, we trouble them! When the enemy tries to avoid battle, we attack! When the enemy retreats, we pursue!❞

—quoted in *Red Star Over China*

The Long March

In 1934 Chiang's troops, with their superior military strength, surrounded the Communist base in Jiangxi and set up a blockade of the stronghold. With the villages behind Chiang's troops, no food or supplies could pass to the Communist base. Chiang even built small forts to prevent Communist raids. However, Mao's army, the People's Liberation Army (PLA), broke through the Nationalist lines and began its famous Long March.

Both Mao and Chiang knew that unless Mao's army could cross the Chang Jiang, it would be wiped out. Mao's army began a desperate race. Moving on foot through mountains, marshes, rivers, and deserts, the army traveled almost 6,000 miles (9,600 km), averaging 24 miles (38 km) each day, to reach the last surviving Communist base in northwest China. All along those miles, Mao's troops had to fight Chiang's army. Many of Mao's troops froze or starved. One survivor of the Long March remembered:

PRIMARY SOURCE

❝As the days went by, there was less and less to eat. After our grain was finished, we ate the horses and then we lived on wild vegetables. When even the wild vegetables were finished, we ate our leather belts. After that we had to march on empty stomachs.❞

—quoted in *A Short History of China*

One year later, Mao's troops reached safety in the dusty hills of northern China. Of the 90,000 troops who had embarked on the journey, only 9,000 remained. In the course of the Long March, Mao Zedong had become the sole leader of the Chinese Communist Party. To people who lived at the time, it must have seemed that the Communist threat to the Nanjing regime was over. To the Communists, however, there remained hope for the future.

✓ **READING PROGRESS CHECK**

Identifying Central Issues Why did the Nationalists and Communists form an alliance?

Mao Zedong (1893–1976)
Mao Zedong was the founding chairman of the Peoples' Republic of China. As a young communist revolutionary, he went to his home in the countryside of Hunan, where he saw political unrest growing among the peasants. He realized that the Soviet-style communism that he and others were pursuing—focusing on factory workers in cities—was not a perfect fit for China. Instead, he decided to organize a revolution of rural peasants. Mao sought to adapt communism to fit the conditions, culture, and traditions of China. Mao was largely responsible for laying the groundwork for a modern, self-sufficient China, but at an extreme cost. Many of his later policies, such as the Great Leap Forward and the Cultural Revolution, brought enormous suffering and political repression.

▶ **CRITICAL THINKING**
Predicting Consequences Why was it important that Mao focused on the revolutionary potential among the peasants in rural China rather than the factory workers in the cities?

guerrilla tactics the use of unexpected maneuvers like sabotage and subterfuge to fight an enemy

The New China

GUIDING QUESTION *What characterized the new China?*

Even while trying to root out Mao's Communist forces, Chiang was trying to build a new Chinese nation. He publicly declared his commitment to Sun Yat-sen's plans for a republican government. But first, a transitional period would occur. In Sun's words:

PRIMARY SOURCE

❝China . . . needs a republican government just as a boy needs school. As a schoolboy must have good teachers and helpful friends, so the Chinese people, being for the first time under republican rule, must have a farsighted revolutionary government for their training. This calls for the period of political tutelage, which is a necessary transitional stage from monarchy to republicanism. Without this, disorder will be unavoidable.❞

—quoted in *Sources of Chinese Tradition*

In keeping with Sun's program, Chiang announced a period of political tutelage (training) to prepare the Chinese people for a final stage of

▼ Rural peasants toil in the fields in 1930s China.

▶ **CRITICAL THINKING**
Contrasting How was life different in urban and rural China in the 1930s?

constitutional government. Even the humblest peasant would be given time to understand the country's problems and the new government. In the meantime, the Nationalists used their dictatorial power to carry out a land-reform program and the modernization of the urban industrial sector.

A Class Divide

It would take more than plans on paper to create a new China, however. Years of neglect and civil war had severely weakened the political, economic, and social fabric of the nation. Faint signs of an impending industrial revolution were appearing in the major urban centers. However, most of the people who lived in the countryside were drained by warfare and civil strife. Rural peasants—up to 80 percent of China's population—were still poor and overwhelmingly illiterate.

Meanwhile, a Westernized middle class began to form in the cities. It was here that the new Nanjing government found much of its support. However, the new Westernized elite were concerned with the middle-class Western values of individual advancement and material accumulation. They had few links with the peasants in the countryside or with the rickshaw (a small, two-wheeled cart that usually carried one passenger and was pulled by a person) driver, "running in this world of suffering," in the words of a Chinese poet. In the cities, observers would have believed that Chiang Kai-shek had lifted China into the modern world. Young people in cities wore European clothes; they went to the movies and listened to the radio.

Innovations and Traditions

Chiang Kai-shek was aware of the problem of introducing foreign ideas into a population that was still culturally conservative. Thus, while attempting to build a modern industrial state, he tried to bring together modern Western innovations with traditional Confucian values of hard work and obedience. With his U.S.-educated wife Soong Mei-ling, Chiang set up a "New Life Movement." Its goal was to promote traditional Confucian social ethics, such as integrity, propriety, and righteousness. Four ancient Confucian virtues would serve as guides for living: Li (courtesy), I (duty), Lien (honesty), and Chih (honor). At the same time, it rejected what was viewed as the excessive individualism and material greed of Western capitalist values.

Unfortunately for Chiang Kai-Shek, Confucian ideas had been widely discredited when the traditional system failed to provide answers to China's decline. Moreover, Chiang Kai-shek faced a host of other problems. The Nanjing government had total control over only a handful of provinces in the Chang Jiang valley. Also, the Japanese threatened to gain control of northern China. The Great Depression also was having an ill effect on China's economy. All of these problems created difficulties for Chiang.

Limited Progress

In spite of these problems, Chiang did have some success. He undertook a massive road-building project and repaired and extended much of the country's railroad system as well. More than 50,000 miles (80,467 km) of highways were built around and through the coastal areas. New factories, mostof which the Chinese owned, were opened. Through a series of agreements,the foreign powers ended many of their leases, gave up extra-territorial rights, and returned the customs service to Chinese control. Chiang established a national bank and improved the education system.

Analyzing PRIMARY SOURCES

The New Life Movement

"The new life movement is based upon the preservation of these four virtues [courtesy, duty, honesty, and honor], and it aims to apply them to actual, existing conditions, in order that the moral character of the nation shall attain the highest possible standard."

—Madame Chiang Kai-shek, quoted in *War Messages and Other Selections*

DBQ DRAWING CONCLUSIONS

What were the goals of the New Life Movement?

The government was also repressive. Fearing Communist influence, Chiang suppressed all opposition and censored free expression. In so doing, he alienated many intellectuals and political moderates. Because Chiang's support came from the rural landed gentry as well as the urban middle class, he did not push for programs that would lead to a **redistribution of wealth,** the shifting of wealth from a rich minority to a poor majority. A land-reform program was enacted in 1930, but it had little effect on the country. For the peasants and poor townspeople, no real improvement occurred under the Nanjing government.

Sun Fo, Sun Yat-sen's son, expressed disapproval of the Nanjing government:

redistribution of wealth
the shifting of wealth from a rich minority to a poor majority

PRIMARY SOURCE

❝We must frankly admit the fact that in these twenty years the machinery and practice of the Kuomintang [Chinese Nationalist Party] have turned in a wrong direction, inconsistent with the party constitution drafted by Dr. Sun Yat-sen in 1923 and contrary to the spirit of democracy. The practice of the revolutionary party has subsequently become the same as that of a bureaucratic regime.❞

—quoted in *China*, 1946

Chiang Kai-shek's government had a little more success in promoting industrial development. Between 1927 and 1937, industrial growth in China averaged only about one percent per year. Much of the national wealth was in the hands of the so-called "four families," a group of senior officials and close subordinates of the ruling elite. Military expenses took up approximately half of the budget. Little money was left for social and economic development.

The new government, then, had little success in dealing with the deep-seated economic and social problems that affected China during the interwar years. This was especially true when internal disintegration and foreign pressure were occurring during the virtual collapse of the global economic order during the Great Depression. In addition, militant political forces in Tokyo were determined to extend Japanese influence and power in an unstable China.

✓ READING PROGRESS CHECK

Drawing Conclusions Why did Chiang Kai-shek believe a period of political tutelage was necessary for China?

LESSON 3 REVIEW

Reviewing Vocabulary
1. *Paraphrasing* Describe Mao Zedong's guerrilla tactics.

Using Your Notes
2. *Synthesizing* Using your notes, list the Confucian values that Chiang Kai-shek used to bring modern Western ideas into a culturally conservative population. Why do you think Chiang Kai-shek used those particular values to introduce Western culture to China?

Answering the Guiding Questions
3. *Identifying Central Issues* What was the relationship between the Nationalists and the Communists?

4. *Analyzing Information* What characterized the new China?

Writing Activity
5. **NARRATIVE** Imagine that you are a young person living in China. Choose a year covered in this lesson and then choose where in China you live. Write a diary entry describing the events that are happening in your home town. Be sure to use specific details and events as you write.

networks

There's More Online!

☑ **CHART/GRAPH** Great Depression in Latin America

☑ **CHART/GRAPH** Goods Exported from Latin America, 1937–1938

☑ **IMAGE** Good Neighbor Policy

☑ **IMAGE** United Fruit Company Workers

☑ **INTERACTIVE SELF-CHECK QUIZ**

☑ **SLIDE SHOW** Modern Art of Latin America

☑ **VIDEO** Nationalism in Latin America

PHOTO: (l to r)©Jacob J. Gayer/National Geographic Society/Corbis, Library of Congress Prints & Photographs Division, Library of Congress, ©Christie's Images/SuperStock, Library of Congress Prints & Photographs Division.

Reading **HELP**DESK CCSS

Academic Vocabulary
- **investor** - **establish**

Content Vocabulary
- **oligarchy**

TAKING NOTES:

Key Ideas and Details

Summarizing Use the following graphic organizer to identify countries and regions in Latin America and their primary exports.

Country or Region	Export
Argentina	
Brazil	
Chile	
Central America	
Caribbean	

LESSON 4
Nationalism in Latin America

ESSENTIAL QUESTIONS
- How can political control lead to nationalist movements?
- How does economic exploitation lead to nationalist movements?

IT MATTERS BECAUSE

During the 1920s, investors in the United States poured funds directly into Latin American businesses. The Great Depression devastated Latin America's economy and created instability. This turmoil led to the creation of military dictatorships and authoritarian states in Latin America in the 1930s.

The Latin American Economy

GUIDING QUESTION *What factors influenced the Latin American economy during the 1920s and 1930s?*

In the early twentieth century, the Latin American economy was based largely on the export of foodstuffs and raw materials. Some countries relied on only one or two products for sale abroad. Argentina, for example, exported beef and wheat; Chile, nitrates and copper; Brazil, coffee and cotton; Caribbean nations, such as Cuba, sugar; and Central America, bananas. A few reaped large profits from these exports. For most of the people, however, the returns were small.

Role of the United States

Beginning in the 1920s, the United States began to replace Great Britain as the major **investor** in Latin America. British investors had put money into stocks and other forms of investment that did not give them direct control of the companies. U.S. investors, however, put their funds directly into production facilities and ran companies themselves. In this way, large segments of Latin America's export industries fell into U.S. hands. A number of smaller Central American countries became independent republics, but their economies often depended on wealthy nations. The U.S.-owned United Fruit Company, for example, owned land, packing plants, and railroads in Central America. American firms also gained control of the copper-mining industry in Chile and Peru, as well as of the oil industry in Mexico, Peru, and Bolivia.

investor a person or entity that commits money to earn a financial return

Many Latin Americans resented U.S. control of Latin American industries. A growing nationalist awareness led many of them to view the United States as an imperialist power. It was not difficult for Latin American nationalists to show that profits from U.S. businesses were sometimes used to keep ruthless dictators in power. In Venezuela, for example, U.S. oil companies had close ties to the dictator Juan Vicente Gómez.

The United States had always cast a large shadow over Latin America. It had intervened militarily in Latin American affairs for years. This was especially true in Central America and the Caribbean. Many Americans considered both regions vital to U.S. security.

The United States made some attempts to change its relationship with Latin America in the 1930s. In 1933 President Franklin D. Roosevelt announced the Good Neighbor policy, rejecting the use of U.S. military force in Latin America. The president then withdrew the last U.S. Marines from Haiti in 1934. For the first time in 30 years, no U.S. troops were stationed in Latin American countries.

Impact of the Great Depression

The Great Depression was a disaster for Latin America's economy. Weak U.S. and European economies meant less demand for Latin American exports, especially coffee, sugar, metals, and meat. The total value of Latin American exports in 1930 was almost 50 percent below the figures for the years 1925 through 1929. The countries that depended on the export of only one product were especially hurt.

The Great Depression, however, had one positive effect on the Latin American economy. When exports declined, Latin American countries could no longer buy manufactured goods from abroad. Thus their governments began to encourage the development of new industries to produce manufactured goods. The hope was that industrial development would bring greater economic independence.

Often, however, individuals could not start new industries because capital was scarce in the private sector. Governments then invested in the new industries. This led to government-run steel industries in Chile and Brazil and government-run oil industries in Argentina and Mexico.

✓ **READING PROGRESS CHECK**

Contrasting How did the U.S. method of investing differ from that of Great Britain?

▼ Workers load bananas at a United Fruit Company farm in Central America.

▶ **CRITICAL THINKING**
Evaluating Who reaped most of the profits from the export of bananas?

Authoritarian Rule

GUIDING QUESTION *Who controlled politics in Latin America?*

Most Latin American countries had republican forms of government. In reality, however, a relatively small group of church officials, military leaders, and large landowners ruled each country. This elite group controlled the masses of people, who were mostly poor peasants. Military forces were crucial in keeping these special-interest groups in power. Indeed, military leaders often took control of the government.

This trend toward authoritarianism increased during the 1930s, largely because of the impact of the Great Depression. Domestic instability caused by economic crises led to the creation of many military dictatorships in the early 1930s. This trend was especially evident in Argentina, Brazil, and Mexico. Together, these nations possessed more than half of the land and wealth of Latin America.

Argentina

Argentina was controlled by an **oligarchy**, a government in which a select group of people exercises control. This oligarchy of large landowners who had grown wealthy from the export of beef and wheat failed to realize the growing importance of industry and cities in their country. This group also ignored the growing middle class, which reacted by forming the Radical Party in 1890.

In 1916 Hipólito Irigoyen (ee • PAW • lee • TOH IHR • ih • GOH • YEHN), leader of the Radical Party, was elected president of Argentina. The Radical Party, however, feared the industrial workers, who were using strikes to improve their conditions. The party thus drew closer to the large landowners and became more corrupt.

The military also was concerned with the rising power of the industrial workers. In 1930 the Argentine army overthrew President Irigoyen and reestablished the power of the large landowners. Through this action, the military hoped to continue the old export economy and thus stop the growth of working-class power that would come with more industrialization.

During World War II, restless military officers formed a new organization, the Group of United Officers (GOU). They were unhappy with the Argentinian government and overthrew it in June 1943.

Brazil

In 1889 the army overthrew the Brazilian monarchy and **established** a republic. It was controlled chiefly by the landed elites, who had become wealthy from large coffee plantations.

By 1900, three-fourths of the world's coffee was grown in Brazil. As long as coffee prices remained high, the ruling oligarchy was able to maintain its power. The oligarchy largely ignored the growth of urban industry and the working class that came with it.

The Great Depression devastated the coffee industry. By the end of 1929, coffee prices had hit a record low. In 1930 a military coup made Getúlio Vargas, a wealthy rancher, president of Brazil. Vargas ruled Brazil from 1930 to 1945. Early in his rule, he appealed to workers by establishing an eight-hour day and a minimum wage.

Faced with strong opposition in 1937, Vargas made himself dictator. Beginning in 1938 he established his New State. It was basically an authoritarian state with some fascist-like features. Political parties were outlawed, and civil rights were restricted. Secret police silenced Vargas's opponents.

oligarchy "the rule of the few;" a form of government in which a select group of people exercises control

establish to set up permanently; to found

Cárdenas in his first report
to Congress in 1935:

❝The exploitation of oil in
Mexico has, for many years,
taken place in a way
characteristic of foreign
companies; that is to say, our
country, though independent
and enjoying advanced social
ideas, permits the extraction
of its wealth and natural
resources by the foreigner
without preserving for itself
any permanent benefit.❞

—quoted in *Oil and Politics in Latin
America: Nationalist Movements and
State Companies*

DBQ **ANALYZING
INFORMATION** How
did Cárdenas attempt to address
the injustice that he perceived in
this relationship?

Vargas also pursued a policy of stimulating new industries. The
government established the Brazilian steel industry and set up a company
to explore for oil. By the end of World War II, Brazil had become Latin
America's chief industrial power. In 1945 the army, fearing that Vargas
might prolong his power illegally after calling for new elections, forced him
to resign.

Mexico

Mexico was not an authoritarian state, but neither was it truly democratic.
The Mexican Revolution of the early twentieth century was the first significant effort in Latin America to overturn the system of large landed estates
and raise the living standards of the masses. Out of the revolution emerged
a relatively stable political order.

The government was democratic in form. However, the official political
party of the Mexican Revolution, known as the Institutional Revolutionary
Party, or PRI, controlled the major groups within Mexican society. Every six
years, party bosses of the PRI chose the party's presidential candidate. That
candidate was then dutifully elected by the people.

A new wave of change began with Lázaro Cárdenas (KAHR • duhn • AHS),
president of Mexico from 1934 to 1940. He moved to fulfill some of the
original goals of the revolution. His major step was to distribute 44 million
acres (17.8 million ha) of land to landless Mexican peasants. This action
made him enormously popular with the peasants.

President Cárdenas also took a strong stand with the United States over
oil. By 1900, Mexico was known to have enormous oil reserves, especially
in the Gulf of Mexico. Over the next 30 years, oil companies from Britain
and, in particular, the United States, made large investments in the Mexican
oil industry. After a dispute with the foreign-owned oil companies over
workers' wages, the Cárdenas government seized control of the oil fields
and the property of the foreign-owned oil companies.

The U.S. oil companies were furious and asked President Franklin
D. Roosevelt to intervene. He refused, reminding them of his promise in the
Good Neighbor policy not to send U.S. troops into Latin America. Mexicans
cheered Cárdenas as the president who stood up to the United States.

Eventually, the Mexican government did pay the oil companies for their
property. It then set up PEMEX, a national oil company, to run the oil
industry. PEMEX did not do well at first, however, because exports fell.
Still, for many, PEMEX was a symbol of Mexican independence.

✔ **READING PROGRESS CHECK**

Specifying How was the Mexican government democratic in form but not
in practice?

Culture in Latin America

GUIDING QUESTION *How was Latin American culture influenced by European art?*

During the early twentieth century, European artistic and literary movements began to penetrate Latin America. In major cities, such as Buenos
Aires, Argentina, and São Paulo, Brazil, wealthy elites expressed interest in
the work of modern artists.

Latin American artists went abroad to Europe and brought back
modern techniques, which they often adapted to their native roots. Many
artists and writers used their work to promote the emergence of a new
national spirit. An example was the Mexican artist Diego Rivera. Rivera

had studied in Europe, where he was especially influenced by fresco painting in Italy. After his return to Mexico, he developed a monumental style that filled wall after wall with murals. Rivera's wall paintings can be found in such diverse places as the Ministry of Education and the Social Security Hospital. His works were aimed at the masses of people, many of whom could not read.

Rivera sought to create a national art that would portray Mexico's past, especially its Aztec legends, as well as Mexican festivals and folk customs. His work also carried a political and social message. Rivera did not want people to forget the Mexican Revolution, which had overthrown the large landowners and the foreign interests that supported them.

☑ **READING PROGRESS CHECK**

Explaining To which subjects did Diego Rivera turn to create a national art of Mexico?

PHOTO: ©The Gallery Collection/Corbis

◀ This detail from Diego Rivera's *The Conquest or Arrival of Hernán Cortés in Veracruz* is part of a series of frescoes on pre-Hispanic and colonial Mexico painted on the inner courtyard walls of the National Palace in Mexico City.

▶ **CRITICAL THINKING**
Identifying How does Rivera portray Cortés and his men?

LESSON 4 REVIEW (CCSS)

Reviewing Vocabulary
1. *Explaining* Write a paragraph in which you explain the role of U.S. investors in Latin American economies and the role of the oligarchy in Argentina and Brazil.

Using Your Notes
2. *Summarizing* Use your notes to write a paragraph identifying five countries or regions in Latin America and their primary exports as well as what those exports have in common.

Answering the Guiding Questions
3. *Identifying Central Issues* What factors influenced the Latin American economy during the 1920s and 1930s?

4. *Evaluating* Who controlled politics in Latin America?

5. *Making Connections* How was Latin American culture influenced by European art?

Writing Activity
6. **INFORMATIVE/EXPLANATORY** How did U.S. and British companies influence the development of nationalism in Latin American countries?

Directions: On a separate sheet of paper, answer the questions below. Make sure you read carefully and answer all parts of the questions.

Lesson Review

Lesson 1

1 **SUMMARIZING** What factors led to the decline of the Ottoman Empire after World War I?

2 **SPECULATING** What might have happened differently if Arabs had been able to unite as one nation after the war?

Lesson 2

3 **EXPLAINING** Why did so many African nations demand independence after World War I?

4 **ANALYZING ETHICAL ISSUES** What were the advantages and disadvantages of Gandhi's strategy for gaining independence for India?

Lesson 3

5 **IDENTIFYING CENTRAL ISSUES** Why did the Nationalist Party and the Communist Party in China form an alliance?

6 **DESCRIBING** Why did Chiang Kai-shek believe the Communists were more dangerous than the Japanese?

Lesson 4

7 **MAKING CONNECTIONS** What effect did the economic crises of the 1930s have on many Latin American governments?

8 **DRAWING CONCLUSIONS** What subjects did Diego Rivera favor in his art?

21st Century Skills

9 **CREATE AND ANALYZE ARGUMENTS AND DRAW CONCLUSIONS** What was the Comintern? Why were colonized peoples attracted to it?

10 **IDENTIFYING CAUSE AND EFFECT** Why did a segment of the Japanese people push for military expansion so soon after World War I?

Exploring the Essential Questions

11 **CATEGORIZING** Work with a partner to create a cause-and-effect chart on poster board that lists at least one nationalist movement from each lesson and some specific causes of the movement. The poster should pay particular attention to political control and economic exploitation. Include visuals such as maps, sketches, and photos or art.

DBQ Analyzing Historical Documents

Use the document to answer the following questions.

This cartoon shows England carrying a bundle that represents its commercial interests in the Orient. An Ottoman Turk advances on Armenia, who is begging for England's help.

12 **ANALYZING** What message is the cartoonist trying to convey?

13 **MAKING INFERENCES** How is Armenia portrayed in the cartoon? Do you think the cartoonist supports the Armenians?

Extended-Response Question

14 **INFORMATIVE/EXPLANATORY** Discuss the personalities of at least three leaders and how they affected the success of their independence movements.

Need Extra Help?

If You've Missed Question	**1**	**2**	**3**	**4**	**5**	**6**	**7**	**8**	**9**	**10**	**11**	**12**	**13**	**14**
Go to page	314	317	319	322	325	326	332	334	321	324	314	336	336	315

World War II and the Holocaust

1939–1945

ESSENTIAL QUESTIONS • Why do political actions often lead to war?
• How does war impact society and the environment?

net.w⊙rks

There's More Online! about World War II and the Holocaust.

CHAPTER 17

The Story Matters...

From 1933 to 1945, the Nazis fought two wars: one against the Allies and another for "racial purity." At first, the Nazis sent European Jews to concentration camps. Later, they developed horribly efficient killing centers such as Auschwitz and Treblinka. By the time Allied forces liberated the death camps in 1945, the Nazis had murdered nearly two out of every three European Jews during the Holocaust.

◄ These prisoners at Auschwitz were liberated by the Soviets in January 1945. Victims of the Holocaust suffered cruelty at the hands of their Nazi captors. Those who survived were ill or dying of starvation and maltreatment.

World War II was the most devastating war in history. Germany and Japan achieved stunning territorial victories between 1939 and 1942. In 1941 the United States and the Soviet Union entered the war, turning the tide against fascist expansion. New military technology, such as aerial photography, informed the military strategies of both the Axis and Allied powers and changed the way the war was fought.

Step Into the Place

Read the quotes and look at the information presented on the map.

 Analyzing Historical Documents How did the Allies use aerial photographs for strategic purposes during the war in Europe?

PRIMARY SOURCE

"Aerial photos were the only solid, irrefutable evidence of where an enemy was, what he was doing and what he had with which to do it. Intelligence was a 'force multiplier,' permitting our side to put resources or air strikes on the most critical ground, and aerial photographic intelligence was the most reliable source."

—Colonel Roy M. Stanley, United States Air Force, *Asia from Above*

PRIMARY SOURCE

"These [36-inch cameras mounted on the belly of the aircraft] produced 3-D views of the areas being photographed, which were then examined by our intelligence people. Details as small as a golf ball were detectable. We also carried a smaller camera in the port side of the aircraft, and with this we could take oblique pictures. Some of the trips involved low-level photographs, and this required flying at tree-top level. On 15 May [1943] we were jumped by six Bf 109s [German fighter planes] while flying photo runs over Oslo...We were able to do ever decreasing turns and avoid their gunfire. We were also able to inch our way over to Sweden. The Swedes will never know how grateful we were to them as they opened up with every flak [anti-aircraft] battery on their coast."

—Flight Lieutenant Bill White, Royal Air Force, recalling a reconnaissance mission to find a German battleship harbored in Norway, quoted in *Mosquito Photo-Reconnaissance Units of World War 2*

PHOTO: (l)©Hulton-Deutsch Collection/Corbis, (r)Stringer/Keystone/Hulton Archive/Getty Images.

Step Into the Time

Determining Importance
Choose an event from the time line and explain why it was an important development in the Second World War.

	1939	1940	1941
EUROPEAN AND NORTH AFRICAN THEATER			
PACIFIC THEATER			

September 1, 1939 German invasion of Poland

September 3, 1939 Britain and France declare war on Germany

June 1940 France falls to Germany

1941 Germany invades the Soviet Union

1939 Japan shocked by signing of Nazi-Soviet Nonaggression Pact

1940 Japan demands rights to resources in French Indochina

1941 Japan acquires Chinese territory in Second Sino-Japanese War

networks

There's More Online!

☑ **MAP** Explore the interactive version of this map on Networks.

☑ **TIME LINE** Explore the interactive version of the time line on Networks.

World War II in Europe and North Africa 1941–1945

Legend:
→ Allied offensive
✳ Major battle with date

Map labels:

NORWAY · FINLAND · Leningrad · SWEDEN · ESTONIA · Moscow · LATVIA · LITH. · SOVIET UNION

North Sea · Baltic Sea · DEN. · *Warsaw Aug. 1944–Jan. 1945* · *Minsk July 1944*

UNITED KINGDOM · IRELAND · *Battle of Britain July–Oct. 1940* · *Berlin Apr.–May 1945* · Berlin · Warsaw · *Kursk July 1943* · Volga R.

London · NETH. · GERMANY · POLAND · Stalingrad

English Channel · *Normandy June 1944* · BELG. · Paris · UKRAINE · *Stalingrad Aug. 1942–Feb. 1943*

ATLANTIC OCEAN · FRANCE · *Battle of the Bulge Dec. 1944–Jan. 1945* · SWITZ. · Munich · SLOVAKIA · HUNGARY · CRIMEA · CAUCASUS · Caspian Sea

VICHY FRANCE · CROATIA · SERBIA · ROMANIA · Black Sea

PORTUGAL · SPAIN · Corsica Fr. · ITALY · MONT. · BULGARIA · TURKEY · IRAN

GIBRALTAR U.K. · *Balearic Is. Sp.* · *Anzio Jan.–Mar. 1944* · Sardinia It. · ALBANIA · GREECE

Sicily It. · MOROCCO Vichy France · *North Africa Landing Nov. 1942* · TUNISIA Vichy France · *Sicily July 1943* · Malta U.K. · Crete Gr.

Mediterranean Sea · ALGERIA Vichy France · *El Alamein Oct.–Nov. 1942* · Alexandria

LIBYA · EGYPT · AFRICA

0 400 miles / 0 400 km
Lambert Azimuthal Equal-Area projection

Time line

1942–1943 Allies and Germany battle for control over North Africa

June 6, 1944 Allies under U.S. General Dwight D. Eisenhower launch D-Day invasion

May 7, 1945 Germany surrenders

March 1945 Allies cross the Rhine after the Battle of the Bulge

1942 · **1943** · **1944** · **1945**

December 7, 1941 Japanese attack Pearl Harbor

1942 Japanese conquer Thailand, Philippines, Malaya

1942 United States Navy defeats Japanese at Battle of Midway Island

May 1943 Japanese launch offensive in central China

December 8, 1944 U.S. Air Force begins bombardment of Iwo Jima

August 1945 United States drops atomic bombs on Japan

August 14, 1945 Japan surrenders

World War II and the Holocaust **339**

Reading **HELP**DESK ⓒⓒⓈⓈ

Academic Vocabulary

• **dominate** • **violation**

Content Vocabulary

• **demilitarized**
• **appeasement**
• **sanctions**

TAKING NOTES:

Key Ideas and Details

Categorizing As you read, create a chart like the one below listing examples of Japanese and German aggression prior to the outbreak of World War II.

Japanese Aggression	German Aggression

LESSON 1
World War II Begins

ESSENTIAL QUESTIONS • *Why do political actions often lead to war?*
• *How does war impact society and the environment?*

IT MATTERS BECAUSE

In the 1930s, Germany and Japan invaded neighboring countries to gain resources and land. Hitler allied with Italy, annexed Austria, and occupied the Sudetenland. Japan made a quick conquest of Manchuria. At first, other world powers allowed these acts of aggression. They wanted to avoid war—yet the path to war was already paved.

The German Path to War

GUIDING QUESTIONS *What was Hitler's motivation for German expansion? What alliances and events contributed to the outbreak of World War II?*

World War II in Europe had its beginnings in the ideas of Adolf Hitler. He believed that Germans belonged to a so-called Aryan race that was superior to all other races and nationalities. Consequently, Hitler believed that Germany was capable of building a great civilization. To be a great power, however, he thought that Germany needed more land to support a larger population.

Already in the 1920s, Hitler had indicated that a Nazi regime would find this land to the east—in the Soviet Union. Germany therefore must prepare for war with the Soviet Union. After the Soviet Union had been conquered, according to Hitler, its land would be resettled by German peasants. The Slavic peoples could be used as slave labor to build an Aryan racial state that Hitler thought would **dominate** Europe for a thousand years.

Hitler Violates Treaty

After World War I, the Treaty of Versailles had limited Germany's military power. As chancellor, Hitler, posing as a man of peace, stressed that Germany wished to revise the unfair provisions of the treaty by peaceful means. Germany, he said, only wanted its rightful place among the European states.

On March 9, 1935, however, Hitler announced the creation of a new air force. One week later, he began a military draft that would expand Germany's army from 100,000 to 550,000 troops. These steps were in direct **violation** of the Treaty of Versailles. France, Great Britain, and Italy condemned Germany's actions and warned against future aggressive steps. In the midst of the Great Depression, however, these nations were distracted by their own internal problems and did nothing further.

Hitler was convinced that the Western states had no intention of using force to maintain the Treaty of Versailles. Hence, on March 7, 1936, he sent German troops into the Rhineland. The Rhineland was part of Germany, but, according to the Treaty of Versailles, it was a **demilitarized** area. That is, Germany was not allowed to have weapons or fortifications there. France had the right to use force against any violation of this provision but would not act without British support.

Great Britain did not support the use of force against Germany. The British government viewed the occupation of German territory by German troops as a reasonable action by a dissatisfied power. *The London Times* noted that the Germans were "only going into their own back garden." Great Britain thus began to practice a policy of **appeasement**. This policy was based on the belief that if European states satisfied the reasonable demands of dissatisfied powers, the dissatisfied powers would be content, and stability and peace would be achieved in Europe.

New Alliances

Meanwhile, Hitler gained new allies. Benito Mussolini of Italy had long dreamed of creating a new Roman Empire. In October 1935, Mussolini's forces invaded Ethiopia. Angered by French and British opposition to his invasion, Mussolini welcomed Hitler's support. He began to draw closer to the German dictator.

In 1936 both Germany and Italy sent troops to Spain to help General Francisco Franco in the Spanish Civil War. In October 1936, Mussolini and Hitler made an agreement recognizing their common interests. One month later, Mussolini spoke of the new alliance between Italy and Germany, called the Rome-Berlin Axis. Also in November, Germany and Japan signed the Anti-Comintern Pact, promising a common front against communism.

Union With Austria

By 1937, Germany was once more a "world power," as Hitler proclaimed. He was convinced that neither France nor Great Britain would provide much opposition to his plans. In 1938 he decided to pursue one of his goals: *Anschluss* (AHN • shloos), or union, with Austria, his native land.

dominate   to influence or control

violation   a disregard of rules or agreements

demilitarized   elimination or prohibition of weapons, fortifications, and other military installations

appeasement   satisfying reasonable demands of dissatisfied powers in an effort to maintain peace and stability

GEOGRAPHY CONNECTION

Germany expanded its borders from 1935–1939.

1 THE WORLD IN SPATIAL TERMS *Which countries did Germany take land from during this time period?*

2 HUMAN SYSTEMS *What was Germany's rationale for expansion?*

German Expansion 1935–1939

0   400 miles
0   400 km
Lambert Azimuthal Equal-Area projection

Germany, 1935
German occupation, 1936
German acquisitions, 1938–1939

By threatening Austria with invasion, Hitler forced the Austrian chancellor to put Austrian Nazis in charge of the government. The new government promptly invited German troops to enter Austria and "help" in maintaining law and order. One day later, on March 13, 1938, after his triumphal return to his native land, Hitler annexed Austria to Germany.

Demands and Appeasement

Hitler's next objective was the destruction of Czechoslovakia. On September 15, 1938, he demanded that Germany be given the Sudetenland, an area in northwestern Czechoslovakia that was inhabited largely by Germans. He was willing to risk "world war" to achieve his objective.

At a hastily arranged conference in Munich, British, French, German, and Italian representatives did not object to Hitler's plans but instead reached an agreement that met virtually all Hitler's demands. German troops were allowed to occupy the Sudetenland. The Czechs, abandoned by their Western allies, stood by helplessly.

The Munich Conference was the high point of Western appeasement of Hitler. When Neville Chamberlain, the British prime minister, returned to England from Munich, he boasted that the agreement meant "peace for our time." One British statesman, Winston Churchill, warned instead that the settlement at Munich was "a disaster of the first magnitude." Hitler, however, had promised Chamberlain that he would make no more demands. Like many others, Chamberlain believed Hitler's promises.

In fact, Hitler was more convinced than ever that the Western democracies would not fight. Increasingly, he was sure that he could not make a mistake, and he had by no means been satisfied at Munich.

In March 1939, Hitler invaded and took control of Bohemia and Moravia in western Czechoslovakia. In the eastern part of the country, Slovakia became a puppet state controlled by Nazi Germany. On the evening of March 15, 1939, Hitler triumphantly declared in Prague that he would be known as the greatest German of them all.

At last, the Western states reacted to the Nazi threat. Hitler's aggression had made clear that his promises were worthless. When Hitler began to demand the Polish port of Danzig, Great Britain saw the danger and offered to protect Poland in the event of war. At the same time, both France and Britain realized that only the Soviet Union was powerful enough to help contain Nazi aggression. They began political and military negotiations with Joseph Stalin, the Soviet dictator.

Hitler and the Soviets

Meanwhile, Hitler continued to believe that the West would not fight over Poland. He now feared, however, that the West and the Soviet Union might make an alliance. Such an alliance could mean a two-front war for Germany. To prevent this, Hitler made his own agreement with Stalin.

On August 23, 1939, Germany and the Soviet Union signed the Nazi-Soviet Nonaggression Pact. In it, the two nations promised not to attack each other. To get the nonaggression pact, Hitler offered Stalin control of eastern Poland and the Baltic states. Because he expected to fight the Soviet Union anyway, it did not matter to Hitler what he promised—he was accustomed to breaking promises.

▲ After the Munich Conference, Adolf Hitler, Nevile Henderson, Neville Chamberlain, and Joachim von Ribbentrop (left to right) at the Munich airport on September 29, 1938.

▶ CRITICAL THINKING

Evaluating Why is the Munich Conference an oft-used example of the failure of appeasement?

WONDER HOW LONG THE HONEYMOON WILL LAST?

▲ This political cartoon depicts Adolf Hitler and Joseph Stalin as a newlywed couple after the signing of the Nazi-Soviet Nonaggression Pact.

PHOTO: (t)Popperfoto/Getty Images, (b)Corbis; TEXT: Winston Churchill, "A Total and Unmitigated Defeat" House of Commons, October 5, 1938, Reproduced with permission of Curtis Brown Ltd, London on behalf of the Estate of Sir Winston Churchill. Copyright © Winston S. Churchill.

Hitler shocked the world when he announced the treaty. Hitler was now free to attack Poland. He told his generals, "Now Poland is in the position in which I wanted her . . . . I am only afraid that at the last moment some swine will yet submit to me a plan for mediation."

Hitler need not have worried. On September 1, German forces invaded western Poland. Two days later, Britain and France declared war on Germany.

✓ **READING PROGRESS CHECK**

Determining Cause and Effect How did World War I affect European leaders' attitudes toward international aggression?

The Japanese Path to War

GUIDING QUESTION *Why did Japan want to seize other countries?*

On the night of September 18, 1931, Japanese soldiers, disguised as Chinese soldiers, blew up a small section of the Manchurian Railway near the city of Mukden. Japan owned this area, and the Japanese soldiers wanted to blame the "Mukden incident" on the Chinese. The Japanese army used this incident to justify its taking all of Manchuria in a series of rapid military advances.

Manchuria offered many resources the Japanese needed. After this conquest, the Japanese army became committed to an expansionist policy— a policy of enlarging the Japanese Empire.

By September 1932, the Japanese army had formed Manchuria into a separate state and renamed it Manchukuo. They placed a puppet ruler, Henry Pu Yi, on the throne. As an infant, Henry Pu Yi had been China's "last emperor." He had abdicated that throne, however, following the revolution of 1911 in China.

Worldwide protests against the Japanese seizure of Manchuria led the League of Nations to send in investigators. When the investigators issued a report condemning the seizure, Japan withdrew from the League. The United States refused to recognize the Japanese takeover of Manchuria but was unwilling to threaten force.

Over the next several years, Japan continued its expansion and established control over the eastern part of Inner Mongolia and areas in north China around Beijing. Neither Emperor Hirohito nor government leaders could control the army. In fact, it was the army that established Japanese foreign policy. The military held the upper hand. By the mid-1930s, militants connected to the government and the armed forces had gained control of Japanese politics.

▲ During the Sino-Japanese War, the Japanese air force bombed Shanghai.

▶ **CRITICAL THINKING**
Making Inferences What role did the Sino-Japanese War play in the Chinese civil war?

War With China

Chiang Kai-shek tried to avoid a conflict with Japan so that he could deal with what he considered the greater threat, the Chinese Communists. When clashes between Chinese and Japanese troops broke out, he sought to appease Japan by allowing it to govern areas in north China.

As Japan moved steadily southward, protests against Japanese aggression grew stronger in Chinese cities. In December 1936, Chiang ended his military efforts against the Communists and formed a new united front

PHOTO: Keystone/Staff/Hulton Archive/Getty Images

against the Japanese. In July 1937, Chinese and Japanese forces clashed south of Beijing and hostilities spread.

Although Japan had not planned to declare war on China, the 1937 incident turned into a major conflict. Japan seized the Chinese capital of Nanjing in December. The Japanese Army destroyed the city and massacred more than 100,000 civilians and prisoners of war. The event was so brutal it became known as the "Rape of Nanjing." Chiang Kai-shek refused to surrender and moved his government upriver, first to Hankou, then to Chongqing. Temporarily defeated, the Chinese continued to resist.

The New Asian Order

Japanese military leaders had hoped to force Chiang to agree to join a New Order in East Asia, comprising Japan, Manchuria, and China. Japan would attempt to establish a new system of control in Asia with Japan guiding its Asian neighbors to prosperity.

Part of Japan's plan was to seize Soviet Siberia, with its rich resources. During the late 1930s, Japan began to cooperate with Nazi Germany. Japan assumed that the two countries would ultimately launch a joint attack on theSoviet Union and divide Soviet resources between them.

When Germany signed the nonaggression pact with the Soviets in August 1939, Japanese leaders had to rethink their goals. Because Japan lacked the resources to defeat the Soviet Union, it looked to South Asia for raw materials for its military machine.

Japan Launches Attack

A move southward would risk war with the European powers and the United States. Japan's attack on China had already aroused strong criticism, especially in the United States. Still, in the summer of 1940, Japan demanded the right to exploit economic resources in French Indochina.

sanctions restrictions intended to enforce international law

The United States objected. It warned Japan that it would apply economic **sanctions** unless Japan withdrew from the area and returned to its borders of 1931. Japan badly needed the oil and scrap iron it was getting from the United States. Should these resources be cut off, Japan would have to find them elsewhere. This would threaten Japan's long-term objectives.

Japan was now caught in a dilemma. To guarantee access to raw materials in Southeast Asia, Japan had to risk losing them from the United States. After much debate, Japan decided to launch a surprise attack on U.S. and European colonies in Southeast Asia.

☑ **READING PROGRESS CHECK**

Summarizing What regions did Japan consider in its search for natural resources?

LESSON 1 REVIEW

Reviewing Vocabulary

1. *Explaining* What is the connection between national sovereignty and demilitarization?

Using Your Notes

2. *Comparing* Use your graphic organizer to compare how German and Japanese aggression affected the United States.

Answering the Guiding Questions

3. *Summarizing* What was Hitler's motivation for German expansion?

4. *Distinguishing* What alliances and events contributed to the outbreak of World War II?

5. *Analyzing* Why did Japan want to seize other countries?

Writing Activity

6. **ARGUMENT** Write a paragraph that argues for or against the following statement: The British policy of appeasement was the main cause for Germany's aggressive actions.

networks

There's More Online!

☑ **BIOGRAPHY** Franklin D. Roosevelt

☑ **BIOGRAPHY** Hideki Tōjō

☑ **CHART/GRAPH** The Axis and the Allies, 1939–1945

☑ **IMAGE** Battle of Midway Island

☑ **INFOGRAPHIC** Pearl Harbor

☑ **INTERACTIVE SELF-CHECK QUIZ**

☑ **MAP** WWII in Asia and the Pacific, 1941–1942

☑ **MAP** WWII in Europe and North Africa, 1939–1942

☑ **VIDEO** World War II

Reading **HELP**DESK   CCSS

Academic Vocabulary

• **resolve** • **involvement**

Content Vocabulary

• **blitzkrieg** • **isolationism**
• **neutrality**

TAKING NOTES:
Key Ideas and Details

Determining Cause and Effect As you read, use a chart like the one below to list key events during World War II and their effect on the course of the war.

Event	Effect

LESSON 2
World War II

ESSENTIAL QUESTIONS • *Why do political actions often lead to war?*
• *How does war impact society and the environment?*

IT MATTERS BECAUSE

In the first years of World War II, Hitler, with his blitzkrieg, had gained control of much of western and central Europe. Victories over Britain and Russia remained elusive, however. When the United States entered the war, the Allies agreed to fight until the Axis Powers surrendered unconditionally.

Europe at War

GUIDING QUESTION *What were Germany's gains and losses during the early years of the war?*

Hitler stunned Europe with the speed and efficiency of the German attack on Poland. His **blitzkrieg**, or "lightning war," used armored columns, called panzer divisions, supported by airplanes. Each panzer division was a strike force of about 300 tanks with accompanying forces and supplies.

The forces of the blitzkrieg broke quickly through Polish lines and encircled the bewildered Polish troops. Regular infantry units then moved in to hold the newly conquered territory. Within four weeks, Poland had surrendered. On September 28, 1939, Germany and the Soviet Union divided Poland.

Hitler's Early Victories

After a winter of waiting, Hitler resumed the attack on April 9, 1940, with another blitzkrieg against Denmark and Norway. One month later, Germany launched an attack on the Netherlands, Belgium, and France. The main assault was through Luxembourg and the Ardennes Forest. German panzer divisions broke through weak French defensive positions there and raced across northern France.

French and British forces were taken by surprise. Anticipating a German attack, France had built a defense system, called the Maginot (MA • zhuh • NOH) Line, along its border with Germany. The line was a series of concrete and steel fortifications armed with heavy artillery. The Germans, however, decided not to cross the Maginot Line. Instead, they went around it and attacked France from its border with Belgium.

blitzkrieg German for "lightning war"; a swift and sudden military attack; used by the Germans during World War II

resolve determination; a fixed purpose

isolationism a policy of national isolation by abstention from alliances and other international political and economic relations

neutrality refusal to take sides or become involved in wars between other nations

By going around the Maginot Line, the Germans split the Allied armies, trapping French troops and the entire British army on the beaches of Dunkirk. Only by the heroic efforts of the Royal Navy and civilians in private boats did the British manage to evacuate 338,000 Allied (mostly British) troops. An English skipper described the scene:

PRIMARY SOURCE

❝The soldiers were coming off the beach clinging to bits of wood and wreckage and anything that would float. As we got close enough we began . . . picking up as many as we could . . . [and taking] them off to one of the ships lying off in the deep water.❞

—quoted in *Blood, Tears and Folly,* 1993

The French signed an armistice on June 22, 1940. German armies now occupied about three-fifths of France. An authoritarian regime under German control was set up over the remainder of the country. It was known as Vichy France and was led by an aged French hero of World War I, Marshal Henri Pétain. Germany was now in control of western and central Europe, but Britain had still not been defeated. In fact, after Dunkirk, the British **resolve** heightened. Especially helpful in rallying the British people were the stirring speeches of Winston Churchill, who had become prime minister in May 1940.

President Franklin D. Roosevelt denounced the aggressors, but the United States followed a strict policy of **isolationism**. A series of **neutrality** acts, passed in the 1930s, prevented the United States from taking sides or becoming involved in any European wars. Many Americans felt that the United States had been drawn into World War I due to economic **involvement** in Europe, and they wanted to prevent a recurrence. Roosevelt was convinced that the neutrality acts actually encouraged Axis aggression and were gradually relaxed as the United States supplied food, ships, planes, and weapons to Britain.

The Battle of Britain

Hitler realized that an amphibious (land-sea) invasion of Britain could succeed only if Germany gained control of the air. At the beginning of August 1940, the Luftwaffe (LOOFT • vah • fuh)—the German air force—launched a major offensive. German planes bombed British air and naval bases, harbors, communication centers, and war industries.

The British fought back with determination. They were supported by an effective radar system that gave them early warning of German attacks. Nevertheless, the British air force suffered critical losses.

In September, in retaliation for a British attack on Berlin, Hitler ordered a shift in strategy. Instead of bombing military targets, the Luftwaffe began massive bombing of British cities. Hitler hoped in this way to break British morale. Instead, because military targets were not being hit, the British were able to rebuild their air strength quickly. Soon, the British air force was inflicting major losses on Luftwaffe bombers. Hitler postponed the invasion of Britain indefinitely.

Attack on the Soviet Union

Although he had no desire for a two-front war, Hitler became convinced that Britain was remaining in the war only because it expected Soviet support. If the Soviet Union were smashed, Britain's last hope would be eliminated. Moreover, Hitler had convinced himself that the Soviet Union had a pitiful army and could be defeated quickly.

PHOTO: ©Culver Pictures, Inc./SuperStock

WWII in Europe and North Africa 1939–1941

Legend:
- Germany, 1941
- Other Axis powers
- Axis-controlled territory
- Vichy France and territories
- Allied powers
- Allied-controlled territory
- Neutral nations
- Ardennes Forest
- Maginot Line
- Axis offensives

GEOGRAPHY CONNECTION

By 1941, Germany had conquered most of continental Europe.

1 PLACES AND REGIONS *What offensive did the Axis powers carry out in Africa?*

2 THE USES OF GEOGRAPHY *Why was it significant that Germany failed to control Moscow by 1941?*

Hitler's invasion of the Soviet Union was scheduled for the spring of 1941, but the attack was delayed because of problems in the Balkans. Hitler had already gained the political cooperation of Hungary, Bulgaria, and Romania. However, the failure of Mussolini's invasion of Greece in 1940 had exposed Hitler's southern flank to British air bases in Greece. To secure his Balkan flank, Hitler seized both Greece and Yugoslavia in April.

Reassured, Hitler invaded the Soviet Union on June 22, 1941. He believed that the Russians could still be decisively defeated before the brutal winter weather set in. The massive attack stretched out along a front some 1,800 miles (about 2,900 km) long. German troops advanced rapidly, capturing 2 million Russian soldiers. By November, one German army group had swept through the Ukraine. A second army was besieging the city of Leningrad, while a third approached within 25 miles (about 40 km) of Moscow, the Soviet capital.

An early winter and fierce Soviet resistance, however, halted the German advance. Certain of quick victory, the Germans had not planned for winter uniforms. For the first time in the war, German armies had been stopped. A counterattack in December 1941 by a Soviet army came as an ominous ending to the year for the Germans.

✔ **READING PROGRESS CHECK**

Predicting Consequences What assumptions did Hitler make about invading the Soviet Union? Do you think the invasion would have gone differently if he had not made those assumptions?

Japan at War

GUIDING QUESTION *What brought the United States into the war?*

On December 7, 1941, Japanese aircraft attacked the U.S. naval base at Pearl Harbor in Hawaii. The surprise attack damaged or destroyed more than 350 aircraft, damaged or sunk 18 ships, and killed or wounded more than 3,500 Americans. The same day, the Japanese attacked the Philippines and advanced on Malaya. Later, they invaded the Dutch East Indies and occupied several islands in the Pacific Ocean. By the spring of 1942, almost all of Southeast Asia and much of the western Pacific had fallen to the Japanese.

A triumphant Japan now declared the creation of a "community" of nations: the Greater East Asia Co-Prosperity Sphere. The entire region would now be under Japanese direction. Japan also announced its intention to liberate areas of Southeast Asia from Western colonial rule. For the moment, however, Japan needed the resources of the region for its war machine and treated the countries under its rule as conquered lands.

Japanese policy was now largely dictated by Prime Minister Hideki Tōjō—formerly a general—who in the course of the war became a virtual military dictator. Tōjō had hoped that Japan's lightning strike at American bases would destroy the U.S. fleet in the Pacific. The Roosevelt administration, he thought, would now accept Japanese domination of the Pacific.

But the Japanese miscalculated. The attack on Pearl Harbor unified American opinion about becoming involved in the war. The United States joined with European nations and Nationalist China in a combined effort to defeat Japan. Believing American **involvement** in the Pacific would make the United States ineffective in the European theater of war, Hitler declared war on the United States four days after Pearl Harbor. As in WWI, another European conflict had turned into a global war.

involvement a commitment or a connection to

✔ **READING PROGRESS CHECK**

Identifying Why did the United States stay out of WWII until the Pearl Harbor attack?

Analyzing PRIMARY SOURCES

Hitler in August 1942

❝As the next step, we are going to advance south of the Caucasus and then help the rebels in Iran and Iraq against the English. Another thrust will be directed along the Caspian Sea toward Afghanistan and India. Then the English will run out of oil. In two years we'll be on the borders of India. Twenty to thirty elite German divisions will do. Then the British Empire will collapse.❞

—quoted in *Spandau*, 1976

DBQ *ANALYZING*
Why was Hitler so optimistic after he captured the Crimea?

The Allies Advance

GUIDING QUESTION *How did the involvement of the United States change the war?*

The entry of the United States into the war created a new coalition, the Grand Alliance. To overcome mutual suspicions, the three major Allies—Great Britain, the United States, and the Soviet Union—agreed to stress military operations and to ignore political differences. At the beginning of 1943, the Allies agreed to fight until the Axis Powers—Germany, Italy, and Japan—surrendered unconditionally, which required the Axis nations to surrender without any favorable condition. This cemented the Grand Alliance by making it nearly impossible for Hitler to divide his foes.

The European Theater

Defeat was far from Hitler's mind at the beginning of 1942. As Japanese forces advanced into Southeast Asia and the Pacific, Hitler and his allies continued fighting the war in Europe against Britain and the Soviet Union.

Until late 1942, it seemed that the Germans might still prevail. In North Africa, German forces broke through the British defenses in Egypt and advanced toward Alexandria. A renewed German offensive in the Soviet Union led to the capture of the entire Crimea in the spring of 1942. However, by the fall of 1942, the war had turned against the Germans.

The Tide Turns

In North Africa, British forces had stopped General Erwin Rommel's troops at El Alamein in the summer of 1942. The Germans then retreated back across the desert. In November 1942, British and American forces invaded French North Africa. They forced the German and Italian troops there to surrender in May 1943.

On the Eastern Front, after the capture of the Crimea, Hitler's generals wanted him to concentrate on the Caucasus and its oil fields. Hitler, however, decided that Stalingrad, a major industrial center on the Volga River, should be taken first. In perhaps the most terrible battle of the war, between November 1942 and February 2, 1943, the Soviets launched a counterattack. German troops were stopped and then encircled, and supply lines were cut off, all in frigid winter conditions. The Germans were forced to surrender at Stalingrad. The entire German Sixth Army, considered the best of the German troops, was lost.

By February 1943, German forces in Russia were back to their positions of June 1942. By the spring, even Hitler knew that the Germans would not defeat the Soviet Union.

The Asian Theater

In 1942 the tide of battle in the East also changed dramatically. In the Battle of the Coral Sea on May 7 and 8, 1942, American naval forces stopped the Japanese advance and saved Australia from being invaded.

The turning point of the war in Asia came on June 4, at the Battle of Midway Island. U.S. planes destroyed four attacking Japanese aircraft carriers. The United States defeated the Japanese navy and established naval superiority in the Pacific.

By the fall of 1942, Allied forces in Asia were gathering for two operations. One, commanded by U.S. general Douglas MacArthur, would move into the Philippines through New Guinea and the South Pacific Islands. The other would move across the Pacific with a combination of U.S. Army, Marine, and Navy attacks on Japanese-held islands. The policy, called "island hopping," was to capture some Japanese-held islands and to bypass others to reach Japan. After engagements near the Solomon Islands from August to November 1942, Japanese fortunes began to fade.

▲ A group of U.S. fighter planes fly over the reefs at Midway Island, November 14, 1942.

▶ **CRITICAL THINKING**
Assessing What Allied strategies helped change the tide of battle in the East?

☑ **READING PROGRESS CHECK**

Summarizing Why was the German assault on Stalingrad a crushing defeat for the Germans?

PHOTO: ©Bettmann/Corbis

LESSON 2 REVIEW (CCSS)

Reviewing Vocabulary
1. *Explaining* What is a blitzkrieg, and what supplies and equipment did it require?

Using Your Notes
2. *Determining Cause and Effect* Use your notes to explain the effects of key events in World War II.

Answering the Guiding Questions
3. *Analyzing Information* What were Germany's gains and losses during the early years of the war?

4. *Determining Cause and Effect* What brought the United States into the war?

5. *Making Generalizations* How did the involvement of the United States change the war?

Writing Activity
6. **NARRATIVE** Research one of the battles described in this lesson. Then write a descriptive account of the battle from the perspective of a soldier fighting in that battle.

netw**o**rks

There's More Online!

- ☑ **IMAGE** American Propaganda Poster
- ☑ **IMAGE** B-29 Superfortresses
- ☑ **IMAGE** Coventry Cathedral After a German Bombing Raid
- ☑ **IMAGE** Soviet Propaganda Poster
- ☑ **IMAGE** Woman at Work in a Munitions Factory
- ☑ **INTERACTIVE SELF-CHECK QUIZ**
- ☑ **VIDEO** The Home Front and Civilians

Reading **HELP**DESK ⒸⒸⓈⓈ

Academic Vocabulary

- **widespread**
- **circumstance**

Content Vocabulary

- **mobilization**
- **kamikaze**
- **blitz**

TAKING NOTES:

Key Ideas and Details

Organizing As you read, complete a chart like this one to show the impact of World War II on the lives of civilians.

Country	Impact on Civilian Lives
Soviet Union	
United States	
Japan	
Germany	

LESSON 3
The Home Front and Civilians

ESSENTIAL QUESTION
- *How does war impact society and the environment?*

IT MATTERS BECAUSE

During World War II, nations mobilized their people and geared their economies to war. While the troops fought, the citizens on the home front made personal sacrifices to produce the materials and supplies needed to fuel the war. Hundreds of thousands lost their lives in bombing raids.

The Mobilization of Four Nations

GUIDING QUESTION *How did countries mobilize for war?*

Even more than World War I, World War II was a total war. Fighting was much more **widespread** and covered most of the world. Economic **mobilization** was more extensive; so, too, was the mobilization of women. The number of civilians killed—almost 20 million—was far higher than those killed in World War I. Many of these victims were children.

World War II had an enormous impact on civilian life in the Soviet Union, the United States, Germany, and Japan. We consider thehome fronts of those four nations next.

The Soviet Union

Known to the Soviets as the Great Patriotic War, the German-Soviet war witnessed the greatest land battles in history, as well as incredible ruthlessness. The initial military defeats suffered by the Soviet Union led to drastic emergency measures that affected the lives of the civilian population. The city of Leningrad (now St. Petersburg), for example, experienced 900 days of siege. Its inhabitants became so desperate for food that they even ate dogs, cats, and mice. Probably 1.5 million people died in the city.

As the German army made its rapid advance into Soviet territory, Soviet workers dismantled and shipped the factories in the western part of the Soviet Union to the interior—to the Urals, western Siberia, and the Volga regions. Machines were placed on the bare ground. As laborers began their work, walls went up around them.

PHOTO: (l to r)Stringer/Hulton Archive/Getty Images, ©akg-images / The Image Works, Corbis, Laski Diffusion/Getty Images News/Getty Images, Library of Congress.

Stalin called the widespread military and industrial mobilization of the nation a "battle of machines." The Soviets won, producing 78,000 tanks and 98,000 artillery pieces. In 1943, 55 percent of the Soviet national income went for war materials, compared with 15 percent in 1940. As a result of the emphasis on military goods, Soviet citizens experienced severe shortages of both food and housing.

Soviet women played a major role in the war effort. Women and girls worked in industries, mines, and railroads. Overall, the number of women working in industry increased almost 60 percent. Soviet women were also expected to dig antitank ditches and to work as air-raid wardens. Also, the Soviet Union was the only country in World War II to use women in battle. Soviet women served as snipers and in aircrews of bomber squadrons.

The United States

The home front in the United States was quite different from that of the other major powers. The United States was not fighting on its own territory. Eventually, the United States became the arsenal of the Allied Powers; it produced much of the military equipment the Allies needed. The height of war production came in November 1943. At that point, the country was building 6 ships a day and 96,000 planes per year.

The mobilization of the American economy and workforce resulted in some social turmoil, however. The construction of new factories created boomtowns. Thousands came there to work but then faced a shortage of houses and schools. Sixteen million men and women were enrolled in the military and moved frequently. Another 16 million, mostly wives and girlfriends of servicemen or workers looking for jobs, also moved around the country.

More than a million African Americans moved from the rural South to the cities of the North and West looking for jobs in industry. The presence of African Americans in areas in which they had not lived before led to racial tensions and sometimes even racial riots. In Detroit in June 1943, for example, white mobs roamed the streets attacking African Americans. One million African Americans joined the military, where they served in segregated units. For some, this treatment later led to a fight for their civil rights.

Japanese Americans faced even more serious issues. On the West Coast, 110,000 Japanese Americans, 65 percent of whom had been born in the United States, were removed to camps surrounded by barbed wire and required to take loyalty oaths. Public officials claimed this policy was necessary for security reasons. California governor Culbert Olson expressed the racism in this policy:

PHOTO: Stringer/Hulton Archive/Getty Images

PRIMARY SOURCE

❝When I look out at a group of Americans of German or Italian descent, I can tell whether they're loyal or not. I can tell how they think and even perhaps what they are thinking. But it is impossible for me to do this with inscrutable Orientals, and particularly the Japanese.❞

—quoted in Spickard, *Japanese Americans: The Formation and Transformation of an Ethnic Group*

widespread widely extended or spread out

mobilization the process of assembling troops and supplies and making them ready for war

▲ An African-American woman works in a U.S. munitions factory during World War II

▶ **CRITICAL THINKING**
Making Inferences How did munitions factories like the one shown above impact U.S. communities?

During World War II, women participated in organizations such as the Women's Army Corps (WACs), where they served in administrative, noncombat positions. In 1948 President Harry S. Truman signed the Women's Armed Services Integration Act, which enabled women to become active members of all branches of the U.S. military. At that time, women made up 2 percent of the armed forces. Today, women make up 15 percent of the military, though they are often excluded from direct combat missions. In 2009 only 6 percent of the Marine Corps was made up of women, while women accounted for 20 percent of the Air Force, 14 percent of the Army, and 15 percent of the Navy.

kamikaze Japanese for "divine wind"; a suicide mission in which young Japanese pilots intentionally flew their airplanes into U.S. fighting ships at sea

Germany

In August 1914, Germans had enthusiastically cheered their soldiers marching off to war. In September 1939, the streets were quiet. Many Germans did not care. Even worse for the Nazi regime, many feared disaster.

Hitler was well aware of the importance of the home front. He believed that the collapse of the home front in World War I had caused Germany's defeat. To avoid a repetition of that experience, he adopted economic policies that may have cost Germany the war.

To maintain the morale of the home front during the first two years of the war, Hitler refused to cut consumer goods production or to increase the production of armaments. Blitzkrieg gave the Germans quick victories and enabled them to plunder the food and raw materials of conquered countries. In this way, they could avoid taking away resources from the civilian economy. After German defeats on the Russian front and the American entry into the war, however, the economic situation in Germany changed.

Early in 1942, Hitler finally ordered a massive increase in armaments production and in the size of the army. Hitler's architect, Albert Speer, was made minister for armaments and munitions in 1942. Speer was able to triple the production of armaments between 1942 and 1943, in spite of Allied air raids.

A total mobilization of the economy was put into effect in July 1944. Schools, theaters, and cafés were closed. By that time, though, total war mobilization was too late to save Germany from defeat.

Nazi attitudes toward women changed over the course of the war. Before the war, the Nazis had worked to keep women out of the job market. As the war progressed and more and more men were called up for military service, this position no longer made sense. In spite of this change, the number of women working in industry, agriculture, commerce, and domestic service increased only slightly. The total number of employed women in September 1944 was 14.9 million, compared with 14.6 million in May 1939. Many women, especially those of the middle class, did not want jobs, particularly in factories.

Japan

Wartime Japan was a highly mobilized society. To guarantee its control over all national resources, the government created a planning board to control prices, wages, labor, and resources. Traditional habits of obedience and hierarchy were used to encourage citizens to sacrifice their resources, and sometimes their lives, for the national cause.

The calls for sacrifice reached a high point in the final years of the war. Young Japanese were encouraged to volunteer to serve as pilots in suicide missions against U.S. fighting ships at sea. These pilots were known as **kamikaze**, or "divine wind."

Japan was reluctant to mobilize women on behalf of Japan's war effort. General Hideki Tōjō, prime minister from 1941 to 1944, opposed female employment. He argued in October 1943:

PRIMARY SOURCE

❝The weakening of the family system would be the weakening of the nation. . . . We are able to do our duties . . . only because we have wives and mothers at home.❞

—quoted in *Valley of Darkness: The Japanese People and World War Two*, 1978

Female employment increased during the war but only in areas such as the textile industry and farming, in which women had traditionally worked. Instead of using women to meet labor shortages, the Japanese government brought in Korean and Chinese laborers.

☑ **READING PROGRESS CHECK**

Contrasting How were war preparations in Germany different from war preparations in the United States?

The Bombing of Cities

GUIDING QUESTION *How did the bombing of cities impact the home front?*

Bombing was used in World War II against military targets, enemy troops, and civilian populations. Bombing made the home front a dangerous place.

Although a few bombing raids had been conducted in the last year of World War I, the aircraft of the time were limited by how far they could fly and by how much they could carry. The bombing of civilians had led to a public outcry, leading many leaders to believe that bombing civilian populations would force governments to make peace. As a result, European air forces began to develop long-range bombers that carried enormous payloads in the 1930s.

Britain

The first sustained use of civilian bombing began in early September 1940. Londoners took the first heavy blows. For months, the German air force bombed London nightly. Thousands of civilians were killed or injured, and enormous damage was done to the buildings of London. In spite of the extensive damage done to lives and property, Londoners' morale remained high.

The **blitz**, as the British called the German air raids, soon became a national experience. The blitz was carried to many other British cities and towns. The ability of Londoners to maintain their morale set the standard for the rest of the British population. The theory that the bombing of civilians would force peace was proved wrong.

Many children were evacuated from cities during the war to avoid the bombing. The British moved about 6 million children and their mothers in 1939. Some British parents even sent their children to Canada and the United States. This, too, could be dangerous. When the ocean liner *Arandora Star* was hit by a German torpedo, it had 77 British children on board. They never made it to Canada.

Germany

The British failed to learn from their own experience, however. Churchill and his advisers believed that destroying German communities would break civilian morale and bring victory. Major bombing raids on German cities began in 1942. On May 31, 1942, Cologne became the first German city to be attacked by 1,000 bombers.

Bombing raids added an element of terror to the dire **circumstances** caused by growing shortages of food, clothing, and fuel. The Germans, too, sought to protect their children from the bombings by evacuating them

blitz the British term for the German air raids on British cities and towns during World War II

▲ The blitz leveled buildings in England. A man stands amid the rubble of what was the Coventry Cathedral in November 1940.

▶ **CRITICAL THINKING**
Drawing Conclusions What effects did the blitz have on England?

circumstance state of affairs

from the cities. They had a program that created about 9,000 camps for children in the countryside. Especially fearful to the Germans were the incendiary bombs, which created firestorms that swept through cities. The ferocious bombing of Dresden from February 13 to 15, 1945, created a firestorm that may have killed as many as 35,000 inhabitants and refugees.

Germany suffered enormously from the Allied bombing raids. Millions of buildings were destroyed; half a million civilians died. Nevertheless, it is highly unlikely that Allied bombing sapped the German morale. Instead, Germans, whether pro-Nazi or anti-Nazi, fought on stubbornly, often driven simply by a desire to live. At times, even young people were expected to fight in the war. In the last years of the war, Hitler Youth members, often only 14 or 15 years old, served in the front lines.

Nor did the bombing destroy Germany's industrial capacity. Production of war materials actually increased between 1942 and 1944, in spite of the bombing. However, the widespread destruction of transportation systems and fuel supplies made it extremely difficult for the new materials to reach the German military.

▲ B-29 Superfortresses fly over Mount Fuji en route to Tokyo.

Japan

Japan was open to air raids toward the end of the war because its air force had almost been destroyed. Moreover, its crowded cities were built of flimsy materials that were especially vulnerable to fire.

Attacks on Japanese cities by the new U.S. B-29 Superfortresses, the biggest bombers of the war, had begun on November 24, 1944. By the summer of 1945, many of Japan's industries had been destroyed, along with one-fourth of its dwellings. To add to the strength of its regular army, the Japanese government decreed the mobilization of all people between the ages of 13 and 60 into a People's Volunteer Corps.

In Japan, the bombing of civilians reached a new level with the use of the first atomic bomb. Fearing high U.S. casualties in a land invasion of Japan, President Truman and his advisers decided to drop atomic bombs in August 1945. The result was the deaths of thousands of Japanese civilians.

 READING PROGRESS CHECK

Drawing Conclusions How did the development of airplanes change the way militaries fought?

PHOTO: © Bettman/CORBIS

LESSON 3 REVIEW (CCSS)

Reviewing Vocabulary

1. *Describing* Describe the social effects of U.S. mobilization for World War II.

Using Your Notes

2. *Comparing and Contrasting* Use your notes to write a paragraph comparing and contrasting the effects of World War II on civilians in the Soviet Union, the United States, Germany, and Japan.

Answering the Guiding Questions

3. *Gathering Information* How did countries mobilize for war?

4. *Identifying Cause and Effects* How did the bombing of cities impact the home front?

Writing Activity

5. **INFORMATIVE/EXPLANATORY** Do research to find out more about the blitz in London or another city in Great Britain. In paragraph form, present a detailed sequence of steps or events that would typically occur for average citizens in their homes from the time planes were sighted until the "all clear" signal. Use transitional words and phrases, and list your source or sources.

networks

There's More Online!

☑ **CHART/GRAPH** Jewish Population in Europe Before and After World War II

☑ **IMAGE** German Prison Camp

☑ **IMAGE** Heinrich Himmler

☑ **IMAGE** Japanese Troops Arriving at Haiphong Port

☑ **INTERACTIVE SELF-CHECK QUIZ**

☑ **MAP** Major Nazi Death Camps

☑ **PRIMARY SOURCE** An Eyewitness to the Holocaust

☑ **VIDEO** The New Order and the Holocaust

Reading **HELP**DESK (CCSS)

Academic Vocabulary
- ethnic
- occupation

Content Vocabulary
- genocide
- collaborator

TAKING NOTES:
Key Ideas and Details

Comparing and Contrasting As you read, use a Venn diagram like the one below to compare and contrast the New Order of Germany with the New Order of Japan.

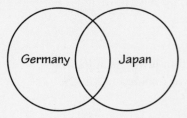

LESSON 4
The New Order and the Holocaust

ESSENTIAL QUESTIONS · Why do political actions often lead to war?
· How does war impact society and the environment?

IT MATTERS BECAUSE

Japan exploited the resources of the nations it conquered. In Germany, the Nazis began a terrifying genocide, carried out by death squads and death camps. Nearly two out of every three European Jews died in the Holocaust.

The New Order in Europe

GUIDING QUESTION *How did Germany establish a New Order in Europe?*

In 1942 the Nazi regime stretched across continental Europe from the English Channel in the west to the outskirts of Moscow in the east. Nazi-occupied Europe was largely organized in one of two ways. Nazi Germany directly annexed some areas, such as western Poland, and made them into German provinces. Most of occupied Europe, however, was run by German military or civilian officials with help from local people who collaborated with the Nazis.

Nazi administration in the conquered lands to the east was especially ruthless. Seen as the "living space" for German expansion, these lands were populated, Nazis thought, by racially inferior Slavic peoples. Hitler's plans for an Aryan racial empire were so important to him that the Nazis began to put their racial program into effect soon after the conquest of Poland.

Heinrich Himmler, the leader of the SS, was in charge of German resettlement plans in the east. Himmler's task was to move the Slavic peoples out and to replace them with Germans. Slavic peoples included Czech, Polish, Serbo-Croatian, Slovene, and Ukrainian people. One million Poles were uprooted and moved to southern Poland. Hundreds of thousands of **ethnic** Germans were brought in to colonize the German provinces in Poland.

The invasion of the Soviet Union made the Nazis even more excited about German colonization. Hitler planned a colossal project of social engineering after the war. Poles, Ukrainians, and Russians would be removed and become slave labor. German peasants would settle on the abandoned lands and "Germanize" them.

"The unit selected for this task would enter a village or city and order the prominent Jewish citizens to call together all Jews for the purpose of resettlement. They were requested to hand over their valuables to the leaders of the unit, and shortly before the execution to surrender their outer clothing. The men, women, and children were led to a place of execution which in most cases was located next to a more deeply excavated anti-tank ditch. Then they were shot, kneeling or standing, and the corpses thrown into the ditch."

—from *Nazi Conspiracy and Aggression*, vol. 5, 1946

DBQ **CLASSIFYING** How do the actions described above exemplify genocide?

ethnic relating to people who have common racial, religious, or cultural origins

occupation the military force occupying a country or the policies carried out by it

genocide the deliberate mass murder or physical extinction of a particular racial, political, or cultural group

By the summer of 1944, more than 7 million European workers labored in Germany. They made up approximately 20 percent of Germany's labor force. Another 7 million workers were forced to labor for the Nazis in their own countries on farms, in industries, and in military camps.

The use of forced labor caused many problems for Germany. Sending so many workers to Germany disrupted industrial production in the occupied countries. Then, too, the brutal way in which Germany recruited foreign workers led more and more people to resist the Nazi **occupation** forces.

☑ **READING PROGRESS CHECK**

Analyzing How did resettlement contribute to the goals of Hitler's New Order?

The Holocaust

GUIDING QUESTION *How did Adolf Hitler's views on race influence the New Order?*

No aspect of the Nazi New Order was more terrifying than the deliberate attempt to exterminate the Jews. Racial struggle was a key element in Hitler's world of ideas. He saw it as a clearly defined conflict of opposites. On one side were the Aryans, who were the creators of human cultural development, according to Hitler. On the other side were the Jews, whom Hitler blamed for Germany's defeat in World War I and the Depression.

Himmler and the SS closely shared Hitler's racial ideas. The SS was given responsibility for what the Nazis called their Final Solution to the Jewish problem. The Final Solution was **genocide** of the Jewish people.

The *Einsatzgruppen*

Reinhard Heydrich, head of the SS's Security Service, had the task of administering the Final Solution. Heydrich created special strike forces, called *Einsatzgruppen*, to carry out Nazi plans. After the defeat of Poland, these forces rounded up all Polish Jews and put them in ghettos set up in many Polish cities. Conditions in the ghettos were horrible. Families were crowded together in unsanitary housing. The Nazis tried to starve residents by allowing only minimal amounts of food. In spite of their suffering, residents carried on, and some organized resistance against the Nazis.

In June 1941, the *Einsatzgruppen* were given the new job acting as mobile killing units. These SS death squads followed the regular army's advance into the Soviet Union. Their job was to round up Jews in their villages, execute them, and to bury them in mass graves.

The Death Camps

The *Einsatzgruppen* probably killed more than 1 million Jews. As appalling as that sounds, it was too slow by Nazi standards. They decided to kill the European Jews in specially built death camps.

Beginning in 1942, Jews from countries occupied by Germany or sympathetic to Germany were rounded up, packed like cattle into freight trains, and shipped to Poland. Six extermination centers were built in Poland for this purpose. The largest was Auschwitz (OWSH • VIHTS).

About 30 percent of the new arrivals at Auschwitz were sent to a labor camp, where many were starved or worked to death. The remainder of the people went to the gas chambers. Some inmates were subjected to cruel and painful "medical" experiments.

By the spring of 1942, the death camps were in full operation. First priority was given to the elimination of the Polish ghettos. By the summer of 1942, Jews were also being shipped from France, Belgium, and Holland.

Major Nazi Death Camps

Legend:
- Concentration camp
- Death camp
- Location of *Einsatzgruppen*
- European boundaries, January 1938

0 — 400 miles
0 — 400 km
Lambert Azimuthal Equal-Area projection

GEOGRAPHY CONNECTION

1 **THE WORLD IN SPATIAL TERMS** *Where were the death camps located?*

2 **HUMAN SYSTEMS** *Why do you think the Einsatzgruppen operated in Eastern Europe and the Soviet Union?*

Even as the Allies were winning the war in 1944, Jews were shipped from Greece and Hungary. In spite of Germany's desperate military needs, even late in the war when Germany was facing utter defeat, the Final Solution often had priority in using railroad cars to ship Jews to the death camps.

The Death Toll

The Germans killed approximately 6 million Jews, more than 3 million of them in the death camps. Even in concentration camps that were not designed specifically for mass murder, large numbers of inmates were worked to death or subjected to deadly medical experiments. Virtually 90 percent of the Jewish populations of Poland, the Baltic countries, and Germany were killed. Overall, the Holocaust was responsible for the death of nearly two out of every three European Jews.

The Nazis were also responsible for the deliberate death by shooting, starvation, or overwork of as many as another 9 to 10 million non-Jewish people. The Nazis considered the Roma, who are sometimes known as Gypsies, to be an alien race. About 40 percent of Europe's Roma were killed in the death camps.

The leading citizens of the Slavic peoples were arrested and killed. Probably an additional 4 million Poles, Ukrainians, and Belorussians lost their lives as slave laborers. Finally, at least 3 to 4 million Soviet prisoners of war were killed.

This mass slaughter of European Jews is known as *Shoah*—a Hebrew word meaning "total destruction." Many Jews attempted to resist the Nazis. Friends and strangers aided some Jews, hiding them or smuggling them to safe areas. A few foreign diplomats saved Jews by issuing exit visas. The nation of Denmark saved almost its entire Jewish population.

Some people did not believe the accounts of death camps because, during World War I, allies had greatly exaggerated German atrocities to arouse enthusiasm for the war. Most often, people pretended not to notice what was happening. Even worse, **collaborators** helped the Nazis hunt down Jews. Although the Allies were aware of the concentration camps and

collaborator a person who assists the enemy

death camps, they chose to concentrate on ending the war. Not until after the war did the full extent of the horror and inhumanity of the Holocaust impress itself upon people's consciousness.

▲ Japanese troops arrive at Haiphong Port in Indochina

✔ **READING PROGRESS CHECK**

Explaining What was the role of the *Einsatzgruppen*?

The New Order in Asia

GUIDING QUESTION *What characterized the New Order in Asia?*

Japan needed its new possessions in Asia to meet its growing need for raw materials, such as tin and oil, and as markets for its manufactured goods. To organize these possessions, Japanese leaders included them in the Greater East Asia Co-Prosperity Sphere. This economic community supposedly would provide mutual benefits to the occupied areas and to Japan.

The Japanese had conquered Southeast Asia under the slogan "Asia for the Asiatics." Japanese officials in occupied territories promised that local governments would be established under Japanese control. In fact, real power rested with Japanese military authorities in each territory. In turn, the Army General Staff in Tokyo controlled the local Japanese military command. Japan used the economic resources of its colonies for its war machine and recruited the native peoples to serve in local military units or in public works projects. In some cases, these policies brought severe hardships to the native peoples. In Vietnam more than a million people starved in 1944 and 1945 when Japan forcibly took their rice to sell abroad.

At first, many Southeast Asian nationalists took Japanese promises at face value and agreed to cooperate. Eventually, the nature of Japanese occupation policies became clear, and sentiment turned against Japan. Japanese officials provoked such attitudes by their contempt for local customs. Like the Germans, Japanese military forces often had little respect for the lives of their subject peoples. To help their war effort, the Japanese used labor forces composed of both prisoners of war and local peoples.

This behavior created a dilemma for many nationalists. They had no desire to see the return of the colonial powers, but they did not like what the Japanese were doing. Some turned against the Japanese. Others simply did nothing. Some nationalists tried to have it both ways. Indonesian patriots pretended to support Japan while actually sabotaging them.

✔ **READING PROGRESS CHECK**

Assessing As part of its New Order, how did Japan treat the peoples it conquered?

PHOTO: Keystone-France/Gamma-Keystone/Getty Images

LESSON 4 REVIEW (CCSS)

Reviewing Vocabulary

1. ***Expressing*** Explain how some collaborators helped make genocide possible.

Using Your Notes

2. ***Contrasting*** Use your notes to write a paragraph contrasting the New Order of Germany with the New Order of Japan.

Answering the Guiding Questions

3. ***Analyzing*** How did Germany establish a New Order in Europe?

4. ***Identifying Cause and Effect*** How did Adolf Hitler's views on race influence the New Order?

5. ***Summarizing*** What characterized the New Order in Japan?

Writing Activity

6. **INFORMATIVE/EXPLANATORY** Using a variety of sources, research and analyze the causes and consequences of the Holocaust. Be careful to use only reputable sources. Be sure to include information on the role of anti-Semitism.

netw⊙rks

There's More Online!

- ☑ **IMAGE** Bombing of Hiroshima
- ☑ **IMAGE** Invasion at Omaha Beach
- ☑ **IMAGE** Prison Camp Liberation
- ☑ **INTERACTIVE SELF-CHECK QUIZ**
- ☑ **MAP** World War II in Asia and the Pacific, 1943–1945
- ☑ **PRIMARY SOURCE** Churchill's Iron Curtain Speech
- ☑ **TIME LINE** The Final Months of World War II
- ☑ **VIDEO** World War II Ends

Reading **HELP**DESK **CCSS**

Academic Vocabulary
- **ideological** • **assure**

Content Vocabulary
- **partisan** • **Cold War**

TAKING NOTES:
Key Ideas and Details

Listing As you read, use a table like the one below to list three of the major military events that brought an end to World War II and where they took place.

Event	Location

LESSON 5
World War II Ends

ESSENTIAL QUESTIONS • *Why do political actions often lead to war?*
• *How does war impact society and the environment?*

IT MATTERS BECAUSE

By 1943, the Allies had strengthened their strategies and stopped the advances of both the Germans and the Japanese. Germany surrendered on May 7, 1945, and Japan surrendered on August 14. When the war ended, political tensions, suspicions, and conflicts of ideas led to a new struggle—the Cold War.

Last Years of the War

GUIDING QUESTION *How did the tide of battle turn against Germany, Italy, and Japan?*

By the beginning of 1943, the tide of battle had turned against Germany, Italy, and Japan. Axis forces in Tunisia surrendered on May 13, 1943. The Allies then crossed the Mediterranean and carried the war to Italy, an area that Winston Churchill, prime minister of Great Britain, called the "soft underbelly" of Europe. After taking Sicily, the Allies began an invasion of mainland Italy in September.

The European Theater

After Sicily fell, King Victor Emmanuel III of Italy arrested Mussolini, but in a daring raid the Germans liberated him. He was then made the head of a German puppet state in northern Italy as German troops moved in and occupied much of Italy.

The Germans set up defense lines in the hills south of Rome. The Allies advanced up the peninsula with heavy casualties, but they took Rome on June 4, 1944. By then, the Italian war was secondary as the Allied forces opened their long-awaited "second front" in western Europe.

Since the autumn of 1943, the Allies had planned an invasion of France from Great Britain, across the English Channel. Finally, on June 6, 1944 (D-Day), Allied forces under U.S. general Dwight D. Eisenhower landed on the Normandy beaches in history's greatest naval invasion. The Allies fought their way past hidden underwater mines, treacherous barbed wire, and horrible machine

gun fire. Believing the battle was a diversion and the real invasion would occur elsewhere, the Germans responded slowly. This gave the Allied forces time to set up a beachhead. Within three months, the Allies had landed 2 million men and 500,000 vehicles. Allied forces then began pushing inland and broke through German defensive lines.

Allied troops liberated Paris by the end of August 1944. In December, with Allied aircraft grounded, the Germans launched a counteroffensive to regain the seaport of Antwerp in Belgium. The Battle of the Bulge was named for the "bulge" the German attack caused in Allied lines. By January 1945, both sides had suffered heavy losses, but the Allied lines held. In March 1945, the Allied forces crossed the Rhine River and advanced into Germany. At the end of April 1945, Allied armies in northern Germany moved toward the Elbe River, where they linked up with the Soviets.

The Soviets had come a long way since the Battle of Stalingrad in 1943. The Soviets had soundly defeated the German forces at the Battle of Kursk (July 5 to 12), the greatest tank battle of World War II. Soviet forces now began a steady advance westward. Reoccupying the Ukraine by the end of 1943, they moved into the Baltic states by early 1944. Advancing along a northern front, Soviet troops occupied Warsaw in January 1945 and entered Berlin in April. Meanwhile, Soviet troops along a southern front swept through Hungary, Romania, and Bulgaria.

As the Allied forces advanced into Nazi-occupied Europe, they also liberated the concentration camps and death camps. Although the Nazis tried to destroy some of the evidence, the Allies were able to see for themselves the crimes against humanity carried out by the Nazis.

By January 1945, Adolf Hitler had moved into a bunker 55 feet (almost 17 m) under the city of Berlin. In his final political testament, Hitler, consistent to the end in his anti-Semitism, blamed the Jews for the war. He wrote:

PRIMARY SOURCE

❝Above all I charge the leaders of the nation and those under them to scrupulous observance of the laws of race and to merciless opposition to the universal poisoner of all peoples, international Jewry.❞

—from Hitler's Final Will and Testament, April 29, 1945

▲ On D-Day, June 6, 1944, Allied troops departed landing craft and moved inland. This map of Omaha Beach was created on April 21, 1944, in preparation for the Normandy invasion.

▶ CRITICAL THINKING
Determining Cause and Effect Why is the Normandy invasion considered a turning point in the war?

partisan a resistance fighter in World War II

Hitler committed suicide on April 30, two days after Italian **partisans**, or resistance fighters, shot Mussolini. On May 7, 1945, Germany surrendered. The war in Europe was finally over.

The Asian Theater

The war in Asia continued. Beginning in 1943, U.S. forces went on the offensive and advanced across the Pacific. Along with their allies, the U.S. forces continued their island-hopping campaign. At the beginning of 1945, the acquisition of Iwo Jima and Okinawa helped the Allied military power draw even closer to the main Japanese islands. The islands of Iwo Jima and Okinawa were of great strategic importance. Iwo Jima was essential to the air war on Japan. This small volcanic island had two airfields used by the Japanese to attack Allied aircraft and to support their naval forces. The Allies felt capturing Iwo Jima would lessen the Japanese threat and could aid in the invasion of the Japanese mainland. The Allies hoped that controlling Okinawa would also provide them with a base near the mainland.

The Allies were victorious in both battles, but the victories came at a great cost. Casualties were great on both sides, and many began to fear even more losses if the war in the Pacific continued. This left Harry S. Truman, who had become president after Roosevelt died in April, with a difficult decision to make. Scientists, including Enrico Fermi, worked on a top secret project called the Manhattan Project. Their efforts led to the development of the atomic bomb. Should he use newly developed atomic weapons to bring the war to an end? If the United States invaded Japan, Truman and his advisers were convinced that American troops would suffer heavy casualties. There were only two bombs; no one knew how effective they would be.

GEOGRAPHY CONNECTION

1. **THE WORLD IN SPATIAL TERMS** *From which islands did Allied air operations begin?*

2. **HUMAN SYSTEMS** *What strategy did Allied forces use to advance on Japan?*

World War II in Asia and the Pacific 1943–1945

▲ Of Hiroshima's 350,000 inhabitants, 190,000 died—some immediately and others after suffering the effects of radiation.

▶ CRITICAL THINKING
Determining Cause and Effect What effects did the bombings of Hiroshima and Nagasaki have on Japan?

Cold War the period of political tension following World War II and ending with the fall of Communism in the Soviet Union at the end of the 1980s

ideological based on a set of beliefs

assure to make certain of something; to guarantee

Truman decided to use the bombs. The first bomb was dropped on the Japanese city of Hiroshima on August 6. Of the city's 350,000 inhabitants, 190,000 died—some immediately and others after suffering the effects of radiation. Three days later, a second bomb was dropped on Nagasaki. Both cities were leveled. Thousands of people died immediately after the bombs were dropped. Thousands more died in later months from radiation. The devastation led Emperor Hirohito to accept the Allied forces' demands for unconditional surrender on August 14, 1945.

World War II was finally over. Seventeen million had died in battle. Perhaps 20 million civilians had perished as well. Some estimates place total losses at 60 million.

The dropping of the atomic bombs in Japan also marked the beginning of the Nuclear Age. After the world had witnessed the deadly potential of nuclear energy, other countries raced to build their own nuclear weapons. In August 1949, the Soviet Union set off its first atomic bomb, starting an arms race with the United States that lasted for 40 years.

☑ **READING PROGRESS CHECK**

Identifying What was the strategic importance of the "second front" that the Allies opened in western Europe?

Peace and a New War

GUIDING QUESTION *What led to the Cold War?*

No real peace but a period of political tensions, known as the **Cold War,** followed the total victory of the Allies in World War II. An **ideological** conflict between the United States and the Soviet Union, the Cold War dominated world affairs until the end of the 1980s.

Stalin, Roosevelt, and Churchill were the leaders of the Big Three (the Soviet Union, the United States, and Great Britain) of the Grand Alliance. They met at Tehran in November 1943 to discuss strategy. Their major tactical decision had concerned the final assault on Germany—an American-British invasion through France scheduled for the spring of 1944.

The acceptance of this plan had important consequences. It meant that Soviet and British-American forces would meet in defeated Germany along a north-south dividing line. Most likely, Soviet forces would liberate Eastern Europe. The Allies also agreed to a partition of postwar Germany.

The Big Three powers met again at Yalta in southern Russia in February 1945. By then, the defeat of Germany was **assured.** The Western powers, having once believed that the Soviets were in a weak position, now faced the reality of 11 million Soviet soldiers taking possession of Eastern Europe and much of central Europe.

Stalin was deeply suspicious of the Western powers. He wanted a buffer to protect the Soviet Union from possible future Western aggression. This meant establishing pro-Soviet governments along the Soviet Union's borders. Roosevelt favored the idea of self-determination for Europe. This involved a pledge to help liberated Europe create "democratic institutions of their own choice" through free elections. Roosevelt also agreed to Stalin's price for military aid against Japan: Sakhalin and the Kuril Islands, ruled by Japan, as well as two warm-water ports and railroad rights in Manchuria.

The creation of the United Nations was a major American concern. Both Churchill and Stalin accepted Roosevelt's plans for the establishment of the United Nations and set the first meeting for San Francisco in April 1945.

The issues of Germany and Eastern Europe were treated less decisively. After Germany surrendered, the Big Three agreed to divide Germany into four zones, one each for the United States, Great Britain, France, and the Soviet Union to occupy and to govern. Stalin compromised and agreed to free elections in Poland. However, it was clear that Stalin might not honor this provision for other Eastern European countries. The issue of free elections caused a serious split between the Soviets and Americans. This split became more evident when the Big Three next met at Potsdam, Germany.

The Potsdam Conference of July 1945 began in a cloud of mistrust. President Harry S. Truman, having succeeded Roosevelt, demanded free elections in Eastern Europe. Stalin responded, "A freely elected government in any of these East European countries would be anti-Soviet, and that we cannot allow." Stalin sought absolute security for the Soviets. Free elections would threaten his goal of controlling Eastern Europe. Short of an invasion by Western forces, nothing would undo developments in Eastern Europe. After the war's most destructive conflict had just ended, very few supported a policy of invasion.

The Allies agreed that trials should be held of leaders who had committed crimes against humanity during the war. In 1945 and 1946, Nazi leaders were tried and condemned at war crimes trials in Nuremberg, Germany. War crimes trials were also held in Japan and Italy.

As the war slowly receded into the past, a new struggle was already beginning. Many in the West thought Soviet policy was part of a worldwide Communist conspiracy. The Soviets viewed Western, and especially American, policy as nothing less than global capitalist expansionism.

In March 1946, in a speech to an American audience, the former British prime minister Winston Churchill declared that "an iron curtain" had "descended across the continent," dividing Europe into two hostile camps. Stalin branded Churchill's speech "a call to war on the USSR." Only months after the world's most devastating conflict had ended, the world seemed to be bitterly divided once again.

▲ Austrian SS chief Ernst Kaltenbrunner addresses the court during his trial for war crimes at Nuremberg.

▶ **CRITICAL THINKING**
Analyzing Why is it important that war crimes trials were held?

✓ **READING PROGRESS CHECK**

Identifying Central Issues What was the major disagreement between the United States and the Soviet Union at the conclusion of World War II?

LESSON 5 REVIEW

Reviewing Vocabulary
1. *Defining* Write a paragraph in which you answer the question: *What was the central ideological conflict of the Cold War?* Be sure to define the terms *ideological* and *Cold War* in your discussion.

Using Your Notes
2. *Identifying* Use your notes to identify three of the major military events that brought an end to World War II and where they took place. Briefly explain the significance of each event.

Answering the Guiding Questions
3. *Analyzing* How did the tide of battle turn against Germany, Italy, and Japan?

4. *Explaining* What led to the Cold War?

Writing Activity
5. **ARGUMENT** Imagine that you are an adviser to President Truman. You must persuade him to use or not to use the atomic bomb against Japan. Which position do you take? How do you make your case?

Directions: On a separate sheet of paper, answer the questions below. Make sure you read carefully and answer all parts of the questions.

Lesson Review

Lesson 1

1 **EXPLAINING** What was Hitler's master plan for creating an Aryan racial empire?

2 **SPECULATING** Why did world powers try to appease or ignore Germany's and Japan's expansionist policies at first?

Lesson 2

3 **MAKING INFERENCES** What new tactic did Hitler use to conquer much of Europe early in the war?

4 **SUMMARIZING** How and where did the Allies turn the tide in the Asian theater of operations?

Lesson 3

5 **SPECIFYING** What effects did war have on civilians in the Soviet Union, the United States, Germany, and Japan?

6 **IDENTIFYING CENTRAL ISSUES** What was the goal of bombing cities and was it successful?

Lesson 4

7 **CATEGORIZING** What methods did the Nazis use in their genocide?

8 **EVALUATING PERSPECTIVES** How did the slogan "Asia for the Asiatics" differ from the reality?

Lesson 5

9 **HYPOTHESIZING** Could the Allies have beaten Germany without a "second front" in Europe?

10 **INTERPRETING** What political tensions, suspicions, and conflict of ideologies led to the Cold War?

21st Century Skills

11 **ECONOMICS** What resources was Japan looking for when it attacked Southeast Asia? What dilemma did Japan face?

12 **UNDERSTANDING RELATIONSHIPS AMONG EVENTS** Define and describe the effects of the Nazis' Final Solution.

Exploring the Essential Questions

13 **SYNTHESIZING** Working with a small group, find a map of the world showing borders before and after World War II. Mark four borders that changed because of the war, and write labels explaining how political decisions contributed to those changes.

DBQ Analyzing Historical Documents

Use the document to answer the following questions.

After the United States dropped the first atomic bomb, the White House released a statement announcing the bombing of Hiroshima.

PRIMARY SOURCE

❝ Sixteen hours ago an American airplane dropped one bomb on Hiroshima and destroyed its usefulness to the enemy. That bomb had more power than 20,000 tons of TNT. It had more than two thousand times the blast power of the British 'Grand Slam' which is the largest bomb ever yet used in the history of warfare.

The Japanese began the war from the air at Pearl Harbor. They have been repaid many fold. And the end is not yet. ❞

—from a White House press release, August 6, 1945

14 **ANALYZING** How does Truman refer to Japan? How does the use of the term support his claim and America's actions?

15 **EVALUATING** Based on what you learned in Lesson 5, is the press release from the White House accurate?

Extended-Response Question

16 **ARGUMENT** Write a paragraph comparing and contrasting Germany's and Japan's goals when they expanded. How did their treatment of people in occupied regions differ?

Need Extra Help?

If You've Missed Question	1	2	3	4	5	6	7	8	9	10	11	12	13	14	15	16
Go to page	340	341	345	349	350	353	356	358	359	362	348	356	362	364	364	341

The Cold War

1945–1989

ESSENTIAL QUESTION
How does conflict influence political relationships?

networks

There's More Online! about the Cold War.

CHAPTER 18

Lesson 1
The Cold War Begins

Lesson 2
China After World War II

Lesson 3
Cold War Conflicts

The Story Matters ...

In 1957 when the Soviets launched the first satellite into space, both the USSR and the United States possessed nuclear missiles. By the time Vice President Richard Nixon visited the Soviet Union in 1959, relations between the two countries were already extremely tense. During Nixon's trip, he and Soviet Premier Nikita Khrushchev participated in a heated debate about capitalism and communism. Their argument illustrates the nature of the growing rivalry between the two nations.

◀ During an impromptu "kitchen debate," Soviet Premier Nikita Khrushchev and U.S. Vice President Richard Nixon argued about politics at the American National Exhibit in Moscow, 1959. They are pictured here, quarrelling in the kitchen of a model suburban American home.

PHOTO: Howard Sochurek/Time & Life Pictures/Getty Images

Place and Time: U.S. and USSR 1945–1975

The United States and the Soviet Union were allies during World War II, but enemies after 1945 until 1989, a period known as the Cold War. The world came to be divided into United States-aligned, Soviet Union-aligned, and non-aligned camps. While the United States and the Soviet Union avoided direct military confrontation, they intervened in proxy wars and influenced foreign policy in other nations. Especially in the early years of the Cold War, both sides saw the struggle between them as one between communism and capitalism.

Step Into the Place

Read the quotes and look at the information presented on the map.

 Analyzing Historical Documents How did Soviet and American views of the spread of the Soviet system differ?

PRIMARY SOURCE

❝When we say that the socialist system will win in the competition between the two systems—the capitalist and the socialist—this by no means signifies that its victory will be achieved through armed interference by the socialist countries in the internal affairs of the capitalist countries. Our certainty of the victory of communism is based on the fact that the socialist mode of production possesses decisive advantages over the capitalist mode of production. Precisely because of this, the ideas of Marxism-Leninism are more and more capturing the minds of the broad masses of the working people in the capitalist countries, just as they have captured the minds of millions of men and women in our country and the People's Democracies.❞

—Premier Nikita Khrushchev, from the Report to the Twentieth Party Congress, February, 1956

PRIMARY SOURCE

❝International Communism, of course, seeks to mask its purposes of domination by expressions of good will and by superficially attractive offers of political, economic and military aid. But any free nation, which is the subject of Soviet enticement, ought, in elementary wisdom, to look behind the mask.
Remember Estonia, Latvia and Lithuania! . . .

Soviet control of the satellite nations of Eastern Europe has been forcibly maintained in spite of solemn promises of a contrary intent, made during World War II. . . .❞

—President Dwight D. Eisenhower, Special Message to the Congress on the Situation in the Middle East, January 5, 1957

PHOTO: (l)Library of Congress, (r)©Bettmann/CORBIS.

Step Into the Time

Making Connections Choose an event from the time line and explain how it shows an important development in the Cold War.

THE USSR & THE U.S.

THE WORLD

1945 | **1955**

1945 World War II ends

1947 U.S. president Truman establishes Truman Doctrine

1949 NATO forms

1955 Warsaw Pact forms

September 1949 Mao Zedong takes control of China

June 1950 Korean War begins

July 1954 Geneva Accords divide Vietnam

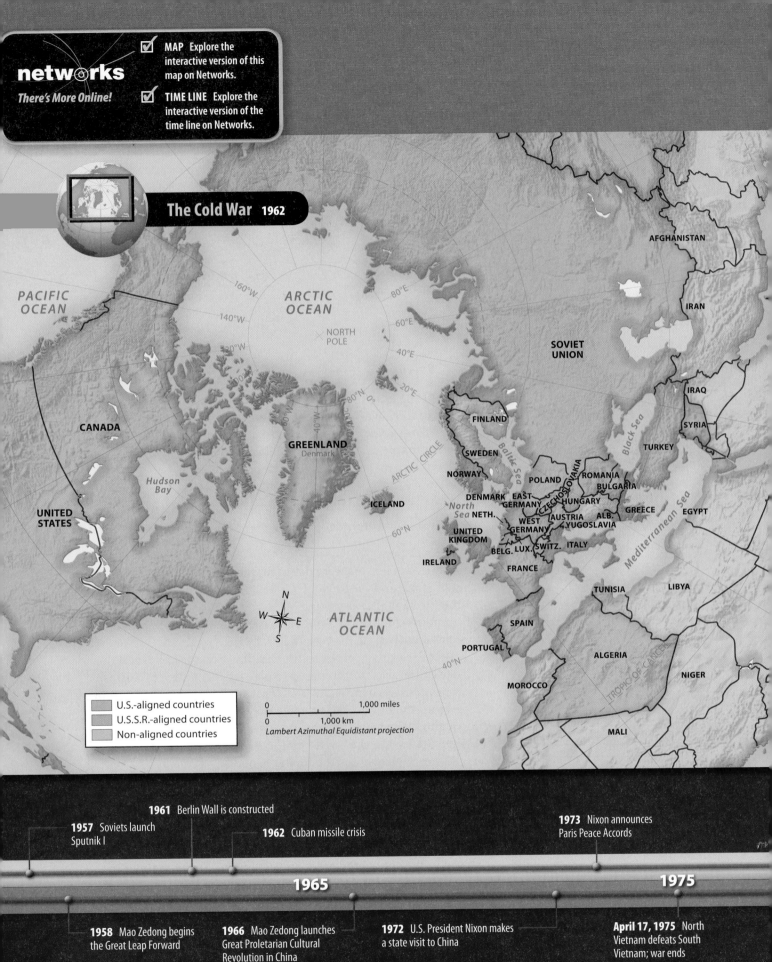

networks
There's More Online!

☑ **MAP** Explore the interactive version of this map on Networks.

☑ **TIME LINE** Explore the interactive version of the time line on Networks.

The Cold War 1962

AFGHANISTAN

IRAN

PACIFIC
OCEAN

160°W

ARCTIC
OCEAN

140°W

80°E

60°E

NORTH
POLE

120°W

40°E

20°E

SOVIET
UNION

IRAQ

100°W

80°N

0°

FINLAND

Black Sea

SYRIA

CANADA

GREENLAND
Denmark

60°W

40°W

20°E

SWEDEN

Baltic Sea

TURKEY

ARCTIC CIRCLE

NORWAY

POLAND

ROMANIA

Hudson
Bay

ICELAND

DENMARK

EAST
GERMANY

CZECHOSLOVAKIA

HUNGARY

BULGARIA

GREECE

Mediterranean Sea

EGYPT

North
Sea

NETH.

UNITED
STATES

60°N

UNITED
KINGDOM

WEST
GERMANY

AUSTRIA

ALB.

YUGOSLAVIA

BELG. LUX. SWITZ. ITALY

IRELAND

FRANCE

TUNISIA

LIBYA

N

W   E

S

ATLANTIC
OCEAN

SPAIN

PORTUGAL

ALGERIA

NIGER

40°N

TROPIC OF CANCER

MOROCCO

U.S.-aligned countries

U.S.S.R.-aligned countries

Non-aligned countries

0   1,000 miles

0   1,000 km

Lambert Azimuthal Equidistant projection

MALI

1961 Berlin Wall is constructed

1957 Soviets launch
Sputnik I

1962 Cuban missile crisis

1973 Nixon announces
Paris Peace Accords

1965

1975

1958 Mao Zedong begins
the Great Leap Forward

1966 Mao Zedong launches
Great Proletarian Cultural
Revolution in China

1972 U.S. President Nixon makes
a state visit to China

April 17, 1975 North
Vietnam defeats South
Vietnam; war ends

netw⊙rks
There's More Online!

- ☑ **BIOGRAPHY** Harry S. Truman
- ☑ **BIOGRAPHY** Nikita Khrushchev
- ☑ **CHART/GRAPH** Postwar Economic Plans
- ☑ **CHART/GRAPH** The Nuclear Arms Race
- ☑ **IMAGE** Building the Berlin Wall
- ☑ **IMAGE** Sputnik I
- ☑ **IMAGE** The Marshall Plan
- ☑ **INTERACTIVE SELF-CHECK QUIZ**
- ☑ **MAP** NATO and Warsaw Pact Members, 1949–1955
- ☑ **VIDEO** The Cold War Begins

Reading **HELP**DESK (CCSS)

Academic Vocabulary
- liberate   • nuclear

Content Vocabulary
- satellite state
- policy of containment
- arms race   • deterrence

TAKING NOTES:

Key Ideas and Details

Determining Cause and Effect As you read, create a chart like the one below listing U.S. actions and the Soviet response to them.

U.S. Action	Soviet Response

LESSON 1

The Cold War Begins

ESSENTIAL QUESTION
How does conflict influence political relationships?

IT MATTERS BECAUSE

At the end of World War II, a new conflict erupted in the Western world as the two new superpowers, the United States and the Soviet Union, competed for political domination of the world. Europeans were forced to become supporters of one side or the other.

Balance of Power After World War II

GUIDING QUESTION *Why did the United States and the Soviet Union become political rivals after World War II?*

After the Axis Powers were defeated, the differences between the United States and the Soviet Union came to the front. Stalin still feared the capitalist West, and Western leaders still had a great fear of communism. It should not surprise us that two such different systems would come into conflict.

Because of its need to feel secure on its western border, the Soviet Union was not prepared to give up its control of Eastern Europe after Germany's defeat. Nor were American leaders willing to give up the power and prestige the United States had gained throughout the world. Suspicious of each other's motives, the United States and the Soviet Union soon became rivals.

Eastern Europe was the first area of disagreement. The United States and Great Britain believed that the **liberated** nations of Eastern Europe should freely determine their own governments. Stalin, however, fearful that these nations would be anti-Soviet if they were permitted to have free elections, opposed the West's plans. Having freed Eastern Europe from the Nazis, the Soviet army stayed in the conquered areas and set up pro-Soviet regimes in Poland, Romania, Bulgaria, and Hungary.

A civil war in Greece created another area of conflict between the superpowers. The Communist People's Liberation Army and anti-communist forces supported by Great Britain fought for control of reece in 1946. However, Britain had its own economic problems, which caused it to withdraw its aid from Greece.

PHOTO: (l to r)Edward Miller/Keystone/Getty Images, NASA, ©Bettmann/CORBIS, Robert Lackenbach/Time & Life Pictures/Getty Images

The Truman Doctrine and the Marshall Plan

President Harry S. Truman of the United States, alarmed by British weakness and the possibility of Soviet expansion into the eastern Mediterranean, responded with the Truman Doctrine. This doctrine, created in 1947, said that the United States would provide money to countries (in this case, Greece and Turkey) that were threatened by communist expansion. If the Soviet Union was not stopped in Greece and Turkey, the Truman argument ran, then the United States would have to face the spread of communism throughout the free world. As Dean Acheson, U.S. undersecretary of state, explained on February 29, 1947:

liberate to free

PRIMARY SOURCE

❝Like apples in a barrel infected by one rotten one, the corruption of Greece would infect Iran and all to the east. It would also carry infection to Africa through Asia Minor and Egypt, and to Europe . . .❞

— from *Present at the Creation: My Years in the State Department*

satellite state a country that is economically and politically dependent on another country

The Truman Doctrine was soon followed by the European Recovery Program. Proposed in June 1947 by General George C. Marshall, U.S. secretary of state, it is better known as the Marshall Plan. Marshall believed that communism was only successful in countries that had economic problems. Thus, to prevent the spread of communism, the Marshall Plan provided close to $13 billion to rebuild war-torn Europe.

The Marshall Plan did not intend to exclude the Soviet Union or its economically and politically dependent Eastern European **satellite states**. Those states refused to participate, however. According to the Soviet view, the Marshall Plan guaranteed "American loans in return for the relinquishing by the European states of their economic and later also their political independence." The Soviets saw the Marshall Plan as an attempt to buy the support of the smaller European countries.

In 1949 the Soviet Union responded to the Marshall Plan by founding the Council for Mutual Economic Assistance (COMECON) for the economic cooperation of the Eastern European states. COMECON largely failed, however, because the Soviet Union was unable to provide much financial aid.

By 1947, the split in Europe between the United States and the Soviet Union had become a fact of life. In July 1947, George Kennan, a well-known U.S. diplomat with much knowledge of Soviet affairs, argued for a **policy of containment** to keep communism within its existing boundaries and to prevent further Soviet aggressive moves. Containment of the Soviet Union became formal U.S. policy.

▲ Goods sent as part of the Marshall Plan arrive at Royal Victoria Dock in London, England, on February 3, 1949.

▶ CRITICAL THINKING
Analyzing What was the goal of the Marshall Plan?

The Division of Germany and the Berlin Airlift

The fate of Germany also became a source of heated contention between the Soviets and the West. At the end of World War II, the Allied Powers had divided Germany into four zones, each occupied by one of the Allies—the United States, the Soviet Union, Great Britain, and France. The city of Berlin, located deep inside the Soviet zone, was also divided into four zones.

policy of containment a plan to keep something, such as communism, within its existing geographical boundaries and prevent further aggressive moves

PHOTO: Edward Miller/Keystone/Getty Images

The foreign ministers of the four occupying powers met repeatedly in an attempt to arrive at a final peace treaty with Germany but had little success. At the same time, Great Britain, France, and the United States gradually began to merge their zones economically. By February 1948, Great Britain, France, and the United States were making plans to unify the three Western sections of Germany (and Berlin) and create a West German government.

The Soviets reacted with a blockade of West Berlin, which allowed neither trucks, nor trains, nor barges to enter the city's three Western zones. Food and supplies could no longer get through to the 2.5 million people in these zones. The Russians hoped to secure economic control of all Berlin and force the Western powers to halt the creation of a separate West German state.

The Western powers faced a dilemma. No one wanted to risk World War III. Therefore, an attempt to break through the Soviet blockade with tanks and trucks was ruled out. However, how could the people in the Western zones of Berlin be kept alive when the whole city was blockaded inside the Soviet zone? The solution was the Berlin Airlift—supplies would be flown in by American and British airplanes. For more than 10 months, more than 200,000 flights carried 2.3 million tons (1.4 million t) of supplies. At the height of the Berlin Airlift, 13,000 tons (11,800 t) of supplies were flown daily to Berlin. The Soviets, also not wanting war, finally gave in and lifted the blockade in May 1949.

The blockade of Berlin increased tensions between the United States and the Soviet Union. It also brought the separation of Germany into two states. In September 1949, the Federal Republic of Germany, or West Germany, was formally created. Its capital was Bonn. Less than a month later, a separate East German state, the German Democratic Republic, was set up by the Soviets. East Berlin became its capital. Berlin was now divided into two parts, a reminder of the division between West and East.

✅ **READING PROGRESS CHECK**

Comparing What did the Marshall Plan and COMECON have in common?

The Spread of the Cold War

GUIDING QUESTION *What was the result of increased tensions between the superpowers?*

In 1949 the Cold War spread from Europe to the rest of the world. The victory of the Chinese Communists in the Chinese civil war created a new Communist regime and strengthened fears in the United States about the spread of communism.

▼ German children cheer an American cargo plan airlifting supplies to Berlin in 1948.

▶ **CRITICAL THINKING**
Sequencing What were the effects of the Berlin airlift?

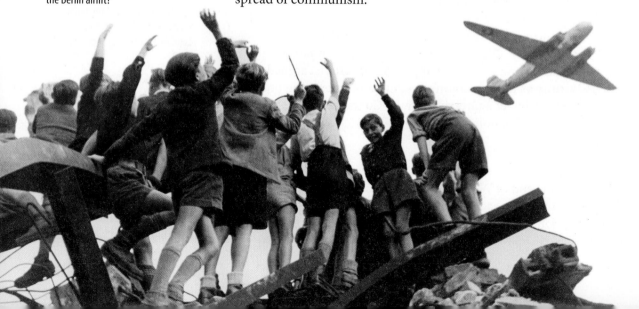

NATO and Warsaw Pact Members 1949–1955

- North Atlantic Treaty Organization (NATO) member nations, 1949
- Nations joining NATO as of 1955
- Warsaw Pact members as of 1955

New Military Alliances

The search for security during the Cold War led to the formation of new military alliances. The North Atlantic Treaty Organization (NATO) was formed in April 1949 when Belgium, Luxembourg, France, the Netherlands, Great Britain, Italy, Denmark, Norway, Portugal, and Iceland signed a treaty with the United States and Canada. These powers agreed to provide mutual help if any one of them was attacked. A few years later, Greece and Turkey joined, followed by West Germany.

The Eastern European states soon followed suit with a military alliance. In 1955 the Soviet Union joined with Albania, Bulgaria, Czechoslovakia, East Germany, Hungary, Poland, and Romania in a formal military alliance known as the Warsaw Pact. Europe was once again divided into hostile alliance systems, just as it had been before World War I.

New military alliances spread to the rest of the world after the United States became involved in the Korean War. The war began in 1950 as an attempt by the Communist government of North Korea, which was allied with the Soviet Union, to take over South Korea. The Korean War confirmed American fears of communist expansion. More determined than ever to contain Soviet power, the United States extended its military alliances around the world. By the mid-1950s, the United States was in military alliances with 42 states around the world.

The Arms Race Begins

By the mid-1950s, the United States and the Soviet Union had become involved in a growing **arms race**, in which both countries built up their armies and increased the size of their weapons arsenals. **Nuclear** weapons added an increasingly frightening element to the arms race as each super-power raced to build deadlier bombs and farther-reaching delivery systems.

GEOGRAPHY CONNECTION

1 THE WORLD IN SPATIAL TERMS *How could geographic factors have determined which alliance a country joined?*

2 PLACES AND REGIONS *Create a chart listing all the NATO and Warsaw Pact countries as of 1955.*

arms race building up armies and stores of weapons to keep up with an enemy

nuclear being a weapon whose destructive power comes from a nuclear reaction

The Cold War **371**

Also by the mid-1950s, the United States feared that the Soviet Union was gaining ground in the arms race. The Soviet Union had set off its first atomic bomb in 1949. In the early 1950s, the Soviet Union and the United States developed the deadlier hydrogen bomb. By the late-1950s, both had intercontinental ballistic missiles (ICBMs), which made them capable of sending bombs anywhere.

The United States and the Soviet Union now worked to build up stockpiles of nuclear weapons. The search for security soon took the form of **deterrence**. This policy held that huge arsenals of nuclear weapons on both sides prevented war. The belief was that neither side would launch a nuclear attack, because both knew that the other side would be able to strike back with devastating power.

In 1957 the Soviets sent *Sputnik I*, the first human-made space satellite, to orbit Earth. New fears seized the American public. Was there a "missile gap" between the United States and the Soviet Union? Could the Soviet Union build a military base in outer space from which it could dominate the world? One American senator said, "It was time... for Americans to be prepared to shed blood, sweat and tears if this country and the free world are to survive."

A Wall in Berlin

Nikita Khrushchev (kroosh • CHAWF), who emerged as the new leader of the Soviet Union in 1955, tried to take advantage of the American concern over missiles to solve the problem of West Berlin. West Berlin remained a "Western island" of prosperity in the midst of the relatively poverty-stricken East Germany. Many East Germans, tired of Communist repression, managed to escape East Germany by fleeing through West Berlin.

Khrushchev realized the need to stop the flow of refugees from East Germany through West Berlin. In August 1961, the East German government began to build a wall separating West Berlin from East Berlin. Eventually it became a massive concrete block wall 15 feet (4.5 m) high topped with barbed wire. Hundreds of machine-gun watchtowers lined the wall, which stretched 28 miles (45km) through the city. Another 75-mile- (120.7 km) long section of wall separated West Berlin from the surrounding East German countryside. The Berlin Wall became a striking symbol of the division between the two superpowers.

✓ **READING PROGRESS CHECK**

Making Connections How were the theory of deterrence and the arms race related?

▲ The Soviet Union launched *Sputnik I,* the first artificial satellite, on October 4, 1957.

▶ **CRITICAL THINKING**
Explaining What was the significance of the *Sputnik I* launch?

deterrence during the Cold War, the U.S. and Soviet policies of holding huge arsenals of nuclear weapons to prevent war; each nation believed that neither would launch a nuclear attack since both knew that the other side could strike back with devastating power

---

LESSON 1 REVIEW

Reviewing Vocabulary
1. *Applying* Explain how the United States and the Soviet Union used nuclear weapons as a form of deterrence.

Using Your Notes
2. *Identifying* Use your notes to write a paragraph explaining how the Soviets responded to U.S. actions.

Answering the Guiding Questions
3. *Analyzing* Why did the United States and the Soviet Union become political rivals after World War II?

4. *Drawing Conclusions* What was the result of increased tensions between the superpowers?

Writing Activity
5. **ARGUMENT** Write an essay arguing whether using nuclear weapons as a form of deterrence was an effective strategy for preventing conflict between the West and the Soviet Union.

networks

There's More Online!

- ☑ **CHART/GRAPH** Grain Production in China, 1950–1970
- ☑ **IMAGE** Cultural Revolution Propaganda
- ☑ **IMAGE** The Little Red Book
- ☑ **IMAGE** The Red Guard
- ☑ **INTERACTIVE SELF-CHECK QUIZ**
- ☑ **MAP** China Since 1945
- ☑ **PRIMARY SOURCE** Life During China's Cultural Revolution
- ☑ **PRIMARY SOURCE** The Little Red Book
- ☑ **VIDEO** China After World War II

Reading **HELP**DESK (CCSS)

Academic Vocabulary
- **final**
- **source**

Content Vocabulary
- **commune**
- **permanent revolution**

TAKING NOTES:

Key Ideas and Details

Categorizing As you read, use a chart like the one below to list communism's effects on China's international affairs.

Communism →

LESSON 2
China After World War II

ESSENTIAL QUESTION
How does conflict influence political relationships?

IT MATTERS BECAUSE

In 1949 Chiang Kai-shek finally lost control of China, and the Communist Mao Zedong announced the formation of the People's Republic of China. Mao's victory strengthened U.S. fears about the spread of communism. To build his socialist society in China, Mao Zedong launched the Great Leap Forward and the Great Proletarian Cultural Revolution. Neither program was especially successful at achieving its goals.

Civil War in China

GUIDING QUESTIONS *How did Mao use economic policies to try and establish a classless society? Why did Mao believe permanent revolution was necessary?*

At the end of World War II, two Chinese governments existed side by side. The Nationalist government of Chiang Kai-shek, based in southern and central China, was supported by the United States. The Communists, led by Mao Zedong, had built a strong base in northern China. By the end of World War II, 20 to 30 million Chinese were living under Communist rule. The People's Liberation Army of the Communists included nearly 1 million troops.

When efforts to form a coalition government in 1946 failed, a full-scale civil war broke out between the Nationalists and the Communists. In the countryside, promises of land attracted millions of peasants to the Communist Party. Many joined Mao's People's Liberation Army. In the cities, middle-class Chinese, who were alienated by Chiang's repressive policies, supported the Communists. Chiang's troops began to defect to the Communists. Sometimes whole divisions—officers and ordinary soldiers—changed sides.

By 1948, the People's Liberation Army had surrounded Beijing. The following spring it crossed the Chang Jiang (Yangtze River) and occupied Shanghai. During the next few months, Chiang Kai-shek and 2 million followers fled to the island of Taiwan.

The Cold War **373**

On October 1, 1949, Mao Zedong mounted the rostrum of the Gate of Heavenly Peace in Beijing and made a victory statement to the thousands gathered in the square before him. "The Chinese people have stood up," he said, "nobody will insult us again."

The Great Leap Forward

The Communist Party, under the leadership of its chairman, Mao Zedong, now ruled China. In 1955 the Chinese government launched a new program to build a socialist society. Virtually all private farmland was collectivized. Peasant families were allowed to keep small plots for their private use, but they worked chiefly in large collective farms. In addition, most industry and commerce was nationalized.

Chinese leaders hoped that collective farms would increase food production, allowing more people to work in industry. Food production, however, did not grow. Meanwhile, China's vast population continued to expand. By 1957, China had approximately 657 million people living within its borders.

In 1958 Mao began a more radical program known as the Great Leap Forward. Under this program, more than 700,000 existing collective farms, normally the size of a village, were combined into 26,000 vast **communes**. Each commune contained more than 30,000 people who lived and worked together. Since they had communal child care, more than 500,000 Chinese mothers worked beside their husbands in the fields by mid-1958.

Mao Zedong hoped his Great Leap Forward program would mobilize the people for a massive effort to speed up economic growth and reach the **final** stage of communism—the classless society—before the end of the twentieth century. The Communist Party's official slogan promised the following to the Chinese people: "Hard work for a few years, happiness for a thousand."

Despite such slogans, the Great Leap Forward was an economic disaster. Bad weather, which resulted in droughts and floods, and the peasants' hatred of the new system, drove food production down. As a result, nearly 15 million people died of starvation. Many peasants were reportedly reduced to eating the bark off trees and, in some cases, to allowing infants to starve. In 1960 the government made some changes. It began to break up the communes and return to collective farms and some private plots.

The Cultural Revolution

Despite opposition within the Communist Party and the commune failure, Mao still dreamed of a classless society. In Mao's eyes, only **permanent revolution**, an atmosphere of constant revolutionary fervor, could enable the Chinese to overcome the past and achieve the final stage of communism.

In 1966 Mao launched the Great Proletarian Cultural Revolution. The Chinese name literally meant "great revolution to create a proletarian (working class) culture." A collection of Mao's thoughts, called the *Little Red Book*, became a sort of bible for the Chinese Communists. It was hailed as the most important **source** of knowledge in all areas. The book was in every hotel, in every school, and in factories, communes, and universities. Few people conversed without first referring to the *Little Red Book*.

commune in China during the 1950s, a group of collective farms, which contained more than 30,000 people who lived and worked together

final the last in a series, process, or progress

▼ A Chinese woman and child hold up Mao's *Little Red Book* during the Cultural Revolution.

▶ CRITICAL THINKING
Describing What one word would you use to describe the *Little Red Book* during the Cultural Revolution? Why?

PHOTO: Sally and Richard Greenhill/Alamy

To further the Cultural Revolution, the Red Guards were formed. These were revolutionary groups composed of unhappy party members and discontented young people. They were urged to take to the streets to cleanse Chinese society of impure elements guilty of taking the capitalist road. In June 1966, all schools and universities in China were closed for six months to prepare for a new system of education based on Mao's ideas. Mao had launched China on a new forced march toward communism.

The Red Guards set out across the nation to eliminate the "Four Olds"—old ideas, old culture, old customs, and old habits. The Red Guards destroyed temples, books written by foreigners, and foreign music. They tore down street signs and replaced them with ones carrying revolutionary names. The city of Shanghai even ordered that red (the revolutionary color) traffic lights would indicate that traffic could move, not stop.

Destruction of property was matched by vicious attacks on individuals who had supposedly deviated from Mao's thought. Those so accused were humiliated at public meetings, where they were forced to admit their "crimes." Many were brutally beaten, often fatally. Intellectuals and artists accused of being pro-Western were especially open to attack. Red Guards broke the fingers of one pianist for the "crime" of playing the works of Frederic Chopin, the nineteenth-century European composer. Nien Cheng, who worked for the British-owned Shell Oil Company in Shanghai, was imprisoned for seven years. She told of her experience in *Life and Death in Shanghai.*

From the start of its socialist revolution, the Communist Party had wanted to create a new kind of citizen, one who would give the utmost for the good of all China. In Mao's words, the people "should be resolute, fear no sacrifice, and surmount every difficulty to win victory."

During the 1950s and 1960s, the Chinese government made some basic changes. Women could now take part in politics and had equal marital rights—a dramatic shift. Mao feared that loyalty to the family would interfere with loyalty to the state. During the Cultural Revolution, for example, children were encouraged to report negative comments their parents made about the government.

Mao found during the Cultural Revolution, however, that it is not easy to maintain a permanent revolution, or constant mood of revolutionary enthusiasm. Key groups, including Communist Party members and many military officers, did not share Mao's desire for permanent revolution. Many people, disgusted by the actions of the Red Guards, began to turn against the movement. In September 1976, Mao Zedong died at the age of 82. A group of practical-minded reformers, led by Deng Xiaoping (DUHNG SHYOW • PIHNG), seized power and soon brought the Cultural Revolution to an end.

✅ **READING PROGRESS CHECK**

Drawing Conclusions Why did the Red Guards specifically target intellectuals and artists?

大力支援农业

▲ This poster urges the Chinese people to give energetic support to agriculture.

▶ **CRITICAL THINKING**
Making Inferences Why was agricultural reform particularly important to the Chinese Communists?

permanent revolution
an atmosphere of constant revolutionary fervor favored by Mao Zedong to enable China to overcome the past and achieve the final stage of communism

source a document or primary reference book that gives information

China and the Cold War

GUIDING QUESTION *How was China affected by the Cold War?*

In 1949 the Cold War spread from Europe to Asia when the Chinese Communists won the Chinese civil war and set up a new Communist regime. American fears about the spread of communism intensified, especially when the new Chinese Communist leaders made it clear that they supported "national wars of liberation"—or movements for revolution—in Africa, Asia, and Latin America. When Communist China signed a pact of friendship and cooperation with the Soviet Union in 1950, some Americans began to speak of a Communist desire for world domination. When war broke out in Korea, the Cold War had arrived in Asia.

China's involvement in the Korean War led to renewed Western fears of China. In turn, China became even more isolated from the major Western powers. The country was forced to rely almost entirely on the Soviet Union for technological and economic aid. Even that became more difficult as relations between China and the Soviet Union began to deteriorate in the late 1950s.

Several issues divided China and the Soviet Union. For one thing, the Chinese were not happy with the amount of economic aid provided by the Soviets. A more important issue, however, was their disagreement over the Cold War. The Chinese wanted the Soviets to go on the offensive to promote world revolution. Specifically, China wanted Soviet aid in retaking Taiwan from Chiang Kai-shek. The Soviets, however, were trying to improve relations with the West and refused.

In the 1960s, the dispute between China and the Soviet Union broke into the open. Military units on both sides of the frontier clashed on a number of occasions. Faced with internal problems and a serious security threat from the Soviets on its northern frontier, some Chinese leaders decided to improve relations with the United States. In 1972 President Richard Nixon made a state visit to China. The two sides agreed to improve relations. China's long isolation from the West was coming to an end.

The end of the Cultural Revolution also affected Chinese foreign policy. In the late 1970s, under Deng Xiaoping, China sought to improve relations with the Western states. Diplomatic ties were established with the United States in 1979. In the 1980s, Chinese relations with the Soviet Union also gradually improved. By the 1990s, China emerged as an independent power and began to play an increasingly active role in Asian affairs.

▲ During Nixon's visit to China, the United States and China competed in ping pong.

▶ **CRITICAL THINKING**
Evaluating What was the significance of Nixon's "ping pong diplomacy"?

☑ **READING PROGRESS CHECK**

Analyzing Why did Chinese-Soviet relations change after the Korean War?

PHOTO: Time Life Pictures/Getty Images

LESSON 2 REVIEW (CCSS)

Reviewing Vocabulary
1. *Making Connections* How did the Red Guard help sustain Mao's permanent revolution?

Using Your Notes
2. *Drawing Conclusions* Use your notes to describe how communism affected China's foreign policy.

Answering the Guiding Questions
3. *Summarizing* How did Mao use economic policies to try and establish a classless society?

4. *Identifying* Why did Mao believe permanent revolution was necessary?

5. *Analyzing* How was China affected by the Cold War?

Writing Activity
6. **NARRATIVE** Imagine you are a Chinese peasant who was sent to a commune during the Great Leap Forward. Write an essay describing how this event has affected your life.

networks

There's More Online!

☑ **IMAGE** 38th Parallel

☑ **IMAGE** Khrushchev and Castro

☑ **INTERACTIVE SELF-CHECK QUIZ**

☑ **MAP** Cuban Missile Crisis, October 1962

☑ **MAP** Korean War, 1950–1953

☑ **MAP** Vietnam War, 1968–1975

☑ **VIDEO** Cold War Conflicts

Reading **HELP**DESK ⓒⓒⓢⓢ

Academic Vocabulary

• temporary   • emerge

Content Vocabulary

• proxy war
• domino theory

TAKING NOTES:

Key Ideas and Details

Categorizing As you read, use a chart like the one below to list the different proxy wars fought by the United States and the Soviet Union.

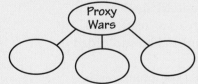

LESSON 3
Cold War Conflicts

ESSENTIAL QUESTION
How does conflict influence political relationships?

IT MATTERS BECAUSE

In the decades after World War II, the Cold War between the United States and the Soviet Union spread, creating military alliances and defining the postwar era. The competition between the superpowers also affected "hot" wars, especially in Korea and Vietnam.

The United States and the Soviet Union

GUIDING QUESTIONS *What common factor triggered the "hot" wars in Asia during the Cold War? How did nuclear weapons influence political relationships during the Cold War?*

World War II destroyed European supremacy in world affairs, and Europe did not recover from this. As the Cold War conflict between the world's two superpowers—the United States and the Soviet Union—grew stronger, the European nations were divided into two armed camps dependent upon one or the other of these two major powers. This division, however, also spread to the rest of the world. The United States and the Soviet Union, whose rivalry brought the world to the brink of nuclear war, seemed to hold the survival of the world in their hands.

Neither power, however, ever went to war directly with the other. Instead, the United States and the Soviet Union fought a series of proxy wars. A **proxy war** occurs when two powers in conflict use substitutes instead of fighting each other directly. Proxy wars were common during the Cold War. Armed with devastating nuclear arsenals, neither the United States nor the Soviet Union wanted to fight each other directly. However, both nations were willing to support opposing sides in local wars in the ongoing struggle between their two worldviews.

Each superpower used military and economic aid to win the support of other nations. In addition to NATO in Europe, the United States also built alliances in other parts of the world. To stem Communist aggression in the East, the United States, Great Britain, France, Pakistan, the Philippines, Australia, and New Zealand

proxy war a war in which the powers in conflict use third parties as substitutes instead of fighting each other directly

formed the Southeast Asia Treaty Organization (SEATO). The Central Treaty Organization (CENTO), which included Turkey, Iraq, Iran, Pakistan, Great Britain, and the United States, was meant to prevent Soviet expansion into the Middle East. The Soviet Union also created a series of alliances.

Two major conflicts of the Cold War were the wars that broke out in Korea and Vietnam. The Soviet Union and the United States each sent military support to prevent the other side from expanding its influence. In addition, a Cold War proxy conflict almost turned into a major nuclear war over the small island of Cuba.

☑ **READING PROGRESS CHECK**

Comparing What did NATO, SEATO, and CENTO have in common?

The Korean War

GUIDING QUESTION *What common factor triggered the "hot" wars in Asia during the Cold War?*

Japan controlled Korea until 1945. In August 1945, the Soviet Union and the United States agreed to divide Korea into two zones at the 38th parallel. The plan was to hold elections after World War II to reunify Korea.

As American-Soviet relations grew worse, however, two separate governments emerged in Korea—Communist in the north and anti-Communist in the south.

Tension between the two governments increased. With the apparent approval of Joseph Stalin, Communist North Korean troops invaded South Korea on June 25, 1950. President Harry S. Truman of the United States, seeing this as yet another example of Communist aggression and expansion, gained the approval of the United Nations (UN) and sent U.S. troops to repel the invaders. Several other countries sent troops as well. In October, UN forces—mostly American—marched across the 38th parallel with the aim of unifying Korea. Greatly alarmed, the Chinese sent hundreds of thousands of troops into North Korea and pushed UN forces back across the 38th parallel.

Three more years of fighting led to no final victory. An armistice was finally signed in 1953. The 38th parallel remained, and remains today, the boundary line between North Korea and South Korea. The division of Korea was reaffirmed. To many Americans, the policy of containing communism had succeeded in Asia, just as it had earlier in Europe.

▲ United Nations forces withdraw from P'yŏngyang, North Korea, recrossing the 38th parallel, the dividing line between North and South Korea.

The Korean War also confirmed American fears of communist expansion. The United States was now more determined than ever to contain Soviet power. In the mid-1950s, the administration of President Dwight D. Eisenhower adopted a policy of massive retaliation. Any Soviet advance, even a ground attack in Europe, would be met with the full use of American nuclear bombs. Moreover, it was after the Korean War that American military alliances were extended around the world. As President Eisenhower explained, "The freedom we cherish and defend in Europe and in the Americas is no different from the freedom that is imperiled in Asia."

☑ **READING PROGRESS CHECK**

Determining Cause and Effect What effects did the Korean War have on U.S. foreign policy in the mid-1950s?

The Cuban Missile Crisis

GUIDING QUESTION *How did nuclear weapons influence political relationships during the Cold War?*

During the administration of John F. Kennedy, the Cold War confrontation between the United States and the Soviet Union reached frightening levels. In 1959 a left-wing revolutionary named Fidel Castro overthrew the Cuban dictator Fulgencio Batista and set up a Soviet-supported totalitarian regime in Cuba. Having a socialist regime with Communist contacts so close to the mainland was considered to be a threat to the security of the United States.

President Kennedy feared that if he moved openly against Castro, then the Soviets might retaliate by moving against Berlin. As a result, the stage might be set for the two superpowers to engage in a nuclear war.

For months, Kennedy considered alternatives. He finally approved a plan that the CIA had proposed. Exiled Cuban fighters would invade Cuba at the Bay of Pigs. The purpose of the invasion was to cause a revolt against Castro. The invasion, which began on Sunday, April 16, 1961, was a disaster. By Wednesday, the exiled fighters began surrendering. One hundred and fourteen died; the rest were captured by Castro's troops.

After the Bay of Pigs, the Soviet Union sent advisers to Cuba. In 1962 Khrushchev began to place nuclear missiles in Cuba, which were meant to counteract U.S. nuclear weapons placed in Turkey. Khrushchev said: "Your rockets are stationed in Turkey. You are worried over Cuba . . . because it lies at a distance of 90 miles across the sea from the shores of the United States. However, Turkey lies next to us."

ANALYZING PRIMARY SOURCES (CCSS)

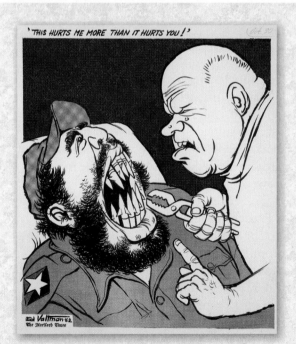

'THIS HURTS ME MORE THAN IT HURTS YOU!'

Ed Valtman '62
The Hartford Times

▲ This American political cartoon was published on October 30, 1962. Khrushchev is depicted as a dentist removing Castro's teeth, which appear as missiles.

The Cuban Missile Crisis

The Cuban missile crisis brought the United States and the Soviet Union to the brink of nuclear war. It was, perhaps, the most frightening moment of the Cold War. These sources focus on Khrushchev's agreement to remove Soviet missiles from Cuba.

❝I appreciate your assurance that the United States will not invade Cuba. Hence, we have ordered our officers to stop building bases, dismantle the equipment, and send it back home.

We must not allow the situation to deteriorate, (but) eliminate hotbeds of tension, and we must see to it that no other conflicts occur which might lead to a world nuclear war.❞

—Letter from Nikita Khrushchev to President John F. Kennedy, October 28, 1962

DBQ Analyzing Historical Documents

❶ *Analyzing Primary Sources* What does the letter to President Kennedy suggest about Khrushchev's reaction to the crisis?

❷ *Drawing Conclusions* Look at the caption of the cartoon on the left. What point is the cartoonist making about the Cuban missile crisis?

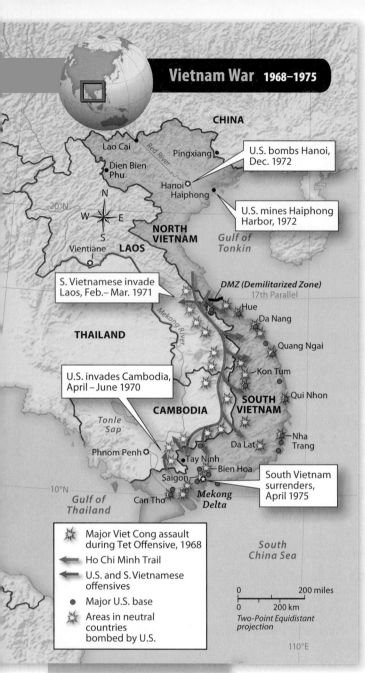

Vietnam War 1968–1975

CHINA

Lao Cai

Pingxiang

Dien Bien Phu

U.S. bombs Hanoi, Dec. 1972

Hanoi ⊕
Haiphong

20°N

N
W E
S

U.S. mines Haiphong Harbor, 1972

NORTH VIETNAM

Vientiane **LAOS**

Gulf of Tonkin

S. Vietnamese invade Laos, Feb.– Mar. 1971

DMZ (Demilitarized Zone)
17th Parallel

Hue

Da Nang

THAILAND

Quang Ngai

U.S. invades Cambodia, April – June 1970

Kon Tum

Qui Nhon

SOUTH VIETNAM

CAMBODIA

Tonle Sap

Phnom Penh ⊕

Da Lat

Nha Trang

South Vietnam surrenders, April 1975

Tay Ninh

Bien Hoa

Saigon ⊕

10°N

Gulf of Thailand

Can Tho

Mekong Delta

South China Sea

✸ Major Viet Cong assault during Tet Offensive, 1968

← Ho Chi Minh Trail

← U.S. and S. Vietnamese offensives

● Major U.S. base

✸ Areas in neutral countries bombed by U.S.

0   200 miles
0   200 km
Two-Point Equidistant projection

110°E

GEOGRAPHY CONNECTION

1 THE USES OF GEOGRAPHY
What suggests that the war widened in the early 1970s?

2 THE WORLD IN SPATIAL TERMS *What neutral countries were bombed by the United States?*

The United States was not willing to allow nuclear weapons within such close striking distance of its mainland. In October 1962, Kennedy found out that Soviet ships carrying missiles were heading to Cuba. He decided to blockade Cuba to prevent the fleet from reaching its destination. This approach gave each side time to find a peaceful solution. Khrushchev agreed to turn back the fleet and remove Soviet missiles from Cuba if Kennedy pledged not to invade Cuba.

The Cuban missile crisis seemed to bring the world frighteningly close to nuclear war. Indeed, in 1992 a high-ranking Soviet officer revealed that short-range rockets armed with nuclear devices would have been used against U.S. troops if the United States had invaded Cuba, an option that Kennedy fortunately had rejected. The realization that the world might have been destroyed in a few days had a profound influence on both sides. A hotline communications system between Moscow and Washington, D.C., was installed in 1963. The two superpowers could now communicate quickly in times of crisis.

☑ **READING PROGRESS CHECK**

Summarizing How was the Cuban missile crisis resolved?

The Vietnam War

GUIDING QUESTION *What common factor triggered the "hot" wars in Asia during the Cold War?*

By 1963, the United States had been drawn into a new struggle that had an important impact on the Cold War—the Vietnam War. After World War II, most states in Southeast Asia gained independence from their colonial rulers. The Philippines became independent of the United States in 1946. Great Britain also ended its colonial rule in Southeast Asia. France refused, however, to let go of Indochina. This led to a long war in Vietnam.

Leading the struggle against French colonial rule was the local Communist Party, headed by Ho Chi Minh. In August 1945, the Vietminh, an alliance of forces under Communist leadership, seized power throughout most of Vietnam. Ho Chi Minh was elected president of a new republic in Hanoi. Refusing to accept the new government, France seized the southern part of the country. For years, France fought Ho Chi Minh's Vietminh for control of Vietnam without success. In 1954, after a huge defeat at Dien Bien Phu, France agreed to sign the Geneva Peace Accords. Because of the Korean War, China and the Soviet Union wanted to avoid another conflict with the United States. They pressured Vietnam to agree to a **temporary** partition of Vietnam. This was meant to save French pride and satisfy the Americans. Vietnam was divided into two parts. In the north were the Communists, based in Hanoi; in the south, the non-Communists, based in Saigon.

Both sides agreed to hold elections in two years to create a single government. Instead, the conflict continued, and Vietnam soon became part of the Cold War. The United States, opposed to the spread of communism, aided South Vietnam under nationalist leader Ngo Dinh Diem. In spite of this aid, the Viet Cong, South Vietnamese Communist guerrillas supported by North Vietnam, were on the verge of seizing control of the entire country by early 1965. Their forces also received military aid from China.

In March 1965, President Johnson sent troops to South Vietnam to keep the Communist regime of North Vietnam from gaining control of South Vietnam. U.S. policy makers saw the conflict in terms of a **domino theory** concerning the spread of communism. If the Communists succeeded in South Vietnam, the argument went, all the other countries in Asia that were freeing themselves from colonial domination would likewise fall (like dominoes) to communism.

North Vietnam responded to the American troops by sending more forces into the south. Despite the massive superiority in equipment and firepower of the American forces, the United States failed to defeat the North Vietnamese. The growing number of American troops in Vietnam soon produced an antiwar movement in the United States, especially among college students of draft age. The mounting destruction of the conflict, seen on television, also turned public opinion against the war.

President Johnson, condemned for his handling of the costly and indecisive war, decided not to run for reelection. Former vice president Richard M. Nixon won the election with his pledge to stop the war and bring the American people together. Finally, in 1973, President Nixon reached an agreement with North Vietnam in the Paris Peace Accords that allowed the United States to withdraw its forces. Within two years after the American withdrawal, Communist armies from the North had forcibly reunited Vietnam.

Despite the success of the North Vietnamese Communists, the domino theory proved to be unfounded. A noisy split between Communist China and the Soviet Union put an end to the Western idea that there was a single form of communism directed by Moscow. Under President Nixon, American relations with China were resumed. New nations in Southeast Asia also managed to avoid Communist governments. Above all, Vietnam helped show the limitations of American power. By the end of the Vietnam War, a new era in American-Soviet relations had begun to **emerge**.

temporary lasting for a limited time; not permanent

domino theory idea that if one country falls to communism, neighboring countries will also fall

emerge to come into being through evolution

✔ **READING PROGRESS CHECK**

Applying Why is the Vietnam War sometimes understood as a proxy war?

LESSON 3 REVIEW CCSS

Reviewing Vocabulary
1. ***Identifying*** Why did the domino theory cause the United States to become involved in Vietnam?

Using Your Notes
2. ***Classifying*** Use your notes to identify the proxy wars the United States was involved in during the Cold War.

Answering the Guiding Questions
3. ***Making Generalizations*** What common factor triggered the "hot" wars in Asia during the Cold War?

4. ***Analyzing*** How did nuclear weapons influence political relationships during the Cold War?

Writing Activity
5. **INFORMATIVE/EXPLANATORY** Pick one of the proxy wars discussed in the lesson and write a short paragraph explaining why the United States decided it was important to fight the war.

Directions: On a separate sheet of paper, answer the questions below. Make sure you read carefully and answer all parts of the questions.

Lesson Review

Lesson 1

1 **IDENTIFYING CAUSE AND EFFECT** What was the North Atlantic Treaty Organization? Why was it formed?

2 **SUMMARIZING** What events led to the Berlin Airlift? How did the Soviets react?

Lesson 2

3 **EXPLORING ISSUES** What steps did Mao Zedong take to increase food production? What were their effects?

4 **DESCRIBING** Who were the Red Guards? What did the Red Guards do to enforce the Cultural Revolution?

Lesson 3

5 **EXPLAINING** What is a proxy war? What two proxy wars were the Soviet Union and the United States involved in during the Cold War?

6 **DRAWING CONCLUSIONS** How did the Cuban missile crisis ultimately create common ground between the Soviet Union and the United States?

21st Century Skills

7 **TIME, CHRONOLOGY, AND SEQUENCING** How long did the Great Proletarian Cultural Revolution last? How did it come to an end?

8 **UNDERSTANDING RELATIONSHIPS AMONG EVENTS** When and how did the Cold War spread from Europe to Asia?

9 **DECISION MAKING** How did Cold War fears help lead to the partition of Vietnam? Did the partition have the intended effect? Explain how the United States responded.

10 **ANALYZING ARGUMENTS** Some U.S. policy makers believed in the domino theory—if the Communists conquered South Vietnam, then other countries in that region would eventually be conquered as well. Did the theory turn out to be valid? Explain.

Exploring the Essential Questions

11 **GATHERING INFORMATION** Write a five-paragraph essay explaining how conflict influenced the political relationship between the Soviet Union and the United States during the Cold War. Make sure you write about several events throughout the chapter that caused conflict and describe how each event positively or negatively influenced the relationship. Create a graphic organizer showing the events cited.

DBQ Analyzing Historical Documents

Use the document to answer the following questions.

After World War II, Berlin was divided into four sectors, one each for the British, the French, the Americans, and the Soviets.

12 **READING MAPS** What does this map tell you about postwar Berlin?

13 **PREDICTING CONSEQUENCES** How might the separation of East and West Berlin by the wall have affected the economic life of the city?

Extended-Response Question

14 **INFORMATIVE/EXPLANATORY** Compare and contrast U.S. foreign policy that conflicted with the Soviet Union and China throughout the Cold War.

Need Extra Help?

If You've Missed Question	**1**	**2**	**3**	**4**	**5**	**6**	**7**	**8**	**9**	**10**	**11**	**12**	**13**	**14**
Go to page	371	370	374	375	377	379	374	376	380	381	368	382	382	368

Independence and Nationalism in the Developing World

1945–1993

ESSENTIAL QUESTIONS · *How can political change cause conflict?*
· *How can political relationships affect economic relationships?*

netw**o**rks

There's More Online! about independence and nationalism in the developing world.

CHAPTER 19

The Story Matters...

In 1950 the South African government passed laws segregating black Africans from white Africans. This system of legalized racism is known as apartheid. Opposition and resistance to apartheid came from leaders within South Africa, such as Nelson Mandela. Mandela, head of the African National Congress, was imprisoned for 27 years because of his protests. Following his release, Mandela led negotiations to transform the South African government into one based on equality. In 1994 he became South Africa's first democratically elected black president.

◄ In 1993 Mandela received the Nobel Peace Prize. He is shown here just after his release from prison in 1990.

PHOTO: © Louise Gubb/Corbis SABA

Place and Time: Africa and Asia 1945–1993

After World War II, the map of the world was dramatically transformed as colonies in Africa and Asia won their independence from European powers. But even after these nations gained their independence, they struggled to maintain balanced economies and political stability.

Step Into the Place

Read the quote and look at the information presented on the map.

 Analyzing Historical Documents What were the goals of nationalist leaders?

PRIMARY SOURCE

❝For centuries, Europeans dominated the African continent. The white man arrogated to himself the right to rule and to be obeyed by the non-white; his mission, he claimed, was to 'civilise' Africa. Under this cloak, the Europeans robbed the continent of vast riches and inflicted unimaginable suffering on the African people. All this makes a sad story . . . All we ask of the former colonial powers is their goodwill and co-operation to remedy past mistakes and injustices and to grant independence to the colonies in Africa.❞

—Kwame Nkrumah, from *I Speak of Freedom*, 1961

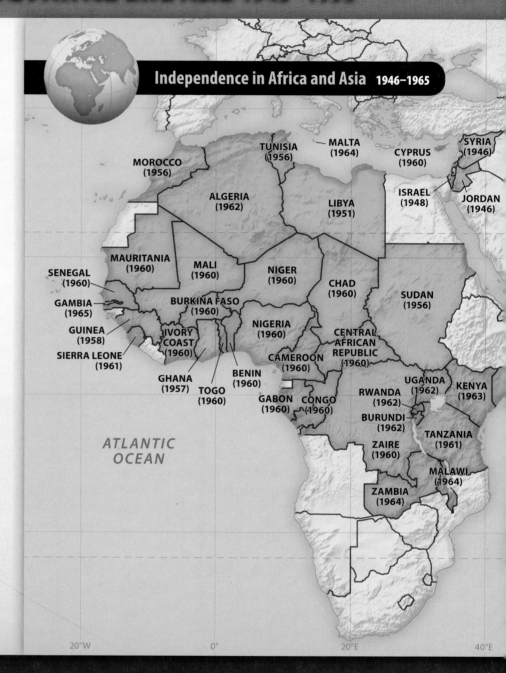

Independence in Africa and Asia 1946–1965

MOROCCO (1956)
TUNISIA (1956)
MALTA (1964)
CYPRUS (1960)
SYRIA (1946)
ALGERIA (1962)
LIBYA (1951)
ISRAEL (1948)
JORDAN (1946)
MAURITANIA (1960)
MALI (1960)
NIGER (1960)
CHAD (1960)
SUDAN (1956)
SENEGAL (1960)
GAMBIA (1965)
BURKINA FASO (1960)
GUINEA (1958)
NIGERIA (1960)
CENTRAL AFRICAN REPUBLIC (1960)
SIERRA LEONE (1961)
IVORY COAST (1960)
CAMEROON (1960)
GHANA (1957)
TOGO (1960)
BENIN (1960)
UGANDA (1962)
KENYA (1963)
GABON (1960)
CONGO (1960)
RWANDA (1962)
BURUNDI (1962)
TANZANIA (1961)
ZAIRE (1960)
MALAWI (1964)
ZAMBIA (1964)

ATLANTIC OCEAN

20°W   0°   20°E   40°E

Step Into the Time

Classifying Choose an event from the time line and explain how it illustrates the struggle for independence or the growth of nationalism in the developing world.

AFRICA AND ASIA

1947 India and Pakistan become independent nations

1949 Netherlands recognizes the Republic of Indonesia

1957 Ghana becomes first British colony to gain independence

THE WORLD

1945   1955

1946 Juan Perón is elected president of Argentina

1959 Fidel Castro seizes power in Cuba

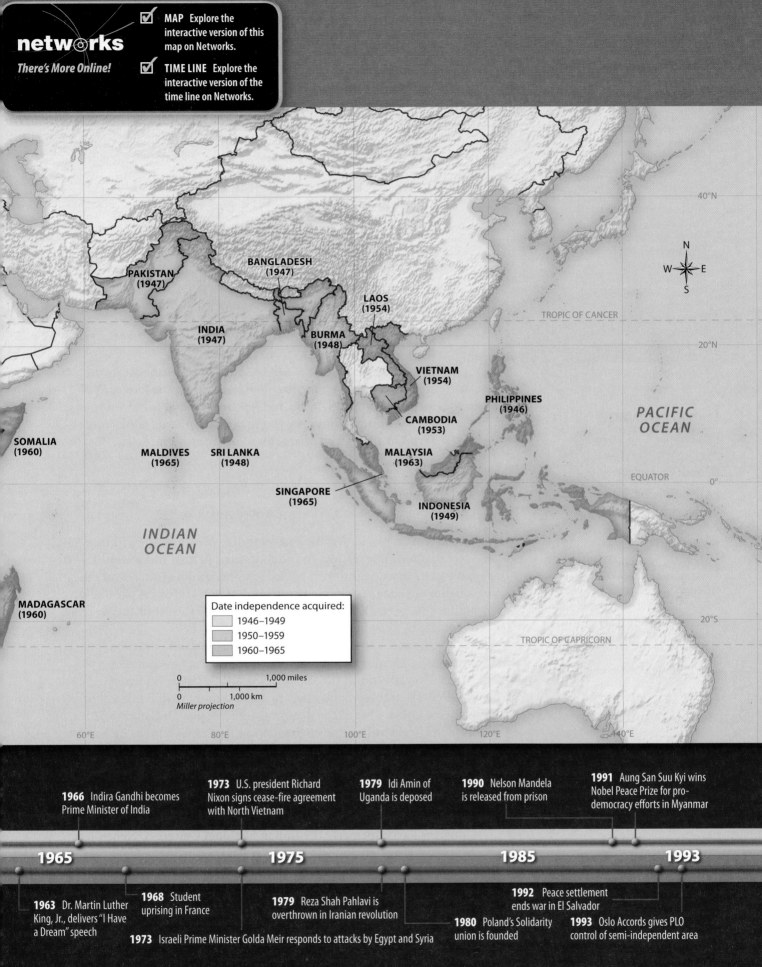

networks

There's More Online!

☑ **MAP** Explore the interactive version of this map on Networks.

☑ **TIME LINE** Explore the interactive version of the time line on Networks.

PAKISTAN
(1947)

BANGLADESH
(1947)

INDIA
(1947)

LAOS
(1954)

BURMA
(1948)

VIETNAM
(1954)

PHILIPPINES
(1946)

CAMBODIA
(1953)

SOMALIA
(1960)

MALDIVES
(1965)

SRI LANKA
(1948)

MALAYSIA
(1963)

SINGAPORE
(1965)

INDONESIA
(1949)

TROPIC OF CANCER

40°N

20°N

PACIFIC
OCEAN

EQUATOR

0°

INDIAN
OCEAN

MADAGASCAR
(1960)

20°S

TROPIC OF CAPRICORN

Date independence acquired:

☐ 1946–1949
☐ 1950–1959
☐ 1960–1965

0   1,000 miles

0   1,000 km

Miller projection

60°E   80°E   100°E   120°E   140°E

1966 Indira Gandhi becomes Prime Minister of India

1973 U.S. president Richard Nixon signs cease-fire agreement with North Vietnam

1979 Idi Amin of Uganda is deposed

1990 Nelson Mandela is released from prison

1991 Aung San Suu Kyi wins Nobel Peace Prize for pro-democracy efforts in Myanmar

1965   **1975**   **1985**   **1993**

1963 Dr. Martin Luther King, Jr., delivers "I Have a Dream" speech

1968 Student uprising in France

1979 Reza Shah Pahlavi is overthrown in Iranian revolution

1992 Peace settlement ends war in El Salvador

1980 Poland's Solidarity union is founded

1993 Oslo Accords gives PLO control of semi-independent area

1973 Israeli Prime Minister Golda Meir responds to attacks by Egypt and Syria

Independence and Nationalism in the Developing World **385**

networks

There's More Online!

☑ **BIOGRAPHY** Indira Gandhi

☑ **BIOGRAPHY** Jawaharlal Nehru

☑ **BIOGRAPHY** Mother Teresa

☑ **CHART/GRAPH** Religion in India

☑ **IMAGE** Aung San Suu Kyi

☑ **IMAGE** Refugees Migrate Between India and Pakistan

☑ **IMAGE** Student Activists in the Philippines

☑ **INTERACTIVE SELF-CHECK QUIZ**

☑ **MAP** The Partition of India, 1947

☑ **VIDEO** South and Southeast Asia

Reading **HELP**DESK (CCSS)

Academic Vocabulary

- **transfer**
- **role**

Content Vocabulary

- **principle of nonalignment**
- **discrimination**

TAKING NOTES:

Key Ideas and Details

Categorizing As you read, use a web diagram like the one below to identify challenges India faced after gaining independence.

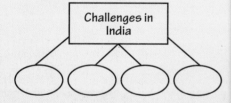

LESSON 1

South and Southeast Asia

ESSENTIAL QUESTIONS • *How can political change cause conflict?*
• *How can political relationships affect economic relationships?*

IT MATTERS BECAUSE

Following World War II, many South and Southeast Asian states gained their independence. British India was split into two nations—India and Pakistan. While some Southeast Asian countries have moved toward democracy, they have faced some serious obstacles along that path.

India Divided

GUIDING QUESTION *How did India emerge as an independent country?*

At the end of World War II, British India's Muslims and Hindus were divided. The leaders in India decided British India would have to be divided into two countries, one Hindu (India) and one Muslim (Pakistan). Pakistan consisted of two regions separated by India. One part, West Pakistan, was to the northwest of India. The other, East Pakistan, was to the northeast.

On August 15, 1947, India and Pakistan became independent. Millions of Hindus and Muslims fled across the new borders, Hindus toward India and Muslims toward Pakistan. Violence resulted from these mass migrations, and more than a million people were killed. One of the dead was well known. On January 30, 1948, a Hindu militant assassinated Mohandas Gandhi as he was going to morning prayer. India's new beginning had not been easy.

The New India

Having worked closely with Mohandas Gandhi for Indian independence, Jawaharlal Nehru (juh • WAH • huhr • LAHL NEHR • oo) led the Congress Party, formerly the Indian National Congress. Nehru admired the socialist ideals of the British Labour Party. His goal was a parliamentary government led by a prime minister and a moderate socialist economy. Under Nehru's leadership, the state took ownership of major industries, utilities, and transportation. Private enterprise was allowed at the local level, and farmland was left in private hands. The Indian government also sought to avoid

PHOTO: (l to r)Sandro Tucci/Getty Images News/Getty Images, ©Bettmann/Corbis, ©Bettmann/Corbis, ©Henri Bureau/Sygma/Corbis.

dependence on foreign investment. India developed a large industrial sector, and industrial production almost tripled between 1950 and 1965.

Nehru also guided India's foreign policy according to a **principle of nonalignment**. Concerned about military conflict between the United States and the Soviet Union and about the influence of former colonial powers, Nehru refused to align India with either bloc. Rather, he joined other developing countries in the idea that they should not take sides in the growing Cold War.

After Nehru's death, the Congress Party selected his daughter, Indira Gandhi (not related to Mohandas Gandhi), as prime minister. She held office for most of the time between 1966 and 1984. India faced many problems during this period. In the 1950s and 1960s, India's population grew by 2 percent a year, contributing to widespread poverty. Millions lived in vast city slums. It was in the slums of Kolkata (formerly Calcutta) that Mother Teresa, a Catholic nun, helped the poor, sick, and dying Indian people.

Growing ethnic and religious strife presented another major problem. One conflict involved the Sikhs, followers of a religion based on both Hindu and Muslim ideas. Many Sikhs lived in the Punjab, a northern province. Militant Sikhs demanded that this province be independent from India. Gandhi refused and in 1984 used military force against Sikh rebels. More than 450 Sikhs were killed. Seeking revenge, two Sikh members of Gandhi's personal bodyguard assassinated her later that year.

Conflict between Hindus and Muslims also continued. Religious differences fueled a long-term dispute between India and Pakistan over Kashmir, a territory between the two nations.

Gandhi's son Rajiv replaced his mother as prime minister and began to move the government in new directions. Private enterprise was encouraged, as well as foreign investment. His successors continued to **transfer** state-run industries into private hands and to rely on the free market. This led to a noticeable growth in the middle class.

Rajiv Gandhi was prime minister from 1984 to 1989. While campaigning for reelection in 1991, he was assassinated. In the following years, the Congress Party lost its leadership position and had to compete with new political parties.

principle of nonalignment Jawaharlal Nehru's refusal to align India with any bloc or alliance

transfer to take over the control of

▼ During partition, nearly 2 million refugees fled to either India or Pakistan.

▶ **CRITICAL THINKING**
Making Inferences Why are the people in the photograph sitting on top of train cars?

PHOTO: ©Bettmann/Corbis

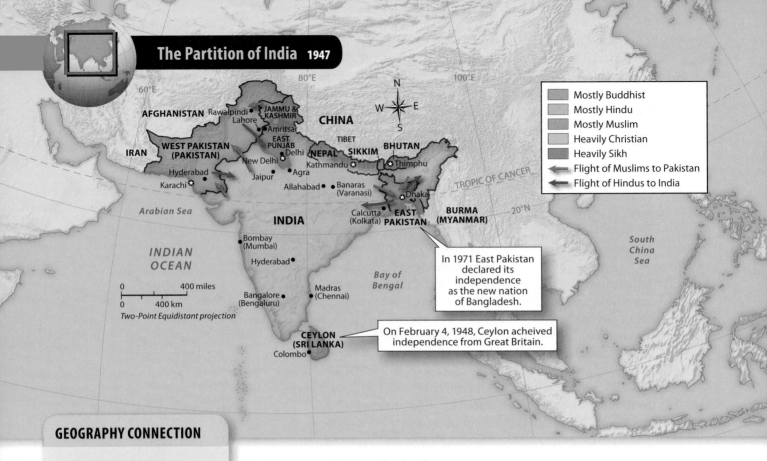

The Partition of India 1947

AFGHANISTAN
Rawalpindi
JAMMU &
KASHMIR
Lahore
Amritsar
CHINA
WEST PAKISTAN
(PAKISTAN)
EAST
PUNJAB
TIBET
BHUTAN
IRAN
Delhi
NEPAL
SIKKIM
New Delhi
Kathmandu
Thimphu
Hyderabad
Jaipur
Agra
Karachi
Allahabad
Banaras
(Varanasi)
Dhaka
Arabian Sea
INDIA
Calcutta
(Kolkata)
EAST
PAKISTAN
BURMA
(MYANMAR)
TROPIC OF CANCER
20°N
INDIAN
OCEAN
Bombay
(Mumbai)
South
China
Sea
Hyderabad
Bay of
Bengal
0   400 miles

0   400 km
Bangalore
(Bengaluru)
Madras
(Chennai)
Two-Point Equidistant projection

In 1971 East Pakistan declared its independence as the new nation of Bangladesh.

CEYLON
(SRI LANKA)
Colombo
On February 4, 1948, Ceylon acheived independence from Great Britain.

Legend:
- Mostly Buddhist
- Mostly Hindu
- Mostly Muslim
- Heavily Christian
- Heavily Sikh
- Flight of Muslims to Pakistan
- Flight of Hindus to India

GEOGRAPHY CONNECTION

1 HUMAN SYSTEMS *To what areas did India's Muslims flee? Why?*

2 PLACES AND REGIONS *The Kashmir region has experienced conflict until the present day. Why do you think this is?*

Pakistan and Bangladesh

Unlike its neighbor India, Pakistan was a completely new nation when it attained independence in 1947. The growing division between East and West Pakistan, separate regions with different geographical features, caused internal conflicts. Many in East Pakistan felt that the government, based in West Pakistan, ignored their needs. In 1971 East Pakistan declared its independence from Pakistan. After a brief civil war, it became the new nation of Bangladesh.

Both Bangladesh and Pakistan (formerly West Pakistan) have remained very poor. They also have had difficulty establishing stable governments. Military officials have often seized control of the civilian government.

☑ **READING PROGRESS CHECK**

Determining Cause and Effect What were the immediate effects of the partition of British India?

Southeast Asia

GUIDING QUESTION *What experiences did independence bring to new Southeast Asian countries?*

After World War II, most states in Southeast Asia gained independence from their colonial rulers. The process varied considerably across the region, however. In July 1946, the United States granted total independence to the Philippines. Great Britain was also willing to end its colonial rule in Southeast Asia. In 1948 Burma became independent from Great Britain.

In the beginning, many of the leaders of the newly independent states in Southeast Asia admired Western political and economic practices. They hoped to form democratic, capitalist states like those in the West. By the end of the 1950s, however, hopes for rapid economic growth had failed. Internal disputes weakened the new democratic governments, opening the door to both military and one-party autocratic regimes.

Indonesia and Myanmar

The Netherlands was less willing than Great Britain to abandon its colonial empire in Southeast Asia. The Netherlands tried to suppress a new Indonesian republic proclaimed by Achmed Sukarno. When the Indonesian Communist Party attempted to seize power, however, the United States pressured the Netherlands to grant independence to Sukarno and his non-Communist Nationalist Party. In 1949 the Netherlands recognized the new Republic of Indonesia.

In 1950 the new leaders created a parliamentary system and Sukarno was elected the first president. In the late 1950s, however, he dissolved the constitution and tried to rule on his own through what he called "guided democracy." Sukarno also nationalized foreign-owned enterprises and sought economic aid from China and the Soviet Union. Military officers overthrew Sukarno and established a military government under General Suharto. Democracy had failed.

In Burma, which is now the nation of Myanmar, the military has been in complete control since the early 1960s. The people of Myanmar have continued to fight for democracy, however. Leading the struggle is Aung San Suu Kyi, the daughter of Aung San, who led the Burma Independence Army in 1947. Educated abroad, Suu Kyi returned to Myanmar in 1988 and became involved in the movement for democracy. Her party won a landslide victory in 1990, but the military rulers refused to hand over power. Instead, Suu Kyi was placed under house arrest for many years. In 1991 Suu Kyi won the Nobel Peace Prize for her pro-democracy efforts.

Vietnam and Cambodia

By 1975, North Vietnamese Communist armies had forcibly reunited Vietnam and begun the process of rebuilding that shattered land. The reunification of Vietnam under Communist rule had an immediate impact on the region. By the end of 1975, both Laos and Cambodia had Communist governments. In Cambodia, Pol Pot, leader of the Khmer Rouge, massacred more than 1 million Cambodians. Conflict continued in Cambodia throughout the 1980s. It was not until 1993 that Cambodians held free UN-sponsored elections. Meanwhile, the government in Vietnam remained suspicious of Western-style democracy and repressed any opposition to the Communist Party's guiding **role** over the state.

▲ Aung San Suu Kyi, Myanmar's pro-democracy opposition leader.

role a socially-expected behavior pattern

The Philippines

In more recent years, some Southeast Asian societies have shown signs of moving again toward more democratic governments. One example is the Philippines. There, President Ferdinand Marcos came to power in 1965. Fraud and corruption became widespread in the Marcos regime. In the early 1980s, Marcos was accused of involvement in the killing of a popular opposition leader, Benigno Aquino. Corazon Aquino, wife of the murdered leader, became president in 1986 and worked for democratic reforms. Nevertheless, she soon proved unable to resolve many of the country's chronic economic and social problems.

▲ Filipino students hold a political rally during the funeral procession of Benigno Aquino.

▶ **CRITICAL THINKING**
Speculating Why are these men featured on the poster?

discrimination prejudicial treatment usually based on race, religion, class, sex, or age

PHOTO: Sandro Tucci/Getty Images News/Getty Images

Women in South and Southeast Asia

Across South and Southeast Asia, the rights and roles of women have changed. In India, women's rights expanded after independence. Its constitution of 1950 forbade **discrimination** based on gender and called for equal pay for equal work. Child marriage was also outlawed. Women were encouraged to attend school and to enter the labor market. In Southeast Asia, virtually all the newly independent states granted women full legal and political rights. Women have become more active in politics and occasionally hold senior political or corporate positions.

☑ **READING PROGRESS CHECK**

Comparing What challenges did Indonesia and Myanmar confront following independence?

LESSON 1 REVIEW

Reviewing Vocabulary
1. *Applying* How did the Cold War influence India's principle of nonalignment?

Using Your Notes
2. *Identifying* Use your notes to identify some of the problems India faced after its independence.

Answering the Guiding Questions
3. *Analyzing* How did India emerge as an independent country?

4. *Drawing Conclusions* What experiences did independence bring to new Southeast Asian countries?

Writing Activity
5. ARGUMENT Pretend you are a citizen of a South or Southeast Asian country that gained its independence. Write an essay about your experiences.

390

netw⚙️rks

There's More Online!

- ☑ **BIOGRAPHY** Gamal Abdel Nasser
- ☑ **BIOGRAPHY** Golda Meir
- ☑ **IMAGE** Protest During the Iranian Revolution
- ☑ **IMAGE** Women in Dubai
- ☑ **INTERACTIVE SELF-CHECK QUIZ**
- ☑ **MAP** Arab-Israeli Disputes, 1947–1993
- ☑ **PRIMARY SOURCE** Cairo Trilogy
- ☑ **TIME LINE** Arab-Israeli Relations
- ☑ **VIDEO** The Middle East

Reading **HELP**DESK (CCSS)

Academic Vocabulary

- **issue**
- **parallel**
- **revenue**

Content Vocabulary

- **Pan-Arabism**
- **intifada**

TAKING NOTES:

Key Ideas and Details

Sequencing As you read, create a table like the one below and list events in the history of Arab-Israeli conflicts.

Year	Event

LESSON 2
The Middle East

ESSENTIAL QUESTIONS • How can political change cause conflict?
• How can political relationships affect economic relationships?

IT MATTERS BECAUSE

Since 1948, Israelis and Arabs have often been in conflict in the Middle East. In Iran a revolution established an Islamic Republic while war broke out in Afghanistan. Iraq's conquest of Kuwait led to war in the Middle East.

The Mideast Crisis

GUIDING QUESTION *What events led to the dispute between Israel and its Arab neighbors?*

In the Middle East, as in Asia and Africa, a number of new nations emerged after World War II. Syria and Lebanon gained their independence just before the end of the war. Jordan achieved complete self-rule soon afterward. These new states in the Middle East were predominantly Muslim.

The Question of Palestine

In the years between the two world wars, many Jews had immigrated to the Palestine Mandate, which is their historic homeland and religious center. Tensions between Jews and Arabs had intensified during the 1930s. Great Britain, which governed Palestine under a League of Nations mandate, had limited Jewish immigration into the area and had rejected proposals for an independent Jewish state. The Muslim states agreed with Great Britain's position.

The Zionists wanted the land of ancient Israel to be a home for the Jewish people. Many people had been shocked at the end of World War II when they learned about the deliberate killing of 6 million European Jews in Nazi death camps. As a result, sympathy for the Jewish cause grew. In 1947 a United Nations (UN) resolution proposed that the Palestine Mandate should be divided into a Jewish state and an Arab state. The Jews then proclaimed the State of Israel on May 14, 1948.

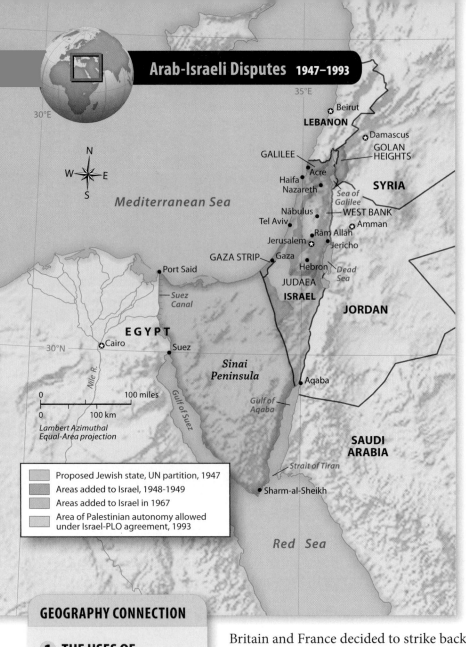

Arab-Israeli Disputes 1947–1993

30°E 35°E

Beirut
LEBANON
Damascus
GOLAN HEIGHTS
GALILEE
Acre
Haifa
Nazareth *Sea of Galilee* **SYRIA**
Nābulus **WEST BANK**
Tel Aviv Amman
Jerusalem Rām Allāh
GAZA STRIP Gaza Jericho
Port Said Hebron *Dead Sea*
Suez Canal **JUDAEA**
ISRAEL **JORDAN**
Mediterranean Sea
EGYPT
30°N Cairo Suez
Nile R. *Sinai Peninsula* Aqaba
0 100 miles *Gulf of Aqaba*
0 100 km *Gulf of Suez*
Lambert Azimuthal Equal-Area projection **SAUDI ARABIA**
Strait of Tiran
Sharm-al-Sheikh
Red Sea

Proposed Jewish state, UN partition, 1947
Areas added to Israel, 1948-1949
Areas added to Israel in 1967
Area of Palestinian autonomy allowed under Israel-PLO agreement, 1993

GEOGRAPHY CONNECTION

1 **THE USES OF GEOGRAPHY** *What is the strategic importance of the Sinai Peninsula?*

2 **PLACES AND REGIONS** *What was a result of the 1993 Oslo Peace Accords?*

issue *a vital or unsettled matter*

Pan-Arabism *Arab unity, regardless of national boundaries*

revenue *the yield of sources of income that a nation or state collects and deposits into its treasury for public use*

Its Arab neighbors saw the creation of Israel as a betrayal of the Palestinian Arabs, a majority of whom were Muslim. Outraged, several Arab countries invaded Israel. The invasion failed, but the Arab states refused to recognize the state of Israel. As a result, hundreds of thousands of Palestinian Arabs fled to neighboring Arab countries, and lived in refugee camps. Others became citizens of Israel. An equal number of Jews fled Arab countries and moved to Israel. Creating a Palestinian state remains an important **issue** in the Middle East today.

Nasser and Pan-Arabism

In Egypt, a new leader arose who played an important role in the Arab world. Colonel Gamal Abdel Nasser took control of the Egyptian government in the early 1950s. He blockaded Israeli shipping and on July 26, 1956, Nasser seized the Suez Canal Company, which had been under British and French administration since the 1800s.

Great Britain and France were upset by this threat to their world positions. The Suez Canal was an important waterway linking the Mediterranean Sea to Asia. Great Britain and France decided to strike back against Egypt, and Israel quickly joined them. The three nations launched a joint attack on Egypt, starting the Suez War of 1956.

The United States and the Soviet Union joined in supporting Nasser. Both countries opposed French and British influence in the Middle East. They forced Britain, France, and Israel to withdraw from Egypt.

Nasser emerged from the conflict as a powerful leader. He began to promote **Pan-Arabism**, or Arab unity. In February 1958, Egypt formally united with Syria in the United Arab Republic (UAR). Nasser was named the first president of the new state. Egypt and Syria hoped that the union would eventually include all Arab states.

Many other Arab leaders were suspicious of Pan-Arabism. Oil-rich Arab states were concerned they would have to share **revenues** with poorer states in the Middle East. In Nasser's view, Arab unity meant that wealth derived from oil, which currently flowed into a few Arab states or to foreign interests, could be used to improve the standard of living throughout the Middle East.

In 1961 Syrian military leaders took over Syria and withdrew the country from its union with Egypt. Nasser continued to work on behalf of Arab interests.

The Arab-Israeli Dispute

In the late 1950s and 1960s, the dispute between Israel and its Arab neighbors intensified. In 1967 Nasser imposed a blockade against Israeli shipping through the Gulf of Aqaba. He declared: "We are now ready to confront Israel … We are [now] ready to deal with the entire Palestine question."

Fearing attack by Egypt and other Arab states, on June 5, 1967, Israel launched air strikes against Egypt and several of its Arab neighbors. Israeli warplanes wiped out most of the Egyptian air force. Then, the Israeli army broke the blockade and gained the Sinai Peninsula. Israel took control of territory on the West Bank of the Jordan River, East Jerusalem, and the Golan Heights. During this Six-Day War, Israel tripled the size of the territory under its control. As a result, million Palestinians now lived in areas under Israeli control, most on the West Bank.

Over the next few years, Arab states continued to demand the return of the West Bank and Gaza. Nasser died in 1970, and Anwar el-Sadat succeeded him. On October 6, 1973 (the Jewish holiday of Yom Kippur), Egypt and Syria launched a coordinated surprise attack against Israel. Golda Meir, Israel's first female prime minister, had little time to mobilize troops. Soon, however, Israeli forces went on the offensive and pushed into Egypt. A UN-negotiated cease-fire on October 22 stopped the fighting. An agreement in 1974 officially ended the conflict, but tensions remained.

Meanwhile, however, the war was having indirect results in Western nations. In 1960 several oil-producing states had formed OPEC, the Organization of the Petroleum Exporting Countries, to control the price of oil. During the Yom Kippur War, some OPEC nations announced large increases in the price of oil to foreign countries. The price hikes, coupled with cuts in oil production, led to oil shortages and serious economic problems in the West.

In 1977 U.S. President Jimmy Carter began to press for a compromise peace between Arabs and Israelis. In September 1978, President Carter met with President Sadat of Egypt and Israeli prime minister Menachem Begin (BAY • gihn) at Camp David in the United States. The result was the Camp David Accords, an agreement to sign an Israeli-Egyptian peace treaty. The treaty, signed by Sadat and Begin in March 1979, led to a complete Israeli withdrawal from the Sinai Peninsula and ended the state of war between Egypt and Israel. Many Arab countries, however, continued to refuse to recognize Israel.

In 1964 the Egyptians took the lead in forming the Palestine Liberation Organization (PLO) to represent Palestinian interests. The PLO believed that only the Palestinian Arabs should have a state in the Palestine region. At the same time, a guerrilla movement called al-Fatah, headed by the PLO political leader Yasir Arafat, began to launch attacks on Israeli territory. These terrorist attacks continued for decades.

During the 1980s, Palestinian Arabs, frustrated by their failure to achieve self-rule, grew more militant. This militancy led to a movement called an **intifada**, or uprising, in the West Bank and Gaza Strip. Finally, in the Oslo Accords of 1993, an interim agreement for future negotiations, Israel and the PLO agreed that the Palestinians would control a semi-independent area and the PLO recognized Israel and renounced terrorism.

☑ **READING PROGRESS CHECK**

Sequencing Place the events of the Six-Day War in order.

BIOGRAPHY

Golda Meir (1898–1978)

Golda Meir was born in Kiev, Russia, but immigrated with her family to Milwaukee, Wisconsin, at the age of eight. In her early 20s, she moved to Palestine, where she was active in politics and the Zionist movement. Meir signed Israel's declaration of independence in 1948. She was subsequently elected to parliament and later served as both labor and foreign minister. In 1969 Meir became the prime minister of Israel and led her country during the Yom Kippur War. During her career, she attempted to establish peace with neighboring Arab states and fostered diplomacy with foreign powers.

DBQ *DRAWING CONCLUSIONS*
How do you think Meir's upbringing affected her foreign policy decisions?

intifada "uprising"; militant movement that arose during the 1980s among supporters of the Palestine Liberation Organization living in the West Bank and Gaza

Iran, Iraq, and Afghanistan

GUIDING QUESTION *How has the move for self-rule led to turmoil among the countries of the Middle East?*

The conflict between Israel and the Palestinians is one of many challenges in the Middle East. As in other parts of the world, a few people are rich while many are poor. Some countries prosper because of oil, but others remain in poverty. A response to these problems is the growth of movements based on Islam. Many of these groups believe that Muslims must return to a pure Islamic culture and values to build prosperous societies. Some are willing to use violence to bring about an Islamic revolution. Such a revolution took place in Iran.

The Iranian Revolution

The leadership of Reza Shah Pahlavi and revenue from oil helped make Iran a rich country. Iran was also an ally of the United States in the Middle East in the 1950s and 1960s.

However, there was much opposition to the shah in Iran. Many Muslims looked with distaste at the new Iranian society. In their eyes, it was based on greed and materialism, which they identified with American influence. Leading the opposition to the shah was the Ayatollah Ruhollah Khomeini (ko • MAY • nee), a member of the Muslim clergy. By the late 1970s, many Iranians had begun to respond to Khomeini's words. In 1979 the shah's government collapsed and was replaced by an Islamic republic.

The new government, led by the Ayatollah Khomeini, moved to restore Islamic law. Supporters of the shah were executed or fled Iran. Anti-American feelings erupted when militants seized 52 Americans in the United States embassy in Tehran and held them hostage for more than a year.

After Khomeini's death in 1989, a more moderate government allowed some civil liberties. Some Iranians were dissatisfied with the government's economic performance. Others, especially young people, pressed for more freedoms and an end to the rule of conservative Muslim clerics.

▼ A pro-Khomeini demonstration during the Iranian Revolution, December 1978.

▶ **CRITICAL THINKING**
Analyzing Visuals How would you describe the participants in this demonstration?

PHOTO: ©Alain Keler/Sygma/Corbis

The Iran-Iraq War

To the west of Iran was a militant and hostile Iraq, led by Saddam Hussein since 1979. Iran and Iraq have long had an uneasy relationship. Religious differences have fueled their disputes. Although both are Muslim nations, the Iranians are mostly Shia Muslims. The Iraqi leaders under Saddam Hussein, on the other hand, were mostly Sunni Muslims. Iran and Iraq have fought over territory, too, especially over the Strait of Hormuz. Strategically very important, the strait connects the Persian Gulf and the Gulf of Oman.

In 1980 Saddam Hussein launched a brutal war against Iran. During the Iran-Iraq War children were used to clear dangerous minefields. Saddam Hussein used poison gas against soldiers and civilians, especially the Kurds, an ethnic minority in the north who wanted their own state. In 1988, Iran and Iraq signed a cease-fire without resolving the war's basic issues.

The Persian Gulf War

In August 1990, Saddam Hussein sent his troops across the border to seize Kuwait, an oil-rich country on the Persian Gulf. The invasion began the Gulf War. The United States led the international forces that freed Kuwait. Hoping an internal revolt would overthrow Hussein, the allies imposed harsh economic sanctions on Iraq. The overthrow of Saddam Hussein, however, did not happen.

Afghanistan and the Taliban

After World War II, the king of Afghanistan, in search of economic assistance for his country, developed close ties with the Soviet Union. Internal fighting was followed in 1979 by a full-scale invasion of Afghanistan by the Soviets, who occupied the country for 10 years. Anti-Communist Islamic forces (known collectively as the mujahideen), supported by the United States and Pakistan, eventually ousted them. When the Soviets left, the Islamic groups began to fight for control of Afghanistan. One of these, the Taliban, seized the capital city of Kabul in 1996. By the fall of 1998, the Taliban controlled more than two-thirds of the country.

Backed by conservative religious forces in Pakistan, the Taliban provided a base of operations for Osama bin Laden. Bin Laden came from a wealthy family in Saudi Arabia and used his wealth to support the Afghan resistance. In 1988 bin Laden founded al-Qaeda, or "the base," which recruited Muslims to drive Westerners out of nations with a largely Muslim population. After the Taliban seized control of much of Afghanistan, bin Laden used bases there to train al-Qaeda recruits.

✔ **READING PROGRESS CHECK**

Identifying Central Issues What role did religious differences play in the Iranian revolution and the Iran-Iraq War?

Society and Culture

GUIDING QUESTION *How has Islam influenced society and culture in the Middle East?*

In recent years, conservative religious forces in the Middle East have tried to replace foreign culture and values with Islamic forms of belief and behavior. This movement is called Islamic fundamentalism or Islamic activism. For some Islamic leaders, Western values and culture are based on materialism, greed, and immorality. Extremists want to remove all Western influence in Muslim countries. These extremists give many Westerners an unfavorable impression of Islam.

▲ Women ride an escalator at an upscale shopping center in Dubai.

▶ CRITICAL THINKING

Describing How does this photograph show the contrast between tradition and modernity in the contemporary Middle East?

parallel having the same direction or course; similar

Islamic fundamentalism began in Iran under the Ayatollah Khomeini. There the return to traditional Muslim beliefs reached into clothing styles, social practices, and the legal system. These ideas and practices spread to other Muslim countries. In Egypt, for example, militant Muslims assassinated President Sadat in 1981.

At the beginning of the twentieth century, women's place in Middle Eastern society had changed little for hundreds of years. Early Muslim women had participated in the political life of society and had extensive legal, political, and social rights. Cultural practices in many countries had overshadowed those rights, however.

In the nineteenth and twentieth centuries, Muslim scholars debated issues surrounding women's roles in society. Many argued for the need to rethink outdated interpretations and cultural practices that prevented women from realizing their potential. Until the 1970s, the general trend in urban areas was toward a greater role for women. Beginning in the 1970s, however, there was a shift toward more traditional roles for women. This trend was especially noticeable in Iran.

The literature of the Middle East since 1945 has reflected a rise in national awareness, which encouraged interest in historical traditions. Writers also began to deal more with secular themes for broader audiences, not just the elite. For example, *Cairo Trilogy* by Egyptian writer Naguib Mahfouz tells about a merchant family in Egypt in the 1920s. The changes in the family **parallel** the changes in Egypt. Mahfouz was the first writer in Arabic to win the Nobel Prize in Literature (in 1988).

☑ READING PROGRESS CHECK

Making Connections Why was there a turn toward more traditional roles for Iranian women beginning in the 1970s?

PHOTO: ©Atlantide Phototravel/Corbis

LESSON 2 REVIEW

Reviewing Vocabulary

1. *Identifying* How did concern over revenue help lead to suspicion of Pan-Arabism?

Using Your Notes

2. *Sequencing* Use your notes to list specific events in the Arab-Israeli conflict.

Answering the Guiding Questions

3. *Analyzing* What events led to the dispute between Israel and its Arab neighbors?

4. *Drawing Conclusions* How has the move for self-rule led to turmoil among the countries of the Middle East?

5. *Making Generalizations* How has Islam influenced society and culture in the Middle East?

Writing Activity

6. INFORMATIVE/EXPLANATORY Research Golda Meir and find out how she became a leader of Israel. What did a woman rising to this position of power say about the State of Israel at that time?

networks

There's More Online!

- ☑ **BIOGRAPHY** Jomo Kenyatta
- ☑ **BIOGRAPHY** Nelson Mandela
- ☑ **CHART/GRAPH** Trends in Africa: Population, Poverty, and Water
- ☑ **IMAGE** African Art
- ☑ **IMAGE** Africa's First Democratic Election
- ☑ **IMAGE** Slums Outside of Nairobi
- ☑ **INTERACTIVE SELF-CHECK QUIZ**
- ☑ **MAP** Independent Africa
- ☑ **VIDEO** Africa

Reading HELPDESK (CCSS)

Academic Vocabulary
- **goal**
- **diverse**
- **theme**

Content Vocabulary
- **apartheid**
- **HIV/AIDS**
- **Pan-Africanism**

TAKING NOTES:
Key Ideas and Details

Categorizing As you read, complete a chart like the one below identifying the different economic views held by African leaders after independence.

African Leader	Country	Economic Views

PHOTO: (l to r)©David Turnley/Corbis, Keystone/Stringer/Hulton Archive/Getty Images, ©Peter Turnley/Corbis, ©David Turnley/Corbis.

LESSON 3
Africa

ESSENTIAL QUESTIONS · *How can political change cause conflict?*
· *How can political relationships affect economic relationships?*

IT MATTERS BECAUSE

Africa's road to independence has not been an easy one. Free from colonial rule, many African nations faced serious political, economic, social, and health challenges.

Independence and New Nations

GUIDING QUESTION *What challenges did newly independent African countries face? What challenges have been overcome by African countries?*

After World War II, Europeans realized that colonial rule in Africa would have to end. The Charter of the United Nations supported this belief. It stated that all colonial peoples should have the right to self-determination. In the late 1950s and 1960s, most African nations achieved independence.

In 1957 the Gold Coast, renamed Ghana and under the guidance of Kwame Nkrumah, was the first British colony to gain independence. In 1960 the Belgian Congo (renamed Zaire, now Democratic Republic of the Congo) and Nigeria gained their independence from the Belgians and the British respectively. Many other nations followed, including Uganda, Kenya, and Botswana. Portugal finally surrendered Mozambique and Angola in 1975.

In North Africa, the French granted full independence to Morocco and Tunisia in 1956. Because Algeria was home to a million French settlers, France chose to keep control there. However, Algerian nationalists began a guerrilla war to liberate their homeland. The French leader, Charles de Gaulle, granted Algeria its independence in 1962.

South Africa and Apartheid
In South Africa, where whites dominated the political system, the process was more complicated. Blacks began organizing against white rule and formed the African National Congress in 1912. Its **goal** of economic and political reform met with little success.

goal an aim or a purpose

apartheid "apartness"; the system of racial segregation in South Africa from the 1950s until 1991

At the same time, by the 1950s, South African whites (descendants of the Dutch, known as Afrikaners) had strengthened the laws separating whites and blacks. The result was a system of racial segregation known as **apartheid** ("apartness").

Blacks demonstrated against these laws, but the white government brutally repressed the demonstrators. In 1960 police opened fire on people who were leading a peaceful march in Sharpeville, killing 69 people, two-thirds of whom were shot in the back. After the arrest of African National Congress (ANC) leader Nelson Mandela in 1962, members of the ANC called for armed resistance to the white government.

New Nations and New Leaders

The African states that achieved independence in the 1950s, 1960s, and 1970s still faced many problems. The leaders of these states, as well as their citizens, dreamed of stable governments and economic prosperity. Many of these dreams have yet to be realized.

Most leaders of the newly independent states came from the urban middle class. They had studied in Europe or the U.S. and knew European languages. They believed in using the Western democratic model in Africa.

diverse varied and not alike

The views of these African leaders on economics were somewhat more **diverse.** Some, such as Jomo Kenyatta of Kenya and General Mobutu Sese Seko of the present-day Democratic Republic of the Congo, believed in Western-style capitalism. Leaders in Angola and Mozambique followed Soviet-style communism. Other leaders, such as Julius Nyerere of Tanzania, Kwame Nkrumah of Ghana, Sékou Touré of Guinea, and Patrice Lumumba of the Republic of Congo, preferred an "African form of socialism."

Pan-Africanism
the unity of all black Africans, regardless of national boundaries

The African form of socialism was not like that practiced in the Soviet Union or Eastern Europe. Instead, it was based on African traditions of community in which ownership of the country's wealth would be put into the hands of the people. As Nyerere declared in 1967, "The basis of socialism is a belief in the oneness of man and the common historical destiny of mankind. Its basis … is human equality."

Some African leaders believed in the dream of **Pan-Africanism**—the unity of all black Africans, regardless of national boundaries. In the view of Pan-Africanists, all black African peoples shared a common identity. Several of the new African leaders, including Léopold Senghor of Senegal, Kwame Nkrumah, and Jomo Kenyatta, supported Pan-Africanism.

Analyzing CCSS
PRIMARY SOURCES

Nelson Mandela on Democracy

"During my lifetime I have dedicated myself to this struggle of the African people. I have fought against white domination, and I have fought against black domination. I have cherished the ideal of a democratic and free society in which all persons live together in harmony and with equal opportunities. It is an ideal which I hope to live for and to achieve. But if needs be, it is an ideal for which I am prepared to die."

—Nelson Mandela, statement at the Rivonia Trial, April 20, 1964, from *In His Own Words*

DBQ ***IDENTIFYING POINTS OF VIEW*** How did Mandela's words challenge the idea of apartheid?

Nkrumah in particular hoped that a Pan-African union would join all the new countries of the continent in a broader community. His dream never became reality. However, the Organization of African Unity (OAU), founded by the leaders of 32 African states in 1963, was a concrete result of the belief in Pan-Africanism. The OAU gave support to African groups fighting against colonialism. The group also presented a united front against the influence of the United States and the Soviet Union during the Cold War. Some African countries were part of the non-aligned movement and did not take sides in the Cold War.

Economic and Political Challenges

Independence did not bring economic prosperity to the new African nations. Most still relied on the export of a single crop or natural resource. Liberia, for example, depended on the export of rubber; Nigeria, on oil. When prices dropped, their economies suffered. To make matters worse, Africa depended on foreign investment. Most African states imported

TEXT: "Nelson Mandela's Statement from the Dock at the Opening of the Defense Case in the Rivonia Trial", Pretoria Supreme Court, 20 April 1964. www.nelsonmandela.org

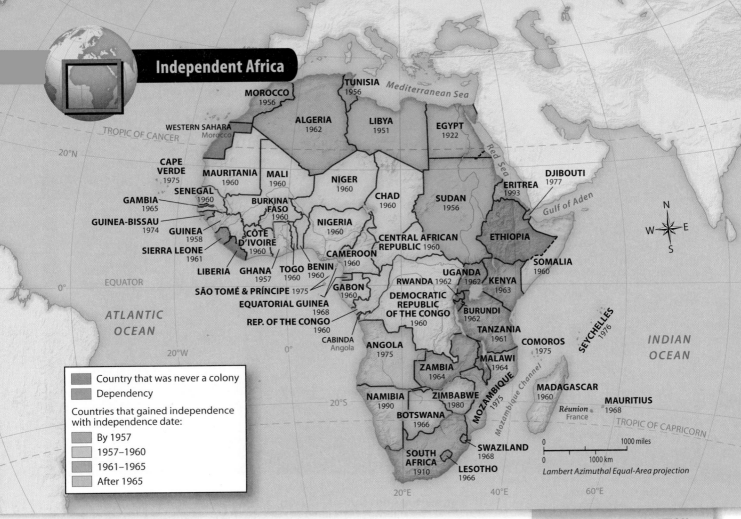

Country that was never a colony
Dependency
Countries that gained independence with independence date:
By 1957
1957–1960
1961–1965
After 1965

MOROCCO 1956
WESTERN SAHARA Morocco
TUNISIA 1956
Mediterranean Sea
ALGERIA 1962
LIBYA 1951
EGYPT 1922
CAPE VERDE 1975
MAURITANIA 1960
MALI 1960
NIGER 1960
DJIBOUTI 1977
ERITREA 1993
Red Sea
SENEGAL 1960
GAMBIA 1965
BURKINA FASO 1960
CHAD 1960
SUDAN 1956
Gulf of Aden
GUINEA-BISSAU 1974
GUINEA 1958
NIGERIA 1960
ETHIOPIA
SIERRA LEONE 1961
CÔTE D'IVOIRE 1960
CENTRAL AFRICAN REPUBLIC 1960
SOMALIA 1960
LIBERIA
GHANA 1957
TOGO 1960
BENIN 1960
CAMEROON 1960
UGANDA 1962
RWANDA 1962
KENYA 1963
SÃO TOMÉ & PRÍNCIPE 1975
EQUATORIAL GUINEA 1968
REP. OF THE CONGO 1960
GABON 1960
DEMOCRATIC REPUBLIC OF THE CONGO 1960
BURUNDI 1962
SEYCHELLES 1976
CABINDA Angola
ANGOLA 1975
TANZANIA 1961
COMOROS 1975
INDIAN OCEAN
ZAMBIA 1964
MALAWI 1964
MADAGASCAR 1960
MAURITIUS 1968
ATLANTIC OCEAN
NAMIBIA 1990
ZIMBABWE 1980
MOZAMBIQUE 1975
Mozambique Channel
Réunion France
BOTSWANA 1966
TROPIC OF CAPRICORN
SOUTH AFRICA 1910
SWAZILAND 1968
LESOTHO 1966

1000 miles
1000 km
Lambert Azimuthal Equal-Area projection

TROPIC OF CANCER
20°N
20°W
0°
EQUATOR
20°S
20°E
40°E
60°E

technology and manufactured goods from the West and depended on foreign financial aid to develop their countries.

The new states also sometimes created their own problems. Scarce national resources were spent on military equipment or expensive consumer goods rather than on building the foundations for an industrial economy. Corruption was common.

Droughts and rapid population growth have also slowed economic growth and taxed resources. Since the 1980s, recurring droughts in many African countries, including Djibouti, Eritrea, Ethiopia, Kenya, Somalia, and Uganda have caused starvation and migration.

As a result of these problems, poverty was widespread among both rural and urban dwellers. As cities grew, massive slums populated by displaced rural people surrounded cities, overwhelming sanitation and transportation systems. Pollution and perpetual traffic jams were the result. Millions lived without access to electricity or even clean water. Meanwhile, the fortunate few enjoyed lavish lifestyles. The rich in many East African countries are known as the *wabenzi*, or Mercedes-Benz people.

Diseases, such as **HIV/AIDS**, also presented major challenges to African progress. AIDS is a worldwide epidemic, but Africa is hardest hit. HIV/AIDS has had a serious impact on children and families in Africa. Many children have lost one or both parents to AIDS. Often, relatives are too poor to care for these children. Many orphans thus become heads of households filled with younger siblings. Extended families have been the source of support in difficult times, especially in rural Africa. The HIV/AIDS epidemic, however, has overwhelmed this support system.

GEOGRAPHY CONNECTION

1 **PLACES AND REGIONS**
Which African nations became independent after 1965?

2 **HUMAN SYSTEMS**
Create a table of select African countries that includes the name of the European country that previously controlled it.

HIV/AIDS human immunodeficiency virus/acquired immunodeficiency syndrome; any of the strains of HIV-1 and HIV-2 that infect and destroy the immune system's helper T cells causing a large drop in their numbers, and becomes AIDS when a person has 20 percent or less than the normal level of helper T cells

▲ The modern skyline of Nairobi, Kenya, forms a backdrop to one of the slums that surround the city.

▶ **CRITICAL THINKING**
Contrasting How do the lives of rich and poor African urban dwellers differ?

African nations have taken steps to fight the epidemic. It has proved a tremendous burden, however, because many of these countries do not have the money or health facilities to educate their citizens about the disease and how to protect against it. Nor can they purchase the drugs that would extend the lives of those with HIV.

Africans also faced political challenges. Many people hoped that independence would lead to democracies. They were soon disappointed as democratic governments failed. Between 1957 and 1982, more than 70 leaders were violently overthrown. In the 1980s, either the military or a single party ruled many major African states. In the 1990s multiparty elections increased, but single-party rule still predominated.

Despite the OAU's push for non-alignment in the Cold War, some African nations were drawn into proxy wars as the U.S. and the Soviet Union took opposing sides in political struggles in the newly independent countries, notably in Angola, Somalia, and Zaire. This caused prolonged conflict in some parts of Africa that undermined political development.

Within many African nations, warring ethnic groups undermined the concept of nationhood. This is not surprising, because the colonial powers had drawn the boundaries of African nations arbitrarily. Virtually all these states included widely diverse ethnic, linguistic, and territorial groups.

For example, during the late 1960s, civil war tore Nigeria apart. Conflicts also broke out among ethnic groups in Zimbabwe. Farther north, in central Africa, fighting between the Hutu and Tutsi created unstable governments in Rwanda and Burundi. During the colonial period, Hutu and Tutsi peoples lived together under European control. After independence in 1962, two new countries were created: Rwanda and Burundi. The population in both countries was mixed, but in Rwanda, the

Hutu majority ran the government. They resented the position of the Tutsis, who had gotten the best education and jobs under the Belgians. In 1994 a Hutu rampage left some 500,000 Tutsi dead in Rwanda.

Not all the news in Africa has been bad. Popular demonstrations led to the collapse of one-party regimes and the emergence of democracies in several countries. One case was that of Idi Amin of Uganda. After ruling by terror and brutal repression throughout the 1970s, Amin was deposed in 1979. Dictatorship also came to an end in Ethiopia, Liberia, and Somalia. In these cases, however, the fall of the regime was later followed by bloody civil war. Apartheid also ended in South Africa.

The End of Apartheid

One of the most remarkable events of recent African history was the 1994 election of Nelson Mandela to the presidency of the Republic of South Africa. Imprisoned in 1962 for his activities with the African National Congress, Mandela spent almost 26 years in maximum-security prisons in South Africa. For all those years, Mandela never wavered from his resolve to secure the freedom of his country.

Mandela was offered freedom in 1985, with conditions. Yet he refused to accept a conditional freedom: "Only free men can negotiate. Prisoners cannot enter into contracts.... Your freedom and mine cannot be separated."

Nobel Peace Prize winner (1984) Bishop Desmond Tutu and others worked to free Mandela and to end apartheid. Eventually, worldwide pressure forced the South African government to dismantle apartheid laws. In 1990 Mandela was released from prison. In 1993 the government of F. W. de Klerk agreed to hold democratic national elections—the first in South Africa's history. In 1994 Nelson Mandela became South Africa's first black president. In his presidential inaugural address, he expressed his hopes:

▲ After his release from prison in 1990, Nelson Mandela visits Bishop Desmond Tutu.

PRIMARY SOURCE

❝We shall build the society in which all South Africans, both black and white, will be able to walk tall, without any fear in their hearts, assured of their inalienable right to human dignity—a rainbow nation at peace with itself and the world.❞

—from *In His Own Words*

☑ READING PROGRESS CHECK

Evaluating To what extent were the goals of Pan-Africanism realized in Africa in the years following independence?

Society and Culture

GUIDING QUESTION *What factors have affected African society and culture?*

Africa is a study in contrasts. Old and new, indigenous and foreign, live side by side. One result is a constant tension between traditional ways and Western culture in most African countries.

In general, the impact of the West has been greatest in the cities. After all, the colonial presence was first and most firmly established in the cities. Many cities, including Lagos, Nigeria; Cape Town, South Africa; Brazzaville, Republic of the Congo; and Nairobi, Kenya, are direct products of colonial rule. Most African cities today look like cities elsewhere in the world.

About sixty percent of the population of Africa lives outside the major cities. Modern influence has had less of an impact there. Millions of people throughout Africa live much as their ancestors did—in thatched dwellings

▲ South Africans wait in line to vote in the nation's first democratic election.

theme a subject or topic of artistic work

without modern plumbing and electricity. They farm, hunt, or raise livestock by traditional methods, wear traditional clothing, and practice traditional beliefs. Conditions such as drought or flooding affect the ability of rural Africans to grow crops or to tend herds. Migration to the cities for work is one solution. This can be very disruptive to families and villages. Many urban people view rural people as backward. Rural dwellers view the cities as corrupting and destructive to traditional African values.

After independence, women's roles in African society changed. Almost without exception, women were allowed to vote and run for political office. Some became leaders of their countries. Women still hold few political offices, however. Although women dominate some professions, such as teaching, child care, and clerical work, they do not share in all career opportunities. Most African women are employed in low-paid positions, such as farm laborers, factory workers, and servants. Furthermore, in many rural areas, traditional attitudes toward women, including arranged marriages, prevail.

The tension between traditional and modern and between indigenous and foreign also affects African culture. Africans have kept their local artistic traditions and have adapted them to foreign influences. A dilemma for many contemporary African artists is finding a balance between Western techniques and training on the one hand and the rich heritage of traditional African art forms on the other. In some countries, governments make the artists' decisions. Artists are told to depict scenes of traditional African life. These works are designed to serve the tourist industry.

African writers have often addressed the tensions and dilemmas that modern Africans face. The conflicting demands of town versus country and indigenous versus foreign were the **themes** of most of the best-known works of the 1960s and 1970s. Chinua Achebe, a Nigerian novelist and winner of the Nobel Prize for literature in 1989, writes about the problems of Africans caught up in the conflict between traditional and Western values. In his most famous novel *Things Fall Apart*, Achebe portrays the simple dignity of traditional African village life.

✓ **READING PROGRESS CHECK**

Differentiating How are women's roles different in rural and urban areas in Africa?

PHOTO: ©Peter Turnley/Corbis

LESSON 3 REVIEW

Reviewing Vocabulary
1. *Assessing* How successful was the African National Congress in its goal of reforming the South African government and ending apartheid?

Using Your Notes
2. *Making Connections* Use your notes to identify post-independence African leaders and their economic views.

Answering the Guiding Questions
3. *Identifying* What challenges did newly independent African countries face?

4. *Drawing Conclusions* What challenges have been overcome by African countries?

5. *Making Generalizations* What factors have affected African society and culture?

Writing Activity
6. **INFORMATIVE/EXPLANATORY** Research independence movements in two African nations. Evaluate their success and compare how political ideology, ethnicity, and religion shaped their future governments.

netw⊙rks

There's More Online!

- ☑ **BIOGRAPHY** Fidel Castro
- ☑ **BIOGRAPHY** François Duvalier
- ☑ **BIOGRAPHY** Oscar Romero
- ☑ **CHART/GRAPH** GDP Per Capita in Selected Latin American Countries
- ☑ **IMAGE** Mothers of the Plaza de Mayo
- ☑ **INTERACTIVE SELF-CHECK QUIZ**
- ☑ **MAP** Struggles for Democracy, 1945–1993
- ☑ **PRIMARY SOURCE** One Hundred Years of Solitude
- ☑ **VIDEO** Latin America

Reading **HELP**DESK (CCSS)

Academic Vocabulary

- consent • target

Content Vocabulary

- privatization
- trade embargo
- cartels
- magic realism
- megacity

TAKING NOTES:

Key Ideas and Details

Categorizing As you read, use a table like the one below to list significant events that happened in each country during the Cold War.

Country	Significant Events
Haiti	
El Salvador	
Nicaragua	
Chile	
Colombia	

LESSON 4
Latin America

ESSENTIAL QUESTIONS • *How can political change cause conflict?*
• *How can political relationships affect economic relationships?*

IT MATTERS BECAUSE

After World War II, Latin American countries faced many economic, social, and political challenges. These challenges arose from a rise in population, a large foreign debt, and ongoing foreign military involvement.

General Trends in Latin America

GUIDING QUESTIONS *How did the involvement of the United States and the Soviet Union increase instability in Latin American countries? What economic and political challenges did Latin American countries face during the Cold War?*

Since the 1800s, Latin Americans have exported raw materials and bought manufactured goods from industrialized countries. The Great Depression caused exports to fall, and revenues to buy manufactured goods declined. In response, Latin Americans developed industries to produce their own goods.

By the 1960s, however, Latin American countries were still experiencing economic problems. They depended on the United States, Europe, and Japan, especially for the advanced technology needed for modern industries. Also, many Latin American countries had failed to find markets abroad to sell their manufactured products.

These economic failures led to political instability. In the 1960s, repressive military regimes in Chile, Brazil, and Argentina abolished political parties and returned to export-import economies financed by foreigners. These regimes also encouraged multinational corporations (companies with divisions in more than two countries) to come to Latin America. This made these Latin American countries even more dependent on industrialized nations. In the 1970s, Latin American countries tried to maintain their weak economies by borrowing money. Between 1970 and 1982, debt to foreigners grew from $27 billion to $315.3 billion. A number of Latin American economies began to crumble. Wages fell, and unemployment and inflation skyrocketed. As the economy declined, people continued to move from the countryside into the cities.

GEOGRAPHY CONNECTION

Latin American countries have
moved toward democracy.

**1 PLACES AND
REGIONS** *Of the countries
shown on the map, which has
experienced the longest period
of electoral democracy?*

**2 THE USES OF
GEOGRAPHY** *What
problems did countries with little
experience with electoral
democracy face?*

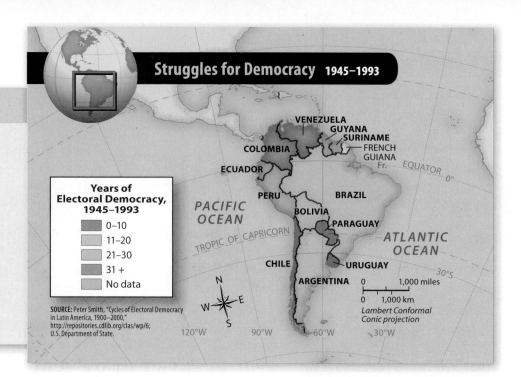

Struggles for Democracy 1945–1993

Years of
Electoral Democracy,
1945–1993

- 0–10
- 11–20
- 21–30
- 31 +
- No data

SOURCE: Peter Smith, "Cycles of Electoral Democracy
in Latin America, 1900–2000,"
http://repositories.cdlib.org/clas/wp/6;
U.S. Department of State.

consent approval

A Move Toward Democracy

With the debt crisis in the 1980s came a movement toward democracy. Some military leaders could not deal with their nations' debt problems. At the same time, many realized that military power without popular **consent** could not maintain a strong state. As a result, a movement toward democracy was the most noticeable trend of the 1980s and the early 1990s in Latin America.

The United States has always played a large role in Latin America. In 1948 the states of the Western Hemisphere formed the Organization of American States (OAS), which called for an end to military action by one state in the affairs of any other state.

The formation of the OAS, however, did not end the interference of the United States in Latin American affairs. As the Cold War developed, so too did the anxiety of U.S. policy makers about the possibility of communist regimes in Central America and the Caribbean. As a result, the United States returned to a policy of taking action when it believed that Soviet agents were trying to set up governments hostile to U.S. interests.

After Fidel Castro created a Marxist state in Cuba, the desire of the United States to prevent "another Cuba" largely determined U.S. policy toward Latin America. In the 1960s, President John F. Kennedy's Alliance for Progress encouraged social reform and economic development in Latin America. It was hoped that economic growth would keep people happy and less inclined to follow radical leaders. The Alliance for Progress failed to work, however. Much of the money intended for economic development ended up in the pockets of the rich.

When Cuba began to start guerrilla wars in other Latin American countries, the United States reacted by sending massive military aid to anti-Communist regimes, regardless of their nature. In the 1980s and 1990s, the United States returned to a policy of direct intervention in Latin American affairs.

☑ READING PROGRESS CHECK

Explaining What was the Alliance for Progress, and why did it fail?

Mexico and the Caribbean

GUIDING QUESTION *What economic and political challenges did Latin American countries face during the Cold War?*

Throughout the twentieth century, Mexico and the Caribbean have experienced political turmoil and economic crises.

Mexico

The Mexican Revolution in the early 1900s created a political order that remained stable for many years. The official political party of the Mexican Revolution—the Institutional Revolutionary Party, or PRI—came to dominate Mexico. Every six years, leaders of the PRI chose the party's presidential candidate, who was then elected by the people. During the 1950s and 1960s, steady economic growth led to real gains in wages in Mexico.

At the end of the 1960s, student protests against Mexico's one-party government system led to change. Two presidents, Luis Echeverría and José López Portillo, made political reforms, and new political parties emerged. Greater freedom of debate in the press and universities was allowed.

In the late 1970s, vast new reserves of oil were discovered in Mexico. The government became more dependent on revenues from foreign oil sales. Then, when world oil prices dropped in the mid-1980s, Mexico was no longer able to make payments on its foreign debt. The government adopted new economic policies. One was **privatization**, the sale of government-owned companies to private firms.

President Carlos Salinas de Gortari sped up privatization to relieve the debt crisis. In 1992 de Gortari began working with the U.S. president and the Canadian prime minister to form the North American Free Trade Agreement (NAFTA). It went into effect in 1994.

The Cuban Revolution

In the 1950s, an opposition movement arose in Cuba. It aimed to overthrow the government of the dictator Fulgencio Batista, who had controlled Cuba since 1933. The leader of the movement was a man named Fidel Castro. In 1954 Fidel and his brother Raúl teamed up with a small band of revolutionaries. As the rebels gained more support, the Batista regime collapsed. Castro's revolutionaries seized Havana on January 3, 1959. Many Cubans who disagreed with Castro fled to the United States.

Relations between Cuba and the United States quickly deteriorated when Castro's regime began to receive aid from the Soviet Union. In October 1960, the United States declared a **trade embargo** with Cuba. Just three months later, all diplomatic relations with Cuba were broken.

After the failure of the Bay of Pigs invasion and the Cuban Missile Crisis, Cuba became less dependent on the Soviet Union and pursued a new strategy of fomenting revolution in the rest of Latin America. Although Cuba's strategy failed, Castro's Marxist regime continued but with mixed results. The Cuban people did secure some social gains, such as free medical services for all citizens. With improvements in education, illiteracy was nearly eliminated.

Haiti

After American troops left Haiti in 1934, the Haitians made several efforts to move toward democracy. In 1957, however, in elections controlled by the military, François Duvalier became president. He created a private militia,

privatization the sale of government-owned companies to private firms

▲ Fidel Castro and two guerillas at their mountain hideout during the insurgency against Cuban dictator Fulgencio Batista.

trade embargo a policy prohibiting trade with a particular country

PHOTO: Corbis

Oscar Romero (1917–1980)

Oscar Romero was appointed Archbishop of San Salvador in part because of his moderate political views. But in his weekly radio broadcasts, he soon began to attack the Salvadoran government's violent practices. Romero quickly became, in the words of his personal aide, "the most loved person and the most hated person" in the country. On March 24, 1980, Romero was murdered while he celebrated mass in a private chapel in San Salvador. His death was the most notable in a 12-year-long civil war in which more than 70,000 Salvadorans died.

▶ **CRITICAL THINKING**

Specifying How did Oscar Romero's political views change?

target something or someone marked for attack

established dictatorial rule, and terrorized the country, killing tens of thousands. After his death in 1971, his son continued to rule Haiti with an iron fist. Growing opposition to his rule led to the collapse of his regime in 1986, followed five years later by a return to democracy with the election of Jean-Bertrand Aristide.

✓ **READING PROGRESS CHECK**

Determining Cause and Effect What immediate effects did the Cuban revolution have on Cuba's relationship with the United States?

Central America

GUIDING QUESTION *What economic and political challenges did Latin American countries face during the Cold War?*

Central America includes seven countries: Costa Rica, Nicaragua, Honduras, El Salvador, Panama, Belize, and Guatemala. Economically, Central America has historically depended on the export of bananas, coffee, and cotton. Prices for these products have varied over time, however, creating economic crises. In addition, a huge gulf between a wealthy elite and poor peasants has created a climate of instability in the region. The U.S. fear of the spread of communism often led to U.S. support for repressive regimes in Central America. The involvement of the United States was especially evident in the nations of Guatemala, El Salvador, and Nicaragua.

Guatemala

In 1954, with support from the United States, Jacobo Arbenz of Guatemala was overthrown. A series of military or military-dominated dictators then ruled the country for years. Guerrilla forces began forming to oppose the government, which responded in the early 1980s by using military action and economic reforms to defeat the guerrillas. As in El Salvador, right-wing death squads began attacking anyone they believed belonged to the opposition, especially the indigenous people of Guatemala, the descendants of the ancient Maya. The government killed as many as 200,000 people, mostly unarmed Maya.

El Salvador

After World War II, the wealthy elite and the military controlled the government in El Salvador. The rise of an urban middle class led to hope for a more democratic government. The army, however, refused to accept the results of free elections that were held in 1972.

World attention focused on El Salvador in the late 1970s and the 1980s when the country was rocked by a bitter civil war. Marxist-led, leftist guerrillas and right-wing groups battled one another. The Catholic Church became a main **target**, and a number of priests were killed or tortured, among them Archbishop Oscar Romero. The United States began to provide weapons and training to the Salvadoran army to defeat the guerrillas. The hope was to bring stability to the country, but the killings continued until a 1992 peace settlement ended the war.

Nicaragua

In Nicaragua, the Somoza family seized control of the government in 1937 and maintained control for the next 43 years. Over most of this period, the Somoza regime had the support of the United States. The Somozas enriched themselves at the expense of the Nicaraguan people and used murder and torture to silence opposition.

By 1979, the United States, under President Jimmy Carter, had grown unwilling to support the corrupt regime. In that same year, Marxist guerrilla forces known as the Sandinista National Liberation Front won a number of military victories against government forces and gained control of the country. Soon, a group opposed to the Sandinistas' policies, called the contras, began to try to overthrow the new government. Worried by the Sandinistas' alignment with the Soviet Union, the United States supported the contras.

The war waged by the contras undermined support for the Sandinistas. In 1990 the Sandinistas, led by Daniel Ortega, agreed to free elections and lost to a coalition headed by Violeta Barrios de Chamorro, who became Nicaragua's first female president.

▲ This Nicaraguan mural depicts the killing of four students at an anti-Somoza protest on July 23, 1959.

 **READING PROGRESS CHECK**

Comparing What experiences did Guatemala, El Salvador, and Nicaragua have in common in the post-World War II period?

South America

GUIDING QUESTION *What economic and political challenges did Latin American countries face during the Cold War?*

Throughout the twentieth century, most South American countries experienced political unrest and had economic and social problems.

Chile

The history of Chile has mirrored the experience of other Latin American countries. However, it took a dramatic step in 1970 when Salvador Allende (ah • YEHN • day), a Marxist, became president.

Allende tried to create a socialist society through constitutional means. His first steps were to increase wages and to nationalize the largest corporations. Allende's policies were not popular with everyone. Nationalization of the copper industry angered the companies' owners in the United States, as well as the U.S. government. However, Allende gained support in the Chilean congress. Afraid of Allende's growing strength, General Augusto Pinochet (PEE • noh • CHEHT) moved to overthrow the government. In September 1973 military forces killed Allende and set up a dictatorship.

The Pinochet regime was one of the most brutal in Chile's history. Thousands of opponents were imprisoned, tortured, or murdered. The regime also outlawed all political parties and did away with the congress. These horrible abuses of human rights led to growing unrest in the mid-1980s. Thousands of Pinochet opponents and other civilians were arrested and were never seen again. Pinochet finally lost in 1989 in free presidential elections.

Argentina

Argentina is Latin America's second-largest country. For years, it had been ruled by a powerful oligarchy whose wealth was based on growing wheat and raising cattle. Support from the army was crucial to the continuing power of the oligarchy.

▲ The Mothers of the Plaza de Mayo, mothers and grandmothers of the *desaparecidos* (the disappeared) of Argentina's "dirty war," demonstrate outside La Casa Rosada in Buenos Aires.

In 1943, during World War II, a group of army officers overthrew the oligarchy. The new regime was not sure how to deal with the working classes. Juan Perón devised a new strategy. Using his position as labor secretary in the military government, Perón sought to win over the workers, known as the *descamisados* (the shirtless ones). He encouraged them to join labor unions and increased job benefits.

In 1946 Juan Perón was elected president of Argentina, with his chief support coming from labor and the urban middle class. His wife, Eva Perón, was adored by many Argentines and was a major part of the Perón regime. Together, the Peróns brought social reforms to Argentina.

To please his supporters from labor and the urban middle class, Perón followed a policy of increased industrialization. He sought to free Argentina from foreign investors. The government bought the railways and took over the banking, insurance, shipping, and communications industries. Perón's regime, however, was also authoritarian. He created Fascist gangs that used violent means to terrify his opponents.

The military overthrew the Argentinean leader in September 1955. Perón went into exile in Spain. Overwhelmed by problems, military leaders later allowed him to return. He was reelected as president in 1973 but died a year later. In 1976 the military once again took over power. The new regime tolerated no opposition. It is believed that 36,000 people were killed.

In April 1982, the military regime invaded the Falkland Islands off the coast of Argentina. Great Britain, which had controlled the islands since the 1800s, sent ships and troops and took the islands back. The loss discredited the military and opened the door to civilian rule in Argentina. When Raúl Alfonsín was elected president in 1983, he restored democracy and prosecuted the former military leaders.

Colombia

Colombia has long had a democratic political system, but a conservative elite led by the owners of coffee plantations has dominated the government. Coffee is an important crop for Colombia, making up about half of the country's legal exports. Yet because the economy relies heavily upon the coffee trade, price fluctuations in either direction can have a negative effect on the overall economy.

In addition to economic problems, political problems troubled Colombia in the twentieth century. After World War II, Marxist guerrilla groups began to organize Colombian peasants. The government responded violently. More than 200,000 peasants had been killed by the mid-1960s. Violence continued in the 1980s and 1990s.

Peasants who lived in poverty turned to a new cash crop—coca leaves, which are used to make cocaine. As the lucrative drug trade grew, two major **cartels** formed in Colombia.

cartels groups of drug businesses

The drug cartels used bribes and violence to force government cooperation in the drug traffic and to dominate the market. Colombia became the major cocaine supplier of the international drug market. Violence increased as rebel guerrillas made deals with the cartels to oppose the government. The government used an aerial eradication program to try to wipe out cocaine fields, but the program did not have much success. Despite the money earned from drug and coffee exports, the Colombian economy remained weak because of high unemployment and the disruption of civil war.

☑ READING PROGRESS CHECK

Explaining How did the invasion of the Falkland Islands affect Argentina?

Latin American Society and Culture

GUIDING QUESTION *How did Latin American society and culture change after World War II?*

Latin America's economic problems have been made worse by its dramatic growth in population. Both Latin America and North America (the United States and Canada) had the same populations in 1950—about 165 million people. By the mid-1980s, however, Latin America's population had exploded to 400 million. That of North America was about 270 million. With the increase in population came a rapid rise in the size of cities. By 1990, there were 29 cities with more than a million people, including Mexico City and Buenos Aires. Analysts refer to such cities as megacities. **Megacities** in Latin America have often grown so fast that regular urban services cannot be provided.

Latin American women's roles have changed. Although the traditional role of homemaker continues, women have also moved into new jobs. In addition to farm labor, women have found jobs in industry and as teachers, professors, doctors, and lawyers.

Twentieth-century Latin American writers and artists have played important roles in their society. Their work is seen as expressing the hopes of the people. Because of this, artists and writers hold high status in Latin American society.

In the 1940s, Latin American writers developed a unique form of expression called magic realism. **Magic realism** brings together realistic events with dreamlike or fantasy backgrounds. The rules of ordinary life are suspended in order to comment on a national or social situation. Perhaps the foremost example of magic realism is *One Hundred Years of Solitude*, a novel by Gabriel García Márquez, a Colombian writer, who won the Nobel Prize in literature in 1982. In this story of the fictional town of Macondo, the point of view slips back and forth between fact and fantasy. According to Márquez, fantasy and fact depend on one's point of view.

Latin American art and architecture were strongly influenced by international styles after World War II. Perhaps the most notable example of modern architecture can be seen in Brasília, the capital of Brazil, which was built in the 1950s and 1960s. Brazilian architect Oscar Niemeyer was appointed chief architect for the new capital.

megacity a very large city

magic realism a form of expression unique to Latin American literature; it combines realistic events with dreamlike or fantasy backgrounds

☑ **READING PROGRESS CHECK**

Defining What problems do megacities cause in Latin America?

LESSON 4 REVIEW

Reviewing Vocabulary
1. *Analyzing* How did the drug cartels in Colombia maintain their control over the cocaine trade?

Using Your Notes
2. *Comparing* Use your notes to describe the similarities among major events in Latin American countries during the Cold War.

Answering the Guiding Questions
3. *Identifying Central Issues* How did the involvement of the United States and the Soviet Union increase instability in Latin American countries?

4. *Making Generalizations* What economic and political challenges did Latin American countries face during the Cold War?

5. *Identifying* How did Latin American society and culture change after World War II?

Writing Activity
6. ARGUMENT The United States has increasingly tried to use economic tools rather than military force to resolve conflicts in Latin America. Research the trade embargo imposed on Cuba. Write a persuasive argument for or against the embargo.

Directions: On a separate sheet of paper, answer the questions below. Make sure you read carefully and answer all parts of the questions.

Lesson Review

Lesson 1

1 **EXPLAINING** After World War II, what decision did Indian Prime Minister Jawaharlal Nehru make in following the principle of nonalignment?

2 **SUMMARIZING** How did women's roles change across South and Southeast Asia after the war?

Lesson 2

3 **ANALYZING** Why has it been difficult to resolve conflict in the Middle East? Give specific examples.

4 **SPECULATING** What might have happened if Pan-Arabism had been more widely accepted among Arab states?

Lesson 3

5 **MAKING INFERENCES** In 1960 two-thirds of the 69 people killed during a peaceful anti-apartheid march were shot in the back. What does this suggest happened?

6 **CONTRASTING** Contrast African cities with rural Africa.

Lesson 4

7 **IDENTIFYING** What political changes occurred in the late 1960s in Mexico?

8 **FINDING THE MAIN IDEA** What happened as a result of the Cuban Revolution?

21st Century Skills

9 **ECONOMICS** How were Western countries affected by the formation of OPEC?

10 **IDENTIFYING CONTINUITY AND CHANGE** What changed for the Philippines after World War II? What were the experiences of this country as a result of this change?

Exploring the Essential Questions

11 **ANALYZING CAUSE AND EFFECT** Create a cause-and-effect diagram with a partner showing the conflicts two or more African states of your choice have encountered as they struggled to gain independence and how their political relationships have affected economic relationships with other countries or states. Illustrate your diagram using other forms of media, such as a photograph, a map, and/or a graph. For example, you could have a photo depicting a demonstration in South Africa and a map showing Rwanda and Uganda.

DBQ Analyzing Historical Documents

Use the document to answer the following questions.

U.S. AGRICULTURAL TRADE WITH NAFTA PARTNERS, 1989–2002

Source: U.S. Department of Agriculture

12 **USING GRAPHS** How did NAFTA affect agricultural trade between the United States, Mexico, and Canada?

13 **COMPARING AND CONTRASTING** Compare and contrast what has happened to the imports and exports between the United States and its NAFTA partners.

Extended-Response Question

14 **INFORMATIVE/EXPLANATORY** Write a multiparagraph essay explaining how religious, political, economic, and ethnic reasons have fueled conflicts in South and Southeast Asia, the Middle East, Africa, and Latin America since World War II. Give one or more examples from each of the four lessons in the chapter to illustrate each reason.

Need Extra Help?

If You've Missed Question	1	2	3	4	5	6	7	8	9	10	11	12	13	14
Go to page	387	390	391	392	398	401	405	405	393	388	397	410	410	386

Life During the Cold War

1945–1989

ESSENTIAL QUESTIONS • *How does war result in change?*
• *What challenges may countries face as a result of war?*

The Story Matters...

During the Cold War, the United States and the Soviet Union had stockpiles of nuclear weapons. When the arms race led to increased hostility between the two nations, the world prepared for the threat of nuclear war. The Soviet Union and United States organized civil defense programs designed to train the civilian population how to react in the event of a nuclear attack. The programs involved "duck and cover" and evacuation drills, as well as widely circulated public safety announcements.

◄ "Duck and cover" drills taught school children how to protect themselves from a nuclear attack. However, these drills would have provided no real protection from the destruction of a bomb or the resulting nuclear radiation.

PHOTO: ©Bettmann/Corbis

411

Place and Time: Europe and the U.S. 1945–1989

During the decades of the Cold War, the tension between the United States and the Soviet Union not only colored foreign affairs but also influenced the nature of daily life. Citizens grew increasingly anxious under the threat of nuclear war. In the United States and Western Europe, students protested political and economic conditions. In the Eastern bloc countries, popular discontent increased when the state did not provide political freedoms or economic security. While the methods of political protest were similar, their goals were different. Furthermore, the level of political freedom in the East and West helped determine the fate of these protest movements.

Step Into the Place

Read the quotes and look at the information presented on the map.

 Analyzing Historical Documents What were the goals of political protests? Which movements do you think were successful?

PRIMARY SOURCE

❝We consider socialist democracy to be a system in which the working man has his own standing and value, his security, his right, and his future. It is based upon human participation, coherence, and cooperation. We wish to meet people's longing for a society in which they can feel to be human among humans. This active, humane, integrating part of socialism, a society without antagonism, that is what we want to realize systematically and gradually, serving the people.❞

—First Secretary Alexander Dubček, from a speech to the Central Committee of the Communist Party of Czechoslovakia, April 1, 1968

PRIMARY SOURCE

❝We are occupying the faculties, you are occupying the factories. Aren't we fighting for the same thing? Higher education only contains 10 percent workers' children. Are we fighting so that there will be more of them, for a democratic university reform? That would a good thing, but it's not the most important. These workers' children would become just like other students. We are not aiming for a worker's son to be a manager. We want to wipe out segregation between workers and management.❞

—The March 22 Movement, "Your Struggle Is Ours," May 21, 1968

PHOTO: (l)Keystone-France/Gamma-Keystone/Getty Images, (r)©Bettmann/Corbis.

Step Into the Time

Predicting Consequences

Choose an event from the time line and explain how it might have affected everyday life in the United States or Europe during the Cold War.

EUROPE AND THE UNITED STATES

THE WORLD

1945 — 1955

1945 World War II ends

1946 Great Britain passes the National Insurance Act and National Health Service Act

1956 Hungarians revolt against Soviets

1960 France explodes its first nuclear bomb

1963 U.S. passes the Equal Pay Act

1948 UN adopts Universal Declaration of Human Rights

1956 Gamal Abdel Nasser takes over Egyptian government

1962 Nikita Khrushchev allows publication of *One Day in the Life of Ivan Denisovich*

1963 Nelson Mandela delivers speech during Rivonia trial

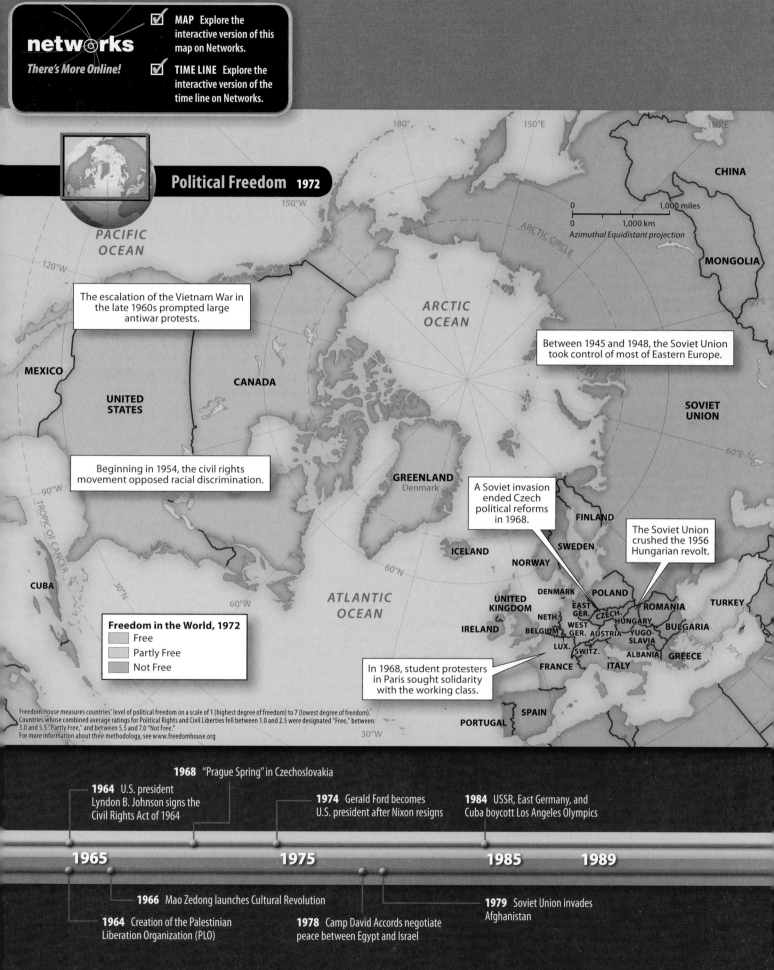

networks
There's More Online!

☑ MAP Explore the interactive version of this map on Networks.

☑ TIME LINE Explore the interactive version of the time line on Networks.

Political Freedom 1972

PACIFIC OCEAN

ARCTIC OCEAN

CHINA

MONGOLIA

The escalation of the Vietnam War in the late 1960s prompted large antiwar protests.

Between 1945 and 1948, the Soviet Union took control of most of Eastern Europe.

MEXICO

CANADA

UNITED STATES

SOVIET UNION

Beginning in 1954, the civil rights movement opposed racial discrimination.

GREENLAND
Denmark

A Soviet invasion ended Czech political reforms in 1968.

FINLAND

The Soviet Union crushed the 1956 Hungarian revolt.

ICELAND

SWEDEN

NORWAY

CUBA

ATLANTIC OCEAN

DENMARK POLAND

UNITED KINGDOM

EAST GER. CZECH. ROMANIA

TURKEY

NETH. HUNGARY

IRELAND BELGIUM WEST GER. AUSTRIA YUGO-SLAVIA BULGARIA

LUX. SWITZ. ALBANIA GREECE

Freedom in the World, 1972
- Free
- Partly Free
- Not Free

FRANCE ITALY

In 1968, student protesters in Paris sought solidarity with the working class.

SPAIN

PORTUGAL

Freedom House measures countries' level of political freedom on a scale of 1 (highest degree of freedom) to 7 (lowest degree of freedom). Countries whose combined average ratings for Political Rights and Civil Liberties fell between 1.0 and 2.5 were designated "Free," between 3.0 and 5.5 "Partly Free," and between 5.5 and 7.0 "Not Free." For more information about their methodology, see www.freedomhouse.org

1968 "Prague Spring" in Czechoslovakia

1964 U.S. president Lyndon B. Johnson signs the Civil Rights Act of 1964

1974 Gerald Ford becomes U.S. president after Nixon resigns

1984 USSR, East Germany, and Cuba boycott Los Angeles Olympics

1965

1975

1985

1989

1966 Mao Zedong launches Cultural Revolution

1964 Creation of the Palestinian Liberation Organization (PLO)

1978 Camp David Accords negotiate peace between Egypt and Israel

1979 Soviet Union invades Afghanistan

networks

There's More Online!

☑ **CHART/GRAPH** The Pay Gap

☑ **CHART/GRAPH** Women's Suffrage by Country and Year

☑ **IMAGE** Equal Rights Amendment Rally in Pittsburgh, 1976

☑ **IMAGE** Family Life in the 1950s

☑ **IMAGE** Integration of Little Rock Central High School

☑ **INTERACTIVE SELF-CHECK QUIZ**

☑ **MAP** European Economic Community, 1989

☑ **VIDEO** Western Europe and North America

Reading **HELP**DESK CCSS

Academic Vocabulary

- shift
- minimal

Content Vocabulary

- **welfare state**
- **bloc**
- **consumer society**
- **women's liberation movement**
- **real wages**

TAKING NOTES:

Key Ideas and Details

Identifying As you read, use a chart like the one below to identify the economic policies of Western countries during the Cold War.

Country	Policies
France	
West Germany	
Great Britain	
United States	
Canada	

LESSON 1
Western Europe and North America

ESSENTIAL QUESTIONS • *How does war result in change?*
• *What challenges may countries face as a result of war?*

IT MATTERS BECAUSE

Most Western European countries recovered rapidly from World War II. The United States experienced an economic boom after World War II but was troubled by social and political issues.

Western Europe

GUIDING QUESTION *How did Western Europe recover from World War II?*

With the economic aid of the Marshall Plan, the countries of Western Europe recovered relatively rapidly from the devastation of World War II. By 1950, industrial output in Europe was 30 percent above prewar levels.

France and de Gaulle

One man—the war hero Charles de Gaulle—dominated the history of France for nearly a quarter of a century after the war. In 1946 de Gaulle helped establish a new government, the Fourth Republic. It, however, was largely ineffective. In 1958 leaders of the Fourth Republic, frightened by bitter divisions caused by a crisis in the French colony of Algeria, asked de Gaulle to form a new government. That year, de Gaulle drafted a new constitution for the Fifth Republic that enhanced the power of the president. The French president would now have the right to choose the prime minister, dissolve parliament, and supervise defense and foreign policy. French voters approved the constitution, and de Gaulle became the first president of the Fifth Republic.

As president, de Gaulle wanted France to be a world power once again. To achieve this, de Gaulle invested heavily in nuclear arms. France exploded its first nuclear bomb in 1960.

During de Gaulle's presidency, the French economy grew at an annual rate of 5.5 percent, faster than the rate of growth in the United States. France became a major industrial producer and exporter, especially of automobiles and weapons. Nevertheless, problems remained. Large government deficits and a rise in the cost

PHOTO: (l to r)Francis Miller/Time & Life Pictures/Getty Images, Barbara Freeman/Hulton Archive/Getty Images, SuperStock, ©Bettmann/Corbis.

of living led to unrest. In May 1968, a series of student protests was followed by a general labor strike. Discouraged, de Gaulle resigned from office in April 1969 and died within a year.

In the 1970s, a deteriorating economic situation caused a political **shift** to the left. By 1981, the Socialists gained power in the National Assembly. Socialist François Mitterrand was elected president. He initiated a number of measures to aid workers—an increased minimum wage, a 39-hour work week, and higher taxes for the rich. The Socialist government also nationalized, or took over, major banks, the steel industry, the space and electronics industries, and insurance firms.

Socialist policies, however, largely failed to work, and France's economic decline continued. In the elections in March of 1993, the Socialists won only 28 percent of the vote. A coalition of conservative parties gained 80 percent of the seats in the National Assembly.

West Germany: The Economic Miracle

The three Western zones of Germany were unified as the Federal Republic of Germany in 1949. From 1949 to 1963, Konrad Adenauer (AHD • uh • NAU • uhr), the leader of the Christian Democratic Union (CDU), served as chancellor (head of state). Adenauer sought respect for West Germany. He cooperated with the United States and other Western European nations, especially France—Germany's longtime enemy.

Under Adenauer, West Germany experienced an "economic miracle." This revival of the West German economy was largely guided by the minister of finance, Ludwig Erhard. Unemployment fell from 8 percent in 1950 to 0.4 percent in 1965. After Adenauer resigned in 1963, Erhard succeeded him as chancellor and largely continued his policies.

An economic downturn in the mid-1960s brought the Social Democratic Party into power in 1969. The Social Democrats, a moderate socialist party, were led by Willy Brandt, mayor of West Berlin. In December 1972, Brandt signed a treaty that led to greater contact between East Germany and West Germany. Economic, cultural, and personal ties between the countries were stronger as a result. For his efforts, Brandt received the Nobel Peace Prize for 1971.

Great Britain

The end of World War II left Great Britain with massive economic problems. In elections held immediately after the war, the Labour Party overwhelmingly defeated Churchill's Conservative Party.

Under Clement Attlee, the new prime minister, the Labour government set out to create a modern **welfare state**, a state in which the government takes responsibility for providing citizens with services and a **minimal** standard of living. In 1946 the new government passed the National Insurance Act and the National Health Service Act. The insurance act provided government funds to help the unemployed, the sick, and the aged. The health act created a system of socialized medicine that ensured medical care for everyone. The British welfare state became the norm for most European states after the war.

Continuing economic problems brought the Conservatives back into power from 1951 to 1964. Although they favored private enterprise, the Conservatives accepted the welfare state and extended it by financing an ambitious building program to improve British housing.

Between 1964 and 1979, power alternated between Great Britain's Conservative Party and Labour Party. In 1979 the Conservatives came to power under Margaret Thatcher, Britain's first female prime minister.

shift a change in direction

welfare state a state in which the government takes responsibility for providing citizens with services such as health care

minimal barely adequate

▲ West German chancellor Willy Brandt

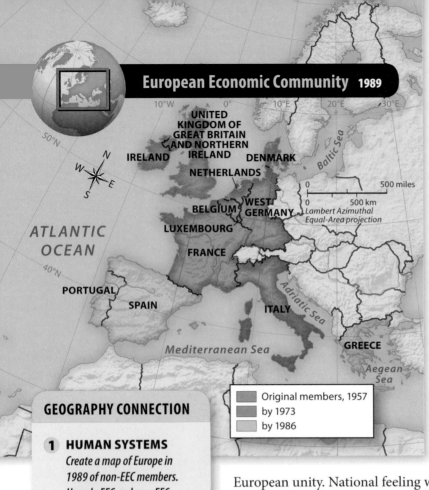

European Economic Community 1989

UNITED KINGDOM OF GREAT BRITAIN AND NORTHERN IRELAND

IRELAND · IRELAND · DENMARK

NETHERLANDS

BELGIUM · WEST GERMANY

LUXEMBOURG

FRANCE

PORTUGAL

SPAIN

ITALY

GREECE

ATLANTIC OCEAN

Mediterranean Sea

Baltic Sea

Adriatic Sea

Aegean Sea

50°N · 40°N · 10°W · 0° · 10°E · 20°E · 30°E

0   500 miles
0   500 km
Lambert Azimuthal Equal-Area projection

Original members, 1957
by 1973
by 1986

GEOGRAPHY CONNECTION

1 HUMAN SYSTEMS
Create a map of Europe in 1989 of non-EEC members. How do EEC and non-EEC countries differ?

2 PLACES AND REGIONS *Create a graph or chart of the expansion of EEC membership.*

bloc a group of nations with a common purpose

Thatcher pledged to limit social welfare, to restrict union power, and to end inflation. Her main focus was privatization. Although she did not eliminate the basic social welfare system, Thatcher broke the power of the labor unions and controlled inflation.

Thatcherism, as her economic policy was termed, improved the British economic situation, but at a price. Business investment and the number of small businesses increased substantially. The south of England, for example, prospered. Old industrial areas elsewhere, however, were beset by high unemployment, poverty, and violence. Thatcher dominated British politics in the 1980s, but in 1990 her popularity fell, and she resigned as prime minister.

The European Economic Community

The destructiveness of two world wars caused many thoughtful Europeans to consider the need for some form of European unity. National feeling was still too powerful, however, for European nations to give up their political sovereignty. As a result, the desire for unity focused chiefly on the economic arena, not the political one.

In 1957 France, West Germany, the Benelux countries (Belgium, the Netherlands, and Luxembourg), and Italy signed the Rome Treaty. This treaty created the European Economic Community (EEC), also known as the Common Market.

The EEC was a free-trade area made up of the six member nations. These six nations would impose no tariffs, or import charges, on each other's goods. However, as a group, they would be protected by a tariff imposed on goods from non-EEC nations. In this way, the EEC encouraged cooperation among the member nations' economies.

By the 1960s, the EEC had become an important trading **bloc** (a group of nations with a common purpose.) In 1973 Britain, Denmark, and Ireland joined the EEC. With a total population of 165 million, the EEC was the world's largest exporter and purchaser of raw materials. By 1986, Spain, Portugal, and Greece had become members. By 1992, the European Economic Community comprised 344 million people and was the world's largest single trading bloc.

✔ **READING PROGRESS CHECK**

Describing How was the Fifth Republic in France different from the Fourth Republic?

The U.S. After the War

GUIDING QUESTION *What social and political issues challenged the United States during the Cold War?*

Between 1945 and 1970, the ideals of Franklin Delano Roosevelt's New Deal largely determined the patterns of American domestic politics. The New Deal brought basic changes to American society. These changes included a dramatic increase in the role and power of the federal government, the rise of organized labor, the beginning of a welfare state, and a realization of the need to deal fairly with the concerns of minorities, especially African Americans.

The New Deal tradition in American politics was reinforced by the election of Democratic presidents—Harry S. Truman in 1948, John F. Kennedy in 1960, and Lyndon B. Johnson in 1964. Even the election of a Republican president, Dwight D. Eisenhower, in 1952 and 1956, did not change the basic direction of the New Deal.

An economic boom followed World War II. A shortage of consumer goods during the war left Americans with extra income and the desire to buy goods after the war. In addition, the growth of labor unions brought higher wages and gave more workers the ability to buy consumer goods. Between 1945 and 1973, **real wages** grew an average of 3 percent per year, the most prolonged advance ever in American history.

real wages the actual purchasing power of income

Prosperity was not the only characteristic of the early 1950s. Cold War struggles abroad led to the widespread fear that Communists had infiltrated the United States. This climate of fear produced a dangerous political agitator, Senator Joseph R. McCarthy of Wisconsin. His charges that hundreds of supposed Communists were in high government positions helped create a massive "Red Scare"—fear of Communist subversion. When McCarthy attacked "Communist conspirators" in the U.S. Army, he was condemned by the Senate in 1954. Very quickly, his anti-Communist crusade came to an end.

The 1960s and Civil Rights

In August 1963, the Reverend Martin Luther King, Jr., leader of a movement for racial equality, led a march on Washington, D.C., to dramatize the African American desire for equality. King's march and his impassioned plea for racial equality had an electrifying effect on the American people. By the end of 1963, a majority of the American people called civil rights the most significant national issue.

After the assassination of John Kennedy, Lyndon B. Johnson became president. Following his landslide victory in 1964, he pursued the cause of equal rights for African Americans. The Civil Rights Act of 1964 created the machinery to end segregation and discrimination in the workplace and all public places. The Voting Rights Act made it easier for African Americans to vote in Southern states.

Laws alone, however, could not guarantee the Great Society that Johnson talked about creating. He soon faced bitter social unrest. In 1968 Martin Luther King, Jr., was assassinated. Riots hit more than 100 cities, including Washington, D.C. The riots led to a "white backlash" (whites became less sympathetic to the cause of racial equality) and continued the racial division of the United States. Antiwar protests also divided the United States as some Americans turned against the Vietnam War.

The combination of antiwar demonstrations and riots in the cities caused many people to call for law and order. This was the appeal used by Richard Nixon, the Republican presidential candidate in 1968. With Nixon's election, a shift to the political right in American politics began.

▼ The Reverend Martin Luther King, Jr., at the March on Washington, August 28, 1963.

▶ **CRITICAL THINKING**
Determining Cause and Effect What do you think was the effect of the March on Washington?

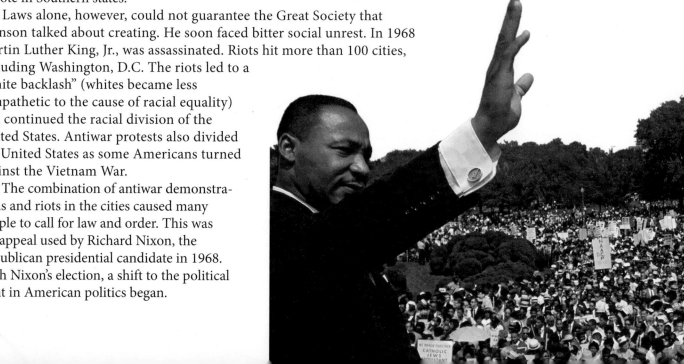

The Voting Rights Act of 1965

66This act flows from a clear and simple wrong. Its only purpose is to right that wrong. Millions of Americans are denied the right to vote because of their color. This law will ensure them the right to vote. . . . I pledge you that we will not delay, or we will not hesitate, or we will not turn aside until Americans of every race and color and origin in this country have the same right as all others to share in the process of democracy.99

—President Lyndon B. Johnson, "Remarks in the Capitol Rotunda at the Signing of the Voting Rights Act," August 6, 1965

DBQ **DRAWING CONCLUSIONS** What is the significance of the Voting Rights Act of 1965?

consumer society a society preoccupied with buying goods

The 1970s and 1980s

As president, Nixon used illegal methods to gain information about his opponents. This led to the Watergate scandal. After lying to the American public about his involvement in the affair, secret tapes of his conversations in the White House revealed the truth. On August 9, 1974, Nixon resigned rather than face possible impeachment.

In the 1976 election, the former governor of Georgia, Jimmy Carter, became president. A crisis abroad erupted when the Iranian government of the Ayatollah Khomeini (koh • MAY • nee) held 52 Americans hostage. Carter's inability to gain the release of the American hostages contributed to his loss to Ronald Reagan in the 1980 election.

Canada

After the war, Canada began developing electronic, aircraft, nuclear, and chemical engineering industries on a large scale. Under Lester Pearson, the Liberal government laid the groundwork for Canada's welfare state. A national social security system and health insurance program were enacted.

When Pierre Trudeau (TROO • DOH) became prime minister in 1968, he supported a vigorous program of industrialization. He was also dedicated to preserving a united Canada. At the same time, he acknowledged the rights of French-speaking Canadians. His government passed the Official Languages Act, which allowed English and French to be used in the federal civil service.

☑ **READING PROGRESS CHECK**

Drawing Conclusions In the United States how was the decade of the 1970s a reaction to the 1960s?

Western Society

GUIDING QUESTION *How did Western society change during the Cold War?*

After World War II, Western society witnessed rapid change. New inventions such as computers, televisions, and jet planes altered the pace and nature of human life.

A New Social Structure

Postwar Western society was marked by a changing social structure. Especially noticeable were changes in the middle class. Traditional middle-class groups were made up of businesspeople, lawyers, doctors, and teachers. A new group of managers and technicians, hired by large companies and government agencies, now joined the middle class.

Changes also occurred among the lower classes. The shift of people from rural to urban areas continued. The number of people in farming declined drastically. By the 1950s, the number of farmers in most parts of Europe dropped by 50 percent. The number of industrial workers declined as white-collar workers increased.

At the same time, a noticeable increase in the real wages of workers made it possible for them to imitate the buying patterns of the middle class. This led to what some observers have called the **consumer society**. Buying on credit became widespread in the 1950s. Workers could now buy such products as televisions, washing machines, refrigerators, and stereos.

Women in the Postwar World

Women's participation in the world wars had resulted in several gains. They had achieved one of the major aims of the nineteenth-century feminist movement—the right to vote.

During World War II, women had entered the workforce in huge numbers. At the war's end, however, they were removed to provide jobs for soldiers returning home. For a time, women fell back into traditional roles. Birthrates rose, creating a "baby boom" in the late 1940s and the 1950s.

By the end of the 1950s, however, the birthrate began to fall and, with it, the size of families. The structure of the workplace changed once again as the number of married women in the workforce increased in Europe and the United States. These women, especially working-class women, faced an old problem. They still earned less than men for equal work. In addition, women still tended to enter traditionally female jobs. Many faced the double burden of earning income and raising a family. Such inequalities led increasing numbers of women to rebel. In the late 1960s came renewed interest in feminism, or the **women's liberation movement**.

In the 1960s and 1970s, the women's movement emerged in the United States and quickly spread to Western Europe. Supporters of the movement wanted to change the basic conditions of women's lives. The United States passed the Equal Pay Act in 1963. It required women to be paid the same as men for performing the same work.

A controversial issue was abortion. In 1973 the U.S. Supreme Court legalized abortion in *Roe* v. *Wade*. Although national health insurance covered abortion in most of Europe, the procedure was debated in the United States.

Student Revolts

Growing discontent among university students led to an outburst of student revolts in the late 1960s. Many protests were an extension of the revolts in American universities, often sparked by student opposition to the Vietnam War. Some students, particularly in Europe, believed that universities failed to respond to their needs or to the realities of the modern world. Others believed they were becoming small cogs in the large and impersonal bureaucratic wheels of the modern world.

☑ **READING PROGRESS CHECK**

Summarizing What was a goal of the women's liberation movement?

▲ Men and women march together at an Equal Rights Amendment (ERA) rally in Pittsburgh, Pennsylvania, in 1976.

▶ **CRITICAL THINKING**
Analyzing Visuals Interpret the meaning of the signs carried at the rally.

women's liberation movement the renewed feminist movement of the late 1960s, which demanded political and economic equality with men

---

LESSON 1 REVIEW (CCSS)

Reviewing Vocabulary
1. *Making Connections* How does the rise of the modern welfare state represent a shift to the left in European nations?

Using Your Notes
2. *Identifying* Use your notes to identify economic policies that Western countries implemented after World War II.

Answering the Guiding Questions
3. *Describing* How did Western Europe recover from World War II?

4. *Analyzing Information* Which social and political issues challenged the United States during the Cold War?

5. *Evaluating* How did Western society change during the Cold War?

Writing Activity
6. INFORMATIVE/EXPLANATORY Pick one of the countries discussed in the lesson and, using information from the lesson and outside research, write a short essay about the postwar reforms implemented in the country and discuss whether they were successful.

Reading **HELP**DESK (CCSS)

Academic Vocabulary

- **enhanced**
- **participation**
- **sole**

Content Vocabulary

- **heavy industry**
- **de-Stalinization**
- **détente**
- **dissidents**

TAKING NOTES:

Key Ideas and Details

Comparing As you read, use a table like the one below to compare the policies of Khrushchev and Brezhnev.

Policies	Khrushchev	Brezhnev

LESSON 2
Eastern Europe and the Soviet Union

ESSENTIAL QUESTIONS • *How does war result in change?*
• *What challenges may countries face as a result of war?*

IT MATTERS BECAUSE

Stalin was a repressive leader who wanted to bring Eastern Europe under Soviet control. Many Communist countries came under Soviet control during this era, including Poland, Hungary, and Czechoslovakia. After Stalin's death, Nikita Khrushchev denounced the most brutal policies of the Stalin regime.

Postwar Soviet Union

GUIDING QUESTION *What political, economic, and social shifts occurred in the Soviet Union during the Cold War?*

World War II devastated the Soviet Union. To create a new industrial base, Stalin returned to the method that he had used in the 1930s. Soviet workers were expected to produce goods for export with little in return for themselves. The incoming capital from abroad could then be used to buy machinery and Western technology.

Economic recovery in the Soviet Union was spectacular in some respects. By 1950, Russian industrial production surpassed prewar levels by 40 percent. New power plants, canals, and giant factories were built. **Heavy industry** increased, chiefly for military benefit. The hydrogen bomb in 1953 and the first space satellite, *Sputnik I,* in 1957 **enhanced** the Soviet Union's reputation as a world power.

Yet the Soviet people were shortchanged. The production of consumer goods did not increase as much as heavy industry, and there was a housing shortage. As a British official in Moscow reported, "Every room is both a living room by day and a bedroom by night."

The Rule of Stalin

Stalin was the undisputed master of the Soviet Union. He distrusted competitors, exercised **sole** power, and had little respect for other Communist Party leaders. He is reported to have said to members of his inner circle in 1952, "You are as blind as kittens. What would you do without me?"

Stalin's suspicions added to the regime's increasing repression. In 1946 the government ordered all literary and scientific work to conform to the state's political needs. Along with this anti-intellectual campaign came political terror. The threat of more purges in 1953 disappeared when Stalin died on March 5, 1953.

The Khrushchev Era

A group of leaders succeeded Stalin, but the new general secretary of the Communist Party, Nikita Khrushchev, soon emerged as the chief Soviet policy maker. After he was in power, Khrushchev took steps to undo some of the worst features of Stalin's regime.

At the Twentieth Congress of the Communist Party in 1956, Khrushchev condemned Stalin for his "administrative violence, mass repression, and terror." The process of eliminating the more ruthless policies of Stalin became known as **de-Stalinization**.

Khrushchev loosened government controls on literary and artistic works. In 1962, for example, he allowed the publication of *One Day in the Life of Ivan Denisovich.* This novel, written by Aleksandr Solzhenitsyn (SOHL • zhuh • NEET • suhn), is a grim portrayal of life in a Siberian labor camp. Many Soviets identified with Ivan as a symbol of the suffering endured under Stalin.

Khrushchev also tried to place more emphasis on producing consumer goods. He attempted to increase agricultural output by growing corn and cultivating vast lands east of the Ural Mountains. The attempt was unsuccessful and damaged Khrushchev's reputation within the party. This failure, combined with increased military spending, hurt the Soviet economy.

heavy industry the manufacture of machines and equipment for factories and mines

enhanced improved

sole being the only one

de-Stalinization the process of eliminating Stalin's more ruthless policies

PHOTO: Neil Beer/Photodisc/Getty Images

ANALYZING PRIMARY SOURCES (CCSS)

Contrasting these depictions of Soviet society

Soviet control over the arts was rigid. Artists had to work within the confines of socialist realist art, which was meant to portray the ideals of Soviet society. Common themes included portraits of Soviet political leaders, people performing manual labor, and industrial progress, such as the sculpture Worker and Kolkhoz [collective farm] Woman *by Vera Mukhina (right). Not everyone worked within these confines, however. Aleksandr Solzhenitsyn was exiled for writing* The Gulag Archipelago, *which revealed life in the forced labor camps to which many political opponents were sent in the 1950s. "Archipelago" was his metaphor for forced labor camps and "Gulag" is an acronym for the agency that supervised the camps.*

❝But the whole central meaning of their existence was identical for serfdom and the Archipelago; they were forms of social organization for the forced and pitiless exploitation of the unpaid labor of millions of slaves.❞

— Aleksandr Solzhenitsyn, from *The Gulag Archipelago*

DBQ Analyzing Historical Documents

1 *Differentiating* How do the text and the sculpture demonstrate differing views of life under the Soviet regime?

2 *Making Inferences* Serfdom was abolished in Russia in 1861. What do you think Solzhenitsyn means when he writes that the "meaning of their existence was identical for serfdom and the Archipelago"?

The industrial growth rate, which had soared in the early 1950s, now declined sharply from 13 percent in 1953 to 7.5 percent in 1964.

Foreign policy failures also damaged Khrushchev's reputation among his colleagues. His rash plan to place missiles in Cuba was the final straw. While he was away on vacation in 1964, a special meeting of the Soviet leaders voted him out of office (because of "deteriorating health") and forced him into retirement.

The Brezhnev Era

When Nikita Khrushchev was removed from office in 1964, two men, Alexei Kosygin and Leonid Brezhnev (BREHZH • nehf) replaced him. Brezhnev emerged as the dominant leader in the 1970s. He was determined to keep Eastern Europe in Communist hands and was not interested in reform. Brezhnev insisted on the Soviet Union's right to intervene if communism was threatened in another Communist state (known as the Brezhnev Doctrine).

détente a phase of relaxed tensions and improved relations between two adversaries

At the same time, Brezhnev benefited from **détente**, a relaxation of tensions and improved relations between the United States and the Soviet Union. In the 1970s, the two superpowers signed SALT I and SALT II (Strategic Arms Limitation Treaties) and the Anti-Ballistic Missile (ABM) Treaty to limit nuclear arms. Because they felt more secure, Soviet leaders relaxed their authoritarian rule and allowed more access to Western music, dress, and art. Of course, **dissidents**—those who spoke out against the regime—were still suppressed. For example, Andrei Sakharov, father of the Soviet hydrogen bomb, was punished for defending human rights.

dissident a person who speaks out against the regime in power

In his economic policies, Brezhnev continued to emphasize heavy industry. Two problems, however, weakened the Soviet economy. First, the government's central planning led to a huge, complex bureaucracy that discouraged efficiency and led to indifference. Second, collective farmers had no incentive to work hard. Many preferred working their own small private plots to laboring in the collective work brigades.

By the 1970s, the Communist ruling class in the Soviet Union had become complacent and corrupt. Party and state leaders, as well as army leaders and secret police (KGB), enjoyed a high standard of living. Brezhnev was unwilling to tamper with the party leadership and state bureaucracy regardless of the inefficiency and corruption that the system encouraged.

participation having a part in or sharing in something

By the 1970s, détente had allowed U.S. grain and consumer goods to be sold to the Soviet Union. However, détente collapsed in 1979 when the Soviet Union invaded Afghanistan. A new period of East-West confrontation began. The Soviet Union wanted to restore a pro-Soviet regime in Afghanistan. The United States viewed this as an act of expansion. To show his disapproval, President Jimmy Carter canceled U.S. **participation** in the 1980 Olympic Games to be held in Moscow. He also placed an embargo on the shipment of U.S. grain to the Soviets.

Relations became even chillier when Ronald Reagan became president of the United States. Calling the Soviet Union an "evil empire," he began a military buildup and a new arms race. Reagan also gave military aid to the Afghan rebels to maintain a war in Afghanistan that the Soviet Union could not win.

☑ **READING PROGRESS CHECK**

Contrasting How were U.S.-Soviet relations different during the Khrushchev and Brezhnev regimes?

Eastern Europe

GUIDING QUESTION *How was Eastern Europe affected by communism after World War II?*

At the end of World War II, Soviet military forces occupied all of Eastern Europe and the Balkans (except for Greece, Albania, and Yugoslavia). All the occupied states came under Soviet control.

Communist Patterns of Control

The timetable of the Soviet takeover varied from country to country. Between 1945 and 1947, Soviet-controlled Communist governments became firmly entrenched in East Germany, Bulgaria, Romania, Poland, and Hungary. In Czechoslovakia, where there was a tradition of democracy and a multi-party system, the Soviets did not seize control of the government until 1948. At that time they dissolved all but the Communist Party.

Albania and Yugoslavia were exceptions to this pattern of Soviet dominance. During the war, both countries had strong Communist movements that resisted the Nazis. After the war, local Communist parties took control. Communists in Albania set up a Stalinist-type regime that grew more and more independent of the Soviet Union.

In Yugoslavia, Josip Broz, known as Tito, had been the leader of the Communist resistance movement. After the war, he created an independent Communist state in Yugoslavia. Stalin hoped to take control of Yugoslavia, just as he had done in other Eastern European countries. Tito, however, refused to give in to Stalin's demands. He gained the support of the people by portraying the struggle as one of Yugoslav national freedom. Tito ruled Yugoslavia until his death in 1980. Although Yugoslavia had a Communist government, it was not a Soviet satellite state.

▲ The head of a destroyed statue of Stalin in the middle of a Budapest street during the Hungarian revolt of 1956.

▶ CRITICAL THINKING
Analyzing Visuals What is the symbolic importance of the fallen statue?

Between 1948 and Stalin's death in 1953, the Eastern European satellite states, directed by the Soviet Union, followed Stalin's example. They instituted Soviet-type five-year plans with emphasis on heavy industry rather than consumer goods. They collectivized agriculture, eliminated all noncommunist parties, and set up the institutions of repression—secret police and military forces.

Revolts Against Communism

Communism did not develop deep roots among the peoples of Eastern Europe. Moreover, the Soviets exploited Eastern Europe economically for their own benefit and made living conditions harsh for most people.

After Stalin's death, many Eastern European states began to pursue a new course. In the late 1950s and 1960s, however, the Soviet Union made it clear—especially in Poland, Hungary, and Czechoslovakia—that it would not allow its Eastern European satellites to become independent of Soviet control.

In 1956 protests erupted in Poland. In response, the Polish Communist Party adopted a series of reforms in October and elected Władysław Gomułka as first secretary. Gomułka declared that Poland had the right to follow its own socialist path. Fearful of Soviet armed response, however, the Poles compromised. Poland pledged to remain loyal to the Warsaw Pact.

Developments in Poland in 1956 led Hungarian Communists to seek the same kinds of reforms. Unrest in Hungary, combined with economic difficulties, led to calls for revolt. To quell the rising rebellion Imre Nagy, the Hungarian leader, declared Hungary a free nation on November 1, 1956, and promised free elections. It soon became clear that this could mean the end of Communist rule in Hungary.

Khrushchev was in no position at home to allow a member of the Communist group of nations to leave, however. Three days after Nagy's declaration, the Soviet Army attacked Budapest. The Soviets reestablished control over the country. Nagy was seized by the Soviet military and executed two years later.

The situation in Czechoslovakia in the 1950s was different. There, Stalin had placed Antonín Novotný, the "Litte Stalin," in power in 1953. By the late 1960s, however, he had alienated many members of his own party. He was especially disliked by Czechoslovakia's writers. A writers' rebellion, which encouraged the people to take control of their own lives, led to Novotný's resignation in 1968.

▲ Soviet tanks left Hungary on October 30, 1956, but the Soviets soon returned, crushing the revolt and reestablishing control.

In January 1968, Alexander Dubček (DOOB • chehk) was elected first secretary of the Communist Party. He introduced a number of reforms, including freedom of speech and press and freedom to travel abroad. He relaxed censorship, began to pursue an independent foreign policy, and promised a democratization of the Czechoslovakian political system. Dubček hoped to create "socialism with a human face." A period of euphoria broke out that came to be known as the "Prague Spring."

The euphoria proved to be short-lived. To forestall the spreading of this "spring fever," the Soviet Army invaded Czechoslovakia in August 1968 and crushed the reform movement. Gustav Husák replaced Dubček, revoked his reforms, and reestablished the old order.

☑ **READING PROGRESS CHECK**

Drawing Conclusions Why was Yugoslavia different from other Eastern European countries during the Cold War?

PHOTO: Keystone-France/Gamma-Keystone/Getty Images

LESSON 2 REVIEW (CCSS)

Reviewing Vocabulary

1. *Making Connections* How did the period of détente between the United States and the Soviet Union lead to a relaxation of authoritarian rule?

Using Your Notes

2. *Comparing and Contrasting* Use your notes to compare and contrast the rule of Khrushchev and Brezhnev.

Answering the Guiding Questions

3. *Drawing Conclusions* What political, economic, and social shifts occurred in the Soviet Union during the Cold War?

4. *Analyzing Information* How were Eastern Europeans affected by communism after World War II?

Writing Activity

5. INFORMATIVE/EXPLANATORY Research and write an essay about the "Prague Spring." What did it hope to achieve, and why was it unsuccessful? Be sure to include a bibliography of the sources you consulted.

Reading HELPDESK CCSS

Academic Vocabulary

• **maintain** • **stable**

Content Vocabulary

• **occupied**
• **state capitalism**

TAKING NOTES:

Key Ideas and Details

Organizing As you read, use a table like the one below to list the key areas of economic development in South Korea, Taiwan, and Singapore.

South Korea	Taiwan	Singapore

PHOTO: (l to r)©Vince Streano/Corbis, John Dominis/Time & Life Pictures/Getty Images, Nigel Hicks/Alamy Images, ©Charles Pertwee/Corbis.

LESSON 3
The Asian Rim

ESSENTIAL QUESTIONS • *How does war result in change?*
• *What challenges may countries face as a result of war?*

IT MATTERS BECAUSE

Japan made a dramatic recovery, transforming itself from the ruins of war to an industrial power. The "Asian tigers" imitated Japan's success and became industrial powerhouses.

The Transformation of Japan

GUIDING QUESTION *How was Japan transformed after World War II?*

In August 1945, Japan was in ruins, and a foreign army occupied its land. A mere 50 years later, Japan emerged as the second-greatest industrial power in the world.

From 1945 to 1952, Japan was **occupied** by Allied military forces under the command of U.S. General Douglas MacArthur. Under his firm direction, Japanese society was remodeled along Western lines. A new constitution renounced war as a national policy. Japan agreed to **maintain** armed forces sufficient only for self-defense. The constitution established a parliamentary system and reduced the power of the emperor (who was forced to announce that he was not a god). It guaranteed basic rights and gave women the right to vote.

On September 8, 1951, a peace treaty restored Japanese independence. Since then, Japan has emerged as an economic giant. The country's dramatic recovery from the war has been described as the "Japanese miracle." How did the miracle occur?

Modeled on the U.S. Constitution, Japan's new constitution guaranteed basic civil and political rights, and it called for universal suffrage and a balance of power among the executive, legislative, and judicial branches of government. However, it retained some of Japan's nineteenth-century political system under the Meiji. An example involves the distribution of political power. Japan has a multiparty system with two major parties—the Liberal Democrats and the Socialists. In practice, however, the Liberal Democrats have dominated the government. A few party leaders decided key issues such as who should be the prime minister.

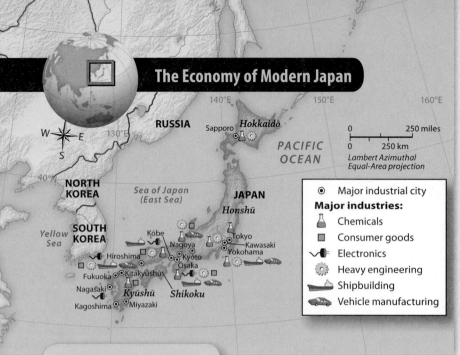

The Economy of Modern Japan

Major industries:
- Chemicals
- Consumer goods
- Electronics
- Heavy engineering
- Shipbuilding
- Vehicle manufacturing

⊙ Major industrial city

occupied held by a foreign power

maintain to keep in an existing state of repair or efficiency

state capitalism an economic system in which the central government plays an active role in the economy, establishing price and wage policies and subsidizing vital industries

The central government plays an active role in the economy. It establishes price and wage policies and subsidizes vital industries. This government role is widely accepted in Japan. Indeed, it is often cited as a key reason for the efficiency of Japanese industry and the emergence of Japan as an industrial giant. Japan's economic system has been described as **state capitalism**.

During their occupation of Japan, Allied officials had planned to dismantle the business conglomerations known as the *zaibatsu*. But with the Cold War, the policy was scaled back. Only the 19 largest companies were affected. Also, the policy did not keep companies from forming ties with each other, which basically gave rise to another *zaibatsu* system.

The occupation administration had more success with its land-reform program. Half of the population lived on farms, and half of all farmers were tenants of large landowners. Under the reform program, lands were sold on easy credit terms to the tenants. The reform program created a strong class of independent farmers.

At the end of the Allied occupation in 1952, the Japanese gross national product was one-third that of Great Britain or France. By the 1980s, it was larger than both combined. After several decades of impressive growth, Japan was considered a model of economic success.

During the occupation, Allied planners tried to eliminate the aggressiveness that had been part of Japanese behavior. A new educational system stressed individualism and removed references to patriotism and loyalty to the emperor. Efforts to remake Japanese behavior through laws were only partly successful, however. Many characteristics of traditional society have persisted. Emphasis on the work ethic, for example, remained strong. The tradition of hard work is stressed in the educational system.

Women's roles are another example of the difficulty of social change. After the war, women gained the vote and were encouraged to enter politics. However, the subordinate role of women has not been eliminated. Women are legally protected against discrimination in employment, yet very few have reached senior levels in business, education, or politics. Most women are employed in retail or service occupations. Also, their average salary is only about 60 percent that of men.

✓ **READING PROGRESS CHECK**

Hypothesizing How did the Japanese "miracle" occur?

The "Asian Tigers"

GUIDING QUESTION *What changes did the Asian Rim countries experience after World War II?*

Sometimes called the "Asian tigers," South Korea, Taiwan, Singapore, and Hong Kong have imitated Japan in creating successful industrial societies. Australia and New Zealand, to the south and east of Asia, now have closer trade relations with their Asian neighbors.

In 1953 the Republic of Korea (South Korea), was under the dictatorial president Syngman Rhee. Rhee ruled harshly. In the spring of 1960, demonstrations broke out in Seoul. Rhee was forced to retire. A coup d'état in 1961 put General Park Chung Hee in power. Two years later, Park was elected president and began to strengthen the South Korean economy. South Korea gradually emerged as a major industrial power in East Asia. The key areas for industrial development were chemicals, textiles, ship-building, and automobile production.

Like many other countries in the region, South Korea was slow to develop democratic principles. Park ruled by autocratic means and suppressed protest. However, after his assassination, democratic elections were restored by the early 1990s.

Defeated by the Communists, Chiang Kai-shek and his followers established their capital at Taipei on Taiwan. Chiang Kai-shek said that the Republic of China was the legitimate government of all Chinese people. Of course, the Communist government on the mainland claimed to rule all of China, including Taiwan. With the protection of American military forces, Chiang Kai-shek's regime focused on economic growth with no worries about a Communist invasion.

Making good use of foreign aid and the efforts of its people, the Republic of China built a modern industrialized society. A land-reform program, which put farmland in the hands of peasants, doubled food production. Local manufacturing and commerce also expanded. Prosperity did not at first lead to democracy. Chiang Kai-shek ruled by decree and did not allow new political parties to form. After his death in 1975, the Republic of China slowly moved toward a more representative form of government.

Singapore, once a British colony and briefly a part of the state of Malaysia, is now an independent state. Under the leadership of Prime Minister Lee Hsien Loong, Singapore developed a free-market economy based on banking, shipbuilding, oil refineries, and electronics. The authoritarian political system created a **stable** environment for economic growth. Its citizens, however, began to demand more political freedoms.

Like Singapore, Hong Kong became an industrial powerhouse with high standards of living. Having ruled Hong Kong for more than 150 years, Great Britain returned control of Hong Kong to mainland China in 1997. China, in turn, promised that, for the next 50 years, Hong Kong would enjoy a high degree of economic freedom under a capitalist system.

▲ The busy port of Singapore, full of containers and container ships, is an international trading hub.

stable not changing or fluctuating; steady

☑ READING PROGRESS CHECK

Comparing During the initial post-World War II period, in what ways were the "Asian tigers" similar?

PHOTO: ©Charles Pertwee/Corbis

LESSON 3 REVIEW

Reviewing Vocabulary
1. ***Gathering Information*** Why was Japan allowed to maintain their armed forces?

Using Your Notes
2. ***Making Connections*** Use your notes to identify how South Korea, Taiwan, and Singapore grew their economies after the war.

Answering the Guiding Questions
3. ***Identifying*** How was Japan transformed after World War II?

4. ***Making Generalizations*** What changes did the Asian Rim countries experience after World War II?

Writing Activity
5. **INFORMATIVE/EXPLANATORY** Do additional research on Japan and the "Asian tigers" and explain in an essay why these countries have been so successful.

Directions: On a separate sheet of paper, answer the questions below. Make sure you read carefully and answer all parts of the questions.

Lesson Review

Lesson 1

1 **EXPLAINING** What did West Berlin mayor Willy Brandt receive in 1971? Why?

2 **MAKING INFERENCES** What aspect of Prime Minister Thatcher's economic policy might have caused old industrial areas to suffer?

Lesson 2

3 **FINDING THE MAIN IDEA** What was Stalin's main goal for the Soviet Union after World War II, and how did he achieve it?

4 **IDENTIFYING** What were the effects of détente in the Soviet Union?

Lesson 3

5 **SUMMARIZING** After World War II, what changes and reforms did the Allied occupation administration lead Japan to make? How successful were the reforms?

6 **COMPARING AND CONTRASTING** How were South Korea, Taiwan, the Republic of China, and Singapore the same as Japan in the years after World War II? How were they different from Japan?

21st Century Skills

7 **TIME, CHRONOLOGY, AND SEQUENCING** Explain the formation and purpose of the European Economic Community. How did it change from the time of its inception until 1986?

8 **UNDERSTANDING RELATIONSHIPS AMONG EVENTS** Which events was Richard Nixon taking advantage of when he appealed to "law and order" during his presidential campaign in 1968?

9 **IDENTIFYING CAUSE AND EFFECT** What were some of the causes of economic changes in the United States after World War II? What impact did these changes have on American society?

Need Extra Help?

Exploring the Essential Questions

10 **MAKING CONNECTIONS** Choose one of the regions discussed in this chapter and write a multi-paragraph essay explaining how World War II created changes and identifying the challenges countries faced because of the war. For each paragraph, include a photo or map depicting an event or a challenge described in the paragraph; for example, a map of Eastern European countries under Soviet control after the war or a photo of Communist leader Tito.

DBQ Analyzing Historical Documents

Use the document to answer the following questions.
American recording artist Bob Dylan expressed the feeling of the younger generation with his song "The Times They Are A-Changin'," released in 1964.

PRIMARY SOURCE

> **The Times They Are A-Changin'**
> *Come gather 'round people*
> *Wherever you roam*
> *And admit that the waters*
> *Around you have grown*
> *And accept it that soon*
> *You'll be drenched to the bone*
> *If your time to you*
> *Is worth savin'*
> *Then you better start swimmin'*
> *Or you'll sink like a stone*
> *For the times they are a-changin'* . . .

11 **THEORIZING** To whom was Bob Dylan directing "come gather 'round people"?

12 **MAKING INFERENCES** What did Dylan mean when he wrote "admit that the waters around you have grown"?

Extended-Response Question

13 **INFORMATIVE/EXPLANATORY** Explain in one paragraph or more why Communist rule was met with so much resistance in most Eastern European satellite states.

If You've Missed Question	**1**	**2**	**3**	**4**	**5**	**6**	**7**	**8**	**9**	**10**	**11**	**12**	**13**
Go to page	415	416	420	422	425	425	416	417	417	414	428	428	423

A New Era Begins

1989–Present

ESSENTIAL QUESTIONS · What motivates political change?
· How can economic and social changes affect a country?

The Story Matters...

The Berlin Wall stood as a potent symbol of the division of the world into two hostile camps during the Cold War. From 1961 to 1989, the Berlin Wall separated West and East Berlin, dividing families and limiting travel across the border. In a major Cold War speech in 1987, U.S. president Ronald Reagan stood in front of the Brandenburg Gate of the Berlin Wall as he challenged the Soviet leader: "Mr. Gorbachev, tear down this wall!" In 1989 the East German government finally ended the political division between West and East.

◄ A child peers through a hole in the Berlin Wall after its destruction in 1989. The fall of the Berlin Wall reunited Germany and marked the beginning of a new era of diplomacy between the Soviet Union and the West.

Place and Time: Eastern Europe 1989–Present

In July 1989, the Soviet premier Mikhail Gorbachev announced that countries in the Warsaw Pact were free to determine their own futures. In November the Berlin Wall fell, symbolizing the end of the Cold War era. Revolutions both peaceful and violent erupted in the following months as Central and Eastern European countries declared their independence. By the end of 1991, the Soviet Union had virtually dissolved, resulting in the formation of 15 newly independent states.

Step Into the Place

Read the quotes and look at the information presented on the map.

 Analyzing Historical Documents What details in these primary sources tell us that perestroika and glasnost led to independence movements in the USSR and Soviet satellite states? How does Gorbachev's statement compare to the letter?

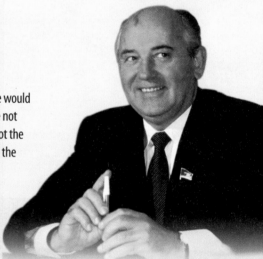

PRIMARY SOURCE

❝Our perestroika led us to the conclusion that the revolutionary course would not receive the support of the working class if [its] living standards were not improving. But it turned out that the problem of sausage and bread is not the only one. The people demand a new social atmosphere, more oxygen in the society, especially because we are talking about the socialist regime... It is important not to miss our chance here. The party should have its own position on these issues, its own clear policy in this respect also. Life itself will punish us if we are late.❞
—Mikhail Gorbachev, statement on October 7, 1989

PRIMARY SOURCE

❝Thanks to glasnost, the mass media have told us a great deal about the past. We learned about the persecution of talented people, who either were victims of repressions or were forced to emigrate abroad, but still remained patriots of their country. We found out a lot about the genocide carried out by the 'Father of All Peoples [Stalin],' about the significant mistakes made before and during the Great Patriotic War, and the truth about the Afghanistan war. We learned about environmental problems, although sometimes too late (the Chernobyl tragedy, for example).... How could the mood of the people be good after all that?❞
—Letter to the editor of *Ogonyok* Magazine (Moscow), May 15, 1989

Step Into the Time

Making Connections

Choose an event from the time line and explain the role it played in bringing the Cold War to an end.

EASTERN EUROPE AND CENTRAL ASIA

THE WORLD

1990

1990 Nobel Peace Prize recipient Lech Walesa elected president of Poland

1992 Yugoslavia disintegrates; Bosnian crisis follows

1989 Fall of the Berlin Wall

1991 Soviet Union dissolves

1989 Tiananmen Square protests

1991 Persian Gulf War

1994 North Atlantic Free Trade Agreement goes into effect

1990 Iraq invades Kuwait

1990 Sandinistas defeated in elections in Nicaragua

networks

There's More Online!

☑ **MAP** Explore the interactive version of this map on Networks.

☑ **TIME LINE** Explore the interactive version of the time line on Networks.

The Fall of Communism 1989–1991

ARCTIC OCEAN

40°E   60°E   80°E   100°E   120°E

80°N

EAST GERMANY (1990)

Baltic Sea

Barents Sea

Kara Sea

CZECHO-SLOVAKIA (1990)

LITHUANIA (1990)

POLAND (1990)

ESTONIA (1991)

LATVIA (1990)

HUNGARY (1990)

BELARUS (1991)

ARCTIC CIRCLE

YUGOSLAVIA (1990)

MOLDOVA (1991)

ALBANIA (1991)

ROMANIA (1992)

BULGARIA (1990)

UKRAINE (1991)

RUSSIA

Mediterranean Sea

Black Sea

Volga R.

Kama R.

Ural R.

GEORGIA (1991)

KAZAKHSTAN (1991)

Aral Sea

Irtysh R.

Yenisey R.

ARMENIA (1991)

AZERBAIJAN (1991)

Lake Balkhash

Caspian Sea

TURKMENISTAN (1991)

UZBEKISTAN (1991)

KYRGYZSTAN (1991)

TAJIKISTAN (1991)

N
W   E
S

(1990) Date of Independence from the Soviet Union

(1990) Date of first multi-party elections in former Soviet satellites

━━ Border of the former Soviet Union

── National boundary

0 _____ 600 miles
0 _____ 600 km
Lambert Conformal Conic projection

2004 Chechen rebels seize Russian school; many children die

2006 Slobodan Milosevic dies while on trial for war crimes

2008 Kosovo declares its independence

2000 Vladimir Putin is elected president of Russia

| 1995 | 2000 | 2005 | 2010 |

1995 Terrorists release deadly chemicals in Tokyo subway

2001 China joins the World Trade Organization

2011 Popular uprisings erupt in Tunisia, Egypt, Bahrain, and Libya

1995 Fourth World Conference on Women, Beijing

2001 Al-Qaeda-led terrorist attacks in the United States on September 11

2012 Barack Obama is reelected president of the United States.

A New Era Begins **431**

Reading HELPDESK (CCSS)

Academic Vocabulary
- demonstration
- collapse

Content Vocabulary
- perestroika
- glasnost
- ethnic cleansing
- autonomous

TAKING NOTES:

Key Ideas and Details

Categorizing As you read, use a table like the one below to identify events that happened after the fall of communism in Poland, Czechoslovakia, and Romania.

Poland	Czechoslovakia	Romania

LESSON 1
End of the Cold War

ESSENTIAL QUESTIONS • *What motivates political change?*
• *How can economic and social changes affect a country?*

IT MATTERS BECAUSE

After 40 years of the Cold War, the new division of Europe between West and East seemed to be permanent. Then a revolutionary upheaval in the Soviet Union and Eastern Europe brought an end to the Cold War and to this division.

Gorbachev and Perestroika

GUIDING QUESTION *How did Mikhail Gorbachev's reforms change the Soviet Union?*

By 1980, the Soviet Union was ailing. It had a declining economy, a rise in infant mortality rates, a dramatic surge in alcoholism, and poor working conditions. Within the Communist Party, a small group of reformers emerged. One was Mikhail Gorbachev. When the party chose him as leader in March 1985, a new era began.

From the start, Gorbachev preached the need for radical reforms based on **perestroika** (PEHR • uh • STRAWIH • kuh), or restructuring. At first, this meant restructuring economic policy. Gorbachev envisioned a market economy more responsive to consumers. It was to have limited free enterprise so that some businesses would be privately owned and operated. He realized, however, that reforming the economy would not work without political reform. He hoped to achieve this through **glasnost**, or openness, a policy that encouraged Soviet citizens and officials to discuss openly the strengths and weaknesses of the Soviet Union.

At the 1988 Communist Party conference, Gorbachev set up a new Soviet parliament of elected members, the Congress of People's Deputies. It met in 1989. He then created a new state presidency. Under the old system, the first secretary of the Communist Party (Gorbachev's position) had been the most important in the Soviet Union. In March 1990, Gorbachev became the Soviet Union's first—and last—president.

Mikhail Gorbachev's accession to power in 1985 also eventually brought a dramatic end to the Cold War. His willingness to rethink Soviet foreign policy led to stunning changes.

Gorbachev made an agreement with the United States in 1987, the Intermediate-Range INF Treaty, to eliminate intermediate-range nuclear weapons. Both Gorbachev and U.S. president Ronald Reagan wanted to slow down the arms race. They sought to reduce their military budgets to solve domestic problems. Gorbachev hoped to focus resources on social and economic change. The United States wanted to cut its national debt, which had tripled during the Reagan presidency.

Gorbachev also stopped giving Soviet military support to Communist governments in Eastern Europe. This opened the door to the overthrow of Communist regimes. A mostly peaceful revolutionary movement swept through Eastern Europe in 1989. The reunification of Germany on October 3, 1990, was a powerful symbol of the end of the Cold War. In 1991 the Soviet Union itself was dissolved. The long rivalry between the two superpowers was over.

✓ **READING PROGRESS CHECK**

Describing How did Gorbachev's reforms affect Soviet foreign relations?

Revolutions in Eastern Europe

GUIDING QUESTIONS *How did popular revolutions help end Communist regimes in Eastern Europe?*

When Gorbachev decided the Soviets would no longer send troops to support the governments of the satellite countries, revolutions broke out throughout Eastern Europe. A look at three Eastern European states shows how the process worked.

Workers' protests led to demands for change in Poland. In 1980, a worker named Lech Wałesa (lehk vah • LEHN • suh) organized a national trade union known as Solidarity. Solidarity gained the support of the workers and of the Roman Catholic Church, which was under the leadership of Pope John Paul II, the first Polish pope. Even when Wałesa was arrested, the movement continued. Finally, in 1988, the Polish regime agreed to free parliamentary elections—the first free elections in Eastern Europe in 40 years. A new government was elected, ending 45 years of Communist rule.

In December 1990, Wałesa was chosen as president. Poland's new path, however, was not easy. Rapid free-market reforms led to severe unemployment. Aleksander Kwasniewski, who succeeded Wałesa, continued Poland's move toward an increasingly prosperous free-market economy and democracy. Recent presidents have emphasized the need to combine modernization with tradition.

The Soviets crushed and then repressed the Czechoslovakian reform movement of 1968. Writers and other intellectuals continued to oppose the government, but they at first had little success. Then in 1988 and 1989, mass **demonstrations** took place throughout Czechoslovakia. By November 1989, crowds as large as 500,000 were forming in Prague.

In December 1989, the Communist government **collapsed**. At the end of, that month, Václav Havel (VAHT • SLAHF HAH • vehl), a writer who had played an important role in bringing down the Communist government, became the new president. Havel was an eloquent spokesperson for Czech democracy and a new order in Europe.

The new government soon faced old ethnic conflicts. The Czechs and Slovaks agreed to a peaceful division of Czechoslovakia, which split into the Czech Republic and Slovakia. Havel became the first president of the Czech Republic, and Michal Kovác became the first president of Slovakia.

BIOGRAPHY

Lech Wałesa (1943–)

In 1980 during protests at the shipyards in Gdansk, Poland, Lech Wałesa, a former electrician turned labor activist, was elected leader of a strike committee. As a result of his successful negotiations with Poland's Communist government, workers won the right to form the national labor organization known as Solidarity. Although Solidarity was soon outlawed and its leadership arrested, Wałesa won the 1983 Nobel Peace Prize for his efforts. Deteriorating economic conditions later forced the government to accept Solidarity; and in 1990 voters elected Wałesa president.

▶ **CRITICAL THINKING**
Drawing Conclusions What different factors contributed to Wałesa's success?

perestroika fundamental restructuring of the Soviet economy; a policy introduced by Gorbachev

glasnost a Soviet policy permitting open discussion of political and social issues

demonstration a public display of group feeling toward a person or cause

demonstration a public display of group feeling toward a person or cause

collapse to break down completely; to suddenly lose force or effectiveness

What Caused the Collapse of the Soviet Union?

International affairs expert Zbigniew Brzezinski attributed the collapse of communism to its failure to "deliver on the material level while its political practices compromised—indeed, discredited—its moral claims." What did Brzezinski mean? What other causes (such as nationalism, for example) do you think might have contributed? Use the Internet to find reliable sources about the various factors that contributed to the fall of the Soviet Union.

Under its second president, Václav Klaus, the Czech Republic has one of the most stable and prosperous economies of the post-Communist Eastern European states. Slovakia has managed to make the transition from a centrally planned economy to a market economy.

Communist leader Nicolae Ceauşescu (nee • kaw • LY chau • SHEHS • koo) ruled Romania with an iron grip, using secret police to crush all dissent. Nonetheless, opposition grew. His economic policies led to a sharp drop in living standards. Food shortages caused rationing. In December 1989, the secret police murdered thousands of people who were peacefully demonstrating. Finally, the army refused to support any more repression. Ceauşescu and his wife were captured and executed. A new government was quickly formed.

Former Communists dominated the government until 1996. The current president, Traian Basescu, leads a country that is just beginning to show economic growth and the rise of a middle class.

✔ **READING PROGRESS CHECK**

Identifying What role did protestors play in the new governments that formed after the fall of Communism in Eastern Europe?

End of the Soviet Union

GUIDING QUESTION *How did Mikhail Gorbachev's reforms change the Soviet Union?*

The Soviet Union was made of 15 separate republics that included 92 ethnic groups and 112 different languages. As Gorbachev released the iron grip of the Communist Party, centered in Moscow, old ethnic tensions came to the fore. Nationalist movements began. In 1989 and 1990, calls for independence came first in Soviet Georgia and then in the Baltic States (Latvia, Lithuania, and Estonia), Moldova, Uzbekistan, and Azerbaijan.

The conservative leaders of the traditional Soviet institutions—the army, government, KGB, and military industries—were worried that the breakup of the Soviet Union would end their privileges. On August 19, 1991, a group of these conservative leaders arrested Gorbachev and tried to seize power. The attempt failed, however, when Boris Yeltsin, president of the Russian Republic, and thousands of Russians bravely resisted the rebel forces in Moscow.

The Soviet republics now moved for complete independence. Ukraine voted for independence on December 1, 1991. A week later, the leaders of Russia, Ukraine, and Belarus announced that the Soviet Union had "ceased to exist."

✔ **READING PROGRESS CHECK**

Analyzing Why was President Gorbachev arrested on August 19, 1991?

The New Russia

GUIDING QUESTION *What are political, economic, and social challenges faced by the new Russia?*

Gorbachev resigned on December 25, 1991. He turned over his responsibilities as commander-in-chief to Boris Yeltsin, the new president of Russia. By the end of 1991, one of the largest empires in world history had ended.

Boris Yeltsin was committed to introducing a free market economy as quickly as possible, but the transition was not easy. Economic hardships and social disarray were made worse by a dramatic rise in organized crime.

Breakup of the Soviet Union 1991

Border of the former Soviet Union
National boundary

Lambert Conformal Conic projection

GEOGRAPHY CONNECTION

1 PLACES AND REGIONS *Create a table of the newly independent states.*

2 HUMAN SYSTEMS *Why might regional trade be more difficult after the breakup?*

Another problem Yeltsin faced was in Chechnya, a province in the south that wanted to secede from Russia and become independent. Yeltsin used brutal force against the Chechens (CHEH • chuhnz) to keep the province as part of Russia.

At the end of 1999, Yeltsin resigned and was replaced by Vladimir Putin, who was elected president in 2000. Putin, a former KGB officer, was widely seen as someone who wanted to keep a tight rein on government power. In July 2001, Putin launched reforms to boost growth and budget revenues. The reforms included the free sale and purchase of land and tax cuts. In spite of these changes, the business climate remained uncertain, which stifled foreign investment.

Since Putin's reforms Russia has experienced a budget surplus and a growing economy. Russia can attribute much of its economic growth to its oil and gas exports. The country has an estimated 6 percent of the world's oil deposits and about 30 percent of the world's natural gas deposits.

The new president also vowed to return the breakaway state of Chechnya to Russian authority and to adopt a more assertive role in international affairs. Fighting in Chechnya continued throughout 2000, nearly reducing the republic's capital city of Grozny to ruins.

Despite economic gains, Russia still faces challenges. Rising alcoholism, criminal activities, and the decline of the traditional family system give Russians concern.

In 2008 Dmitry Medvedev became president of Russia. Putin could not run for reelection because of limits in Russia's constitution, but he became prime minister. However, since Russia's contitution only limits consecutive terms, Putin won the presidency again in 2012. Putin will be eligible to run for reelection in 2018.

✔ **READING PROGRESS CHECK**

Describing What were the effects of Russia's transition to a market economy?

The Disintegration of Yugoslavia

GUIDING QUESTION *How did the fall of the Soviet Union impact Eastern Europe?*

Yugoslavia had a Communist government but was never a Soviet satellite state. After World War II, its dictatorial leader, Josip Broz Tito, worked to keep together the six republics and two provinces that made up Yugoslavia. By 1990, however, the Communist Party collapsed.

The Yugoslav political scene was complex. Slobodan Miloševic (slaw • BAW • dahn muh • LOH • suh • VIHCH), leader of Serbia, rejected efforts toward independence. In Miloševic's view, the republics' borders first needed to be redrawn to form a new Greater Serbian state. When negotiations failed, Slovenia and Croatia declared their independence in June 1991. In September 1991, the Yugoslav army attacked Croatia. Increasingly, Serbia dominated the Yugoslav army. Serbian forces captured one-third of Croatia's territory before the conflict ended.

The Serbs next attacked Bosnia-Herzegovina and acquired 70 percent of Bosnian territory. Many Bosnians were Muslims. The Serbs followed a policy called **ethnic cleansing** toward Bosnians—killing or forcibly emoving them from their lands. Ethnic cleansing revived memories of Nazi atrocities in World War II. In 1995, with support from NATO air attacks, Bosnian and Croatian forces regained considerable territory lost to Serbian forces. The Serbs signed a formal peace treaty that split Bosnia into a Serb republic and a Muslim-Croat federation.

A new war erupted in 1998 over Kosovo, an **autonomous**, or self-governing province within Yugoslavia. After Slobodan Miloševic stripped Kosovo of its autonomy in 1989, groups of ethnic Albanians founded the Kosovo Liberation Army (KLA) and began a campaign against Serbian rule. To crush the KLA, Serb forces massacred ethnic Albanians. The United States and NATO allies worked on a settlement that would end the killing. The Albanians in Kosovo regained their autonomy in 1999. Miloševic's rule ended in 2000. While on trial for his role in the massacre of Kosovo civilians, Miloševic died in 2006.

The last political vestiges of Yugoslavia ceased to exist in 2004 when the government officially renamed the country Serbia and Montenegro. The people of Montenegro voted for independence in 2006; and in 2008, Kosovo declared its independence. Thus, all six republics that formed Yugoslavia in 1918 were again independent nations, and a new one (Kosovo) was born.

✓ READING PROGRESS CHECK

Describing What role did NATO play in the conflicts in the former Yugoslavia?

---

ethnic cleansing
a policy of killing or forcibly removing an ethnic group from its lands; used by the Serbs against the Muslim minority in Bosnia

autonomous self-governing

▼ A police building destroyed during NATO air strikes in Pristina

LESSON 1 REVIEW

Reviewing Vocabulary
1. *Making Inferences* How did the policies of perestroika and glasnost lead to the end of the Soviet Union?

Using Your Notes
2. *Comparing* Use your notes to identify similarities among the countries of Eastern Europe after the fall of communist regimes.

Answering the Guiding Questions
3. *Making Generalizations* How did Mikhail Gorbachev's reforms change the Soviet Union?

4. *Drawing Conclusions* How did popular revolutions help end Communist regimes in Eastern Europe?

5. *Assessing* What are the political, economic, and social challenges faced by the new Russia?

6. *Analyzing* How did the fall of the Soviet Union impact Eastern Europe?

Writing Activity
7. **INFORMATIVE/EXPLANATORY** Research and write an essay about how life has changed in Russia since the fall of the Soviet Union.

Reading **HELP**DESK (CCSS)

Academic Vocabulary
- currency
- symbol

Content Vocabulary
- **budget deficit**
- **postmodernism**
- **popular culture**
- **cultural imperialism**

TAKING NOTES:
Key Ideas and Details

Organizing As you read, use a flow chart like the one below to identify events that led to the reunification of Germany.

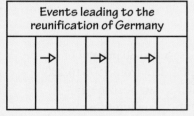

Events leading to the reunification of Germany			
→	→	→	

LESSON 2
Western Europe and North America

ESSENTIAL QUESTIONS • *What motivates political change?*
• *How can economic and social changes affect a country?*

IT MATTERS BECAUSE
During the last decade of the twentieth century and the first decade of the twenty-first century, the leaders of Western European and North American countries faced many economic challenges. Western culture has continued to influence many parts of the world.

Winds of Change in Western Europe

GUIDING QUESTION *What were the political, social, and cultural trends in Western Europe and North America since the end of the Cold War?*

In the course of the 1980s, Western European economies recovered, but problems remained. Unemployment was still high. Despite their economic woes, however, the Western European states seemed quite capable of prospering.

Especially important in that respect was the European Community (EC), which was chiefly an economic union. The Treaty on European Union, which went into effect on November 1, 1993, turned the EC into the European Union (EU). One of the EU's first goals was to establish a common **currency**, the euro. By January 2010, the euro had officially replaced 17 national currencies and served approximately 327 million people. A major crisis for the euro emerged in the same year, when the public debts of Greece and Ireland threatened bankruptcy for those countries and financial disaster for the euro.

Between 2004 and 2007, the EU expanded, by adding 12 new members, mostly from Eastern Europe. These included nations that became independent after the collapse of the Soviet Union. The end of the Soviet Union also had a major impact on the fate of Germany.

Reunification of Germany
In 1982 the Christian Democratic Union of Helmut Kohl formed a new, more conservative government in West Germany. Kohl was a smart politician who benefited greatly from an economic boom in the mid-1980s. Then events in East Germany led to the unexpected reunification of the two Germanies in 1990.

currency coins, for example, that are in circulation and used as a medium of exchange

symbol something that stands for something else by way of association; a visible sign of something invisible

Erich Honecker, head of the Communist Party in East Germany, ruled harshly. While many East Germans fled their country, others led mass demonstrations against the regime in 1989. When the Communist government opened its entire border with the West, thousands of East Germans swarmed across the border to reunite with their families and friends. The Berlin Wall, long a **symbol** of the Cold War, was torn down. The reunification of Germany took place on October 3, 1990. What had seemed almost impossible became a reality—the countries of West and East Germany had formed one Germany.

With a population of 79 million people, the new Germany became the leading power in Europe. The joy over reunification soon faded as new problems arose. It became clear that the rebuilding of eastern Germany would take far more money than had been thought.

Kohl's government was soon forced to raise taxes. In addition, the virtual collapse of the economy in eastern Germany had led to extremely high unemployment and severe discontent. One result was a return to power for the Social Democrats, who were victorious in the 1998 elections. However, the Social Democrats had little success in solving Germany's economic woes. In 2005 Angela Merkel, leader of the Christian Democrats, became the first female chancellor in German history.

The collapse of the German economy also led to increasing attacks on foreigners. For years, illegal immigrants and foreigners seeking refuge had found haven in Germany because of its very liberal immigration laws. Increased unemployment and economic problems caused tensions between some Germans and immigrant groups.

▲ East Germans take sledgehammers to the Berlin Wall, dismantling it piece by piece.

▶ **CRITICAL THINKING**
Analyzing Why was the Berlin Wall such a potent symbol of the Cold War?

Great Britain

After Margaret Thatcher resigned as prime minister in 1990, the Conservative Party, now led by John Major, failed to capture the imagination of most Britons. In new elections in 1997, the Labour Party won a landslide victory. Moderate Tony Blair became prime minister. However, his ongoing support of the U.S. war in Iraq, when most Britons opposed it, caused his popularity to plummet. Another member of the Labour Party, Gordon Brown, became prime minister in June 2007. New elections in May 2010 led to Conservative David Cameron becoming prime minister.

France

In the elections of 1993, a coalition of conservative parties gained 80 percent of the seats in the National Assembly. Jacques Chirac was president from 1995 to 2007.

By 1995, resentment against foreign-born residents had become a growing political reality. Especially noticeable were the growing tensions between the Muslim community and the remainder of the French population. These tensions helped elect Nicolas Sarkozy president in 2007.

France did not escape the financial woes of the euro crisis. Amid the failing economy and low approval ratings, Sarkozy lost his reelection bid in a run-off election in May 2012. He was defeated by François Hollande of France's Socialist Party.

✓ **READING PROGRESS CHECK**

Determining Cause and Effect What happened after the Berlin Wall was dismantled?

The United States and Canada

GUIDING QUESTION *What were the political, social, and cultural trends in Western Europe and North America since the end of the Cold War?*

As the Cold War was coming to a close, U.S. politics oscillated between the right and left as economic issues became a focus. Canadians were also concerned about economic problems and the status of Quebec.

The United States

The Reagan Revolution, as it has been called, sent U.S. policy in new directions. Reagan reduced welfare policies by cutting spending on food stamps, school lunch programs, and job programs. At the same time, Reagan oversaw the largest peacetime military buildup in U.S. history.

Total federal spending rose from $631 billion in 1981 to over a trillion dollars by 1987. The spending policies of the Reagan administration produced record government **budget deficits**. A budget deficit exists when the government spends more than it collects in revenues. In the 1970s, the total deficit was $420 billion. Between 1981 and 1987, budget deficits were three times that amount.

George Bush, Reagan's vice president, succeeded him as president. Bush's inability to deal with the federal deficit and an economic downturn, however, allowed Democrat Bill Clinton to be elected president in 1992. Clinton claimed to be a new kind of Democrat, one who favored several Republican policies of the 1980s. A lengthy economic revival won Clinton popular support, but his second term was overshadowed by charges of presidential misconduct. Clinton's problems helped Republican George W. Bush, son of the first President Bush, to win the presidency in 2000.

The Bush administration was largely occupied with the war on terrorism and the U.S.-led war on Iraq. Bush and Congress passed tax cuts to boost the economy but also helped to produce record deficits. From 2004 to 2008, Bush's popularity fell due to growing discontent over the Iraq War and a significant downturn in the economy caused in part by problems in the home mortgage industry. These key issues in the 2008 presidential race led to a change in American politics with the election of Barack Obama, the first African American president. In 2009 Obama moved to deal with the worst economic recession since the Great Depression, the passage of national healthcare legislation, and the war in Afghanistan. He was reelected in 2012.

Canada

In 1993 Canada approved the North American Free Trade Agreement (NAFTA), along with the United States and Mexico, to make trade easier and more profitable. Because many Canadians thought the agreement was too favorable to the United States, prime minister Brian Mulroney lost popularity. Jean Chrétien served as prime minister from 1993 to 2003. However, with a Conservative victory in 2006, Stephen Harper became the new prime minister.

The status of the French-speaking Quebec province has been an issue for decades. In 1995 Quebec voters only narrowly rejected secession. The debate still divides Canadians.

☑ **READING PROGRESS CHECK**

Describing What role did the economy play in U.S. presidential administrations in the first two decades of the 2000s?

▲ U.S. president Barack Obama faced economic challenges in the United States and around the globe during this two terms in the White House.

budget deficit the state that exists when a government spends more than it collects in revenues

PHOTO: Saul Loeb/AFP/Getty Images

▲ *Cold Dark Matter: An Exploded View* (1991) by the English sculptor Cornelia Parker is a postmodern art installation.

postmodernism an artistic movement that emerged in the 1980s; its artists do not expect rationality in the world and are comfortable with many "truths"

popular culture entertainment created for a profit and for a mass audience

cultural imperialism referring to Western nations' control of other world cultures similar to how they had controlled colonial governments

Society and Culture in the West

GUIDING QUESTION *What were the political, social, and cultural trends in Western Europe and North America since the end of the Cold War?*

Among the effects of globalization is the spread of culture, and Western culture has expanded to and influenced most parts of the world.

The Women's Movement

In the 1990s, there was a backlash against the women's movement. Some women urged a return to traditional gender roles. Other women rejected these ideas and continued to find ways to balance career and family. While there have been gains in the women's movement in the 2000s, women continue to do most of the child rearing and domestic work in most homes.

Art and Popular Culture

The United States dominated the art world after World War II. Abstractionism, especially abstract expressionism, dominated modern art after 1945. Abstract artists focused on conveying emotion and feeling. By the 1980s, **postmodernism** emerged. Postmodern artists often create works that include elements of film, performance, popular culture, and sculpture. Today's artists use digital cameras and computer programs to produce interactive art forms.

Music, movies, television, sports—all are part of our **popular culture**. Known throughout the world, American performers and filmmakers help spread American popular culture. From early rock 'n' roll to multimillion-dollar musical acts, the world participates in America's musical pop culture. Films also play a big role in spreading Western culture.

Television and sports have created a sense that Americans and Europeans share a culture. Europeans watch American shows and become familiar with American brand names—and American attitudes about family, work, and money. As a cultural export, sports have become big business. Some nations' peoples worry that American entertainment weakens their own language and culture. Critics refer to this as **cultural imperialism**. Although Western music and movies may still dominate, trends in the opposite direction are developing. One trend is that non-Western music has large Western audiences. For example, the reggae music native to Jamaica has an enormous following, and Latin pop has become so popular that there have been Latin Grammy awards since 1999.

✔ **READING PROGRESS CHECK**

Drawing Conclusions Why has the spread of American popular culture led some critics to be concerned about U.S. cultural imperialism?

LESSON 2 REVIEW

Reviewing Vocabulary

1. *Identifying* What happened to budget deficits in the United States from the 1970s to the 1980s?

2. *Making Connections* How is American popular culture related to the idea of cultural imperialism?

Using Your Notes

3. *Sequencing* Use your notes to list the events that led to the reunification of Germany.

Answering the Guiding Questions

4. *Making Generalizations* What were the political, social, and cultural trends in Western Europe and North America since the end of the Cold War?

Writing Activity

5. **NARRATIVE** Write an essay describing how popular culture has affected your life. Be sure to include examples of music, film, television, and art and how it impacted you.

networks
There's More Online!

- ☑ **CHART/GRAPH** North Korean Conflicts
- ☑ **CHART/GRAPH** Oil Production and Consumption in China
- ☑ **CHART/GRAPH** Population Distribution in Japan
- ☑ **IMAGE** Border Between North Korea and South Korea
- ☑ **IMAGE** Chinese Household in the 1990s
- ☑ **IMAGE** Deng Xiaoping
- ☑ **INTERACTIVE SELF-CHECK QUIZ**
- ☑ **VIDEO** China, Japan, and the Koreas

Reading **HELP**DESK

Academic Vocabulary
- unify
- sector

Content Vocabulary
- per capita
- one-child policy
- deflation

TAKING NOTES:
Key Ideas and Details

Organizing As you read, use a chart to list the actions Deng Xiaoping took to help modernize China's industry and agriculture.

Industry	Agriculture

PHOTO: (l to r)©Reuters/Corbis, ©Reuters/Corbis, ©Xiaoyang Liu/Corbis, ©Fritz Hoffmann/In Pictures/Corbis, EPA/ASAHI SHIMBUN,

LESSON 3
China, Japan, and the Koreas

ESSENTIAL QUESTIONS · *What motivates political change?*
· *How can economic and social changes affect a country?*

IT MATTERS BECAUSE
Although the Chinese Communist Party has managed to retain power, China has taken giant steps toward becoming an economic world power. Meanwhile, Japan's economy has suffered in recent decades. There is an uneasy peace between North Korea and South Korea, which are vastly different countries.

China After Mao

GUIDING QUESTION *What political and social changes has China undergone in the late twentieth and early twenty-first centuries?*

Under the leadership of Deng Xiaoping (DUHNG SHYOW · PIHNG), the new Chinese government after the death of Mao Zedong called for Four Modernizations—new policies in industry, agriculture, technology, and national defense. For more than 20 years, China had been isolated from the technological advances taking place elsewhere in the world. To make up for lost time, the government invited foreign investors to China. The government also sent thousands of students abroad to study science, technology, and modern business techniques.

A new agricultural policy began. Collective farms could now lease land to peasants who paid rent to the collective. Anything produced above the value of the rent could be sold for profit. Peasants were also allowed to make goods to sell.

By adopting this practical approach, China began to make great strides in ending its problems of poverty and underdevelopment. **Per capita** (per person) income, including farm income, doubled during the 1980s. Housing, education, and sanitation improved. Both agriculture and industrial output skyrocketed. Clearly, China had begun to enter the Industrial Age.

Despite such achievements, many complained that Deng Xiaoping's program had not achieved a fifth modernization—democracy.

▲ A demonstrator stands in front of the tanks at Tiananmen Square.

▶ **CRITICAL THINKING**

Reasoning Why do you think the Chinese government responded with such overwhelming force?

per capita per person

unify to make into a unit or whole; unite

People could not directly criticize the Communist Party. Those who called for democracy were often sentenced to long terms in prison.

The problem intensified in the late 1980s. More Chinese studied abroad and learned about the West. As the economy prospered, students and other groups wanted better living conditions and greater freedom. In the late 1980s, rising inflation led to growing discontent among salaried workers, especially in the cities. Corruption and special treatment for officials and party members led to increasing criticism as well. In May 1989, student protesters called for an end to the corruption and demanded the resignation of China's aging Communist Party leaders. These demands received widespread support from people in the cities. Discontent led to massive demonstrations in Tiananmen Square in Beijing.

Deng Xiaoping believed the protesters were calling for an end to Communist rule. He ordered tanks and troops into the square to crush the demonstrators. Between 500 and 2,000 were killed and many more injured. Democracy was a dream.

Throughout the 1990s and into the 2000s, China's human rights violations, its determination to **unify** with Taiwan, and its increasing military power created international concern. China's neighbors, especially Japan, India, and Russia, fear the increasingly active role China is playing in its area of the world. To Chinese leaders, however, such actions represent China's rightful role in the region.

For now, a strong patriotism seems to be on the rise. This is encouraged by the government as a means of holding the country together. When China was selected to host the 2008 Olympic Games, the Chinese celebrated enthusiastically. The event seemed to symbolize China's emergence as a major national power on the world stage.

Problems remain, however. For example, unrest is growing among China's national minorities. This is especially true in Tibet, where the Chinese government has violently suppressed Tibetan culture.

☑ **READING PROGRESS CHECK**

Identifying What is the "fifth modernization," and how has China failed to achieve it?

Chinese Society and Economy

GUIDING QUESTIONS *What political and social changes has China undergone in the late twentieth and early twenty-first centuries? How has modern China become a world economic power?*

From the start, the Communist Party wanted to create a new kind of citizen, one who would give the utmost for the good of all China. In Mao's words, the people should "be resolute, fear no sacrifice, and surmount every difficulty to win victory."

During the 1950s and 1960s, the Chinese government began to allow women to take part in politics and gave them equal marital rights—a dramatic shift. After Mao's death, family traditions returned. People now had more freedom in everyday matters and had better living conditions.

Married couples who had been given patriotic names chose more elegant names for their own children. Clothing choices were no longer restricted to a baggy "Mao suit." Today, young Chinese people wear jeans and athletic shoes.

Mao's successors have followed one of his goals to the present day—the effort to control population growth. In 1979 the state began advocating a **one-child policy**. Incentives such as education benefits, child care, and housing were offered to couples who limited their families to one child. Although criticized as oppressive, the policy has continued, with a few exceptions for rural areas and some minorities. One effect is that China's population growth rate has declined from 2.2 percent in 1970–1975 to an estimated 0.6 percent in 2005–2010. Another effect has been an aging population. Life expectancy is increasing, but the birth rate remains low.

After the Tiananmen Square demonstrations, the Chinese government adopted a policy of promoting rapid economic growth while cracking down harshly on political dissenters. Especially noticeable was the attempt to win middle-class support in the cities by guaranteeing more consumer goods.

During the 1990s, growth rates in industry remained high, leading to predictions that China would become one of the economic superpowers of the twenty-first century. Domestic capital in China became available to compete with the growing presence of foreign enterprises. The government also shut down inefficient state enterprises. By the early 2000s, the private **sector** accounted for more than 10 percent of the nation's gross domestic product. A stock market opened. At the same time, China was strengthening international trade relations. China joined the World Trade Organization in 2001 and normalized trade relations with the United States in 2002.

Rapid economic change, however, never comes without cost. Workers in Chinese factories complain about poor working conditions and low salaries, leading to labor unrest. Many farmers are also unhappy. They earn only about half the salary of urban workers. In desperation, millions flee to the big cities, where they are forced to live in pitiful conditions in tenements.

✔ **READING PROGRESS CHECK**

Summarizing What negative effects has rapid economic change had on China?

Japan

GUIDING QUESTION *What changes have occurred in Japan from the 1990s to the present?*

Between 1950 and 1990, Japan became the greatest exporting nation in the world. It also developed the world's largest economy after that of the United States. Some economists even predicted that Japan would pass the United States as the world's largest economy by 2010. At the end of the 1980s, however, a collapse of the Japanese real estate market sent the economy into a tailspin.

By the 1990s, the Japanese economy had slipped into a recession that has largely continued until the present day. Job security declined as large numbers of workers were laid off. Many older Japanese saw their savings decline. Retirement programs were increasingly strained by the demands of a rapidly aging population. Japan today has the highest proportion of people more than age 65 of any industrialized country in the world—17 percent of the country's total population of about 130 million.

one-child policy China's effort, beginning in 1979, to control population growth; incentives such as education benefits, child care, and housing are offered to couples who limit their families to one child

sector a sociological, economic, or political subdivision of society

▲ China joined the WTO in 2001 after 15 years of negotiations, becoming the 143rd member.

deflation a contraction in the volume of available money or credit that results in a general decline in prices

For more than 20 years, Japan has witnessed slow economic growth and a decline in prices, known as **deflation**. A crisis of confidence has led to deep pessimism about the future and a decline in spending, especially among young Japanese who have now known nothing other than economic decline.

In recent years, Japanese consumers have also complained about a decline in the quality of some domestic products. One government official accused Japanese firms of "sloppiness." Even the Japanese automaker Toyota was faced with quality problems in its best-selling fleet of cars.

The country's economic decline was evident when China passed Japan in the second quarter of 2010 as the world's second-largest economy behind the United States. Despite government attempts to stimulate the economy in 2010, Japan faced a growing government debt and increasing rates of poverty.

On March 11, 2011, Japan received another crushing economic blow as a result of a devastating natural catastrophe. An offshore earthquake produced a gigantic tsunami, or tidal wave, that destroyed cities and farmland on the northeast coast. Recorded at 9.0 on the Richter scale, it was the most powerful quake to hit a country that was accustomed to periodic earthquakes. Thousands of people were killed, and hundreds of thousands were left homeless.

▲ The 2011 tsunami devastated towns like Natori, Japan. The tsunami also led to rising radiation levels from the damaged Fukushima Daiichi nuclear plant.

▶ CRITICAL THINKING

Theorizing Do you think the damage at the Fukushima Daiichi nuclear plant will limit the development of new nuclear power plants in the United States? Why or why not?

Authorities began a massive rescue and recovery effort. A month after the disaster, the official death toll was over 12,000, and nearly 15,000 people remained missing.

The tsunami also damaged the nuclear power plant at Fukushima Daiichi and created the worst nuclear disaster since the accident at Chernobyl in Ukraine in 1986. Leaks of radioactive gas into the atmosphere not only endangered the lives of many Japanese but also brought threats of radioactive contamination to Japan's food supplies. Japanese officials worked overtime to contain the damage.

✓ READING PROGRESS CHECK

Making Connections What factors have affected Japan's economy since the 1990s?

The Koreas

GUIDING QUESTION *What are the major differences between North Korea and South Korea?*

Although the Korean War ended in 1953, political tensions between North Korea and South Korea continue to threaten the peace between the two countries, primarily due to North Korea's nuclear weapons program. At the same time, South Korea has become one of the strongest economies in Asia.

North Korea

Since 1990, North Korea remained an isolated country under a military dictatorship led by Kim Jong Il. Only the second leader since the formation of North Korea in 1953, Kim Jong Il attempted to secure his country by creating a nuclear program. Multinational negotiations to persuade the regime to suspend its nuclear program reached a fragile agreement in 2008.

Internal problems continue to plague North Korea. Droughts and famines during the 1990s led North Korea to seek help from the United Nations and the United States. Economic problems forced the North Korean government to devalue its currency in 2009. The World Food Program estimates that one in five North Korean children is underweight. After Kim Jong Il died in December 2011, his son Kim Jong Un became North Korea's leader. At 29, he is the youngest head of state in the world. He continues his father's legacy in his role as leader of North Korea.

South Korea

Since 1990, South Korea has experienced a growing democracy. National elections held since 1989 removed former military leaders from power, replacing them with civilian leaders.

North Korea's nuclear program continues to cause tension between the two countries. President Lee Myung-bak, elected in 2007, pushed for North Korea to abandon its nuclear program. Tensions have risen between North and South Korea following the 2010 sinking of a military ship killing 46 soldiers. South Korea has blamed North Korea for the attack. Conflict continued in late 2010 between the two countries following the live-artillery firing on an island off the coast of South Korea.

South Korea has also faced economic problems as a result of the Asian financial crises of 1997 following the collapse of Taiwan's banking industry. But South Korea's strong educational institutions and economic policies enabled South Korea to weather the 2008 global economic crisis with an unemployment rate of 3.8 percent in 2009.

Culturally, South Korea is changing rapidly as almost every household has high-speed Internet and cell phones. South Korean television and movies have great popularity throughout Asia, and education remains the number one priority. The third largest group of foreign students in the United States comes from South Korea.

▲ North Korean and South Korean soldiers guard the demilitarized zone, which is a constant reminder of tensions between the two countries.

✓ READING PROGRESS CHECK

Identifying What has led to increased tensions between North Korea and South Korea in recent decades?

LESSON 3 REVIEW (CCSS)

Reviewing Vocabulary

1. *Making Connections* What is deflation, and how did it hurt the Japanese economy?

Using Your Notes

2. *Identifying* Use your notes to identify the policies of Deng Xiaoping that were intended to help modernize China.

Answering the Guiding Questions

3. *Making Generalizations* What political and social changes has China undergone in the late twentieth and early twenty-first centuries?

4. *Drawing Conclusions* How has modern China become a world economic power?

5. *Analyzing Information* What changes have occurred in Japan from the 1990s to the present?

6. *Contrasting* What are the major differences between North Korea and South Korea?

Writing Activity

7. **NARRATIVE** Imagine you are a foreign exchange student attending a Beijing university in 1989. You witness the demonstration at Tiananmen Square. Write a letter to a friend describing what you saw.

Reading **HELP**DESK CCSS

Academic Vocabulary
- **evolve**
- **evident**

Content Vocabulary
- **jurisdiction**
- **corruption**

TAKING NOTES:
Key Ideas and Details

Summarizing As you read, use a chart to list the major events in these regions since the end of the Cold War.

Middle East & North Africa	Africa South of the Sahara

South & Southeast Asia	Latin America

LESSON 4
Regions After the Cold War

ESSENTIAL QUESTION · *What motivates political change?*
· *How can economic and social changes affect a country?*

IT MATTERS BECAUSE
After the end of the Cold War, significant developments were occurring throughout the Middle East, Africa, Asia, and Latin America. A movement toward democracy and a desire for a better life led to increasing political participation.

Middle East and North Africa

GUIDING QUESTION *What changes have occurred in the Middle East and North Africa since the 1990s?*

Many countries in these regions have been plagued with political instability, ethnic tensions, high unemployment, growing poverty rates, poor education, and limited civil liberties.

Region Overview

Efforts to reach a peace agreement between the Israelis and the Palestinians, represented by the PLO (Palestinian Liberation Organization), have failed due to continued terrorist attacks and disputes over territory, especially Jerusalem.

Iran, an oil-rich country, remains under the control of Muslim clerics, who enforce strict adherence to Islamic law. They limit the rights of women, and the right to free assembly and a free press. In 2009, following the re-election of Mahmoud Ahmadinejad, hundreds of thousands of Iranians protested the outcome and declared the election a fraud. The violent oppression of the protestors by the Iranian military was captured on cell phones and posted on the Internet.

After the terrorist attacks on the World Trade Center on September 11, 2001, the United States invaded Afghanistan in 2001 and Iraq in 2003. Under the control of the Taliban, Afghanistan was harboring Osama bin Laden, the head of al-Qaeda, who claimed responsibility for the attacks. In 2011 U.S. forces killed bin Laden in Pakistan. After the invasion of Iraq, the country fell into civil war between the Shia Muslims, who controlled southern Iraq, and the Sunni Muslims, who controlled central Iraq. Elections held in 2010 led to the election of Prime Minister Nuri Kamal al-Maliki eight months later. Protests also swept across Iraq in 2011 as people sought better government services.

Revolutionary Upheaval

North Africa and the Middle East were rocked by an immense uprising that led to a regime change in Tunisia and Egypt. Most countries in the region have a high percentage of young people; more than half of Egypt's 80 million people are under the age of 25. Most of these young people are unemployed. After 23 years of oppressive government, Tunisian president Zine el-Abidine Ben Ali fled the country following mass protests that began in December 2010. Other protests in the region soon followed.

In Egypt an oppressive regime under President Hosni Mubarak maintained power through a large security force, which used torture and brutality to suppress any political opposition. By January 28, 2011, hundreds of thousands of Egyptians, including women, from all walks of life flooded Tahrir (Liberation) Square in downtown Cairo. Protesters used social networking to organize protests. After 18 days of sometimes violent retaliation by Mubarak's secret police forces, the Egyptian army sided with the protesters, forcing Mubarak to leave the country. Since the uprising, Egypt has sentenced its former president to life in prison. Elections were held in June 2012, and Egyptians elected Muslim Brotherhood candidate Mohammed Morsi as president.

In Libya, protesters rebelled against the authoritarian regime of Colonel Muammar al-Qaddafi. After Colonel Qaddafi's troops began to use force against the protesters, the UN Security Council voted to authorize military action. In March 2011, American and European forces began airstrikes against the Qaddafi regime. Libyan rebel forces took control of Tripoli in August, ousting Qaddafi from power. It was not until Qaddafi was killed in October, however, that the creation of a new Libya could begin in earnest. On July 7, 2012, Libya held its first free election since 1952. Libya's new Prime Minister Mustafa Abushagur faces ongoing political unrest as parties struggle for control of the country and anti-America protests make headlines around the world.

Protests spread throughout the entire region to Algeria, Yemen, Jordan, Bahrain, Oman, Morocco, Saudi Arabia, and Syria. Despite the successes in Tunisia and Egypt, the protests in these other nations have been met with force. Nevertheless, after decades of conflict, political oppression, and exploitation, the revolutionary upheaval led by young people has brought a new beginning to the Middle East and North Africa.

☑ **READING PROGRESS CHECK**

Comparing and Contrasting How are the uprisings in Egypt and Libya similar? How are they different?

▲ Antigovernment demonstrators In Tahrir Square in Cairo demand the resignation of Egyptian president Hosni Mubarak.

▶ **CRITICAL THINKING**
Analyzing Visuals What words would you use to describe the demonstrators?

Africa South of the Sahara

GUIDING QUESTION *What challenges have confronted countries in Africa south of the Sahara since the end of the Cold War?*

African societies have not yet begun to overcome the challenges they have faced since independence. Most African states are still poor, and African concerns continue to carry little weight in the international community. There are signs of progress toward political stability in some countries. Other nations, however, are still racked by civil war or ruled by brutal dictatorships.

Region Overview

Africans have found ways to address their political problems, to cooperate with one another, and to protect and promote their own interests. In 1991 the Organization of African Unity (OAU) agreed to establish the African Economic Community (AEC). This group is intended to provide greater political and economic integration throughout Africa on the pattern of the EU. In 2001 the African Union (AU) replaced the OAU. The new organization has already sought to mediate several of the conflicts in the region. The AU also promotes democracy and economic growth in Africa.

As Africa **evolves**, it is important to remember that economic and political change is often a slow and painful process. Introduced to industrialization and ideas of Western democracy only a century ago, African societies are still looking for ways to graft Western political institutions and economic practices onto indigenous structures still influenced by traditional values and attitudes.

African countries face many social and economic problems. Rapid population growth has slowed economic growth. In the first decade of the 2000s, Africa's population growth rate was 2.3 percent compared to 1.24 percent in the rest of the world. As a result, poverty remains widespread. Cities have grown tremendously. By 2007, approximately 39 percent of Africans lived in urban areas where there are massive slums and high levels of pollution.

Moreover, AIDS remains a serious concern in Africa. More than two-thirds (22.9 million) of all persons infected with HIV are living in Africa south of the Sahara. In this area during 2010, 1.9 million people became infected with HIV and more than 1.2 million died of AIDS.

Some African nations have mounted an impressive effort to fight AIDS. In Uganda President Yoweri Museveni involved a wide range of natural leaders in Ugandan society as well as international health and social service agencies. Uganda has made significant progress in its fight against AIDS. The numbers of cases of HIV in Uganda stabilized in the early 2000s.

Politically, Africa has witnessed a number of women as leaders of their countries. For example, Luisa Diogo became prime minister of Mozambique in 2004. There has also been a trend toward multi-party elections. In Senegal, for example, national elections held in the summer of 2000 brought an end to four decades of rule by the once-dominant Socialist Party.

Religion has played a role in dividing parts of Africa. An Islamic resurgence was evident in a number of African countries. It surfaced in Ethiopia where Muslim tribespeople rebelled against a Marxist regime and eventually established an independent Eritrea.

More recently, in Nigeria and other nations of West Africa, divisions between Muslims and Christians have erupted into violence. In the early 2000s, riots between Christians and Muslims broke out in several northern cities as a result of the decision by Muslim local officials to apply Islamic law throughout their **jurisdictions**. The violence has lessened as local officials managed to craft compromise policies that limit some of the harsher aspects of Muslim law. Nevertheless, the dispute continues to threaten the fragile unity of Nigeria, Africa's most populous country.

Côte d'Ivoire

The religious tensions that erupted in Nigeria have spilled over into neighboring states. Under its first president, Felix Houphouet-Boigny, Côte d'Ivoire (Ivory Coast) was often seen as a model of religious and ethnic harmony. But his death in 1993 led to an outbreak of long-simmering resentment between

evolve develop; work out

▲ A health counselor teaches South African students about HIV/AIDS prevention.

jurisdiction the limits or territory within which authority may be exercised

Christians in the south and Muslim immigrants in the north. Elections held in 2000 resulted in the election of a Christian president. The elections were marked by violence and widespread charges of voting irregularities.

In 2002, an armed uprising split the nation into a Muslim, rebel-dominated north and a Christian, government-controlled south. A power sharing deal brought temporary peace in 2007. It was also believed that a presidential election in November 2010 might bring a new unity. Laurent Gbagbo, who had been president since 2000, lost to Alassane Ouattara, who was declared the winner by the United Nations. Gbagbo used the army in an attempt to stay in power, while UN peacekeeping forces guarded Ouattara. Gbagbo's forces terrorized civilians in order to remain in power. A peaceful march of unarmed women, for example, was stopped by machine gun fire from Gbagbo's armed followers. In November 2011, Gbagbo was arrested and sentenced to prison for crimes against humanity.

As in other African countries, civil war has devastated the economy of Côte d'Ivoire. The city of Abidjan once had a shining downtown. Now it is a jungle of darkened high-rise windows. Jobs have disappeared; 4 million men are out of work in a country of 21 million. Banks and businesses have closed, and food shortages are widespread.

✅ **READING PROGRESS CHECK**

Analyzing What role has religion played in recent African conflicts?

▲ A suburb of Abidjan shows the aftermath of the fighting that followed the 2010 election in Côte d'Ivoire.

▶ **CRITICAL THINKING**
Describing Write a sentence or two that describes the scene in this photograph.

South and Southeast Asia

GUIDING QUESTION *What different economic and political issues have affected the countries of South and Southeast Asia since the 1990s?*

South Asia comprises the states of India, Pakistan, Bangladesh, Nepal, Bhutan, Sri Lanka, and the Maldives. Important developments in South Asia since the 1990s are the growing economic power of India, the continuing rivalry between India and Pakistan, and the instability in Pakistan.

Region Overview

During the early 1990s, the Congress Party remained the leading party in India. Its powerful hold, however, began to decline. New parties, such as the militantly Hindu Bharata Janata Party (BJP), competed with the Congress Party for control of the central and state governments. Growing political instability was accompanied by rising tensions between Hindus and Muslims. After a series of coalition governments headed by the BJP leader A. B. Vajpayee between 1996 and 2004, the Congress Party returned to power at the head of a coalition government based on a commitment to maintain economic growth and carry out reforms in rural areas. These reforms included public works projects and hot lunch programs for all primary school children. Manmohan Singh, who had carried out economic reforms in India in 1991 as finance minister, became prime minister. He was reelected in 2009 and has become highly regarded by other world leaders.

India's economy has emerged as one of the world's largest and fastest growing. Economic reforms in 1991 fostered foreign investment and began to move India toward a market-based economy. Although agriculture is still the occupation of many Indians, the service and industrial sectors now account for much of India's GDP. Many economists believe that India is a rising economic superpower and may have the world's third largest economy by 2035.

▲ A General Motors plant in India

▶ **CRITICAL THINKING**
Hypothesizing Why do you think jobs in the automotive industry have moved to India?

evident apparent

corruption impairment of integrity, virtue, or moral principle

Conflict between Hindus and Muslims has continued, and religious differences have fueled a long-term dispute between India and Pakistan over Kashmir, a territory between the two countries. The danger escalated in 1998 when both countries tested nuclear warheads. Border conflicts in 2002 led to threats of war, but in 2003 the countries agreed to a cease-fire and restored diplomatic relations.

Since 1990, most countries in Southeast Asia have experienced strong economic growth. Especially strong economies are **evident** in the Philippines, Indonesia, Malaysia, Singapore, Thailand, and Vietnam. Myanmar, Cambodia, and Laos have not kept pace.

In recent years, some Southeast Asian societies have once again moved toward democracy. However, serious troubles remain. The financial crisis of the 1990s aroused political unrest in Indonesia. Myanmar remains isolated and mired in brutal military rule. Although the Philippines is democratic, terrorism remains a challenge. Muslim rebels on the island of Mindanao, for example, have used terror to promote their demands for independence. Regional cooperation, however, has continued through the Association of Southeast Asia Nations (ASEAN), which fosters trade among Asian states.

Pakistan

After her dismissal by the military on charges of corruption, Benazir Bhutto was reelected as president in 1993. She attempted to crack down on opposition forces but was removed once again in 1997 amid renewed charges of corruption. Her successor, too, was ousted in 1999 by a military coup led by General Pervez Musharraf, who promised to restore honest government.

In September 2001, Pakistan became the focus of international attention when a coalition of forces arrived in Afghanistan to overthrow the Taliban regime. Despite considerable support for the Taliban among the local population, President Musharraf pledged his help in bringing terrorists to justice.

By 2003, problems had escalated. As Musharraf sought to fend off challenges from radical Muslim groups, secular opposition figures criticized his regime's authoritarian nature. Exiled, Bhutto planned her return.

PRIMARY SOURCE

❝God willing, I will return to my homeland and once again lead the forces of democracy in electoral battle against the entrenched power of dictators, generals, and extremists. This is my destiny.❞

—from *Daughter of Destiny: An Autobiography,* April 2007

She did return to Pakistan early in 2008 to run for president, but she was assassinated. This led to widespread suspicions of official involvement. In September 2008, amid growing political turmoil, Bhutto's widower, Asif Ali Zardari, was elected president of Pakistan. He remains in power, despite accusations of **corruption** and misuse of public funds.

✔ **READING PROGRESS CHECK**

Describing What political changes have India and Pakistan experienced in recent decades?

Latin America

GUIDING QUESTION *How have economic issues affected Latin American countries since the end of the Cold War?*

For much of Latin America's history, Latin Americans have struggled to free themselves from oppressive rule, civil war, poverty, and economic dependence on foreign countries. Since 1990, many countries have created democratic governments and reformed their social and economic structures.

Region Overview

Programs for increased public education and greater economic growth have helped to alleviate Latin America's greatest challenge, income inequality, or the large gap between rich and poor. However, countries in South America have fared better than in Central America, where many countries remain poverty stricken and are often involved in deadly drug wars.

At the end of the 1900s and beginning of the 2000s, a noticeable political trend in Latin America has been the election of left-wing governments. This is evident in the election of Hugo Chavez in Venezuela in 1998; Luiz Inácio Lula da Silva in Brazil in 2002 and his successor, Dilma Rousseff, in 2010; Michelle Bachelet in Chile in 2006; and Daniel Ortega in Nicaragua in 2007 and 2011.

Most, but not all, of these countries have pushed for democratic freedoms, social reforms, and economic growth. While Nicaragua remains poverty stricken, Brazil and Chile have seen unprecedented economic growth. In Brazil Lula da Silva pursued a policy of increased trade and educational reform. He expanded the middle class and created new consumers while continuing to increase exports. In Chile Bachelet used revenue from copper resources to fund social programs for women and children.

Drug Wars in Mexico

High poverty rates, illiteracy, high unemployment, and political corruption have led to a violent drug war in Mexico. More than 35,000 people have been killed since President Felipe Calderón, elected in 2006, ordered a military response against the country's drug gangs.

Colombia is the world's biggest producer of cocaine. Mexico serves as the gateway into the United States, which is the largest market for the drug. Mexican drug cartels, or criminal organizations whose chief purpose is to promote and control drug trafficking operations, began to transport drugs for the Colombians. More recently, however, they have taken over the distribution of drugs in the United States. This has led to considerable violence on the border of Mexico and the United States.

Mexican drug cartels recruit their members from a pool of soldiers who had served in the armies of several countries, including Guatemala and El Salvador. Increasingly, Mexican drug cartels also rely upon young people of Central America, who are poor and unemployed. These teenagers are willing to transport drugs, watch kidnap victims, and perform other low-level tasks.

☑ **READING PROGRESS CHECK**

Describing How do Mexican drug cartels traffic in drugs?

PHOTO: Marcelo Hernandez/LatinContent/Getty Images

LESSON 4 REVIEW (CCSS)

Reviewing Vocabulary

1. *Making Generalizations* Why are leaders who are charged with corruption sometimes forced out of office?

Using Your Notes

2. *Contrasting* Use your notes to find differences among major events in the regions in this lesson since the end of the Cold War.

Answering the Guiding Questions

3. *Identifying Central Issues* What changes have occurred in the Middle East and North Africa since the 1990s?

4. *Analyzing* What challenges have confronted countries in Africa south of the Sahara since the end of the Cold War?

5. *Identifying* What different economic and political issues have affected the countries of South and Southeast Asia since the 1990s?

6. *Determining Causes and Effects* How have economic issues affected Latin American countries since the end of the Cold War?

Writing Activity

7. ARGUMENT Do you think the uprisings in North Africa in 2009 and 2010 would have been as effective without the use of social networking sites? Why or why not?

Directions: On a separate sheet of paper, answer the questions below. Make sure you read carefully and answer all parts of the questions.

Lesson Review

Lesson 1

1 **MAKING INFERENCES** Why do you think Gorbachev believed that in order for his economic reforms to be successful, there would also need to be a policy of glasnost?

2 **IDENTIFYING** What has greatly helped Russia's economic growth?

Lesson 2

3 **IDENTIFYING CAUSE AND EFFECT** What events led to the reunification of the two Germanies in the 1990s?

4 **DESCRIBING** How has Western culture influenced other parts of the world?

Lesson 3

5 **EVALUATING** Do you think the one-child policy in China is oppressive? Why or why not?

6 **MAKING CONNECTIONS** How have nuclear weapons affected North Korea and South Korea?

Lesson 4

7 **DETERMINING CAUSE AND EFFECT** What happened in Libya in 2011, and how did the international community respond?

8 **SEQUENCING** Describe the leadership changes in Pakistan from the years 1993 through 2008. What accounted for these changes in leadership?

21st Century Skills

9 **GEOGRAPHY SKILLS** What happened to Yugoslavia by 2009?

10 **ECONOMICS** Why did the euro go through a major crisis in 2010?

11 **CREATE AND ANALYZE ARGUMENTS** What are some possible reasons for the decline in the Japanese economy?

12 **CREATING AND USING GRAPHS** Research the HIV/AIDS epidemic in Africa. Create a graph that illustrates the social impact of the disease.

Exploring the Essential Questions

13 **SYNTHESIZING** With a partner or in a small group select a country or region discussed in the chapter, and create a chronological multimedia presentation showing political, economic, and social changes that have occurred in that country or region over the past 30 or so years. Be sure to include how the country or region was affected.

DBQ Analyzing Historical Documents

Use the document to answer the following questions.

The following is an excerpt of Yeltsin's resignation speech in which he addresses the many challenges he faced during his presidency.

> **PRIMARY SOURCE**
>
> ❝ I want to ask for your forgiveness for the fact that many of the dreams we shared did not come true. And for the fact that what seemed simple to us turned out to be tormentingly difficult. I ask forgiveness for not justifying some hopes of those people who believed that at one stroke, in one spurt, we could leap from the gray, stagnant, totalitarian past in to the light, rich, civilized future. ❞
>
> —Boris Yeltsin, December 31, 1999

14 **ANALYZING** Did Yeltsin believe he succeeded in transforming post-Soviet Russia? Cite evidence to support your answer.

15 **EVALUATING** Why might moving from a totalitarian government to a successful and prosperous country "in one spurt" not have been a reasonable hope? Explain.

Extended-Response Question

16 **INFORMATIVE/EXPLANATORY** Compare and contrast the revolutions that occurred in Poland, Czechoslovakia, and Romania. Discuss their causes, outcomes, and long-term effects.

Need Extra Help?

If You've Missed Question	1	2	3	4	5	6	7	8	9	10	11	12	13	14	15	16
Go to page	432	435	437	440	443	445	447	450	436	437	443	448	432	452	452	433

Contemporary Global Issues

1989–Present

ESSENTIAL QUESTIONS · *What influences global political and economic relationships?* · *How do social and environmental issues affect countries differently?*

PHOTO: ©Phillipe Lissac/Godong/Corbis

netw⬤rks

There's More Online! about contemporary global issues.

CHAPTER 22

Lesson 1
Political Challenges in the Modern World

Lesson 2
Social Challenges in the Modern World

Lesson 3
Global Economies

Lesson 4
Science, Technology, and the Environment

The Story Matters...

The world faces a daunting array of challenges in the twenty-first century. Some of these, such as nuclear proliferation and cyberterrorism, are relatively new. Other problems, such as war, poverty, hunger, and disease, have a long history. Creative solutions are needed to address these problems. Microcredit loans are one example. Microcredit banks make small loans to individual entrepreneurs, the majority of them women, enabling them to start small businesses and to escape from poverty.

◄ Photographed in 2001, this woman is a Rwandan refugee now living in Nairobi, Kenya. She was able to set up her business as a seamstress with a loan from a microcredit bank.

Place and Time: The World 1989–Present

One of the most significant parts of the human story has been the growth of cities. Civilization began with the first cities 5,000 years ago. Urbanization greatly accelerated with the Industrial Revolution. If current trends in population growth and economic development continue, the human future will be a story of megacities. A megacity is an urban area with more than 10 million inhabitants. In 1950 there were only two megacities—New York City and Tokyo. Today, the United Nations estimates that there are 26 megacities.

Step Into the Place

Read the quotation and look at the information presented on the map.

DBQ **Analyzing Historical Documents** What will be the biggest challenge facing megacities?

PRIMARY SOURCE

"Over the next two decades, the world will see a burst of urban expansion at a speed and on a scale never before witnessed in human history. But not all the world will take part. When you hear about the coming urban age, it's really a story about rising Asia and the two countries that will define this new era of the megacity: China and India. Half of Asia will become urbanized, and nearly a billion people will shift from countryside to cityscape. Trillions of dollars will need to be spent on roads, trains, power plants, water systems, and social services. And it's going to happen in less than half the time that it took the West."

—Richard Dobbs, from "Megacities," *Foreign Policy*, Sept./Oct. 2010

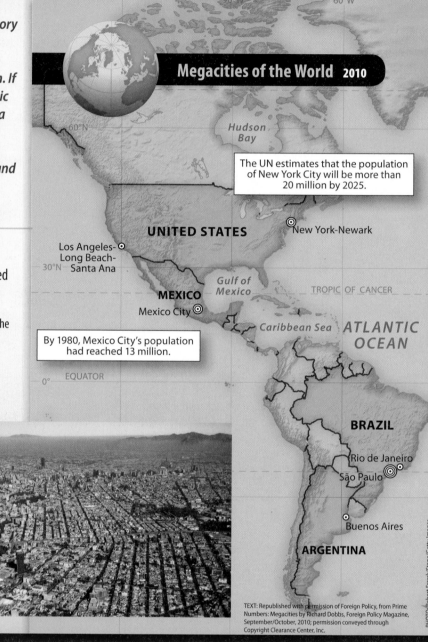

Megacities of the World 2010

Hudson Bay

The UN estimates that the population of New York City will be more than 20 million by 2025.

UNITED STATES

New York-Newark

Los Angeles-Long Beach-Santa Ana

Gulf of Mexico

MEXICO

TROPIC OF CANCER

Mexico City

Caribbean Sea

ATLANTIC OCEAN

By 1980, Mexico City's population had reached 13 million.

EQUATOR

BRAZIL

Rio de Janeiro

São Paulo

Buenos Aires

ARGENTINA

TEXT: Republished with permission of Foreign Policy, from Prime Numbers: Megacities by Richard Dobbs, Foreign Policy Magazine, September/October, 2010; permission conveyed through Copyright Clearance Center, Inc.

PHOTO: Robert Frerck/Stone/Getty Images

Step Into the Time

Making Generalizations

Select several events from the time line and use them as evidence for a generalization about world population patterns.

1990 The number of megacities in the world reaches 10

1995 India has three megacities— Mumbai, Delhi, and Kolkata

MEGACITIES

THE WORLD

1989 1990

1995

1990 World Wide Web created

1995 World Trade Organization (WTO) begins operations

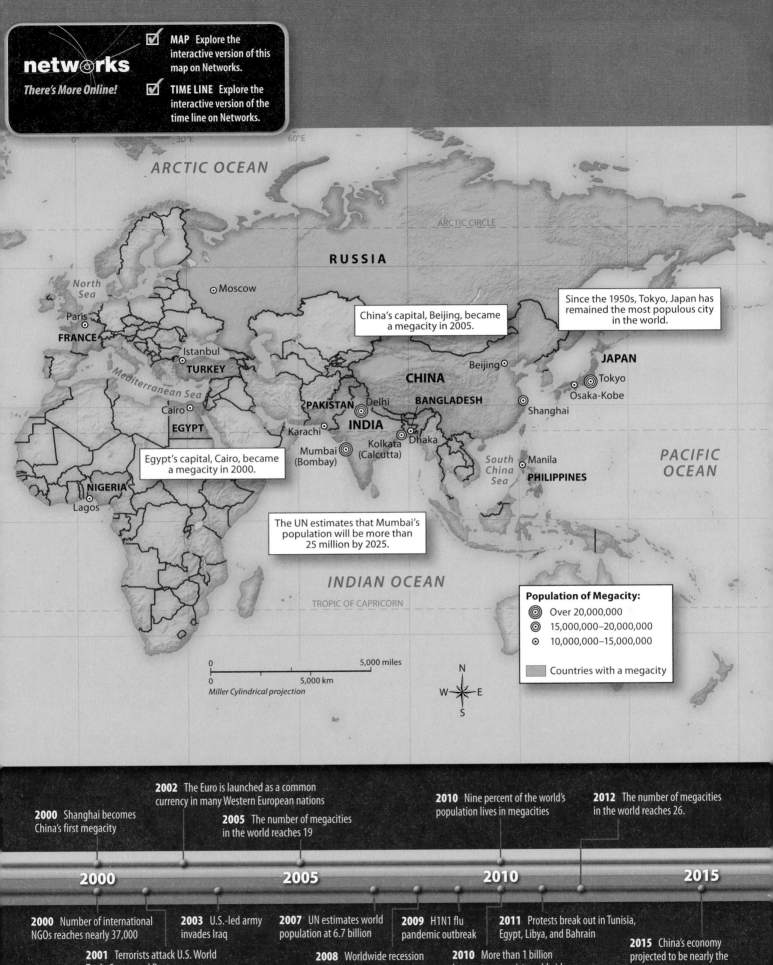

networks
There's More Online!

☑ **MAP** Explore the interactive version of this map on Networks.

☑ **TIME LINE** Explore the interactive version of the time line on Networks.

ARCTIC OCEAN

ARCTIC CIRCLE

RUSSIA

○ Moscow

North Sea

Paris ◎
FRANCE

Istanbul ◎
TURKEY

Mediterranean Sea

Cairo ◎
EGYPT

NIGERIA
Lagos ○

China's capital, Beijing, became a megacity in 2005.

Since the 1950s, Tokyo, Japan has remained the most populous city in the world.

Beijing ○

JAPAN
◎ Tokyo
Osaka-Kobe

CHINA

BANGLADESH

◎ Shanghai

PAKISTAN Delhi ◎
Karachi ○ **INDIA**
Mumbai ◎ Kolkata ◎ Dhaka
(Bombay) (Calcutta)

South China Sea

○ Manila
PHILIPPINES

PACIFIC OCEAN

Egypt's capital, Cairo, became a megacity in 2000.

The UN estimates that Mumbai's population will be more than 25 million by 2025.

INDIAN OCEAN

TROPIC OF CAPRICORN

Population of Megacity:
◎ Over 20,000,000
◎ 15,000,000–20,000,000
○ 10,000,000–15,000,000

▢ Countries with a megacity

0   5,000 miles
0   5,000 km
Miller Cylindrical projection

N W E S

2000 Shanghai becomes China's first megacity

2002 The Euro is launched as a common currency in many Western European nations

2005 The number of megacities in the world reaches 19

2010 Nine percent of the world's population lives in megacities

2012 The number of megacities in the world reaches 26.

2000   **2005**   **2010**   **2015**

2000 Number of international NGOs reaches nearly 37,000

2001 Terrorists attack U.S. World Trade Center and Pentagon

2003 U.S.-led army invades Iraq

2007 UN estimates world population at 6.7 billion

2008 Worldwide recession

2009 H1N1 flu pandemic outbreak

2010 More than 1 billion Internet users exist worldwide

2011 Protests break out in Tunisia, Egypt, Libya, and Bahrain

2015 China's economy projected to be nearly the world's largest

Reading **HELP**DESK

Academic Vocabulary

- **chemical**
- **drama**
- **arbitrarily**

Content Vocabulary

- **peacekeeping forces**
- **nuclear proliferation**
- **bioterrorism**

TAKING NOTES:

Key Ideas and Details

Summarizing As you read, use a table like the one below to identify important political events that have occurred in modern Africa, Asia, and Latin America.

Africa	Asia	Latin America

LESSON 1
Political Challenges in the Modern World

ESSENTIAL QUESTION
What influences global political and economic relationships?

IT MATTERS BECAUSE

In today's world, problems in one part of the world can affect people all over the globe. Terrorism, civil war, and ethnic conflict are some of the most difficult political challenges of the modern world.

The United Nations

GUIDING QUESTION *What are the structure and goals of the United Nations?*

In recent decades, many nations have become convinced that there are significant problems that can be solved only by working with other nations. Today, the United Nations (UN) is one of the most visible symbols of the new globalism. The UN was founded in 1945 at the end of World War II. Two of the UN's goals are peace and human dignity. Its members pledged:

PRIMARY SOURCE

❝to save succeeding generations from the scourge of war…to reaffirm faith in fundamental human rights…and to promote social progress and better standards of life in larger freedom.❞

—from the Preamble to the United Nations Charter, June 26, 1945

The General Assembly of the United Nations is made of representatives from all member nations. It has the power to discuss any important question and to recommend action. The Security Council advises the General Assembly and passes resolutions that require the organization to act. Five nations have permanent seats on the Security Council: the United States, Russia, Great Britain, France, and China. Ten other members are chosen by the General Assembly and serve for limited terms. Because each permanent member can veto a decision, deliberations can often end in stalemate. The UN Secretariat, an administrative body, is headed by the secretary-general. The International Court of Justice (sometimes referred to as the World Court) is the judicial body of the UN.

UN programs and specialized agencies work to address economic and social problems and to organize conferences on important issues such as women's rights and the environment. UN **peacekeeping forces** settle conflicts and supervise truces in "hot spots" around the globe.

✓ READING PROGRESS CHECK

Contrasting How do the UN General Assembly and the UN Security Council differ?

International Security

GUIDING QUESTION *What international security issues confront the post-Cold War world?*

Despite the efforts of the United Nations, numerous challenges remain in the effort to provide security in today's world.

Weapons of Mass Destruction

Modern technology has led to frightening methods of mass destruction: nuclear, biological, and **chemical** weapons. The end of the Cold War reduced the risk of nuclear conflict between the United States and the Soviet Union. However, nuclear weapons still exist and nuclear conflicts remain possible.

The UN established the International Atomic Energy Agency (IAEA) in 1957. This agency is a safeguard system against **nuclear proliferation**—the spread of nuclear weapons production technology and knowledge to nations without that capability. A great risk comes from countries that have not joined the Nuclear Nonproliferation Treaty (NPT)—India, Pakistan, Israel, and North Korea—and from countries that have violated the NPT, such as Iran. In 1998 India and Pakistan exploded nuclear devices underground. North Korea performed its first nuclear test in October 2006, and Iran refused to shelve its nuclear enrichment program.

Since 2000, there has also been an increased awareness of the threat from biological and chemical weapons. Biowarfare, the use of disease and poison against civilians and soldiers in wartime, is not new. For example, chemical weapons were used extensively in World War I and during the Iran-Iraq war in the 1980s. Governments have agreed to limit the research, production, and use of weapons of mass destruction, but these agreements are difficult to enforce. Furthermore, these measures have not prevented terrorists from practicing **bioterrorism**, the use of biological and chemical weapons in terrorist attacks.

The Challenge of Terrorism

Acts of terror have become a regular feature of modern society. Terrorists often kill civilians and take hostages to achieve their political goals. Beginning in the late 1970s and 1980s, many countries placed their concern about terrorism at the top of foreign policy agendas. Terrorist acts have received considerable media attention. When Palestinian terrorists kidnapped and killed 11 Israeli athletes at the Munich Olympic Games in 1972, hundreds of millions of people watched the **drama** unfold on television.

Some terrorists are militant nationalists who want separatist states. The Irish Republican Army (IRA), for example, wants to unite Northern Ireland with the Irish Republic. IRA leaders now seem more willing to open normal relations with the police of Northern Ireland after decades of violence. The group Basque Fatherland and Liberty (ETA) employs violence as a tool to free the Basque region in the western Pyrenees from Spanish control.

A radical Communist guerrilla group in Peru, known as Shining Path, also used terrorist violence. Aiming to create a classless society, Shining Path killed mayors, missionaries, priests, and peasants across Peru.

Analyzing
PRIMARY SOURCES

Nuclear Proliferation

❝The threat of nuclear terrorism is real and current... the existence of a nuclear threat anywhere is a threat everywhere, and as a global community, we will win or lose this battle together.❞

—Dr. Mohamed ElBaradei, Director General, IAEA, November 8, 2004

DBQ *DRAWING CONCLUSIONS*
Why does the Director General argue that stopping nuclear terrorism requires a global effort?

peacekeeping forces
military forces drawn from neutral members of the United Nations to settle conflicts and supervise truces

chemical used in or produced by chemistry

nuclear proliferation the spread of nuclear weapons production technology and knowledge to nations without that capability

bioterrorism the use of biological and chemical weapons in terrorist attacks

drama state of intense conflict

PHOTO: BETH A. KEISER/AFP/Getty Images

▲ Fire and rescue workers search for surviviors amid the rubble of the World Trade Center two days after the September 11, 2001, attacks.

▶ **CRITICAL THINKING**
Describing What was the immediate response to the attacks of September 11, 2001?

One of the most destructive acts of terrorism occurred on September 11, 2001. Al-Qaeda terrorists directed by Osama bin Laden hijacked four commercial jets in Boston, Newark, and Washington, D.C., flying two into the World Trade Center and one into the Pentagon. Almost 3,000 people were killed. President George W. Bush vowed to wage war on terrorism. This process began in Afghanistan in October 2001. President Barack Obama announced a major U.S. victory against al-Qaeda in 2011, when U.S. forces killed bin Laden at his hideout in Pakistan.

Worldwide, one of the most noticeable changes in public policies since September 11, 2001, has been increased security at airports. Many European and Asian governments have also begun working more closely together in their intelligence and police activities to track down terrorists.

Challenges in the Middle East

The war on terrorism spread to the Middle East when the United States attacked Iraq in March 2003. President Bush claimed that Iraq's leader, Saddam Hussein, had chemical and biological weapons of mass destruction and that Saddam had close ties to al-Qaeda. Both claims turned out to be mistaken and the United States soon became bogged down in a war in which Hussein's supporters, foreign terrorists, and Islamic militants all battled the American-led forces.

By 2006, Iraq seemed to be descending into a widespread civil war, especially between the Shia, who controlled southern Iraq, and the Sunnis, who controlled central Iraq. An American troop surge in 2007 helped stabilize conditions within a year. The U.S. and Iraqi governments then agreed to a complete withdrawal of American troops by 2011. President Obama fulfilled this promise. After more than nine years in Iraq, all remaining American troops left the country on December 18, 2011.

Much of the terrorism in the Middle East is aimed against the West. One reason Middle Eastern terrorists have targeted Westerners can be traced to Western investment in the Middle East oil industry, which began in the 1920s. This industry brought wealth to ruling families in some Middle Eastern kingdoms, but most citizens remained very poor. They often blamed the West, especially the United States, for supporting the ruling families.

The oil business increased Middle Eastern contact with the West. Some Muslims feared that this contact would weaken their religion and their way of life. Some Muslims began organizing to overthrow their pro-Western governments. Muslims who support these movements are called fundamentalist militants. They promote their own vision of what a pure Islamic society should be. Most Muslims around the world do not share this vision, do not support terrorism, and some are terror victims.

☑ **READING PROGRESS CHECK**

Determining Cause and Effect How have governments responded to terrorism since September 11, 2001?

Civil War, Ethnic Conflict, and New Democracies

GUIDING QUESTIONS *How have civil war, ethnic conflict, and genocide affected some nations in the post-Cold War period, and how have governments and nongovernmental organizations responded to them? Where have new democracies emerged in the late twentieth and early twenty-first centuries?*

Ethnic and religious conflicts, which often lead to civil war, have plagued many developing nations and some developed nations in Europe. In Northern Ireland, Protestants and Catholics have frequently clashed. The Serbs used ethnic cleansing in the 1990s to kill Bosnian Muslims during the war in Bosnia. After Cyprus achieved independence, fighting between Greek and Turkish Cypriots led to a division of the island.

Some conflicts that stem from regional, ethnic, and religious differences in the 1990s and 2000s have led to the creation of new countries with fledgling democracies. Several states of the former Yugoslavia and East Timor became independent democratic states in recent years.

Africa

Within many African nations, warring ethnic groups undermined the concept of nationhood. This is not surprising because the colonial powers had **arbitrarily** drawn the boundaries of African nations. Virtually all of these states included widely different ethnic, linguistic, and territorial groups. In central Africa, fighting between the Hutu and the Tutsi created unstable governments. In Rwanda, brutal civil war broke out in 1994 as Hutu militias began a campaign of genocide against Tutsis, killing at least 500,000. As thousands of Rwandan refugees died in camps, the United States began a relief operation in conjunction with the UN. In 1997 a UN-sponsored war crimes tribunal began in Tanzania. In 1998 the tribunal sentenced the former Rwandan prime minister to life imprisonment for genocide.

Ethnic violence also plagued Sudan, Africa's largest nation. In the western province of Darfur, Arab militias attacked African ethnic groups with the support of the Arab-led government. Entire villages were burned, more than 200,000 people died, and more than 2 million fled their homes. The UN took over a struggling peacekeeping operation from the African Union at the end of 2007. In 2008 the International Criminal Court issued an arrest warrant for the sitting Sudanese president, Omar Hassan al-Bashir, for genocide, war crimes, and crimes against humanity. In a 2011 referendum, southern Sudan voted to become independent from the north.

Desire for more democratic government led to a series of protests in Egypt and surrounding countries in 2011. Working to end nearly 30 years of autocratic rule, protesters demanded that Egyptian president Hosni Mubarak step down. After days of continued unrest, Mubarak resigned.

arbitrarily at one's discretion; randomly

▼ A poll worker counts ballots for the 2007 election in East Timor.

Asia

Several areas in Asia and Southeast Asia experienced ethnic and religious conflict, including Tibet, East Timor, and Sri Lanka. Tibet seeks independence from the Chinese government that has suppressed dissent among ethnic minorities. The Dalai Lama led the government of Tibet in exile from India since 1959 but stepped down in 2011.

In 1999 the people of East Timor voted to become free of Indonesian rule, which was followed by violence between Christians and Muslims on the island. Nearly 10,000 died from the conflict. In 2002 East Timor (Timor-Leste) was internationally recognized as an independent country. In 2007, with the help of the UN, East Timor held mostly peaceful democratic elections.

In Sri Lanka, there has been tension and violence since 1983 between the majority Sinhalese (who are mostly Buddhist) who lead the government and the minority Tamils (who are mostly Hindu). A 2002 ceasefire halted the violence temporarily, but it ended with renewed violence in 2008. The military conflict ended in 2010.

Latin America

In recent years, democracy has also begun to flourish in Latin America. With the debt crisis in Latin America in the 1980s came a movement toward democracy as people realized that military power without popular consent could not maintain a strong state.

In Brazil the military leadership opened the door to a return to democracy in 1985. In the 1990s, democratic presidents restored some stability to the economy, but the gap between rich and poor remained wide. This led to the election of Luiz Inacio Lula da Silva in 2002, Brazil's first left-wing president in four decades. He was successful in promoting rapid economic growth.

A series of military dictators ruled Venezuela during the first half of the twentieth century. Hugo Chavez became a folk hero to the Venezuelan people when he opposed the military government. As a result, he was elected as president in 1998 in a landslide victory and reelected in 2006. In 2007 Chavez began to nationalize energy and communications firms, reducing foreign influence in its economy. Critics charge that he has taken away the freedom of the press. Chavez was reelected in October 2012.

☑ **READING PROGRESS CHECK**

Explaining How did governments and international organizations respond to the conflicts in Rwanda and Darfur?

LESSON 1 REVIEW

Reviewing Vocabulary

1. *Making Inferances* Why have countries sought to stop nuclear proliferation and the use of chemical and biological weapons?

Using Your Notes

2. *Comparing* Use your notes to compare the political challenges faced in Africa, Asia, and Latin America.

Answering the Guiding Questions

3. *Identifying* What are the structure and goals of the United Nations?

4. *Drawing Conclusions* What international security issues confront the post-Cold War world?

5. *Assessing* How have civil war, ethnic conflict, and genocide affected some nations in the post-Cold War period, and how have governments and nongovernmental organizations responded to them?

6. *Stating* Where have new democracies emerged in the late twentieth and early twenty-first centuries?

Writing Activity

7. ARGUMENT Research a place where the United Nations has deployed peacekeeping forces, and write an essay on whether or not those forces have been effective at promoting the UN's goals.

Reading **HELP**DESK (CCSS)

Academic Vocabulary

- projection
- migration

Content Vocabulary

- pandemic
- nongovernmental organization

TAKING NOTES:

Key Ideas and Details

Organizing As you read, use a chart like the one below to identify factors that can cause world hunger.

World Hunger

LESSON 2
Social Challenges in the Modern World

ESSENTIAL QUESTIONS • *What influences global political and economic relationships?* • *How do social and environmental issues affect countries differently?*

IT MATTERS BECAUSE

More and more people are becoming aware of the global nature of our contemporary problems. Those problems include world hunger, global health pandemics, human rights and equality for women, and population and migration trends. At the same time, new transnational grassroots social movements have arisen to address these problems.

Global Poverty

GUIDING QUESTION *What is the social impact of poverty, hunger, and health pandemics in developing nations?*

Developing nations confront many serious problems, not the least of which is extreme poverty. About 1 billion people in developing nations live on less than 1 dollar a day, which can cause poor health, illness, and even death. About 18 million people a year worldwide die from poverty-related causes. Poverty is a complex problem that creates many other challenges for developing nations. It can keep children from attending school, limit access to clean water and sanitation, cause people to live in unsafe housing, and is a primary cause of worldwide hunger.

World Hunger

Growing or purchasing enough food for more and more people creates a severe problem in many developing countries. An estimated 1 billion people worldwide suffer from hunger. About 75 percent of the hungry live in rural areas of developing countries, and 25 percent of them are children.

The effects of hunger and malnutrition are devastating. Every year, more than 10 million people die of hunger and hunger-related diseases. The long-term health problems caused by malnutrition are severe. Undernourished infants and children suffer from blindness, mental retardation, and increased susceptibility to disease.

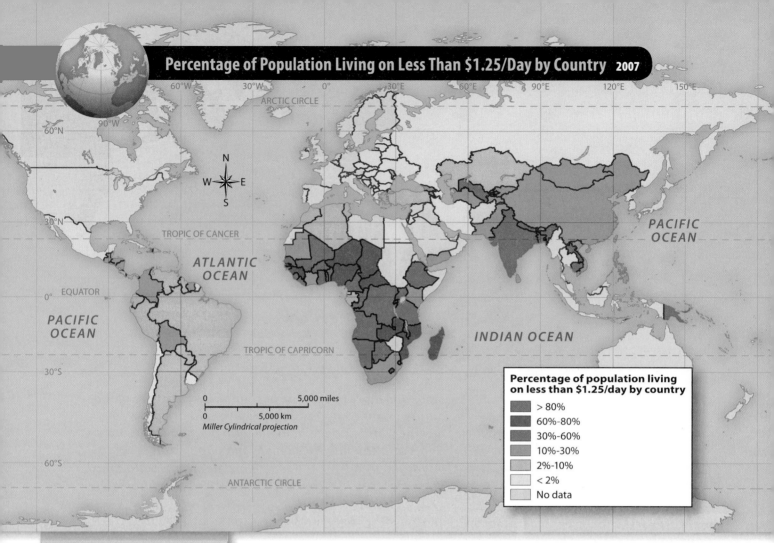

Percentage of Population Living on Less Than $1.25/Day by Country 2007

Percentage of population living on less than $1.25/day by country

- > 80%
- 60%-80%
- 30%-60%
- 10%-30%
- 2%-10%
- < 2%
- No data

0   5,000 miles

0   5,000 km

Miller Cylindrical projection

pandemic a widespread outbreak of a disease

Among the many causes of worldwide hunger, poverty and economic factors are by far the major ones. The poor do not have enough money to produce or buy an adequate amount of food. For those living in poverty, food is costly. Food prices increased 45 percent from the end of 2006 to 2008. Prices for corn, wheat, and rice reached record highs, due in part to increasing demand from developing economies, rising biofuel production, drought conditions, and higher costs to produce these foods.

Natural disasters can also bring about hunger. Droughts, earthquakes, hurricanes, floods, and tsunamis cause many to go without food, at least on a short-term basis. Poor farming practices, deforestation, and overgrazing can also lead to hunger if land becomes depleted and can no longer produce as much food.

Food shortages can also result from civil war. War disrupts normal farming, and warring groups often try to limit their enemies' access to food. For example, in Sudan, 1.3 million people starved when combatants of a civil war in the 1980s interrupted the food supply.

Global Health Pandemics

The fear of a global swine flu **pandemic** in 2009 made people aware that in a global age, infectious diseases can easily spread as a result of international interactions. Global infectious diseases, such as HIV and AIDS, have raised concerns in recent decades. In 2010 nearly 1.8 million people died of AIDS and 2.7 million were newly infected with HIV. Africa has been especially devastated. According to the UN, more than two-thirds of the 34 million people living with HIV are in Africa south of the Sahara. AIDS has had a serious impact on children and families in Africa. Many children have lost one or both parents to AIDS. Often, relatives are too poor to care for these children. Many orphans thus become heads of households filled with younger siblings.

Still, there has been some good news: Global AIDS deaths have declined and the percentage of the world's population living with HIV has stabilized. Organizations, such as UNAIDS, continue to sponsor initiatives to educate the public, to prevent HIV infection, to provide AIDS treatment, and to search for a cure.

☑ READING PROGRESS CHECK

Making Connections How are problems of poverty and world hunger related?

Human Rights and Equality for Women

GUIDING QUESTION *How have problems involving human rights and gender inequality been addressed in the late twentieth and early twenty-first centuries?*

The United Nations took the lead in affirming the basic human rights of all people. On December 10, 1948, the UN General Assembly adopted the Universal Declaration of Human Rights (UDHR). This declaration is a set of basic human rights and standards for government that has been agreed to by almost every country in the world. It affirms everyone's right to life, liberty, and security of person as well as the right to freedom of movement and the freedom of opinion and expression.

Since the adoption of the UDHR, the human rights movement has achieved much success in freeing political prisoners and bringing economic and political change around the world. Nevertheless, human rights violations still occur worldwide.

Governments themselves often carry on the violence. Dictators and military regimes punish people who disagree with their views. In Cuba, Chile, Myanmar, Iraq, Iran, and other countries, people have been persecuted for opposing repressive governments. In other countries, such as Bosnia and Rwanda, ethnic, religious, and racial hatreds have led to the mass murder of hundreds of thousands of people.

In the social and economic spheres of the Western world, the gap that once separated men and women has been steadily narrowing. More and more women are joining the workforce, and they make up half the university graduates in Western countries. Many countries have laws that require equal pay for women and men doing the same work, and some laws prohibit promotions based on gender. Nevertheless, women in many Western countries still do not hold many top positions in business or government.

Bound to their homes and families and subordinate to men, women in developing nations face considerable difficulties. They are often unable to obtain education, property rights, or decent jobs. Indeed, one of the UN Millennium Development Goals is to "promote gender equality and empower women." Still, some women in developing nations have become leaders of their countries, such as Ellen Johnson Sirleaf, who became president of Liberia in 2006, and Joyce Hilda Banda, who became Malawi's first female vice president in 2009.

☑ READING PROGRESS CHECK

Evaluating What effect has the Universal Declaration of Human Rights had on the movement for human rights around the world?

TEXT: Millennium Development Goal 3 from UN Millennium Campaign. http://www.undp.org/mdg/goal3.shtml

Analyzing **CCSS**
PRIMARY SOURCES

Universal Declaration of Human Rights, 1948

"All human beings are born free and equal in dignity and rights. . . . Everyone is entitled to all the rights and freedoms set forth in this Declaration, without distinction of any kind, such as race, colour, sex, language, religion, political or other opinion, national or social origin, property, birth or other status. . . . Everyone has the right to life, liberty and security of person. . . . Everyone has the right to freedom of movement. . . Everyone has the right to freedom of opinion and expression."

—from the Universal Declaration of Human Rights, adopted by the UN General Assembly on December 10, 1948

DBQ *PARAPHRASING*
Describe the human rights listed above in your own words.

Population and Migration Trends

GUIDING QUESTION *How have population and migration trends affected developed and developing nations?*

projection an estimate or a calculation

Estimates by the Population Reference Bureau put the 2010 world population at about 6.9 billion. Their **projections** estimate that the global population could reach 9.4 billion by 2050. The world population is expected to increase approximately one-third over the next four decades.

Almost all population growth is from the developing nations. The most populous have taken steps to decrease growth. China has a one-child policy, and India promotes a national family welfare program but has had limited success. By 2050, India will have surpassed China in population and will likely remain the most populous country in the world thereafter.

Meanwhile, many wealthy regions, such as Western Europe, are declining in population. In fact, by 2050, the United States is expected to be the only wealthy nation with a growing population. The developed nations are also "graying"—a larger percentage of the population is reaching retirement age. In the more developed regions, more than one-fifth of the population is aged 60 or over. By 2050, it is expected to reach one-third.

The global age distribution is shifting toward older people because of increases in life expectancies, lower birthrates, and lower death rates. The number of people aged 80 and over and those who live beyond 100 is rising, placing increased demands on the economies of developed nations.

Developing countries face different problems. Between 2010 and 2050, the population in developing countries is expected to grow from 6.8 billion to 8.1 billion. Also, the trend of increased urbanization is expected to continue. Because many cities lack the infrastructure to support larger populations, concerns are rising about future international health and environmental problems, especially in developing nations.

migration the movement of people from one country, place, or locality to another

Connected to population growth is the problem of global **migrations**. In 2010 there were about 214 million international migrants. Although about 60 percent of migrants live in more developed countries, the remainder relocated from one developing country to another.

There are several reasons people migrate. Persecution for political reasons and brutal civil wars in Asia, Africa, the Middle East, and Europe has led millions of refugees to seek safety in neighboring countries. Many have migrated for economic reasons. For example, guest workers from Turkey, India, Pakistan, and North Africa entered more prosperous

CHARTS/GRAPHS

The world population is projected to reach over 9 billion by 2050.

1 *Problem-Solving* By what percent is the world population expected to increase from 1980 to 2020?

2 *Interpreting* In which decade is there projected to be the smallest population increase?

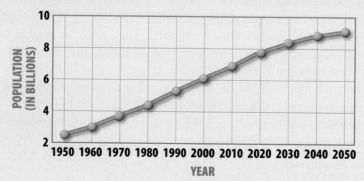

WORLD POPULATION GROWTH, 1950–2050

Source: United Nations Population Division, 2010

European countries. But foreign workers often become scapegoats when countries face economic problems. Political parties in France and Norway in the 1990s, for example, called for the removal of blacks and Arabs to protect the ethnic purity of their nations.

☑ **READING PROGRESS CHECK**

Contrasting How do population issues affect developed and developing countries differently?

Transnational Organizations

GUIDING QUESTION *What role do transnational and non-governmental organizations play in the international arena?*

Global awareness has led to new social movements that focus on problems that nations share. These problems include areas such as the environment, gender inequality, child labor, the appropriate use of technology, and the promotion of peace.

Groups such as the International Red Cross and Red Crescent Movement draw their membership from different countries. Other groups have members in one country. Many individuals act at the grassroots level, that is, in their own community. A favorite slogan of grassroots groups is "Think globally, act locally."

Another movement that addresses world problems is the growth of **nongovernmental organizations** (NGOs). NGOs are often represented at the United Nations. They include professional, business, and cooperative organizations, as well as foundations. Also included are religious, peace, and disarmament groups that work to limit the size of military forces and weapons stocks. Other NGOs protect the welfare of women and children and include environmental and human rights groups.

American educator Elise Boulding promoted NGOs. She believed they can educate people to consider problems globally. She said that all NGOs are expected "to define problems in global terms, to take account of human interests and needs as they are found in all parts of the planet." The number of international NGOs increased from 176 in 1910 to nearly 37,000 in 2000.

☑ **READING PROGRESS CHECK**

Describing How are grassroots organizations related to NGOs?

▲ An international NGO builds a well to provide safe drinking water for a village in Zimbabwe.

nongovernmental organization an organization that has no government ties and works to address world problems

PHOTO: Neil Cooper/Alamy

LESSON 2 REVIEW (CCSS)

Reviewing Vocabulary

1. *Drawing Conclusions* Why are pandemics a concern in an increasingly globalized world?

Using Your Notes

2. *Identifying* Use your notes to identify the causes of worldwide hunger.

Answering the Guiding Questions

3. *Making Generalizations* What is the social impact of poverty, hunger, and health pandemics in developing nations?

4. *Evaluating* How have problems involving human rights and gender inequality been addressed in the late twentieth and early twenty-first centuries?

5. *Differentiating* How have population and migration trends affected developed and developing nations?

6. *Analyzing* What role do transnational and nongovernmental organizations play in the international arena?

Writing Activity

7. **INFORMATIVE/EXPLANATORY** Choose one non-governmental organization to research. Write an essay about the organization's mission, goals, accomplishments, and challenges it faces.

Reading **HELP**DESK (CCSS)

Academic Vocabulary

- **currency**
- **dynamic**

Content Vocabulary

- **multinational corporation**
- **globalization**
- **collateralized debt obligation**
- **subprime investments**

TAKING NOTES:

Key Ideas and Details

Organizing As you read, use a table like the one below to identify global economic organizations and regional trade organizations.

Global Economic Organizations	Regional Trade Organizations

LESSON 3
Global Economies

ESSENTIAL QUESTIONS
- *What influences global political and economic relationships?*
- *How do social and environmental issues affect countries differently?*

IT MATTERS BECAUSE
The technology revolution has tied people and nations closely together and contributed to globalization. Economically, globalization has taken the form of a global economy.

Global Economic Organizations

GUIDING QUESTION *What are the roles of global economic organizations in the world economy?*

The global economy began to develop after World War II and gained momentum in the 1980s and 1990s. After World War II, the United States and other nations set up the World Bank and the International Monetary Fund (IMF) as a means of expanding global markets and avoiding economic crises. The World Bank is actually a group of five international organizations, largely controlled by developed countries. It provides grants, loans, and advice for economic development in developing countries. The World Bank's stated goal is "a world free of poverty." The IMF, founded in 1945, is now an "organization of 184 countries." Its goal is to oversee the global financial system. To achieve its goal, the IMF watches exchange rates and offers financial and technical assistance to developing nations.

Multinational corporations are another reflection of the global economy. Prominent examples of multinational corporations include Siemens, General Motors, Exxon Mobil, Mitsubishi, and the Sony Corporation. These companies are among the 200 largest multinational corporations, which are responsible for more than half the world's industrial production. In addition, these supercorporations dominate much of the world's investment capital, technology, and markets. A recent comparison of corporate sales and national gross domestic product revealed that only 49 of the world's 100 largest economic entities are nations. The remaining 51 are corporations. For this reason, some people believe that economic globalization might best be called "corporate globalization."

There is also a downside to the growing number of multinational corporations. As they increasingly tie one country to another in a global economy, an economic downturn in one country can create stagnant conditions in other countries. We live in an economically interdependent world.

Global trade is another important component of the global economy. Over the years, many nations joined in talks to make trade between countries free and easy. These talks led to the General Agreement on Trade and Tariffs (GATT). In 1995 the nations that had signed the GATT treaties agreed to create the World Trade Organization (WTO). Made of more than 150 member nations, the WTO arranges trade agreements and settles trade disputes.

multinational corporation a company with divisions in more than two countries

✓ **READING PROGRESS CHECK**

Contrasting How are the World Bank and International Monetary Fund different?

WORLD'S LARGEST MULTINATIONAL CORPORATIONS, 2010				
Rank/Company	**Country of Origin**	**Industry**	**Sales ($bil)**	**Profits ($bil)**
1. JPMorgan Chase	United States	Banking	115.63	11.65
2. General Electric	United States	Conglomerates	156.78	11.03
3. Bank of America	United States	Banking	150.45	6.28
4. ExxonMobil	United States	Oil & Gas Operations	275.56	19.28
5. ICBC	China	Banking	71.86	16.27
6. Banco Santander	Spain	Banking	109.57	12.34
7. Wells Fargo	United States	Banking	98.64	12.28
8. HSBC Holdings	United Kingdom	Banking	103.74	5.83
9. Royal Dutch Shell	Netherlands	Oil & Gas Operations	278.19	12.52
10. BP	United Kingdom	Oil & Gas Operations	239.27	16.58
11. BNP Paribas	France	Banking	101.06	8.37
12. PetroChina	China	Oil & Gas Operations	157.22	16.8

Source: www.forbes.com

CHARTS/GRAPHS

In 2010 many of the largest multinational corporations were in the banking and the oil and gas operations industries and had their headquarters in the United States.

▶ **CRITICAL THINKING**

1 **Transferring Knowledge** Create a bar graph that displays the multinational corporations with profits over $12 billion.

2 **Interpreting** Create a circle graph that summarizes the country of origin of the 12 largest multinational corporations.

Regional Trade Organizations

GUIDING QUESTION *What are the effects of regional trade organizations on national and regional economies?*

Groups of nations have also joined together to form trading blocs to foster regional prosperity. Mercosur, for example, is an economic union of Argentina, Brazil, Paraguay, and Uruguay.

NAFTA

In 1992 the Mexican president Carlos Salinas de Gortari began to work with U.S. president George H. W. Bush and the Canadian prime minister Brian Mulroney to form the North American Free Trade Agreement (NAFTA). It was ratified and put into effect in the beginning of 1994. It created a free-trade area for Canada, the United States, and Mexico. Some economists have argued that it has been beneficial to business owners but harmful to others. Farmers in Mexico, for example, saw prices for their food products drop as cheap American foodstuffs were imported. Industrial workers in

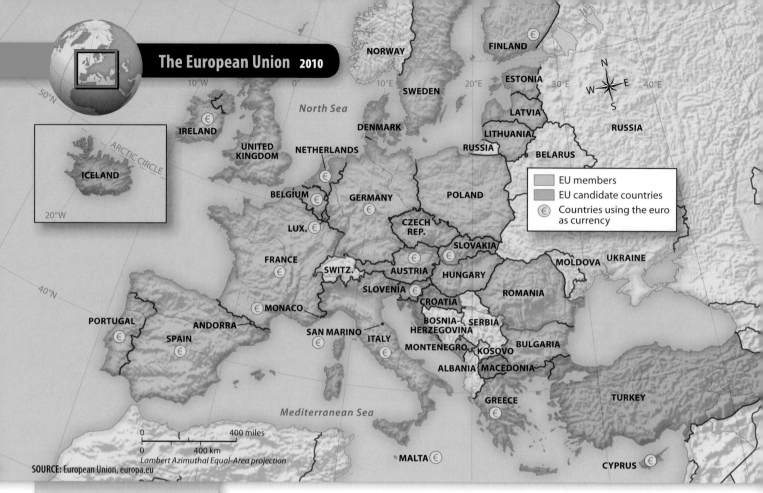

The European Union 2010

NORWAY
FINLAND
SWEDEN
ESTONIA
North Sea
LATVIA
RUSSIA
DENMARK
LITHUANIA
IRELAND
RUSSIA
BELARUS
UNITED KINGDOM
NETHERLANDS
BELGIUM
GERMANY
POLAND
LUX.
CZECH REP.
SLOVAKIA
FRANCE
SWITZ.
AUSTRIA
HUNGARY
MOLDOVA
UKRAINE
SLOVENIA
CROATIA
ROMANIA
MONACO
PORTUGAL
ANDORRA
SAN MARINO
ITALY
BOSNIA-HERZEGOVINA
SERBIA
SPAIN
MONTENEGRO
KOSOVO
BULGARIA
ALBANIA
MACEDONIA
Mediterranean Sea
GREECE
TURKEY
MALTA
CYPRUS
ICELAND
ARCTIC CIRCLE

Legend:
- EU members
- EU candidate countries
- € Countries using the euro as currency

0   400 miles
0   400 km
Lambert Azimuthal Equal-Area projection
SOURCE: European Union, europa.eu

GEOGRAPHY CONNECTION

1 PLACES AND REGIONS
What percent of EU members are using the euro?

2 THE WORLD IN SPATIAL TERMS *Which countries of the former Yugoslavia are candidates for EU membership?*

currency *coins, for example, that are in circulation and used as a medium of exchange*

the United States lost jobs as American companies outsourced jobs to Mexico in order to use cheap labor. A similar agreement called CAFTA (Central America-U.S. Free Trade Agreement) was created by the United States and six Central American nations in the mid-1990s.

European Union

The European Community (EC) was chiefly an economic union. By 1992, it comprised 344 million people and was the world's largest single trading bloc. The Treaty on European Union was an attempt to create a true economic and monetary union of all EC members. On January 1, 1994, the EC renamed itself the European Union (EU). One of the EU's first goals was to establish a common **currency**, called the euro, adopted by 12 EU nations early in 1999. On June 1, 1999, a European Central Bank was created, and by January 2010, the euro had officially replaced 16 national currencies. The euro serves approximately 327 million people and has become the world's second largest reserve currency after the U.S. dollar.

In addition to having a single internal market for its members and a common currency, the European Union also established a common agricultural policy. It provides subsidies to farmers to enable them to sell their goods competitively on the world market. The policy also provides aid to the EU's poorest countries and subsidies for job training, education, and modernization programs.

The EU has been less successful in setting common foreign policy goals. Individual nations still see foreign policy as a national right and are reluctant to give it up. Although EU foreign ministers meet periodically, they usually do not draw up a uniform policy. Nevertheless, the EU did create a military force of 60,000 to be used chiefly for peacekeeping purposes.

In 2009 the European Union ratified the Lisbon Treaty, which created a full-time presidential post and a new voting system that reflected each country's population size. It also provided more power for the European Parliament in an effort to promote the EU's foreign policy goals.

☑ **READING PROGRESS CHECK**

Classifying Would you describe the European Union as solely an economic entity?

Aspects of Globalization

GUIDING QUESTION *What are the costs and benefits of globalization?*

Globalization is the process by which people and nations have become more interdependent. Politically and socially, globalization has led to the emergence of citizen groups and other transnational organizations that work across national boundaries to bring solutions to common problems. Not everyone, however, is happy with the globalization of the economy.

Protests

Global economic organizations have come under attack. Both the World Bank and the IMF have been criticized for forcing inappropriate Western economic practices on non-Western nations. Critics also argue that World Bank and IMF policies aggravate the poverty and debt of developing nations. The WTO has been criticized for ignoring environmental and health concerns and for leaving out small and developing countries.

There have also been direct protests against globalization. Critics of globalization have accused multinational corporations of maximizing profits by supporting pitiful workers' wages and working conditions and ignoring environmental concerns. Anti-globalization protesters have clashed with police when trying to disrupt meetings of the IMF and World Bank in cities around the world.

Another challenge to globalization stems from the wide gap between rich and poor nations. Rich nations, or developed nations, are located mainly in the Northern Hemisphere. They include countries such as the United States, Canada, Germany, and Japan, which have well-organized industrial and agricultural systems, advanced technologies, and effective educational systems. The poor nations, or developing nations, include many nations in Africa, Asia, and Latin America. They are often primarily agricultural nations with little technology and income inequality.

Global Financial Crisis

The global economy experienced worldwide financial troubles beginning in 2007 following the collapse of the U.S. housing market. Spurred by low interest rates in the early 2000s, easily available mortgages drove up housing values. In response, investors began selling financial investments called **collateralized debt obligations** (CDOs), or investments based upon bundled mortgages. Banks in New York sold CDOs to banks in Europe and elsewhere, spreading the wealth and the risk of investment. Many of these mortgages had been to borrowers with a low credit rating and high rate of default. As the initial rates on the mortgages ended, default rates increased and securities began to lose their value. By September 2008, a number of insurance and mortgage companies, investment firms, and banks fell into bankruptcy. Stock values fell by almost $8 trillion from mid-September to November.

In effect, the crash of the United States housing market in 2008 led to a worldwide recession. As the American economy slowed, trade decreased

Widespread use of the term *globalization* to refer to the movement toward a more integrated and interdependent world economy is relatively recent. How old do you think globalization is as a historical phenomenon? For example, do you think it dates back to the rise of global trading empires that began during the Age of Exploration? Historians differ on whether the concept of globalization should be applied only to the modern era. Use your school library to locate secondary sources from two different historians with conflicting interpretations of this concept.

globalization the movement toward a more integrated and interdependent world economy

collateralized debt obligation a security guaranteed by a pool of, bonds, loans, and other types of debt

▼ Anti-globalization activists protest outside World Bank headquarters in Washington, D.C.

worldwide because the American consumer, who had been consuming because of higher home values, could no longer do so. Production in Asia decreased and commodity prices fell, especially that of oil, making an impact on both Middle Eastern countries and Russia.

The United States responded to the financial crisis with an emergency program to recapitalize financial institutions and a stimulus package to support growth and to curb unemployment. Europe faced less severe problems than the United States, although European banks with exposure to **subprime investments** required government assistance to recapitalize. In Eastern Europe, recent free market economies experienced a drastic devaluation of their currencies as investors fled to the stronger dollar and euro. Governmental measures prevented a total failure of the world financial system. However, high unemployment and weak consumption will probably plague Western nations for years to come.

subprime investments investments based on loans that have an interest rate that is higher than a prime rate and is extended especially to low-income borrowers

Emerging Economic Powers

China and India are experiencing economic growth on a scale rarely seen before. For the past 20 years, China's growth rate has been 9.5 percent a year; India's, 6 percent. Both have the potential for such growth rates to continue for decades. Some economists predict that China's economy will overtake that of the United States by 2050.

The economies of China and India are not the same. China is supreme in mass manufacturing. India is a growing power in design services and software. Multinational corporations have their products built in China with software designed in India. One major result is the outsourcing of jobs from the United States to both India and China, much to the concern of U.S. political leaders who seem helpless to stop the trend.

But both countries have serious problems. Poverty is still prevalent for hundreds of millions of people in India and China. Moreover, environmental problems are growing. Fertile land is in increasingly short supply while the rate of air pollution, especially in China, is 10 times the level in the United States, contributing to growing health concerns. Smog smothers the air in both Shanghai, China, and Mumbai, India. Finally, no one is sure that both countries can continue on their **dynamic** rate of economic growth. Per capita income in the United States is six times as high as in China. In India, an estimated 350 million Indians earn less than one U.S. dollar a day.

dynamic an activity or change that is continuous and productive

✓ **READING PROGRESS CHECK**

Analyzing Why have some individuals protested the practices of global economic organizations?

LESSON 3 REVIEW

Reviewing Vocabulary

1. *Drawing Conclusions* How does the large number of multinational corporations reflect increasing globalization?

Using Your Notes

2. *Identifying* Use your notes to identify different global and regional trade and economic organizations.

Answering the Guiding Questions

3. *Making Generalizations* What are the roles of global economic organizations in the world economy?

4. *Evaluating* What are the effects of regional trade organizations on national and regional economies?

5. *Differentiating* What are the costs and benefits of globalization?

Writing Activity

6. **ARGUMENT** Write an essay arguing whether free trade agreements are a good idea or a bad idea. Be sure to focus on the costs and benefits to both developed and developing countries.

networks

There's More Online!

☑ **CHART/GRAPH** Mobile Phone and Internet Use, 2009

☑ **IMAGE** Destruction of Rainforests in South America

☑ **IMAGE** International Space Station

☑ **IMAGE** Technology in the Classroom

☑ **INTERACTIVE SELF-CHECK QUIZ**

☑ **MAP** Desertification in Africa

☑ **PRIMARY SOURCE** Newspaper Article About the Kyoto Protocol

☑ **VIDEO** Science, Technology, and the Environment

Reading **HELP**DESK (CCSS)

Academic Vocabulary

- intense
- manipulation

Content Vocabulary

- **microchip**
- **ecology**
- **deforestation**
- **desertification**
- **greenhouse effect**
- **sustainable development**

TAKING NOTES:

Key Ideas and Details

Summarizing As you read, use a table like the one below to identify important technological advances discussed in this lesson.

Communication, Transportation, and Space	Health Care	Agriculture

---

LESSON 4

Science, Technology, and the Environment

ESSENTIAL QUESTION
How do social and environmental issues affect countries differently?

IT MATTERS BECAUSE

In the twenty-first century, science and technology continue to build a global community connected by the Internet. Scientific advances have brought benefits in communications, transportation, space exploration, health care, and agriculture. Unfortunately, they have also produced environmental challenges.

Technological Revolution

GUIDING QUESTION *How have scientific discoveries and technological innovations transformed society?*

Since World War II, but especially since the 1970s, a stunning array of changes has created a technological revolution. Like the first and second Industrial Revolutions, this revolution is also having a profound effect on people's daily lives and on entire societies. This technological revolution is also closely interrelated with new scientific discoveries.

Communication, Transportation, and Space

Global transportation and communication systems are transforming the world community. People are connected and "online" throughout the world as they have never been before. Space exploration and orbiting satellites have increased our understanding of our world and of solar systems beyond our world.

Since the 1970s, jumbo jet airliners have moved millions of people around the world each year. A flight between London and New York took half a day in 1945. Now that trip takes only five or six hours. The Internet—the world's largest computer network—provides quick access to vast quantities of information. The World Wide Web, developed in the 1990s, has made the Internet even more accessible to people everywhere. Satellites, cable television, cellular telephones, and computers enable people to communicate with one another practically everywhere in the world. Communication and transportation systems have made the world a truly global village.

The computer may be the most revolutionary of all technological inventions of the twentieth century. The first computer was really a product of World War II. British mathematician Alan Turing designed the first electronic computer to crack enemy codes. Turing's machine did calculations faster than any human. IBM of the United States made the first computer with stored memory in 1948. These early computers used thousands of vacuum tubes to function and took up considerable space. The development of the transistor and the silicon chip produced a revolutionary new approach to computers.

Then, in 1971, the microprocessor was invented and paved the way for the personal computer. Both small and powerful, the personal computer became a regular fixture in businesses, schools, and homes by the 1990s. The computer made many routine tasks easier and has become important in nearly every area of modern life. Other tools and machines, such as those that help fly airplanes, depend on computers to function.

Through their personal computers, people can access the Internet, a huge web of linked computer networks. The Internet was introduced to the public for the first time in 1972. That same year, electronic mail, or e-mail, was introduced. The system mushroomed, and by the early 1990s, a new way of sending Internet information, called hypertext transfer protocol (http), had been developed. This, combined with the invention of Web browsers, made it easier for people to use the Internet. By 2010, there were more than 1 billion Internet users worldwide.

As Web capabilities increased, new forms of communication began to emerge with Twitter, a communications platform that allows people to send instant updates from their computers or cell phones to their followers. Facebook, a social networking site, and YouTube, an Internet video site that provides instant visual access to many events, are also important.

Advances in telecommunications led to cellular, or mobile, phones. Though cellular phones existed in the 1970s and the 1980s, it was not until the invention of the **microchip**, a small semiconductor used to relay information, that cell phones became truly portable. Cell phones have since become enormously important. Cell phones are everywhere, and their ability to transfer data electronically has made text messaging a global communications craze. Text and instant messaging have revolutionized written language, as shorthand script has replaced complete sentences for the purposes of relaying brief messages.

microchip also called an integrated circuit; a tiny assembly of electronic components and their connections that is produced in or on a tiny bit of material, usually silicon

intense marked by great zeal, energy, determination, or concentration

---

CHARTS/GRAPHS

▶ CRITICAL THINKING

1 *Drawing Conclusions* How do developed and developing countries differ in their access to technology?

2 *Contrasting* Which country has the most mobile phone and Internet users? Which has the least?

MOBILE PHONE AND INTERNET USE, 2009

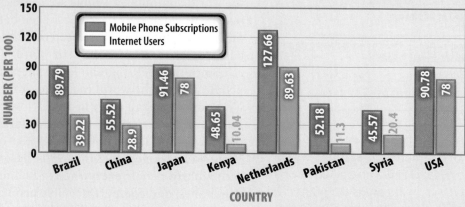

Mobile Phone Subscriptions
Internet Users

NUMBER (PER 100)

Brazil: 89.79, 39.22
China: 55.52, 28.9
Japan: 91.46, 78
Kenya: 48.65, 10.04
Netherlands: 127.66, 89.63
Pakistan: 52.18, 11.3
Syria: 45.57, 20.4
USA: 90.78, 78

COUNTRY

Source: International Telecommunications Union, 2010

Technological developments have also improved our ability to explore space. Ever since Neil Armstrong and Buzz Aldrin landed on the moon in 1969, the exploration of space has continued. Space probes have increased our understanding of distant planets.

Today hundreds of satellites orbit Earth. Some are used to predict the weather, and others help navigate ships, aircraft, and cars. Communications satellites are used to relay radio, television, and telephone signals.

Launched in 1990, the Hubble Space Telescope (HST), a large astronomical observatory, orbits about 375 miles (603 km) above Earth's surface. Thus, the HST avoids the distorting effects of the Earth's atmosphere and provides clear views of our solar system and distant galaxies.

The National Aeronautics and Space Administration (NASA) sent two rovers, called *Spirit* and *Opportunity*, to the planet Mars in 2004. Based on the minerals that the rovers found in Mars's rocks, NASA scientists determined that the now-barren planet once had abundant supplies of water. NASA continues its Mars Exploration Program, analyzing data transmissions from rovers to Earth via the *Odyssey* orbiter, which was launched in 2001. Such data includes radiation risks for potential future human exploration of Mars.

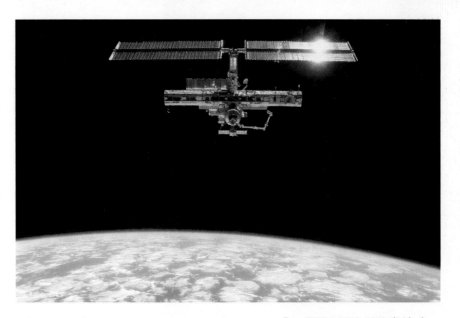

▲ From 2000 to 2010, 196 individuals from eight different countries have visited the International Space Station.

▶ **CRITICAL THINKING**
Speculating There have been over 100 launches to the space station. Which two countries do you think have sent the most vehicles? Why?

manipulation skillful or artful management

Health Care

New technologies in health care have allowed people to live longer and more productive lives. For example, doctors use mechanical valves and pumps for the heart and transplant organs. New medicines can treat both physical and mental illness. Scientific research has also led to improvements. From 1990 to 2003, the Human Genome Project unlocked the secrets of DNA, leading to new ways to diagnose and treat genetic diseases. The discovery of DNA itself—the molecule that carries genetic information from one generation to another—was the work of James Watson, Francis Crick, and Maurice Wilkins, who received a joint Nobel Prize for Medicine in 1962.

These new technologies have broadened the field of bioethics, which deals with moral choices in medical research. There are concerns that genetic engineering, or the altering of genetic information of cells to produce new variations, could create deadly strains of bacteria. The possibility of human cloning, along with stem-cell research (using stem cells from human embryos to research cures for certain diseases), has caused **intense** debate in many countries.

Agriculture

In agriculture, the development of new strains of rice, corn, and other grains, known as genetically engineered (GE) foods, have resulted in greater yields. Scientists and world leaders disagree over the use of GE foods, which are created by the **manipulation** of the DNA of plants to improve crops. Some experts see GE foods as a way to solve hunger crises in developing countries, although others worry about the effects GE foods have on the health of

Connections to
TODAY

Medical Advancements

Many medical advancements that have had a major impact on our lives today were developed during World War II. For example, Charles R. Drew, an African-American physician, started the American Red Cross blood banking program to assist soldiers. Today, nearly 3 percent of the U.S. population donates blood, which is used to save military and civilian lives across the country. Likewise, Dr. Jonas Salk developed vaccines for flu and polio. Today, mass vaccinations prevent many childhood illnesses each year, and polio is close to being eradicated globally.

▲ A farmer clears an area of the Amazon rain forest.

▶ **CRITICAL THINKING**
Determining Cause and Effect
What may be the global effects of deforestation on the environment?

ecology the study of the relationships between living things and their environment

deforestation the clearing of forests

desertification formation of degraded soil, turning semi-arid lands into nonproductive deserts

individuals and the ecosystem. Huge quantities of chemical fertilizers, which many farmers cannot afford, are needed to grow these new strains of foods.

The growing concern with chemical pesticides has led to an increase in organic farming in industrialized countries and the profitable export of organically grown crops by developing nations. Organic farming rejects the use of chemical fertilizers and pesticides, growth hormones, and livestock feed additives. Its goal is to maintain a healthy and sustainable environment.

☑ **READING PROGRESS CHECK**

Identifying Points of View What are the arguments for and against the use of GE foods?

Environmental Challenges

GUIDING QUESTION *What are the environmental challenges of the twenty-first century and how have governments and citizens responded to them?*

In *Silent Spring*, published in 1962, Rachel Carson, an American scientist, argued that the buildup of pesticides—chemicals sprayed on crops to kill insects—was having unforeseen results. Insects were dying, but so too were birds, fish, and other wild animals. Also, the pesticide residue on food harmed humans.

Carson's warnings alarmed many scientists and gave rise to the new science of **ecology**, the study of the relationship between living things and their environment. Since then, scientific research studies have shown that dangers to the environment have many sources.

Impact of Population Growth

Some fear that population is growing too fast for Earth's resources to support it. **Deforestation** is one by-product of a growing population. Forests and jungles have been cut down to provide more farmland, firewood, and timber.

Especially worrisome is the rapid destruction of tropical rain forests near Earth's equator. Although tropical rain forests cover only 6 percent of Earth's surface, they support 50 percent of the world's species of plants and animals. The tropical rain forests are also crucial to human survival because they remove carbon dioxide from the air and return oxygen to it.

Desertification is another by-product of population growth. Overgrazing, poor cultivation practices, and destruction of vegetation in semiarid lands are human-caused factors that destroy the soil's productivity. More than 250 million people are directly affected by desertification.

Chemical Wastes and Disasters

Chemical wastes pose another danger to the environment. The release of chlorofluorocarbons—gases used in aerosol cans, refrigerators, and air conditioners—destroys the ozone layer. This thin layer in the upper atmosphere shields Earth from the sun's ultraviolet rays. Acid rain results when sulfur from factories mixes with moisture in the air. Acid rain is responsible for killing forests and damaging buildings.

Ecological disasters also leave long-lasting consequences. Toxic fumes from a chemical plant at Bhopal, India, in 1984; a nuclear accident at Chernobyl, Ukraine, in 1986; an oil spill from the *Exxon Valdez* in Alaska in 1989; and an oil platform explosion in the Gulf of Mexico in 2010 caused ecological and health problems that can still be seen today.

Yet another threat to the environment is global climate change, which has the potential to create a worldwide crisis. Many of the world's scientists agree that the **greenhouse effect**, the warming of Earth due to the buildup of carbon dioxide in the atmosphere, is contributing to devastating droughts and storms, the melting of the polar ice caps, and rising sea levels that could flood coastal regions in the second half of the twenty-first century. Also alarming is the potential loss of biodiversity. Seven out of ten biologists believe the planet is now experiencing a surprising extinction of both plant and animal species.

In an attempt to reduce carbon emissions, more than 150 nations have signed the Kyoto Protocol, which calls on countries to cut air pollution. The United States did not ratify the treaty, saying that the required changes would be too costly.

A number of nations, however, have already begun to reduce their dependence on fossil fuels by introducing geothermal and hydroelectric power plants. Another clear source of energy is wind. Scientists estimate that one-third of the world's electricity could be supplied by wind generators by 2050. That would be enough to prevent 113 billion metric tons of carbon dioxide from entering the atmosphere each year. Wind farms have sprouted around the world—including in the United States.

Sustainable Development

Economic development that does not limit the ability of future generations to meet their basic needs is known as **sustainable development**. In promoting sustainable development, the United Nations urges countries to work to conserve all natural resources. Many countries have already enacted recycling and water conservation programs, along with curbing the dumping of toxic materials. A limited water supply affects 4 out of every 10 people globally. People without access to a source of clean water often get sick with cholera, typhoid, and diarrhea. More than 5 million people die every year from the lack of water or from drinking untreated water.

greenhouse effect
global warming caused by the buildup of carbon dioxide in the atmosphere

sustainable development
economic development that does not limit the ability of future generations to meet their basic needs

▼ Rooftop gardens, like the one below, help the environment by insulating the roof which helps save energy.

✓ **READING PROGRESS CHECK**

Summarizing How have nations responded to global environmental challenges?

LESSON 4 REVIEW (CCSS)

Reviewing Vocabulary
1. ***Drawing Conclusions*** How can sustainable development prevent deforestation and desertification?

Using Your Notes
2. ***Identifying*** Use your notes to identify the technological breakthroughs discussed in this lesson.

Answering the Guiding Questions
3. ***Evaluating*** How have scientific discoveries and technological innovations transformed society?

4. ***Identifying Central Issues*** What are the environmental challenges of the twenty-first century, and how have governments and citizens responded to them?

Writing Activity
5. **NARRATIVE** Identify a technology discussed in the lesson and write an essay about how this technology has affected your life. The essay should also include thoughts on how your life would be different without this technology.

Directions: On a separate sheet of paper, answer the questions below. Make sure you read carefully and answer all parts of the questions.

Lesson Review

Lesson 1

1 **IDENTIFYING CENTRAL ISSUES** What is the main reason that terrorism in the Middle East has been aimed against Westerners?

2 **DRAWING CONCLUSIONS** Has Africa benefited from being split up into countries with arbitrary boundaries?

Lesson 2

3 **SUMMARIZING** What are some of the causes of worldwide hunger?

4 **MAKING INFERENCES** Why are people living longer in developed nations?

Lesson 3

5 **EXPLAINING** How has NAFTA impacted farmers in Mexico and industrial workers in the United States?

6 **ANALYZING CAUSE AND EFFECT** How did the collapse of the United States housing market in 2008 contribute to a worldwide recession?

Lesson 4

7 **IDENTIFYING** What technological advances have helped the world become a global village?

8 **DEFENDING** What arguments might you use to convince others that genetically engineered foods are a good idea?

21st Century Skills

9 **COMPARE AND CONTRAST** Explain how equality for women has been the same and how it has been different over the past several decades in developed and developing countries.

10 **DECISION MAKING** Do you think that the huge media attention terrorist acts have received has helped reduce or increase those acts? Explain your answer.

Exploring the Essential Questions

11 **SYNTHESIZING** Write a multiparagraph essay describing at least four events that have influenced global political and economic relationships since World War II. Cite at least two examples for each event to show how it has influenced countries worldwide.

DBQ Analyzing Historical Documents

Use the document to answer the following questions.

At the United Nations Millennium Summit in 2000, world leaders agreed to work together to achieve eight development goals by 2015. These goals include eradicating extreme poverty and hunger, achieving universal primary education, promoting gender equality, reducing child mortality, and combating diseases.

> **PRIMARY SOURCE**

> 66 We will have time to reach the Millennium Development Goals . . . but only if we break with business as usual. . . . Success will require sustained action. . . . It takes time to train the teachers, nurses and engineers; to build the roads, schools and hospitals; to grow the small and large businesses able to create the jobs and income needed. So we must start now. And we must more than double global development assistance over the next few years. Nothing less will help to achieve the Goals. 99

> —Kofi Annan, former UN Secretary-General, June 7, 2005

12 **SUMMARIZING** According to Kofi Annan, how can the goals be achieved?

13 **ASSESSING** What role does the UN play in achieving these goals, and why is this role important?

Extended-Response Question

14 **INFORMATIVE/EXPLANATORY** Find two or more primary sources on the conflict between Tutsis and Hutus. Write an analysis of the causes and effects of the conflict.

Need Extra Help?

If You've Missed Question	**1**	**2**	**3**	**4**	**5**	**6**	**7**	**8**	**9**	**10**	**11**	**12**	**13**	**14**
Go to page	457	459	461	464	467	469	471	473	463	457	456	476	476	459

CONTENTS

What Did Ancient Societies Believe About Creation?

How were ancient creation accounts similar and different? The ancient peoples of Mesopotamia, Egypt, and Israel had different accounts of the creation of the world. Although each society worshiped different gods for different reasons, there are several similarities in their creation accounts.

What do creation accounts reveal about religious beliefs? Religion played a central role in the lives of ancient peoples. Creation accounts describe the gods or God they worshiped and help explain how ancient societies interpreted the world around them.

Creation accounts provide insights into the cultures of the people who developed them. Read the excerpts and study the painting to find out what the Babylonians, Israelites, and Egyptians believed about the creation of the world.

PRIMARY SOURCE

The Babylonian story of creation is part of an epic poem titled *Enûma elish.*

The lord [**Marduk**[1]] trod upon the hinder part of **Tiâmat**[2],
And with his unsparing club he split her skull. . . .
He split her open like a mussel into two parts;
Half of her he set in place and formed the sky therewith as a roof. . . .
He fixed the crossbar and posted guards;
He commanded them not to let her waters escape. . . .
The lord measured the dimensions of the *Apsû*[3],
And a great structure, its counterpart, he established, namely, **Esharra**[4],
The great structure Esharra which he made as a canopy. . . .
As Marduk hears the words of the gods,
His heart prompts him to create ingenious things.
He conveys his idea to **Ea**[5],
Imparting the plan which he had conceived in his heart:
"Blood will I form and cause bone to be;
Then will I set up *lullû*[6], 'Man' shall be his name!
Yes, I will create *lullû*: Man!
Upon him shall the services of the gods be imposed that they may be at rest."

PRIMARY SOURCE

The book of Genesis contains an Israelite account of creation.

In the beginning God created the heavens and the earth. . . .
And God said, "Let there be light," and there was light. God saw that the light was good, and he separated the light from the darkness. God called the light "day," and the darkness he called "night." And there was evening and there was morning—the first day.
And God said, "Let there be an expanse between the waters to separate water from water." So God made the expanse and separated the water under the expanse from the water above it. And it was so. God called the expanse "sky." And there was evening, and there was morning—the second day.
And God said, "Let the water under the sky be gathered to one place, and let dry ground appear." And it was so. God called the dry ground "land," and the gathered waters he called "seas." And God saw that it was good. . . .
Then God said, "Let us make man in our image, in our likeness, and let them rule over the fish of the sea and the birds of the air, over the livestock, over all the earth, and over all the creatures that move along the ground."
So God created man in his own image, in the image of God he created him; male and female he created them.

---

[1] **Marduk:** ruler of the gods in Babylonian mythology

[2] **Tiâmat:** monster goddess; the earliest salt water

[3] *Apsû:* husband of Tiâmat; the earliest freshwater

[4] **Esharra:** a poetic name for the Earth

▲ The sun god, Re, makes his night journey in this drawing and relief from the tomb of Horemheb in Egypt, c. 1300 B.C.

PRIMARY SOURCE

The ancient Egyptians had several creation myths. In one account, Re, the sun god, emerged from an egg that appeared on the surface of the ocean. Re later produced gods of air, earth, and heaven. Afterward, Re made humans and all other beings and objects on Earth. In the above painting, Re, the ram- headed figure, crosses through the under- world in his boat, carrying the spirits of Egyptians who have died. When Re reappears above the horizon at the beginning of each new day, the souls of the dead are reborn into new lives with him.

Egyptians spent every day surrounded by symbols of their religion. They saw gods in the natural world, they had gods important to their hometowns, and they believed in gods of trade, justice, and prosperity. They expected the gods to care for them in the afterlife.

5 **Ea:** god of wisdom and magic; father of Marduk

6 *lullû:* humans

 Analyzing Historical Documents (CCSS)

❶ *Explaining* Why did the Babylonian god Marduk create humans?

❷ *Identifying* In the Israelite account of creation, what was the expanse that separated water from water?

❸ *Analyzing* How does the Egyptian god Re represent the sun?

❹ *Contrasting* How is the depiction of the Israelite deity different from those in the other two creation accounts?

❺ *Comparing* What similar event is found in all three creation accounts?

❻ *Drawing Conclusions* What is the role of humans in each of the three creation accounts?

❼ *Synthesizing* How would you describe the beliefs that ancient societies held about the creation of the world?

What Was the Role of Religion in Aztec Society?

How did the Aztec worship their gods? Religion was an important feature of Aztec life. Prayers, legends, and ceremonies at great temples were all part of Aztec religious practice.

How did outsiders view Aztec religion? After their arrival in Mexico in 1519, the Spanish were shocked by the Aztec religious rituals. The Spaniards immediately worked to convert the Aztec to Christianity.

The Aztec and the Spanish had extremely different viewpoints about Aztec religion. Read the passages and study the illustration to learn more about the role religion played in Aztec society.

PRIMARY SOURCE

The Aztec king Ahuizotl, who ruled from 1486 to 1502, offered the following prayer to the god Huitzilopochtli while celebrating a successful military campaign.

O almighty, powerful lord of All Created
  Things,
You who give us life, and whose **vassals**[1] and
  slaves we are,
Lord of the Day and of the Night, of the Wind
  and the Water,
Whose strength keeps us alive! I give you
  infinite thanks
For having brought me back to your city of
  Mexico
With the victory which you granted me.
I have returned. . . .
Since you did not frown upon my extreme
  youth
Or my lack of strength or the weakness of
  my chest,
You have subjected those remote and
  barbarous nations
To my power. You did all of these things!
All is yours!
All was won to give you honor and praise!
Therefore, O powerful and heroic
  Huitzilopochtli,
You have brought us back to this place which
  was only water
Before, which was enclosed by our ancestors,
And where they built our city.

PRIMARY SOURCE

Spanish conquistador Hernán Cortés wrote the following description of a temple in the Aztec capital in a 1520 letter to the Spanish king, Charles V.

Three halls are in this grand temple, which contain the principal idols; these are of wonderful extent and height, and admirable workmanship, adorned with figures sculptured in stone and wood; leading from the halls are chapels with very small doors . . . In these chapels are the images of idols, although, as I have before said, many of them are also found on the outside; the principal ones, in which the people have greatest faith and confidence, I **precipitated**[2] from their pedestals, and cast them down the steps of the temple, purifying the chapels in which they had stood, as they were all polluted with human blood, shed ill the sacrifices. In the place of these I put images of Our Lady and the Saints, which excited not a little feeling in **Moctezuma**[3] and the inhabitants, who at first **remonstrated**[4], declaring that if my proceedings were known throughout the country, the people would rise against me; for they believed that their idols bestowed on them all **temporal** good, and if they permitted them to be ill-treated, they would be angry and without their gifts, and by this means the people would be deprived of the fruits of the earth and perish with famine. . . .

---

[1] **vassals:** people in a subordinate position

[2] **precipitated:** threw down

[3] **Moctezuma:** the Aztec king in 1520

[4] **remonstrated:** vocally protested

▲ *Tenochtitlán priests sacrifice warriors to the sun god in this Aztec drawing dated after 1519.*

Human sacrifice was a central part of Aztec religion. The Aztec believed their deities, such as the war god Huitzilopochtli, demanded a steady supply of human sacrifices. At the dedication of the great pyramid of Tenochtitlán, for example, Aztec priests sacrificed more than 20,000 people. Most of the Aztec's sacrifice victims were prisoners captured from enemy tribes. For this purpose, Aztec warriors were trained to capture, rather than kill, their enemies in battle.

The above image is an Aztec drawing of a sacrifice ritual. During these ceremonies, priests cut out the victim's heart and held it up to the sun as an offering. As shown in the image, the victim's body was then thrown down the steps of the pyramid temple.

---

5 temporal: relating to earthly life

DBQ Analyzing Historical Documents CCSS

1 *Explaining* Why did King Ahuizotl pray to the god Huitzilopochtli?

2 *Identifying Points of View* How did Cortés's background influence his actions in the Aztec temple?

3 *Drawing Conclusions* What does this image reveal about the Aztec's relationship with their gods?

4 *Contrasting* How would Ahuizotl's description of the scene in the above image have contrasted with Cortés's description of the same image?

5 *Synthesizing* On what points do Ahuizotl and Cortés agree in their description of Aztec religious beliefs?

6 *Recognizing Bias* Consider the question "What was the role of religion in Aztec society?" How would an Aztec have answered that question differently than a Spaniard? Which answer do you think would have been most similar to your own answer to the question?

What Role Did Hobbes and Locke Play in Government?

Who played a major role in England's power struggle during the 1600s? During the struggle for power that dominated English life in the 1600s, the differing political views of Thomas Hobbes and John Locke played significant roles in reinforcing, as well as inflaming, the attitudes of the two sides of the conflict: the monarchy and Parliament.

What happened in England as a result of this political discourse? At the heart of the issue was the ongoing dispute over what kind of monarchy would rule England. Simply put, Hobbes supported an absolute monarchy, in which the king had complete and sole power. Locke believed in a limited monarchy, in which the king and parliament shared power. These different views of government and the political conflicts that resulted from them were very complicated, but the eventual outcome of the dispute was clear and uncomplicated. With the ascension of William and Mary to the throne in 1689, supporters of a limited monarchy had won a permanent victory.

PRIMARY SOURCE

This excerpt from Hobbes's *Leviathan* was published in 1651.

There is a sixth doctrine, plainly, and directly against the essence of a commonwealth, and 'tis this, that the **sovereign**[1] power may be divided. For what is it to divide the power of a commonwealth, but to dissolve it? for powers divided mutually destroy each other. And for these doctrines, men are chiefly **beholding**[2] to some of those, that making profession of the laws, endeavour to make them depend upon their own learning, and not upon the legislative power.

Lastly, when in a warre (forraign, or intestine,) the enemies got a final Victory; so as (the forces of the Common-wealth keeping the field no longer) there is no farther protection of Subjects in their loyalty; then is the Common-wealth DISSOLVED, and every man at liberty to protect himself by such courses as his own discretion shall suggest unto him. For the Soveraign, is the publique Soule, giving Life and Motion to the Common-wealth; which expiring, the Members are governed by it no more, than the Carcasse of a man, by his departed (though Immortal) Soule.

PRIMARY SOURCE

This passage is from Locke's *Two Treatises of Government,* which was published in 1690.

People have not appointed so to do, they make Laws, whom the People have not appointed so to do, they make Laws without Authority, which the People are not therefore bound to obey; by which means they come again to be out of **subjection**[3], and may constitute to themselves a new Legislative, as they think best, being in full liberty to resist the force of those, who without Authority would impose any thing upon them. Everyone is at the disposure of his own Will, when those who had by the delegation of the Society, the declaring of the publick [sic] Will, are excluded from it, and others **usurp**[4] the place who have no such Authority or Delegation. . . . When such a single Person or Prince sets up his own Arbitrary Will in place of the Laws, which are the Will of the Society, declared by the Legislative, then the Legislative is changed.

---

[1] **sovereign:** politically independent

[2] **beholding:** looking upon

[3] **subjection:** to force under one's control

[4] **usurp:** to seize and hold by force or without the right to do so

▲ *The John Trumbull painting,* Declaration of Independence, *depicts the presentation of the Declaration of Independence to John Hancock (seated right), president of the Continental Congress.*

PRIMARY SOURCE

This excerpt from the Declaration of Independence, which was written in 1776, draws on the conventions of Locke's theories of government.

We hold these truths to be self-evident, that all men are created equal, that they are endowed by their Creator with certain unalienable Rights, that among these are Life, Liberty and the pursuit of Happiness.—That to secure these rights, Governments are instituted among Men, deriving their just powers from the consent of the governed, —That whenever any Form of Government becomes destructive of these ends, it is the Right of the People to alter or to abolish it, and to institute new Government, laying its foundation on such principles and organizing its powers in such form, as to them shall seem most likely to effect their Safety and Happiness.

5 **impel:** to urge into action

DBQ Analyzing Historical Documents CCSS

❶ *Comparing and Contrasting* When Hobbes uses the term *legislative power,* to whom is he referring? To whom is Locke referring when he uses the term *Legislative*? Who is the "single Person or Prince" Locke mentions?

❷ *Analyzing Central Ideas* Why does Hobbes believe that power in a commonwealth should not be divided?

❸ *Drawing Conclusions* According to Hobbes, what do people mistakenly assume when they advocate that a division of powers is good for a commonwealth?

❹ *Making Inferences* When Locke says that people are not obligated to obey laws that are made without their authority and have a right to install a new government under such circumstances, what is he implying about their rule in a commonwealth?

❺ *Making Connections* Locke's views on government influenced some of the ideas in the U.S. Declaration of Independence and the U.S. Constitution. What ideas in the excerpt from *Two Treatises* can you find in the Declaration of Independence to support this statement?

❻ *Interpreting* According to the Declaration of Independence, what duty does mankind have to fulfill when faced with a tyrannical government?

Who Should be a Citizen?

What is a citizen? One definition of a citizen is a free person who owes loyalty to a nation and who receives protection, rights, and privileges in return. In the 1700s the meaning of this definition was challenged by both men and women for different reasons.

Who should be a citizen? At the time of the American Revolution only free, white adult males who owned property or paid taxes could vote.

In France, the *Declaration of the Rights of Man and the Citizen* addressed social distinctions, but opinions differed on how to interpret the document. Read the excerpts from Robespierre and d'Aelders and study Fragonard's painting to see how they viewed citizenship and the continuing struggle for rights.

PRIMARY SOURCE

In this speech from October 1789, Maximilien Robespierre stated his view on property requirements for holding office and voting.

All citizens, whoever they are, have the right to aspire to all levels of office-holding. Nothing is more in line with your declaration of rights, according to which all privileges, all distinctions, all exceptions must disappear. The Constitution establishes that **sovereignty**[1] resides in the people, in all the individuals of the people. Each individual therefore has the right to participate in making the law which governs him and in the administration of the public good which is his own. If not, it is not true that all men are equal in rights, that every man is a citizen. If he who only pays a tax **equivalent**[2] to a day of work has fewer rights than he who pays the equivalent to three days of work, and he who pays at the level of ten days has more rights than he whose tax only equals that value of three, then he who enjoys 100,000 livres [French pounds] of **revenue**[3] has 100 times as many rights as he who only has 1,000 livres of revenue. It follows from all your **decrees**[4] that every citizen has the right to participate in making the law and consequently that of being an elector or eligible for office without the distinction of wealth.

PRIMARY SOURCE

Etta Palm d'Aelders was a woman active in a reform group called the Cercle Social (Social Circle). D'Aelders expressed her opinions in "The Injustices of the Laws and Favor of Men at the Expense of Women" (December, 1790).

Do not be just by halves, Gentlemen; . . . justice must be the first virtue of free men, and justice demands that the laws be the same for all beings, like the air and the sun. And yet everywhere, the laws favor men at the expense of women, because everywhere power is in your hands. What! Will free men, an **enlightened**[5] people living in a century of enlightenment and philosophy, will they **consecrate**[6] what has been the abuse of power in a century of ignorance? . . .

The prejudices with which our sex has been surrounded—supported by unjust laws which only accord us a secondary existence in society and which often force us into the humiliating necessity of winning over the **cantankerous**[7] and **ferocious**[8] character of a man, who, by the greed of those close to us has become our master—those prejudices have changed what was for us the sweetest and most saintly of duties, those of wife and mother, into a painful and terrible slavery. . . .

Oh! Gentlemen, if you wish us to be enthusiastic about the happy constitution that gives back men their rights, then begin by being just toward us. From now on we should be your voluntary companions and not your slaves. Let us merit your attachment!

"Speech Denouncing the New Conditions of Eligibility" Spoken by Maximilien Robespierre October 1789. From The French Revolution and Human Rights, edited and translated by Lynn Hunt. Copyright © 1996 by Bedford/St. Martins, pp. 83.

---

1 **sovereignty:** power; authority

2 **equivalent:** same, of equal force

3 **revenue:** income

4 **decrees:** authoritative decisions; declarations

Boissy d'Anglas salutes the head of the deputy Feraud, May 20, 1795, by Alexandre Fragonard.

PRIMARY SOURCE

On May 20, 1795, an angry mob in the Convention hacked the head off deputy Feraud and presented it to the chairman, Boissy d'Anglas, who saluted the head. After this incident, d'Anglas presented measures to prevent the return of the Reign of Terror and to take precautions against anarchy.

Usually the crowds in the balcony were merely rowdy, insulting and threatening the deputies. At times like the one in the painting, they became a mob, invading the chamber and killing deputies with whom they disagreed. Some leaders thought the poor and the uneducated would take over the government, leading to violence and disorder. They feared "mob rule."

5 **enlightened:** knowledgeable, comprehending

6 **consecrate:** make sacred

7 **cantankerous:** having a bad disposition; quarrelsome

8 **ferocious:** brutal, fierce

DBQ Analyzing Historical Documents (CCSS)

1 **Analyzing** What does Robespierre think about basing citizenship on whether a person has property or pays taxes?

2 **Explaining** What does d'Aelders mean by women's "secondary existence in society"?

3 **Making Inferences** What do you think Fragonard's opinion might have been of universal suffrage—the right of all citizens to vote?

4 **Comparing** Although Robespierre was not a supporter of equal rights for women, list some similarities between his and d'Aelders's arguments.

5 **Contrasting** How does d'Aelders's portrayal of women contrast with Fragonard's?

6 **Defending** How would you answer the question "Who should be a citizen?" Which source has a position most like your own? Write a letter to the editor that explains your position on universal suffrage and identifies the source with which you most agree.

Describing the Lives of Workers in the Early 1800s

What hardships did industrialization create for workers? Though it transformed the British economy with the addition of jobs, industrialization had a drastic social impact on the working people of England.

PRIMARY SOURCE

Miner Betty Harris, 37, gave testimony to an 1842 Royal Commission investigating conditions in British mines.

> I was married at 23, and went into a **colliery** when I was married. I . . . can neither read nor write. . . . I am a **drawer**[2], and work from 6 in the morning to 6 at night. Stop about an hour at noon to eat my dinner; have bread and butter for dinner; I get no drink. . . .
>
> I have a belt round my waist, and a chain passing between my legs, and I go on my hands and feet. The road is very steep, and we have to hold by a rope; and when there is no rope, by anything we can catch hold of. There are six women and about six boys and girls in the pit I work in; it is very hard work for a woman. The pit is very wet where I work, and the water comes over our clog-tops always, and I have seen it up to my thighs; it rains in at the roof terribly. My clothes are wet through almost all day long. . . .
>
> My cousin looks after my children in the day time. I am very tired when I get home at night; I fall asleep sometimes before I get washed. . . . the belt and chain is worse when we are **in the family way**[3]. My feller (husband) has beaten me many a times for not being ready.

1 **colliery:** coal mine and its connected buildings

2 **drawer:** worker who pulled coal tubs in a mine; tubs were attached to the drawer's belt with a chain

How did industrialization affect living conditions in cities? The Industrial Revolution not only brought waves of new factories, it caused masses of workers to move to the cities to find jobs at these factories. Both developments had a profound impact on the lives of England's workers.

The Industrial Revolution altered both the working and living conditions of Britain's working class. Read the excerpts and study the illustration to learn more about how industrialization impacted the people of England during the first half of the nineteenth century.

PRIMARY SOURCE

German socialist Friedrich Engels, co-founder of Marxism, described industrial Manchester in his book, *The Condition of the Working-Class in England in 1844.*

> The first court below Ducie Bridge . . . was in such a state at the time of the cholera that the sanitary police ordered it evacuated, swept, and disinfected with **chloride of lime**[4]. . . . At the bottom flows, or rather stagnates, the Irk, a narrow, coal-black, foul-smelling stream, full of debris and refuse, which it deposits on the shallower right bank. . . .
>
> Above the bridge are **tanneries**[5], **bone mills**[6], and gasworks, from which all drains and refuse find their way into the Irk, which receives further the contents of all the neighboring sewers and **privies**[7]. . . . Below the bridge you look upon the piles of debris, the refuse, the filth, and offal from the courts on the steep left bank; here each house is packed close behind its neighbor and a piece of each is visible, all black, smoky, crumbling, ancient, with broken panes and window frames. . . .
>
> Such is the Old Town of Manchester . . . [in] defiance of all considerations of cleanliness, ventilation, and health which characterize the construction of this single district, containing at least twenty to thirty thousand inhabitants.

3 **in the family way:** pregnant

4 **chloride of lime:** bleaching powder

▲ This illustration shows a female drawer—as portrayed by Betty Harris in Parliamentary Papers of 1842—in a coal pit in Little Bolton, England in 1842.

PRIMARY SOURCE

England's Industrial Revolution increased the need for coal. By 1841, more than 200,000 men, women and children were working in the mines. Women and young boys were used to remove the coal from the mines.

The above print of a woman drawer in a coal pit was created to accompany Betty Harris's testimony to the Royal Commission in 1842. The image shows the belt around her waist and the chain between her legs. In Betty's testimony, she claimed that she worked in these conditions with other women and small children.

The Mines Act passed in August 1842, prohibiting femal labor and boys under the age of 10 from working in the mines.

₅ **tanneries:** buildings where skins and hides are tanned

₆ **bone mills:** mills that convert animal bones into fertilizer

₇ **privies:** outhouses

DBQ **Analyzing Historical Documents** **CCSS**

❶ *Calculating* How many hours did Betty Harris work each day?

❷ *Recognizing Bias* How could Engels's background have affected his assessment of Manchester? How might a description of the city written by a factory owner contrast from that written by Engels?

❸ *Integrating Visual Information* How does the above illustration support Harris's testimony about the work experience for women in mines?

❹ *Contrasting* How have working conditions changed in the United States since Industrialization? What laws protect the rights of workers?

❺ *Synthesizing* How could Engels have used Harris's testimony to support his main point about industrialization?

❻ *Problem-Solving* Consider the lives of England's workers in the early 1800s. Suppose you are an adviser to the British government. Write a letter to government leaders recommending changes for work conditions.

What Were the Causes of World War II?

Why did these efforts fail to prevent World War II?

Japan, Italy, and Germany each used its military to occupy foreign territories in the 1930s. Their aggressive moves led to the outbreak of a global conflict by the end of the decade.

After World War I ended in 1918, global leaders resolved to prevent future wars. Nonetheless, only two decades later, the most destructive conflict in human history broke out. Read the excerpts and study the cartoon to learn more about the causes of World War II.

How did the international community try to prevent war?

The League of Nations, disarmament conferences, and mutual defense treaties were efforts used in the 1920s and 1930s by the international community to maintain world peace.

PRIMARY SOURCE

British historian Dr. G.P. Gooch addressed the threat of war in his 1938 article, "The Breakdown of the System of Collective Security."

"Since the Allies declined to scale down their armaments to the German level, Germany was certain to climb towards theirs as soon as she felt strong enough to do so with **impunity**[1].

The Disarmament Conference which opened at Geneva in February 1932 had taken years to prepare, and it met too late. Even the chance of a limited agreement was lost owing to the lack of a strong lead at the outset by a Great Power . . . Each country was **virtuously**[2] ready for reductions in categories which were not of vital importance to itself, but stood out for those which it needed most. Thus Great Britain longed for the abolition of the submarine, which nearly starved us in 1917, while she clung to the **capital ship**[3]. . . . When the Conference adjourned for the summer holidays in 1932, it was clear that it had failed. In the autumn Germany retired, but was brought back by a promise of equality of status. . . . Such a system proved unattainable, and a year later Hitler's Germany withdrew not only from the Conference but from the League [of Nations] itself. . . . Since that moment Germany has been re-arming at feverish speed, and Europe is back again in its pre-War mood when everyone was afraid of Berlin. Our own colossal re-armament programme is the measure of our alarm."

PRIMARY SOURCE

The following passages are from 1938 diary entries of Victor Klemperer, a Jewish professor who lived in Nazi Germany.

The immense act of violence on the [German] **annexation**[4] of Austria, the immense increase in [Germany's] power both internally and externally, the defenseless trembling fear of England, France, etc. We shall not live to see the end of the Third Reich. . . .

The Third Reich will win again—whether by bluff or by force. . . . Chamberlain flies to Hitler for the second time tomorrow. England and France remain calm, in Dresden the **Sudeten German "Freikorps**[5]**"** is almost ready to invade [Czechoslovakia]. And the populace here is convinced that the Czechs alone are to blame and that Hitler loves peace. . . .

Four-power meeting[6] today [September 29] at three in Munich. Czechoslovakia continues to exist, Germany gets the Sudetenland, probably a colony as well. . . . For the populace on the front pages of the German press it is of course the absolute success of Hitler, the prince of peace and brilliant diplomat. . . . No shot is fired, and the [German] troops have been marching in since yesterday. Wishes for peace and friendship have been exchanged with England and France, Russia is cowering and silent, a zero. Hitler is being acclaimed even more extravagantly than in the Austria business.

---

1 **impunity:** freedom from punishment

2 **virtuously:** morally

3 **capital ship:** large class warship, such as a battleship

4 **annexation:** the act of incorporating new territory

▲ The weakness of the League of Nations is illustrated in this 1931 cartoon, "Let Sam Do It," by Winsor McCay.

PRIMARY SOURCE

At the end of World War I, United States president Woodrow Wilson lobbied for the creation of an international organization to help prevent future conflicts. The League of Nations formed in 1919. Many Americans, however, feared that joining the League would drag the country into foreign wars. As a result, the U.S. Senate refused to allow the nation to become a member of the League.

In 1931, the League of Nations faced a major challenge to its ability to maintain world peace when Japan invaded China. Artist Winsor McCay published the above cartoon after Japanese soldiers captured Manchuria from the Chinese. The man standing on the right side of the cartoon, Uncle Sam, represents the United States.

---

5 **Sudeten German "Freikorps":** German guerrilla force that sought to add the Sudetenland region to Germany

6 **Four-power meeting:** meeting of Germany, Italy, France, and Britain to discuss Germany's claims to the Sudetenland

DBQ Analyzing Historical Documents (CCSS)

❶ *Explaining* According to Gooch, why did the Disarmament Conference in Geneva fail?

❷ *Recognizing Bias* What does Klemperer suggest about how most Germans felt about Hitler in 1938? Why do you think the German populace felt that way about Hitler?

❸ *Interpreting* What does McCay believe about the likelihood of stopping the conflict between Japan and China?

❹ *Analyzing* Do Gooch and Klemperer primarily agree or disagree in their assessments of the threat to world peace in 1938?

❺ *Comparing* What common point does each of the three sources make about the international efforts to prevent war in the 1930s?

❻ *Drawing Conclusions* What were the causes of World War II? Do you think the Western powers could have prevented the war? Why or why not?

What Challenges Did Apartheid Create for South Africans?

How did apartheid affect South Africa? For much of the twentieth century, South Africa's white-run government denied political and economic equality to the country's black majority.

What progress have South Africans made in overcoming the effects of apartheid? Despite facing harsh government repression, South Africans carried on a decades-long campaign against apartheid. The nation finally held free elections in 1994, marking the end of apartheid and the beginning of democracy with the election of Nelson Mandela.

Apartheid in South Africa attracted international attention. Read the excerpts and study the cartoon to learn more about how South Africa faced this challenge.

PRIMARY SOURCE

The following passage is from a speech by Desmond Tutu, a black Anglican Archbishop, to the United Nations Security Council on October 23, 1984.

For my beloved country is wracked by division, by alienation, by **animosity¹**, by separation, by injustice, by unavoidable pain and suffering. It is a deeply **fragmented²** society, ridden by fear and anxiety . . . and a sense of desperation, split up into hostile, warring factions. . . .

There is little freedom to disagree with the determinations of the authorities. There is large scale unemployment here because of the drought and the recession that has hit most of the world's economy. And it is such a time that the authorities have increased the prices of various foodstuffs and also of rents in black townships—measures designed to hit hardest those least able to afford the additional costs. . . .

The authorities have not stopped stripping blacks of their South African citizenship. . . . The South African government is turning us into aliens in the land of our birth.

White South Africans are . . . scared human beings, many of them; who would not be, if they were outnumbered five to one? Through this lofty body I wish to appeal to my white fellow South Africans to share in building a new society, for blacks are not intent on driving whites into the sea but on claiming only their rightful place in the sun in the land of their birth.

PRIMARY SOURCE

African National Congress leader Nelson Mandela discussed South Africa's past and future in a speech he gave after his release from prison in 1990.

Today, the majority of South Africans, black and white, recognize that **apartheid³** has no future. It has to be ended by our own decisive mass action in order to build peace and security. The mass campaigns of defiance and other actions of our organizations and people can only **culminate⁴** in the establishment of democracy. The apartheid's destruction on our subcontinent is incalculable. The fabric of family life of millions of my people has been shattered. Millions are homeless and unemployed. Our economy lies in ruins and our people are embroiled in political strife. . . .

We call on our people to seize this moment, so that the process toward democracy is rapid and uninterrupted. . . . We must not allow fear to stand in our way. Universal suffrage on a common voters roll in a united, democratic and non-racial South Africa is the only way to peace and racial harmony. . . .

I have fought against white domination, and I have fought against black domination. I have cherished the ideal of a democratic and free society in which all persons live together in harmony and with equal opportunity. It is an ideal which I hope to live for and to achieve. But, if need be, it is an ideal for which I am prepared to die.

---

¹ **animosity:** resentment

² **fragmented:** broken into pieces

³ **apartheid:** policy of racial segregation

⁴ **culminate:** conclude

(l) Bishop Desmond Tutu, "Statement to UN Security Council" 23 October 1984. From Crying in the Wilderness: The Struggle for Justice in South Africa by Desmond Tutu, Edited by John Webster. Published by W.B. Eerdmans Pub. Co. 1990. Printed with permission from the Bloomsbury Academic Publishing. (c) Bishop Desmond Tutu 1984; (r) Nelson Mandela's Statement from the Dock at the Opening of the Defense Case in the Rivonia Trial, February 11, 1990, Pretoria Supreme Court. Used by permission from The Nelson Mandela Centre of Memory.

▲ *Nelson Mondela was sworn in as South Africa's first democratically elected president in 1994.*

PRIMARY SOURCE

In the 1940s the African National Congress (ANC) formed a Youth League to lead a nonviolent campaign against the apartheid policies of South Africa. In 1960 South African police fired on unarmed demonstrators at Sharpeville, killing 67. A year later the ANC formed an armed wing, Umkhonto we Sizwe, headed by Nelson Mandela to carry out sabotage against government installations.

In 1963 the South African government arrested Mandela and, a year later, sentenced him to life imprisonment. In 1990, amidst growing international and domestic pressure, the government released Mandela. Four years later, he was elected president by voters in South Africa. His **inauguration** marked the end of apartheid.

₅ **inauguration:** ceremonial induction into office

DBQ **Analyzing Historical Documents**

❶ *Explaining* According to Bishop Tutu, what problems did South Africa face in 1984?

❷ *Drawing Conclusions* What do you think Mandela hoped to accomplish with his speech?

❸ *Assessing* What does the cartoon reveal about the state of the South African nation after Mandela gained his freedom?

❹ *Identifying Points of View* How do you think Mandela's experiences influenced the opinions he expressed in his speech?

❺ *Synthesizing* What similarities exist between the messages conveyed by all three sources?

❻ *Defending* What challenges did apartheid create for South Africans? Write a paragraph explaining whether you believe that Mandela and Tutu offered effective ideas to deal with these challenges.

What was Social Media's Role in the Arab Spring?

What was the Arab Spring? In 2011, a wave of democratic popular protests swept across dictatorships in the Muslim nations of North Africa. This movement was called the Arab Spring by journalists covering the events.

How did the use of social media lead to the overthrow of Muslim nations? Protesters used Facebook, Twitter, and YouTube to connect and organize supporters for their cause and build international support in such a way that could not be accomplished through state-run media outlets.

Read the excerpts to learn more about the role of social media in the movement known as the Arab Spring.

PRIMARY SOURCE

This excerpt from New York Times journalist Anthony Shadid describes the Syrian regime's attempts to regain control of Homs amidst a revolution fueled by the use of social media. The article "In Assad's Syria, There is No Imagination", was published on November 8, 2011. Shadid died of an asthma attack in February 2012 while on assignment in Syria.

Bashar seemed to think he was different. . . .

For a time, his seeming humility brought a measure of support his father never enjoyed . . . But Bashar believed his own **aura**[2]. In those days, he declared his state immune from the upheavals of Egypt and Tunisia. He insisted that his foreign policy, built rhetorically on **enmity**[3] with Israel, opposition to American **hegemony**[4] and support for the kind of resistance preached by Lebanon's Hezbollah, reflected the sentiments of an Arab world long humiliated by its impotence.

Even today, eight months after an uprising and a ferocious crackdown that, by the United Nations' count, has killed more than 3,000 people and, by the Arab League's estimate, put more than 70,000 in jail, people who have seen Bashar contend that he still doesn't recognize the severity of the challenge.

As in Iraq, Syria's neighbor to the east, the clichés of superficial analysis that preceded tumult now threaten to come true: Us or chaos. The regime posed as the guardian of Syria's diversity, even as the House of Assad and its lieutenants relentlessly stirred that diversity so as to divide and rule. Pitting community against community, never in a more pronounced way than now, it may finally bring forth the civil war that it long claimed it was the **bulwark**[5] against.

In their ambition at least, the Arab revolts and revolutions were about a positive sort of legitimacy: democracy, freedom, social justice and individual rights. They remain an unfulfilled promise, but no one in Egypt, Tunisia or Libya is really afraid to speak anymore. The **cacophony**[6] that has ensued is the most liberating feature of rejuvenated societies. It already echoes in parts of Syria. When I was in Hama this summer, a city still scarred by memory and for a brief moment freed from security forces, youths embraced their new space by protesting every couple of hours in streets made kinetic by the allure of self-determination. They demonstrated simply because they could. In Homs, a city whose uprising could prove Syria's demise or salvation, youths drawn from an eclectic array of leftists, liberals, nationalists, Islamists and the simply pissed-off articulated the essence of courage: They had come too far to go back.

"In the end, I'm a person now," a young activist named Iyad told me in Homs. "I can say what I want. I love you if I want to love you, I hate you if I want to hate you. I can denounce your beliefs or I can support them. I can agree with your position or disagree with it. But I'm a person now." He dragged on his cigarette, and we shared more tea. "We're not waiting to live our lives until after the fall of the regime," he went on. "We started living them the first day of the protests."

---

1 **rue:** to feel regret

2 **aura:** a distinct atmosphere or quality surrounding a person, place, or thing

3 **enmity:** an extremely unfriendly or hostile feeling toward something

4 **hegemony:** dominance by one country or social group

Yet digital media didn't oust Hosni Mubarak. The committed Egyptians occupying the streets of Cairo did that. As Barack Obama put it, mobile phones and the Internet were the media by which soulful calls for freedom have cascaded across North Africa and the Middle East. Just as the fall of Suharto in Indonesia is a story that involves the creative use of mobile phones by student activists, the falls of Zine El Abidine Ben Ali in Tunisia and Mubarak in Egypt will be recorded as a process of Internet-enabled social **mobilization**[10].

▲ During the Arab Spring protest movement, many in the Middle East used social network sites on the Internet to spread organization plans. These sites also kept the world informed of their actions.

PRIMARY SOURCE

This is an excerpt from an article entitled "The Arab Spring's Cascading Effects."

Over the last few months, social unrest has cascaded across the major urban centers of North Africa and the Middle East. Journalists and communications media are often part of such moments of upheaval. Yet this recent wave of unrest is unlike other discrete periods of rapid political change. Through digital media, the stories of success in Tunisia and Egypt have spread over social networks to many other authoritarian regimes. Digital media has not only caused a cascade of civil disobedience to spread among populations living under the most **unflappable**[7] dictators, it has made for unique new means of civic organizing.

During the heady days of protests in Cairo, one activist **succinctly**[8] tweeted about why digital media was so important to the organization of political unrest. "We use Facebook to schedule the protests, Twitter to coordinate, and YouTube to tell the world," she said. The protesters openly acknowledge the role of digital media as a fundamental **infrastructure**[9] for their work. Moammar Gadhafi's former aides have advised him to submit his resignation through Twitter.

DBQ Analyzing Historical Documents

❶ **Contrasting** Based on the context clues provided, what do you think Howard meant when he referred to "discrete periods" of political change? How was this different from the Arab Spring?

❷ **Identifying** According to Shadid, what was the primary ambition of the Arab revolts?

❸ **Analyzing** What reasoning does Shadid use as evidence to the protestors' "essence of courage" in the face of opposition? What event in American History could be related to such a statement?

❹ **Identifying** What evidence did Bashar ignore that signified the challenges in his country might be insurmountable?

❺ **Comparing** What ideal is expressed in both accounts?

❻ **Drawing Conclusions** Based on the photographs of the protestors, what conclusions can you make about the participants in the Arab Spring and the connection to social media? How is this form of communication different from traditional media?

5 **bulwark:** support or protection

6 **cacophony:** harsh unpleasant noise

7 **unflappable:** not easily upset or bothered

8 **succinctly:** concisely

9 **infrastructure:** underlying foundation or basic framework

10 **mobilization:** to make ready for action

▲ *This rendition of an Egyptian father teaching his son is on the wall of the Tomb of Sennedjem.*

PHOTO: DEA/G. DAGLI ORTI/De Agostini Picture Library/Getty Images; TEXT: The Instruction of the Vizier Ptah-hotep: "An Egyptian Father's Advice to His Son," from James Pritchard, Ancient Near Eastern Texts Relating to the Old Testament-Third Edition with Supplement, © 1950, 1955, 1969, renewed 1978 by Princeton University Press.

fraud
to deceive with dishonest methods

inclines
"leans toward" or persuades

astray
off the correct path

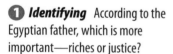

DBQ Analyzing Historical Documents **CCSS**

❶ *Identifying* According to the Egyptian father, which is more important—riches or justice?

❷ *Determining Word Meanings* Use the context clues from the excerpt to determine whether the word "wretched" has a positive or negative connotation.

❸ *Evaluating* Does any part of the Egyptian father's advice have value today for sons or daughters? Be specific and support your answer.

An Egyptian Father's Advice to His Son

Upper-class Egyptians enjoyed compiling collections of wise sayings to provide guidance for leading an upright and successful life. This excerpt from The Instruction of the Vizier Ptah-hotep *dates from around 2450 B.C.*

Then he said to his son:

If you are a leader commanding the affairs of the many, seek out for yourself every good deed, until it may be that your own affairs are without wrong. Justice is great, and it is lasting; it has been disturbed since the time of him who made it, whereas there is punishment for him who passes over its laws. Wrongdoing has never brought its undertaking into port. It may be that it is **fraud** that gains riches, but the strength of justice is that it lasts . . . .

If you are a man of standing who is pleasing to god, if he is correct and **inclines** toward your ways and listens to your instruction, while his manners in your house are fitting, and if he takes care of your property as it should be, seek out for him every useful action. He is your son, . . . you should not cut your heart off from him.

If he [the son] goes **astray** and does not carry out your instruction, so that his manners in your household are wretched, and he rebels against all that you say, while his mouth runs on in the most wretched talk, quite apart from his experience, while he possesses nothing, you should cast him off: he is not your son at all. He was not really born to you . . . He is one whom god has condemned in the very womb.

▲ China's emperor's used book burnings to destroy all history and potential influence from previous dynasties.

The Burning of Books

Li Su was a chief minister of the First Qin Emperor. A follower of Legalism, he hoped to eliminate all rival theories of government.

Your servant suggests that all books in the **imperial archives**, save the memoirs of Qin, be burned. All persons in the empire, except members of the Academy of Learned Scholars, in possession of the Book of Odes, the Book of History, and **discourses** of the hundred philosophers [including Confucius] should take them to the local governors and have them burned. Those who dare to talk to each other about the Book of Odes and the Book of History should be executed and their bodies exposed in the market place. Anyone referring to the past to criticize the present should, together with all members of his family, be put to death. Officials who fail to report cases that have come under their attention are equally guilty. After thirty days from the time of issuing the **decree**, those who have not destroyed their books are to be branded and sent to build the Great Wall. Books not to be destroyed will be those on medicine and pharmacy, agriculture and arboriculture [the cultivation of trees and shrubs]. People wishing to pursue learning should take the officials as their teachers.

VOCABULARY

imperial
relating to the empire or the emperor

archives
official documents that are preserved for historical or public use

discourse
discussion

decree
an order that has the force of law

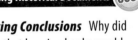

DBQ **Analyzing Historical Documents** CCSS

❶ *Drawing Conclusions* Why did Li Su think that burning books would eliminate all rival theories of government?

❷ *Identifying* Which books were saved? Why were these books not burned?

❸ *Argument* Do you agree or disagree with burning or banning books with what some consider objectionable content? Why or why not? What amendment protects this right? Write a paragraph defending your position.

▲ The plague affected all classes of men. Athenian statesman Pericles died in 429 B.C. after becoming infected by the plague that killed nearly one-third of all Athenians.

PHOTO: Time & Life Pictures/Getty Images

VOCABULARY

livid
bruised and disolored

calamity
an event that brings great harm

profane
to treat something that is sacred with disrespect

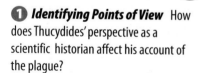

DBQ Analyzing Historical Documents (CCSS)

❶ *Identifying Points of View* How does Thucydides' perspective as a scientific historian affect his account of the plague?

❷ *Analyzing* Why were the sick—and the dead—gathered around the fountains? How could this have potentially made things worse?

❸ *Identifying* What hardships did newcomers to Athens face during the time of the plague?

Plague in Athens

Thucydides (471–c. 400 B.C.) is regarded as the first scientific historian. In his account of the plague that broke out in Athens in 430 B.C., Thucydides simply presents the facts, describing the disease's symptoms and impact on the city itself.

. . . Externally, the body was not so very warm to the touch; it was not pale, but reddish, **livid**, and breaking out in small blisters and ulcers. But internally it was consumed by such a heat that the patients could not bear to have on them the lightest coverings or linen sheets. . . .

The Athenians suffered further hardships owing to the crowding into the city of the people from the country districts; and this affected the new arrivals especially. For since no houses were available for them and they had to live in huts that were stifling in the hot season, they perished in wild disorder. Bodies of dying men lay one upon another, and half-dead people rolled about in the streets and, in their longing for water, near all the fountains. . . . The **calamity** which weighed upon them was so overpowering that men became careless of all law, sacred as well as **profane**. And the customs which they had hitherto observed regarding burial were all thrown into confusion, and they buried their dead each one as he could. . . .

The Justinian Code

The Justinian Code stands as a monumental document in all of Western culture because it recorded the common understanding of law within the Roman Empire for the previous 1000 years, as well as of current law. The recording of all Roman laws had never been attempted before. The Justinian Code clarified the accepted laws of the Roman Empire. The Justinian Code is made up of four parts: the Codex, the Digest, the Institutes, and the Novels which set the standard for Roman law until the empire ceased to exist in 1453.

Civil law is thus distinguished from the law of nations. Every community governed by laws and customs uses partly its own law, partly laws common to all mankind. The law which a people makes for its own government belongs exclusively to that state and is called the civil law, as being the law of the particular state. But the law which natural reason appoints for all mankind obtains equally among all nations, because all nations make use of it. The people of Rome, then, are governed partly by their own laws, and partly by the laws which are common to all mankind. We will take notice of this **distinction** as occasion may arise.

—From Book II, Natural, Common and Civil Law, 527–565

A person who takes a thing belonging to another by force is liable to an action of theft, for who can be said to take the property of another more against his will than he who takes it by force? And he is therefore rightly said to be an *improbus fur*. The **praetor**, however, has introduced a peculiar action in this case, called *vi bonorum raptorum*; by which, if brought within a year after the robbery, quadruple the value of the thing taken may be recovered; but if brought after the expiration of a year, then the single value only may be brought even against a person who has only taken by force a single thing, and one of the most trifling value. But this quadruple of the value is not altogether a penalty, as in the action *furtum manifestum*; for the thing itself is included, so that, strictly, the penalty is only three times the value. And it is the same, whether the robber was or was not taken in the actual commission of the crime. For it would be ridiculous that a person who uses force should be in a better condition than he who secretly commits a theft.

—From Book IV, Goods Taken by Force, 527–565

DBQ Analyzing Historical Documents CCSS

❶ Analyzing How is civil law different from the law of nations?

❷ Identifying Why does the code mention both civil law and the law of nations?

❸ Identifying Continuity and Change Is the position of the Justinian Code on the law of nations and civil law similar to or different from the modern law in the United States? Explain your answer.

The Magna Carta

The Magna Carta, sealed by King John of England in 1215, marked a decisive step forward in the development of English constitutional government. Later, it served as a model for the colonists, who carried the Magna Carta's guarantees of political rights to America.

"John, by the grace of God, king of England, lord of Ireland, duke of Normandy and Aquitaine, and count of Anjou; to the archbishops, bishops, abbots, earls, barons, justiciaries, foresters, sheriffs, reeves, ministers, and all bailiffs, and others his faithful subjects, greeting. . . .

1. We have, in the first place, granted to God, and by this our present charter, confirmed for us and our heirs forever that the English church shall be free. . . .
9. Neither we nor our bailiffs shall seize any land or rent for any debt so long as the debtor's chattels are sufficient to discharge the same. . . .
12. No scutage [tax] or aid shall be imposed in our kingdoms unless by the common counsel thereof. . . .
14. For obtaining the common counsel of the kingdom concerning the assessment of aids . . . or of scutage, we will cause to be summoned, severally by our letters, the archbishops, bishops, abbots, earls, and great barons; we will also cause to be summoned generally, by our sheriffs and bailiffs, all those who hold lands directly of us, to meet on a fixed day . . . and at a fixed place. . . .
20. A free man shall be amerced [punished] for a small fault only according to the measure thereof, and for a great crime according to its magnitude. . . . None of these achievements shall be imposed except by the oath of honest men of the neighborhood.
21. Earls and barons shall be amerced only by their peers and only in proportion to the measure of the offense. . . .
38. In the future no bailiff shall upon his own unsupported accusation put any man to trial without producing credible witnesses to the truth of the accusation.
39. No free man shall be taken, imprisoned, disseised [seized], outlawed, banished, or in any way destroyed, nor will we proceed against or prosecute him, except by the lawful judgment of his peers and by the law of the land.
40. To no one will we sell, to none will we deny or delay, right or justice. . . .
42. In the future it shall be lawful . . . for anyone to leave and return to our kingdom safely and securely by land and water, saving his fealty to us. Excepted are those who have been imprisoned or outlawed according to the law of the land. . . .
61. Whereas we, for the honor of God, and the amendment of our realm, and in order the better to allay the discord arisen between us and our barons, have granted all these things aforesaid. . . .
63. Wherefore we will, and firmly charge that all men in our kingdom shall have and hold all the aforesaid liberties, rights, and concessions . . . fully, and wholly to them and their heirs . . . in all places ever. . . . It is moreover sworn, as well on our part as on the part of the barons, that all these matters aforesaid will be kept in good faith and without deceit. Witness the above named and many others. Given by our hand in the meadow which is called Runnymeade. . . ."

DBQ Analyzing Historical Documents CCSS

❶ *Identifying* Which paragraph discusses the idea of a punishment "fitting" a crime?

❷ *Citing Text Evidence* What are the similarities between the Magna Carta and the Bill of Rights? Provide at least one specific example from the text of the Magna Carta to support your comparison.

❸ *Assessing* Which paragraphs address an individual's right to a trial by jury?

The English Bill of Rights

In 1689 William of Orange and his wife Mary became joint rulers of England after accepting a list of conditions that later became known as the English Bill of Rights. This document assured the English people of certain basic civil rights and limited the power of the English monarchy.

An act declaring the rights and liberties of the subject and settling the succession of the crown. Whereas the lords spiritual and temporal and commons assembled at Westminster lawfully, fully, and freely representing all the estates of the people of this realm did upon the thirteenth day of February in the year of our Lord one thousand six hundred eighty-eight [nine] present unto their majesties . . . William and Mary prince and princess of Orange . . . a certain declaration in writing made by the said lords and commons in the words following viz [namely]:

Whereas the late king James the second, by the assistance of **divers** evil counsellors, judges and ministers employed by him did endeavor to subvert and **extirpate** the Protestant religion and the laws and liberties of this kingdom.

By assuming and exercising a power of dispensing with and suspending of laws and the execution of laws without consent of parliament. . . .

By levying money for and to the use of the crown by pretence of **prerogative** for other time and in other manner than the same was granted by parliament.

By raising and keeping a standing army within this kingdom in time of peace without consent of parliament and quartering soldiers contrary to law. . . .

By violating the freedom of election of members to serve in parliament. . . .

And excessive bail hath been required of persons committed in criminal cases to elude the benefit of the laws made for the liberty of the subjects.

And excessive fines have been imposed.

And illegal and cruel punishments inflicted . . .

And thereupon the said lords spiritual and temporal and commons . . . do . . . declare that the pretended power of suspending of laws or the execution of laws by regal authority without consent of parliament is illegal.

That levying money for or to the use of the crown . . . without grant of parliament for longer time or in other manner than the same is or shall be granted is illegal.

That it is the right of the subjects to petition the king and all commitments and protections for such petitioning are illegal.

That the raising or keeping a standing army within the kingdom in time of peace unless it be with consent of parliament is against law. . . .

That election of members of parliament ought to be free. . . .

That excessive bail ought not to be required nor excessive fines imposed nor cruel and unusual punishments inflicted. . . .

The said lords . . . do resolve that William and Mary, prince and princess of Orange, be declared king and queen of England, France, and Ireland. . . .

VOCABULARY

divers
various

extirpate
to destroy

prerogative
a special right or privilege given because of one's rank or position

DBQ Analyzing Historical Documents

1 *Defending* The document states that King James II "raised a standing army . . . and quartered soldiers contrary to law". What was unlawful about these actions?

2 *Recognizing Bias* How does the author's point of view affect the tone of the document?

3 *Determining Meaning* How did the English Bill of Rights settle "the succession of the crown"?

▲ *Christine de Pizan writes at her desk.*

PHOTO: Leemage/Universal Images Group/Getty Images; TEXT: "A Woman May Need to Have the Heart of a Man," from Christine de Pisan, The Treasure of the City of Ladies, translated by Sarah Lawson (Penguin Classics, 1985). Reprinted by Permission of Penguin Books Ltd

Analyzing Historical Documents (CCSS)

1 *Identifying* What are some of the duties and responsibilities of the medieval gentlewoman, according to Christine de Pizan's account?

2 *Describing* Based on the excerpt, how would you describe Pizan's opinion of barons and their responsibilities?

3 *Narrative* Suppose you are a widow in the 1400s? How would you support your family? Write a journal entry detailing your plans.

A Woman May Need to Have the Heart of a Man

Christine de Pizan was widowed at age 25. She supported her three children by copying manuscripts, compiling a manual of instructions for knights, and writing books. The following is from her 1405 work, The Treasure of the City of Ladies.

It is the responsibility of every baron to spend the least possible time at his manors and his own estate, for his duties are to bear arms, to attend the court of his prince and to travel. Now, his lady stays behind and must take his place. . . . Her men should be able to rely on her for all kinds of protection in the **absence** of their lord. . . . She ought to know how to use weapons and be familiar with everything that pertains to them, so that she may be ready to command her men if the need arises. She should know how to launch an attack or to defend against one.

In addition she will do well to be a very good manager of the estate. . . . She will busy herself around the house; she will find plenty of orders to give. She will have the animals brought in at the right time [and] take care how the shepherd looks after them. . . .

In the winter-time, she will have her men cut her willow groves and make vine props to sell in the season. She will never let them be idle. . . . She will employ her women . . . to attend to the livestock, . . . [and] to weed the courtyards. . . . There is a great need to run an estate well, and the one who is most diligent and careful about it is more than wise and ought to be highly praised.

▲ Martin Luther

▲ Ulrich Zwingli

A Reformation Debate

In 1529 Martin Luther and Ulrich Zwingli debated over the sacrament of the Lord's Supper, or Communion.

LUTHER: Although I have no intention of changing my mind, which is firmly made up, I will nevertheless present the grounds of my belief and show where the others are in error. . . . Your basic **contentions** are these: In the last analysis you wish to prove that a body cannot be in two places at once, and you produce arguments about the unlimited body which are based on natural reason. I do not question how Christ can be God and man and how the two natures can be joined. For God is more powerful than all our ideas, and we must submit to his word.

Prove that Christ's body is not there where the **Scripture** says, "This is my body!" God is beyond all mathematics and the words of God are to be **revered** and carried out in awe. It is God who commands, "Take, eat, this is my body." I request, therefore, valid scriptural proof to the contrary.

ZWINGLI: I insist that the words of the Lord's Supper must be **figurative**. This is ever apparent, and even required by the article of faith; "taken up into heaven, seated at the right hand of the Father." Otherwise, it would be absurd to look for him in the Lord's Supper at the same time that Christ is telling us that he is in heaven. One and the same body cannot possibly be in different places. . . .

LUTHER: I call upon you as before: your basic contentions are shaky. Give way, and give glory to God!

ZWINGLI: And we call upon you to give glory to God and to quit begging the question! The issue at stake is this: Where is the proof of your position?

LUTHER: It is your point that must be proved, not mine. But let us stop this sort of thing. It serves no purpose.

ZWINGLI: It certainly does! It is for you to prove that the passage in John 6 speaks of a physical meal.

LUTHER: You express yourself poorly. . . . You're going nowhere.

PHOTO: (l) SuperStock/Getty Images; (r) Popperfoto/Getty Images

contention
point made in an argument

Scripture
passage from the Bible

revered
honored or respected

figurative
describing something in terms normally used for another

DBQ Analyzing Historical Documents

❶ *Citing Text Evidence* Do you think that Martin Luther's beliefs about communion could be changed? Cite text evidence to support your answer.

❷ *Analyzing* What is the basis for the disagreement between Luther and Zwingli?

❸ *Drawing Conclusions* Was a conclusion reached in the debate presented between Luther and Zwingli?

▲ *Silk in China has been woven on hand looms for many years.*

PHOTO: Glow Images

VOCABULARY

lowly
low rank or position in society

hemp
a fiber from the mulberry bush

loom
a frame or machine for weaving yarns or threads in order to make cloth

DBQ Analyzing Historical Documents CCSS

❶ Differentiating How was clothing used to establish class in Chinese society?

❷ Identifying Points of View Which class of Chinese society do you suppose the narrator belongs to? Provide evidence from the excerpt to support your conclusion.

❸ Listing According to Sung Ying-Hsing, from what sources was all clothing made?

❹ Narrative Is class division apparent in the clothing of modern American society? Write a journal entry that describes your impression of clothing and class in your school. Are the two related?

The Silk Industry in China

.During the 1600s Sung Ying-Hsing wrote a book on Chinese industry called T'ien-kung K'ai-wu (Chinese Technology in the Seventeenth Century), *which included sections on the production of silk.*

. . . Members of the aristocracy are clothed in flowing robes decorated with patterns of magnificent mountain dragons, and they are rulers of the country. Those of **lowly** stations would be dressed in **hempen** jackets and cotton garments to protect themselves from the cold winter and cover their nakedness in summer, in order to distinguish themselves from the birds and beasts. Therefore nature has provided the materials for clothing. Of these, the vegetable [plant] ones are cotton, hemp, meng hemp, and creeper hemp; those derived from birds, animals, and insects are furs, woolens, silk, and spun silk. . . .

But, although silk **looms** are to be found in all parts of the country, how many persons have actually seen the remarkable functioning of the draw-loom: Such words as "orderly government" [chih, i.e., the word used in silk reeling], "chaos" [luan, i.e., when the fibers are entangled], "knowledge or good policy" [ching-lun, i.e., the warp thread and the woven pattern] are known by every schoolboy, but is it not regrettable that he should never see the actual things that gave rise to these words?

from The Wealth of Nations

Adam Smith's most influential work was The Wealth of Nations. *In this excerpt, Smith argues that even though business leaders and investors are motivated to build businesses to make money for themselves, their work helps society as well. The "invisible hand" is an image Smith made famous as an explanation of why this happens.*

It is only for the sake of profit that any man employs a **capital** in the support of industry; and he will always, therefore, endeavor to employ it in the support of that industry of which the produce is likely to be of the greatest value, or to exchange for the greatest quantity either of money or of other goods.

But the annual revenue of every society is always precisely equal to the exchangeable value of the whole annual produce of its industry, or rather is precisely the same thing with that exchangeable value. As every individual, therefore, **endeavors** as much as he can both to employ his capital in the support of domestic industry, and so to direct that industry that its produce may be of the greatest value; every individual necessarily labors to render the annual revenue of the society as great as he can. He generally, indeed, neither intends to promote the public interest, nor knows how much he is promoting it. By preferring the support of domestic to that of foreign industry, he intends only his own security; and by directing that industry in such a manner as its produce may be of the greatest value, he intends only his own gain, and he is in this, as in many other cases, led by an invisible hand to promote an end which was no part of his intention. Nor is it always the worse for the society that it was no part of it. By pursuing his own interest he frequently promotes that of the society more effectually than when he really intends to promote it.

VOCABULARY

capital
In this context, Smith refers to money used for investment.

endeavors
to attempt to achieve

DBQ Analyzing Historical Documents

❶ *Analyzing* How does Smith portray the nature of businessmen or investors?

❷ *Identifying* What is the difference, according to Smith, between domestic and foreign industry?

▲ *Madame Aubry, Olympe de Gouges*

VOCABULARY

utility
something useful or designed for use

imprescriptible
cannot be taken away by law

rigorous
extremely strict

Declaration of the Rights of Woman and the Female Citizen

Olympe de Gouges composed her own Declaration of the Rights of Woman and the Female Citizen *in 1791. Following are excerpts.*

1. Woman is born free and lives as equal to man in her rights. Social distinctions can be based only on the common **utility**.

2. The purpose of any political association is the conservation of the natural and **imprescriptible** rights of woman and man; these rights are liberty, property, security, and especially resistance to oppression. . . .

3. Liberty and justice consist of restoring all that belongs to others; thus, the only limits on the exercise of the natural rights of woman are perpetual male tyranny; these limits are to be reformed by the laws of nature and reason. . . .

4. The law must be . . . the same for all: male and female citizens. . . .

5. No woman is an exception; she is accused, arrested, and detained in cases determined by law. Women, like men, obey this **rigorous** law. . . .

6. The free communication of thoughts and opinions is one of the most precious rights of woman, since that liberty assured the recognition of children by their fathers. . . .

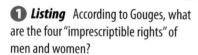

DBQ Analyzing Historical Documents **CCSS**

❶ *Listing* According to Gouges, what are the four "imprescriptible rights" of men and women?

❷ *Analyzing* What does Gouges blame for the limits on the rights of women?

❸ *Defending* Olympe de Gouges states that free communication of thoughts is one of the most precious rights of women. Do you agree or disagree? Write a paragraph defending your position.

504

▲ 19th century portrait of Russian Czar Alexander II

▲ On March 1, 1881 Alexander II was assassinated. This magazine Illustration shows the Russian Chief of the Police escorting the czar's body to the Winter Palace.

Imperial Decree to Free the Serfs

In 1861 the Russian czar Alexander II issued the Emancipation Manifesto, *an imperial decree to free his country's serfs.*

By the grace of God, we, Alexander II, Emperor and **Autocrat** of all the Russias, King of Poland, Grand Duke of Finland, etc., to all our faithful subjects, make known: Examining the condition of classes and professions comprising the state, we became convinced that the present state legislation favors the upper and middle classes, . . . but does not equally favor the serfs. . . . These facts had already attracted the attention of our **predecessors**, and they had adopted measures aimed at improving the conditions of the peasants. But decrees on free farmers and serfs have been carried out on a limited scale only.

We thus came to the conviction that the work of a serious improvement of the condition of the peasants was a sacred inheritance **bequeathed** to us by our ancestors, a mission which, in the course of events Divine Providence called upon us to fulfill. . . .

In virtue of the new dispositions above mentioned, the peasants attached to the soil will be invested within a term fixed by the law with all the rights of free cultivators. . . .

At the same time, they are granted the right of purchasing their **close**, and, with the consent of the proprietors, they may acquire in full property the arable lands and other appurtenances [rights of way] which are allotted to them as a permanent holding. By the acquisition in full property of the quantity of land fixed, the peasants are free from their obligations towards the proprietors for land thus purchased, and they enter definitely into the condition of free peasants-landholders

VOCABULARY

autocrat
a monarch who rules with unlimited authority

predecessors
a person who has held a certain position or office before another

bequeathed
to leave property or possessions to someone in a will

close
an enclosed area of land

DBQ Analyzing Historical Documents (CCSS)

❶ *Identifying* What new right did the decree give to serfs?

❷ *Predicting Consequences* What affect do you think the decree had on the relationship between the classes?

❸ *Explaining* Why does Czar Alexander II free the serfs?

⟰ Women worked long hours around heavy equipment for very little pay. This illustration shows a woman examining a power loom in a textile factory.

The Unfortunate Situation of Working Women

This article was published in L'Atelier, *a Parisian workingman's newspaper, in 1842.*

Although women's work is less productive for society than that of men, it does, nevertheless, have a certain value, and, moreover, there are professions that only women can practice. For these, women are indispensable. . . . It is these very workers in all these necessary trades who earn the least and who are subject to the longest layoffs. Since for so much work they earn only barely enough to live from day to day, it happens that during times of unemployment they sink into **abject** poverty.

Who has not heard of the women silkworkers' dirty, unhealthy, and badly paid work; of the women in the spinning and weaving factories working fourteen to sixteen hours (except for one hour for both meals); always standing, without a single minute for **repose**, putting forth an enormous amount of effort. And many of them have to walk a **league** or more, morning and evening, to get home. Nor should we neglect to mention the danger that exists merely from working in these large factories, surrounded by wheels, gears, enormous leather belts that always threaten to seize you and pound you to pieces.

The existence of women who work as day laborers, and are obliged to abandon . . . the care of their children to indifferent neighbors is no better. . . . We believe that the condition of women will never really improve until workingmen can earn enough to support their families, which is only fair. Woman is so closely linked to man that the position of the one cannot be improved without reference to the position of the other.

VOCABULARY

abject
existing in a low state or condition

repose
to rest

league
a measure of distance between approximately 2.4 and 4.6 miles

DBQ Analyzing Historical Documents (CCSS)

❶ *Paraphrasing* Using your own words, explain the author meant by "indifferent neighbors." How does this word choice convey the author's opinion about working women?

❷ *Describing* How would you describe working conditions for women?

❸ *Identifying Points of View* What is the attitude of the *L'Atelier* writer toward women and women's work? Is the author of the article likely to be a woman or a man? What makes you think so?

▲ *Dadabhai Naoroji was an outspoken Indian nationalist and a critic of Britain's economic policies in India. In his speech* Poverty and Un-British Rule in India, *he argued that Britain was overtaxing India.*

The Impact of British Rule in India

In 1871 Dadabhai Naoroji commented on the benefits and the problems of British rule in India.

Benefits of British Rule:

In the Cause of Humanity: Abolition of suttee and **infanticide**. Civilization: Education, both male and female. . . . **Resuscitation** of India's own noble literature. Politically: Peace and order. Freedom of speech and liberty of the press. . . . Improvement of government in the native states. Security of life and property. Freedom from oppression. . . . Materially: Loans for railways and irrigation. Development of a few valuable products, such as indigo, tea, coffee, silk, etc. Increase of exports. Telegraphs.

The Detriments of British Rule:

In the Cause of Humanity: Nothing. Civilization: [T]here has been a failure to do as much as might have been done. Politically: Repeated breach of pledges to give the natives a fair and reasonable share in the higher administration of their own country, . . . an utter disregard of the feelings and views of the natives. Financially: [N]ew modes of taxation, without any adequate effort to increase the means of the people to pay.

Summary:

British rule has been: morally, a great blessing; politically, peace and order on one hand, **blunders** on the other; materially, **impoverishment**. . . . Our great misfortune is that you do not know our wants. When you will know our real wishes, I have not the least doubt that you would do justice. The genius and spirit of the British people is fair play and justice.

VOCABULARY

infanticide
killing an infant

resuscitation
restoration or renewal

blunders
mistakes

impoverishment
to make poor or to take riches from someone

DBQ Analyzing Historical Documents

❶ *Explaining* According to Naoroji, did British rule improve certain ways of life for Indian men, women, or both? Explain your answer.

❷ *Listing* What natural resources of India were developed under British rule? How could the development of natural resources cause problems for the two countries?

❸ *Defending* Were the benefits of British rule in India worth the disadvantages? Write a paragraph explaining your position. Use evidence from the excerpt to defend your position.

▲ *Allied soldiers went "Over the Top" in the 1916 Battle of the Somme to battle German forces.*

An American Soldier Remembers World War I

Arthur Guy Empey reflects upon his experiences during World War I in the trenches in France. This is an excerpt from his book Over the Top.

Suddenly, the earth seemed to shake and a thunderclap burst in my ears. I opened my eyes,—I was splashed all over with sticky mud, and men were picking themselves up from the bottom of the trench. The **parapet** on my left had toppled into the trench, completely blocking it with a wall of tossed-up earth. The man on my left lay still. . . . A German "Minnie" (trench mortar) had exploded in the [trench].

. . . Stretcher-bearers came up the trench on the double. After a few minutes of digging, three still, muddy forms on stretchers were carried down the communication trench to the rear. Soon they would be resting "somewhere in France," with a little wooden cross over their heads. They had done their bit for King and Country, had died without firing a shot. . . . I was dazed and motionless. Suddenly a shovel was pushed into my hands, and a rough but kindly voice said: "Here, my lad, lend a hand clearing the trench, but keep your head down, and look out for **snipers**. . . ."

Lying on my belly on the bottom of the trench, I filled sandbags with the sticky mud.

. . . The harder I worked, the better I felt.

Occasionally a bullet would crack overhead, and a machine gun would kick up the mud on the bashed-in parapet. At each crack I would duck and shield my face with my arm. One of the older men noticed this action of mine, and whispered: "Don't duck at the crack of a bullet, Yank; the danger has passed,—you never hear the one that wings you. Always remember that if you are going to get it, you'll get it, so never worry." . . . [Days later] we received the cheerful news that at four in the morning we were to go over the top and take the German frontline trench. My heart turned to lead.

VOCABULARY

parapet
wall of earth piled on top of a trench

snipers
people who shoot at exposed individuals from a concealed location

DBQ Analyzing Historical Documents (CCSS)

❶ *Using Context Clues* The title of the excerpt tells the reader that the narrator is American. What clue from the excerpt also reveals this fact?

❷ *Integrating Visual Information* Study the photograph. Does it convey the mood of the excerpt? How?

❸ *Expressing* How does Arthur Guy Empey uses sarcasm in the final paragraph?

PHOTO: Time & Life Pictures/Getty Images

▲ *Mohandas Gandhi led a campaign of nonviolent resistance against British rule in India until his assassination in 1948.*

Gandhi Takes the Path of Civil Disobedience

Mohandas Gandhi explains why British rule in India must end.

Before embarking on **civil disobedience** and taking the risk I have dreaded to take all these years, I would fain approach you and find a way out.

My personal faith is absolutely clear. I cannot intentionally hurt anything that lives, much less fellow human beings, even though they may do the greatest wrong to me and mine. Whilst, therefore, I hold the British rule to be a curse, I do not intend harm to a single Englishman or to any legitimate interest he may have in India.

. . . Though I hold the British rule in India to be a curse, I do not, therefore, consider Englishmen in general to be worse than any other people on earth. I have the privilege of claiming many Englishmen as dearest friends. Indeed much that I have learned of the evil of British rule is due to the writings of frank and courageous Englishmen who have not hesitated to tell the truth about that rule.

And why do I regard British rule as a curse? It has impoverished the ignorant millions by a system of progressive **exploitation** and by a ruinously expensive military and civil administration which the country can never afford.

It has reduced us politically to serfdom. It has sapped the foundations of our culture. And, by the policy of cruel **disarmament**, it has degraded us spiritually. Lacking the inward strength, we have been reduced . . . to a state bordering on cowardly helplessness. . . .

VOCABULARY

civil disobedience
refusal to obey government demands

exploitation
unfair use for one's own advantage

disarmament
reducing or eliminating weapons

DBQ Analyzing Historical Documents (CCSS)

1 *Making Inferences* Using what you know about the relationship between Britain and India and the concept of serfdom, explain what Gandhi meant when he stated that India had been "reduced . . . to serfdom."

2 *Determining Word Meanings* Based on the context clues provided in the text, how would you define the word "frank?"

3 *Analyzing* Why do you think Gandhi believed that nonviolent civil disobedience would encourage the British to free India? Write a short "letter to the editor" of a British newspaper in support of the policies of either Britain or Ghandi. Provide examples to defend your position.

▲ Children gather behind a barbed-wire fence while imprisoned at Auschwitz concentration camp in Poland in 1945.

▲ These railroad tracks brought thousands of Jews to Auschwitz Millions of Jewish men, women, and children were killed at this camp during World War II.

PHOTOS: (l) Galerie Bilderwelt/Hulton Archive/Getty Images (r) Hulton Archive/Archive Photos/Getty Images; TEXT: Nazism, 1919-1945 Volume 3 Foreign policy, War, and Racial

VOCABULARY

indescribable
impossible to explain or describe

jostling
pushing around

squashed
to end or stop something by using force

distorted
to unnaturally twist

 DBQ Analyzing Historical Documents **CCSS**

❶ Identifying Points of View What is the French doctor's point of view about the events he describes at the Auschwitz-Birkenau death camp?

❷ Using Context Clues Which words or phrases from the excerpt provide evidence that the doctor was horrified by the event?

❸ Analyzing Visual Information Study the photographs from the concentration camp. How do the photographs convey the mood of the excerpt?

The Holocaust—The Camp Victims

A French doctor describes the victims of one of the gas chambers at Auschwitz-Birkenau during the Holocaust.

It is mid-day, when a long line of women, children, and old people enter the yard. The senior official in charge . . . climbs on a bench to tell them that they are going to have a bath and that afterwards they will get a drink of hot coffee. They all undress in the yard. . . . The doors are opened and an **indescribable jostling** begins. The first people to enter the gas chamber begin to draw back. They sense the death which awaits them. The SS men put and end to the pushing and shoving with blows from their rifle butts beating the heads of the horrified women who are desperately hugging their children. The massive oak double doors are shut. For two endless minutes one can hear banging on the walls and screams which are no longer human. And then—not a sound. Five minutes later the doors are opened. The corpses, **squashed** together and **distorted**, fall out like a waterfall. The bodies which are still warm pass through the hands of the hairdresser who cuts their hair and the dentist who pulls out their gold teeth. . .

▲ John Glenn, Jr., was the first American to orbit the Earth and the third American in space.

Progress Never Stops

In 1962 John J. Glenn, Jr., was commander of the first U.S. crewed spacecraft to orbit the earth. Glenn spoke to a joint meeting of Congress six days after he returned from orbit.

What did we learn from the flight? . . . The Mercury spacecraft and systems design concepts are sound and have now been verified during **manned** flight. We also proved that man can operate intelligently in space and can adapt rapidly to this new environment.

Zero G or weightlessness appears to be no problem. As a matter of fact, lack of gravity is a rather fascinating thing. Objects within the cockpit can be parked in midair. For example, at one time during the flight, I was using a hand-held camera. Another system needed attention; so it seemed quite natural to let go of the camera, take care of the other chore, then reach out, grasp the camera, and go back about my business.

There seemed to be little **sensation** of speed although the craft was traveling at about five miles per second—a speed that I too find difficult to comprehend.

The view from that altitude defies description. The horizon colors are brilliant and sunsets are spectacular. It is hard to beat a day in which you are permitted the luxury of seeing four sunsets. . . .

Our efforts today and what we have done so far are but small building blocks in a huge pyramid to come.

But questions are sometimes raised regarding the immediate payoffs from our efforts. Explorations and the pursuit of knowledge have always paid dividends in the long run— usually far greater than anything expected at the **outset**. Experimenters with common, green mold, little dreamed what effect their discovery of penicillin would have.

We are just probing the surface of the greatest advancements in man's knowledge of his surroundings that has ever been made.

. . . Knowledge **begets** knowledge. Progress never stops.

VOCABULARY

manned
supplying people for a service or a ship

sensation
a bodily feeling caused by the senses or excitement

outset
the beginning

begets
causes

DBQ **Analyzing Historical Documents**

❶ *Listing* According to Glenn, what knowledge was gained by the mission?

❷ *Identifying Points of View* Why did Glenn choose to explain that the ship moved at "a speed that *I too* find difficult to comprehend?"

❸ *Identifying Central Ideas* What are the immediate and long-term "payoffs" of John Glenn's 1962 space mission, according to his report to Congress?

▲ *Nelson Mandela visits the jail cell where he served a twenty-seven year sentence for opposition to apartheid. He became the first democratically elected president of South Africa in 1994.*

VOCABULARY

reserves
a reservation; land set aside for use by a particular group

squatters
those who settle on public land without rights or permission

domination
to hold a commanding position or controlling power over something or someone

DBQ Analyzing Historical Documents CCSS

1 *Analyzing* According to Mandela, what role does soil play in South Africa's divided society?

2 *Identifying* What argument do poor South Africans make regarding the country's laws?

3 *Explaining* What ideal does Nelson Mandela discuss?

An Ideal for Which I am Prepared to Die

Nelson Mandela delivered his speech "I am the First Accused" during the Rivonia Trial in Pretoria, South Africa on April 20, 1964. Following the trial, he was sentenced to life in prison. The following is an excerpt from his speech.

. . . The whites enjoy what may well be the highest standard of living in the world, whilst Africans live in poverty and misery. Forty percent of the Africans live in hopelessly overcrowded and, in some cases, drought-stricken **reserves**, where soil erosion and the overworking of the soil make it impossible for them to live properly off the land. Thirty percent are labourers, labour tenants, and **squatters** on white farms . . . The other thirty percent live in towns where they have developed economic and social habits which bring them closer, in many respects, to white standards. Forty-six percent of all African families in Johannesburg do not earn enough to keep them going. . . .

. . . The complaint of Africans, however, is not only that they are poor and whites are rich, but that the laws which are made by the whites are designed to preserve this situation. . . .

. . . During my lifetime I have dedicated my life to this struggle of the African people. I have fought against white **domination**, and I have fought against black domination. I have cherished the ideal of a democratic and free society in which all persons live together in harmony with equal opportunities. It is an ideal which I hope to live for, and to see realized. It is an ideal which I hope to live for and to achieve. But if needs be, it is an ideal for which I am prepared to die.

from "A new chapter in China's reform and opening"

World Trade Organization Director-General Pascal Lamy, in a speech at a forum in Beijing on 11 December 2011 commemorating the 10th anniversary of China's inclusion in the WTO.

Ten years is a long minute in China's **millenary** history. And yet these ten years have witnessed an unprecedented transformation of China's economy and society.

My first trip to China was in the 1980s, accompanying the then President of the European Commission on his first visit to Deng Xiaoping. Bicycles in ChangAn Street were the rule. . . . Ten years later, the streets of Beijing are crowded with family cars, not bicycles. . . . Millions of Chinese farmers have moved to the cities, employed by a rapidly expanding industrial sector, including multinational corporations which have come into China at unprecedented speed since 2001 and played a key part in creating a network of global value chains. . . .

China's accession to the WTO proved decisive in several respects.

The goal to become a WTO member acted as a lever for the process of domestic modernization. . . .

WTO membership also underpinned Chinese export-led growth with a strong insurance policy against **protectionism**.

. . . And yet the lesson learnt from the recent global economic crisis is that the WTO has a significant role to play as a bulwark against protectionism. This is particularly true of China which would have been much more severely affected by protectionist measures, given its prominence in world trade. The WTO has so far protected China against high intensity protectionism during the crisis.

Looking into the future, as a key member of the WTO family, China's role and influence will be vital in our collective endeavour to advance trade opening and global trade regulation. . . .

Today, the Chinese economy and its influence are greater and stronger than ten years ago. As a global power, it is only natural that the expectations of other countries on China have also grown. China's participation and support are vital in any collective action to address global challenges. With today's economic difficulties across the world, resolve and leadership are in desperate need. We all need a **proactive** China. . . .

On this tenth anniversary, and as we look forward for the next decade, I have two wishes that I would like to express.

The first is that China's involvement in the WTO helps us all in keeping this organization on the move towards more open and fairer trade.

The second is that the WTO's relevance for China keeps growing and helps this country to address its reform challenges.

VOCABULARY

millenary
relating to 1,000 years

protectionism
an economic system that aims to encourage growth of domestic business and industry by placing restrictions on foreign imports

proactive
to anticipate and devise plans to solve future problems

DBQ Analyzing Historical Documents

1 *Analyzing* How does Pascal Lamy view the global role of China now and going forward?

2 *Identifying* What has changed in China's economy since it was granted admission into the World Trade Organization?

President Bush's Address to Joint Session of Congress, September 20, 2001

On September 11, 2001, terrorists crashed airplanes into the World Trade Center in New York City and the Pentagon in Washington, D.C. Thousands of people were killed. In his address, President George W. Bush announced a new kind of war against terrorism.

". . . On September the eleventh, enemies of freedom committed an act of war against our country. . . . Americans have known surprise attacks—but never before on thousands of civilians. All of this was brought upon us in a single day—and night fell on a different world, a world where freedom itself is under attack. . . .

The evidence we have gathered all points to a collection of loosely **affiliated** terrorist organizations known as al-Qaeda. . . . Our war on terror begins with al-Qaeda, but it does not end there. It will not end until every terrorist group of global reach has been found, stopped and defeated.

Americans are asking: Why do they hate us? They hate what we see right here in this chamber—a democratically elected government.

Their leaders are self-appointed. They hate our freedoms. . . . By sacrificing human life to serve their radical visions—by abandoning every value except the will to power—they follow in the path of **fascism**, and Nazism, and totalitarianism. And they will follow that path all the way, to where it ends: in history's unmarked grave of discarded lives.

. . . We will direct every resource at our command—every means of diplomacy, every tool of intelligence, every instrument of law enforcement, every financial influence, and every necessary weapon of war—to the disruption and defeat of the global terror network.

I know there are struggles ahead, and dangers to face. But this country will define our times, not be defined by them. . . . Great harm had been done to us. We have suffered great loss. And in our grief and anger we have found our mission and our moment. . . . Our Nation—this generation—will lift a dark threat of violence from our people and our future. We will rally the world to this cause, by our efforts and by our courage. We will not tire, we will not **falter**, and we will not fail."

VOCABULARY

affiliated
to connect closely with as a member or associate

fascism
a government led by a dictator that controls business and labor and opposition is not permitted

falter
to hesitate in action or purpose

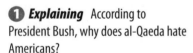

DBQ Analyzing Historical Documents CCSS

❶ *Explaining* According to President Bush, why does al-Qaeda hate Americans?

❷ *Interpreting* What did President Bush mean when he said "night fell on a different world"?

❸ *Making Connections* President Bush's speech was delivered on September 20, 2001. In your opinion, has the passage of time affected the political stance described here or the public's opinion of this tragic event? Write a paragraph explaining your thoughts.

from Tawakkol Karman's Nobel Peace Prize Speech

In 2011, Tawakkol Kaman gave her acceptance speech in receipt of the Nobel Peace Prize. She spoke about the democratic movement, known as the Arab Spring, that was affecting her home country of Yemen.

"Your Majesties, Highnesses, Excellencies, Distinguished Committee of the Nobel Peace Prize, Arab spring and revolution youth in the arena of freedom and change, and all free people of the world,

Peace upon you from the Nobel Peace **rostrum**.

. . . Alfred Nobel's dream of a world, where peace prevails and wars disappear, has not been achieved yet, but the hope to make it come true has grown large, and the effort to achieve it has doubled. The Nobel Peace Prize still offers this hope spiritual and conscientious momentum. For more than a hundred years, this award has stood as proof of the values of peaceful struggle for rights, justice and freedom, and also as proof of how wrong violence and wars are with all their backfiring and devastating results.

I have always believed that resistance against repression and violence is possible without relying on similar represson and violence. I have always believed that human civilization is the fruit of the effort of both women and men. So, when women are treated unjustly and are deprived of their natural right in this process, all social deficiencies and cultural illnesses will be unfolded, and in the end the whole community, men and women, will suffer. The solution to women's issues can only be achieved in a free and democratic society in which human energy is liberated, the energy of both women and men together. Our civilization is called human civilization and is not attributed only to men or women.

. . . At this moment, as I speak to you here, young Arab people, both women and men, march in peaceful demonstrations demanding freedom and dignity from their rulers. They go forward on this noble path armed not with weapons, but with faith in their right to freedom and dignity. They march in a dramatic scene which embodies the most beautiful of the human spirit of sacrifice and the **aspiration** to freedom and life, against the ugliest forms of selfishness, injustice, and the desire to hold on to power and wealth.

. . . The democratic world, which has told us a lot about the virtues of democracy and good governance, should not be indifferent to what is happening in Yemen and Syria, and happened before that in Tunisia, Egypt, and Libya, and happens in every Arab and non-Arab country aspiring for freedom. All of that is just hard labour during the birth of democracy which requires support and assistance, not fear and caution.

Allow me, ladies and gentlemen, to share my belief that peace will remain the hope of mankind forever, and that the best hope for a better future for mankind will always drive us to speak noble words and do noble deeds. Together, we will push the horizons, one after another, towards a world of true human perfection. . . .

VOCABULARY

rostrum
a stage or platform for public speaking

aspiration
the desire to achieve a goal

DBQ **Analyzing Historical Documents**

❶ *Analyzing* What is Kaman's view about the equality of men and women?

❷ *Identifying* How does Kaman believe democracies in the West should react to the protests that made up the Arab Spring movement?

Manmohan Singh addresses the Indian Science Congress

In January 2012, Indian Prime Minister Manmohan Singh spoke before the 99th Annual Session of the Indian Science Congress in Bhubneshwar, India.

"I have often spoken about the commitment of our Government to give a boost to the science and technology sector in the country. We have taken several steps towards this end.

- We have greatly expanded the higher education **infrastructure** for Science and Technology by establishing new institutions. . . .
- We have introduced a large number of scholarships; most notably, the Innovation in Science Pursuit for Inspired Research or INSPIRE scheme which gives awards to one million science students.

. . . The university research system is also showing signs of rejuvenation. In 2008, I gave away incentive awards to 14 universities under the Promotion of University Research and Scientific Excellence (PURSE) scheme. In 2010, 30 more universities have qualified under the same criteria. . . .

. . . Things are changing but we cannot be satisfied with what has been achieved. We need to do much more to change the face of Indian science. . . . While it is true that science and engineering continue to attract some of our best students, many of them later opt for other careers because of relatively poorer prospects in science.

. . . An occasion like the present one should be used to revisit a fundamental question: what is the role of science in a country like India? There is no simple answer. But for a country grappling with the challenges of poverty and development, the **over-riding** objective of a comprehensive and well-considered policy for science, technology and innovation should be to support the national objective of faster, sustainable and inclusive development.

There is much that the scientific community can do to achieve these objectives. Research should be directed to providing **'frugal'** solutions to our chronic problems of providing food, energy and water security to our people. Science should help us understand how to give practical meaning to the concept of sustainable development and green growth. Science should help us shift our mindsets from the allocation of resources to their more efficient use. Technology and process engineering should help us reach the benefits of development to those who need it most. . . .

In the final analysis, the pursuit of science is a process of unlocking the human mind. It is an exploration of the mystery, beauty and method in the universe by stretching the frontiers of our imagination. We need to invoke the power of science in every sphere of our economy and way of life.

VOCABULARY

infrastructure
an organization's structure or plan for forward progress

over-riding
chief, most important; the main focus

frugal
sparing; using resources carefully and economically

DBQ Analyzing Historical Documents (CCSS)

 Analyzing Why, according to the prime minister, is a focus on the development of science education and increasing the number of trained scientists, a necessary goal?

2 **Identifying** What specific examples are cited that indicate that India has been targeting ways to improve the development of scientists within the nation?

from the "World Economic Outlook"

Olivier Blanchard was the Economic Counsellor of the International Monetary Fund, a group of 188 countries whose aim is to encourage stable global economic activity and global economic growth. In this segment of the World Economic Outlook report, Blanchard discusses the economic crisis that hit the European Union economies in the first decade of the twenty-first century.

Soon after the September 2011 *World Economic Outlook* went to press, the euro area went through another **acute** crisis. . . . With the value of some of [Spain and Italy's] banks' assets now in doubt, questions arose as to whether those banks would be able to convince investors to roll over their loans. Worried about funding, banks froze credit. Confidence decreased, and activity slumped.

Strong policy responses turned things around. Elections in Spain and the appointment of a new prime minister in Italy gave some reassurance to investors. The adoption of a fiscal compact showed the commitment of EU members to dealing with their deficits and debt. . . .

With the passing of the crisis, and some good news about the U.S. economy, some optimism has returned. It should remain **tempered**. Even absent another European crisis, most advanced economies still face major brakes on growth. . . .

[There are] two main brakes on growth: fiscal consolidation and **bank deleveraging**. Both reflect needed adjustments, but both decrease growth in the short term. . . .

Emerging economies are not immune to these developments. Low advanced economy growth has meant lower export growth. And financial uncertainty, together with sharp shifts in risk appetite, has led to volatile capital flows. For the most part, however, emerging economies have enough policy room to maintain solid growth. . . .

Turning to policies aimed at reducing risks, the focus is clearly on Europe. . . . Measures should be taken to decrease the links between sovereigns and banks, from the creation of euro level deposit insurance and bank resolution to the introduction of limited forms of Eurobonds, such as the creation of a common euro bill market. These measures are urgently needed and can make a difference were another crisis to take place soon.

Taking one step back, perhaps the highest priority, but also the most difficult to achieve, is to durably increase growth in advanced economies, and especially in Europe. . . . For the moment, the focus should be on measures that increase demand. Looking forward, however, the focus should also be on measures that increase potential growth. The Holy Grail would be measures that do both. There are probably few of those. More realistically, the search must be for reforms that help in the long term but do not depress demand in the short term. Identifying these reforms, and addressing their potentially adverse short-term effects, should be very high on the policy agenda.

International Monetary Fund 2012. World Economic Outlook, April 2012, Olivier Blanchard, Economic Counsellor. Used by permission of the International Monetary Fund.

VOCABULARY

acute
characterized by severity or size of problem

tempered
qualifying or adjusting a point of view, not jumping to a conclusion

bank deleveraging
the action of a bank reducing its amount of debt, in proportion to its amount of fiscal assets

DBQ Analyzing Historical Documents

❶ *Analyzing* How can bank deleveraging help in the context of the fiscal crisis that was being battled in Europe?

❷ *Identifying* What is meant by the recommendation to "decrease the links between sovereigns and banks"?

CONTENTS

World Population, A.D. 1–2010

Source: United Nations Population Division, 2006.
Note: Populations are estimates.

Population by Continent, 2012

Continent	Population, 2010	Projected Population 2050
Asia	4.133 billion	5.167 billion
Africa	1.015 billion	2.138 billion
Europe	734 million	671 million
North America	539 million	739 million
South America	396 million	520 million
Australia/Oceania	35 million	49 million

Source: www.census.gov

Life Expectancy

Country	Years
Japan	83.91
Andorra	82.50
France	81.46
Israel	81.07
New Zealand	80.71
United Kingdom	80.17
United States	78.49
Chile	78.10
China	74.84
Egypt	72.93
Brazil	72.79
India	67.14
Russia	66.46
Mozambique	52.02
South Africa	49.41

Source: *The World Factbook*, 2012, CIA

Infant Mortality

Country	Infant Deaths per 1,000 Live Births
South Africa	43
India	46
Egypt	24
Brazil	21
China	16
Russia	10
Chile	8
United States	6
South Korea	4
United Kingdom	5
Canada	5
Germany	4
France	3
Japan	2

Source: *The World Factbook*, 2012, CIA

Most Populous Countries

Country	Population
China	1,340,000,000
India	1,200,000,000
United States	314,000,000
Indonesia	249,000,000
Brazil	200,000,000
Pakistan	190,000,000
Nigeria	170,000,000
Bangladesh	161,000,000
Russia	143,000,000
Japan	127,000,000

Source: *The World Factbook*, 2012, CIA

World's Richest Countries

Country	Gross National Income per Capita (in U.S. dollars)
Liechtenstein	141,000
Qatar	104,300
Luxembourg	81,100
Bermuda	69,900
Singapore	60,500
Jersey	57,000
Falkland Islands	55,400
Norway	54,200
Brunei	50,000
Hong Kong	49,800

Source: *The World Factbook,* 2012, CIA

World's Poorest Countries

Country	Gross National Income per Capita (in U.S. dollars)
The Democratic Republic of Congo	400
Liberia	500
Zimbabwe	500
Burundi	600
Somalia	600
Eritrea	700
Niger	800
Central African Republic	800
Madagascar	900
Malawi	900

Source: *The World Factbook,* 2012, CIA

Highest Inflation Rates

Country	Rate of Inflation (percent)
Belarus	52.40
Ethiopia	33.20
Venezuela	26.10
Iran	22.50
Argentina	22.00
Yemen	20.00
Eritrea	20.00
Suriname	19.50
Uganda	18.70
Vietnam	18.70

Source: *The World Factbook,* 2012, CIA

Lowest Inflation Rates

Country	Rate of Inflation (percent)
Bahrain	-0.40
Japan	-0.30
Kiribati	0.20
Switzerland	0.20
Liechtenstein	0.30
Saint Maarten	0.70
United Arab Emirates	0.90
Vanuatu	0.90
French Polynesia	1.10

Source: *The World Factbook,* 2012, CIA

World's Ten Largest Economies

Economy	GDP (Purchasing Power Parity in U.S. Dollars)
European Union	15.7 trillion
United States	15.3 trillion
China	11.4 trillion
India	4.5 trillion
Japan	4.5 trillion
Germany	3.1 trillion
Russia	2.4 trillion
Brazil	2.3 trillion
United Kingdom	2.3 trillion
France	2.2 trillion

Source: *The World Factbook,* 2012, CIA

Regional Water and Sanitation

Region	Access to Improved Water	Access to Improved Sanitation
World	87	61
Middle East and North Africa	87	84
Latin America and Caribbean	93	79
Europe and Central Asia	95	89
East Asia and Pacific	88	59
South Asia	87	36
Sub-Saharan Africa	60	31

Source: *The World Factbook,* 2012, CIA

Highest Adult Literacy Rates

Country	Rate of Literacy (percent)
Andorra	100
Finland	100
Greenland	100
Liechtenstein	100
Norway	100
Cuba	99.8
Estonia	99.8
Azerbaijan	99.8
Georgia	99.7

Source: *The World Factbook,* 2012, CIA

Lowest Adult Literacy Rates

Country	Rate of Literacy (percent)
Burkina Faso	21.8
South Sudan	27
Afghanistan	28.1
Niger	28.7
Chad	34.5
Sierra Leone	35.1
Somalia	37.8
Senegal	39.3
Guinea	41

Source: *The World Factbook,* 2012, CIA

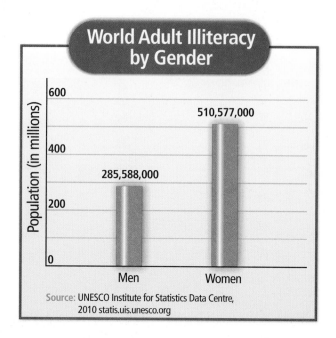

World Adult Illiteracy by Gender

- Men: 285,588,000
- Women: 510,577,000

Source: UNESCO Institute for Statistics Data Centre, 2010 statis.uis.unesco.org

Years, by Country, in Which Women Gained the Right to Vote

Year	Country	Year	Country
1893	New Zealand	1945	Italy
1902	Australia	1945	Japan
1913	Norway	1947	Argentina
1918	United Kingdom	1947	Mexico
1918	Canada	1950	India
1919	Germany	1952	Greece
1920	United States	1956	Egypt
1930	South Africa	1963	Kenya
1934	Brazil	1971	Switzerland
1944	France	1980	Iraq

Source: *The World Factbook*, 2012, CIA

Highest Military Expenditures

Country	GDP	Billions of U.S. Dollars per Year	Percentage of Gross Domestic Product (GDP)
United States	15.29	626.89	4.1
China	11.44	491.92	4.3
France	2.246	58.36	2.6
Japan	4.497	3.5976	0.8
United Kingdom	2.29	61.83	2.7
Germany	3.139	47.085	1.5
Italy	1.871	33.678	1.8
South Korea	1.574	42.498	2.7
India	4.515	112.87	2.5
Saudi Arabia	691.5	691.5	10.0

Source: *The World Factbook*, 2012, CIA

Nuclear Weapons Capability

Country	Date of First Test
United States	1945
Russia (Soviet Union)	1949
United Kingdom	1952
France	1960
China	1964
India	1974
Pakistan	1998
North Korea	2006

Source: U.S. Department of State and *TIME* magazine

REFERENCE ATLAS

ATLAS KEY

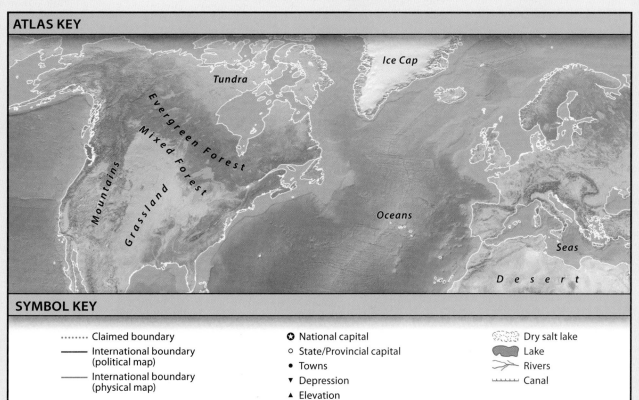

SYMBOL KEY

.... Claimed boundary	✪ National capital	🌫 Dry salt lake
——— International boundary (political map)	○ State/Provincial capital	🗺 Lake
——— International boundary (physical map)	● Towns	🏞 Rivers
	▼ Depression	⊬⊬⊬⊬ Canal
	▲ Elevation	

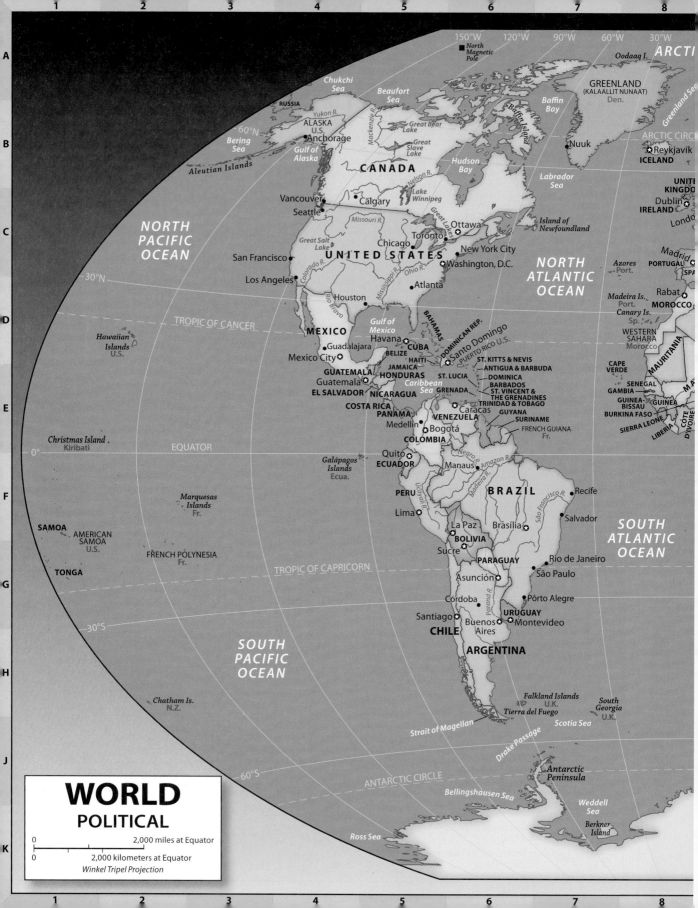

WORLD
POLITICAL

0 2,000 miles at Equator
0 2,000 kilometers at Equator
Winkel Tripel Projection

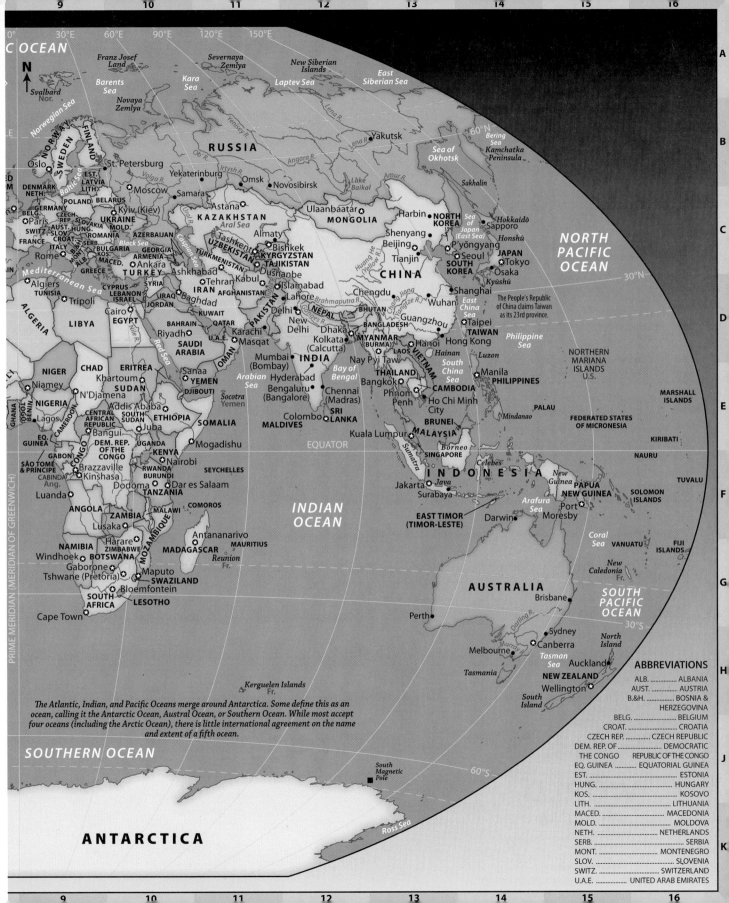

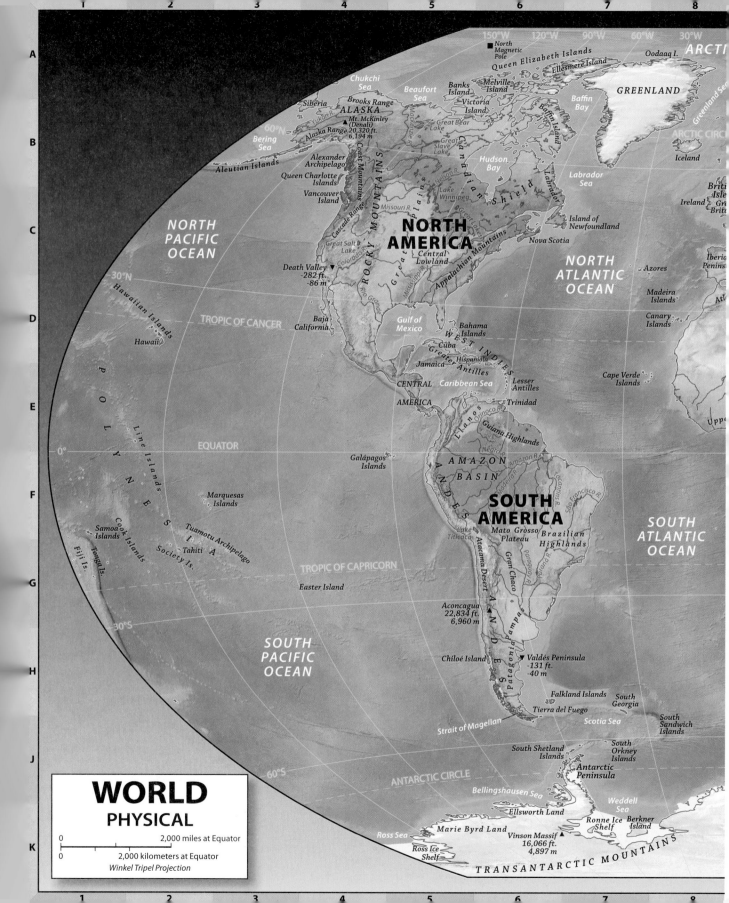

WORLD

PHYSICAL

0		2,000 miles at Equator
0		2,000 kilometers at Equator

Winkel Tripel Projection

Map labels:

ARCTI

North Magnetic Pole

Queen Elizabeth Islands
Oodaaq I.
Ellesmere Island
GREENLAND
ARCTIC CIRCL

Chukchi Sea
Siberia
Beaufort Sea
Banks Island
Melville Island
Victoria Island
Baffin Bay
Baffin Island
Greenland Sea

Brooks Range
ALASKA
Mt. McKinley (Denali) 20,320 ft. 6,194 m
Great Bear Lake
Mackenzie R.
Great Slave Lake
Hudson Bay
Labrador Sea
Iceland

Bering Sea
Aleutian Islands
Alaska Range
Yukon R.
Nelson R.
Canadian Shield
Labrador

Alexander Archipelago
Queen Charlotte Islands
Vancouver Island
Coast Mountains
Great Plains
Lake Winnipeg
Missouri R.

NORTH PACIFIC OCEAN

Cascade Range
ROCKY MOUNTAINS
NORTH AMERICA
Island of Newfoundland
Nova Scotia

Briti Isle
Ireland Gr Brita

Great Salt Lake
Central Lowland
Appalachian Mountains
NORTH ATLANTIC OCEAN
Azores
Iberia Penins

Death Valley -282 ft. -86 m
Colorado R.
Mississippi R.
Madeira Islands

Hawaiian Islands
Baja California
Rio Grande
Gulf of Mexico
Bahama Islands
WEST INDIES
TROPIC OF CANCER
Canary Islands

Hawaii
Cuba
Greater Antilles
Hispaniola
Cape Verde Islands
Atl

Jamaica
CENTRAL
Caribbean Sea
Lesser Antilles

AMERICA
Trinidad

P O L Y N E S I A
Line Islands

Galápagos Islands
Llanos
Orinoco R.
Guiana Highlands
Upper

EQUATOR
Negro R.
AMAZON BASIN
Amazon R.

Marquesas Islands
ANDES
SOUTH AMERICA
SOUTH ATLANTIC OCEAN

Tuamotu Archipelago
Madeira R.
Tocantins R.
São Francisco R.

Samoa Islands
Cook Islands
Society Is.
Tahiti
Lake Titicaca
Mato Grosso Plateau
Brazilian Highlands

Fiji Is.
Tonga Is.
TROPIC OF CAPRICORN
Atacama Desert
Gran Chaco
Paraguay R.
Paraná R.

Easter Island
Aconcagua 22,834 ft. 6,960 m
Pampas

SOUTH PACIFIC OCEAN
Chiloé Island
Valdés Peninsula -131 ft. -40 m

Patagonia
ANDES

Falkland Islands
South Georgia

Tierra del Fuego
Scotia Sea
South Sandwich Islands

Strait of Magellan

South Shetland Islands
South Orkney Islands

Antarctic Peninsula

ANTARCTIC CIRCLE
Bellingshausen Sea
Weddell Sea

Ellsworth Land
Ronne Ice Shelf
Berkner Island

Ross Sea
Marie Byrd Land
Vinson Massif 16,066 ft. 4,897 m

Ross Ice Shelf
TRANSANTARCTIC MOUNTAINS

150°W 120°W 90°W 60°W 30°W
60°N
30°N
0°
30°S
60°S

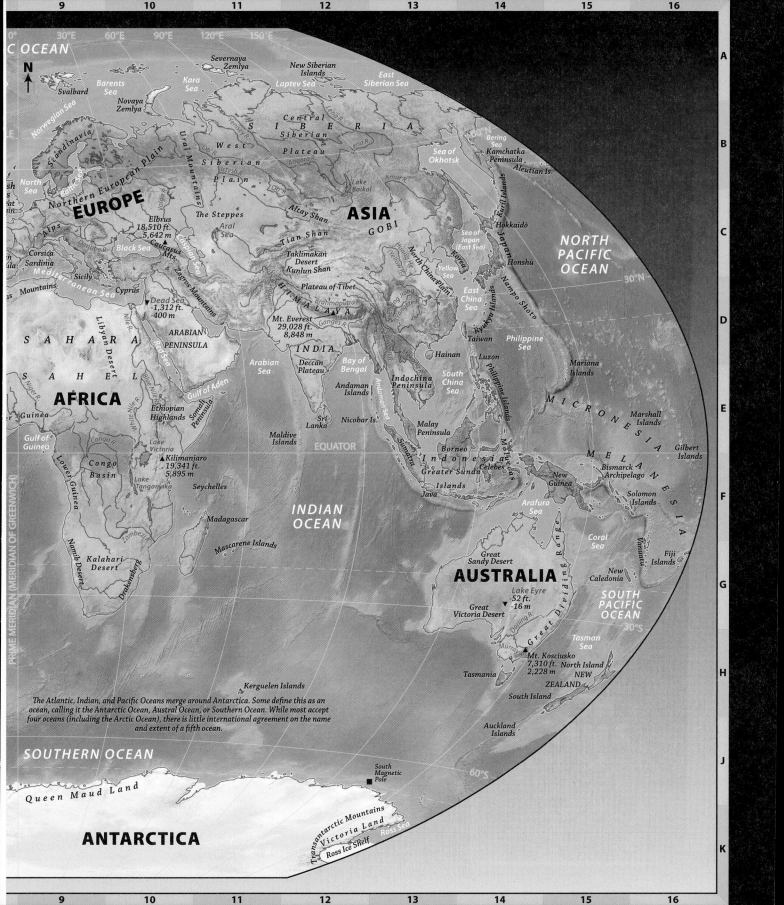

ARCTIC OCEAN

N

EUROPE

Svalbard

Norwegian Sea

Barents Sea

Novaya Zemlya

Kara Sea

Severnaya Zemlya

New Siberian Islands

Laptev Sea

East Siberian Sea

Scandinavia

North Sea

Baltic Sea

Northern European Plain

Ural Mountains

Ob' R.

West Siberian Plain

C e n t r a l Siberian Plateau

Yenisey R.

Lena R.

Bering Sea

Kamchatka Peninsula

Aleutian Is.

NORTH PACIFIC OCEAN

Alps

The Steppes

Volga R.

Elbrus 18,510 ft. 5,642 m

Caucasus Mts.

Irtysh R.

Ob' R.

Angara R.

Lake Baikal

Amur R.

Sea of Okhotsk

S I B E R I A

ASIA

Altay Shan

GOBI

Sea of Japan (East Sea)

Hokkaidō

Kuril Islands

Japan

Honshū

Corsica

Sardinia

Sicily

Mediterranean Sea

Black Sea

Cyprus

Caspian Sea

Zagros Mountains

Tian Shan

Taklimakan Desert

Kunlun Shan

Plateau of Tibet

Huang He (Yellow R.)

Yangtze R.

North China Plain

Korea

Yellow Sea

Nampo Shoto

30°N

Mountains

Dead Sea -1,312 ft. -400 m

Red Sea

ARABIAN PENINSULA

Nile R.

H I M A L A Y A

Mt. Everest 29,028 ft. 8,848 m

Brahmaputra R.

Ganges R.

Mekong R.

Xi Jiang

Hainan

East China Sea

Taiwan

Ryukyu Islands

Luzon

Philippine Sea

Mariana Islands

SAHARA

Libyan Desert

SAHEL

AFRICA

Niger R.

White Nile R.

Blue Nile R.

Ethiopian Highlands

Gulf of Aden

Somali Peninsula

INDIA

Deccan Plateau

Arabian Sea

Bay of Bengal

Andaman Islands

Andaman Sea

Indochina Peninsula

South China Sea

Philippine Islands

MICRONESIA

Gulf of Guinea

Guinea

Sri Lanka

Nicobar Is.

Malay Peninsula

Marshall Islands

Gilbert Islands

Lake Victoria

Kilimanjaro 19,341 ft. 5,895 m

Maldive Islands

EQUATOR

Sumatra

Borneo

I n d o n e s i a

Greater Sunda

Moluccas

Celebes

New Guinea

Bismarck Archipelago

MELANESIA

Lower Guinea

Congo R.

Congo Basin

Lake Tanganyika

Seychelles

Java

Islands

Solomon Islands

Namib Desert

Madagascar

Mascarene Islands

INDIAN OCEAN

Arafura Sea

Coral Sea

Vanuatu

New Caledonia

Fiji Islands

Kalahari Desert

Drakensberg

Zambezi R.

Great Sandy Desert

AUSTRALIA

Great Dividing Range

SOUTH PACIFIC OCEAN

30°S

Great Victoria Desert

Lake Eyre -52 ft. -16 m

Darling R.

Tasman Sea

Murray R.

Mt. Kosciusko 7,310 ft. 2,228 m

North Island

Tasmania

NEW ZEALAND

South Island

Kerguelen Islands

Auckland Islands

The Atlantic, Indian, and Pacific Oceans merge around Antarctica. Some define this as an ocean, calling it the Antarctic Ocean, Austral Ocean, or Southern Ocean. While most accept four oceans (including the Arctic Ocean), there is little international agreement on the name and extent of a fifth ocean.

SOUTHERN OCEAN

South Magnetic Pole

60°S

Queen Maud Land

ANTARCTICA

Transantarctic Mountains

Victoria Land

Ross Ice Shelf

Ross Sea

PRIME MERIDIAN (MERIDIAN OF GREENWICH)

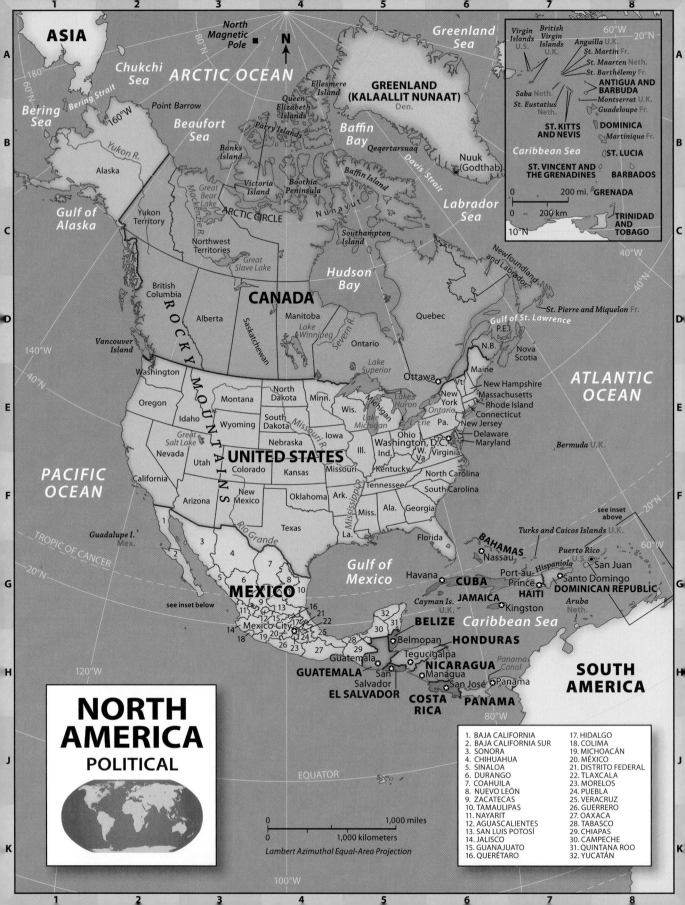

NORTH AMERICA
POLITICAL

ASIA

Chukchi Sea

ARCTIC OCEAN

North Magnetic Pole

N

Greenland Sea

Bering Strait

Point Barrow

Beaufort Sea

Ellesmere Island

Queen Elizabeth Islands

GREENLAND (KALAALLIT NUNAAT) Den.

Bering Sea

Alaska

Yukon R.

Banks Island

Parry Islands

Baffin Bay

Qeqertarsuaq

Nuuk (Godthab)

Gulf of Alaska

Yukon Territory

Victoria Island

Boothia Peninsula

Baffin Island

Davis Strait

Great Bear Lake

ARCTIC CIRCLE

Mackenzie R.

Northwest Territories

Nunavut

Southampton Island

Labrador Sea

Great Slave Lake

Hudson Bay

Newfoundland and Labrador

Vancouver Island

British Columbia

CANADA

ROCKY MOUNTAINS

Alberta

Saskatchewan

Manitoba

Lake Winnipeg

Severn R.

Ontario

Quebec

St. Pierre and Miquelon Fr.

Gulf of St. Lawrence

P.E.I.

N.B.

Nova Scotia

Washington

Oregon

Idaho

Montana

Wyoming

North Dakota

South Dakota

Minn.

Wis.

Lake Superior

Michigan

Lake Huron

L. Ontario

Maine

New Hampshire

Massachusetts

ATLANTIC OCEAN

Ottawa

New York

Vt.

Rhode Island

Connecticut

New Jersey

Lake Michigan

L. Erie

Pa.

PACIFIC OCEAN

Nevada

Great Salt Lake

Utah

UNITED STATES

Colorado

Nebraska

Iowa

Ill.

Ind.

Ohio

W. Va.

Washington, D.C.

Delaware

Maryland

Virginia

Bermuda U.K.

California

Kansas

Missouri

Kentucky

North Carolina

Arizona

New Mexico

Oklahoma

Ark.

Tennessee

South Carolina

TROPIC OF CANCER

Guadalupe I. Mex.

Texas

Miss.

Ala.

Georgia

Rio Grande

Mississippi R.

La.

Florida

Gulf of Mexico

BAHAMAS

Turks and Caicos Islands U.K.

Puerto Rico U.S.

San Juan

Nassau

Hispaniola

Havana

Port-au-Prince

Santo Domingo

see inset above

MEXICO

see inset below

CUBA

JAMAICA

HAITI

DOMINICAN REPUBLIC

Aruba Neth.

Cayman Is. U.K.

Kingston

Mexico City

BELIZE

Caribbean Sea

Belmopan

HONDURAS

Tegucigalpa

NICARAGUA

Panama Canal

SOUTH AMERICA

Guatemala

GUATEMALA

San Salvador

EL SALVADOR

Managua

San José

COSTA RICA

Panama

PANAMA

EQUATOR

North Magnetic Pole
North

Virgin Islands U.S.

British Virgin Islands U.K.

Anguilla U.K.

St. Martin Fr.

St. Maarten Neth.

St. Barthélemy Fr.

ANTIGUA AND BARBUDA

Saba Neth.

St. Eustatius Neth.

Montserrat U.K.

Guadeloupe Fr.

ST. KITTS AND NEVIS

DOMINICA

Martinique Fr.

Caribbean Sea

ST. LUCIA

ST. VINCENT AND THE GRENADINES

BARBADOS

0   200 mi.   GRENADA

0   200 km

10°N

TRINIDAD AND TOBAGO

1. BAJA CALIFORNIA
2. BAJA CALIFORNIA SUR
3. SONORA
4. CHIHUAHUA
5. SINALOA
6. DURANGO
7. COAHUILA
8. NUEVO LEÓN
9. ZACATECAS
10. TAMAULIPAS
11. NAYARIT
12. AGUASCALIENTES
13. SAN LUIS POTOSÍ
14. JALISCO
15. GUANAJUATO
16. QUERÉTARO
17. HIDALGO
18. COLIMA
19. MICHOACÁN
20. MÉXICO
21. DISTRITO FEDERAL
22. TLAXCALA
23. MORELOS
24. PUEBLA
25. VERACRUZ
26. GUERRERO
27. OAXACA
28. TABASCO
29. CHIAPAS
30. CAMPECHE
31. QUINTANA ROO
32. YUCATÁN

0   1,000 miles

0   1,000 kilometers

Lambert Azimuthal Equal-Area Projection

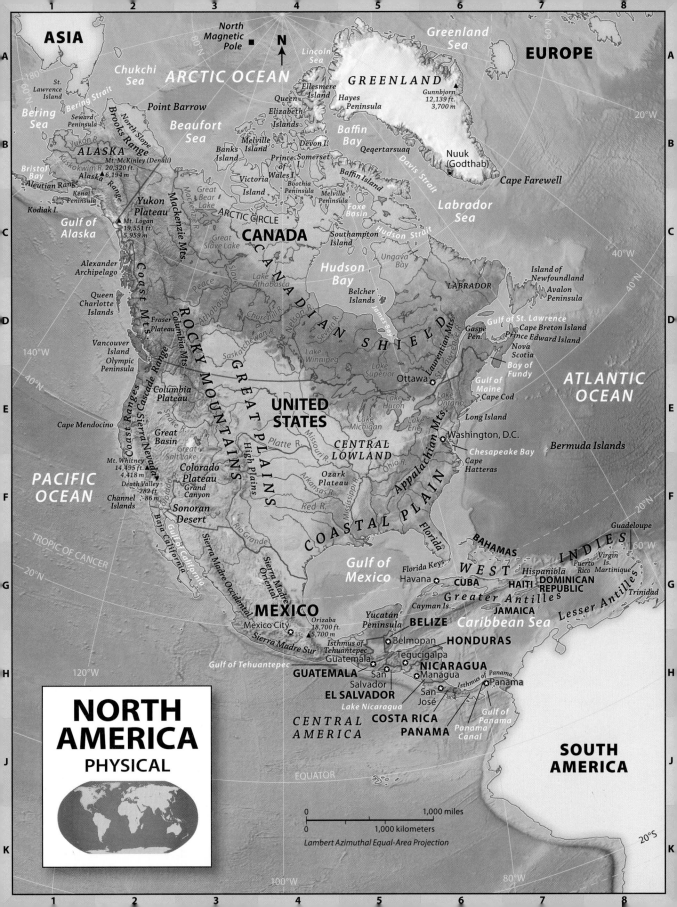

NORTH AMERICA
PHYSICAL

Lambert Azimuthal Equal-Area Projection

0 — 1,000 miles
0 — 1,000 kilometers

SOUTH AMERICA
POLITICAL

Caribbean Sea

N

0   1,000 miles
0   1,000 kilometers
Lambert Azimuthal Equal-Area Projection

Santa Marta
Barranquilla
Cartagena
Maracaibo
Caracas
Valencia
VENEZUELA
Ciudad Guayana
GUYANA
Georgetown
SURINAME
Paramaribo
Cayenne
FRENCH GUIANA
Fr.
Bucaramanga
San Cristóbal
Medellín
Bogotá
Lake Maracaibo
Orinoco R.
Boundary claimed by Suriname

Malpelo I. Col.
Cali
COLOMBIA
Boa Vista
Rio Negro
Marajó Island

Esmeraldas
Quito
ECUADOR
Guayaquil
0°
A M A Z O N
Amazon R.
Manaus
Santarém
Belém
São Luís
EQUATOR
0°

Iquitos
Marañón R.
B A S I N
Amazon R.
Fortaleza
Teresina

PERU
Ucayali R.
Purus R.
Madeira R.
Tapajós R.
Xingu R.
Campina Grande
Natal
Recife

Callao
Lima
Ayacucho
Machu Picchu
Cuzco
Río Branco
Pôrto Velho
Araguaia R.
Tocantins R.
São Francisco R.
BRAZIL
Salvador

Arequipa
Arica
Iquique
Oruro
La Paz
BOLIVIA
Sucre
Santa Cruz
Trinidad
Lake Titicaca
Brasília
Goiânia
Uberlândia
Campo Grande
Uberaba
Belo Horizonte

20°S
TROPIC OF CAPRICORN
Antofagasta
Tarija
Salta
PARAGUAY
Londrina
Paraguay R.
Paraná R.
Campinas
São Paulo
Nova Iguaçu
Rio de Janeiro
Santos
20°S

San Félix I. *San Ambrosio I.*
Chile
CHILE
San Miguel de Tucumán
Asunción
Curitiba

La Serena
Coquimbo
Córdoba
Uruguaiana
Santa Maria
Pôrto Alegre

Juan Fernández Is.
Chile
Valparaíso
Santiago
Mendoza
Rosario
URUGUAY
Montevideo
ATLANTIC OCEAN

Concepción
ARGENTINA
Buenos Aires
La Plata
Mar del Plata
Río de la Plata
Colorado R.
Negro R.
Bahía Blanca

PACIFIC OCEAN
Puerto Montt
40°S
40°S

Comodoro Rivadavia

*Falkland Islands
(Islas Malvinas)*
Stanley
Administered by United Kingdom
Claimed by Arg.

Río Gallegos
Punta Arenas
Ushuaia
Strait of Magellan
Cape Horn
South Georgia Island
U.K.

100°W   80°W   60°W   40°W   20°W

80°W   60°W   40°W

Caribbean Sea

N

0   1,000 miles
0   1,000 kilometers
Lambert Azimuthal Equal-Area Projection

VENEZUELA
Caracas
GUYANA
SURINAME
Georgetown
Paramaribo
Cayenne
FRENCH GUIANA

Lake Maracaibo
Orinoco R.
LLANOS
Bogotá
Angel Falls
Total drop
3,212 ft. 979 m
GUIANA HIGHLANDS

COLOMBIA

Boundary claimed
by Suriname

Marajó Island

EQUATOR

Quito
ECUADOR
Rio Negro
A M A Z O N
Amazon R.

Marañón R.

S e l   v   a   s
B   A   S   I   N

PERU
Amazon R.
Ucayali R.
Purus R.
Madeira R.
Tapajós R.
Xingu R.
Araguaia R.
Tocantins R.
São Francisco R.

BRAZIL

Lima
Machu Picchu
Lake Titicaca
La Paz
BOLIVIA
Sucre
Altiplano
Salar de Uyuni

MATO GROSSO PLATEAU

Brasília

B   R   A   Z   I   L   I   A   N
H   I   G   H   L   A   N   D   S

C H A C O
Paraguay R.
Paraná R.

PARAGUAY
Asunción
Iguazú Falls

G R A N
P A M P A S
Paraná R.
Uruguay R.

CHILE

Aconcagua
22,834 ft.
6,960 m
Santiago
Buenos Aires
URUGUAY
Montevideo
Rio de la Plata

San Ambrosio I.
San Félix I.

Juan Fernández Is.

ARGENTINA

Colorado R.
Negro R.

ATLANTIC OCEAN

Chiloé Island
Valdés Peninsula
-131 ft.
-40 m

Taitao Peninsula

P A T A G O N I A

PACIFIC OCEAN

Wellington I.

Falkland Islands
(Islas Malvinas)
Stanley

Strait of Magellan
Cape Horn
Tierra del Fuego

South Georgia Island

Malpelo I.

SOUTH AMERICA
PHYSICAL

80°W   60°W   40°W
0°   20°S   40°S

TROPIC OF CAPRICORN

100°W   80°W   60°W   40°W   20°W

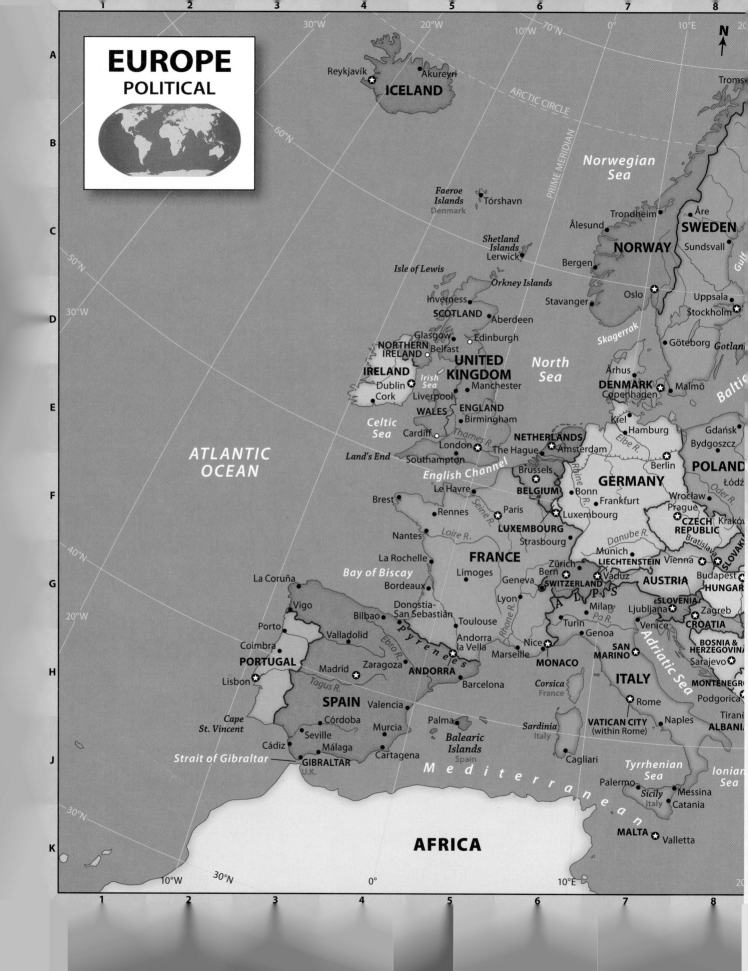

EUROPE
POLITICAL

EUROPE
PHYSICAL

Grid references (top): 1 2 3 4 5 6 7 8

Grid references (left): A B C D E F G H J K

Reykjavík
ICELAND

ARCTIC CIRCLE

PRIME MERIDIAN

Norwegian Sea

Faeroe Islands

Shetland Islands

NORWAY

SCANDINA...

Gulf...

Outer Hebrides

Orkney Islands

Oslo

SWEDEN

British Isles

Highlands

Stockholm

Edinburgh

Skagerrak

Kattega...

Gotlan...

50°N

30°W

Belfast

UNITED KINGDOM

North Sea

Jutland

Zealand

DENMARK

Copenhagen

Baltic...

IRELAND

Dublin

Irish Sea

Great Britain

Elbe R.

Berlin

Celtic Sea

Cardiff

London

Thames R.

NETHERLANDS

Amsterdam

ATLANTIC OCEAN

Land's End

English Channel

Brussels

BELGIUM

Rhine R.

GERMANY

N... POLAND

Brittany

Paris

Seine R.

Luxembourg

LUXEMBOURG

Prague

CZECH REPUBLIC

Loire R.

Danube R.

Bratislava

SLOVAK...

40°N

20°W

FRANCE

LIECHTENSTEIN

Vienna

Budapest

Bay of Biscay

Bern

Vaduz

AUSTRIA

HUNGAR...

SWITZERLAND

Mont Blanc 15,771 ft. 4,807 m

SLOVENIA

Massif Central

ALPS

Ljubljana

Zagreb

Cantabrian Mountains

Andorra la Vella

Rhône

Po R.

A p e n...

CROATIA

IBERIAN

Douro R.

Pyrenees

ANDORRA

Riviera

MONACO

SAN MARINO

Adriatic Sea

BOSNIA & HERZEGOVIN...

Madrid

SPAIN

Corsica

ITALY

Sarajevo

Lisbon

PORTUGAL

Tagus R.

Rome

VATICAN CITY (within Rome)

MONTENEGRO

Podgorica

Cape St. Vincent

PENINSULA

Baetic Mountains

Balearic Islands

Sardinia

Tirane

ALBANI...

30°N

Strait of Gibraltar

GIBRALTAR

Mediterranean

Tyrrhenian Sea

Ionia... Sea...

Sicily

Etna 10,902 ft. 3,323 m

MALTA

Valletta

AFRICA

10°W

30°N

0°

10°E

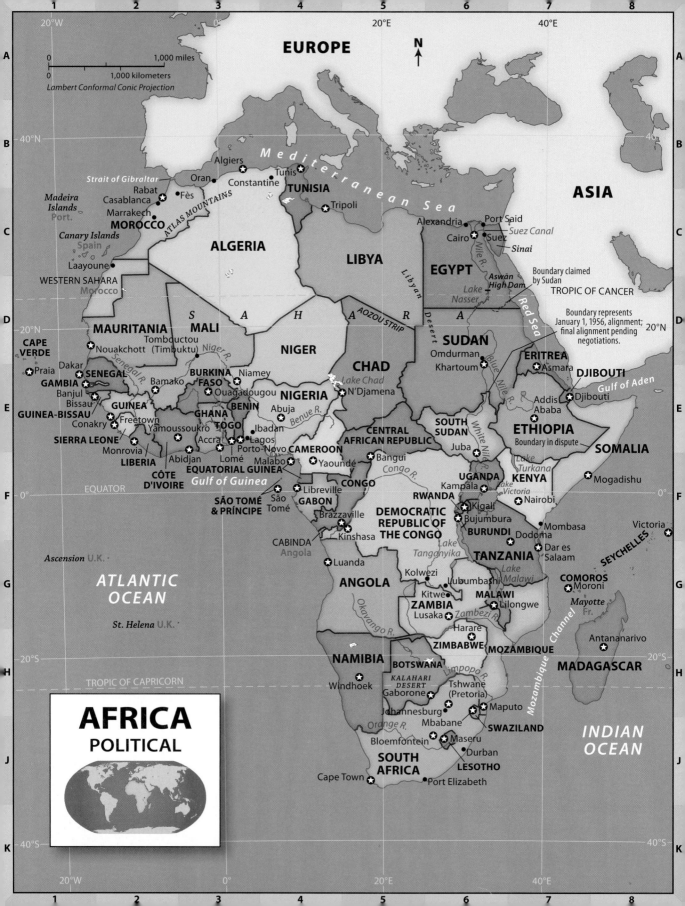

AFRICA
POLITICAL

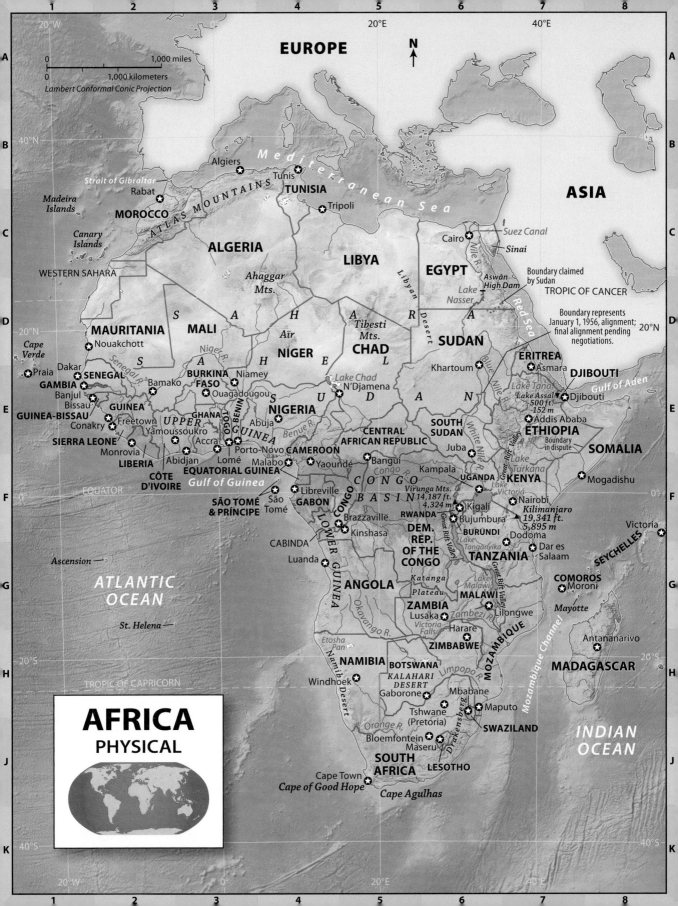

AFRICA
PHYSICAL

EUROPE

ASIA

ATLANTIC OCEAN

INDIAN OCEAN

N

0   1,000 miles
0   1,000 kilometers
Lambert Conformal Conic Projection

20°W 0° 20°E 40°E

Mediterranean Sea

Strait of Gibraltar

Madeira Islands

Canary Islands

Algiers
Tunis
TUNISIA
Tripoli
Rabat
MOROCCO
ATLAS MOUNTAINS
ALGERIA
LIBYA
Cairo
Suez Canal
Sinai
Boundary claimed by Sudan
TROPIC OF CANCER
EGYPT
Aswân High Dam
Lake Nasser
Nile R.
Red Sea

WESTERN SAHARA

Boundary represents January 1, 1956, alignment; final alignment pending negotiations.

Cape Verde

MAURITANIA
Nouakchott
MALI
Ahaggar Mts.
Aïr
NIGER
Tibesti Mts.
CHAD
Libyan Desert
SUDAN
Khartoum
Blue Nile
Lake Tana
ERITREA
Asmara
DJIBOUTI
Djibouti
Gulf of Aden
Lake Assal -500 ft. -152 m

S A H A R A

Praia
Dakar
SENEGAL
Senegal R.
Niger R.
Bamako
BURKINA FASO
Niamey
Ouagadougou
Lake Chad
N'Djamena
NIGERIA
Abuja
CENTRAL AFRICAN REPUBLIC
SOUTH SUDAN
Juba
White Nile R.
Addis Ababa
ETHIOPIA
Boundary in dispute
SOMALIA

GAMBIA
Banjul
Bissau
GUINEA-BISSAU
Conakry
GUINEA
Freetown
SIERRA LEONE
Monrovia
LIBERIA
GHANA
Yamoussoukro
Accra
Abidjan
CÔTE D'IVOIRE
UPPER GUINEA
Benue R.
TOGO
BENIN
Porto-Novo
Lomé
Malabo
EQUATORIAL GUINEA
CAMEROON
Yaoundé
Bangui
Kampala
UGANDA
Lake Turkana
KENYA
Mogadishu

EQUATOR
Gulf of Guinea
SÃO TOMÉ & PRÍNCIPE
São Tomé
Libreville
GABON
CONGO
LOWER GUINEA
Brazzaville
Kinshasa
RWANDA
Kigali
Bujumbura
BURUNDI
Dodoma
Nairobi
Kilimanjaro 19,341 ft. 5,895 m
CONGO BASIN
Virunga Mts. 14,187 ft. 4,324 m
Lake Victoria
Great Rift Valley
Congo R.
SEYCHELLES
Victoria

CABINDA
Luanda
ANGOLA
DEM. REP. OF THE CONGO
Katanga Plateau
Lake Tanganyika
TANZANIA
Dar es Salaam
COMOROS
Moroni
Mayotte

Ascension

St. Helena

Okavango R.
Lake Malawi
ZAMBIA
Lusaka
MALAWI
Lilongwe
Antananarivo
MADAGASCAR

Victoria Falls
Zambezi R.
Harare
ZIMBABWE
MOZAMBIQUE
Mozambique Channel

TROPIC OF CAPRICORN
Etosha Pan
Namib Desert
Windhoek
NAMIBIA
BOTSWANA
KALAHARI DESERT
Gaborone
Limpopo R.
Mbabane
Maputo
SWAZILAND

Tshwane (Pretoria)
Orange R.
Bloemfontein
Maseru
LESOTHO
Drakensberg
SOUTH AFRICA
Cape Town
Cape of Good Hope
Cape Agulhas

20°N
20°N
EQUATOR
20°S
20°S
40°S

40°N
40°N
20°W   0°   20°E   40°E

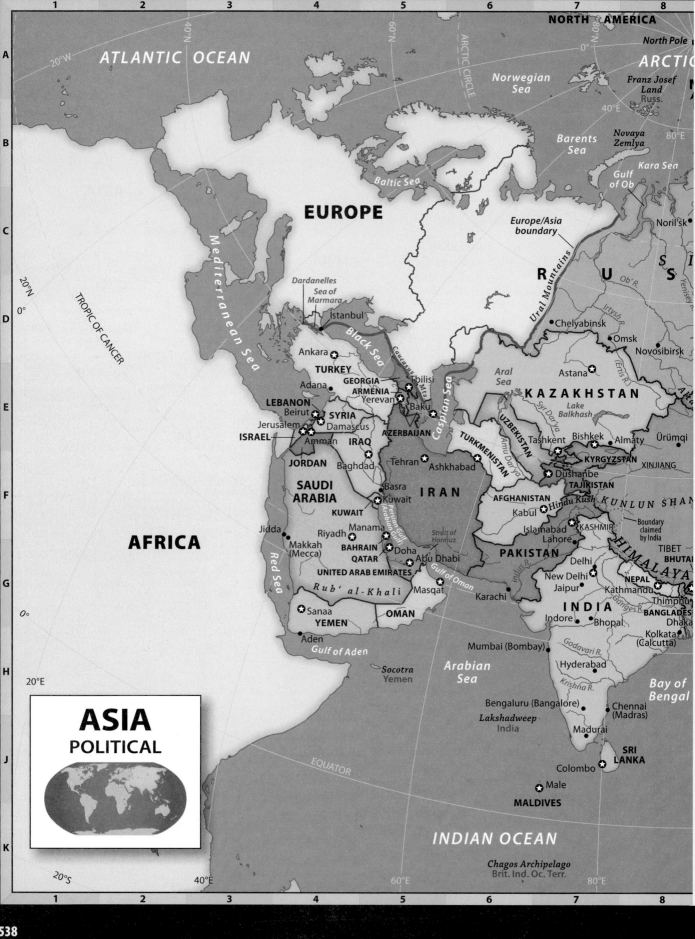

ASIA
POLITICAL

NORTH AMERICA

North Pole

ARCTIC

ATLANTIC OCEAN

Norwegian Sea

Franz Josef Land Russ.

Novaya Zemlya

Barents Sea

Kara Sea

Gulf of Ob

Noril'sk

EUROPE

Baltic Sea

Europe/Asia boundary

R U S S I

Ob' R.

Ural Mountains

Chelyabinsk

Omsk

Irtysh R.

Novosibirsk

Mediterranean Sea

Dardanelles
Sea of Marmara

İstanbul

Ankara

Black Sea

TURKEY

Tbilisi

Caucasus Mts.

GEORGIA

Adana

ARMENIA

Yerevan

Baku

Astana

Aral Sea

KAZAKHSTAN

Lake Balkhash

Syr Darya

LEBANON

Beirut

SYRIA

Damascus

Caspian Sea

AZERBAIJAN

UZBEKISTAN

Tashkent

Bishkek

Almaty

Ürümqi

Jerusalem

Amman

ISRAEL

IRAQ

Baghdad

Tehran

TURKMENISTAN

Amu Darya

Dushanbe

KYRGYZSTAN

XINJIANG

JORDAN

SAUDI ARABIA

Basra

Kuwait

IRAN

Ashkhabad

TAJIKISTAN

KUNLUN SHAN

KUWAIT

Jidda

Makkah (Mecca)

Riyadh

Manama

BAHRAIN

QATAR

Doha

Persian Gulf
Arabian Gulf

Strait of Hormuz

AFGHANISTAN

Kabul

Hindu Kush

Islamabad

Lahore

KASHMIR

Boundary claimed by India

TIBET

BHUTA

HIMALAYA

Red Sea

Rub' al-Khali

UNITED ARAB EMIRATES

Abu Dhabi

Masqat

Gulf of Oman

PAKISTAN

Delhi

New Delhi

Jaipur

Indus R.

Karachi

Kathmandu

NEPAL

Thimphu

BANGLADES

Dhaka

AFRICA

Sanaa

YEMEN

Aden

Gulf of Aden

OMAN

Socotra Yemen

Arabian Sea

Indore

Bhopal

INDIA

Godavari R.

Ganges R.

Kolkata (Calcutta)

Mumbai (Bombay)

Hyderabad

Krishna R.

Bay of Bengal

Bengaluru (Bangalore)

Lakshadweep India

Chennai (Madras)

Madurai

SRI LANKA

EQUATOR

Colombo

Male

MALDIVES

INDIAN OCEAN

Chagos Archipelago Brit. Ind. Oc. Terr.

TROPIC OF CANCER

20°N

0°

20°E

0°

20°S

20°W

40°N

40°E

80°E

60°N

0°

80°E

60°E

40°E

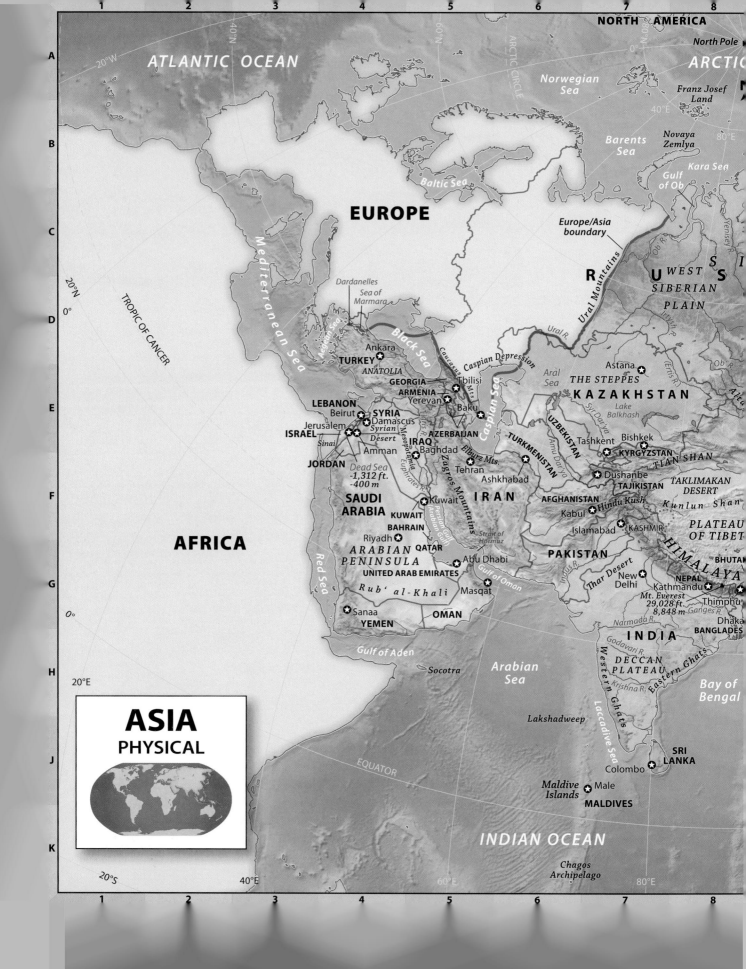

ASIA
PHYSICAL

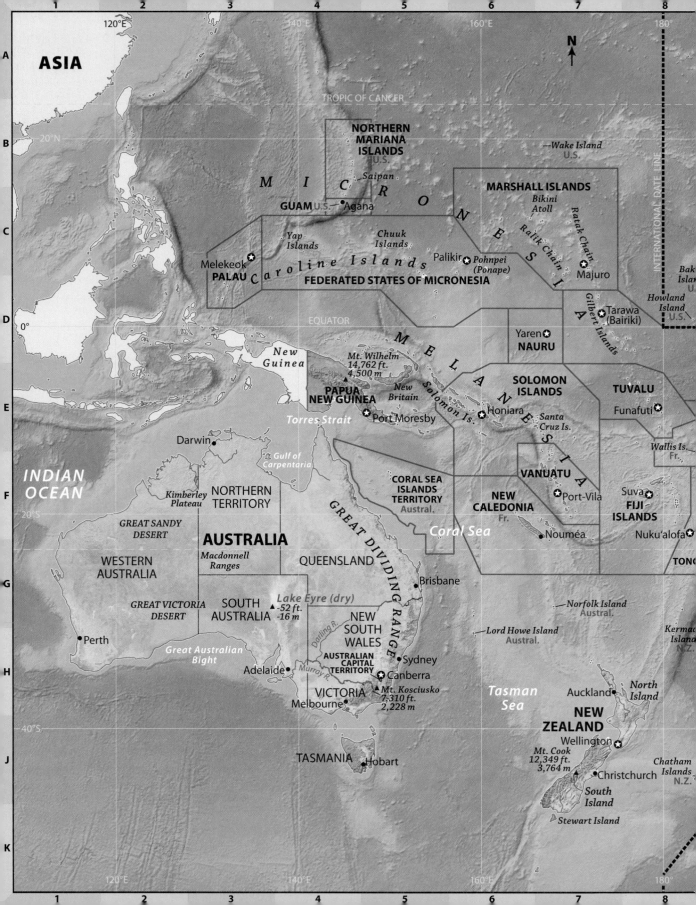

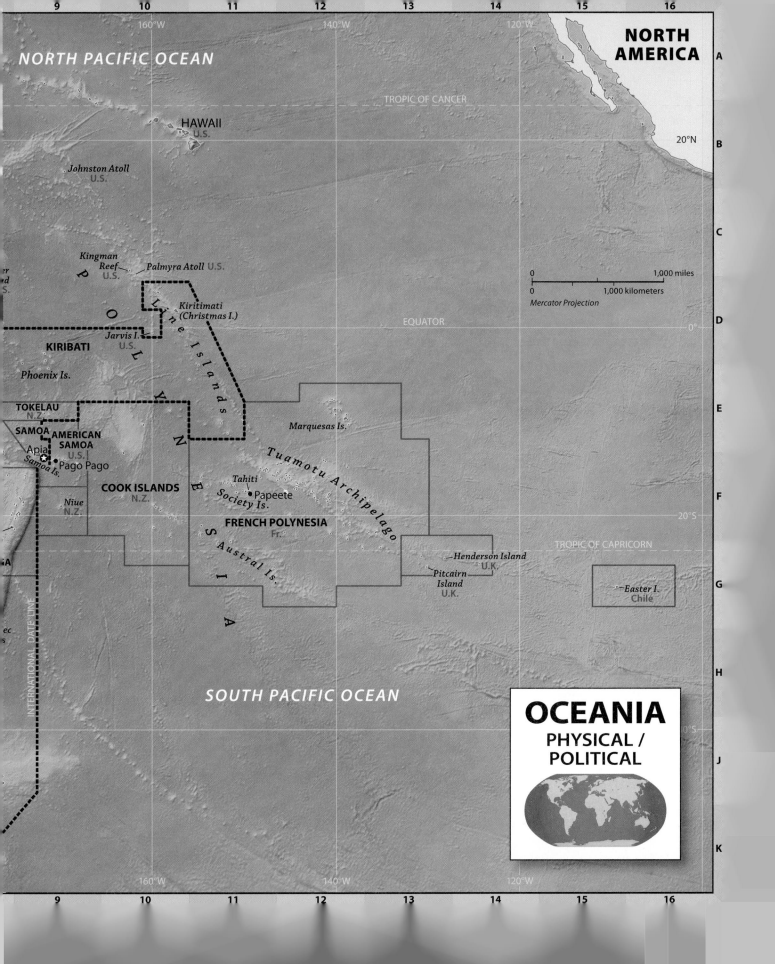

NORTH PACIFIC OCEAN

NORTH AMERICA

TROPIC OF CANCER

20°N

HAWAII
U.S.

Johnston Atoll
U.S.

Kingman
Reef
U.S.

Palmyra Atoll U.S.

Kiritimati
(Christmas I.)

EQUATOR

0°

Jarvis I.
U.S.

KIRIBATI

Phoenix Is.

TOKELAU
N.Z.

SAMOA

AMERICAN
SAMOA
U.S.

Apia

Pago Pago

Samoa Is.

COOK ISLANDS
N.Z.

Niue
N.Z.

Marquesas Is.

Tahiti

Papeete

Society Is.

FRENCH POLYNESIA
Fr.

Tuamotu Archipelago

TROPIC OF CAPRICORN

20°S

Austral Is.

Henderson Island
U.K.

Pitcairn
Island
U.K.

Easter I.
Chile

POLYNESIA

Line Islands

INTERNATIONAL DATE LINE

SOUTH PACIFIC OCEAN

160°W

140°W

120°W

0
1,000 miles

0
1,000 kilometers

Mercator Projection

OCEANIA
PHYSICAL /
POLITICAL

PACIFIC RIM
PHYSICAL / POLITICAL

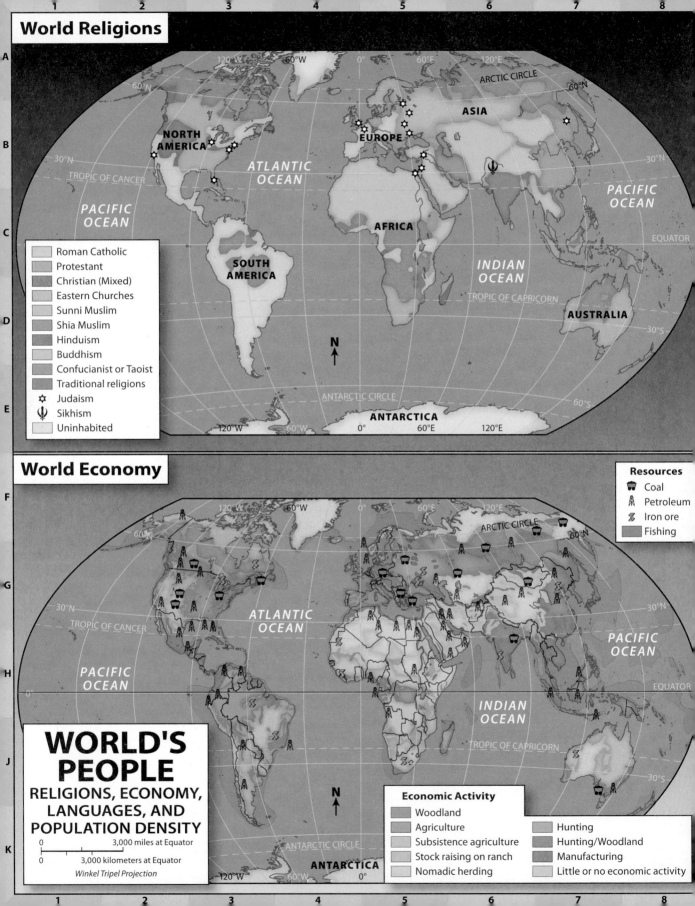

World Religions

A

120°W   60°W   0°   60°E   120°E

ARCTIC CIRCLE

60°N   60°N

ASIA

NORTH
AMERICA

EUROPE

B

30°N   30°N

ATLANTIC
OCEAN

TROPIC OF CANCER

PACIFIC
OCEAN

PACIFIC
OCEAN

AFRICA

C

EQUATOR

SOUTH
AMERICA

INDIAN
OCEAN

Roman Catholic
Protestant
Christian (Mixed)
Eastern Churches
Sunni Muslim
Shia Muslim
Hinduism
Buddhism
Confucianist or Taoist
Traditional religions
☆ Judaism
Ѱ Sikhism
Uninhabited

TROPIC OF CAPRICORN

AUSTRALIA

D

30°S

N
↑

E

60°S

ANTARCTIC CIRCLE

120°W   60°W   0°   60°E   120°E

ANTARCTICA

World Economy

Resources
🜨 Coal
🛢 Petroleum
⚒ Iron ore
Fishing

F

120°W   60°W   0°   60°E   120°E

ARCTIC CIRCLE

60°N   60°N

G

TROPIC OF CANCER   30°N   30°N

ATLANTIC
OCEAN

PACIFIC
OCEAN

PACIFIC
OCEAN

H

0°   EQUATOR

INDIAN
OCEAN

WORLD'S
PEOPLE
RELIGIONS, ECONOMY,
LANGUAGES, AND
POPULATION DENSITY

TROPIC OF CAPRICORN

30°S

J

N
↑

Economic Activity

Woodland
Agriculture   Hunting
Subsistence agriculture   Hunting/Woodland
Stock raising on ranch   Manufacturing
Nomadic herding   Little or no economic activity

0   3,000 miles at Equator

0   3,000 kilometers at Equator

Winkel Tripel Projection

K

ANTARCTIC CIRCLE

120°W   60°W   0°

ANTARCTICA

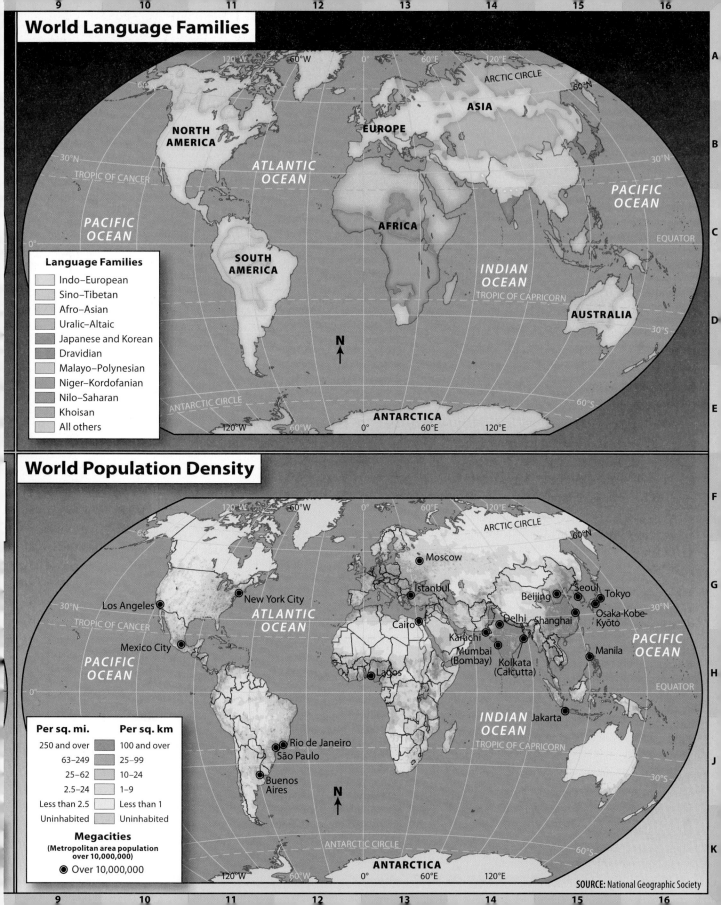

World Language Families

Language Families

- Indo–European
- Sino–Tibetan
- Afro–Asian
- Uralic–Altaic
- Japanese and Korean
- Dravidian
- Malayo–Polynesian
- Niger–Kordofanian
- Nilo–Saharan
- Khoisan
- All others

NORTH AMERICA

SOUTH AMERICA

EUROPE

ASIA

AFRICA

AUSTRALIA

ANTARCTICA

ATLANTIC OCEAN

PACIFIC OCEAN

PACIFIC OCEAN

INDIAN OCEAN

ARCTIC CIRCLE

TROPIC OF CANCER

EQUATOR

TROPIC OF CAPRICORN

ANTARCTIC CIRCLE

N

World Population Density

Per sq. mi.	Per sq. km
250 and over	100 and over
63–249	25–99
25–62	10–24
2.5–24	1–9
Less than 2.5	Less than 1
Uninhabited	Uninhabited

Megacities
(Metropolitan area population over 10,000,000)
- ◉ Over 10,000,000

Los Angeles
New York City
Mexico City
Rio de Janeiro
São Paulo
Buenos Aires
Lagos
Cairo
Istanbul
Moscow
Karachi
Mumbai (Bombay)
Delhi
Kolkata (Calcutta)
Beijing
Shanghai
Seoul
Tokyo
Osaka-Kobe-Kyōto
Manila
Jakarta

ATLANTIC OCEAN

PACIFIC OCEAN

PACIFIC OCEAN

INDIAN OCEAN

ARCTIC CIRCLE

TROPIC OF CANCER

EQUATOR

TROPIC OF CAPRICORN

ANTARCTIC CIRCLE

ANTARCTICA

N

SOURCE: National Geographic Society

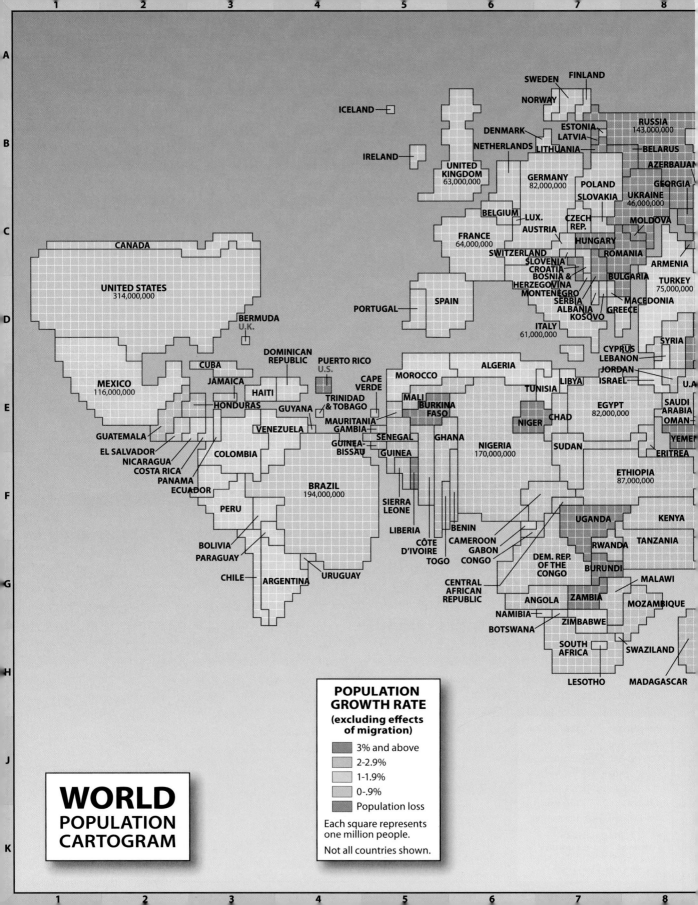

WORLD
POPULATION
CARTOGRAM

POPULATION GROWTH RATE
(excluding effects of migration)

- 3% and above
- 2-2.9%
- 1-1.9%
- 0-.9%
- Population loss

Each square represents one million people.

Not all countries shown.

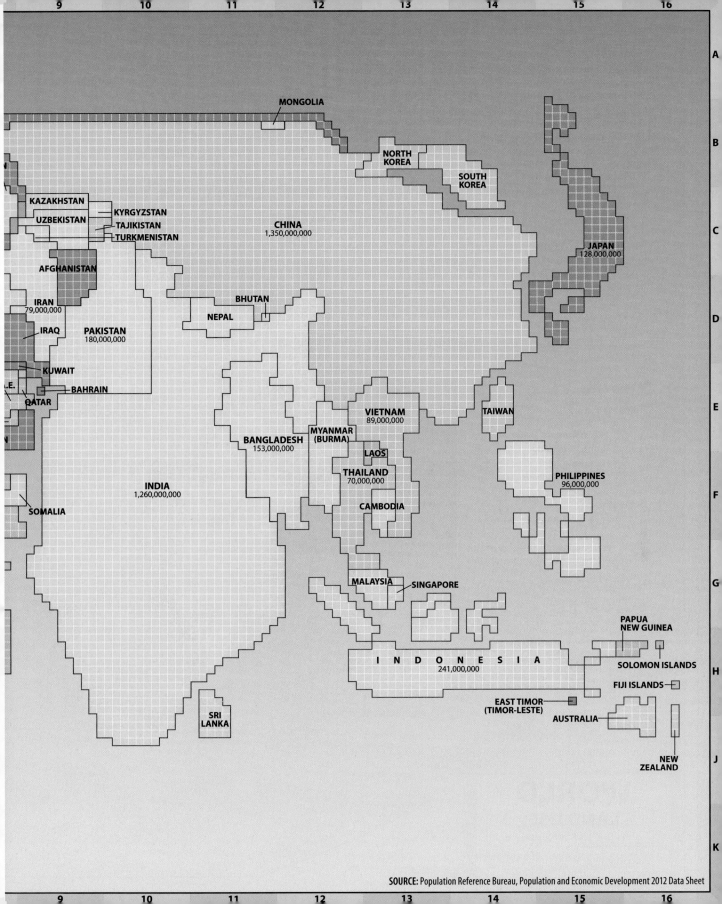

MONGOLIA

NORTH KOREA

SOUTH KOREA

KAZAKHSTAN

KYRGYZSTAN

UZBEKISTAN

TAJIKISTAN

TURKMENISTAN

CHINA
1,350,000,000

JAPAN
128,000,000

AFGHANISTAN

IRAN
79,000,000

IRAQ

PAKISTAN
180,000,000

BHUTAN

NEPAL

KUWAIT

U.A.E.

BAHRAIN

QATAR

VIETNAM
89,000,000

TAIWAN

BANGLADESH
153,000,000

MYANMAR
(BURMA)

LAOS

THAILAND
70,000,000

PHILIPPINES
96,000,000

INDIA
1,260,000,000

CAMBODIA

SOMALIA

MALAYSIA

SINGAPORE

PAPUA
NEW GUINEA

I N D O N E S I A
241,000,000

SOLOMON ISLANDS

FIJI ISLANDS

EAST TIMOR
(TIMOR-LESTE)

SRI
LANKA

AUSTRALIA

NEW
ZEALAND

SOURCE: Population Reference Bureau, Population and Economic Development 2012 Data Sheet

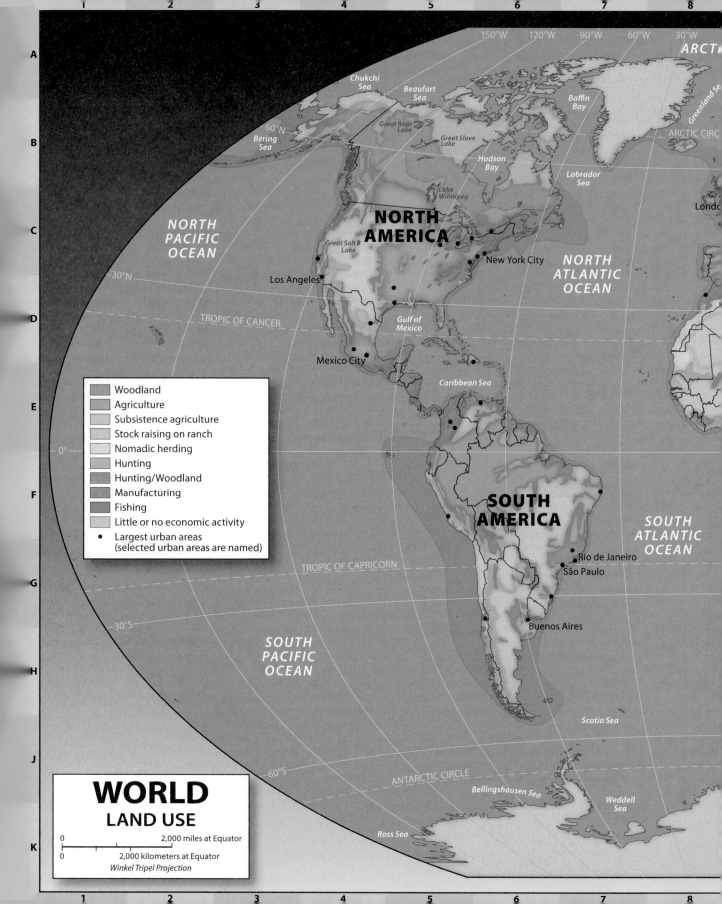

WORLD
LAND USE

Woodland
Agriculture
Subsistence agriculture
Stock raising on ranch
Nomadic herding
Hunting
Hunting/Woodland
Manufacturing
Fishing
Little or no economic activity
• Largest urban areas
(selected urban areas are named)

0   2,000 miles at Equator
0   2,000 kilometers at Equator
Winkel Tripel Projection

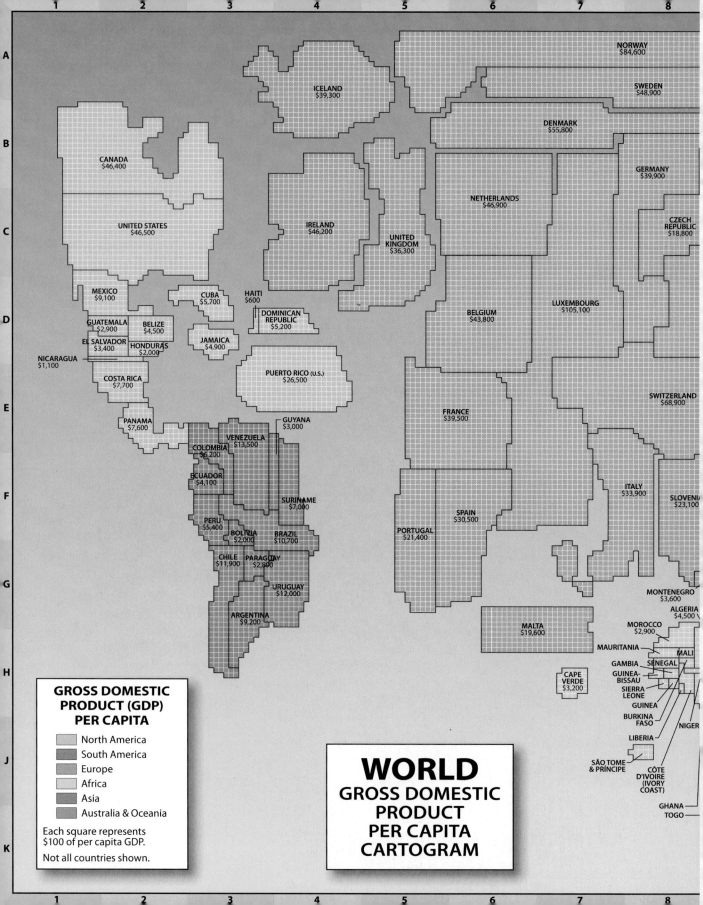

WORLD
GROSS DOMESTIC
PRODUCT
PER CAPITA
CARTOGRAM

GROSS DOMESTIC
PRODUCT (GDP)
PER CAPITA

- North America
- South America
- Europe
- Africa
- Asia
- Australia & Oceania

Each square represents
$100 of per capita GDP.

Not all countries shown.

NORWAY $84,600
SWEDEN $48,900
ICELAND $39,300
DENMARK $55,800
GERMANY $39,900
CANADA $46,400
NETHERLANDS $46,900
CZECH REPUBLIC $18,800
UNITED STATES $46,500
IRELAND $46,200
UNITED KINGDOM $36,300
MEXICO $9,100
CUBA $5,700
HAITI $600
DOMINICAN REPUBLIC $5,200
BELGIUM $43,800
LUXEMBOURG $105,100
GUATEMALA $2,900
BELIZE $4,500
EL SALVADOR $3,400
HONDURAS $2,000
JAMAICA $4,900
NICARAGUA $1,100
COSTA RICA $7,700
PUERTO RICO (U.S.) $26,500
SWITZERLAND $68,900
PANAMA $7,600
GUYANA $3,000
VENEZUELA $13,500
COLOMBIA $6,200
FRANCE $39,500
ECUADOR $4,100
SURINAME $7,000
ITALY $33,900
SLOVENIA $23,100
PERU $5,400
BOLIVIA $2,000
BRAZIL $10,700
SPAIN $30,500
CHILE $11,900
PARAGUAY $2,800
PORTUGAL $21,400
URUGUAY $12,000
MONTENEGRO $3,600
ARGENTINA $9,200
ALGERIA $4,500
MALTA $19,600
MOROCCO $2,900
MAURITANIA
MALI
GAMBIA SENEGAL
CAPE VERDE $3,200
GUINEA-BISSAU
SIERRA LEONE
GUINEA
BURKINA FASO
NIGER
LIBERIA
SÃO TOME & PRÍNCIPE
CÔTE D'IVOIRE (IVORY COAST)
GHANA
TOGO

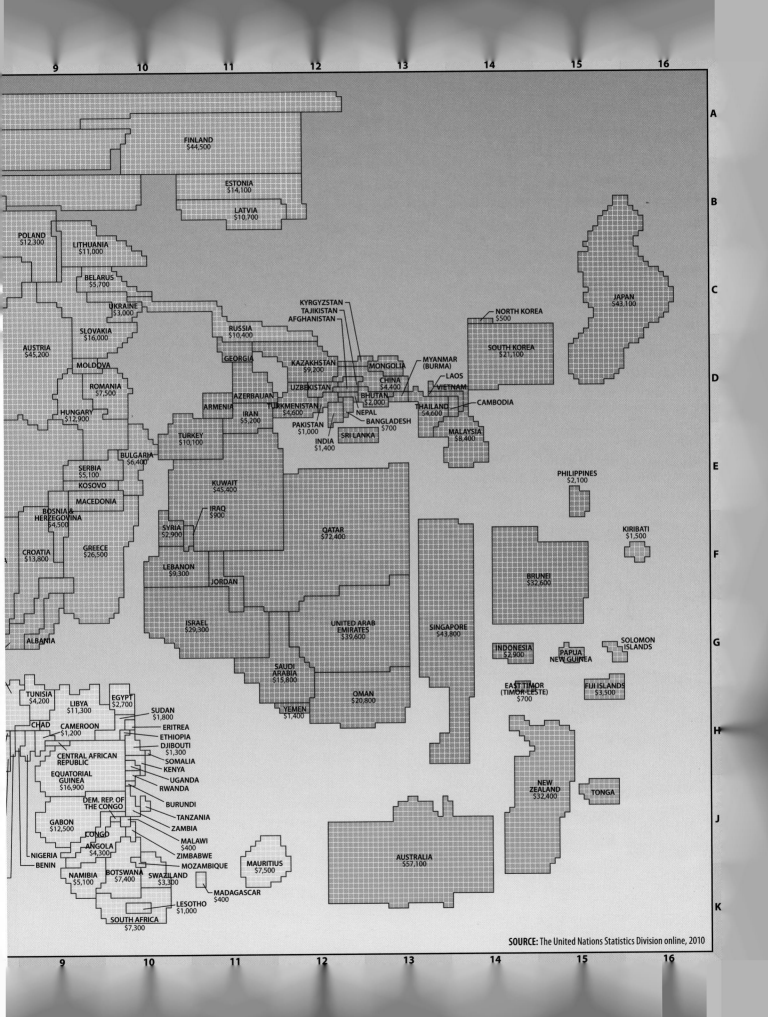

SOURCE: The United Nations Statistics Division online, 2010

How do I study Geography?

Geographers have tried to understand the best way to teach and learn about geography. In order to do this, geographers created the *Five Themes of Geography*. The themes acted as a guide for teaching the basic ideas about geography to students like yourself.

People who teach and study geography, though, thought that the Five Themes were too broad. In 1994, geographers created 18 national geography standards. These standards were more detailed about what should be taught and learned. The Six Essential Elements act as a bridge connecting the Five Themes with the standards.

These pages show you how the Five Themes are related to the Six Essential Elements and the 18 standards.

5 Themes of Geography

1 Location

Location describes where something is. Absolute location describes a place's exact position on the Earth's surface. Relative location expresses where a place is in relation to another place.

2 Place

Place describes the physical and human characteristics that make a location unique.

3 Regions

Regions are areas that share common characteristics.

4 Movement

Movement explains how and why people and things move and are connected.

5 Human-Environment Interaction

Human-Environment Interaction describes the relationship between people and their environment.

6 Essential Elements   # 18 Geography Standards

I. The World in Spatial Terms

Geographers look to see where a place is located. Location acts as a starting point to answer "Where is it?" The location of a place helps you orient yourself as to where you are.

1 How to use maps and other tools.

2 How to use mental maps to organize information.

3 How to analyze the spatial organization of people, places, and environments.

II Places and Regions

Place describes physical characteristics such as landforms, climate, and plant or animal life. It might also describe human characteristics, including language and way of life. Places can also be organized into regions. **Regions** are places united by one or more characteristics.

4 The physical and human characteristics of places.

5 How people create regions to interpret Earth's complexity.

6 How culture and experience influence people's perceptions of places and regions.

III. Physical Systems

Geographers study how physical systems, such as hurricanes, volcanoes, and glaciers, shape the surface of the Earth. They also look at how plants and animals depend upon one another and their surroundings for their survival.

7 The physical processes that shape Earth's surface.

8 The distribution of ecosystems on Earth's surface.

9 The characteristics, distribution, and migration of human populations.

10 The complexity of Earth's cultural mosaics.

11 The patterns and networks of economic interdependence.

IV. Human Systems

People shape the world in which they live. They settle in certain places, but not in others. An ongoing theme in geography is the movement of people, ideas, and goods.

12 The patterns of human settlements.

13 The forces of cooperation and conflict.

14 How human actions modify the physical environment.

V. Environment and Society

How does the relationship between people and their natural surroundings influence the way people live? Geographers study how people use the environment and how their actions affect the environment.

15 How physical systems affect human systems.

16 The meaning, use, and distribution of resources.

VI. The Uses of Geography

Knowledge of geography helps us understand the relationships among people, places, and environments over time. Applying geographic skills helps you understand the past and prepare for the future.

17 How to apply geography to interpret the past.

18 How to apply geography to interpret the present and plan for the future.

GEOGRAPHY SKILLS HANDBOOK

CONTENTS

Geography Skills Handbook

Throughout this text, you will discover how geography has shaped the course of events in history. Landforms, waterways, climate, and natural resources all have helped or hindered human activities. Usually people have learned either to adapt to their environments or to transform it to meet their needs. The resources in this Geography Skills Handbook will help you get the most out of your textbook—and provide you with skills you will use for the rest of your life.

Geographers use a wide array of tools to collect and analyze information to help them understand the Earth. The study of geography is more than knowing a lot of facts about places. Rather, it has more to do with asking questions about the Earth, pursuing their answers, and solving problems. Thus, one of the most important geographic tools is inside your head: the ability to think geographically.

Globes and Maps

A **globe** is a scale model of the Earth. Because Earth is round, a globe presents the most accurate depiction of geographic information such as area, distance, and direction. However, globes show little close-up detail. A printed **map** is a symbolic representation of all or part of the planet. Unlike globes, maps can show small areas in great detail.

From 3-D to 2-D

Think about the surface of the Earth as the peel of an orange. To flatten the peel, you have to cut it into segments that are still connected as one piece. To create maps that are not interrupted, mapmakers, or **cartographers**, use mathematical formulas to transfer information from the three-dimensional globe to the two-dimensional map. However, when the curves of a globe become straight lines on a map, distortion of size, shape, distance, or area occurs.

Great Circle Routes

A straight line of true direction—one that runs directly from west to east, for example—is not always the shortest distance between two points. This is due to the curvature of the Earth. To find the shortest distance, stretch a piece of string around the globe from one point to the other. The string will form part of a *great circle*, an imaginary line that follows the curve of the Earth. Ship captains and airline pilots use these **great circle routes** to reduce travel time and conserve fuel.

The idea of a great circle route in an important difference between globes and maps. A round globe accurately shows a great circle route, as indicated on the top right map. However, the flat map below it shows the great circle distance (dotted line) between Tokyo and Los Angeles to be far longer than the true direction distance (solid line). In fact, the great circle distance is 315 miles (506 km) shorter.

VOCABULARY

globe
a scale model of the Earth

maps
a symbolic representation of all or part of the planet

cartographers
mapmakers

great circle route
a straight line of true direction on a globe

GEOGRAPHY CONNECTION

1 *Explain* the significance of: globe, map, cartographer, great circle route.

2 *Describe* the problems that arise when the curves of a globe become straight lines on a map.

3 *Use* a Venn diagram like the one below to identify the similarities and differences between globes and maps.

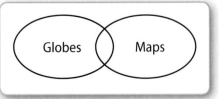

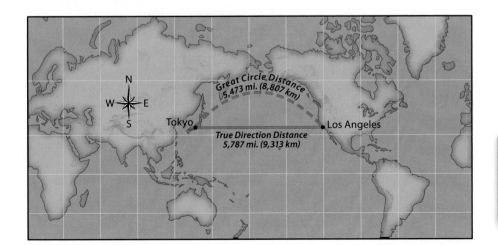

Projections

To create maps, cartographers project the round Earth onto a flat surface—making a **map projection.** Distance, shape, direction, or size may be distorted by a projection. As a result, the purpose of the map usually dictates which projection is used. There are many kinds of map projections, some with general names and some named for the cartographers who developed them. Three basic categories of map projections are shown here: **planar, cylindrical,** and **conic**.

Planar Projection

A planar projection shows the Earth centered in such a way that a straight line coming from the center to any point represents the shortest distance. Also known as an azimuthal projection, it is most accurate at its center. As a result, it is often used for maps of the Poles.

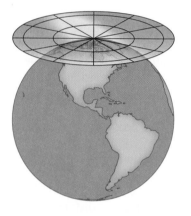
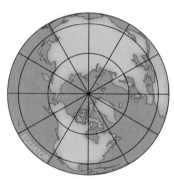

Cylindrical Projection

A cylindrical projection is based on the projection of the globe onto a cylinder. This projection is most accurate near the Equator, but shapes and distances are distorted near the Poles.

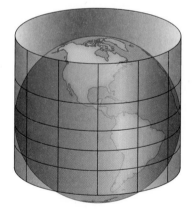

Conic Projection

A conic projection comes from placing a cone over part of the globe. Conic projections are best suited for showing limited east-west areas that are not far from the Equator. For these uses, a conic projection can indicate distances and directions fairly accurately.

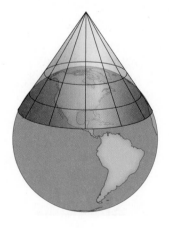

Common Map Projections

Each type of map projection has advantages and some degree of inaccuracy. Four of the most common projections are shown here.

Winkel Tripel Projection

Most general reference world maps are the Winkel Tripel projection. It provides a good balance between the size and shape of land areas as they are shown on the map. Even the polar areas are depicted with little distortion of size and shape.

Robinson Projection

The Robinson projection has minor distortions. The sizes and shapes near the eastern and western edges of the map are accurate, and outlines of the continents appear much as they do on the globe. However, the polar areas are flattened.

Goode's Interrupted Equal-Area Projection

An interrupted projection looks something like a globe that has been cut apart and laid flat. Goode's Interrupted Equal-Area projection shows the true size and shape of Earth's landmasses, but distances are generally distorted.

Mercator Projection

The Mercator projection increasingly distorts size and distance as it moves away from the Equator. However, Mercator projections do accurately show true directions and the shapes of landmasses, making these maps useful for sea travel.

GEOGRAPHY CONNECTION

① **Explain** the significance of: map projection, planar, cylindrical, conic.

② **How** does a cartographer determine which map projection to use?

③ **How** is Goode's Interrupted Equal-Area projection different from the Mercator projection?

④ **Which** of the four common projections described above is the best one to use when showing the entire world? Why?

⑤ **Use** a Venn diagram like the one below to identify the similarities and differences between the Winkel Tripel and Mercator projections.

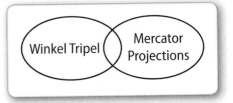

VOCABULARY

grid system
a pattern of lines on a map or globe that determine exact locations on Earths' surface

hemisphere
one of the halves that geographers divide the Earth into

latitude
lines that circle the Earth parallel to the Equator

longitude
lines that circle the Earth from Pole to Pole

Prime Meridian
the line of longitude set at 0°

absolute location
a global address determined by the intersection of longitude and latitude lines

Determining Location

Geography is often said to begin with the question: *Where?* The basic tool for answering the question is *location*. Lines on globes and maps provide information that can help you locate places. These lines cross one another forming a pattern called a **grid system**, which helps you find exact places on the Earth's surface.

A **hemisphere** is one of the halves into which the Earth is divided. Geographers divide the Earth into hemispheres to help them classify and describe places on Earth. Most places are located in two of the four hemispheres.

Latitude

Lines of **latitude**, or parallels, circle the Earth parallel to the Equator and measure the distance north or south of the Equator in degrees. The Equator is measured at 0° latitude, while the Poles lie at latitudes 90°N (north) and 90°S (south). Parallels north of the Equator are called north latitude. Parallels south of the Equator are called south latitude.

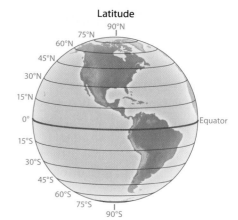

Latitude

Longitude

Lines of **longitude**, or meridians, circle the Earth from Pole to Pole. These lines measure distance east or west of the **Prime Meridian** at 0° longitude. Meridians east of the Prime Meridian are known as east longitude. Meridian west of the Prime Meridian are known as west longitude. The 180° meridian on the opposite side of the Earth is called the International Date Line.

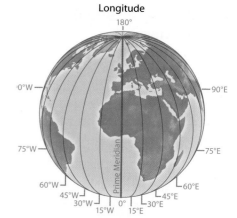

Longitude

The Global Grid

Every place has a global address, or **absolute location**. You can identify the absolute location of a place by naming the latitude and longitude lines that cross exactly at that place. For example, Tokyo, Japan is located at 36°N latitude and 140°E longitude. For more precise readings, each degree is further divided into 60 units called minutes.

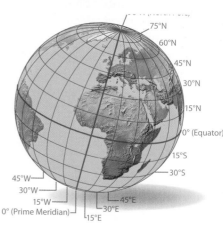

Northern and Southern Hemispheres

The diagram below shows that the Equator divides the Earth into the Northern and Southern Hemispheres. Everything north of the Equator is in the **Northern Hemisphere**. Everything south of the Equator is in the **Southern Hemisphere**.

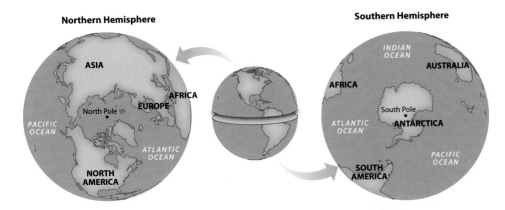

Eastern and Western Hemispheres

The Prime Meridian and the International Date Line divide the Earth into the Eastern and Western Hemispheres. Everything east of the Prime Meridian for 180° is in the **Eastern Hemisphere**. Everything west of the Prime Meridian for 180° is in the **Western Hemisphere**.

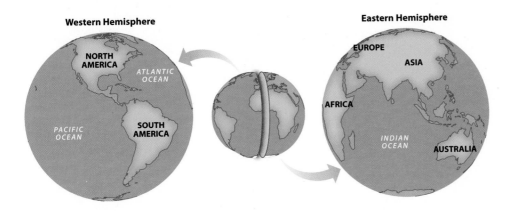

VOCABULARY

Northern Hemisphere
the half of the globe north of the Equator

Southern Hemisphere
the half of the globe south of the Equator

Eastern Hemisphere
the half of the globe east of the Prime Meridian for 180°

Western Hemisphere
the half of the globe west of the Prime Meridian for 180°

GEOGRAPHY CONNECTION

❶ *Explain* the significance of: location, grid system, hemisphere, Northern Hemisphere, Southern Hemisphere, Eastern Hemisphere, Western Hemisphere, latitude, longitude, Prime Meridian, absolute location.

❷ *Why* do all maps label the Equator 0° latitude and the Prime Meridian 0° longitude?

❸ *Which* lines of latitude and longitude divide the Earth into hemispheres?

❹ *Using* the Reference Atlas maps, fill in a chart by writing the latitude and longitude of three world cities. Have a partner try to identify the cities listed in your chart.

❺ *Use* a chart like the one below to identify the continents in each hemisphere. Some may be in more than one hemisphere.

Hemisphere	Continents
Northern	
Southern	
Eastern	
Western	

Reading a Map

In addition to latitude and longitude, maps feature other important tools to help you interpret the information they contain. Learning to use these map tools will help you read the symbolic language of maps more easily.

Key
The key lists and explains the symbols, colors, and lines used on the map. The key is sometimes called a legend.

Title
The title tells you what kind of information the map is showing.

Boundary Lines
On political maps of large areas, boundary lines highlight the borders between different countries or states.

Compass Rose
The compass rose indicates directions. The four cardinal directions—north, south, east, and west—are usually indicated with arrows or the points of a star. The intermediate directions—northeast, northwest, southeast, and southwest—may also be shown.

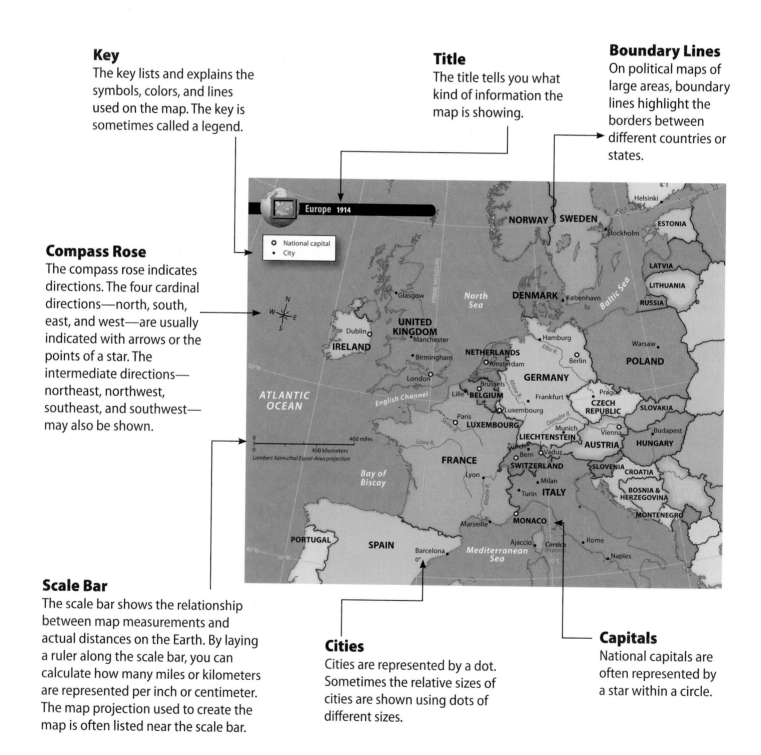

Scale Bar
The scale bar shows the relationship between map measurements and actual distances on the Earth. By laying a ruler along the scale bar, you can calculate how many miles or kilometers are represented per inch or centimeter. The map projection used to create the map is often listed near the scale bar.

Cities
Cities are represented by a dot. Sometimes the relative sizes of cities are shown using dots of different sizes.

Capitals
National capitals are often represented by a star within a circle.

Using Scale

All maps are drawn to a certain scale. **Scale** is a consistent, proportional relationship between the measurements shown on the map and the measurement of the Earth's surface.

Small-Scale Maps A small-scale map, like this political map of France, can show a large area but little detail. Note that the scale bar on this map indicates that about 1 inch is equal to 200 miles.

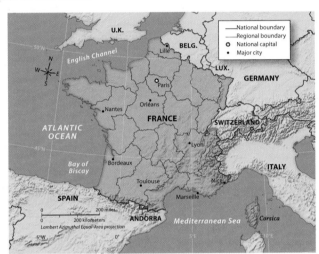

Large-Scale Maps A large-scale map, like this map of Paris, can show a small area with a great amount of detail. Study the scale bar. Note that the map measurements correspond to much smaller distances than on the map of France.

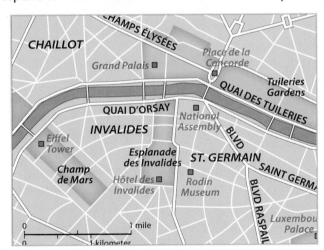

Absolute and Relative Location

Absolute location is the exact point where a line of latitude crosses a line of longitude. Another way to indicate location is by **relative location**, or the location of one place in relation to another. To find relative location, find a reference point—a location you already know—on a map. Then look in the appropriate direction for the new location. For example, locate Paris (your reference point) on the map of France above. The relative location of Lyon can be described as southeast of Paris.

VOCABULARY

Scale
a consistant, proportional relationship between measurements shown on a map and measurements of the Earth's surface

relative location
the location of one place in relation to another

GEOGRAPHY CONNECTION

❶ *Explain* the significance of: key, compass rose, cardinal directions, intermediate directions, scale bar, scale, relative location.

❷ *Describe* the elements of a map that help you interpret the information displayed on the map.

❸ *How* does the scale bar help you determine distances on the Earth's surface?

❹ *Describe* the relative location of your school in two different ways.

❺ *Use* a Venn diagram to identify the similarities and differences of small-scale maps and large-scale maps.

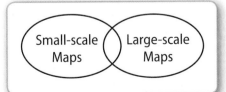

physical map
a map that shows the location and shape of the Earth's physical features

political map
a map that shows the boundaries and locations of political units such as countries, states, and cities

Physical and Political Maps

Physical and political are the two main types of maps in this book. A **physical map** shows the location and the topography, or shape of the Earth's physical features. A study of an area's physical features often helps explain its historical development. A **political map** shows the boundaries and locations of political units such as countries, states, and cities. Non subject area is usually shown in a different color to set it apart from the main area of the map. This nonsubject area gives you a context for the region you are studying.

Physical Maps

Physical maps use shading and texture to show general relief—the differences in elevation or height, of landforms. Landforms are physical features such as plains, mountains, plateaus, and valleys. Physical maps show rivers, streams, lakes, and other water features.

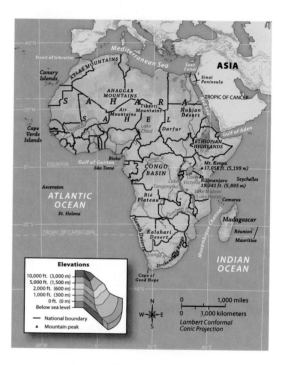

Political Maps

Many features on a political map are human-made, or determined by humans rather than by nature. Some human-made features are boundaries, capital cities, and roads. Political maps may also show physical features such as mountains and rivers.

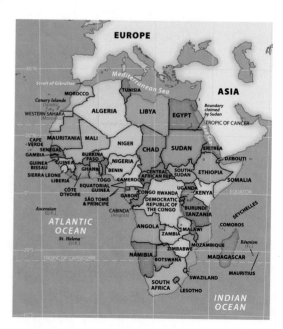

Thematic Maps

Maps that emphasize a particular kind of information or a single idea are called **thematic maps**. This textbook includes thematic maps that show civilizations, migrations, natural resources, war, trade, and exploration.

VOCABULARY

thematic maps
maps focused on a kind of information or a single idea

Qualitative Maps

Maps that use colors, symbols, lines, or dots to show information related to a specific idea are called qualitative maps.

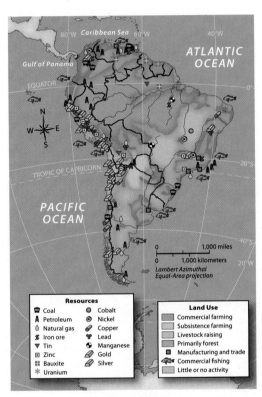

Flow-Line Maps

Maps that use arrows to show the movement of people, ideas, or physical systems are called flow-line maps.

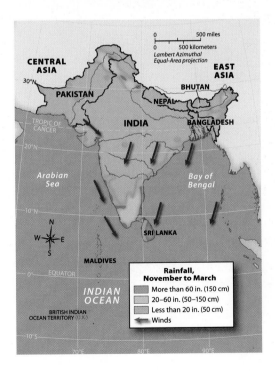

GEOGRAPHY CONNECTION

❶ *Explain* the significance of: physical map, political map, thematic map, qualitative map, flow-line map.

❷ *Complete* a Venn diagram like the one below to compare physical and political maps.

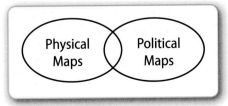

VOCABULARY

ecosystem
a community of plants and animals that depend upon one another and their surroundings for survival

Biodiversity
the variation of lifeforms within an ecosystem

Ecosystems and Biodiversity

An **ecosystem** is a community of plants and animals that depend upon one another and their surroundings for survival. There are many different ecosystems on Earth. Plants, animals, and micro-organisms interact within an ecosystem. **Biodiversity** is the variation of life forms within an ecosystem.

Rain forests are one type of ecosystem. Nowhere is biodiversity more apparent than in tropical rain forests, which harbor at least half of all animal and plant species on Earth. Although the world's largest remaining tropical rain forests are in Brazil, there are temperate rain forests from North America to Australia, as seen in the photograph.

Desert climates occur in just under one-third of the Earth's total land area. The natural vegetation of a desert ecosystem consists of scrub and cactus, plants that tolerate low and unreliable precipitation, low humidity, and wise temperate ranges. This arid landscape is in Arizona.

GEOGRAPHY CONNECTION

❶ **Explain** the significance of: ecosystem, biodiversity.

❷ **Complete** a table like the one below to list some of the types of interactions in the physical systems.

Hemisphere	Interactions
Atmosphere	
Hydrosphere	
Lithosphere	

Biodiversity at Risk As the human communities expand, they threaten natural ecosystems. Because the Earth's land, air, and water are interrelated, what effects one part of the system affects all the other parts—including humans and other living things. The photograph shows deforestation, in this case clear-cutting of the Brazilian rain forest.

Geographic Information Systems

Modern technology has changed the way maps are made. Most cartographers use computers with software programs called **geographic information systems** (GIS). A GIS is designed to accept data from different sources—maps, satellite images, printed text, and statistics. The GIS converts the data into a digital code, which arranges it in a database. Cartographers then program the GIS to process the data and produce maps. With GIS, each kind of information on a map is saved as a separate electronic layer.

VOCABULARY

geographic information systems
a software program used by cartographers that arranges a variety of data in a database and uses those data layers to produce maps

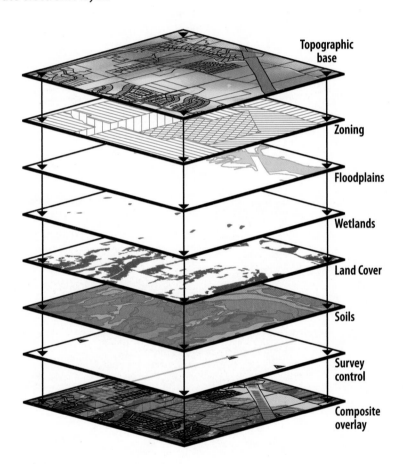

- Topographic base
- Zoning
- Floodplains
- Wetlands
- Land Cover
- Soils
- Survey control
- Composite overlay

GEOGRAPHY CONNECTION

1 *How* does GIS allow cartographers to create maps and make changes to maps quickly and easily?

2 *Complete* a chart like the one below by identifying the different types of layers available in a GIS to make more *informative maps.*

Layers

archipelago   a group of islands

basin   area of land drained by a given river and its branches; area of land surrounded by lands of higher elevations

bay   part of a large body of water that extends into a shoreline, generally smaller than a gulf

canyon   deep and narrow valley with steep walls

cape   point of land that extends into a river, lake, or ocean

channel   wide strait or waterway between two landmasses that lie close to each other; deep part of a river or other waterway

cliff   steep, high wall of rock, earth, or ice

continent   one of the seven large landmasses on the Earth

delta   flat, low-lying land built up from soil carried downstream by a river and deposited at its mouth

divide   stretch of high land that separates river systems

downstream   direction in which a river or stream flows from its source to its mouth

escarpment   steep cliff or slope between a higher and lower land surface

glacier   large, thick body of slowly moving ice

gulf   part of a large body of water that extends into a shoreline, generally larger and more deeply indented than a bay

harbor   a sheltered place along a shoreline where ships can anchor safely

highland   elevated land area such as a hill, mountain, or plateau

hill   elevated land with sloping sides and rounded summit; generally smaller than a mountain

island   land area, smaller than a continent, completely surrounded by water

isthmus   narrow stretch of land connecting two larger land areas

lake   a sizable inland body of water

lowland   land, usually level, at a low elevation

mesa   broad, flat-topped landform with steep sides; smaller than a plateau

mountain   land with steep sides that rises sharply (1,000 feet or more) from surrounding land; generally larger and more rugged than a hill

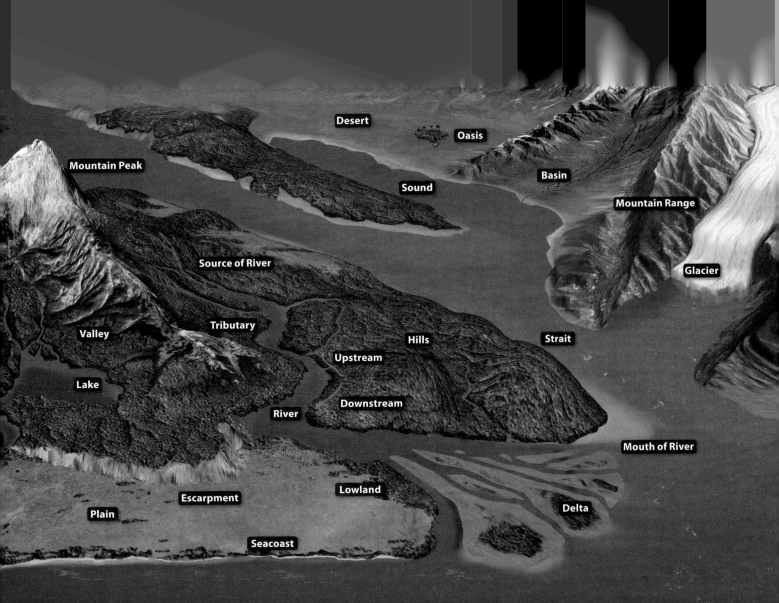

Mountain Peak

Desert

Oasis

Basin

Sound

Mountain Range

Source of River

Glacier

Tributary

Valley

Hills

Strait

Upstream

Lake

Downstream

River

Mouth of River

Lowland

Escarpment

Delta

Plain

Seacoast

mountain peak pointed top of a mountain

mountain range a series of connected mountains

mouth (of a river) place where a stream or river flows into a larger body of water

oasis small area in a desert where water and vegetation are found

ocean one of the four major bodies of salt water that surround the continents

ocean current stream of either cold or warm water that moves in a definite direction through an ocean

peninsula body of land jutting into a lake or ocean, surrounded on three sides by water

physical feature characteristic of a place occurring naturally, such as a landform, body of water, climate pattern, or resource

plain area of level land, usually at low elevation and often covered with grasses

plateau area of flat or rolling land at a high elevation, about 300 to 3,000 feet (90 to 900 m) high

river large natural stream of water that runs through the land

sea large body of water completely or partly surrounded by land

seacoast land lying next to a sea or an ocean

sound broad inland body of water, often between a coastline and one or more islands off the coast

source (of a river) place where a river or stream begins, often in highlands

strait narrow stretch of water joining two larger bodies of water

tributary small river or stream that flows into a large river or stream; a branch of the river

upstream direction opposite the flow of a river; toward the source of a river or stream

valley area of low land usually between hills or mountains

volcano mountain or hill created as liquid rock and ash erupt from inside the Earth

TERMS

animism—belief that spirits inhabit natural objects and forces of nature

atheism—disbelief in the existence of any god

monotheism—belief in one God

polytheism—belief in more than one god

secularism—belief that life's questions can be answered apart from religious belief

sect—a subdivision within a religion that has its own distinctive beliefs and/or practices

tenet—a belief, doctrine, or principle believed to be true and held in common by members of a group

A *religion* is a set of beliefs in an ultimate reality and a set of practices used to express those beliefs. Religion is a key component of culture.

Each religion is defined and set apart from other religions by its own special celebrations and worship styles. Most religions also have their own sacred texts, sacred symbols, and sacred sites. All of these aspects of religion help to unite followers of that faith regardless of where in the world they live.

The religions examined in this World Religions Handbook all have these sacred elements, celebrations, and worship styles. Examining these characteristics provides insight into each of these religions.

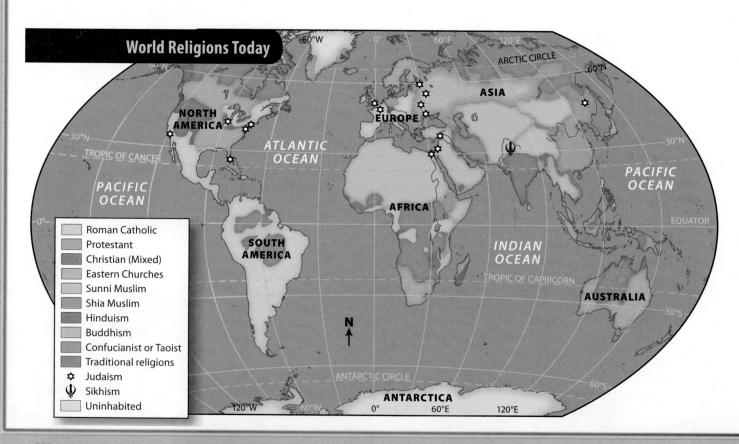

World Religions Today

Legend:
- Roman Catholic
- Protestant
- Christian (Mixed)
- Eastern Churches
- Sunni Muslim
- Shia Muslim
- Hinduism
- Buddhism
- Confucianist or Taoist
- Traditional religions
- ✡ Judaism
- ☬ Sikhism
- Uninhabited

We study religion because it is an important component of culture, shaping how people interact with one another, dress, and eat. Religion is at the core of the belief system of a religion's culture.

The diffusion of religion throughout the world has been caused by a variety of factors including migration, missionary work, trade, and war. Buddhism, Christianity, and Islam are the three major religions that spread their religion through missionary activities. Religions such as Hinduism, Sikhism, and Judaism are associated with a particular culture group. Followers are usually born into these religions. Sometimes close contract and differences in beliefs have resulted in conflict between religious groups.

Percentage of World Population

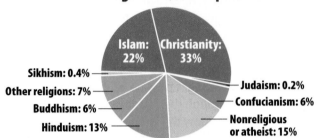

Islam: 22%
Christianity: 33%
Sikhism: 0.4%
Other religions: 7%
Buddhism: 6%
Hinduism: 13%
Judaism: 0.2%
Confucianism: 6%
Nonreligious or atheist: 15%

Note: Total exceeds 100% because numbers were rounded.
Sources: www.cia.gov, The World Factbook 2006; www.adherents.com.

Early Diffusion of Major World Religions

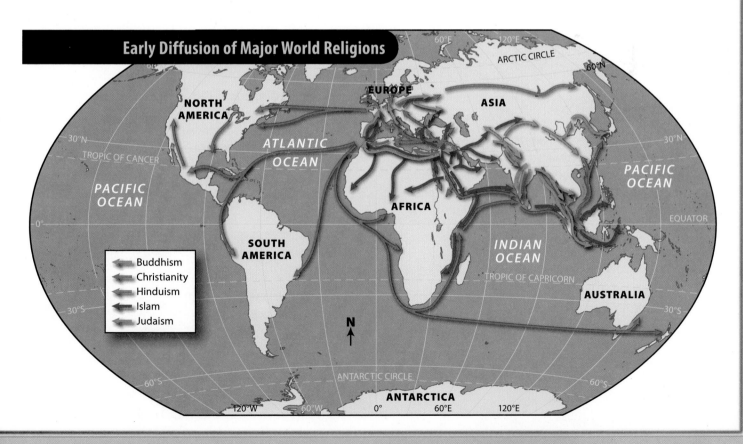

Buddhism

Siddhartha Gautama, known as the Buddha ("the Awakened") after his enlightenment at the age of 35, was born some 2,500 years ago in what is now Nepal. The Buddha's followers adhere to his teachings (dharma, meaning "divine law"), which aim to end suffering in the world. Buddhists call this goal Nirvana; and they believe that it can be achieved only by understanding the Four Noble Truths and by following the 4th Truth, which says that freedom from suffering is possible by practicing the Eightfold Path. Through the Buddha's teachings, his followers come to know the impermanence of all things and reach the end of ignorance and unhappiness.

Over time, as Buddhism spread throughout Asia, several branches emerged. The largest of these are Theravada Buddhism, the monk-centered Buddhism which is dominant in Sri Lanka, Burma, Thailand, Laos, and Cambodia; and Mahayana, a complex, more liberal variety of Buddhism that has traditionally been dominant in Tibet, Central Asia, Korea, China, and Japan.

Statue of the Buddha, Siddhartha Gautama

Sacred Text ▼

For centuries the Buddha's teachings were transmitted orally. For Theravada Buddhists, the authoritative collection of Buddhist texts is the Tripitaka ("three baskets"). These texts were first written on palm leaves in a language called Pali. This excerpt from the *Dhammapada*, a famous text within the Tripitaka, urges responding to hatred with love:

> " *Never in this world is hate*
> *Appeased by hatred.*
> *It is only appeased by love—*
> *This is an eternal law.* "
> —*Dhammapada 1.5*

Sacred Symbol ▼

The *dharmachakra* ("wheel of the law") is a major Buddhist symbol. Among other things, it signifies the overcoming of obstacles. The eight spokes represent the Eightfold Path—right view, right intention, right speech, right action, right livelihood, right effort, right mindfulness, right concentration—that is central for all Buddhists.

Sacred Site ▲

Buddhists believe that Siddhartha Gautama achieved enlightenment beneath the Bodhi Tree in Bodh Gayā, India. Today, Buddhists from around the world flock to Bodh Gayā in search of their own spiritual awakening.

Worship and Celebration ▶

The ultimate goal of Buddhists is to achieve Nirvana, the enlightened state in which individuals are free from ignorance, greed, and suffering. Theravada Buddhists believe that monks are most likely to reach Nirvana because of their lifestyle of renunciation, moral virtue, study, and meditation.

Christianity

Christianity claims more members than any of the other world religions. It dates its beginning to the death of Jesus in A.D. 33 in what is now Israel. It is based on the belief in one God and on the life and teachings of Jesus. Christians believe that Jesus, who was born a Jew, is the son of God and is fully divine and human. Christians regard Jesus as the Messiah (Christ), or savior, who died for humanity's sins. Christians feel that people are saved and achieve eternal life by faith in Jesus.

The major forms of Christianity are Roman Catholicism, Eastern Orthodoxy, and Protestantism. All three are united in their belief in Jesus as savior, but have developed their own individual theologies.

Sacred Text ▾

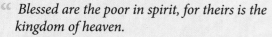

The Christian Bible is the spiritual text for all Christians and is considered to be inspired by God. This excerpt, from Matthew 5:3-12, is from Jesus' Sermon on the Mount.

Stained glass window depicting Jesus

> " *Blessed are the poor in spirit, for theirs is the kingdom of heaven.*
> *Blessed are those who mourn, for they shall be comforted.*
> *Blessed are the meek, for they shall inherit the earth.*
> *Blessed are those who hunger and thirst for righteousness, for they shall be satisfied.*
> *Blessed are the merciful, for they shall obtain mercy.*
> *Blessed are the pure in heart, for they shall see God.*
> *Blessed are the peacemakers, for they shall be called sons of God.*
> *Blessed are those who are persecuted for righteousness' sake, for theirs is the kingdom of heaven.*
> *Blessed are you when men revile you and persecute you and utter all kinds of evil against you falsely on my account.*
> *Rejoice and be glad, for your reward is great in heaven, for so men persecuted the prophets who were before you.* "

Sacred Symbol ▾

Christians believe that Jesus died for their sins. His death *redeemed* those who follow his teachings. The statue *Christ the Redeemer,* located in Rio de Janeiro, Brazil, symbolizes this fundamental belief.

Sacred Site ▸

The Gospels affirm that Bethlehem was the birthplace of Jesus. Consequently, it holds great importance to Christians. The Church of the Nativity is located in the heart of Bethlehem. It houses the spot where Christians believe Jesus was born.

Worship and Celebration ▾

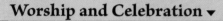

Christians celebrate many events commemorating the life and death of Jesus. Among the most widely known and observed are Christmas, Good Friday, and Easter. Christmas is often commemorated by attending church services to celebrate the birth of Jesus. As part of the celebration, followers often light candles.

Confucianism

onfucianism began more than 2,500 years ago in China. Although considered a religion, it is actually a philosophy. It is based upon the teachings of Confucius, which are grounded in ethical behavior and good government.

The teachings of Confucius focused on three areas: social philosophy, political philosophy, and education. Confucius taught that relationships are based on rank. Persons of higher rank are responsible for caring for those of lower rank. Those of lower rank should respect and obey those of higher rank. Eventually his teachings spread from China to other East Asian societies.

Students study Confucianism, Chunghak-dong, South Korea

Sacred Symbol ▾

Yin-yang, associated with both Confucianism and Daoism, symbolizes the harmony offered by the philosophies. The light half represents *yang,* the creative, firm, strong elements in all things. The dark half represents *yin,* the receptive, yielding, weak elements. The two act together to balance one another.

Sacred Text ▾

Confucius was famous for his sayings and proverbs. These teachings were gathered into a book called the *Analects* (see image above) after Confucius's death. Below is an example of Confucius's teachings:

Confucius said:

❝ To learn and to practice what is learned time and again is pleasure, is it not? To have friends come from afar is happiness, is it not? To be unperturbed when not appreciated by others is gentlemanly, is it not? ❞

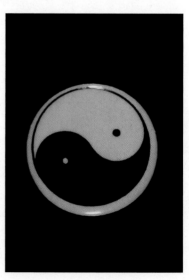

先师功德垂青史

念孔子二千五百五十五年诞辰
COMMEMORATE THE 2555TH ANNIVERSARY OF CONFUCIUS BIRTHDAY

Sacred Site ▲

The temple at Qufu is a group of buildings dedicated to Confucius. It is located on Confucius's ancestral land. It is one of the largest ancient architectural complexes in China. Every year followers gather at Qufu to celebrate the birthday of Confucius.

Worship and Celebration ▶

Confucianism does not have a god or clergy, but there are temples dedicated to Confucius, the spiritual leader. Those who follow his teachings see Confucianism as a way of life and a guide to ethical behavior and good government.

Hinduism

Hinduism is the oldest of the world's major living religions. It developed among the cultures in India as they spread out over the plains and forests of the subcontinent. It has no single founder or founding date. Hinduism is complex; it has numerous sects and many different divinities are honored. Among the more famous Hindu gods are Brahma, Vishnu, and Shiva, who represent respectively the creative, sustaining, and destructive forces in the universe. Major Hindu beliefs are reincarnation, karma, and dharma.

Hindus believe the universe contains several heavens and hells. According to the concept of rebirth or reincarnation, which is central to their beliefs, souls are continually reborn. In what form one is reborn is determined by the good and evil actions performed in his or her past lives. Those acts are karma. A soul continues in the cycle of rebirth until release is achieved.

Sacred Text ▾

The Vedas consist of hymns, prayers, and speculations composed in ancient Sanskrit. They are the oldest religious texts in an Indo-European language. The Rig Veda, Sama Veda, Yajur Veda, and Atharva Veda are the four great Vedic collections. Together, they make up one of the most significant and authoritative Hindu religious texts.

Statue of Vishnu

> " *Now, whether they perform a cremation for such a person or not,*
> *people like him pass into the flame,*
> *from the flame into the day,*
> *from the day into the fortnight of the waxing moon*
> *from the fortnight of the waxing moon into the six months when the sun moves north,*
> *from these months into the year, from the year into the sun,*
> *from the sun into the moon, and from the moon into the lightning.*
> *Then a person who is not human—he leads them to Brahman.*
> *This is the path to the gods, the path to Brahman.*
> *Those who proceed along this path do not return to this human condition.* "
> —The Chandogya Upanishad 4:15.5

Sacred Symbol ▾

One important symbol of Hinduism is actually a symbol for a sound. "Om" is a sound that Hindus often chant during prayer, mantras, and rituals.

Sacred Site ▶

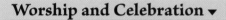

Hindus believe that when a person dies his or her soul is reborn. This is known as reincarnation. Many Hindus bathe in the Ganges and other sacred rivers to purify their soul and to be released from rebirth.

Worship and Celebration ▼

Holi is a significant North Indian Hindu festival celebrating the triumph of good over evil. As part of the celebration, men, women, and children splash colored powders and water on each other. In addition to its religious significance, Holi also celebrates the beginning of spring.

Islam

Followers of Islam, known as Muslims, believe in one God, whom they call Allah. The word *Allah* is Arabic for "the god." The spiritual founder of Islam, Muhammad, began his teachings in Makkah (Mecca) in A.D. 610. Eventually the religion spread throughout much of Asia, including parts of India to the borders of China, and substantial portion of Africa. According to Muslims, the Quran, their holy book, contains the direct word of God, revealed to their prophet Muhammad sometime between A.D. 610 and A.D. 632. Muslims believe that God created nature and without his intervention, there would be nothingness. God serves four functions: creation, sustenance, guidance, and judgment.

Central to Islamic beliefs are the Five Pillars. These are affirmation of the belief in Allah and Muhammad as his prophet; group prayer; tithing, or the giving of money to charity; fasting during Ramadan; and a pilgrimage to Makkah once in a lifetime if physically and financially able. Within Islam, there are two main branches, the Sunni and the Shia. The differences between the two are based on the history of the Muslim state. The Shia believed that the rulers should descend from Muhammad. The Sunni believed that the rulers need only be followers of Muhammad. Most Muslims are Sunni.

The Dome of the Rock, Jerusalem

The Quran

Sacred Text ▾

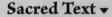

The sacred text of Islam is the Quran. Preferably, it is written and read only in Arabic, but translations have been made into many languages. The excerpt below is a verse repeated by all Muslims during their five daily prayers.

> " In the Name of Allah, the Compassionate, the Merciful,
> Praise be to Allah, the Lord of the World,
> The Compassionate, the Merciful,
> Master of the Day of Judgment,
> Only You do we worship, and only You
> Do we implore for help.
> Lead us to the right path,
> The path of those you have favored
> Not those who have incurred
> Your wrath or
> Have gone astray. "
>
> —The Quran

Sacred Symbol ▾

Islam is often symbolized by the crescent moon. It is an important part of Muslim rituals, which are based on the lunar calendar.

PHOTOS: (t) Design Pics/Natural Selection Ralph Curtin; (m) ©GOODSHOOT/Alamy; (b) Martin Moos/Lonely Planet Images/Getty Images; TEXT: Reprinted with the permission of MBI, Inc.

Sacred Site ▶

Makkah is a sacred site for all Muslims. One of the Five Pillars of Islam states that all who are physically and financially able must make a hajj, or pilgrimage, to the holy city once in their life. Practicing Muslims are also required to pray facing Makkah five times a day.

Worship and Celebration ▼

Ramadan is a month-long celebration commemorating the time during which Muhammad received the Quran from Allah. It is customary for Muslims to fast from dawn until sunset all month long. Muslims believe that fasting helps followers focus on spiritual rather than bodily matters and creates empathy for one's fellow men and women. Ramadan ends with a feast known as Eid-al-Fitr, or Feast of the Fast.

Judaism

Judaism is a monotheistic religion. In fact, Judaism was the first major religion to believe in one God. Jews trace their national and religious origins back to God's call to Abraham. Jews have a covenant with God. They believe that God, who expects them to pursue justice and live ethical lives, will one day usher in an era of universal peace.

Over time Judaism has separated into branches, including Orthodox, Reform, Conservative, and Reconstructionist. Orthodox Jews are the most traditional of all the branches.

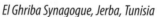

El Ghriba Synagogue, Jerba, Tunisia

The Torah scroll

Sacred Text ▾

The Torah is the five books of Moses, which tell the story of the origins of the Jews and explain Jewish laws. The remainder of the Hebrew Bible contains the wriitngs of the prophets, Psalms, and ethical and historical works.

> " I am the Lord your God, who brought you out of the land of Egypt, out of the house of slavery; you shall have no other gods before me. "
>
> —Exodus 20:2

Sacred Symbol ▾

The menorah is used in the celebration of Hanukkah, commemorating the rededication of the Temple of Jerusalem following the Maccabees' victory over the Syrian Greeks.

Sacred Site ◄

The Western Wall is what remains of the structure surrounding the Second Jerusalem Temple, built after the Jews' return from the Babylonian captivity. It is considered a sacred spot in Jewish religious tradition. Prayers are offered at the wall morning, afternoon, and evening.

Worship and Celebration ▼

The day-long Yom Kippur service ends with the blowing of the ram's horn (shofar). Yom Kippur is the holiest day in the Jewish calendar. During Yom Kippur, Jews do not eat or drink for 25 hours. The purpose is to reflect on the past year and gain forgiveness from God for one's sins. It falls in September or October, ten days after Rosh Hashanah, the Jewish New Year.

Sikhism

Sikhism emerged in the mid-1500s in the Punjab, in northwest India, rising from the religious experience and teachings of Guru Nanak. The religion exhibits influences from Islam and Hinduism, but it is distinct from both. Sikh traditions teach that Nanak encountered God directly and was commissioned by Him to be His servant.

Sikhs ("students, disciples") believe in one, almighty god who is formless and without qualities (*nirguna*) but can be known through meditation and heard directly. Sikhism forbids discrimination on the basis of class, color, religion, caste, or gender. While over 80 percent of the world's 23 million Sikhs live in the Punjab, Sikhism has spread widely as many Sikhs have migrated to new homes around the world.

Sikh men often wear long beards and cover their heari with turbans.

Guru Nanak.

Sacred Text ▾

The great authoritative sacred text for Sikhs is the Adi Granth ("Principal Book," also known as the Guru Granth Sahib). Compiled from the mid-1500s through the 1600s, it includes contributions from Sikh gurus and from some persons also claimed as saints by Hindus and Muslims, such as Namdev, Ravidas, and Kabir.

> " *Enshrine the Lord's Name within your heart. The Word of the Guru's Bani prevails throughout the world, through this Bani, the Lord's name is obtained.* "
> —Guru Amar Das, page 1066

Sacred Symbol ▾

The sacred symbol of the Sikhs is the *khanda*. It is composed of four traditional Sikh weapons: the *khanda* or double-edged sword (in the center), from which the symbol takes its name; the *cakkar* (disk), and two curved daggars (*kirpan*) representing temporal and spiritual power, respectively Piri and Miri.

Sacred Site ▶

Amritsar is the spiritual capital of Sikhism. The Golden Temple (*Harimandir Sahib*) in Amritsar is the most sacred of Sikh shrines.

Worship and Celebration ▼

Vaisakhi is a significant Punjabi and Sikh festival in April celebrating the new year and the beginning of the harvest season. Celebrations often take place along riverbanks with participants dancing and wearing brightly colored clothes.

Indigenous Religions

There are many varieties of religious belief that are limited to particular ethnic groups. These local religions are found in Africa as well as isolated parts of Japan, Australia, and the Americas.

Most local religions reflect a close relationship with the environment. Some groups teach that people are a part of nature, not separate from it. Animism is characteristic of many indigenous religions. Natural features are sacred, and stories about how nature came to be are an important part of religious heritage. Although many of these stories have been written down in modern times, they were originally transmitted orally.

Africa The continent of Africa is home to a variety of local religions. Despite their differences, most African religions recognize the existence of one creator in addition to spirits that inhabit all aspects of life. Religious ceremonies are often celebrated with music and dance.

These Turkana men from Kenya are performing a traditional jumping dance.

Rituals are an important part of African religions. These Masai boys are wearing ceremonial dress as part of a ritual.

Masks are a component of ritual and ceremony. This mask from Cameroon is used to celebrate harvest.

Japan Shinto, founded in Japan, is the largest indigenous religion. It dates back to prehistoric times and has no formal doctrine. The gods are known as kami. Ancestors are also revered and worshiped. Its four million followers often practice Buddhism in addition to practicing Shinto.

Shinto shrines, like this one, are usually built in places of great natural beauty to emphasize the relationship between people and nature.

This Shinto priest is presiding over a ritual at a Japanese temple. These priests often live on shrine grounds.

Australia The Australian Aboriginal religion has no deities. It is based upon a belief known as the Dreaming, or Dreamtime. Followers believe that ancestors sprang from the Earth and created all people, plant, and animal life. They also believe that these ancestors continue to control the natural world.

These Aborigine women are blessing a newborn with smoke during a traditional ritual intended to ensure the child's health and good fortune.

Aborigines, like these young girls, often paint their faces with the symbols of their clan or family group.

Indigenous Religions

Native Americans The beliefs of most Native Americans center on the spirit world; however, the rituals and practices of individual groups vary. Most Native Americans believe in a Great Spirit who, along with other spirits, influences all aspects of life. These spirits make their presence known primarily through acts of nature.

The rituals, prayers, and ceremonies of Native Americans are often centered on health and good harvest and hunting. Rituals used to mark the passage through stages of life, including birth, adulthood, and death are passed down as tribal traditions. Religious ceremonies often focus on important points in the agricultural and hunting seasons. Prayers, which are offered in song and dance, also concentrate on agriculture and hunting themes as well as health and well-being.

Rituals are passed down from generation to generation. These Native Americans are performing a ritual dance.

There are many different Native American groups throughout the United States and Canada. This Pawnee is wearing traditional dress during a celebration in Oklahoma.

Totem poles, like this one in Alaska, were popular among the Native American peoples of the Northwest Coast. They were often decorated with mythical beings, family crests, or other figures. They were placed outside homes.

Assessment

Reviewing Vocabulary

Match the following terms with their definitions.

1. sect
2. monotheism
3. polytheism
4. animism
5. atheism

a. belief that spirits inhabit natural objects and forces of nature

b. belief in one God

c. a subdivision within a religion that has its own distinctive belief and/or practices

d. belief in more than one god

e. disbelief in the existence of any god

Reviewing the Main Ideas

World Religions

6. Which religion has the most followers worldwide?

7. On a separate sheet of paper, make a table of the major world religions. Use the chart below to get you started.

Name	Founder	Geographic distribution	Sacred sites
Buddhism			
Christianity			
Confucianism			
Hinduism			
Islam			
Judaism			
Sikhism			
Indigenous			

Buddhism

8. According to Buddhism, how can the end of suffering in the world be achieved?

9. What is Nirvana? According to Buddhists, who is most likely to achieve Nirvana and why?

Christianity

10. In what religion was Jesus raised?

11. Why do Christians regard Jesus as their savior?

Confucianism

12. What is Confucianism based on?

13. What does yin-yang symbolize?

Hinduism

14. Where did Hinduism develop?

15. What role do Hindus believe karma plays in reincarnation?

Islam

16. What are the two branches of Islam? What is the main difference between the two groups?

17. What role does Makkah play in the Islamic faith?

Judaism

18. What is the Torah?

19. What is the purpose of Yom Kippur?

Sikhism

20. Where do most Sikhs live? Why?

21. What religions have contributed to the Adi Granth?

Indigenous Religions

22. Why would local religions feature sacred stories about the creation of people, animals, and plant life?

23. Which of the indigenous religions has the largest membership?

Problem-Solving Activity

24. **Research Project** Use library and Internet sources to research the role of food and food customs in one of the world's major religions. Create a presentation to report your findings to the class.

GLOSSARY/GLOSARIO

- Content vocabulary are words that relate to world history content.
- Words that have an asterisk (*) are academic vocabulary. They help you understand your school subjects.
- All vocabulary words are **boldfaced or highlighted in yellow** in your textbook.

ENGLISH	A	**ESPAÑOL**

abdicate to formally give up control of a country or state (p. 283)

abolitionism a movement to end slavery (p. 191)

absolutism a political system in which a ruler holds total power (p. 81)

***abstract** a style of art, emerging around 1910, that spoke directly to the soul and avoided visual reality by using only lines and color (p. 219)

***administrator** one who manages the affairs of a government or a business (p. 100)

***advocate** support; speak in favor of (p. 211)

***aid** assistance such as money or supplies (p. 283)

***amendment** an alteration proposed or effected by parliamentary or constitutional procedure (p. 147)

anarchy political disorder; lawlessness (p. 100)

annex to incorporate into an existing political unit, such as a city or country (p. 231)

***annual** yearly (p. 294)

annul declare invalid (p. 44)

apartheid "apartness"; the system of racial segregation in South Africa from the 1950s until 1991 (p. 398)

appeasement satisfying reasonable demands of dissatisfied powers in an effort to maintain peace and stability (p. 341)

***approach** the way or method in which one examines or studies an issue or a concept (p. 197)

***appropriate** suitable or compatible; fitting (p. 298)

***arbitrarily** (adverb form of *arbitrary*) at one's discretion; randomly (p. 459)

***arbitrary** at one's discretion; random (p. 137)

archipelago a chain of islands (pp. 80, 122)

---

abdicar renunciar formalmente al control de un país o Estado (pág. 283)

abolicionismo movimiento para acabar con la esclavitud (pág. 191)

absolutismo sistema político en el que el gobernante mantiene un poder total (pág. 81)

***abstracto** estilo artístico que surgió alrededor de 1910; hablaba directamente al alma y evitaba la realidad visual usando sólo líneas y colores (pág. 219)

***administrador** persona que maneja los asuntos de un gobierno o un negocio (pág. 100)

***defender** apoyar; hablar en favor de (pág. 211)

***ayuda** asistencia económica o en especie (pág. 283)

***enmienda** alteración propuesta o realizda por el parlamento o un procedimiento constitucional (pág. 147)

anarquía desorden político; situación al margen de la ley (pág. 100)

anexar incorporar a una unidad política existente, como una ciudad o un país (pág. 231)

anual que sucede una vez al año (pág. 294)

anular declarar no válido (pág. 44)

apartheid "separación"; sistema de segregación racial que se dio en Suráfrica desde la década de 1950 hasta 1991 (pág. 398)

apaciguamiento satisfacer demandas razonables de potencias insatisfechas en un esfuerzo por mantener la paz y la estabilidad (pág. 341)

***enfoque** forma o método para examinar o estudiar un aspecto o un concepto (pág. 197)

***apropiado** adecuado o compatible; que encaja (pág. 298)

***arbitrariamente** (adverbio de arbitrario) a discreción propia; al azar (pág. 459)

***arbitrario** a discreción personal; al azar (pág. 137)

archipiélago cadena de islas (págs. 80, 122)

armada a fleet of warships (p. 74)

armada flota de barcos de guerra (pág. 74)

armistice a truce or an agreement to end fighting (p. 286)

armisticio tregua o acuerdo para poner fin a un combate (pág. 286)

arms race building up armies and stores of weapons to keep up with an enemy (p. 371)

carrera armamentista acumulación de ejércitos y reservas de armas para hacer frente al enemigo (pág. 371)

Aryan a term used to identify people speaking Indo-European languages; Nazis misused the term, treating it as a racial designation and identifying the Aryans with the ancient Greeks and Romans and twentieth-century Germans and Scandinavians (p. 306)

ario término usado para identificar a los hablantes de alguna lengua indoeuropea. Los nazis tergiversaron el uso del término empleándolo como una designación racial e identificaron a los arios con los antiguos griegos y romanos, y con los germanos y escandinavos del siglo XX (pág. 306)

assembly line pioneered by Henry Ford in 1913, a manufacturing method that allowed much more efficient mass production of goods (p. 205)

cadena de montaje método de producción instaurado por Henry Ford en 1913, que permitía una producción masiva de bienes más eficiente (pág. 205)

*assure to make certain of something; to guarantee (p. 362)

*asegurar cerciorarse de algo; garantizar (pág. 362)

*attain to gain or achieve (p. 29)

*obtener ganar o alcanzar (pág. 29)

*attitude a mental position regarding a fact or state (p. 301)

*actitud posición mental con respecto a un hecho o un estado (pág. 301)

*authority power; person in command (pp. 81, 103)

*autoridad poder; persona a cargo (págs. 81, 103)

autonomous self-governing (p. 436)

autónomo que se gobierna a sí mismo (pág. 436)

B

baroque an artistic style of the seventeenth century characterized by complex forms, bold ornamentation, and contrasting elements (p. 87)

Barroco estilo artístico del siglo XVII caracterizado por formas complejas, una decoración recargada y elementos que contrastan (pág. 87)

bioterrorism the use of biological and chemical weapons in terrorist attacks (p. 457)

bioterrorismo uso de armas biológicas y químicas en ataques terroristas (pág. 457)

blitz the British term for the German air raids on British cities and towns during World War II (p. 353)

bombardeo aéreo término con que los británicos designaron los ataques aéreos alemanes sobre las ciudades y los pueblos británicos durante la Segunda Guerra Mundial (pág. 353)

blitzkrieg German for "lightning war"; a swift and sudden military attack; used by the Germans during World War II (p. 345)

blitzkriegk en alemán, "guerra relámpago"; ataque militar rápido y sorpresivo; usado por los alemanes durante la Segunda Guerra Mundial (pág. 345)

bloc a group of nations with a common purpose (p. 416)

bloque grupo de naciones con un propósito común (pág. 416)

bourgeoisie the middle class, including merchants, industrialists, and professional people (pp. 153, 206)

burguesía la clase media, que incluye comerciantes, industriales y profesionales (págs. 153, 206)

boyar a Russian noble (p. 84)

boyar noble ruso (pág. 84)

budget deficit the state that exists when a government spends more than it collects in revenues (p. 439)

déficit presupuestario estado que tiene lugar cuando los gastos de un gobierno superan los ingresos que recauda (pág. 439)

ENGLISH	ESPAÑOL
bureaucracy an administrative organization that relies on nonelective officials and regular procedures (p. 122)	**burocracia** organización administrativa que se basa en funcionarios que no son elegidos y en procedimientos habituales (pág. 122)
burgher a member of the middle class who lived in a city or town (p. 26)	**burgués** miembro de la clase media que vivía en una ciudad o un pueblo (pág. 26)

C

ENGLISH	ESPAÑOL
caliph a successor of Muhammad as spiritual and temporal leader of the Muslims (p. 316)	**califa** sucesor de Mahoma como líder espiritual y temporal de los musulmanes (pág. 316)
***caliphate** the office of caliph (p. 316)	***califato** junsdicción del calafa (pág. 316)
***capable** having or showing ability (p. 165)	***capaz** que tiene o demuestra habilidad (pág. 165)
capital money available for investment (p. 176)	**capital** dinero disponible para invertir (pág. 176)
caravel a small, fast, maneuverable ship that had a large cargo hold and usually three masts with lateen sails (p. 53)	**carabela** embarcación pequeña, rápida y maniobrable con una gran capacidad de carga y que por lo general tenía tres mástiles con velas latinas (pág. 53)
cartel a group of drug businesses (p. 408)	**cartel** grupo dedicado al narcotráfico (pág. 408)
cash crop a crop that is grown for sale rather than for personal use (p. 195)	**cultivo comercial** cultivo destinado a la venta, no para el uso personal (pág. 195)
caudillo in post-revolutionary Latin America, a strong leader who ruled chiefly by military force, usually with the support of the landed elite (p. 194)	**caudillo** en la América Latina posrevolucionaria, líder fuerte que gobernaba principalmente mediante la fuerza militar, por lo general con el apoyo de la élite latifundista (pág. 194)
Cavaliers supporters of King Charles I in the English Civil War (p. 78)	**caballeros** partidarios del rey Carlos I durante la Guerra Civil Inglesa (pág. 78)
***cease** to come to an end (p. 325)	***cesar** terminar (pág. 325)
***chemical** used in or produced by chemistry (p. 457)	***producto químico** que se usa o es producido por productas química (pág. 457)
Christian humanism a movement that developed in northern Europe during the Renaissance combining classical learning (humanism) with the goal of reforming the Catholic Church (p. 38)	**humanismo cristiano** movimiento desarrollado en el norte de Europa durante el Renacimiento, que combina el aprendizaje clásico (humanismo) con el objetivo de reformar la Iglesia católica (pág. 38)
***circumstance** a determining condition (p. 32); a state of affairs (p. 353)	***circunstancia** condición determinante (pág. 32); estado de un asunto (pág. 353)
***civil** involving the general public or civic affairs (pp. 170, 238)	***civil** que implica asuntos relacionados con el público o los asuntos cívicos (págs. 170, 238)
civil disobedience refusal to obey laws that are considered to be unjust (p. 322)	**desobediencia civil** negativa a obedecer leyes que se consideran injustas (pág. 322)
clan a group of related families (p. 114)	**clan** grupo de familias relacionadas (pág. 114)
***classical** authoritative, traditional; relating to the literature, art, architecture, and ideals of the ancient Greek and Roman world (p. 8)	***clásico** fidedigno, tradicional; relativo a la literatura, el arte, la arquitectura y los ideales del antiguo mundo grecorromano (pág. 8)

Cold War the period of political tension following World War II and ending with the fall of Communism in the Soviet Union at the end of the 1980s (p. 362)

collaborator a person who assists the enemy (p. 357)

*collapse to break down completely; to suddenly lose force or effectiveness (p. 433)

collateralized debt obligation a debt security collateralized by a variety of debt obligations including bonds and loans of different maturities and credit quality (p. 469)

collective bargaining the right of unions to negotiate with employers over wages and hours (p. 297)

collectivization a system in which private farms are eliminated and peasants work land owned by the government (p. 303)

colony a settlement of people living in a new territory, linked with the parent country by trade and direct government control (p. 56)

commodities agricultural, mined, and mass-produced marketable goods (p. 259)

*commonwealth a republic (p. 78)

commune in China during the 1950s, a group of collective farms which contained more than 30,000 people who lived and worked together (p. 374)

*community a group of people with common interests and characteristics living together within a larger society (pp. 45, 117)

*compensation payment (p. 320)

*complex having many intricate parts (p. 271)

concentration camp a camp where prisoners of war, political prisoners, or members of minority groups are confined, typically under harsh conditions (p. 306)

concession a political compromise (p. 261)

*conflict opposition; a fight, battle, or war (p. 73)

*conform to adhere to rules or standards; to fit in (p. 100)

conquistador a leader in the Spanish conquest of the Americas (p. 55)

conscription military draft (p. 271)

*consent approval (p. 404)

conservatism a political philosophy based on tradition and social stability, favoring obedience to political authority and organized religion (p. 169)

Guerra Fría periodo de tensión política posterior a la Segunda Guerra Mundial, que terminó con la caída del comunismo en la Unión Soviética, a finales de la década de 1980 (pág. 362)

colaborador persona que ayuda al enemigo (pág. 357)

*colapsar desplomarse por completo; perder fuerza o efectividad de manera repentina (pág. 433)

obligaciones de deuda colateralizada valor garantizado por un conjunto de bonos, préstamos y otros tipos de deuda (pág 469)

negociación colectiva derecho de los sindicatos a negociar con los empleadores los salarios y horarios de trabajo (pág. 297)

colectivización sistema en el cual se eliminan las granjas privadas y los campesinos trabajan la tierra que pertenece al gobierno (pág. 303)

colonia asentamiento de personas que viven en un nuevo territorio y que guardan un vínculo con su país de origen por el comercio y el control directo del gobierno (pág. 56)

bienes de consumo bienes comercializables agrícolas, mineros y de producción masiva (pág. 259)

*mancomunidad república (pág. 78)

comuna en la China de la década de 1950, grupo de granjas colectivas donde vivían y trabajaban juntas más de 30,000 personas (pág. 374)

*comunidad grupo de personas con intereses y características comunes que viven juntos dentro de una sociedad (págs. 45, 117)

*compensación pago (pág. 320)

*complejo que tiene muchas partes intrincadas (pág. 271)

campo de concentración campo donde se confinaba a los prisioneros de guerra, prisioneros políticos o miembros de grupos minoritarios, por lo general en condiciones inhumanas (pág. 306)

concesión compromiso político (pág. 261)

*conflicto oposición; lucha, batalla o guerra (pág. 73)

*cumplir ceñirse a las normas o estándares; encajar (pág. 100)

conquistador líder en la conquista española de América (pág. 55)

conscripción reclutamiento military (pág. 271)

*consentimiento aprobación (pág. 404)

conservadurismo filosofía política basada en la tradición y la estabilidad social, que apoya la obediencia a la autoridad política y la religión organizada (pág. 169)

Glossary/Glosario

ENGLISH	ESPAÑOL

*constitution the basic principles and laws of a nation, state, or social group that determine the powers and duties of the government and guarantee certain rights to the people in it (p. 171)

*constitución principios y leyes básicos de una nación, Estado o grupo social, que determinan los poderes y deberes del gobierno y garantizan algunos derechos a sus habitantes (pág. 171)

consulate the government established in France after the overthrow of the Directory in 1799, with Napoleon as first consul in control of the entire government (p. 164)

Consulado el gobierno establecido en Francia después del derrocamiento del Directorio en 1799, con Napoleón como el primer cónsul a cargo de todo el gobierno (pág. 164)

*consumer one who consumes or uses economic goods (p. 153)

*consumidor quien consume o usa bienes económicos (pág. 153)

consumer society a society preoccupied with buying goods (p. 418)

sociedad de consumo sociedad que se preocupa por comprar bienes (pág. 418)

*context the circumstances surrounding a situation or event (p. 264)

*contexto circunstancias que rodean una situación o evento (pág. 264)

*controversy a dispute or quarrel (p. 217)

*controversia disputa o discrepancia (pág. 217)

*convert to change from one belief to another (p. 79)

*convertirse cambiar de una creencia a otra (pág. 79)

*cooperation a common effort (p. 287)

*cooperación esfuerzo común (pág. 287)

*core the basic or essential part (p. 30)

*núcleo parte básica o esencial (pág. 30)

corruption impairment of integrity, virtue, or moral principle (p. 450)

corrupción falta de integridad, virtud o principios morales (pág. 450)

cottage industry a method of production in which tasks are done by individuals in their rural homes (p. 177)

industria artesanal método de producción en el cual los individuos realizan el trabajo en sus hogares rurales (pág. 177)

coup d'état a sudden overthrow of the government (p. 162)

golpe de Estado derrocamiento repentino de un gobierno (pág. 162)

*creative imaginative (p. 89)

*creativo imaginativo (pág. 89)

creole a person of European descent born in Latin America and living there permanently (pp. 64, 192)

criollo persona de ascendencia europea nacida en América Latina y que vive allí permanentemente (págs. 64, 192)

Crusades military expeditions carried out by European Christians in the Middle Ages to regain the Holy Land from the Muslims (p. 15)

Cruzadas expediciones militares llevados a cabo por los cristianos europeos durante la Edad Media con el fin de recuperar la Tierra Santa que estaba en manos de los musulmanes (pág. 15)

cultural imperialism referring to Western nations' control of other world cultures similar to how they had controlled colonial governments (p. 440)

imperialismo cultural relativo al control que ejercen las naciones occidentales sobre otras culturas, semejante a la manera en que estas naciones controlaban los gobiernos de las colonias (pág. 440)

*culture the customary beliefs, social forms, and material traits of a racial, religious, or social group (pp. 4, 58)

*cultura creencias, formas sociales y rasgos materiales tradicionales de un grupo racial, religioso o social (págs. 4, 58)

*currency coins, for example, that are in circulation and used as a medium of exchange (pp. 437, 468)

*moneda billetes y monedas, por ejemplo, que están en circulación y se usan como medio de intercambio (págs. 437, 468)

*cycle a series of events that recur regularly and usually lead back to the starting point (p. 7)

*ciclo serie de eventos que se repiten con regularidad y que por lo general llevan de nuevo al punto departida (pág. 7)

czar Russian for *caesar;* the title used by Russian emperors (p. 84)

zar "césar" en ruso; título adoptado por los emperadores rusos (pág. 84)

Glossary/Glosario

D

daimyo "great names"; the head of noble families in Japan who controlled vast landed estates and relied on samurai for protection (p. 116)

daimio "gran nombre"; jefe de una familia noble japonesa que controlaba grandes propiedades de tierra y dependía de la protección de los samuráis (pág. 116)

*decline a change to a lower state or level (pp. 24, 86)

*descenso cambio a un estado o nivel inferior (págs. 24, 86)

deficit spending when a government pays out more money than it takes in through taxation and other revenues, thus going into debt (p. 297)

gasto deficitario cuando un gobierno paga más dinero del que recibe por concepto de impuestos y otros ingresos, y por lo tanto se endeuda (pág. 297)

deflation a contraction in the volume of available money or credit that results in a general decline in prices (p. 444)

deflación reducción en el volumen de dinero o crédito disponible que lleva a una caída general en los precios (pág. 444)

deforestation the clearing of forests (p. 474)

deforestación devastación de los bosques (pág. 474)

deism an eighteenth-century religious philosophy based on reason and natural law (p. 135)

deísmo filosofía religiosa del siglo XVIII basada en la razón y la ley natural (pág. 135)

demilitarized elimination or prohibition of weapons, fortifications, and other military installations (p. 341)

desmilitarización eliminación o prohibición de usar armas, fortalezas u otras instalaciones militares (pág. 341)

democratic governed by the "rule of many," or by the people, either directly or through their elected representatives (p. 8)

democrático cuando los pueblos son regidos por el "gobierno de muchos," o por las personas, directamente o por intermedio de representantes elegidos (pág. 8)

*demonstration a public display of group feeling toward a person or cause (p. 433)

*manifestación expresión pública de los sentimientos de un grupo hacia una persona o causa (pág. 433)

depression a period of low economic activity and rising unemployment (p. 295)

depresión periodo de baja actividad económica y aumento del desempleo (pág. 295)

*derived obtained from, came from (p. 178)

*derivación obtenido de; vino de (pág. 178)

desertification formation of degraded soil, turning semi-arid lands into nonproductive deserts (p. 474)

desertificación formación de suelo degradado que transforma tierras semiáridas en desiertos improductivos (pág. 474)

de-Stalinization the process of eliminating Stalin's more ruthless policies (p. 421)

desestalinización proceso de eliminación de las políticas más despiadadas de Stalin (pág. 421)

détente a phase of relaxed tensions and improved relations between two adversaries (p. 422)

détente fase de alivio de las tensiones y mejoramiento de las relaciones entre dos adversarios (pág. 422)

deterrence during the Cold War, the U.S. and Soviet policies of holding huge arsenals of nuclear weapons to prevent war; each nation believed that neither would launch a nuclear attack since both knew that the other side could strike back with devastating power (p. 372)

disuasión durante la Guerra Fría, política de Estados Unidos y la Unión Soviética que consistía en poseer enormes arsenales de armas nucleares para evitar la guerra; cada nación creía que ninguna de ellas lanzaría un ataque nuclear porque ambas sabían que la contraparte podría responder con una fuerza devastadora (pág. 372)

direct rule colonial government in which local elites are removed from power and replaced by a new set of officials brought from the colonizing country (p. 229)

gobierno directo gobierno colonial en el cual se retira del poder a las élites locales y las reemplaza un nuevo grupo de funcionarios del país colonizador (pág. 229)

discrimination prejudicial treatment usually based on race, religion, class, sex, or age (p. 390)

discriminación tratamiento que va en detrimento de las personas por razones de raza, religión, clase social, sexo o edad (pág. 390)

dissident a person who speaks out against the regime in power (p. 422)

disidente persona que habla en contra del régimen en el poder (pág. 422)

*diverse varied and not alike (p. 398)

*diverso variado, diferente (pág. 398)

Glossary/Glosario

ENGLISH	ESPAÑOL
divine right of kings the belief that the kings receive their power from God and are responsible only to God (p. 77)	**derecho divino de los reyes** creencia de que los reyes reciben su poder de Dios y son responsables solo ante Él (pág. 77)
dollar diplomacy the diplomacy that seeks to strengthen the power of a country or effect its purposes in foreign relations by the use of its financial resources (p. 243)	**diplomacia del dólar** diplomacia que busca fortalecer el poder de un país o alcanzar sus propósitos en las relaciones internacionales mediante el uso de sus recursos financieros (pág. 243)
***domain** a territory over which control is exercised (p. 96)	***dominio** territorio sobre el cual se ejerce control (pág. 96)
***domestic** relating to or originating within one's country (p. 59)	***interno** relativo al país de una persona o que se origina allí (pág. 59)
***dominate** to influence or control (pp. 22, 340)	***dominar** influir o controlar (págs. 22, 340)
domino theory the idea that if one country falls to communism, neighboring countries will also fall (p. 381)	**teoría del efecto dominó** idea según la cual si un país cede al comunismo, los países vecinos también lo harán (pág. 381)
draft to select for some purpose; to conscript (p. 66)	**reclutar** elegir para algún propósito; conscribir (pág. 66)
***drama** a composition that tells a story usually involving conflicts and emotions through action and dialogue and typically designed for the theater (p. 88); state on intense conflict (p. 725)	***drama** composición que cuenta una historia que usualmente implica conflictos y emociones mediante la acción y el uso de diálogos; por lo general se crea para el teatro (pág. 88); estado de conflicto intenso (pág. 457)
Duma the Russian legislative assembly (p. 215)	**duma** Asamblea Legislativa de Rusia (pág. 215)
***dynamic** an activity or change that is continuous and productive (p. 438)	***dinámica** actividad o cambio que es continuo y productivo (pág. 438)

E

ecology the study of the relationships between living things and their environment (p. 474)	**ecología** estudio de las relaciones entre los seres vivos y su medioambiente (pág. 474)
elector an individual qualified to vote in an election (p. 162)	**elector** un individuo calificado para votar en una elección (pág. 162)
***element** a distinct group within a larger group (p. 315)	***elemento** un grupo distinto dentro de un grupo más grande (pág. 315)
emancipation the act of setting free (p. 190)	**emancipación** acción de poner en libertad (pág. 190)
***emerge** to become manifest; to become known (p. 83); to come into being through evolution; to develop (p. 381)	***emerger** hacerse manifiesto; darse a conocer (pág. 83); surgir por evolución; desarrollar (pág. 381)
encomienda a system of labor the Spanish used in the Americas; Spanish landowners had the right, as granted by Queen Isabella, to use Native Americans as laborers (p. 66)	**encomienda** sistema de mano de obra usado por los españoles en América; los terratenientes españoles tenían derecho, concedido por la Reina Isabel, de emplear a indígenas americanos como mano de obra (pág. 66)
***enhanced** improved (p. 420)	***aumentado** mejorado (pág. 420)
enlightened absolutism a system in which rulers tried to govern by Enlightenment principles while maintaining their full royal powers (p. 140)	**despotismo ilustrado** sistema en el cual los gobernantes trataron de dirigir siguiendo los principios de la Ilustración, pero en el que conservaban todas sus facultades reales (pág. 140)
entrepreneur a person who finds new business opportunities and new ways to make profits (p. 176)	**empresario** persona interesada en hallar nuevas oportunidades comerciales y formas de obtener ganancias (pág. 176)

*erupt to suddenly become active or violent (p. 195)

*establish to set up permanently; to found (p. 333)

estate a landed property with a large house (p. 241); one of the three classes into which French society was divided before the revolution: the clergy (First Estate), the nobles (Second Estate), and the townspeople (Third Estate) (p. 152)

eta Japan's outcast class whose way of life was strictly regulated by the Tokugawa (p. 118)

*ethnic relating to people who have common racial, religious, or cultural origins (p. 355)

ethnic cleansing a policy of killing or forcibly removing an ethnic group from its lands; used by the Serbs against the Muslim minority in Bosnia (pp. 315, 436)

*eventually in the end (pp. 142, 326)

*evident apparent (p. 450)

*evolve develop; work out (p. 448)

*exclusion barred from inclusion or participation in (p. 155)

*exclusive limited to a single individual or group (p. 253)

*exploit to make use of meanly or unfairly for one's own advantage (p. 229)

*export to send a product or service for sale to another country (pp. 59, 229)

*external not intrinsic or essential (p. 39)

extraterritoriality living in a section of a country set aside for foreigners but not subject to the host country's laws (p. 252)

*estallar entrar en actividad o tornarse violento repentinamente (pág. 195)

*establecer instalar permanentemente; fundar (pág. 333)

latifundio propiedad de tierra con una casa grande (pág. 241); una de las tres clases en las que se dividía la sociedad francesa antes de la revolución: el clero (Primer estado), los nobles (Segundo estado) y el pueblo (Tercer estado) (pág. 152)

eta clase japonesa fuera del sistema de castas cuya forma de vida estaba estrictamente regulada por los Tokugawa (pág. 118)

*étnico relativo a las personas que tienen un origen racial, religioso o cultural común (pág. 355)

limpieza étnica política que consiste en asesinar o sacar a la fuerza de sus tierras a un grupo étnico; la usaron los serbios contra la minoría musulmana en Bosnia (págs. 315, 436)

*con el tiempo al final (págs. 142, 326)

*evidente aparente (pág. 450)

*evolucionar desarrollar; elaborar (pág. 448)

*exclusión prohibición de incluir o participar (pág. 155)

*exclusivo limitado a un individuo o grupo (pág. 253)

*explotar hacer uso de manera cruel o injusta para beneficio propio (pág. 229)

*exportar enviar un producto o servicio para venderlo en otro país (págs. 59, 229)

*exterior no es intrínseco o esencial (pág. 39)

extraterritorialidad vivir en una sección de un país destinada a las personas extranjeras, pero que no está sujeta a las leyes del país anfitrión (pág. 252)

F

fascism a political philosophy that glorifies the state above the individual by emphasizing the need for a strong central government led by a dictatorial ruler (p. 300)

federal system a form of government in which power is shared between the national and state governments (p. 147)

feminism the movement for women's rights (p. 211)

feudalism political and social order that developed during the Middle Ages when royal governments were no longer able to defend their subjects; nobles offered protection and land in return for service (p. 15)

*final the last in a series, process, or progress (p. 374)

fascismo filosofía política que exalta al Estado por encima del individuo, poniendo énfasis en la necesidad de un gobierno central fuerte liderado por un dictador (pág. 300)

sistema federal forma de gobierno en la cual el poder se comparte entre los gobiernos nacional y estatal (pág. 147)

feminismo movimiento que lucha por los derechos de las mujeres (pág. 211)

feudalismo orden política y social que se desarrolló durante la Edad Media, cuando los gobiernos monárquicos ya no podían defender a sus súbditos; los nobles ofrecían protección y tierras a cambio de servicios (pág. 15)

*final último en una serie, proceso o progreso (pág. 374)

Glossary/Glosario

ENGLISH	ESPAÑOL
fresco painting done on fresh, wet plaster with water-based paints (p. 31)	**fresco** pintura elaborada sobre yeso fresco y húmedo con pinturas a base de agua (pág. 31)
*fundamental basic or essential (p. 38)	***fundamental** básico o esencial (pág. 38)

G

*generation a group of individuals born and living at the same time (p. 137)	***generación** grupo de individuos que nacen y viven durante la misma época (pág. 137)
genocide the deliberate mass murder or physical extinction of a particular racial, political, or cultural group (pp. 315, 356)	**genocidio** asesinato masivo o exterminio físico deliberado de un grupo racial, político o cultural específico (págs. 315, 356)
geocentric Earth-centered; a system of planetary motion in which the sun, moon, and other planets revolve around the Earth (pp. 129, 156)	**geocéntrico** con centro en la Tierra; sistema de movimiento de los planetas en el cual el Sol, la Luna y otros planetas orbitan la Tierra (págs. 129, 156)
ghetto formerly a district in a city in which Jews were required to live (p. 46)	**gueto** antiguo distrito en una ciudad en el cual se obligaba a vivir a los judíos (pág. 46)
glasnost a Soviet policy permitting open discussion of political and social issues (p. 432)	**glasnot** política soviética que permitió el debate abierto de temas políticos y sociales (pág. 432)
globalization the movement toward a more integrated and interdependent world economy (p. 469)	**globalización** movimiento hacia una economía mundial más integrada e interdependiente (pág. 469)
*goal an aim or a purpose (p. 397)	***meta** objetivo o propósito (pág. 397)
grand vizier the Ottoman sultan's chief minister who carried the main burdens of the state and who led the council meetings (p. 96)	**gran visir** primer ministro del sultán otomano responsable de las principales tareas del Estado, que encabezaba las reuniones del consejo (pág. 96)
greenhouse effect global warming caused by the buildup of carbon dioxide in the atmosphere (p. 475)	**efecto invernadero** calentamiento global ocasionado por la acumulación de dióxido de carbono en la atmósfera (pág. 475)
guarantee to assure fulfillment of a condition (p. 147)	**garantizar** asegurar el cumplimiento de una condición (pág. 147)
guerrilla tactics the use of unexpected maneuvers like sabotage and subterfuge to fight an enemy (p. 327)	**táctica de guerrillas** uso de maniobras inesperadas como el sabotaje y el uso de subterfugios para combatir a un enemigo (pág. 327)
gunpowder empire an empire formed by outside conquerors who unified the regions they conquered through their mastery of firearms (p. 95)	**imperio de la pólvora** imperio formado por conquistadores extranjeros que unificaron las regiones que conquistaban gracias a su dominio de las armas de fuego (pág. 95)

H

hans approximately 250 domains into which Japan was divided under the Tokugawa (p. 117)	*han* aproximadamente 250 dominios en los cuales se dividía Japón bajo el dominio de los Tokugawa (pág. 117)
harem "sacred place"; the private domain of an Ottoman sultan, where he and his wives resided (p. 96)	**harén** "lugar sagrado"; dominio privado de un sultán otomano, donde este vivía junto a sus esposas (pág. 96)
heavy industry the manufacture of machines and equipment for factories and mines (p. 420)	**industria pesada** manufactura de maquinaria y equipo para fábricas y minas (pág. 420)

Glossary/Glosario

heliocentric sun-centered; the system of the universe in which the Earth and planets revolve around the sun (p. 129)

heretic one who does not conform to established doctrine (p. 72)

*highlighted centered attention on (p. 250)

HIV/AIDS human immunodeficiency virus/acquired immunodeficiency syndrome; any of the strains of HIV-1 and HIV-2 that infect and destroy the immune system's helper T cells causing a large drop in their numbers, and becomes AIDS when a person has 20 percent or less than the normal level of helper T cells (p. 399)

hostage system a system used by the shogunate to control the daimyo in Tokugawa Japan; the family of a daimyo lord was forced to stay at their residence in the capital whenever the lord was absent from it (p. 117)

humanism an intellectual movement of the Renaissance based on the study of the humanities, which included grammar, rhetoric, poetry, moral philosophy, and history (p. 28)

heliocéntrico con centro en el Sol; sistema del universo en el cual la Tierra y los planetas orbitan el Sol (pág. 129)

hereje persona que no acepta la doctrina establecida (pág. 72)

*destacado algo sobre lo cual se centra la atención (pág. 250)

VIH/sida virus de inmunodeficiencia humana/síndrome de inmunodeficiencia adquirida; cualquiera de las cadenas de VIH-1 y VIH-2 que infectan y destruyen las células T cooperadoras del sistema inmunológico, lo que ocasiona una gran disminución de las mismas. Se convierte en sida cuando el número de células es igual o inferior al 20 por ciento del recuento normal de células T cooperadoras (pág. 399)

sistema de rehenes sistema usado por el shogunato Tokugawa para controlar al señor daimio; la familia del daimio era obligada a permanecer en su residencia en la capital siempre que el señor no se encontraba allí (pág. 117)

humanismo movimiento intelectual del Renacimiento basado en el estudio de las humanidades, que incluían la gramática, la retórica, la poesía, la filosofía moral y la historia (pág. 28)

I

*ideological based on a set of beliefs (p. 362)

imperialism the extension of a nation's power over other lands (p. 226)

*impose to establish or apply (p. 123)

indemnity the payment for damages (p. 255)

indigenous native to a region (p. 234)

indirect rule a colonial government in which local rulers are allowed to maintain their positions of authority and status (p. 229)

*individuality a total character that distinguishes an individual from others (p. 196)

inductive reasoning the doctrine that scientists should proceed from the particular to the general by making systematic observations and carefully organized experiments to test hypotheses or theories, a process that will lead to correct general principles (p. 132)

indulgence a release from all or part of punishment for sin by the Catholic Church, reducing time in purgatory after death (p. 39)

industrial capitalism an economic system based on industrial production or manufacturing (p. 180)

*ideológico que se basa en una serie de creencias (pág. 362)

imperialismo extensión del poder de una nación sobre otras tierras (pág. 226)

*imponer establecer o aplicar (pág. 123)

indemnización pago para compensar un daño (pág. 255)

indígena nativo de una región (pág. 234)

gobierno indirecto forma de gobierno colonial en la cual se permitía a los gobernantes mantener sus cargos de autoridad y su estatus (pág. 229)

*individualidad carácter total que distingue a un individuo de otros (pág. 196)

razonamiento inductivo doctrina según la cual los científicos deben ir de lo particular a lo general haciendo observaciones sistemáticas y experimentos organizados cuidadosamente para probar hipótesis o teorías, un proceso que llevará a los principios generales correctos (pág. 132)

indulgencia exoneración total o parcial del castigo por un pecado que concede la Iglesia católica, la cual reduce el tiempo en el purgatorio después de morir (pág. 39)

capitalismo industrial sistema económico basado en la producción o manufactura industrial (pág. 180)

Glossary/Glosario

ENGLISH	ESPAÑOL
infidel an unbeliever; a term applied to the Muslims during the Crusades (p. 75)	**infiel** persona no creyente; término que se aplicó a los musulmanes durante las cruzadas (pág. 75)
inflation a rapid increase in prices (p. 75)	**inflación** aumento rápido de los precios (pág. 75)
***insecure** uncertain, shaky; not adequately covered or sustained (p. 216)	***inseguro** incierto, flojo; que no está cubierto o sostenido adecuadamente (pág. 216)
***intelligent** having a high degree of understanding and mental capacity (p. 102)	***inteligente** que tiene un alto grado de comprensión y capacidad mental (pág. 102)
***intense** marked by great zeal, energy, determination, or concentration (p. 473)	***intenso** marcado por gran fervor, energía, determinación o concentración (pág. 473)
***intensity** extreme degree of strength, force, energy, or feeling (p. 221)	***intensidad** grado extremo de resistencia, fuerza, energía o sentimiento (pág. 221)
***intervention** the involvement in a situation to alter the outcome (p. 194)	***intervención** participación en una situación para alterar el resultado (pág. 194)
intifada "uprising"; a militant movement that arose during the 1980s among supporters of the Palestine Liberation Organization living in Israel (p. 393)	*intifada* movimiento militante que se generó en la década de 1980 entre quienes apoyaban a la Organización para la Liberación de Palestina, y que Vivian en Cisjordania y Gaza (pág. 393)
***involvement** a commitment or a connection to (p. 346)	***participación** compromiso o conexión con algo (pág. 346)
isolationism a policy of national isolation by abstention from alliances and other international political and economic relations (p. 346)	**aislacionismo** política de aislamiento nacional llevada a cabo absteniéndose de establecer alianzas y otras relaciones políticas y económicas internacionales (pág. 346)
isolationist a policy of national isolation by abstention from alliances and other international political and economic relations (p. 121)	**aislacionista** política de aislamiento nacional según la cual se evitan alianzas y otras relaciones políticas y económicas internacionales (pág. 121)
***issue** a vital or an unsettled matter (p. 392)	***asunto** tema esencial o por resolver (pág. 392)
***investor** a person or an entity that commits money to earn a financial return (p. 331)	***inversionista** persona o entidad que compromete dinero para obtener un rendimiento financiero (pág. 331)

J

janissary a soldier in the elite guard of the Ottoman Turks (p. 95)	**jenízaro** soldado en la guardia principal de los turcos otomanos (pág. 95)
jurisdiction the limits or territory within which authority may be exercised (p. 448)	**jurisdicción** límites o territorio dentro del cual se puede ejercer autoridad (pág. 448)
justification the process of being justified, or deemed worthy of salvation, by God (p. 44)	**justificación** proceso mediante el cual Dios declara que alguien es justo o digno de salvación (pág. 44)

K

kaiser German for "caesar"; the title of the emperors of the Second German Empire (p. 189)

kamikaze Japanese for "divine wind"; a suicide mission in which young Japanese pilots intentionally flew their airplanes into U.S. fighting ships at sea (p. 352)

káiser en alemán, "césar"; título de los emperadores del Segundo Imperio Alemán (pág. 189)

kamikaze en japonés, "viento divino"; misión suicida en la cual jóvenes pilotos japoneses estrellaban sus aviones intencionalmente contra los barcos de combate estadounidenses que estaban en el mar (pág. 352)

L

labor people with all their abilities and efforts (p. 66); work performed by people that provides the goods or services in an economy (p. 176)

laissez-faire the concept that the state should not impose government regulations but should leave the economy alone (p. 136)

landed aristocrat an upper class whose wealth is based on land whose power is passed on from one generation to another (p. 14)

*legislature an organized body that makes laws (p. 314)

*liberal broad-minded; associated with ideals of the individual, especially economic freedom and greater participation in government (p. 166)

liberalism a political philosophy originally based largely on Enlightenment principles, holding that people should be as free as possible from government restraint and that civil liberties—the basic rights of all people—should be protected (p. 170)

liberate to free (p. 368)

lineage group an extended family unit within a larger community (p. 12)

Lutheranism the religious doctrine that Martin Luther developed; it differed from Catholicism in the doctrine of salvation, which Luther believed could be achieved by faith alone, not by good works; Lutheranism was the first Protestant faith (p. 41)

mano de obra personas con todas sus capacidades y esfuerzos (pág. 66); trabajo realizado por personas, que proporciona los bienes y servicios en una economía (pág. 176)

laissez-faire concepto según el cual el Estado no debe imponer regulaciones gubernamentales, sino que debe haber libertad en la economía (pág. 136)

aristocracia terrateniente clase alta cuya riqueza se basa en la tierra y cuyo poder se transmite de generación en generación (pág. 14)

*Legislativo cuerpo organizado que hace las leyes (pág. 314)

*liberal de mente abierta; asociado con ideales de los individuos, en especial la libertad económica y una mayor participación en el gobierno (pág. 166)

liberalismo filosofía política basada originalmente en los principios de la Ilustración, que sostiene que las personas deben estar tan libres como sea posible de las restricciones impuestas por el gobierno y que las libertades civiles, es decir los derechos fundamentales de las personas, se deben proteger (pág. 170)

liberar poner en libertad (pág. 368)

grupo de linaje unidad de familia extensa que se integra en una comunidad más grande (pág. 12)

luteranismo doctrina religiosa desarrollada por Martín Lutero; se diferencia del catolicismo en la doctrina de la salvación, la cual según Lutero se podía alcanzar solo por la fe, no por las buenas obras. El luteranismo fue el primer credo protestante (pág. 41)

M

magic realism a form of expression unique to Latin American literature; it combines realistic events with dreamlike or fantasy backgrounds (p. 409)

mainland states a part of a continent, as distinguished from peninsulas or offshore islands (p. 122)

*maintain to keep in an existing state of repair or efficiency (p. 425)

realismo mágico forma de expresión propia de la literatura latinoamericana; combina sucesos reales con trasfondos irreales o fantásticos (pág. 409)

Estados del territorio continental parte de un continente, en oposición a las penínsulas o islas mar adentro (pág. 122)

*mantener conservar en buen estado de funcionamiento o eficiencia (pág. 425)

Glossary/Glosario

ENGLISH	ESPAÑOL
mandate a territory temporarily governed by another nation on behalf of the League of Nations (p. 289)	**mandato** territorio gobernado temporariamente por un país en nombre de la Liga de las Naciones (pág. 289)
Mandate of Heaven the claim by Chinese kings of the Zhou dynasty that they had direct authority from heaven to rule and keep order in the universe (p. 7)	**mandato divino** afirmanción de los reyes de la dinastía Zhou según la cual ellos tenían autoridad proveniente directamente del cielo para gobernar y mantener el orden en el universo (pág. 7)
*****manipulation** skillful or artful management (p. 473)	*****manipulación** manejo hábil o astuto (pág. 473)
Mannerism an artistic movement that emerged in Italy in the 1520s and 1530s; it marked the end of the Renaissance by breaking down the principles of balance, harmony, and moderation (p. 86)	**manierismo** movimiento artístico surgido en Italia en las décadas de 1520 y 1530; marcó el fin del Renacimiento al romper los principios de balance, armonía y moderación (pág. 86)
mass production production of goods in quantity usually by machinery (p. 205)	**producción masiva** producción de bienes en cantidad por lo general mediante el uso de maquinaria (pág. 205)
*****media** channels or systems of communication (p. 301)	*****medios de comunicación** canales o sistemas de comunicación (pág. 301)
megacity a very large city (p. 409)	**megaciudad** una ciudad muy grande (pág. 409)
mercantilism a set of principles that dominated economic thought in the seventeenth century; it held that the prosperity of a nation depended on a large supply of gold and silver (p. 58)	**mercantilismo** conjunto de principios que dominaban el pensamiento económico en el siglo XVII. Planteaba que la prosperidad de una nación dependía de una abundante acumulación de oro y plata (pág. 58)
mercenary a soldier who fights primarily for pay (p. 23)	**mercenario** soldado que combate principalmente a cambio de un pago (pág. 23)
mestizo a person of mixed European and Native American descent (pp. 65, 193)	**mestizo** persona que desciende de un europeo y un indígena americano (págs. 65, 193)
microchip also called an integrated circuit; a tiny assembly of electronic components and their connections that is produced in or on a tiny bit of material, usually silicon (p. 472)	**microchip** conocido también como circuito integrado; diminuto ensamblaje de componentes electrónicos y sus conexiones, producido en (o sobre) un trozo pequeño de material, por lo general silicio (pág. 472)
Middle Passage the forced voyage of enslaved Africans across the Atlantic Ocean to the Americas (p. 62)	**travesía intermedia** viaje obligado de los africanos esclavizados a través del océano Atlántico hasta América (pág. 62)
*****migration** the movement of people from one country, place, or locality to another (p. 464)	*****migración** movimiento de personas de un país, lugar o área a otra (pág. 464)
militarism the reliance on military strength (p. 188)	**militarismo** dependencia del poderío militar (pág. 188)
*****military** relating to the armed forces or to soldiers, arms, or war (p. 271)	*****militar** relativo a las fuerzas armadas o a los soldados, las armas o la guerra (pág. 271)
*****minimal** barely adequate (p. 415)	*****mínimo** apenas adecuado (pág. 415)
ministerial responsibility the idea that the prime minister is responsible to the popularly elected legislative body and not to the king or president (p. 213)	**responsabilidad ministerial** idea según la cual el primer ministro es responsable ante el órgano legislador elegido popularmente y no ante el rey o el presidente (pág. 213)
mita a labor system that the Spanish administrators in Peru used to draft native people to work in the Spanish landowners' silver mines (p. 66)	**mita** sistema de mano de obra usado por los administradores españoles en Perú, que solían reclutar indígenas para trabajar en las minas de plata de los terratenientes españoles (pág. 66)

Glossary/Glosario

mobilization the process of assembling troops and supplies and making them ready for war (pp. 273, 350)

modernism a movement in which writers and artists between 1870 and 1914 rebelled against the traditional literary and artistic styles that had dominated European cultural life since the Renaissance (p. 218)

monothesim the belief in one God, rather than many (p. 6)

*motive a reason to take action (p. 258)

mulatto a person of mixed African and European descent (p. 65)

multinational corporation a company with divisions in more than two countries (p. 466)

multinational empire an empire in which people of many nationalities live (p. 184)

movilización proceso de reunir tropas y provisiones y prepararlas para la guerra (págs. 273, 350)

modernismo movimiento en el cual los escritores y artistas entre 1870 y 1914 se rebelaron contra los estilos literarios y artísticos tradicionales que predominaban en la vida cultural de Europa desde el Renacimiento (pág. 218)

monoteísmo creencia en un solo Dios, no en varios (pág. 6)

*motivo razón para actuar (pág. 258)

mulato persona que desciende de un africano y un europeo (pág. 65)

empresa multinacional compañía con divisiones en más de dos países (pág. 466)

imperio multinacional imperio en el cual viven personas de muchas nacionalidades (pág. 184)

N

nationalism the unique cultural identity of a people based on common language, religion, and national symbols (p. 167)

natural rights rights with which all humans are born, including the rights to life, liberty, and property (p. 80)

natural selection the principle set forth by Charles Darwin that some organisms are more adaptable to the environment than others; in popular terms, "survival of the fittest" (p. 198)

Nazi shortened form of the German *Nazional,* or the National Socialist German Workers' Party; a member of such party (p. 305)

*network an interrelated or interconnected group or system (p. 122)

neutrality the refusal to take sides or become involved in wars between other nations (p. 346)

nongovernmental organization an organization that has no government ties and works to address world problems (p. 465)

*nuclear being a weapon whose destructive power comes from a nuclear reaction (p. 371)

nuclear proliferation the spread of nuclear weapons production technology and knowledge to nations without that capability (p. 457)

nacionalismo identidad cultural exclusiva de un pueblo que comparte su lengua, su religión y sus símbolos nacionales (pág. 167)

derechos naturales derechos con los cuales nacen los seres humanos, como el derecho a la vida, la libertad y la propiedad (pág. 80)

selección natural principio establecido por Charles Darwin según el cual algunos organismos se adaptan mejor que otros al medioambiente; en términos populares se conoce como "la supervivencia del más fuerte" (pág. 198)

nazi abreviatura del alemán *Nazional,* relativo al Partido Nacional Socialista Obrero Alemán; miembro de ese partido (pág. 305)

*red grupo o sistema interrelacionado o interconectado (pág. 122)

neutralidad negativa a tomar partido o involucrarse en guerras entre otras naciones (pág. 346)

organización no gubernamental organización que no tiene vínculos con el gobierno y que trabaja para tratar problemas mundiales (pág. 465)

*nuclear arma cuyo poder destructivo proviene de una reacción nuclear (pág. 371)

proliferación nuclear expansión de la tecnología de producción y los conocimientos de armas nucleares a naciones que no tienen esa capacidad (pág. 457)

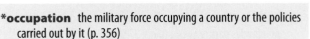

ENGLISH		ESPAÑOL

O

*occupation the military force occupying a country or the policies carried out by it (p. 356)

*ocupación cuando las fuerzas militares se apoderan de un país; políticas derivadas de esta acción (pág. 356)

occupied held by a foreign power (p. 425)

ocupado en poder de una potencia extranjera (pág. 425)

oligarchy "the rule of the few"; a form of government in which a select group of people exercises control (pp. 4, 333)

oligarquía "gobierno de pocos"; forma de gobierno en la cual un grupo selecto de personas ejerce control (págs. 4, 333)

one-child policy China's effort, beginning in 1979, to control population growth; incentives such as education benefits, child care, and housing are offered to couples who limit their families to one child (p. 443)

política de un solo hijo iniciativa de China, que comenzó en 1979, para controlar el aumento de su población; las parejas que limitan sus familias a un solo hijo reciben incentivos como beneficios educativos, cuidado de los niños y vivienda (pág. 443)

Open Door policy a policy, proposed by U.S. secretary of state John Hay in 1899, that stated all powers with spheres of influence in China would respect equal trading opportunities with China and not set tariffs giving an unfair advantage to the citizens of their own country (p. 255)

política de Puertas Abiertas política propuesta por el Secretario de Estado estadounidense John Hay en 1899, según la cual las potencias con esferas de influencia en China debían respetar las mismas condiciones comerciales con ese país y no fijar aranceles que dieran una ventaja desleal a los ciudadanos de su país (pág. 255)

orthodoxy traditional beliefs, especially in religion (p. 100)

ortodoxia creencias tradicionales, especialmente religiosas (pág. 100)

*overseas beyond or across the sea (p. 52)

*de ultramar más allá del mar o al otro lado del mar (pág. 52)

P

Pan-Africanism the unity of all black Africans, regardless of national boundaries (pp. 321, 398)

panafricanismo unión de todos las personas africanas negras sin importar sus fronteras nacionales (págs. 321, 398)

Pan-Arabism Arab unity, regardless of national boundaries (p. 392)

panarabismo unión de todos los pueblos árabes sin importar sus fronteras nacionales (pág. 392)

pandemic a widespread outbreak of a disease (p. 462)

pandemia brote generalizado de una enfermedad (pág. 462)

*parallel having the same direction or course; similar (p. 396)

*paralelo que tiene la misma dirección o curso; semejante (pág. 396)

*participation having a part in or sharing in something (p. 422)

*participación que tiene parte en algo o comparte la propiedad de algo (pág. 422)

partisan a resistance fighter in World War II (p. 360)

partisano combatiente de la resistencia durante la Segunda Guerra Mundial (pág. 360)

pasha an appointed official of the Ottoman Empire who collected taxes, maintained law and order, and was directly responsible to the sultan's court (p. 96)

pachá funcionario del imperio otomano que recaudaba impuestos, mantenía la ley y el orden y era responsable directamente ante la corte del sultán (pág. 96)

peacekeeping forces military forces drawn from neutral members of the United Nations to settle conflicts and supervise truces (p. 457)

fuerzas de paz fuerzas militares conformadas por miembros neutrales de las Naciones Unidas para resolver conflictos y supervisar las treguas (pág. 457)

peninsulare a person born on the Iberian Peninsula; typically, a Spanish or Portuguese official who resided temporarily in Latin America for political and economic gain and then returned to Europe (pp. 64, 192)

peninsular persona nacida en la Península Ibérica; por lo general, un funcionario español o portugués que vivía temporalmente en América Latina para obtener beneficios políticos y económicos y luego regresaba a Europa (págs. 64, 192)

per capita per person (p. 441)

*percent a part of a whole divided into 100 parts (p. 160)

perestroika the fundamental restructuring of the Soviet economy; a policy introduced by Gorbachev (p. 432)

permanent revolution an atmosphere of constant revolutionary fervor favored by Mao Zedong to enable China to overcome the past and achieve the final stage of communism (p. 374)

perspective artistic techniques used to give the effect of three-dimensional depth to two-dimensional surfaces (p. 31); viewpoint (p. 111)

*phase a part in the development cycle (p. 257)

philosophe French for "philosopher"; applied to all intellectuals during the Enlightenment (p. 135)

*philosopher a person who seeks wisdom or enlightenment; a scholar or a thinker (p. 129)

planned economy an economic system directed by government agencies (p. 278)

plantation a large agricultural estate (p. 60)

plebiscite a popular vote (p. 189)

pogrom the organized massacre of a minority group, especially Jews (p. 221)

*policy an overall plan embracing the general goals and acceptable procedures of a governmental body (p. 74)

policy of containment a plan to keep something, such as communism, within its existing geographical boundaries and prevent further aggressive moves (p. 369)

popular culture entertainment created for a profit and for a mass audience (p. 440)

porcelain a ceramic made of fine clay baked at very high temperatures (p. 113)

postmodernism an artistic movement that emerged in the 1980s; its artists do not expect rationality in the world and are comfortable with many "truths" (p. 440)

predestination the belief that God has determined in advance who will be saved (the elect) and who will be damned (the reprobate) (p. 44)

prefecture in the Japanese Meiji Restoration, a territory governed by its former daimyo lord (p. 262)

per cápita por persona (pág. 441)

*porcentaje parte de un todo dividido entre 100 (pág. 160)

perestroika reestructuración de los fundamentos de la economía soviética; política introducida por Mijaíl Gorbachov (pág. 432)

revolución permanente atmósfera de fervor revolucionario constante promovida por Mao Tse-Tung para permitir que China superara el pasado y llegara a la etapa final del comunismo (pág. 374)

perspectiva técnicas artísticas usadas para dar a las superficies bidimensionales el efecto de profundidad tridimensional (pág. 31); punto de vista (pág. 111)

*fase parte en el ciclo de desarrollo (pág. 257)

philosophe término francés para "filósofo"; se aplicaba a todos los intelectuales durante la Ilustración (pág. 135)

*filósofo persona que busca la sabiduría o la ilustración; académico o pensador (pág. 129)

economía dirigida sistema económico dirigido por agencias del gobierno (pág. 278)

plantación gran propiedad agrícola (pág. 60)

plebiscito voto popular (pág. 189)

pogromo masacre organizada de una minoría, especialmente los judíos (pág. 221)

*política plan general que comprende los objetivos generales y los procedimientos aceptables de un organismo gubernamental (pág. 74)

política de contención plan para mantener algo, como el comunismo, dentro de los límites geográficos existentes y evitar movimientos radicales en el futuro (pág. 369)

cultura popular entretenimiento creado con fines de lucro y dirigido a una audiencia masiva (pág. 440)

porcelana cerámica elaborada con arcilla fina cocida a temperaturas muy elevadas (pág. 113)

posmodernismo movimiento artístico surgido en la década de 1980; los artistas que lo practican no esperan encontrar racionalidad en el mundo y están a gusto con muchas "verdades" (pág. 440)

predestinación creencia de que Dios ha determinado de antemano quiénes se salvarán (los elegidos) y quiénes se condenarán (los réprobos) (pág. 44)

prefectura durante la Restauración Meiji en Japón, territorio gobernado por su antiguo señor daimio (pág. 262)

Glossary/Glosario

ENGLISH	ESPAÑOL
*principle a fundamental law or idea; when said of people (e.g., someone is highly principled), it means a devotion to high codes or rules of conduct (p. 103)	***principio** ley o idea fundamental; cuando se refiere a una persona (p. ej. alguien de sólidos principios), significa fidelidad a altos códigos o normas de conducta (pág. 103)
principle of intervention the idea that great powers have the right to send armies into countries where there are revolutions to restore legitimate governments (p. 170)	**principio de intervención** idea según la cual las grandes potencias tienen derecho a enviar ejércitos a países donde se presenta una revolución para restaurar los gobiernos legítimos (pág. 170)
principle of nonalignment Jawaharlal Nehru's refusal to align India with any bloc or alliance (p. 387)	**principio de no alineación** negativa del líder Jawaharlal Nehru a alinear India con ningún bloque o alianza (pág. 387)
privatization the sale of government-owned companies to private firms (p. 405)	**privatización** venta de compañías del gobierno a firmas privadas (pág. 405)
*process a series of actions or operations necessary to meet a specified end (p. 116)	***proceso** serie de acciones u operaciones necesarias para lograr un fin específico (pág. 116)
*prohibit to prevent or to forbid (p. 308)	***prohibir** evitar o impeder (pág. 308)
*projection an estimate or a calculation (p. 464)	***proyección** estimación o cálculo (pág. 464)
proletariat the working class (p. 206)	**proletariado** clase trabajadora (pág. 206)
propaganda ideas spread to influence public opinion for or against a cause (p. 274)	**propaganda** ideas difundidas con el fin de influenciar a la opinión pública a favor o en contra de una causa (pág. 274)
*prosper to succeed in an activity; to have economic success (p. 12)	***prosperar** tener éxito en una actividad; tener éxito económico (pág. 12)
protectorate a political unit that depends on another government for its protection (p. 228)	**protectorado** unidad política que depende de otro gobierno para su protección (pág. 228)
provincial local; of or relating to a province (p. 256)	**provincial** local; de una provincia o relativo a ella (pág. 256)
proxy war a war in which the powers in conflict use third parties as substitutes instead of fighting each other directly (p. 377)	**guerra subsidiaria** guerra en la cual las potencias en conflicto usan a terceros como sustitutos en lugar de combatir entre ellos directamente (pág. 377)
psychoanalysis a method by which a therapist and patient probe deeply into the patient's memory; by making the patient's conscious mind aware of repressed thoughts, healing can take place (p. 220)	**psicoanálisis** método por el cual un terapeuta y un paciente exploran en lo profundo de la memoria del paciente; se puede obtener una cura trayendo al consciente del paciente los pensamientos reprimidos (pág. 220)
*psychological mental; directed toward the will or mind (p. 285)	***psicológico** mental; que se dirige a la voluntad o la mente (pág. 285)
*publish to print for distribution (p. 44)	***publicar** imprimir para la distribución (pág. 44)
puddling the process in which coke derived from coal is used to burn away impurities in crude iron to produce high quality iron (p. 178)	**pudelación** proceso en el cual se usa coque derivado del carbón para quemar las impurezas del hierro bruto para producir hierro de alta calidad (pág. 178)
Puritans English Protestants who felt that the Church of England needed further reform and sought to simplify and regulate forms of worship (p. 77)	**puritanos** protestantes ingleses que sentían que la Iglesia de Inglaterra necesitaba una reforma más profunda y buscaban simplificar y regular las formas de culto (pág. 77)

Glossary/Glosario

Q

queue the braided pigtail that was traditionally worn by Chinese males (p. 112)

coleta mechón de cabello trenzado que usaban tradicionalmente los hombres chinos (pág. 112)

R

racism the belief that race determines a person's traits and capabilities (p. 227)

racismo creencia de que la raza determina los rasgos y capacidades de una persona (pág. 227)

*radical relating to a political group associated with views, practices, and policies of extreme change (p. 183)

*radical relativo a un grupo político asociado con opiniones, prácticas y políticas de cambio extremo (pág. 183)

rationalism a system of thought expounded by René Descartes based on the belief that reason is the chief source of knowledge (p. 132)

racionalismo sistema de pensamiento expuesto por René Descartes, que se basa en la creencia de que la razón es la fuente principal del conocimiento (pág. 132)

realism a mid-nineteenth century movement that rejected romanticism and sought to portray lower- and middle-class life as it actually was (p. 199)

Realismo movimiento de mediados del siglo XIX que se oponía al Romanticismo y buscaba representar la vida de las clases baja y media tal como era (pág. 199)

real wages the actual purchasing power of income (p. 417)

salario real poder adquisitivo real de los ingresos (pág. 417)

redistribution of wealth the shifting of wealth from a rich minority to a poor majority (p. 330)

redistribución de la riqueza paso de la riqueza de una minoría rica a una mayoría pobre (pág. 330)

*regime the government in power (pp. 59, 190)

*régimen gobierno que está en el poder (págs. 59, 190)

reparation a payment made to the victor by the vanquished to cover the costs of war (p. 287)

reparación pago que el vencido hace al vencedor para cubrir los gastos de la guerra (pág. 287)

republic a form of government in which the leader is not a king and certain citizens have the right to vote (pp. 9, 23)

república forma de gobierno en la cual el líder no es un rey y algunos ciudadanos tienen derecho al voto (págs. 9, 23)

*require to demand as being necessary (p. 308)

*exigir demandar como algo necesario (pág. 308)

*resolve determination; a fixed purpose (p. 346)

*resolución determinación; propósito fijo (pág. 346)

*restoration a bringing back to a former position or condition (p. 78)

*restauración regreso a una posición o condición anterior (pág. 78)

*revenue the yield of sources of income that a nation or state collects and deposits into its treasury for public use (p. 392)

*renta producto de diversas fuentes de ingresos que una nación o Estado recauda y deposita en su tesoro para destinarlo al gasto público (pág. 392)

revisionist a Marxist who rejected the revolutionary approach, believing instead in evolution by democratic means to achieve the goal of socialism (p. 207)

revisionista marxista que se oponía al enfoque revolucionario, y en cambio, creía en la evolución por medios democráticos para alcanzar los objetivos del socialismo (pág. 207)

*revival renewed attention to, or interest in, something (p. 15)

*renacimiento atención o interés renovados en algo (pág. 15)

*revolution an overthrow of government (p. 281)

*revolución derrocamiento de un gobierno (pág. 281)

*rigid inflexible, unyielding (p. 141)

*rígido inflexible, que no cede (pág. 141)

rococo an artistic style that replaced baroque in the 1730s; it was highly secular, emphasizing grace, charm, and gentle action (p. 139)

Rococó estilo artístico que reemplazó al Barroco en la década de 1730; altamente seglar, con énfasis en la gracia, el encanto y las acciones gentiles (pág. 139)

*role a socially-expected behavior pattern (p. 389)

*conducta patrón de comportamiento socialmente esperado (pág. 389)

Glossary/Glosario

ENGLISH	ESPAÑOL
romanticism an intellectual movement that emerged at the end of the eighteenth century in reaction to the ideas of the Enlightenment; it stressed feelings, emotion, and imagination as sources of knowing (p. 196)	**Romanticismo** movimiento intelectual surgido a finales del siglo XVIII como reacción a las ideas de la Ilustración. Ponía énfasis en los sentimientos, las emociones y la imaginación como fuentes de conocimiento (pág. 196)
Roundheads supporters of the Parliament in the English Civil War (p. 78)	**cabezas redondas** partidarios del Parlamento durante la Guerra Civil Inglesa (pág. 78)

S

ENGLISH	ESPAÑOL
salons the elegant urban drawing rooms where, in the eighteenth century, writers, artists, aristocrats, government officials, and wealthy middle-class people gathered to discuss the ideas of the philosophes (p. 138)	**salón** elegante recinto urbano donde, durante el siglo XVIII, escritores, artistas, aristócratas, funcionarios del gobierno y personas acaudaladas de la clase media se reunían a analizar las ideas de los filósofos (pág. 138)
salvation the state of being saved (that is, going to heaven) through faith alone or through faith and good works (p. 39)	**salvación** salvarse (es decir, ir al cielo) a través de la fe solamente o por la fe y las buenas obras (pág. 39)
sanctions restrictions intended to enforce international law (p. 344)	**sanciones** restricciones cuyo propósito es hacer cumplir las leyes internacionales (pág. 344)
sans-culottes "without breeches"; members of the Paris Commune who considered themselves ordinary patriots (in other words, they wore long trousers instead of the fine knee-length breeches of the nobles) (p. 157)	**sans-culottes** "sin pantalón corto"; miembros de la comuna de París que se consideraban patriotas comunes (es decir, usaban pantalones largos en lugar de los finos pantalones hasta la rodilla que usaban los nobles) (pág. 157)
satellite state a country that is economically and politically dependent on another country (p. 369)	**nación satélite** país que dependen política y económicamente de otro país (pág. 369)
scientific method a systematic procedure for collecting and analyzing evidence that was crucial to the evolution of science in the modern world (p. 132)	**método científico** procedimiento sistemático para recolectar y analizar evidencias, que fue fundamental para la evolución de la ciencia en el mundo moderno (pág. 132)
***sector** a sociological, economic, or political subdivision of society (pp. 245, 443)	***sector** subdivisión sociológica, económica o política de la sociedad (págs. 245, 443)
secularization indifference to or rejection of religion or religious consideration (p. 198)	**secularización** indiferencia o rechazo hacia la religión o las consideraciones religiosas (pág. 198)
self-strengthening a policy promoted by reformers toward the end of the Qing dynasty under which China would adopt Western technology while keeping its Confucian values and institutions (p. 253)	**autofortalecimiento** política promovida por los reformistas hacia el final de la dinastía Qing, en la cual China adoptaba la tecnología occidental, pero mantenía sus valores e instituciones confucianos (pág. 253)
separation of powers a form of government in which the executive, legislative, and judicial branches limit and control each other through a system of checks and balances (p. 135)	**separación de poderes** forma de gobierno en la cual las ramas ejecutiva, legislativa y judicial se limitan y controlan entre sí mediante un sistema de equilibrio de poderes (pág. 135)
sepoy an Indian soldier hired by the British East India Company to protect the company's interests in the region (p. 237)	***cipayo** soldado indio contratado por la Compañía Británica de las Indias Orientales para proteger sus intereses en la región (pág. 237)
***series** a group of related things or events (p. 111)	***serie** grupo de cosas o eventos relacionados (pág. 111)
shāh the ruler of Iran or Persia (p. 99)	**sha** gobernante de Irán o Persia (pág. 99)
***shift** a change in direction (p. 415)	***desplazamiento** cambio de dirección (pág. 415)

social contract the concept proposed by Rousseau that an entire society agrees to be governed by its general will, and all individuals should be forced to abide by the general will since it represents what is best for the entire community (p. 137)

Social Darwinism theory used by Western nations in the late nineteenth century to justify their dominance; it was based on Charles Darwin's theory of natural selection, "the survival of the fittest," and applied to modern human activities (p. 221)

socialism a system in which society, usually in the form of the government, owns and controls the means of production (p. 181)

***sole** being the only one (p. 420)

***source** a document or primary reference book that gives information (p. 374)

soviets Russian councils composed of representatives from the workers and soldiers (p. 281)

***sphere** any of the concentric, revolving, spherical transparent shells in which, according to ancient astronomy, the stars, sun, planets, and moon are set (p. 129)

spheres of influence areas in which foreign powers have been granted exclusive rights and privileges, such as trading rights and mining privileges (p. 253)

***stability** the state of being stable; strong enough to endure (p. 81)

***stable** not changing or fluctuating; steady (p. 427)

state capitalism an economic system in which the central government plays an active role in the economy, establishing price and wage policies and subsidizing vital industries (p. 426)

***style** having a distinctive quality or form (p. 31)

subprime investments investments based on loans that have an interest rate that is higher than a prime rate and is extended especially to low-income borrowers (p. 470)

***subsidy** a government payment to encourage or protect a certain economic activity (p. 263)

***successor** one who follows, especially one who takes over a throne, title, estate, or office (pp. 95, 141)

suffrage the right to vote (p. 211)

contrato social concepto planteado por Rousseau según el cual una sociedad accede a ser gobernada por su voluntad general, y todos los individuos deben ser obligados a acatar la voluntad general ya que esta representa lo que es mejor para toda la comunidad (pág. 137)

darwinismo social teoría de finales del siglo XIX con la cual las naciones occidentales justificaban su dominación; se basaba en la teoría de la selección natural de Charles Darwin, "la supervivencia del más fuerte", aplicada a las actividades humanas modernas (pág. 221)

socialismo sistema en el cual la sociedad, por lo general representada por el gobierno, posee y controla los medios de producción (pág. 181)

***exclusivo** que es único (pág. 420)

***fuente** documento o libro usado como referencia primaria para aportar información (pág. 374)

sóviets consejos rusos conformados por representantes de los obreros y los soldados (pág. 281)

***esfera** cualquiera de las capas concéntricas, giratorias, esféricas y transparentes en las cuales, según la astronomía antigua, están distribuidas las estrellas, el Sol, los planetas y la Luna (pág. 129)

esferas de influencia áreas en las cuales se concede a las potencias extranjeras derechos y privilegios exclusivos, como derechos comerciales y privilegios para la explotación minera (pág. 253)

***estabilidad** propiedad de estable; suficientemente fuerte como para resistir (pág. 81)

***estable** que no cambia ni fluctúa; invariable (pág. 427)

capitalismo de Estado sistema económico en el cual el gobierno central desempeña un rol activo en la economía, estableciendo las políticas de precios y salarios, y subsidiando las industrias vitales (pág. 426)

***estilo** que tiene un modo o una forma que lo distingue (pág. 31)

inversiones de alto riesgo inversiones basadas en préstamos que tienen una tasa de interés más alta que la tasa preferencial y se otorgan especialmente a prestatarios de bajos ingresos (pág. 470)

***subsidio** pago del gobierno para estimular o proteger una actividad económica determinada (pág. 263)

***sucesor** el que sigue, especialmente el que asume el trono o un título, una propiedad, o recibe una herencia o un cargo (págs. 95, 141)

sufragio derecho al voto (pág. 211)

Glossary/Glosario

ENGLISH	ESPAÑOL
sultan "holder of power"; the military and political head of state under the Seljuk Turks and the Ottomans (p. 95)	**sultán** "quien posee el poder"; jefe político y militar de Estado durante los gobiernos de los turcos selyúcidas y los otomanos (pág. 95)
sultanate a state whose military and political power is held by the sultan (p. 14)	**sultanato** estado en el cual el poder militar y político lo ejerce el sultán (pág. 14)
surrealism an artistic movement that seeks to depict the world of the unconscious (p. 298)	**Surrealismo** movimiento artístico que busca representar el mundo del inconsciente (pág. 298)
sustainable development an economic development that does not limit the ability of future generations to meet their basic needs (p. 475)	**desarrollo sostenible** desarrollo económico que no limita la capacidad de las generaciones futuras de satisfacer sus necesidades básicas (pág. 475)
suttee the Hindu custom of cremating a widow on her husband's funeral pyre (p. 103)	**satí** tradición hindú de cremar a una viuda en la pira funeraria de su esposo (pág. 103)
*symbol something that stands for something else by way of association; a visible sign of something invisible (p. 438)	***símbolo** algo que representa otra cosa por asociación; signo visible de algo invisible (pág. 438)

T

ENGLISH	ESPAÑOL
taille an annual direct tax, usually on land or property, that provided a regular source of income for the French monarchy (p. 152)	**talla** impuesto directo anual, usualmente sobre la tierra o las propiedades, que proveía una fuente habitual de ingresos a la monarquía francesa (pág. 152)
*target something or someone marked for attack (pp. 276, 406)	***objetivo** algo o alguien marcado para un ataque (págs. 276, 406)
*temporary lasting for a limited time; not permanent (pp. 183, 380)	***temporal** de duración limitada; que no es permanente (págs. 183, 380)
*theme a subject or topic of artistic work (p. 402)	***tema** materia o asunto de una obra artística (pág. 402)
totalitarian state a government that aims to control the political, economic, social, intellectual, and cultural lives of its citizens (p. 299)	**Estado totalitario** gobierno que intenta controlar la vida política, económica, social, intelectual y cultural de sus ciudadanos (pág. 299)
total war a war that involved the complete mobilization of resources and people, affecting the lives of all citizens in the warring countries, even those remote from the battlefield (p. 278)	**guerra total** guerra que implica la movilización total de recursos y personas, y afecta la vida de todos los ciudadanos de las naciones en conflicto, aun aquellas alejadas del campo de batalla (pág. 278)
trade embargo a policy prohibiting trade with a particular country (p. 405)	**embargo comercial** política que prohíbe comercializar con un país en particular (pág. 405)
traditional established; customary (p. 14)	**tradicional** establecido; acostumbrado (pág. 14)
*traditions the established customs of a people (p. 235)	***tradiciones** costumbres establecidas de un pueblo (pág. 235)
*transfer to take over the control of (p. 387)	***traspasar** asumir el control (pág. 387)
*transition changeover; the move from one form, stage, or style to another (p. 206)	***transición** conversión; pasar de una forma, etapa o estilo a otra (pág. 206)
trench warfare fighting from ditches protected by barbed wire, as in World War I (p. 275)	**guerra de trincheras** combatir desde zanjas protegidas por alambre de púas, como en la Primera Guerra Mundial (pág. 275)

Glossary/Glosario

U

ulema a group of religious advisors to the Ottoman sultan; this group administered the legal system and schools for educating Muslims (p. 96)

uncertainty principle the idea put forth by Werner Heisenberg in 1927 that the behavior of subatomic particles is uncertain, suggesting that all of the physical laws governing the universe are based on uncertainty (p. 298)

*uncharted not mapped; unknown (p. 233)

*unification the act, process, or result of making into a coherent or coordinated whole; the state of being unified (p. 187)

*unify to make into a unit or whole; to unite (p. 442)

universal law of gravitation one of Newton's three rules of motion; it explains that planetary bodies continue in elliptical orbits around the sun because every object in the universe is attracted to every other object by a force called gravity. (p. 130)

universal male suffrage the right of all males to vote in elections (p. 183)

*unrestricted having no restrictions or bounds (p. 277)

utopian socialists individuals who believe that social ownership of the means of production can be achieved by the voluntary and peaceful surrender of property (p. 181)

ulema grupo de consejeros religiosos del sultán otomano; este grupo administraba el sistema legal y las escuelas donde se educaban los musulmanes (pág. 96)

principio de incertidumbre idea planteada por Werner Heisenberg en 1927 según la cual el comportamiento de las partículas subatómicas es incierto, lo cual sugiere que las leyes físicas que gobiernan el universo se basan en la incertidumbre (pág. 298)

*inexplorado no cartografiado; desconocido (pág. 233)

*unificación acción, proceso o resultado de conformar un todo coherente o coordinado; estar unificado (pág. 187)

*unificar hacer un todo; unir (pág. 442)

ley de la gravitación universal una de las tres leyes del movimiento de Newton; explica que los cuerpos planetarios siguen órbitas elípticas alrededor del Sol porque todos los objetos del universo son atraídos entre sí por una fuerza llamada gravedad. (pág. 130)

sufragio universal masculino derecho de todos los hombres a votar en las elecciones (pág. 183)

*irrestricto que no tiene restricciones o límites (pág. 277)

socialistas utópicos individuos que piensan que la propiedad social de los medios de producción se lograr mediante la renuncia voluntaria y pacífica a la propiedad (pág. 181)

V

*valid well-grounded or justifiable (p. 40)

vernacular the language of everyday speech in a particular region (p. 29)

viceroy a governor who ruled as a representative of a monarch (p. 238)

*violation a disregard of rules or agreements (p. 341)

*volunteer one who enters the military voluntarily (p. 319)

*válido bien fundamentado o justificable (pág. 40)

vernácula lengua cotidiana que se habla en una región en particular (pág. 29)

virrey gobernante que regía como representante de un monarca (pág. 238)

*violación desprecio de las reglas o acuerdos (pág. 341)

*voluntario persona que entra al ejército voluntariamente (pág. 319)

Glossary/Glosario

ENGLISH — W — ESPAÑOL

war communism in World War I Russia, the government control of banks and most industries, the seizing of grain from peasants, and the centralization of state administration under Communist control (p. 284)

comunismo de guerra durante la Primera Guerra Mundial en Rusia, control gubernamental de bancos y la mayoría de industrias, la incautación de los granos y la centralización de la administración del Estado bajo el control comunista (pág. 284)

war of attrition a war based on wearing down the other side with constant attacks and heavy losses, such as World War I (p. 276)

guerra de desgaste guerra que consiste en desgastar a la contraparte con ataques constantes y pérdidas numerosas, como en la Primera Guerra Mundial (pág. 276)

welfare state a state in which the government takes responsibility for providing citizens with services such as health care (p. 415)

estado de bienestar estado en el cual el gobierno asume la responsabilidad de proveer a los ciudadanos servicios como la atención en salud (pág. 415)

*whereas although (p. 244)

*en tanto que aunque (pág. 244)

*widespread widely extended or spread out (p. 350)

*generalizado muy ampliado o difundido (pág. 350)

women's liberation movement the renewed feminist movement of the late 1960s, which demanded political and economic equality with men (p. 419)

movimiento de liberación femenina movimiento feminista renovado de finales de la década de 1960, que exigía la igualdad política y económica con los hombres (pág. 419)

— Z —

zaibatsu in the Japanese economy, a large financial and industrial corporation (p. 323)

zaibatsu en la economía japonesa, sociedad financiera e industrial grande (pág. 323)

zamindar a local official in Mogul India who received a plot of farmland (p. 103)

zamindar funcionario local durante el imperio mogol en la India, que recibía una parcela de tierra para la labranza (pág. 103)

Zionism an international movement originally for the establishment of a Jewish national homeland in Palestine and later for the support of modern Israel (p. 221)

sionismo movimiento internacional en apoyo del establecimiento de un territorio judío en Palestina, donde de ubicaba el antiguo Israel, y luego en apoyo del Israel modern (pág. 221)

The following abbreviations are used in the index: *m* = map; *f* = feature (photograph, picture, painting, cartoon, chart); *t* = table; *q* = quote.

A

Index

Index

Index

Index

Index

Index

Index

Index

Index

Index

Index